FINANCIAL FUTURES AND OPTIONS MARKETS

CONCEPTS AND STRATEGIES

ROBERT T. DAIGLER

Florida International University

HarperCollins*CollegePublishers*

DEDICATION

To my family and friends
Especially to my daughters Wendy and Shaina
And to my wife Joyce

IN MEMORIUM

To Charles Ascencio
An Honest Person, a Patriot,
A Unique Individual who was enthusiastic about life
Why do the good ones die young?

Sponsoring Editor: Kirsten D. Sandberg
Editorial Assistant: Edward Yarnell
Project Coordination: Ruttle, Shaw & Wetherill, Inc.
Cover Design: Heather Ziegler
Compositor: Beacon Graphics Corporation
Printer and Binder: R. R. Donnelley & Sons Company
Cover Printer: The Lehigh Press, Inc.

For permission to use copyrighted material, grateful acknowledgment is made to the copyright holders on pp. 621–623, which are hereby made part of this copyright page.

Financial Futures and Options Markets: Concepts and Strategies

Copyright © 1994 by HarperCollins College Publishers

Library of Congress Cataloging-in-Publication Data

Daigler, Robert T.
    Financial futures and options markets: concepts and strategies /
  Robert T. Daigler.
        p.   cm.
    Includes bibliographical references and index.
    ISBN 0-06-501011-6
    1. Financial futures. 2. Options (Finance) I. Title.
HG6024.3.D34 1993
332.64′5—dc20

93-23241
CIP

95 96 9 8 7 6 5 4 3 2

CONTENTS

PART I   FUTURES MARKETS: CONCEPTS AND USES

PART II ADVANCED FUTURES PRICING AND HEDGING ISSUES

PREFACE

Students look forward to taking a course in futures and options markets. There is a mystery to these markets associated with their uniqueness and the possibility of becoming a millionaire by a few correct speculative decisions! In addition, the study of futures and options is directly associated with real-world uses and strategies such as "hedging" and "arbitrage." Moreover, few abstract theories are needed to explain futures and options concepts: The tools and explanations used here are employed by those working on Wall Street and in the investment and financial firms on Main Street, U.S.A. Overall, futures and options are more exciting than those "other" classes.

Unfortunately, there is no magic way to earn a million dollars in these markets without knowledge of what will happen to the underlying asset. However, this book will show how these markets are best used when the speculator has information (or strong beliefs) about the security or index being priced by the futures or options contract. Perhaps more important, this book examines how to manage risk by using futures and options. A speculator is willing to increase risk in order to obtain a higher return. A pension fund or company treasurer often wants to decrease risk by hedging. Investment managers are willing to take risk-free profits above the T-bill interest rate by engaging in arbitrage transactions. Therefore, risk management becomes a key focus in the use of futures and options contracts. Once the key concepts related to risk management (i.e., hedging, the pricing of these contracts, and arbitrage) are mastered, one can expect a rewarding career in using these instruments in the financial community.

This book is readable by anyone having at least one course in finance. However, it is recommended that a second finance course be taken to obtain more familiarity with how to solve finance numerical problems, to be exposed to a wider finance vocabulary, and to obtain practice in interpreting graphs. Those who have taken an Investments or Financial Markets course that has introduced futures and options markets will find the initial chapter(s) on these topics mostly a review. However, others need only put additional time into this material to "catch up." The book is appropriate for both upper level undergraduates and graduate students who want a conceptual and practical examination of futures and options.

I have tried to limit the coverage of futures and options material to the "essential" topics. However, there is much to know about these markets and there is a wide range of opinions on what material should be taught in a course on futures and options. Therefore, this text is difficult to cover in its entirety in one semester or one quarter. I strongly recommend that most of the material in Parts I (Futures) and III (Options) be covered for a futures and options course. (Those who want to concentrate on futures may wish to use the companion book *Financial Futures Markets* by Robert T. Daigler, Harper Collins Publishers, 1993.) Chapters from Parts II and IV can then be chosen based on time available and the interest of the instructor/class. Appendixes provide more in-depth study of given topic areas and are generally geared for more advanced students.

FEATURES OF THIS BOOK

- The mathematics used in this book is limited to what is needed for the futures and options markets. More advanced models and proofs can be found in the appendixes.
- The unique overview and terminology sections appear at the *beginning* of each chapter to provide a general background to the material before reading the chapter. Bulleted lists are given throughout to serve as a quick reference and review.
- "Focus" boxes provide insights into what happens in the financial world.
- Important material not found elsewhere, or given in rudimentary fashion, provides a greater depth to the coverage of these markets. For example, see the sections/chapters on market microstructure, the futures "pits," the options trading floor, financial engineering, and exotic options. Moreover, futures pricing of specific instruments (Chapters 8 and 9), duration and immunization (Chapter 10), applications of futures (Chapter 17), options sensitivities (Chapter 14), options on futures (Chapter 18), and currency options (Chapter 19) are covered in more detail than in most competing texts.
- Numerous figures, examples, exhibits, and tables provide insights and clarification to the material. In particular, the three-dimensional figures in the options chapters provide a unique perspective to the coverage of options.
- Most end-of-chapter problems are consistent with the chapter examples so that students can refer to the text material to help them understand the concepts.
- Empirical evidence shows that the concepts are relevant to real-world experience.
- PC options programs are discussed to make the options material more realistic and useful.

ORGANIZATION AND TOPICS

This book is organized to provide flexibility in the coverage of futures and options markets. After reading Chapter 1, either futures (Part I, and if desired Part II) or options (Part III, and if desired Part IV) can be covered. If futures markets are discussed first, then the instructor can use one type of contract, such as stock index futures, to explain the quotations and concepts given in Chapters 2 and 3. Alternatively, the quotations for all of the futures contracts in Chapter 2 can be discussed before proceeding to Chapter 3. On the other hand, if options are taken before futures, then the reader may want to review the quotations and basic concepts of cash markets in parts of Chapter 2.

Part I examines the important concepts relating to futures markets. The topics covered include: the quotations and characteristics of futures and related cash markets, terminology and concepts, pricing and arbitrage, how the trading "pits" work, and hedging concepts and techniques.

Part II provides specific information on how stock index and interest rate futures are priced and how arbitrage is executed. In addition, Chapter 10 discusses duration for bonds, immunization, and how duration is used with futures for hedging.

Part III provides coverage of options concepts, pricing, and strategies. Topics include the quotation of stock options, payoff diagrams of options, pricing concepts and models, the sensitivities of the option prices, and the option strategies of speculating, hedging and spreading.

Part IV provides applications of futures and options markets. Futures applications include methods for adjusting risk, such as portfolio insurance, and the ways in which financial institutions use futures. Options topics include options on futures, currency options, and exotic options. The basic concepts of financial engineering are also covered.

SUPPLEMENTS

Supplemental material is available to help the instructor best structure a course in futures and options markets. In addition, these supplements are now available for the companion text *Financial Futures Markets*.

- The Instructor's Manual provides answers to the problems at the back of the chapters, as well as additional problems and answers for students who want the extra practice. These additional problems can also be used by the instructor as exam questions. The Instructor's Manual also provides recommendations on the values of each problem and other suggestions relating to the course.

- Overhead transparency masters that summarize the important information in each chapter are available to adopters. The Instructor's Manual includes samples of the overhead transparency masters. These masters can be used for preparation, class coverage of the material, and/or for student use to minimize the need for note taking.

- Multiple choice and true-false questions covering the material in the chapters are available both in hard copy format and by using "Testmaster" software for the PC. Testmaster allows automatic test generation once the questions are chosen.

- Spreadsheet templates covering the important numerical problems in the text are available for adopters. These templates can be used as a substitute for manual calculation of the answers to check whether the manual calculations are correct. In addition, many of the spreadsheets provide graphs that help the student better comprehend the material. The spreadsheets are set up with a menu structure so that students with only a minimal understanding of a spreadsheet can use them. See the Instructor's Manual for more information on the spreadsheets.

- A complete bibliography on futures and options markets is available to adopters. The bibliography is an integrated version of the bibliographies that appear in *The Journal of Futures Markets*, plus additional option entries. Every article that relates to futures and futures options (and most articles on other options) is segregated into the type of market and into subheadings according to topic area.

ACKNOWLEDGMENTS

The quality of the options chapters of this book has been improved immeasurably by the generosity of Mark Rubinstein. When I was a Visiting Scholar at Stanford University, Mark Rubinstein graciously allowed me to attend his class offered by the University of California, Berkeley. His insights into the options markets helped me to solidify and coordinate my thinking concerning options. In addition, his organization of the material and presentation of notes to the class ranks him as the best instructor I know.

These notes are the source of many of the option tables on prices used in this text. Mark also provided me with a beta version of his PC software "Options and Futures Simulator" to create the three-dimensional graphs, many of the two-dimensional options graphs, and printouts of screens in the program. All of this material is referenced in the text. This material has allowed me to bring to finance two tools that I have told my students will be part of the future finance curriculum: three-dimensional surface graphs to help explain complicated relationships and sophisticated PC programs that bring reality to the classroom. I greatly appreciate Mark's generosity.

There are many other individuals who have helped improve the quality, readability, and completeness of this textbook. Reviewers of this book noted important areas for improvement and clarification. Students in my undergraduate and graduate classes in futures and options markets politely pointed out confusing passages and helped to clarify the end-of-chapter problems and answers. Officials at the Exchanges and financial institutions graciously provided information and ideas concerning the markets that helped to make this book more relevant to the users. Finally, my experiences as a Visiting Scholar at the Graduate School of Business at Standord allowed me to clarify issues related to futures and options markets and how models are employed on Wall Street. The gracious hospitality provided by the faculty at Stanford is appreciated and will remain a fond memory. I thank all of the above individuals, but retain the responsibility for the mistakes contained here.

My contacts and the Exchanges and institutions who helped me in many respects to find important information are:

Patrick Catania	The Chicago Board of Trade
Ted Doukas	The Chicago Board of Trade
Ira Kawaller	The Chicago Mercantile Exchange
William Mullen	Loomis-Sayles, Inc.
Todd Petzel	The Chicago Mercantile Exchange
Mark Powers	Powers Research Inc. and *The Journal of Futures Markets*
Juliet Reinert	The Chicago Board of Trade
Joseph Sweeney	The Chicago Board of Trade

The Chicago Board of Trade has been kind to me and other academicians over the years, providing sponsored research, educational programs, and funding. Much of my practical knowledge of how the markets and pits work is due to their effors. I thank them on behalf of all of us who have participated in their programs. The Chicago Mercantile Exchange, and Dr. Ira Kawaller in particular, have also greatly aided the academic community through their previous support of research and Ira's constant involvement with the academic community.

Those who read most or all of the futures material and provided extremely helpful suggestions and ideas are:

Robert E. Brooks	The University of Alabama
Andrew H. Chen	Southern Methodist University
Ted Doukas	The Chicago Board of Trade
David Emanuel	The University of Texas-Dallas
Shantaram P. Hegde	The University of Connecticut
Daniel R. Pieptea	(deceased)
Thomas V. Schwarz	Southern Illinois University

Those who read the options chapters and provided equally helpful advice are:

Amy Adams	Templeton Worldwide, Inc.
Robert E. Brooks	The University of Alabama
Anthony F. Herbst	The University of Texas, El Paso
Avraham Kamara	The University of Washington
Ronnie M. Karanjia	Fordham University
George W. Kutner	Marquette University
Renee Schwartz	Formerly, American Express
Joseph D. Vu	DePaul University

There are many individuals at Stanford University to whom I owe a debt of gratitude and thanks. All of the faculty and staff were very kind to me during my stay at Stanford as a Visiting Scholar. In particular, I would like to thank the following: Darrell Duffie, Allan Kleidon, Anne Peck, Paul Pfleiderer, and Kenneth Singleton.

At Harper Collins, Kirsten Sandberg is always enthusiastic about her job as Finance editor. Her ideas are present in both this book and *Financial Futures Markets*. She finally managed to get me to put all the pieces together to come up with a finished product. Tom Conville at Ruttle, Shaw & Wetherill pushed this project through the production process, trying to overcome delays and my anxieties. His efforts are also appreciated.

Last, but certainly not least are those who helped me obtain information, prepare the manuscript, and make typing corrections. Many student assistants worked long and hard for slave wages, while Carole Johnson and Ruth Chapman typed the answers to the problems with cheer and accuracy. Chi-Chin Yen and Brian Bickford played a major role in developing the spreadsheets, while Edward Newman set up the quotations in Chapter 2.

As I found in *Financial Futures Markets,* despite diligence and care, errors occur at various stages of such a complicated project as this one. I would appreciate knowing about any errors so that they can be corrected. In addition, comments on the structure, material included/excluded, and level of presentation would be appreciated.

Finally, I would like to thank my family for enduring yet another book. Shaina, my lovable seven-year-old, had a particularly difficult time understanding why her dad was always at the computer. Now it's time to do something other than books!

Robert T. Daigler
Department of Finance
Florida International University
Miami, Florida

Chapter 1

FUTURES AND OPTIONS MARKETS: AN INTRODUCTION

Overview

This chapter examines the concepts of forward, futures, and options contracts. In particular, the ability of forwards, futures, and options to adjust the risk and return of a portfolio provides benefits not obtained solely by dealing in the cash market. The history and importance of futures and options help to explain why these markets exist. The chapter discusses the differences between forward and futures transactions and examines the criteria used to determine the usefulness of a futures contract. The important criteria for futures are price discovery and hedging effectiveness. Options markets provide information on volatility. In addition, the discussion of the advantages and criticisms of futures and options markets serves as a preview to an examination of the uses of these markets by traders and hedgers. The chapter concludes by discussing the roles of regulation and education. Overall, this chapter provides a perspective of what futures and options are and how they fit into the financial markets. This knowledge provides a foundation for the concepts examined in the remainder of the book. Appendix 1A provides a primer on interest rates and bond valuation.

Terminology

Reading the definitions provided in the terminology section of each chapter, plus the initial overview, provides a foundation for the concepts in the chapter. Terms are highlighted in boldface type when first discussed in the book.

An asterisk (*) identifies the most important definitions in the chapter. Subsequent terminology lists will identify important terms defined in earlier chapters. The index to the book identifies the location of each definition provided at the beginning of the chapters.

---

*Arbitrage   Obtaining risk-free profits by simultaneously buying and selling identical or similar instruments in different markets. For example, one could buy in the cash market and simultaneously sell in the futures market.

*Contract specifications or characteristics   All the quality, size, pricing, and delivery terms of a futures contract, including which specific cash securities fulfill the delivery obligations of the futures contract.

Dealer   One who functions as a middleman for traders by "making a market" in cash instruments or assets that do not trade on an exchange. The dealer keeps an inventory of the instrument to facilitate buying and selling whenever the market participants need to make a trade.

*Delivery   The seller of the futures contract sends the appropriate cash instrument to the buyer of the futures during the futures expiration period. The buyer pays the futures price. Some futures contracts, such as stock index futures, are settled by a cash payment rather than by the physical delivery of the asset.

*Forward contract   A private agreement made now to purchase a specified amount of a cash asset at a specific price, with the exchange of the funds and the asset taking place at a specific time in the future. A forward contract, unlike futures, has unique quantity, time until maturity, and other characteristics for each separate forward transaction. Forward contracts typically do not trade.

*Futures contract   A standardized agreement between a buyer and seller for a prespecified quantity of an underlying cash asset. Futures trade until the contract expires, allowing traders to profit from price changes without receiving delivery of the cash asset.

*Hedging   Reducing the risk of a cash position by taking a position in the futures instrument to offset the price movement of the cash asset. A broader definition of hedging includes using futures as a temporary substitute for the cash position. (Hedging also is implemented with options and by other techniques.)

Leverage   The magnification of gains and losses by only paying for part of the underlying value of the instrument or asset; the smaller the amount of funds invested, the greater the leverage. For example, buying a house by obtaining a mortgage results in a significant degree of leverage for the owner, since typically the owner pays only 10% to 20% of the purchase price and the mortgage covers the remaining 80% to 90%.

Liquidity   The ability to buy or sell a large number of units of a financial asset in a short time period without significantly affecting the price of the instrument.

Long   A long position exists when one purchases a futures or cash instrument; it is profitable when the price increases.

Options   Contracts that allow the buyer the right (but not the obligation) to purchase (call option) or the right to sell (put option) a given quantity of the cash security at a specific "strike" price for a specified period of time. The strike price of an option is the trade price for the asset if the option is exercised. The strike price distinguishes an option from a futures contract, and results in an initial cost premium over the current value of the option. Options also have a limited loss feature, unlike futures contracts.

*Short   Selling an instrument without owning it; called a "short sale" when it involves a cash asset because the asset is borrowed (not currently owned) with the promise to buy it back. Short sales with cash assets are often difficult or costly to implement, whereas short futures transactions are easy to implement and inexpensive. Shorts are profitable if the instrument declines in price. If one shorts a futures contract, then either the trader repurchases the contract to cover the short or the trader "delivers the underlying cash asset." When a hedger who owns a cash asset sells a futures contract, then the gains in the short position offset losses in the value of the long cash position.

Speculation   Trading in instruments that have the potential for a large profit. Often related to leverage.

Squeeze   A situation in which there is an insufficient amount of the cash asset available to cover all of the probable futures deliveries, thereby causing prices to rise above their economic value. Squeezes create problems for market participants and for the allocation of that asset in the economy.

Synthetic instrument   Creating a new security by trading two or more other securities in an appropriate combination.

Trader   One who buys or sells an instrument; sometimes refers solely to a speculator, but in general means anyone who executes a trade.

*Underlying cash asset   The specific asset that the buyer of the futures contract receives at delivery. The price of the futures contract is a function of this underlying cash asset.

A HISTORY OF FUTURES AND OPTIONS MARKETS

An examination of the history of **forward, futures,** and **options** markets provides an insight into why these markets come into existence and their primary purpose. These factors then are developed into formal definitions, a comparison of these instruments is made, and their use in today's financial markets is explored.

Currently, both futures and options exist on common stock indexes, while options on a large number of individual stocks also trade. Debt futures, more commonly known as interest rate futures, are futures contracts associated with interest-bearing securities. Futures and/or options on currencies, agricultural products, energy products, metals, and foreign securities also trade.

From Agricultural Futures to Financial Futures

Forward contracts came into existence as a means for merchandisers to guarantee the sale *and* price of goods before they were transported to their destination.[1] Agricultural futures markets started in Chicago in the mid 1800s as a means of hedging agricultural products such as wheat. In fact, before these markets existed to promote the storage of grains, farmers would end up dumping wheat in the streets of Chicago because prices would plummet during the excess supply period after harvest. Then, during the winter, prices would soar as the supply became scarce. Forwards and futures allow those who produce and store grains to pass on the risk of price change to others. This practice allows those who produce and store the grain to avoid losses from unexpected price changes.

Viable futures markets were developed in Chicago because of its location as the principal transportation center for wheat, corn, and other agricultural products from the Midwest. Another important aspect of the Chicago market was that it developed standardized trading **characteristics** for its futures contracts, an advantage over the unique characteristics associated with forward contracts. Location also became important for cotton futures, which began trading in New York in 1872. Regulation of these markets was initiated by the Grain Futures Act of 1922 and the Commodity Exchange Act of 1936.

A Brief History of Financial Futures Markets

The Chicago exchanges developed stock options and currency futures in the early 1970s to offset a constantly decreasing volume of trading in agricultural futures. Financial professionals in New York did not believe that these new products would create sufficient interest in the financial markets, so they ignored these efforts by the "hog traders" in Chicago. However, the volume of option trading grew to rival the volume of stocks on the NYSE (New York Stock Exchange). Moreover, subsequent futures contracts on debt instruments and stock indexes also grew to the size of their respective cash markets.

---

[1] Elements of forward contracts existed in India about 2000 B.C. More modern forward agreements appeared in England and France by the fourteenth century, and organized trading markets existed in Japan and Europe by the eighteenth century. Forward trading in tulip bulbs in the 1600s was part of the speculative activity in that commodity that resulted in a collapse of tulip prices. As these markets developed, the grading procedure for the commodity became an important element of the contract process. The procedure for grading cotton is shown today at the cotton exchanges on Front Street in Memphis, Tennessee. Leuthold, Junkus, and Cordier (1989) provide additional details on the history of futures exchanges, especially the development of Chicago as an agricultural and merchandizing hub.

Elimination of fixed exchange rates for currencies generated some interest in futures hedging against currency changes in the 1970s. However, the small volume of international trade in the early 1970s, the isolation of the currency effect to a small segment of the business community, and the existence of active forward contracts in currencies caused limited interest in currency futures contracts.

The major increase in the level and volatility of interest rates in the mid 1970s led to the introduction of interest rate futures starting in 1975. The volatility of interest rates showed the entire financial community the need for risk management tools. What was important only to firms dealing in agricultural products and international currencies now was needed for *all* business firms. After all, interest rates affect every business venture in one way or another. However, most financial institutions and corporations ignored the usefulness of futures markets and followed the traditional procedures of dealing with interest rate risk, at least until October 1979. During October 1979 the Federal Reserve Board changed its policy of controlling interest rates to one of controlling the money supply. The action provided an additional shock to both the level and volatility of interest rates and caused many of the major financial institutions to reevaluate their stance on financial futures as a means of controlling interest rate risk. Information on the use of hedging techniques filled professional meetings and publications. The futures market had finally gained respectability within the business community.

Currently, the most active futures contracts are those for Treasury bond (T-bond) futures and Eurodollar futures; stock index futures are a distant third in volume. T-bond futures trade 250,000 to 500,000 contracts a day, Eurodollar futures trade 150,000 to 400,000 contracts, and stock index futures have a combined total volume of 40,000 contracts a day. Currency futures for major trading countries, Treasury bill futures, Treasury note futures, and Municipal bond futures also exist.

A Brief History of Options Markets

Before 1972 stock options were created and traded by "Over-the-Counter" **dealers**. These options were significantly overpriced, which allowed the dealers to earn large profits from the **speculators** who purchased them. In addition, these options could not be traded once they were purchased, and sometimes the seller defaulted. In 1973 the Chicago Board Options Exchange (CBOE) started to trade call options on individual stocks. That same year, Black and Scholes (1972, 1973) provided a model to determine the appropriate price for a call option. The advantage of CBOE options was that one could buy or sell the options at any time for a fair price. The popularity of exchange traded options caught on and the number of stocks having traded options increased from sixteen to several hundred. Eventually, put options, options on other assets (such as currencies), options on stock market indices, and options on futures contracts started to trade.

The popularity of stock options arose from the interest of individual speculators in "playing the market" with a small amount of cash and with significant leverage. Options on other types of assets have never reached the volume accorded stock options, perhaps because individual speculators have less interest in currency and debt markets. Moreover, the volume in options declined after the 1987 market crash. In the mid to late 1970s, institutions became interested in stock options for hedging purposes. Selling call options, and to a lesser extent buying put options, allowed institutions to hedge their individual stock positions. The interest of institutions in options increased significantly when the S&P 100 options contract started to trade.

Currently, the most active option contracts are the S&P 100 stock index contract, stock options for large industrial companies, some currency options, and options on futures for the following instruments: T-bonds, S&P 500 stock index, German mark, Japanese yen, Eurodollar, crude oil, and gold.

Large industrial stock options trade 2,000 to 10,000 contracts on an active day (each contract is for 100 shares). The S&P 100 Index, as well as the total of all the currency options, trade over 50,000 contracts per day. The active options on futures contracts trade 10,000 to 30,000 contracts per day, with the options on T-bonds futures averaging over 50,000 contracts.

Importance of Financial Futures Markets

Futures markets are important for several reasons:

- Fluctuations in interest rates, currency values, and stock market prices cause severe problems for financial planning and forecasting; futures markets are a tool to help alleviate these problems.
- Financial executives and money managers employ financial futures as risk management tools to reduce significantly the potential losses of a cash position.
- Futures provide speculators a degree of leverage that is not typically available with other instruments and thus allow speculators to change their risk profiles.

During the late 1970s the financial community started to realize the potential of hedging with futures to control risk. Formal identification and evaluation of risk for securities transactions, capital budgeting projects, and other asset and liability decisions had been a major undertaking for the two decades preceding the introduction of financial futures. However, controlling risk for these situations was a difficult proposition. For example, using either betas or portfolio analysis only allows the investor limited flexibility in changing the amount of risk in the portfolio. Moreover, betas and portfolio risk measures change over time. Futures provide a more effective and flexible alternative to adjusting the return and risk characteristics of a cash position. The realization that hedging could revolutionize risk management caused an explosion of research efforts to measure hedging effectiveness, empirical studies on risk measurement, strategies to enhance risk control, and theoretical research on the relationship between hedging and the economy. Therefore, the use of futures for hedging, financial planning, and speculation requires the acquisition of new knowledge concerning how these markets operate, the strategies one can employ, and techniques for using futures markets optimally.

Importance of Options Markets

Option contracts provide the speculator who purchases options with a significant degree of leverage, while limiting the potential loss to the price of the option. A hedger who employs options can partially or completely reduce the downside risk, depending on whether the hedger uses call or put options. The extent of the protection desired and the cost of the options are considerations in this decision.

Options are the preferred trading vehicle for individual speculators because of the combined characteristics of leverage and the limited loss if the speculator is wrong. Some hedgers, particularly in stocks, prefer options because they allow upside gains as well as downside protection, even though the hedger must pay for this protection. Other hedgers can implement strategies with options that provide extra returns when the stock is stable, while also providing some protection on the downside.

The use of options for speculation and hedging requires knowledge concerning the appropriate pricing of options and the risk and return characteristics of strategies that employ option contracts. Risk-return tradeoffs are important for strategies involving options since the value of an option declines as the time until the option expiration approaches.

The Growth of Financial Markets

The explosive growth of the cash stock and debt markets illustrates the need for futures markets for hedging and other purposes. Figure 1-1 illustrates the size and growth of common stock activity by showing the total number of shares and the number of institutional shares traded on the NYSE over the past 20 years. The significant increase in trading by financial institutions shows the need for hedging instruments for these institutions to control the risk of stock ownership.

Figure 1-2 shows the growth in the issuance of *new* government debt, segregated by type of debt instrument. The size and growth of this new debt demonstrates the importance of the government sector of the market. In particular, the T-bill and T-note issuance is substantial, with more than $525 billion and $1250 billion issued in 1990, respectively. The new dollar issuance of T-bonds is smaller than for T-bills or T-notes, but the cumulative effect of the total value of the outstanding T-bonds is significant,

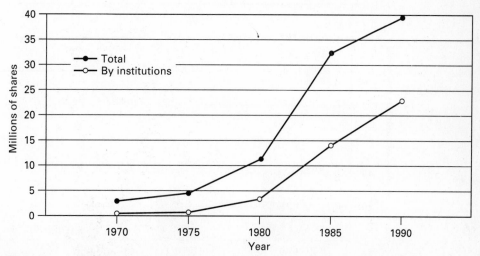

Figure 1-1 NYSE common stock volume. (*Source:* Data from *NYSE Fact Book,* various years.)

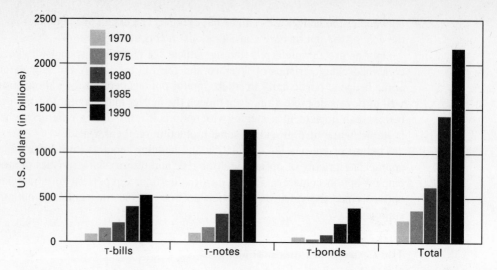

Figure 1-2 Newly issued government debt. (*Source:* Data from Treasury Bulletins.)

given the typical 25- to 30-year maturity for T-bonds. Overall, the growth of these markets indicates the increasing importance of trading activity for government securities over the past decade. Unfortunately, no accurate data on the size of this trading activity are available.

The ability to adjust the risk and return characteristics of a position with futures contracts and the liquidity of futures have made these markets a tremendous success. In fact, the underlying dollar value of futures markets is as large as the corresponding cash markets for common stocks and debt instruments. Figure 1-3 illustrates the significant growth in futures volume that has occurred since 1980, especially for debt futures. The increasing debt of the U.S. government will likely create additional interest

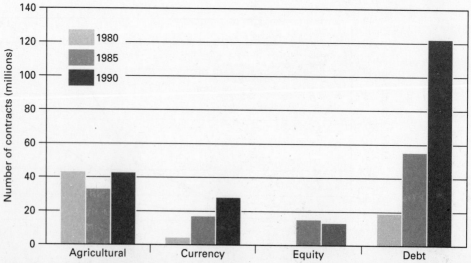

Figure 1-3 Total futures volume by category. (*Source:* Chicago Board of Trade and Chicago Mercantile Exchange Annuals.)

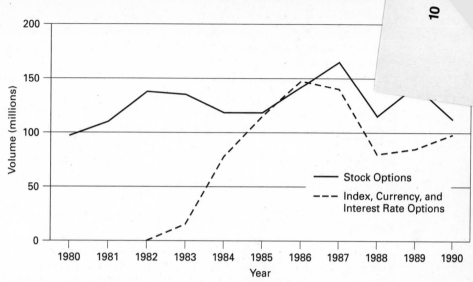

Figure 1-4 Volume of option trading. (*Source:* Options exchanges and The Options Clearing Corporation.)

in futures markets for risk management purposes. Figure 1-4 shows the growth of volume for individual stock and nonstock options since 1980. Notice the drop in option trading after the crash of 1987.

A VIEW OF FORWARD, FUTURES, AND OPTIONS MARKETS

Cash Assets

The instruments discussed in this book are called "derivative securities" since they are a function of cash assets. The value of the cash asset is the most important factor affecting the price of the derivative security. Valuations of stocks and bonds are the subjects of courses in investments and security analysis. Stock valuation is a topic that is beyond the scope of this book. Here we use common stock index prices as an estimate of the value of the current stock market. Appendix 1A reviews bond valuation and interest rate behavior—concepts that are needed to understand which debt strategies are superior under specific conditions.

Forward Contracts

A forward contract is a *private* transaction made now to purchase a specified amount of a cash asset at a specific price with the exchange of funds and asset taking place at an agreed-upon time in the future. Each forward contract typically has unique terms. Forward transactions are completed every day for agricultural commodities, Treasury securities, foreign currencies, and interest rate agreements made in London. For example, a farmer often makes a forward contract with an intermediary (called a "grain elevator") whereby the farmer agrees to sell grain to the elevator after harvesting. This contract specifies the number of bushels of grain, the price per bushel, and the delivery date of the grain. This forward contract allows the farmer to plan for the future with the certainty of a profit, barring a natural weather disaster. An example of a forward transaction for a Treasury bill is an agreement to purchase a cash T-bill in 90 days that will have a 60-day maturity at that time. Thus, the agreement sets the price *now,* with the T-bill and cash changing hands in 90 days and the buyer receiving a T-bill maturing 60 days later. An example of a currency forward transaction is the agreement to receive 10 million yen in one month for a price of 140 yen per dollar ($.00714 per yen). In one month the buyer would receive 1 million yen by paying $71,400. The price of the transaction is set at the time of the original agreement, and is *not* affected by changes in the exchange rate over the subsequent month before the currencies are exchanged. It is interesting to note that the institution that provides the forward contract often hedges its risk in the futures market.

Futures Contracts

Futures contracts standardize the agreement between a buyer and a seller, specifying a trade in an **underlying cash asset** for a given quantity at a specific time. Two important advantages of a futures contract are its tradability and its **liquidity** (i.e., one can trade large positions without affecting prices). In addition, one can profit with a futures contract without having to buy the cash asset. Futures exist because they provide risk and return characteristics that are not available solely by trading cash instruments such as stocks and bonds. Speculators can obtain very high rates of return with futures due

FOCUS 1-1
What Is a Futures Contract?

The concept of a futures contract can be confusing at first. This introductory explanation of a futures contract will help put the first few chapters into perspective.

There is a distinct difference between owning a futures contract and owning the "underlying cash asset." Buying a futures contract obligates the purchaser to complete one of the following actions: (1) sell the futures before the futures stop trading, or (2) receive the underlying cash asset when the futures stop trading. Thus, buying a futures contract *only* creates an obligation to buy the cash asset described by the futures contract *if* the contract is held until the end of its trading life. (Some futures contracts transfer money rather than transfer the cash asset when the futures stop trading.) Before trading ceases, the buyer of the futures can sell the contract to avoid receiving the cash asset (the futures buyer pays or receives only the *change* in price in the futures for the time period the contract is held). In most circumstances the futures buyer does trade the futures contract rather than receive the cash asset.

The "underlying cash asset" simply refers to the asset that will be received by the futures buyer *if* the contract is delivered. The "underlying cash asset" is important because changes in the price of this asset *cause* changes in price of the associated futures contract. Finally, since a futures contract does *not* require the *immediate* purchase or sale of the cash asset, the amount of down payment or "good faith deposit" required is only a fraction of the value of the underlying cash asset (typically 2% to 10% of the cash value).

to the **leverage** effect of magnifying gains (and losses) from a small cash down payment; moreover, holders of cash securities can hedge with futures to eliminate most of the price change risk inherent in their portfolios.

Comparing Forwards and Futures

Examining the differences between forward and futures transactions is important so that one can determine which type of contract is superior for a particular situation. Forward contracts are useful for small transactions, wherein the forward contract is tailored to the individual transaction in terms of the size, expiration date, and type (quality) of the asset, since all terms of the forward contract are negotiable. A futures contract has standardized contract terms for size, date, and quality, terms that often do not meet the needs of the potential smaller user. Another advantage of forward contracts is the lack of cash deposit requirements; that is, cash does not change hands until the asset is delivered.

Futures contracts possess their own set of advantages in relation to forward commitments, and these advantages are often significant for larger market participants. Since each forward contract has its own unique terms, it is typically difficult to trade these instruments.[2] On the other hand, the standardized quantity and time to expiration characteristics of futures contracts make them extremely liquid, a feature that promotes a very active trading environment. Since forward contracts cannot typically be traded, they *require* **delivery** of the cash asset, whereas a futures contract can either be delivered or traded. Another important advantage of futures markets is their substantial safeguards against defaults, including the exchange clearinghouse guarantees, the default fund, and the daily cash adjustments to account balances as prices change. A disadvantage of forward transactions is that the intermediary who issues the contract might default. Although a default is infrequent for forwards, it is not uncommon. The typical result of such a default is bankruptcy for all concerned. In view of the possibility of default, the participants in forward transactions must either have a good credit standing or post a security deposit to cover the change in the price of the asset. Another important advantage of futures is its lower cost; such lower costs arise from lower commissions and the lack of the intermediary's profit and risk premiums. Moreover, forward contracts typically have unique terms that promote delivery, whereas futures contracts actively trade on any business day. Exhibit 1-1 summarizes the characteristics of futures and forward markets.

Overall, the use of a forward versus a futures contract depends on the availability of these instruments for a specific transaction *and* the relative importance of the factors discussed above for the market participant. The significant use of futures markets by a large number of participants shows that many people believe that the benefits of futures far outweigh the disadvantages. More specifically, large forward markets often exist if they were established before futures began to trade or if they provide advisory services not available with futures; in that case, the participants are reluctant to deal with an unknown futures market. In general, traders prefer futures to forward contracts because of their tradability and the virtual elimination of bankruptcy risk. However, the

---

[2] Forward rate agreements on short-term interest rates made in London are an exception to this rule because they have sufficient liquidity for trading.

EXHIBIT 1-1
Characteristics of Forward Versus Futures Contracts

Forward Contracts	Futures Contracts
• All terms negotiable; private transaction	• Standardized terms; traded on an exchange
• Default risk (thus participants must have good credit standing or post a deposit)	• No default risk
• No cash flow requirements	• Daily cash flows as prices change to guarantee performance of contract
• Creating contract often costly because of intermediary's profit	• Low cost
• Cannot trade before delivery	• Can trade contract on an exchange with liquidity
• No price variability or quality risk from negotiated contract	• Risk related to differences between standardized contract and security desired

uses and concepts of forward contracts are very similar to those of futures, and therefore some individuals treat the two instruments as indistinguishable.

Risk Management with Futures Contracts

The discussion of the history and concepts of forward and futures contracts pointed out the most important reason for these instruments to exist: to adjust risk. Pension funds, financial institutions, corporations, insurance companies, and any large organization with an investment portfolio or exposure to interest rate fluctuations want to avoid losses. Hedging with futures provides a tool to reduce the risk associated with potential losses. Hedging with futures provides a method of eliminating most of the fluctuation in the value of the cash asset held by the hedger. For example, the owner of a portfolio of common stocks can *sell* stock index futures if he or she believes that the market is going to decline. If stock prices do decline, then the profits from **shorting** the futures contract offset most of the decline in the value of the common stock. Consequently, hedging with futures provides a means to *control* the risk of price changes.

Futures also provide the means for obtaining a temporary substitute for a cash position. Futures transactions are less costly and can be executed more quickly than dealing solely in the cash market. Numerous strategies involving common stocks use this substitutability characteristic of futures markets.

Speculators also use futures to adjust the risk characteristics of their position, as well as using them as a substitute for trading cash instruments. Speculation involves the purchase (**long**) or sale (**short**) of a futures contract to profit from a change in the price of the contract. Although some individuals consider trading in any asset (such as common stocks) as speculation, futures and similar types of contracts typically are called "speculative instruments" because of the significant degree of leverage inherent in them. Thus, changes in the price of the contract magnify the gains or losses to the speculator (and therefore the risk), since the speculator needs to deposit only a small percentage of the value of the underlying cash instrument.

This book examines the important aspects of the financial futures markets, especially hedging and speculation. Most of the topics discussed are relevant for both speculators and hedgers, since one must understand the motivations of each type of participant in the market to be a successful **trader**.

Options Contracts

An option provides a standardized contract between the buyer and seller, specifying the underlying cash asset and the trade price of the cash asset if the option is exercised by the buyer. Options are popular with speculators who want to profit if the stock, stock market, or underlying asset moves sufficiently in the direction forecasted, but who also want a limited loss if their forecast is wrong. In addition, the cost of an option is only a small percentage of the cost of the underlying asset—that is, options possess leverage. Hedgers also use options to reduce the risk of a position in the associated cash asset. Options traded on exchanges provide tradability and liquidity, at least for the most active options. Focus 1-2 identifies the basic characteristics of an option contract.

Risk Management with Options

Options provide buyers with significant leverage, a limited cost, and a maximum loss equal to the initial cost of the option. These characteristics of options allow speculators to adjust their risk-return profile to a position that is not available when only the cash asset is traded. In fact, price gains in the option depend primarily on the price change of the cash asset, while losses are limited to the cost of the option. Therefore,

FOCUS 1-2
What Is an Option Contract?

A call option gives the buyer the right, but not the obligation, to buy a given quantity of the underlying cash asset at a specific "strike" price for a specific period of time. An example of a call option is an option to buy 100 shares of ABC stock at a strike price of 50 at any time during the next three months; the cost of this option is 4 ($400 for a 100 share option). The call buyer profits if ABC stock rises above 54 (the strike price plus the cost of the option). The most the option buyer can lose is the $400 cost of the option. Buying call options provides significant profits if the underlying asset increases substantially, but only has a limited loss if the asset declines or remains the same.

A put option gives the buyer the right, but not the obligation, to *sell* a given quantity of the underlying cash asset at a specific "strike" price for a specific period of time. Those who purchase put options either are speculating that the asset will decline in price or are hedging against a price decline for an asset currently held in the portfolio.

the return on an option position is magnified by the leverage, while the risk is limited. These characteristics are unique and therefore desired by some speculators, especially when combined with the small cost of an option relative to the cost of the asset.

Some institutions prefer options because of their unique risk and return characteristics. Hence, institutions can purchase a put in order to protect against a potential decline in the asset's price while still retaining the potential profits from any increase in the asset's price. Other institutions sell call options to speculators in order to receive the price of the option; this strategy provides some downside protection while providing an incremental return to the institution. The specific characteristics and implementation of these strategies are covered later in this book; for now, it is important to note that options provide unique advantages and disadvantages that are not available with other types of instruments.

Controlled Chaos

Activity in the futures and options markets is often illustrated by the apparent chaos on the trading floor and the emotions generated by the market participants. People who do not understand these markets are confused by what they see.

The explosion of activity on the exchange floor and the uncertainty that prevails in any trading room of a financial institution creates excitement for both speculators and hedgers. Anyone who has seen an exchange trading floor or a bank trading room, or has had to make a decision on a multimillion-dollar trade, knows that the trading activity is a far cry from the "staid" office environment often associated with financial or bank managers.[3]

The emotional pressure and physical strain occurring during hectic market periods can evoke a wide range of emotions from a trader. Even those who analyze futures and options strategies, examine price movements, and implement hedging procedures are affected by this market activity, since they realize both the potential disastrous effect of inappropriate strategies and the rewards of good models.

Those who do *not* understand futures and options markets often associate these markets with confusion and fear. Horror stories about unsuspecting widows losing their houses and the dumping of truckloads of eggs on a trader's front lawn cause many individuals to recoil at the mention of these "unwholesome dens of inequity." Unfortunately, such isolated events of incompetence have unduly affected the attitudes of uninformed professional financial managers concerning futures and options markets. The stock market crash on "Black Monday: October 19, 1987," when the Dow Jones Industrial Index dropped more than 500 points in one day, also reinforced these attitudes. Various strategies associated with the futures market, such as "program trading" and "portfolio insurance," were blamed for the market crash. Although these strategies could have played a minor part in the market freefall, knowledgeable market participants realize the importance of futures markets in the financial environment. Because

---

[3] An interesting description of a trading room is given in the movie *Rollover,* wherein the world political system collapses as currencies fluctuate wildly in the bank's trading room. The movie is similar in concept to Adam Smith's *Paper Money* (1981), which is an enjoyable and readable description of our financial system. The movie *Trading Places* also portrays a trading floor situation, though with less realism.

of the significant increase in the volatility of interest rates, stock prices, and currency values during the past 15 years, everyone involved in these markets is looking for new tools to reduce risks. Futures and options are such tools.

FUTURES AND OPTIONS MARKETS: CRITERIA, CRITICISMS, AND USES

CFTC Criteria for Futures Markets

The two criteria employed by the Commodity Futures Trading Commission (CFTC), the regulatory agency for futures, to evaluate the potential usefulness of a new futures contract are:

- Price discovery: the ability of futures to provide information on current and future cash prices based on known information.
- Hedging ability: the potential for the futures contract to provide risk reduction capabilities for the cash position.

Some individuals include speculation as a necessary ingredient for futures markets. Although speculation provides liquidity to the markets, speculative interest is not needed for a futures contract to be approved for trading.

The price discovery criteria of a futures contract relates to both the current and future price of the cash asset. Whereas financial markets typically have active cash markets, agricultural and other commodity markets are often less active and/or are private markets where prices are not disseminated widely or constantly throughout the day. For these latter markets, futures provide a price discovery mechanism concerning the current value of the commodity. Even for financial markets the futures markets provide a current price discovery role for dealer markets. For example, the Treasury bond, T-bill, and Eurodollar interest rate markets are dealer and bank dominated. Thus, computer screens provide up-to-the-minute quotes *only* for dealers in these markets; futures show *nondealers* the status of the market. Futures also provide information concerning the stock market; during volatile market periods, for example, the cash stock market index values lag the true value by 15 to 40 minutes because of the effect of the less frequent trading of smaller stocks and the greater liquidity of futures contracts.[4] Thus, stock index futures provide market participants with information on the true current level of the index. In addition, the Major Market Index (MMI) stock index futures opens 15 minutes before the New York Stock Exchange (NYSE), thereby providing important information concerning the behavior of stock prices *before* they start to trade.

The second part of the price discovery criteria relates to the ability of futures markets to provide a consensus estimate of the *future* value of the underlying cash asset. Such an estimate provides useful information for planning purposes. Whereas current and expected future interest rates play a key role in futures pricing, sufficient trading interest from the financial community generates a forecast of the future price based both on current information and the consensus *expectations* of the market participants. An interesting example of the ability of futures to reflect new information (and hence

---

[4] Chapter 8 on pricing stock index futures examines the evidence on the lead of futures prices over stock indexes. Kwaller, Koch, and Koch (1987) conclude that futures lead stock indexes by up to 45 minutes.

to provide price discovery) is the study by Richard Roll (1984), who has determined that orange juice futures are a *better* predictor of severe winter weather than forecasts from the National Weather Bureau.

Finally, financial economists agree that the most important criterion for a futures contract is its usefulness in reducng the risk of a postiion by employing hedging techniques. By hedging, the risk averter substantially reduces any adverse effect of price changes in the associated cash market position. Proper hedging can eliminate most of the potential loss in a cash position when interest rates increase or cash prices fall. Its use reduces the possibility of bankruptcy for a financial institution when short-term interest rates rise significantly or eliminates much of the risk for a dealer who has cash assets to sell. Thus, hedgers shift risk to speculators, thereby "locking in" the price for the hedger. This practice permits better planning and provides a more accurate estimate of costs for hedgers and consequently a more stable price for the product. For example, a construction company that hedges interest rate costs helps to guarantee a stable price for the finished house. Hedging also allows intermediaries to make a forward contract with a producer or user without an undue risk premium, since intermediaries can hedge the resultant risk with futures.

Criticisms of Futures Markets

The critics of futures markets claim that futures do not provide benefits to the economy and society. Moreover, politicians sometimes state that futures actually *cause* many of the economic evils of our society: higher interest rates, greater volatility of prices and rates, scarcity of resources, and a "legalized place to gamble." In the past, Congress has gone so far as to outlaw trading in onion futures because farmers claimed futures were the cause of the large volatility in cash onion prices. More recent examples of volatile markets where futures were blamed are the silver price roller coaster ride associated with the Hunt brothers, who attempted to corner the silver supply in order to create a monopoly, and the stock market crash of October, 1987. These episodes brought new waves of criticism and a move to increase the regulation of the futures markets, including the major policy studies on the silver and stock market crashes authored by several federal agencies.

How valid are the criticisms of the futures markets? Undoubtedly, there are unscrupulous brokers who take advantage of unsuspecting customers by churning accounts in the quest for large commissions. Moreover, powerful groups such as the Hunts attempt to manipulate markets. However, in general, futures markets only reflect the consensus opinions of the market: higher interest rates forecasted by a financial futures market only reflect economists' and business executives' expectations of the economy and government actions. Greater volatility for currencies, stock prices, and interest rates show the markets' concerns for international trade deficits, the economy, and the federal debt. Likewise, some of the other evils attributed to futures markets are unfounded in economic reasoning and evidence. Let us briefly look at the specific criticisms and the benefits of futures.

Rebuttals: Futures and the Economy

Francis (1972) provides a response to the criticisms listed above. The most frequent criticism of futures is that these markets are simply a sophisticated form of gambling. However, gambling is the *artificial creation* of risk, in which something of value is gained or lost on a game of chance or uncertain event. Unlike gambling, the risks from futures markets are not artificially created; rather, they arise naturally from the price fluctuations of the underlying cash market. Hence, futures markets do not create new risk; they simply allow the hedger to shift the risk of price fluctuations to a speculator who is willing to assume the risk and who provides trading volume and liquidity. Other differences from gambling are that futures trading consists of a legal contract with specific conditions, and that government regulatory agencies constantly monitor the markets to prevent manipulation or unfair practices. Finally, speculation is by no means limited to the futures markets (or its cousins, the stock and option markets) but is prevalent in many other areas, such as real estate. In fact, the purchasers of homes in California in the late 1970s were surprised to find out later that they owned one of the most speculative investments of the early 1980s.[5]

The second criticism of futures markets is that they do not provide a useful function to society. In addition to the important aspects of hedging and price discovery discussed above, the rebuttal to this criticism involves a number of factors that show the benefits of futures:

- Speculators' profit motives tend to reduce extreme price fluctuations, providing more stable prices for both the futures *and* cash markets. This result occurs because speculators enter the market when prices become undervalued or overvalued because of an imbalance in either supply or demand. The stability of prices in the futures market is then transmitted to the cash market via their association.

- Futures markets allow a more efficient economy by providing a better flow of funds and goods between different segments of the economy. For example, futures help to allocate agricultural supplies for the season of the year and for geographic usage, inasmuch as commodities are stored to receive a higher price, which is locked in via the futures market, rather than forcing producers to receive a low current cash price.[6]

- Users of commodities are able to guarantee the purchase of the commodities they need at a specific price without paying for the product now; this reduction in potential inventory reduces the cost of business and improves the firm's liquidity, benefits that can be passed on to the consumer.

- Futures markets equalize the bargaining power among the participants by putting the buyer and seller on equal terms; the result is a transaction at the market price rather than at a price dictated by the most powerful participant. Thus, differences in size, amount of cash,

---

[5] Adam Smith in *Paper Money* (1981) advances an interesting hypothesis that homeowners obtaining low fixed-rate mortgages during the 1960s and 1970s were speculating on higher interest rates. Consequently, the eventual reality of higher rates was the main motivating force in the large increases in the value of homes.

[6] The classic example of this benefit, the wheat harvests of the late 1800s, was described earlier in this chapter. All of the farmers would bring their wheat into Chicago at the same time, and thus cash prices were forced down to 10 cents per bushel, thereby causing farmers to dump the grain in the street. Later in the year when wheat was not available, wheat prices rose sharply.

and aggressiveness have less effect in the futures market than in cash and forward market transactions.

- Futures allow the creation of new products, such as "**synthetic** fixed-rate loans" and guaranteed value insurance contracts. Futures provide this opportunity because they allow the institution offering the product to reduce their risk of losing money, and thus the sale of the product to their customers becomes more feasible.

The most often challenged and criticized benefit listed above is the claim that futures markets actually help to stabilize markets. Many critics believe that these markets actually destabilize cash prices. Although the onion futures case mentioned previously is often stated by the uninitiated as an example of how futures increase the volatility of cash prices, the cessation of onion futures trading is a political rather than an economic statement. The evidence by economists concerning the relationship between futures and cash prices is that futures help to *reduce* longer-term cash price fluctuations rather than increase them. Thus, although politicians often wish to blame futures markets for greater volatility in interest rates and cash market prices, the simple truth is that the changing status of the national and international economy is the cause of the variability; futures markets simply mirror the effects. In fact, the success of financial futures is a direct *result* of the greater volatility in cash interest rates, not the cause of the volatility.[7]

Options Markets

Options, like futures, are used for hedging purposes. As examined in our discussion of option hedging, options can reduce downside risk or reduce the variability of asset returns. While options do *not* provide the price discovery of futures contracts, options do provide an estimate of the underlying asset's *future* volatility. This forecast is more accurate than using historical estimates of volatility.

The critics of options markets are less vocal than those of the futures markets. While many critics claim options are equivalent to gambling and that unsuspecting investors lose millions of dollars speculating in options, legitimate exchange-traded options are not actively criticized in the popular press or in Congress. However, unscrupulous brokers have been known to drain naive traders' accounts by speculating in options. In addition, over-the-counter trading in options on commodities (before they started to trade on exchanges) was often done by scam artists who absconded with the traders' money.

Advantages and Disadvantages of Futures and Options Markets

Potential users of futures and options need to understand the advantages and disadvantages of these markets. Exhibit 1-2 summarizes and extends the previous discussions on the advantages and disadvantages of futures markets in relation to cash and

---

[7] For example, Edwards (1988) shows that the introduction of futures contracts did not affect daily stock market and short-term interest rate volatility. However, the evidence for shorter-term volatility, such as within the day, is not conclusive. For example, futures-related program trades for stocks could actually increase volatility. The difficulty in examining intraday behavior is determining whether an increase in volatility is due to fundamental factors, price pressure caused by large trade sizes, or the effect of futures markets.

EXHIBIT 1-2
Advantages and Disadvantages of Futures Markets

Category	Advantages	Reason
Macro	• Increased efficiency	• Centralized market brings together all segments of the market plus standardized contracts provide liquidity
	• Increased flow of information for planning	• Price, volume, expectations (cash market is too thin or information is not available)
Micro	• Less expensive hedging vehicle	• Commissions, bid-ask spreads, and short-sale costs smaller than for cash transactions
	• More convenient forward price	• No calculations needed and intraday data available
	• Built-in safeguards against credit risks	• Clearinghouse fund and daily cash settlement
	• Can create "synthetic securities"	• Cash and futures combinations that would be too expensive in cash market
	• Speculators can enter market	• Significant leverage exists; minimal capital needed
	Disadvantages	**Effects**
Macro	• Control of the market by a few individuals is possible (called a "squeeze")	• Prices rise above economic value, creating allocation problems in the economy
	• Futures *accused* of causing cash prices to be more volatile	• Would affect allocation process, but little evidence exists to support greater volatility claim
Micro	• Futures require cash deposit called "margin"	• Affects cash flow
	• Futures require payment of losses on a daily basis (called "marking-to-market")	• Affects cash flow and earnings on invested funds
	• Hedges are imperfect	• Complete loss might not be covered

forward markets. These advantages and disadvantages include macro- and microfactors. The macrofactors affect all participants in the market as well as the economy, whereas the microfactors primarily affect specific users of the futures markets.

Options provide an alternative type of hedging and speculative contract for a trader. More important, options have different characteristics than futures contracts. Options include a premium in their price that does not exist for a futures contract; however, options have a limited loss equal to the initial price of the option. Thus market participants must choose the specific market that is consistent with their goals and purposes.

A number of factors determine whether one should use a futures or an options market. The importance of specific factors for a particular strategy will become more apparent as we discuss various strategies throughout this book. Meanwhile, the following general uses and benefits of futures and options given by Jaffee (1984) and Stoll and Whaley (1988) in their review articles on stock index futures and options provide a perspective for our introductory overview. Futures are employed:

- To hedge the price risk of a cash asset at a minimum cost.
- To "invest" new cash inflows temporarily until these funds are used to purchase the desired cash assets; that is, futures provide a temporary substitute to invest funds quickly and inexpensively.[8]
- To provide a method for specializing in stock selection by removing the risk of general market movements.
- To provide a means for changing allocations in stocks versus bonds quickly and inexpensively, without affecting the market in the individual assets.

Options markets are employed:

- To adjust the risk and return of a position at a minimum cost.
- To hedge both price and quantity risk; that is, options are preferable to futures when the quantity one wishes to hedge is uncertain.

Finally, Stoll and Whaley (1988) note the three most important benefits of futures to society:

- Futures provide a means of allocating risk.
- Futures summarize price information that is useful in allocating resources.
- Futures allow a more flexible risk-return structuring of the position at a *lower cost* than that available in the cash markets.

MARKET REGULATION OF FUTURES AND OPTIONS

The Commodity Futures Trading Commission (CFTC) is the regulatory body for the futures exchanges. The CFTC approves new contract, conducts economic studies of the markets, and provides regulatory surveillance of market participants. The Securities and Exchange Commission (SEC) regulates options markets. This section briefly discusses some of the functions of the CFTC and SEC and concepts related to regulation. Johnson's *Commodities Regulation* (1982) is the legal bible on futures.

---

[8] For example, futures provide a benefit as a cash substitute when dealing with the asset itself has high trading costs or when it is cumbersome to trade the cash asset. A "cumbersome cash asset" with high trading costs is a portfolio of all the stocks in the Standard & Poor's 500 Index (S&P 500). A futures trade in this portfolio is easy to make, whereas a trade in all 500 stocks is more costly and can be difficult to execute.

Approving New Financial Futures Contracts

The explosion of new financial futures and options on futures contracts over the past 15 years fueled additional requests for other futures contracts. In excess of 50 proposed new futures and options on futures contracts were waiting for approval by the CFTC when a $25,000 fee per contract imposed by the CFTC prompted the exchanges to remove 25 of these proposals from consideration. Only a handful of the remaining proposals ever traded (e.g., the international stock index contracts mentioned in Appendix 2A). Other proposals included futures on the prime rate and housing starts.[9]

The CFTC considers a number of factors before approving a given contract proposal for trading. It weighs the potential difficulties with the specifications of a given contract against the potential benefits for commercial hedging and price discovery. Lately, the CFTC has taken care in approving new contracts, allowing trading to begin only after a judicious review process. However, even though the CFTC examines new contract proposals before approving them, market participants must still investigate thoroughly the characteristics of the futures contracts and the benefits of using these contracts. In particular, before trading in a new futures contract one must examine the prerequisites for an effective futures market. Moreover, examination of the pricing process is a necessity for avoiding costly mistakes. On the other hand, one should not avoid new futures contracts just because they are new. A futures contract possessing sufficient liquidity is beneficial to a hedging or trading program.

Regulatory Surveillance of Futures

The CFTC constantly oversees the futures markets to determine whether a **squeeze** is possible, market manipulation is being undertaken, or irregularities in the trading pit exist. A squeeze occurs when one or more individuals obtain most of the supply of an asset in order to control prices, as was the case with the Hunt brothers' attempted squeeze in the silver market.[10] One method for overseeing the futures markets is to

[9] Potential pitfalls for these futures contracts include the possibility of market manipulation by those who determine the prime rate (financial institutions) or those who have inside information on housing starts. For example, in 1985 the Commerce Department investigated the apparent leaking of gross national product (GNP) values to financial market traders. A second potential difficulty for these contracts is the lack of an underlying cash market. Thus, simply the *expectations* of futures market participants concerning the next announcement of the prime rate or housing starts would affect futures prices. Consequently, the noncontinuous nature of the underlying cash value could cause unusual behavior for futures prices, especially during the expiration period. Since arbitrage is not possible, the pricing process and the variability in price would be uncertain, if not chaotic. Third, although cash settlement has worked well for market traded instruments such as stock index futures, cash settlement for nonmarket instruments suggests the possibility of manipulation of the actual "cash index."

One could argue that the potential leaking of information is also a problem for agricultural crop reports, especially if traders have received such information in the past. However, two important differences exist between financial and agricultural information, especially for the prime rate: (1) crop reports are gathered by an independent government agency rather than dictated by private financial institutions; and (2) those who set the prime rate work for profit-maximizing entities that would benefit by knowledge of what position to take in the futures market. Moreover, there are seldom surprises in the crop reports.

[10] The exchanges also have a responsibility in these areas. In fact, the exchanges are criticized when they do not act appropriately to curtail potential problems, such as the attempted squeezes in silver and Maine potatoes and the floor traders' illegal activity in the S&P 500 futures.

obtain information on the positions of all large market participants. Size limitations on the number of futures contracts held by any one person, or group of related individuals, are called "position limits." The CFTC uses position limits to control potential market manipulation and squeezes. Position limits vary according to the activity in a given market. The CFTC also obtains information from the traders at the exchange to determine whether all trading regulations are being followed. In particular, time stamping of individual trades allows the exchanges and the CFTC to detect market irregularities.

Another example of CFTC regulatory interest is "boiler room" operations. Boiler rooms are telephone sales operations in which "brokers" use high-pressure and fraudulent tactics to convince unwary individuals to place orders. Some of the boiler room operations simply try to get an individual to trade futures without explaining the risks involved. Others promote related schemes, make false statements of "guaranteed" profits, or "churn" (overtrade) the account. In the early 1980s the CFTC was caught unaware when boiler rooms started trading unregulated London commodity options. In fact, these operations often took the individual's money and then closed up shop if the trader actually made profits. When the CFTC banned commodity options (until it later legalized them for exchange trading later in the decade), the boiler room operations started promoting "leverage contracts" for metals, and then "cash metals for deferred delivery." Thus, traders need to be wary of operations that sound "too good to be true."

Option Regulation

The SEC oversees the stock option and option on cash asset markets. The CFTC regulates options on futures markets. The SEC continually monitors trading on stock options to determne whether insider trading based on private information is being conducted in these markets. Vigorous legal sanctions have been undertaken when such insider trading is discovered.

Position limits exist for options, as for futures. While some people believe these position limits restrict volume in options, the purpose of these limits is to guarantee that no one person or group manipulates or controls a particular stock through its options.

EDUCATIONAL INFORMATION

Education is a significant factor that explains the eventual use and trading volume of futures and options since potential hedgers must be comfortable with their applications in these markets. Otherwise, potential hedgers might avoid these markets because the perceived risk of using a poorly understood tool often is larger than the perceived risk of not using the tool at all. For example, a few banks actually have used futures mistakenly to "unhedge" a well-structured balance sheet, creating more risk than originally existed.

The exchanges and various institutions have taken a significant role in educating users of futures and options by conducting seminars in major cities on how to use these markets. Explanatory and research articles increase our knowledge about futures and options markets by providing new ideas and applications, empirical evidence, and theoretical advances. They also suggest alternative strategies for a changing environment. Focus 1-3 provides information on sources involving these markets.

FOCUS 1-3
Publications on Futures and Options

Futures Magazine and *Futures and Options World* publish short, concise reports on various aspects of futures and options markets of interest to speculators and certain professionals. The articles in these magazines are nontechnical features on the market and specific products, with reports on hedging strategies and basic analytical tools. They also have a significant amount of advertising from various aspects of the industry, especially ads catering to the speculator. *Risk Management Magazine* publishes more sophisticated practitioner articles for those with an understanding of the models and strategies of futures, options, and swap markets.

The Journal of Futures Markets (JFM) is a premier professional publication involving futures and options markets and their applications; it began publication in 1981 and has quickly become a respected journal. *JFM* examines hedging applications to industry, empirical evidence involving futures and options markets, and important issues of interest to the industry. Professionals use *JFM* to keep up-to-date on the issues relating to these markets. "Futures Bibliography" is a regular feature in *The Journal of Futures Markets* that lists the research and application articles for futures and options from all publications by subtopic area.

The Review of Futures Markets publishes proceedings of The Chicago Board of Trade's research and industry conferences. Its research articles are similar to other academic journals in their rigor and use of statistical and quantitative tools. The industry proceedings and published commentaries on the research articles in the *Review* provide a rare look into the viewpoints of a cross section of floor traders, exchange staff, regulators, and academicians on a number of interesting questions related to the markets.

Advances in Futures and Options Research is an annual research journal published by Jai Press. It includes academic papers on both futures markets and options. Other academic journals in finance and economics also publish research articles relating to futures. *The Journal of Financial Engineering* is a new journal published by the American Association of Financial Engineers covering futures, options, swaps, and over-the-counter instruments in the derivative markets, as well as how these instruments can be used to develop new trading vehicles. *The Journal of Derivatives* is another new journal, published by Institutional Investor, that covers futures, options, and related markets.

Publication	Publisher	Audience
Futures Magazine	Oster Communications 219 Parkade Cedar Falls, IA 50613	Speculators and traders
Futures and Options World	Park House, Park Terrace Worcester Park Surrey KT47HY England	Speculators and traders
Risk Management Magazine	53 West Jackson Suite 225 Chicago, IL 60604	Professionals and executives

continued next page

continued

Publication	Publisher	Audience
The Journal of Futures Markets	John Wiley & Sons 605 Third Avenue New York, NY 10158	Professionals, executives, academicians
Journal of Financial Engineering	American Association of Financial Engineers Department of Finance St. John's University Jamaica, NY 11439	Professionals, academicians
The Review of Futures Markets	Chicago Board of Trade LaSalle at Jackson Chicago, IL 60604	Financial economists, academicians
Journal of Derivatives	Institutional Investor 488 Madison Avenue New York, NY 10126	Professionals, academicians
Advances in Futures and Options Research	Jai Press 55 Old Post Road #2 P.O. Box 1678 Greenwich, CT 06836	Academicians

SUMMARY AND LOOKING AHEAD

This chapter provides an overview to the financial futures and options markets. In particular, it examines the benefits, importance, and risk management aspects of futures and options. This information provides a general perspective for the rest of Part I and the remainder of the book. Chapter 2 shows how to interpret cash and financial futures quotes for stock indexes and debt instruments; the appendixes to Chapter 2 cover other futures markets. Chapter 3 provides a basic understanding of how these markets work by discussing terminology and presenting an overview of speculation, hedging, spreading, and arbitrage. Chapter 4 examines futures pricing concepts. Chapter 5 examines the operation of exchange "pits" and the behavior of intraday prices. Chapters 6 and 7 cover hedging concepts and techniques. Those who want to skip to options may do so by reading Part III, starting with the quotations and characteristics of options, presented in Chapter 11.

BIBLIOGRAPHY

Black, Fisher and Myron Scholes (1972). "The Valuation of Option Contracts and a Test of Market Efficiency," *Journal of Finance,* Vol. 27, No. 2, May, pp. 399–418.

Black, Fisher and Myron Scholes (1973). "The Pricing of Options and Corporate Liabilities," *Journal of Political Economy,* Vol. 81, No. 3, May/June, pp. 637–654.

Edwards, Franklin (1988). "Futures Trading and Cash Market Volatility: Stock Index and Interest Rate Futures," *The Journal of Futures Markets,* Vol. 8, No. 4, August, pp. 421–439.

Francis, Jack Clark (1972). "Speculative Markets: Valuable Institutions or Dens of Inequity?" *Federal Reserve Bank of Philadelphia Business Review,* July–August.

Jaffee, D. M. (1984). "The Impact of Financial Futures and Options on Capital Formation," *The Journal of Futures Markets,* Vol. 4, No. 3, Fall, pp. 417–447.

Johnson, Philip McBride (1982). *Commodities Regulation,* two volumes. Boston: Little, Brown.

Kawaller, Ira, Paul Koch, and Timothy Koch (1987). "The Temporal Relationship Between S&P Futures and the S&P 500 Index," *Journal of Finance,* Vol. 42, No. 5, December, pp. 1309–1329.

Leuthold, Raymond M., Joan C. Junkus, and Jean E. Cordier (1989). *The Theory and Practice of Futures Markets.* Lexington, MA: Lexington Books.

NYSE Fact Book. New York: New York Stock Exchange, annual.

Roll, Richard (1984). "Orange Juice and Weather," *American Economic Review,* Vol. 74, No. 5, December, pp. 861–880.

Smith, Adam (1981). *Paper Money.* New York: Summit Books.

Stoll, Hans R., and Robert E. Whaley (1988). "Futures and Options on Stock Indexes: Economic Purpose, Arbitrage, and Market Structure," *The Review of Futures Markets,* Vol. 7, No. 2, pp. 224–249.

APPENDIX 1A
A PRIMER ON INTEREST RATES AND BOND PRICES

▬▬▬

Terminology

▬▬▬

▬▬▬▬▬

*Accrued interest   The interest that has been earned, but not yet paid, since the last coupon payment date. Accrued interest must be added to the quoted price of a bond to obtain the total cost of the bond.

Nominal interest rate   The actual market interest rate on fixed-rate securities, which includes the effect of expected inflation. Treasury bills are an example of this rate.

*Real rate of interest   The nominal interest rate less the *actual* inflation rate; the real rate can be positive or negative.

Realized compound yield to maturity (RCYTM)   The actual compound return obtained when the actual reinvestment rates for the cash flows are considered.

*Term structure   The economic relationship between the term to maturity and the default-free forward interest rates.

*Yield curve The graphical depiction of the relationship between government bond yields (*Y*-axis) and time until maturity (*X*-axis).

*Zero-coupon bond A bond that pays only on ending principal payment; it does not pay any intermediate cash flows (coupons). Zeros possess no uncertainty concerning the reinvestment rates of coupons encountered with regular bonds.

INTEREST RATES

The Level of Nominal Interest Rates

A myriad of economic, political, and social forces affect the behavior of interest rates. This section presents a basic conceptual foundation for the underlying factors that determine the level of interest rates. These factors are the pure rate of interest, the expected inflation premium, capital market factors, and the risk premium. Thus, the **nominal interest rate,** which states the actual interest rate on a security, is:

$$\text{Nominal interest rate} = \text{pure rate of interest} + \text{expected inflation premium}$$
$$+ \text{capital market factors} + \text{risk premium} \qquad (1A\text{-}1)$$

The pure rate of interest comprises the basic risk-free, inflation-free exchange rate in the economy. It is directly related to the long-term real rate of growth in the economy and has been estimated to be approximately 2% to 3.5% per year. The supply-and-demand factors affecting the pure rate of interest are the aggregate savings rate in the economy and the basic economic factors of labor, capital, and natural resources.

The expected inflation rate compensates the lender of funds for the loss of purchasing power. The inflation premium considers the inflationary *expectations* regarding future price changes rather than a specified current or past inflation rate. These estimates of the correct premium for expected future inflation vary from one market participant to another and from one time period to another. An accurate forecast is important, since 75% of the variability in T-bill interest rates is associated with changes in the actual rate of inflation.

A difference between the supply and demand for securities is a capital market factor. Capital market factors cause interest rates to deviate from their expected rates. Examples of capital market factors are a large increase in federal government sales of Treasury securities due to an increase in the budget deficit, an unexpected change in monetary policy, or changes in the purchases of U.S. government securities by the Japanese. Since the Japanese now purchase a large portion of newly issued U.S. Treasury bonds, they influence the interest rate on the large Treasury auctions of bonds.

A number of factors influence the size of the risk premium. For example, the price change for default-free securities such as Treasury bonds is directly related to the length of maturity of the bond; the longer the maturity of the bond, the greater the change in price for a given change in interest rates. Another major risk factor is default risk; non-federal government bonds have varying degrees of default risk, requiring an additional premium to compensate for this risk.

Nominal and Real Interest Rates

The Concepts.   If there are no default or price risk premiums to consider, then the pure rate of interest, expected inflation premium, and capital market factors create the nominal *risk-free rate*. A Treasury bill is the typical example of the nominal risk-free rate. Thus, the nominal risk-free rate is free of default risk, but includes the risk of changing interest rates at the maturity of the T-bill caused by changes in the expected inflation premium. In addition, T-bonds have a price risk as interest rates change, and corporate bonds have a potential default risk.

The **real rate of interest** is the nominal interest rate less the *actual* ex-post inflation rate for the period in question:

$$\text{Real rate of interest} = \text{nominal rate} - \text{actual inflation rate} \qquad (1A-2)$$

Since the actual inflation rate typically differs from the expected inflation rate, the real rate of interest is either positive or negative and it fluctuates significantly over time.

The History of Real Rates.   During much of the inflationary period from the early 1970s until the early 1980s, investors' after-tax real rate of return from debt instruments was negative. However, the Fed's policies to control inflation in conjunction with the capital market influences of the deficit financing by the government caused large positive real rates starting in 1982. In other words, actual inflation fears declined while expected inflation fears and capital market factors kept nominal rates high. This situation in turn created an unusually strong U.S. dollar until 1985, as foreign investors purchased dollars to obtain interest rates in T-bills and T-bonds that were significantly above the actual U.S. inflation rate. From 1982 until early 1990, the U.S. economy remained strong, inflation low, and real rates of return positive. By 1991 the United States was in a recession. By 1992 short-term interest rates declined below 4%; inflation remained low. Figure 1A-1 shows the history of short-term and long-term interest rates and their difference. Rates were high in the early and mid 1980s and low in the early 1990s. In the late 1970s and early 1980s, short-term interest rates were extremely volatile and often were higher than long-term rates. Since 1982, long-term rates have been above short-term rates. In conclusion, forecasts of the size and movement of nominal interest rates must consider the major economic, inflationary, and capital market factors that affect the level of interest rates.

Bonds: Pricing and Yields

Basic Bond Concepts

Present Values.   A fundamental relationship of fixed-income securities is that interest rates and prices move in opposite directions. This concept is understood by examining the present value formula for the price of a bond. Equation (1A-3) states the present value formulation for a bond paying interest semiannually:

$$P_0 = \sum_{t=1}^{N} \frac{c/2}{(1 + i/2)^t} + \frac{P_m}{(1 + i/2)^N} \qquad (1A-3)$$

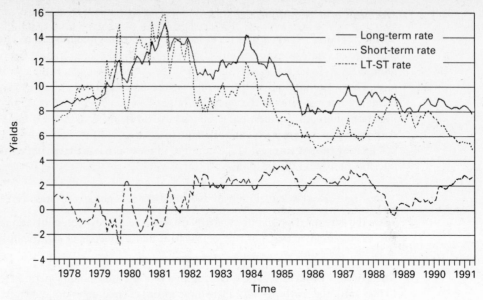

Figure 1A-1 The history of interest rates. (*Source:* Data from Tick Data, Inc.)

where P_0 = current price

   c = dollar coupon amount received per year

   t = the semiannual time period

   P_m = price at maturity (face value)

   N = number of semiannual periods

   i = the market interest rate

Based on algebraic concepts, if the interest rate i declines, then the present values of each coupon payment c and the principal payment P_m are increased, thereby causing the present value (price) of the bond to be larger. Correspondingly, increases in the interest rate cause the present values to be reduced and the price of the bond to decrease.[1]

Yield to Maturity.   One can determine the yield to maturity (YTM) for a bond, given the coupon and the current price. Although the YTM is given in *The Wall Street Journal* for Treasury securities, only the current yield is stated for corporate bonds. The yield to maturity considers both the current coupon yield and the effect on yield of the difference between the current price and the bond's maturity value. The YTM is determined by solving for i in Equation (1A-3):

$$P_0 = \sum_{t=1}^{N} \frac{c/2}{(1 + \text{YTM}/2)^t} + \frac{P_m}{(1 + \text{YTM}/2)^N} \tag{1A-4}$$

[1] The present value of the bond's cash flows is determined by a financial calculator, a computer spreadsheet, present value tables, or the equations for the present values of an annuity and a single amount. The closed-form present value equation for a bond paying interest semiannually with N semiannual periods is

$$P_0 = \frac{c}{2}\left(\frac{1 - [1/(1 + i/2)^N]}{i/2}\right) + \frac{P_m}{(1 + i/2)^N}$$

Yield to maturity is calculated by a trial-and-error method with present value tables, by using a business calculator that computes the yield to maturity automatically, by a computer spreadsheet, or by the closed-form present value equation in conjunction with the trial-and-error procedure. In order to use either the interest factor tables or the closed-form present value equation with semiannual coupons, one must divide the annual coupon by 2 and multiply the number of periods by 2.

Accrued Interest. Interest on T-bonds, T-notes, and most corporate bonds is paid semiannually; the total price for a bond or note between interest payments is the quoted transactions price *plus* the unpaid **accrued interest.** Accrued interest is the amount of interest earned, but not yet paid, since the last interest date. Equation (1A-5) calculates the amount of accrued interest. Note that the calculation of accrued interest uses the actual number of days from the last interest payment to the sale of the bond. Example 1A-1 shows how to calculate accrued interest.

$$\text{Accrued interest} = \frac{(c)(\text{NL})}{\text{NB}} \qquad (1A\text{-}5)$$

where c = the dollar coupon payment amount
NL = the number of days since the last coupon payment
NB = the number of days between coupon payments

EXAMPLE 1A-1
Calculation of Accrued Interest

One determines the accrued interest for a bond by using Equation (1A-5):

   Annual coupon interest rate: 12%

   Coupon date: August 15

   Bond face value: $1000

   Current date: June 9

   Number of days since the last coupon 114

   Number of days between coupon payments: 181

The number of days since the last coupon is calculated as follows (note that interest typically is paid on the 15th of the month for most bonds):

February	13
March	31
April	30
May	31
June	9
	114

$$\text{Accrued interest} = (c)(\text{NL})/\text{NB}$$
$$= (\$60)(114)/181$$
$$= \$37.79$$

FOCUS 1A-1
Information Technology and Bond Management

MarketMaster, more commonly known as the Bloomberg bond system, is the computer system most desired by bond traders and bond portfolio managers. In addition to real-time government and mortgage bond prices and other bond information, the system provides historical graphs and evaluates bond positions. Bond portfolio management, yield analysis when the bond manager exchanges bonds, and hedge positions are examples of the type of analyses performed on the Bloomberg system.

Portfolio managers can obtain a complete bond inventory on the system within 15 seconds. Traders can tell clients the effects of exchanging zero-coupon bonds for Treasuries. The key aspect of the system is the integration of real-time data, graphs, a menu system, and extensive analytical programs to evaluate bonds.

The key to this merger of information technology and financial products is how such a system speeds and improves decision making by bond managers. As such systems proliferate, managers can worry less about calculations and concentrate on ways to meet the objectives of the bond portfolio.

Yield to Maturity Versus Realized Compound Yield to Maturity

The yield to maturity (YTM) shown in Equation (1A-5) is the interest rate that equates the current bond price with the present value of the bond's cash flows. Although this yield to maturity calculation does consider the original coupon yield and the expected change in the bond price as it moves toward par value, it also assumes that coupons will be reinvested *at the YTM*. Thus, the YTM is sometimes referred to as the promised yield, since the reinvestment rate on the coupons is uncertain and the true reinvestment rate changes as interest rates change over time. Consequently, the true rate of return that a portfolio manager earns on a bond portfolio depends on the *reinvestment rate* obtained on the coupons received and reinvested, as well as the original coupon yield and the change in bond price. Hence, another measure is needed to take into account the changing reinvestment rate on intermediate cash flows. The **realized compound yield to maturity (RCYTM)** measures the *total* annual average compound return after all cash flows are reinvested. RCYTM is useful as a more realistic overall rate of return measure *after* the fact, whereas YTM provides a value of the *expected* return.

The RCYTM is determined as follows:

$$RCYTM = (TV/IV)^{1/N} - 1 \qquad (1A\text{-}6)$$

where TV = total final dollar value of the bond portfolio, including coupons and returns from reinvesting coupons

    IV = initial dollar value of the portfolio

    N = number of periods until the bond or bond portfolio matures[2]

---

[2] Note that if N is measured in semiannual periods, then RCYTM represents a six-month yield.

TV/IV often is referred to as the terminal value ratio. Note that if the reinvestment rate equals the yield to maturity for all coupons, then the RCYTM equals the YTM. If the reinvestment rate is greater than the YTM, then RCYTM > YTM, and vice versa. The concepts of reinvestment rates and RCYTM need to be considered when managing large amounts of fixed-income funds.

Zero-Coupon Bonds

A zero-coupon bond is a bond that only pays an ending principal payment (it has no coupons). Since a zero-coupon bond has no intermediate cash flows to reinvest, its RCYTM equals the original YTM. Hence, a zero-coupon bond avoids the uncertainty concerning reinvestment rates that is present for coupon-paying bonds. Zero-coupon bonds exist for Treasury securities and corporate bonds.

Yield Curves

The Bond Yield-Maturity Relationship

The average time until maturity for a fixed-rate portfolio is one of the few factors that can be managed effectively in the bond investment process. Since the maturity effect is directly related to the size and volatility of bond price changes, the maturity of a bond is an important consideration for investment decisions. Consequently, a discussion of **yield curves** (the bond yield-to-maturity versus maturity relationship) is needed to understand specific strategies concerning bonds. The yield curve typically is developed from Treasury securities in order to remove the default risk effect of corporate and municipal bonds.

Shapes of the Yield Curve

Figure 1A-2 shows the four shapes of the yield curves for Treasury securities. Note that the Y-axis is the yield on government bonds, whereas the X-axis indicates the year of the maturity of the given instrument. The upward sloping yield curve depicted in Figure 1A-2(A) was the prevalent shape during the economic expansion of the 1950s and 1960s and much of the 1980s after 1982; hence it is known as the "normal" curve. The upward sloping yield curve generally occurs during periods of low inflation and relatively low interest rates.

The downward sloping yield curve or "inverted curve" depicted in Figure 1A-2(B) often occurs during periods of relatively high inflation and relatively high interest rates. In fact, from the early 1970s to the early 1980s, the downward sloping curve was the prevalent shape of the yield curve. The year 1981 was the last time that a downward sloping curve existed. The downward sloping curve usually is described as indicating a near-term decline in inflation, since the higher short-term rates reflect high short-term inflation forecasts, whereas lower longer-term rates are forecasting a decline in inflation by the intermediate term.[3]

Figures 1A-2(C) and 1A-2(D) show transition yield curves—that is, situations where the shape of the yield curve changes from an upward sloping to a downward sloping curve, or vice versa. Humped curves often occur when the level of interest rates

---

[3] On the other hand, if the general consensus of the markets is that a high long-term inflation rate is likely to continue (such as in a number of South American countries—e.g., Brazil), then the yield curve could be upward sloping, but at a very high interest rate that would reflect both a high inflation rate and the expectation that inflation would exist for the longer term.

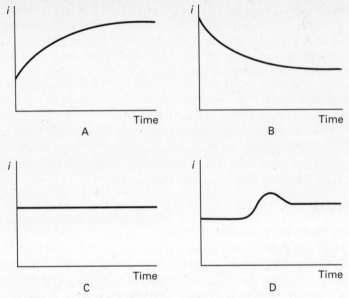

Figure 1A-2 The four yield curves. (A) An upward sloping curve.
(B) A downward sloping curve. (C) A flat transition
curve. (D) A humped transition curve.

is high and the rates are about to decline. In fact, the humped curve shows that the transition from higher to lower rates (or vice versa) has already started to occur in the short-term range, with the intermediate range not yet fully reacting to the change in expectations.[4]

The relationship between maturity and interest rates is a significant factor in the money manager's decision parameters for investing funds. Changing levels of interest rates and changing shapes of the yield curve make decisions concerning the maturity of the investments and the reinvestment rates for short-term investments difficult. In particular, changing yield curve shapes offer significant opportunities *and* risks for the aggressive money manager. Understanding the factors that determine the yield curve shape is critical in determining the appropriate maturity strategy.

In addition to yield curves, the interest rate–maturity relationship is explained by the term structure of interest rates. The term structure uses the forward rates from one time period to the next to generate the term structure graph, while the yield curve uses the yield to maturity for particular bonds. Most analysis on Wall Street now uses the term structure curve. There are four theories concerning the shape of the term structure curve: the expectations hypothesis, the liquidity preference hypothesis, and the segmented markets hypothesis. Investment textbooks discuss the details of these hypotheses. The meaning and calculation of forward rates are discussed in Chapter 4.

---

[4] The humped curve can provide profitable arbitrage trading strategies since one can purchase the lower-priced and sell the higher-priced securities; profits occur when the curve becomes flat and the positions are reversed.

PROBLEMS FOR APPENDIX 1A

*Indicates more difficult problems.

1A-1 T-Bond Price

You wish to purchase a Treasury bond that has an 8% annual coupon (paid semiannually on June 30 and December 31). The bond has a face value of $1000 and matures in 10 years. T-bonds with similar maturities presently yield 10.5%. The current date is May 1. What is the bond's total cost? (Ignore fractions of semiannual periods when calculating the present value.)

*1A-2 T-Bond Interest Payment

A Treasury bond investor received a statement from his broker informing him of accrued interest totaling $6.60 as of 11/22. The bond has a face value of $1000 and pays a 15.01% annual coupon. There are 182 days between interest payments. When was the last time he received an interest payment?

1A-3 Yield to Maturity

In February 1983, Dade Inc. issued 20-year bonds with a par value of $1000. Because of a potential default, the bonds sell for $452.29 in February 1993, creating a yield to maturity of 18%. The bond pays interest semiannually. Find the interest rate at the original issue data. In February 1998 the bond sells for $845.50; find the bond's yield to maturity in 1998.

1A-4 Yield to Maturity Versus Realized Compound Yield to Maturity

	Portfolio A	Portfolio B
Total value	$10,852,700	$10,852,700
Initial value	$10,000,000	$ 8,000,000

The time to maturity of both A and B is five years.
a. Determine the realized compound yield to maturity for portfolio A.
b. Determine the RCYTM for portfolio B.
c. As an investor, which portfolio would you choose? Why?

Chapter 2

QUOTATIONS AND CHARACTERISTICS OF CASH AND FUTURES INSTRUMENTS

Overview

This chapter discusses the trading and quotation procedures for cash and futures contracts. In particular, it examines who stocks and bonds are traded, the key aspects of common stock indexes and cash bonds, and the characteristics of futures markets. The quotations for each important U.S. stock index and interest rate futures contracts are discussed; other futures contracts are covered in the appendixes at the end of the chapter. Graphs of historical price behavior over time show both the need for hedging to reduce risk and the opportunities for speculators to profit by using futures contracts. This chapter enables the reader to comprehend newspaper quotations covering common stock indexes, cash T-bills and T-bonds, and the associated futures contracts. Moreover, it provides the foundation needed to employ futures contracts for various strategies such as speculation, hedging, and arbitrage. Those who want to cover only one type of futures contract at a time can combine the relevant sections, terminology, and examples from Chapters 2 and 3, and then return to the remaining futures contracts later.

Terminology

*Bank discount interest rate   The annualized rate of return based on the *face* value of security. T-bills are quoted on a bank discount basis.

*Basis point   A change in the interest rate of $\frac{1}{100}$ of 1% or .01%. One basis point is written as .01 when 1.0 represents 1%.

Bellwether bond   The most recently issued and most liquid government bond.

*Bond equivalent yield   The annual rate of return on the funds invested in the asset, including both the effect of the interest payment and the capital price change. Bond equivalent yield quotations in the paper assume that no changes in interest rates will occur.

Callable bond   A bond that is redeemable by the issuer of the bond during a specific time period. The bondholder is paid the face value of the bond plus a premium for having the bond called. Thus, the issuer is able to repurchase the bond for a price below the current market value if the level of interest rates has decreased.

Cash   The term "cash" is used in several contexts. Cash or cash instrument refers to the actual asset or the price of the asset, as distinguished from the futures contract; other sources also refer to cash as the "spot" asset. The cash market is where the cash asset trades. Cash settlement is the method for determining the final change in value for certain futures contracts such as stock index futures; that is, cash changes hands rather than having the buyer deliver the asset. Also see "underlying cash asset" in Chapter 1.

Contract specifications or characteristics   See Chapter 1.

Default risk   The possibility that the issuer of the security will not pay the interest payment or the face value of the bond due to a lack of funds.

Eurodollars   A dollar denominated deposit in a bank outside the United States or in an International Banking Facility in the United States.

Money market yield   A simple interest rate that adjusts for the number of days the funds are deposited; no compounding exists for these funds; that is, number of dollars $\times$ interest rate $\times$ number of days held $\div$ number of days in the year.

*Nearby/deferred contracts   The next expiration month is the nearby contract, later expirations are deferred contracts, and futures expiring after one year are distant deferred contracts.

*Open interest   The number of futures contracts that at any given time have both a buyer (long position) and seller (short position). Open interest increases as more positions are taken on both sides of the market; open interest decreases as traders close positions. At expiration, traders settle any remaining open interest positions either by delivery of the asset or by the net cash settlement for contracts not having delivery.

*Program trading   Stock index arbitrage; that is, obtaining risk-free profits when the futures price deviates from the forward price by more than transactions costs. In more general terms, program trading is the use of computer programs to execute the purchase or sale of a basket of stocks in order to obtain liquidity and to lower transaction costs.

Stock index fund   A mutual fund that purchases stock in the same exact proportions as a given cash index—typically, the S&P 500 index.

THE STOCK MARKET

Basics of the Cash Market

Most common stocks of major corporations trade on the New York Stock Exchange (NYSE) or the American Stock Exchange (AMEX). Orders arrive on the floor of the exchange via phone, teletype, and computer terminal. Orders received by the brokerage houses from individual customers are typically given to the floor brokers, who take the order to the specific "post" on the floor of the exchange where the particular stock trades. At the relevant post the broker can trade the stock with another broker or with the specialist assigned to that stock. The specialist's purpose is to keep an orderly and continuous market by buying and selling the stocks that the specialist handles. Block orders, order for 10,000 or more shares of a given stock, typically trade off the exchange via telephone, since the specialists and traders on the floor do not have sufficient capital or motivation to handle such orders. However, block orders still appear on the exchange tape of transactions.

Stock index funds and those dealing simultaneously in futures markets and the stock market often wish to buy or sell shares in a number of different stocks at one time. This is accomplished automatically and almost instantaneously by traders using the NYSE DOT (Designated Order Turnaround) System. The trader merely has to indicate via a computer terminal that a given basket of stocks with a prestated set of shares needs to be purchased or sold. This order is automatically sent to the specialists' computers on the floor of the exchange and executed at that time.[1]

---

[1] There are two systems of trading over-the-counter (OTC) stocks. The National Association of Security Dealers (NASD) has a computer system called NASDAQ (the NASD Automated Quotation System). This system allows brokers who wish to purchase or sell a stock in the system to find the prices that dealers are quoting to buy and to sell the stock. The broker then picks the lowest ask price for the broker's purchase (the dealer's sale) or the highest bid price for the broker's sale (the dealer's purchase). This trade then is executed via several commands on the computer terminal. The second method, which is used for smaller OTC stocks, executes trades via a telephone system to dealers. In this case, the broker must contact the dealer via telephone to determine the dealer's bid and ask price. The broker may have to call several dealers to obtain a reasonable estimate of the true market bid and ask price for that stock before determining which dealer is bidding or offering the best price.

Common Stock Indexes

There are several popular common stock indexes that show the combined behavior of the portfolio of stocks that make up the index. The common stock indexes that have widespread appeal are the Dow Jones Industrial Average, the Standard & Poor's 500 Index, and the NYSE Index. The Dow Jones Industrial Index is determined by adding the prices of 30 large industrial stocks and dividing by the appropriate divisor. The S&P 500 and NYSE Indexes are determined by calculating the total market value for all the relevant firms and dividing by the total market value when the index was started. The equation to determine the Dow Jones Industrial Index is as follows:

$$\text{Dow Jones Index} = \sum_{j=1}^{30} \frac{P_j}{\text{IDIV}} \qquad (2\text{-}1)$$

where P_j = price of each stock j in the index

$j = 1, 2, \ldots, 30$, i.e., j represents each stock in the index

IDIV = the index divisor

Σ represents the summation over the number of stocks in the index

The value-weighted indexes are calculated by the following procedure:

$$\text{S\&P and NYSE indexes} = \frac{\Sigma_j P_{jt} S_{jt}}{\Sigma_j P_{j,\text{base}} S_{j,\text{base}} \times \text{beginning index value}} \qquad (2\text{-}2)$$

where P_{jt} = price of stock j at time t

S_{jt} = number of shares of stock j at time t

$P_{j,\text{base}} S_{j,\text{base}}$ = price (P) and number of shares for each stock (j) for the base time period

The beginning index for the S&P 500 is 10, whereas the NYSE started at 50. The procedures used to calculate these indexes and the related biases in determining the Dow Jones Index are given in most investments and security analysis textbooks; for example, see Reilly (1989, chap. 4).

The common stock index is only a *relative* measure of the value of the "market." Thus, the stock index value does *not* state an average price per share, since the current market value of the stocks in the index is compared to a historical value to determine the index. However, one is able to analyze the performance of an index by determining the *percent change* in the index. Thus, a 50 point change in the Dow Jones Industrials when the Index is at 2000 is, in percentage terms, identical to a 25 point change when the Index is at 1000. Alternatively, one can examine the level of the index over a historical time period. However, since stock indexes seldom correspond to most actual portfolios, one must take care in using these indexes to estimate portfolio performance.[2]

Figure 2-1 illustrates the movement in the S&P 500 index from 1987 through 1991. The 1987 market crash and the 1990 major downward movement are clearly shown on this figure, as well as the general upward movement in the market from late 1987 and numerous smaller changes of 20 index points or more. Both the large and the numerous smaller movements suggest how to employ futures markets in order to benefit the user. Changes of 20 points translate into a speculator's return on deposited funds of 50%. Similarly, hedgers can avoid losses of $10,000 for a 20-point index change for each

---

[2] Some funds do structure their portfolios to correspond exactly to the S&P 500 index.

Figure 2-1 S&P 500 weekly index. (*Source:* Data from Tick Data, Inc.)

futures contract they use. The following section covers the calculations of price changes for futures.

BASIC INFORMATION FOR ALL TYPES OF FUTURES CONTRACTS

The newspaper quotations for all financial futures contracts follow the same general format. Stock index futures quotes are shown in Exhibit 2-1, and debt futures quotations are given later in this chapter. Here we discuss only the general format of the quotation process. The specifics of each futures contract will be covered later.

The months identified at the left of each futures contract represent the expiration months of the futures. The futures contract ceases to trade at some point during the month. During the expiration period, the buyer of a deliverable futures contract receives the underlying **cash** security from the seller and the buyer pays the futures price. However, some futures, such as stock index futures contracts, are settled only with a net cash payment. This "cash settlement" is used for contracts for which delivery of the cash asset would be difficult or cumbersome. Cash settlement also minimizes the cost of settling the futures contract. The expiration months for all of the financial futures contracts except the Major Market stock index futures are March, June, September, and December; these expiration months constitute the financial cycle. The Major Market stock index futures also have expirations in the current and following two months as well as the financial cycle. The **nearby** expiration is the next futures to expire. The **deferred** contracts expire later.

The second through fifth columns of the futures quotations show the opening, high, low, and closing (settle) prices for the day, with the price change in the sixth column

EXHIBIT 2-1
Stock Index Futures Quotations

	Open	High	Low	Settle	Chg	Lifetime High	Lifetime Low	Open Interest
S&P 500 Index (CME) 500 times index								
Mar	416.40	422.50	415.65	421.65	+5.85	422.60	372.90	145,697
June	417.70	423.90	417.10	423.10	+5.95	423.90	374.50	4,010
Sept	419.40	425.40	418.45	424.50	+5.85	425.40	376.25	415
Est vol 55,272; vol Mon 45,848; open int 150,155, −235.								
Index High 420.44; Low 414.32; Close 420.44 +6.10								
NYSE Composite Index (NYFE) 500 times index								
Mar	229.45	232.85	229.05	232.35	+3.20	232.95	205.70	4,766
June	230.00	233.50	229.70	232.85	+3.20	233.50	206.50	365
Sept	231.75	231.75	231.00	233.35	+3.20	232.35	212.55	133
Est vol 7,463; vol Mon 5,738; open int 5,264, −136.								
Index High 231.60; Low 228.45; Close 231.57 +3.10								
Major Market Index (CBT) 500 times index								
Jan	347.50	351.70	345.70	351.00	+4.15	352.00	309.90	4,664
Feb	347.50	351.80	346.00	351.10	+4.20	351.90	311.50	854
Mar	347.00	352.00	346.50	351.30	+4.10	352.00	311.60	109
Est vol 2,500; vol Mon 1,177; open int 5,654, +45.								
Index High 351.54; Low 345.23; Close 350.82 +4.38								

Source: Exchange quotes January 15.

being the difference in price from the previous day's close.[3] The "lifetime high and low" columns reflect the highest and lowest price for that particular contract expiration since it started to trade.

The volume of trading per expiration month is not given in most publications, but the total volume for all expirations for any given day is given at the bottom of the quotations for each futures contract. The final column of the quotations shows the level of **open interest** in the futures contract. For each open interest contract there must be a buyer and a seller, since their combined transactions "create" a contract. Later, the buyer can reverse the position by selling, and vice versa with a seller, thereby eliminating one open interest position. For example, the following illustrates that in period 1 an open interest contract is created when a buyer and seller trade. A contract in period 2 still exists even though a trade occurs. In period 3 the open interest contract disappears.

---

[3] The official opening and closing prices are actually ranges of price transactions, with the midpoint of the range of the first and last minute of trading used for the printed opening and closing values. A committee officially determines the settle, but usually the settle is the midpoint of the closing range; however, for low-volume expiration months, the committee can adjust the settle price to conform to the price structure of the other expiration months so as to obtain the appropriate differences in prices (spreads). When adjustments are necessary, they are typically required because different expiration months have their last trades at different times of the day. For example, the NYFE September contract has a settle price that is greater than the "high" price. Thus, the settle has been adjusted in this case.

Period	Trader 1	Trader 2	Trader 3	Open Interest
0				0
1	Buys	Sells		1
2	Sells		Buys	1
3		Buys	Sells	0

For financial futures contracts the nearby expiration typically has the largest open interest, with the deferred expirations having smaller open interest positions. However, near the termination of trading the open interest for the nearby contract becomes a small number. Agricultural futures have large open interest values for the harvest month expirations. Figure 2-2 shows how the level of open interest changes over the life of the contract, with the September 1991 T-bond futures used as an example. Notice that the open interest builds slowly over time until June 1991 (the expiration month of the nearby futures contract), when the open interest for the September contract increases dramatically. The open interest remains high until the expiration month of September, when it falls dramatically as positions are covered and delivered.

STOCK INDEX FUTURES QUOTATIONS AND CHARACTERISTICS

The following sections present information on futures contracts, including the meaning of the quotes for each stock index futures contract and the relevant **contract characteristics** or **specifications** for each contract. Exhibit 2-1 illustrates stock index futures quotations.

These stock index futures contracts allow speculators and hedgers to trade in futures that mirror the movements of the associated cash market indexes. Thus, pension funds and other large investment portfolios of stocks can avoid large losses by selling stock index futures. These funds also employ stock index futures as a temporary substitute for eventual purchases or sales of stocks, since traders can execute futures transactions quickly and inexpensively. Finally, funds use futures for arbitrage, and therefore the institutions are able to earn risk-free profits from mispriced combinations of stock and

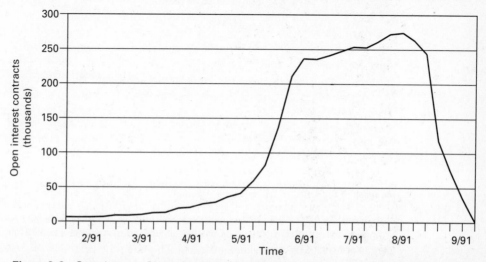

Figure 2-2 Open interest: September 1991 T-bond futures. (*Source:* Data from Tick Data, Inc.)

FOCUS 2-1
Program Trading: Untouched by Human Hands?

The general perception of program trading is that computers control the entire trans-action, from the identification of the arbitrage opportunity between stocks and fu-tures to the execution of the trades. In fact, the *arbitrageur* makes the decision whether or not to execute the trades. Typically, the computer is programmed to identify when the futures price differs sufficiently from the fair price to prompt an examination of the situation. The computer also is programmed to *execute* the cash stock trades once the trader decides to enter the arbitrage. In other words, the com-puterized system at the NYSE allows the trader to program the computer to execute buy or sell orders on a given basket of stocks for a given predetermined number of shares for each stock by simply pressing a designated key on the computer key-board. These orders are then electronically sent to each specialist's desk on the floor of the exchange and are executed immediately. However, the decision to execute the arbitrage transaction in the first place, and the appropriate size of the trade, are made by the arbitrageur.

Scott Hamilton (1987) presents a history and discussion of program trading. His examination of this maligned technique shows its use and advantages, both for futures-related trades and general portfolio management. In its original form, pro-gram trading was simply the orderly purchase or sale of an entire portfolio of secu-rities. Specifically, in the mid 1970s, stock index fund managers needed a method to buy or sell a basket of securities at the closing price of the market since their funds are priced to the public at the close. Since the purpose of an index fund is to track the cash index exactly, and since no security analysis or speculative trading is em-ployed, trading at other times could create prices that would underperform the cash index closing value. Therefore, program trading was devised as a method to trade a basket of stocks at a guaranteed (closing) price. Overall, non–figures-related pro-gram trades constitute more than half of all the program trades.

Program trading developed into a futures arbitrage strategy when liquidity devel-oped in the futures market. Pension funds, corporations, and brokerage houses started to use arbitrage as a means of obtaining a risk-free return above the T-bill rate using short futures arbitrage or to outperform the cash index for long futures arbitrage (by selling stocks currently owned and buying futures). Other uses for fu-tures program trading are to move funds from one market to another (say, from stocks to bonds) or from one money manager to another and to handle large cash inflows or outflows. Some claim these futures-related activities increase the volatil-ity in the market because of the large volume generated by these trades. The issues of volatility and the relationship of program trades to the 1987 market crash are dis-cussed in Chapter 8.

futures transactions. Speculators like stock index futures because they provide a means to buy or sell the entire market with a relatively small cash deposit, a feature that pro-vides a significant degree of leverage. Focus 2-1 tells how trades of large baskets of stocks, called **program trades,** are executed and how they relate to futures trades by financial institutions. Exhibit 2-2 lists the characteristics of each of the stock index futures contracts in a convenient format. The following sections discuss the essential information from this exhibit.

EXHIBIT 2-2
Characteristics of Stock Index Futures Contracts

Futures Contract	Trading Unit	Deliverable Instrument	Price Quotation	Minimum Price Change		Last Trading Day	Last Delivery Day
				Units	Dollars		
S&P 500	500 × index	Cash	Index	.05	$25	(2)	(1)
MMI	500 × index	Cash	Index	.05	$25	3rd Fri. of month	(1)
NYSE	500 × index	Cash	Index	.05	$25	3rd Fri. of month	(1)

(1) No delivery is made since the contract is settled in cash. The cash settlement is made the day following the last trading day.
(2) Thursday before the third Friday of the expiration month.
Note: All stock index futures contracts trade on the March, June, September, and December expiration cycle, except for the Major Market Index. The MMI has expirations in the current month, the next two months, and the March, June, September, and December cycle.

Stock Index Futures

The S&P 500 and NYSE Index contracts began trading in 1982. The Major Market Index began in 1984. The open interest and volume values in Exhibit 2-1 show that the S&P 500 contract is the most active of the stock index futures.

Cash settlement at expiration of the stock index futures works as follows: On the specified day of contract expiration the buyer and seller of the stock index futures settle any *differences* in value in their accounts in cash rather than by delivering or receiving actual stock. The reason for a cash settlement is obvious; for most stock index futures contracts it is impossible to deliver the number of stocks that make up the index or deliver the stock in the proportions required by the index construction. Thus, since the contract is settled in cash, the important aspect of the futures quotation is the *change* in the futures price from the time the futures contract was purchased or sold.

S&P 500 Index.   The S&P 500 Index contract trades on the Chicago Mercantile Exchange (CMEX). The underlying cash "value" of the contract is determined by multiplying the Index by 500. For example, the value of the March expiration month in Exhibit 2-1 is found by multiplying the close (settle) of 421.65 by 500 to obtain $210,825. The minimum change in the Index is .05, which is worth $25. A change of one index point (1.00) is worth $500—that is, 500 × 1.00. The S&P 500 contract has four expiration months trading at one time. However, as shown in Exhibit 2-1, only the first two expirations have much trading activity. The futures stop trading on the Thursday before the third Friday of the expiration month. The growth of the stock index futures markets has been significant. The total S&P 500 futures volume of more than 50,000 contracts, as shown in Exhibit 2-1, totals more than $10 billion in value of the underlying stock. Figure 2-3 illustrates how the open interest for the S&P 500 contract has grown significantly since the inception of this futures contract. Although the level of open interest stagnated from mid 1986 to mid 1990, mostly as a result of the 1987 market crash, the growth in the S&P 500 contract has recently resumed.

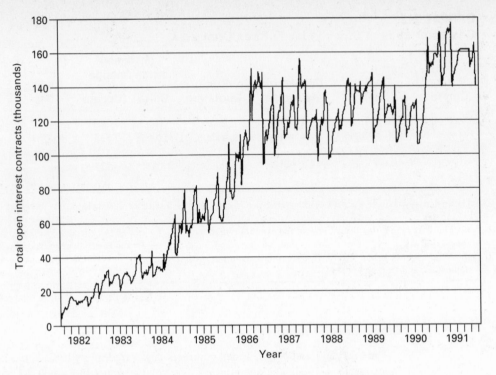

Figure 2-3 S&P 500 futures open interest. (*Source:* Data from Tick Data, Inc.)

Major Market Index. The MMI trades on the Chicago Board of Trade (CBT). The Index includes 20 major companies, with 17 of these firms being part of the Dow Jones Industrial Index; hence, the MMI is comparable to the Dow Jones Industrial Index in terms of volatility. The cash MMI is determined by adding the prices of the 20 stocks and dividing by the appropriate divisor. The divisor as of late 1993 was 3.09984; the divisor changes with stock dividends and substitutions of stock in the Index. The total underlying cash value of the MMI futures is then determined by multiplying the cash index by 500. The minimum change in the Index is .05, which is worth $25. One index point is worth $500. Expirations exist for the current and the next two calendar months, as well as for the financial cycle; however, typically only the first two contract expiration months are actively traded. The futures stop trading on the third Friday of the expiration month. Settlement is in cash.

NYSE Index. The NYSE Composite Futures Index trades on the New York Futures Exchange (NYFE). The Index is equivalent to the cash NYSE Index of all stocks traded on that exchange. The underlying cash value of the contract is 500 times the Index, the minimum change is .05, and the value of this change is $25. One index point is worth $500. Maturities follow on the financial cycle, with the first two expirations being most active. Settlement is in cash. The futures stop trading on the third Friday of the expiration month.

Other Stock Index Futures Contracts. The Value Line Stock Index contract is a low-volume futures, while over-the-counter futures are dormant. No industry or individual stock futures exist, since an agreement between the CFTC and the Securities and Exchange Commission (SEC) allocates authority of all industry and stock products to the SEC. The SEC does not believe that industry futures are appropriate for trading at this time.

SHORT-TERM INTEREST RATE INSTRUMENTS

Cash T-Bills

T-bills are short-term government debt instruments that range in initial maturity from 91 days to one year. The U.S. Treasury sells 91-day T-bills each week, whereas the one-year bills are sold monthly. T-bills are issued at a discount and redeemed at par, the difference being the "interest" paid. The sale is made by sealed competitive auction for large amounts, and institutions who bid the lowest interest rate receive the Treasury bills. Smaller size public requests for T-bills are filled at the average auction rate on a noncompetitive basis, since the Treasury discourages small competitive bids. Once issued, T-bills are traded by banks and dealers. The typical trade in T-bills is $5 million, although $50 million to $100 million trades are not uncommon. The total dollar value of T-bill trades per day is significantly larger than that of the common stock or bond markets, and thus the T-bill market is extremely liquid. Since the U.S. government issues T-bills, traders consider the **default risk** of not paying an upcoming obligation to be nonexistent.

Panel A of Exhibit 2-3 shows how cash T-bills are quoted. In *The Wall Street Journal* these quotes appear at the bottom of the section entitled "Treasury Bonds, Notes & Bills." Panel B of Exhibit 2-3 shows several representative quotes for cash Treasury bills obtained from panel A. The first column in the table shows the maturity month and day for the T-bill. The second column states the number of days until the T-bill matures. The third and fourth columns give the bid-and-ask **bank discount interest rates** for the transaction. The bank discount rate is the annualized simple rate of return based on the *face* (par) value of the security—that is, the value of the T-bill when it is redeemed at maturity, using a 360-day year. The ask price in column 4 refers to the discount interest rate when purchasing a T-bill, whereas the bid price in column 3 refers to the discount rate for a T-bill sale. Since an increase in the interest rate causes fixed-income security prices to decrease (and vice versa), the larger interest rate for the bid means that a *lower* price is received when a T-bill is sold in comparison to buying at the ask price. Note that the dealer for the T-bills buys at the lower bid price and sells at the higher ask price; the trader sells at the bid and buys at the ask price. Thus, the difference between the bid and ask prices is the dealer's commission.

The sixth column in the quotations shows the **bond equivalent yield**—that is, the rate of return on the *amount invested* in terms of the ask price. Since T-bills are sold at a discount from the par value, the return on invested funds (the bond equivalent yield) is larger than the return on the par value (the bank discount interest rate). When a T-bill has a maturity in excess of 182 days, then the yield is adjusted downward to be comparable to T-bonds that pay coupons semiannually (creating a compound interest effect).

EXHIBIT 2-3
T-Bill Quotations

PANEL A: SELECTED DEALER CASH T-BILL QUOTES
Treasury bill quotes in hundredths, quoted on terms of a rate of discount. Days to maturity calculated from settlement date. Yields are to maturity and based on the asked quote. Latest 13-week and 26-week bills are boldfaced.

Maturity	Days to Maturity	Bid	Asked	Ask Chg.	Yld.
Jan 23	7	3.80	3.70	−0.02	3.76
Jan 30	14	3.69	3.59	+0.03	3.65
Feb 06	21	3.77	3.67	+0.05	3.74
Apr 02	77	3.80	3.78	−0.01	3.87
Apr 09	84	3.79	3.77	−0.02	3.87
Apr 16	**91**	**3.82**	**3.80**	....	**3.90**
Apr 23	98	3.83	3.81	....	3.91
Apr 30	105	3.83	3.81	+0.01	3.92
Jul 09	175	3.87	3.85	+0.01	3.99
Jul 16	**182**	**3.87**	**3.85**	....	**3.99**
Jul 30	196	3.87	3.85	....	3.99
Dec 17	336	3.95	3.93	....	4.11
Jan 14	364	3.97	3.95	−0.01	4.14

PANEL B: REPRESENTATIVE QUOTES

(1) Maturity	(2) Days to Maturity	(3) Bid	(4) Ask	(5) Chg	(6) Yield
		Discount			
April 16	91	3.82	3.80	....	3.90
June 18	154	3.83	3.81	−.01	3.94
October 22	280	3.91	3.89	−.01	4.05

Source: Cash T-bill dealers, January 14.

TREASURY BILLS: CALCULATING PRICES AND YIELDS

Equations (2-3) through (2-5) are used for determining, respectively, the price of a T-bill, the bank discount rate, and the bond-equivalent yield for a specific period of time. Note that the bond-equivalent yield uses 365 days for the year while the other formulations employ a 360-day year. The 360-day year for T-bill calculations is the Treasury's procedure for calculating T-bill discounts and prices. Note that the bank discount rate misstates the true yield for two reasons: first, the face value rather than the investment amount is used; and second, a 360-day year is employed rather than the true 365-day year. These simplifications started decades ago to promote ease of use.[4]

$$P = F - \frac{(i_d)(F)(N)}{360} \tag{2-3}$$

$$i_d = \frac{(F - P)}{F} \cdot \frac{360}{N} \tag{2-4}$$

$$BEY = \frac{(F - P)}{P} \cdot \frac{365}{N} \tag{2-5}$$

where P = price of T-bill

i_d = discount interest rate

F = face or par value

N = number of days until maturity

BEY = bond-equivalent yield

Example 2-1 employs the above equations to determine the price and bond-equivalent yield of a cash T-bill. Note that using the bid versus ask rate (whether one is selling or buying the T-bill) provides slightly different results for the price and yield values.

T-Bill Futures

Treasury bill futures contracts started to trade in January 1976 on the International Monetary Market (IMM) of the Chicago Mercantile Exchange. They were the first short-term interest rate futures contracts to trade. Thus, T-bill futures are useful in protecting against short-term interest rate changes, such as for loans where the interest rate is based on a short-term interest rate. The mid 1970s to 1982 proved to be a very volatile period for short-term rates, accounting for the popularity, and to a large extent the very development of, the T-bill futures contract during this time period.

T-bill futures are based on a 90-day cash T-bill instrument with a face value of $1 million. If the futures contract is kept until expiration, then the owner (long position) of the futures receives cash T-bills with a 90-day maturity and a face value of $1 million.[5] The 360-day year convention for cash T-bills is also used for the futures. Each one **basis point** change ($\frac{1}{100}$ of 1% or .01%) in the T-bill futures price index causes a

---

[4] Although the equations given here are those typically presented, they do ignore the compounding effect on the annualized return of reinvesting funds from a maturing T-bill into a new T-bill. Stigum (1981, 1983) provides alternative (complicated) formulations for these equations that consider compounding. Stigum's equations take into account the reinvestment of the coupons one would receive if an equivalent bond issue was held. This coupon effect also needs to be considered for T-bills with maturities in excess of 182 days.

[5] Delivery is possible on any one of three days. Thus, the seller of the futures contract can substitute a 91- or 92-day cash T-bill for the 90-day contract maturity specified by the futures, with the appropriate interest payment (price) adjustment.

EXAMPLE 2-1
Calculating T-Bill Prices and Yields

Equations (2-3) and (2-5) show how to determine the price and bond-equivalent yield of a Treasury bill, given the discount yield. Alternatively, Equation (2-4) calculates the discount rate if the price of the T-bill is known. The following information is employed to determine the price and bond-equivalent yield for a T-bill:

Maturity date: 1/14	Discount ask interest rate: 6.31
Current date: 10/19	Face (maturity) value: $100,000

The ask rate is used since one buys at the ask. Using Equation (2-3) to find the price of the T-bill, we have

$$\text{Price} = \$100,000 - [(.0631)(\$100,000)(87)/360]$$

$$= \$100,000 - \$1524.92$$

$$= \$98,475.08$$

The number of days are calculated as the actual number of days from the current date to maturity; for this example,

October: There are 12 days between October 19 and 31 (the 19th is not counted as a day to receive interest).

November: 30 days.

December: 31 days.

January: 14 days until maturity.

To find the bond-equivalent yield we employ Equation (2-5) as follows:

$$\text{Bond-equivalent yield} = [(\$100,000 - \$98,475.08)/\$98,475.08](365/87)$$

$$= (.0154854)(4.1954023)$$

$$= 6.497$$

$25 change in the value of the contract. Hence, a 1% change in interest rates (a 100 basis point change) creates a $2500 change in value.[6] Exhibit 2-4 illustrates the interest rate futures quotations. The examples used in this chapter are taken from these quotes.

The interest rates associated with T-bill futures are quoted in terms of the bank discount rate, or annualized rate of return on the *face value*, in order to be consistent with the cash T-bill quotations. The T-bill futures "price" is actually an index value, with the index value equal to 100.00 minus the discount interest rate; that is, $I = 100 - D$. This index value system for T-bill futures reduces confusion. The logic of the T-bill futures quotation procedure is for long positions in the futures market to make money when the index increases and to lose money when the index declines. The reason is that

---

[6] The $25 = 1 basis point is determined as follows: 1% of $1 million = $10,000; consequently, 1 basis point ($\frac{1}{100}$ of 1%) = $100; since the contract is for a 90-day T-bill, we have $100 × $\frac{90}{360}$ = $25.

EXHIBIT 2-4
Interest Rate Futures Quotations

	Open	High	Low	Settle	Chg	Yield Settle	Yield Chg	Open Interest
Treasury Bonds (CBT)—$100,000; pts. 32nds of 100%								
Mar	103–19	103–31	102–23	103–10	−16	7.673	+.048	304,584
June	102–17	102–29	101–23	102–90	−16	7.773	+.048	27,327
Sept	101–19	101–28	100–28	101–09	−16	7.872	+.050	7,644
Dec	100–22	100–30	100–01	100–12	−15	7.962	+.047	5,598
Mr	100–05	100–05	99–07	99–18	−14	8.044	+.044	1,280

Est vol 450,000; vol Mon 268,027; op int 346,756, −10,772.

	Open	High	Low	Settle	Chg	Yield Settle	Yield Chg	Open Interest
Treasury Notes (CBT)—$100,000; pts. 32nds of 100%								
Mar	105–07	105–09	103–24	104–20	−25	7.339	+.108	117,817
June	104–06	104–08	102–25	103–19	−25	7.483	+.109	2,502

Est vol 60,000; vol Mon 41,221; open int 120,343, +7,168.

	Open	High	Low	Settle	Chg	Yield Settle	Yield Chg	Open Interest
5 Yr Treas Notes (CBT)—$100,000; pts. 32nds of 100%								
Mar	05–245	105–26	104–27	105–13	−16	6.709	+.115	118,967
June	104–19	104–27	103–30	04–165	−14	6.917	+.102	2,531

Est vol 81,031; vol Mon 26,868; open int 121,498, +6,302.

	Open	High	Low	Settle	Chg	Yield Settle	Yield Chg	Open Interest
2 Yr Treas Notes (CBT)—$200,000, pts. 32nds of 100%								
Mar	104–22	104–24	104–13	04–205	−6	5.517	+.097	17,124

Est vol 1,200; vol Mon 709; open int 17,124, +57.

	Open	High	Low	Settle	Chg	Yield Settle	Yield Chg	Open Interest
Muni Bond Index (CBT)—$1,000; times Bond Buyer MBI								
Mar	96–18	96–27	96–06	96–12	−9	97–20	88–00	20,893
June	96–03	96–03	95–17	95–25	−7	97–02	93–04	145

Est vol 3,000; vol Mon 1,683; open int 21,038, −207.
The index: Close 96–22; Yield 6.68.

	Open	High	Low	Settle	Chg	Interest Rate	Chg	Open Interest
30–Day Interest Rate (CBT)—$5 million; pts. of 100%								
Jan	95.97	95.97	95.96	95.96	−.01	4.04	+.01	1,697
Feb	96.04	96.04	96.01	96.03	−.01	3.97	+.01	2,044
Mar	96.05	96.05	96.02	96.04	−.02	3.96	+.02	1,564

Est vol 1,422; vol Mon 5563; open int 7,612, +73.

	Open	High	Low	Settle	Chg	Interest Rate	Chg	Open Interest
Treasury Bills (IMM)—$1 mil.; pts. of 100%								
Mar	96.17	96.25	96.15	96.21	−.03	3.79	+.03	38,404
June	96.07	96.12	96.97	96.08	−.04	3.92	+.04	14,324
Sept	95.78	95.85	95.63	95.76	−.10	4.24	+.10	2,453
Dec	95.30	95.30	95.20	95.27	−.12	4.73	+.12	446

Est vol 8,771; vol Mon 6,227; open int 55,669, +1,162.

continued next page

						Yield		*continued* Open
	Open	High	Low	Settle	Chg	Settle	Chg	Interest
LIBOR—1 Mo (IMM)—$3,000,000; pts. of 100%								
Feb	95.88	95.91	95.78	95.85	−.07	4.15	+.07	6,841
Mar	95.88	95.90	95.77	95.84	−.06	4.16	+.06	3,438
Apr	95.89	95.91	95.79	95.87	−.06	4.13	+.06	2,202
Est vol 2,441; vol Mon 3,597; open int 22,196, +1,548.								
Eurodollar (IMM)—$1 million; pts of 100%								
Mar	95.83	95.89	95.75	95.83	−.06	4.17	+.06	289,724
June	95.62	95.67	95.49	95.62	−.07	4.38	+.07	209,926
Sept	95.32	95.38	95.11	95.24	−.15	4.76	+.15	160,764
Dec	94.70	94.80	94.51	94.65	−.19	5.35	+.19	108,419
Mr	94.46	94.55	94.27	94.38	−.21	5.62	+.21	92,765
June	94.02	94.11	93.85	93.95	−.21	6.05	+.21	64,700
Sept	93.66	93.72	93.45	93.56	−.21	6.44	+.21	46,292
Dec	93.17	93.21	92.94	93.06	−.22	6.94	+.22	38,190
Mr	93.11	93.17	92.89	92.98	−.23	7.02	+.23	34,788
June	92.88	92.94	92.66	92.74	−.24	7.26	+.24	24,251
Sept	92.67	92.72	92.41	92.52	−.25	7.48	+.25	17,123
Dec	92.30	92.35	92.14	92.15	−.25	7.85	+.25	13,229
Mr	92.38	92.40	92.14	92.17	−.25	7.83	+.25	12,791
June	92.24	92.26	92.00	92.03	−.25	7.97	+.25	9,739
Sept	92.10	92.12	91.87	91.89	−.25	8.11	+.25	8,260
Dec	91.91	91.93	91.69	91.70	−.25	8.30	+.25	7,680
Est vol 442,374; vol Mon 323,817; open int 1,138,641, −11,757								

Source: Exchange quotes, January 15.

interest *rates* change in the *opposite* direction to the price of fixed-rate instruments. Thus, as interest rates go *down* 1 basis point, the index value goes *up* 1 basis point, with long positions making money as the index value increases. The discount change in the next to last column of the table shows the difference in basis points from the previous day's close. Since each contract has a face value of $1 million, the total face value for all T-bill futures contracts traded was in excess of $8.7 billion for this day, with the total open interest (the last column) being in excess of $55 billion. Example 2-2 describes the quotation procedure for the T-bill futures, quotes shown in Exhibit 2-4.

T-bill futures expire according to the financial cycle of March, June, September, and December. Eight expirations (two years of contracts) trade at any one time; however, there is limited activity after the first three expiration months. Trading during the month of expiration ceases on the first day during the month when a 13-week T-bill is issued *and* an originally issued one-year T-bill has 13 weeks *remaining* until maturity. Although this procedure does cause the specific delivery day to change significantly from one expiration month to another since the delivery day must correspond to two separate cash T-bill maturities, it increases the amount of cash T-bills available for

EXAMPLE 2-2
Interpreting T-Bill Futures Quotations

Treasury bill futures: $1 mil; points of 100%

	Settle	Chg	Discount Settle	Chg
Mar	96.21	−.03	3.79	+.03

	Close	Change
Index Settle	96.21	−.03
Discount Settle	3.79	+.03
	100.00	.00

The T-bill index closing value and the discount rate close always add to 100. Thus, 100 minus discount = index, and vice versa. The quote above is for a closing index value of 96.21, and therefore the discount interest rate for the futures contract must be 3.79%.

The change in the index value from the previous day is −.03 or a decline in value of −.03 × $2500 = −$75 for those holding a long position in futures. Since the index and discount values add to 100, the change for the discount value from the previous day must be +.03. Thus, the "changes" for the index and discount values are the same, but they have opposite signs.

Note that the close of 96.21 for the index typically differs from the next day's open. There is no requirement that the close and the next day's open be the same value, since new information overnight and supply-and-demand factors can change the price that traders are willing to pay for the futures contract.

delivery into the futures contract. Exhibit 2-5 summarizes the characteristics of T-bill futures and the other interest rate futures contracts examined below.

Figure 2-4 shows the extent of the fluctuation in T-bill interest rates since the inception of the T-bill futures contract in 1976. The figure shows the significant increase and volatility of short-term interest rates in the late 1970s and early 1980s, with each 1% change in interest rates creating a $2500 gain or loss for each futures contract. In particular, the decline in rates from 15% to almost 6% in late 1979 and early 1980 translates to a profit or loss of almost $22,500 per contract (on a deposit of $1500 per contract). Chapter 3 presents more extensive examples of speculation. In early 1992, short-term T-bill rates dropped below 4%, the lowest level since T-bill futures started to trade.

Eurodollar Time Deposits

Eurodollars are U.S. dollars that are deposited in a bank outside the United States or in an International Banking Facility (IBF) in the United States. Eurodollars are the

EXHIBIT 2-5
Characteristics of Interest Rate Futures Contracts

Futures Contract	Trading Unit	Deliverable Instrument	Price Quotation	Minimum Price Change		Last Trading Day	Last Delivery Day
				Units	Dollars		
T-bills	$1,000,000	90-day T-bill	Index	.01	$25	(1)	(1)
Eurodollar	$1,000,000	Cash	Index	.01	$25	(2)	(3)
1-month LIBOR	$3,000,000	Cash	Index	.01	$25	(2)	(3)
T-bonds	$100,000	(4)	% of par: points and 32nds	$\frac{1}{32}$	$31.25	(5)	Last day of month
T-notes Ten-Year	$100,000	(6)	Same as T-bonds	$\frac{1}{32}$	$31.25	(5)	Last day of month
Five-Year	$100,000	(7)	(8)	$\frac{1}{64}$	$15.625	(5)	Last day of month
Municipals	$1000 × index	Cash	Same as T-bonds	$\frac{1}{32}$	$31.25	(5)	(3)

(1) Trading for T-bill futures ceases on the first day during the month when 13-week T-bill is issued *and* a one-year T-bill has 13 weeks remaining until delivery. The following day is the delivery day.
(2) Second London business day before third Wednesday of the expiration month.
(3) No delivery since contract is settled in cash.
(4) Any cash T-bond that is noncallable and has at least 15 years to maturity on the first day of the delivery month are deliverable; callable bonds with at least 15 years to the first call date are deliverable.
(5) The eighth to last business day of the delivery month.
(6) Any cash T-note maturing in at least 6½ years, but not more than 10 years, from the first day of the delivery month.
(7) Any cash T-note maturing in at least 4¼ years, but not more than 5¼ years, from the first day of the delivery month.
(8) Same as T-bonds and Ten Year T-notes, except that the Five Year Notes are quoted in one-half of ¹⁄₃₂ of a point.
Note: All interest rate contracts trade on a March, June, September, and December expiration cycle.
Source: Exchange pamphlets

most important vehicle for international trade and investment activity. For example, 80% of the trade with Latin America is completed in Eurodollars.[7]

Eurodollar time deposits reflect the short-term interest rate paid for commercial deposits of U.S. dollars by financial institutions operating outside the U.S. banking system. Hence, a Eurodollar time deposit is simply a bank or corporate savings account that pays market interest rates. Similarly, Eurodollar loan rates refer to the cost of borrowing funds from these same financial institutions. The typical Eurodollar deposit or loan is for 30 or 90 days, with interest rates calculated on the basis of a 360-day year.

[7] Financial institutions located in London actively trade in "Eurodollars" because of the importance of the dollar for trade purposes. Offshore branches of United States banks, as well as foreign banks, use Eurodollars both to transact trade financing and as an investment vehicle for short-term funds. International Banking Facility funds are a Eurodollar product that provide Edge Act banks in the United States with a low-risk product possessing substantial trading potential.

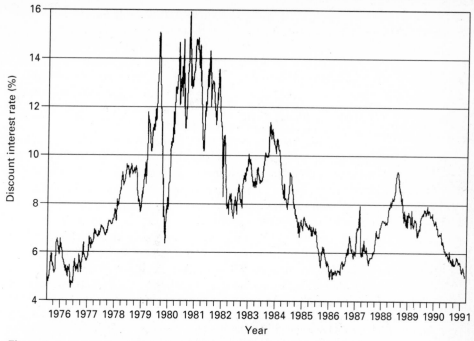

Figure 2-4 T-bill futures interest rate. (*Source:* Data from Tick Data, Inc.)

Eurodollar rates are quoted in terms of a simple **money market yield** basis in terms of a 360-day year. A deposit of $1 million for 90 days at 5% would generate $12,500 of interest ($1,000,000 × .05 × $^{90}/_{360}$). A quote of 5.1–5.2 is the bid-and-ask rates for a Eurodollar deposit and a Eurodollar loan, respectively. These rates are for interbank deposits and loans; corporate loan rates are higher because of the greater risk. Unlike other investments, time deposits are not actively traded in the secondary market.

Eurodollar rates tend to parallel U.S. short-term interest rates; however, they are higher than U.S. rates since some credit risk exists with these institutions and because the non-U.S. financial institutions are not bound by the reserve requirements that restrict U.S. banks.[8] A full range of Eurodollar time deposit maturities is available to traders; selected maturities for Eurodollar deposits are given in the "Money Rates" section of *The Wall Street Journal*, listed as "London Interbank Offer Rates—LIBOR."

Eurodollar Futures

The Chicago Mercantile Exchange added Eurodollar time deposit contracts to its futures list in December 1981. Eurodollar futures are similar to T-bill contracts in concept, since both are based on short-term $1 million contracts and use the financial

---

[8] The existence of reserve requirements for U.S. banks means that they cannot loan out all of their funds, and thus the interest rate they can pay on deposited funds is reduced; non-U.S. banks do not have this restriction. Grabbe (1991) provides an interesting historical development of the Eurodollar market as well as an in-depth discussion of the international financial markets.

cycle months for expirations. Eurodollar futures initiated trading and became popular because of the importance of the U.S. dollar in international trade and the activity of the dollar deposits in the London financial market. This popularity soon made the Eurodollar futures more active than T-bill futures. Eurodollar futures are used to hedge loans based on LIBOR and for other floating-rate obligations such as interest rate swap agreements.

The quoting procedure for Eurodollar futures is similar to the T-bill futures contracts, except that the interest rate is based on a money market yield (with a 360-day year) rather than a bank discount rate in order to correspond with the cash Eurodollar time deposit market. Also note that T-bill futures are based on a specific tradable security, whereas Eurodollar time deposits are not a security and hence are not actively traded. Since Eurodollar time deposits are not a security, Eurodollar futures settle in cash rather than through the delivery of a financial instrument.

Originally six expiration months traded at one time; now 28 expirations (seven years) trade concurrently. Years eight to ten will be added later. Also, a one-year combination of Eurodollar futures for years six and seven will trade. Several years ago, Eurodollar futures surpassed T-bill futures as the most active short-term interest rate contract. Eurodollar futures have a much larger volume than the S&P 500 Stock Index futures and are the only futures contracts to have more than one million contracts of open interest.

One-Month LIBOR Futures

In 1990 the CMEX started to trade 30-day LIBOR Time Deposit futures contracts. The 30-day LIBOR futures are based on a $3-million, 30-day time deposit. Expirations months are the next seven consecutive months, with four to five months being active. Each basis point is worth $25, and the contract settles in cash. This type of futures is most useful for strategies involving overnight to one-month interest rates.[9]

TREASURY BONDS, T-NOTES, AND THEIR FUTURES

Treasury Bonds and Notes

Treasury bonds and notes are long-term debt instruments of the U.S. government. Treasury bonds are originally sold with maturities of ten years or more, while Treasury notes have maturities of one to ten years. Treasury securities trade in excess of $3 billion daily. Government and corporate bond trades of $100,000 or more are transacted via the bond dealer network, with $1-million trades being typical. Such a network developed because of the large increase in the use of debt by the government and by

---

[9] In late 1988 the CBT started to trade futures based on a weighted average of the Federal Reserve (Fed) funds interest rate to date and an *N*-day term interest rate. These futures contracts expire on a monthly cycle. The CBT contract is based on $5 million of Fed funds and is quoted by taking 100 minus the interest rate. The size of each 1 basis point is $41.67, and the contract settles on the last day of the expiration month. The CBT contract has a volume of less than 1000 contracts per day.

corporations over the past 25 years. The debt markets are "over-the-counter" or telephone markets. Transactions are completed by telephone between the market participant wanting to make a trade (say a regional bank) and one of the major bond dealers. Dealers and financial institutions trading in Treasuries concentrate on the **bellwether** bond—that is, the most recently issued Treasury bond with the current coupon. This bond has the greatest liquidity. Noncurrent bonds are called "off-the-run"; the price of such bonds is affected by coupon, maturity, and liquidity differentials from the bellwether bond.

Once one realizes that previously issued fixed-income securities must change in price when the interest rate in the economy changes, then the need to trade these securities to realize gains and to avoid losses becomes evident. If one adds to this situation the necessity for liquidity by many of the market participants, then the potential for debt market instruments becomes apparent.

Quoting Long-Term Treasury Instruments

Exhibit 2-6 presents the quotations of Treasury bonds and notes. Panel A of Exhibit 2-7 selects several of these quotes for discussion. Column 1 in panel A shows the stated annual interest rate on the face value of the bond or note. A stated rate of $9\frac{1}{2}$ means that the bond pays 9.5% interest per year on the face value of the bond. Treasury bonds and notes pay interest on the face value of the bond. Treasury bonds and notes pay interest semiannually and trade in denominations as small as $1000 and as large as hundreds of thousands of dollars. Column 2 indicates the month and year for the maturity of the security. A "p" or "n" after the maturity shows that the instrument is a "note"; otherwise it is a bond. A range of years (e.g., 95–00) indicates a **callable bond;** that is, the bond is initially callable by the government during or after the first year listed (1995). If the bond is not called by the last year shown (2000), then it will mature during that year. Government bonds had a history of not being called until 1991, when the government announced it would call several issues in 1992.

Prices of bonds are given in terms of a *percentage* of par, with the numbers to the right of the colon indicating the number of 32nds. Thus, 109:09 means $109\frac{9}{32}$ as a percentage of par. If par is $1000, then the price would be $1092.81, since $\frac{9}{32} = .281$. A price of 118:24 means $118\frac{24}{32}$ as a percentage of par, or $1187.50 per $1000 bond, since $\frac{24}{32} = .75$. The yield states the bond equivalent yield—that is, the promised rate of return on the investment. A trader buys at the higher ask price and sells at the lower bid price. Bid-ask spreads for liquid bonds typically are $\frac{2}{32}$'s to $\frac{4}{32}$'s.

Appendix 1A covers interest rate and bond price relationships. Recall that bond prices and interest rates move in opposite directions and that the yield to maturity of a bond is the promised annual return from the bond's coupons and price change.

Treasury Bond Futures

The Chicago Board of Trade introduced Treasury Bond futures in August 1977. The T-bond contract is used by speculators and hedgers of long-term interest rates. The huge government bond market could no longer function effectively without T-bond and T-note futures contracts. For example, when the government sells new T-bonds and

EXHIBIT 2-6
Selected T-Bond and T-Note Quotations

Representative over-the-counter quotations based on transactions of $1 million or more. Treasury bond and note quotes are as of mid-afternoon. Colons in bid-and-asked quotes represent 32nds; 101:01 means 101$\frac{1}{32}$. Net changes in 32nds. n = Treasury note. Yields are to maturity and based on the asked quote. For bonds callable prior to maturity, yields are computed to the earliest call date for issues quoted above par and to the maturity date for issues below par.

Rate	Maturity Mo/Yr	Bid	Asked	Chg.	Ask Yld.	Rate	Maturity Mo/Yr	Bid	Asked	Chg.	Ask Yld.
7⅛	Oct 93n	103:23	103:25	−4	4.84	3½	Nov 98	97:28	98:28	−4	3.69
6	Oct 93n	101:26	101:28	−4	4.89	8⅞	Nov 98n	110:29	110:31	−27	6.84
7¾	Nov 93n	104:28	104:30	−3	4.90	6⅜	Jan 99n	97:27	97:29	−25	6.76
8⅝	Nov 93	106:11	106:13	−4	4.92	8⅞	Feb 99n	111:00	111:02	−28	6.88
9	Nov 93n	107:01	107:03	−3	4.90	8½	May 94-99	105:25	106:01	−11	5.70
11¾	Nov 93n	111:26	111:28	−4	4.89	9⅛	May 99n	112:12	112:14	−29	6.93
5½	Nov 93n	100:30	101:00	−4	4.93	8	Aug 99n	106:00	106:02	−27	6.96
5	Dec 93n	100:01	100:03	−4	4.95	7⅞	Nov 99n	105:06	105:08	−29	6.99
7⅝	Dec 93n	104:29	104:31	−3	4.93	7⅞	Feb 95-00	104:07	104:11	−10	6.30
7	Jan 94n	103:25	103:27	−3	4.95	8½	Feb 00n	108:29	108:31	−26	7.03
6⅛	Feb 94n	103:18	103:20	−4	5.02	8⅞	May 00n	111:06	111:08	−28	7.07
8⅞	Feb 94n	107:15	107:17	−4	5.02	8⅜	Aug 95-00	106:09	106:13	−12	6.35
9	Feb 94	107:22	107:26	−4	5.00	8¾	Aug 00n	110:16	110:18	−27	7.09
8½	Mar 94n	107:00	107:02	−6	5.08						
7	Apr 94n	103:30	104:00	−7	5.09		⋮				
4⅛	May 89-94	97:28	98:28	−2	4.64	7⅞	Nov 02-07	104:09	104:13	−26	7.28
7	May 94n	103:28	103:30	−6	5.18	8⅜	Aug 03-08	107:23	107:27	−28	7.36
9½	May 94n	109:09	109:11	−6	5.19	8¾	Nov 03-08	110:18	110:22	−29	7.38
13⅛	May 94n	117:06	117:08	−9	5.17	9⅛	May 04-09	113:27	113:31	−28	7.38
						10⅜	Nov 04-09	124:12	124:16	−26	7.39
	⋮					11¾	Feb 05-10	136:00	136:04	−27	7.39
8½	Apr 97n	108:24	108:26	−19	6.49	10	May 05-10	121:23	121:27	−26	7.40
8½	May 97n	108:24	108:26	−17	6.52	12¾	Nov 05-10	145:25	145:29	−26	7.39
8½	Jul 97n	108:25	108:27	−19	6.56	13⅞	May 06-11	156:20	156:24	−26	7.39
8⅝	Aug 97n	109:10	109:12	−20	6.59	14	Nov 06-11	158:26	158:30	−26	7.39
8¾	Oct 97n	109:28	109:30	−23	6.64	10⅜	Nov 07-12	126:15	126:19	−27	7.48
8⅞	Nov 97n	110:16	110:18	−25	6.66						
7⅞	Jan 98n	105:23	105:25	−23	6.69		⋮				
8⅛	Feb 98n	106:28	106:30	−24	6.72	7½	Nov 16	98:21	98:23	−16	7.62
7⅞	Apr 98n	105:20	105:22	−24	6.74	8⅜	May 17	112:21	112:23	−19	7.61
7	May 93-98	101:13	101:21	−7	5.69	8⅞	Aug 17	114:01	114:03	−20	7.62
9	May 98n	111:10	111:12	−26	6.76	9⅛	May 18	117:02	117:04	−20	7.61
8¼	Jul 98n	107:16	107:18	−27	6.79	9	Nov 18	115:23	115:25	−19	7.61
9¼	Aug 98n	112:24	112:26	−26	6.80	8⅞	Feb 19	114:07	114:09	−19	7.62
7⅛	Oct 98n	101:26	101:28	−28	6.77	8⅛	Aug 19	105:22	105:24	−19	7.62

Source: Bond dealers as reported to the Federal Reserve.

T-notes, all of the dealers hedge their positions in the long-term interest rate futures to reduce the risk of price changes for the billions of dollars of bonds and notes they buy. In addition, the initiation of a night trading session from Sunday through Thursday allows Japanese traders access to the T-bond futures contracts. Since Japanese investors hold significant quantities of U.S. T-bonds, this session becomes useful to Far Eastern traders. Night volume averages 15,000 to 20,000 contracts but can rise to more than 40,000 contracts on active evenings. The total daily open interest and volume values for the T-bond contracts in Exhibit 2-4 show the tremendous success that this contract enjoys. In particular, nearby open interest and total volume values make T-bond futures the most active of all futures contracts.

The yield to maturity in *The Wall Street Journal* for T-bond futures is based on a hypothetical T-bond with an 8% coupon, 20 years to maturity, and a $100,000 face value. In fact, the *WSJ* calculates the *semiannual* bond equivalent yield for the hypothetical 20-year, 8% bond and then simply *doubles* that yield, rather than considering the effect of compounding. However, *any* T-bond with at least 15 years to maturity (or 15 years to the first call date, if callable) can be used for delivery.[10] The benefit of allowing a number of bonds to be delivered is that it increases the liquidity for delivery purposes. A conversion process exists to adjust delivery prices for different bond coupons and maturities, as explained in Chapter 9. The pricing of this futures contract is based on the futures market's perception of the appropriate future long-term interest rate.

T-bond futures quotes are equivalent to cash T-bond quotes in that they trade in 32nds of a point, with the price shown being a percentage of the face value. Hence, the price of 103-10 for the March maturity in Exhibit 2-4 means $103^{10}/_{32}$ as a percent of the $100,000 face value of the contract. Each $1/_{32}$ of a point changes the value of the contract by $31.25, with $^{32}/_{32}$ creating a change of $1000. When interest rates rise above 8%, the prices of the T-bond futures contracts fall below the par value of 100, and vice versa.

Twelve separate futures expirations for the T-bond futures typically are traded at one time; that is, T-bond contracts are traded for the next three years. During the expiration month of the futures, the seller of the T-bond futures decides which day to deliver the cash T-bonds. *Any day* that the exchange is open within the expiration month of the futures can be used for delivery. This feature provides some interesting alternatives for the seller, as discussed in Chapter 9.

---

[10] Current callable cash Treasury bond issues have a five-year call provision. Hence, these bonds would need at least 20 years to maturity to be deliverable into the T-bond futures contract. The maturity requirement for the cash bonds is measured from the first day of expiration of the futures contract. Note that if there were a number of *different* Treasury bond futures contracts that employed special cash bonds with different coupons and/or years to maturity as the underlying cash instrument, a significant dilution in the liquidity and pricing stability of the futures contracts would occur.

EXHIBIT 2-7
Selected Bond Quotations

Panel A: Treasury Bonds and Treasury Notes

(1) Rate	(2) Maturity	(3) Bid	(4) Ask	(5) Yield
9½	May 94 n	109:09	109:11	5.19
8½	May 97 n	118:24	118:26	6.52
7⅞	Feb 95–00	104:07	104:11	6.30

Panel B: Corporate Bonds

Bond	(1) Coupon Rate and Maturity	(2) Current Yield	(3) Vol.	(4) Close	(5) Net Chg.
AT&T	7⅛ 03	7.3	495	98⅛	−⅜
Dow	8⅝ 08	8.5	35	102	…

Source: Exhibits 2-6 and 2-8.

FOCUS 2-2
The Intricacies of the Cash T-Bond Market

A network of dealers and brokers controls the trading in cash T-bonds. There are 39 primary T-bond dealers who serve as intermediaries between the Treasury and investors. Dealers buy T-bonds from the Treasury at regular auctions and then sell them to institutional investors. In fact, the Treasury and the bond dealers are so interrelated that William Niskanen, an economic advisor to Reagan, said "Government debt management has not been and is not substantially independent of the Street." (See Wessel, 1991 for an inside look at this relationship.) The scandal at Solomon Brothers, where Solomon traders cornered the market in at least one issue of new T-notes by circumventing rules on the amount of an issue to be held by one dealer, has caused a reevaluation of the relationship between the Treasury and the primary dealers.

When trading in bonds requires anonymity as well as liquidity, certain brokers serve as intermediaries for the dealers of bonds. The brokers do not hold inventories of bonds, nor do they take positions. Brokers post bids and offers for bonds on trading screens, where the bids and offers are communicated to the brokers by the dealers via telephone. The brokers do *not* reveal the dealer for which they are trading.

There are five major brokers on Wall Street: FBI, RMJ, Garvan, Candor-Fitzgerald, and Mabon Nugent. Position traders for the major dealers keep constant watch on the broker screens in order to change their bids and offers as warranted. These broker screens generally ensure an orderly market in T-bonds. However, on October 20, 1987, the bond market lost liquidity. Traders were unable to determine fair bid and offering levels. Whereas price dispersion normally ranges from ¹⁄₃₂ to ⅛ on active issues, on October 20 there were simultaneous price dispersions of up to 2 points. In fact, the bond markets moved so quickly that many dealers refused to show customers firm bid or offering prices.

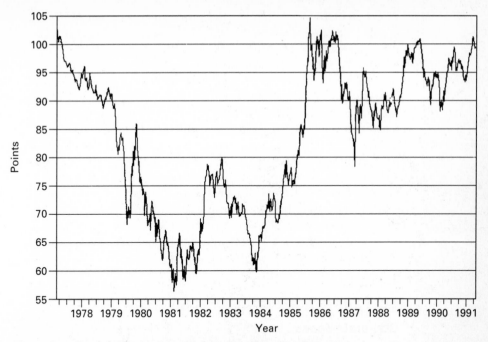

Figure 2-5 T-bond futures prices. (*Source:* Data from Tick Data, Inc.)

Figure 2-5 provides a graphical history of weekly T-bond futures prices. The figure shows that at the peak of long-term interest rates in 1981, T-bond futures prices were as low as 56-0. More important, each 5-point change in price translates to a profit/loss of $5000 per $100,000 par futures contract. The figure shows numerous times when the T-bond futures changed by 5 points or more.

Treasury Note Futures

Ten-Year Notes. The CBT introduced Ten-Year Treasury Note futures in May 1982. These T-note futures are based on a hypothetical T-note with a $100,000 face value, an 8% coupon, and ten years to maturity. Prices are a percentage of par, and each ¹⁄₃₂ of a point change is worth $31.25. T-notes (*not* T-bonds) with maturities of 6½ to 10 years are employed for delivery. These contracts help to fill the gap in maturities between the long-term T-bond futures and the short-term T-bill futures. The shorter maturity of the T-note does cause its price to be less volatile than T-bond futures as interest rates change and thus causes T-note futures to be a better hedging device for those debt portfolios with shorter maturity. The open interest and volume values for the "Treasury Note" futures in Exhibit 2-4 show that this contract has been successful, at least in terms of the nearby contract. Ten-year T-note futures currently trade six expiration months at one time, although only the first three are active.

Five-Year Notes.   The introduction of $100,000, 8% coupon, Five-Year T-note futures in 1988 allows more precise hedging of intermediate-term debt securities by filling in the term structure below the 10-Year T-note futures. Cash T-notes with maturities between $4\frac{1}{4}$ and $5\frac{1}{4}$ years are used for delivery purposes, as long as the original maturity was no more than $5\frac{1}{4}$ years. Thus, only 5-year T-notes issued over the life of the futures contract are deliverable. Consequently, the futures prices the *recently issued* 5-year T-notes. The pricing scheme is similar to the Ten-Year T-note futures, although the 5-year T-note is less volatile in nature. The Five-Year T-note futures are quoted as a percentage of par, with units of *one-half* of $\frac{1}{32}$ of a point. Thus, the June expiration price of 104-165 equals 104 and $^{16.5}\!/_{32}$ as a percentage of par, which is equivalent to $104^{33}\!/_{64}$. Each one-half of $\frac{1}{32}$ is worth $15.625. To date, the nearby contract is most liquid, but the first deferred contract also is tradable. Previous attempts to introduce shorter-term T-note futures were unsuccessful; specifically, a Four- to Six-Year T-note futures in June 1979 and a Two-Year T-note contract in January 1983 did not survive. A 1990 reintroduction of a Two-Year T-note futures has achieved limited volume but reasonable open interest.

CORPORATE AND MUNICIPAL BOND INSTRUMENTS

Corporate Bonds

Corporate bonds are long-term debt instruments issued by corporations. Daily quotations for institutional transactions are available via various data services, such as the Merrill Lynch bond pricing service. Merrill Lynch matrix pricing provides representative quotes for corporate issues even when the particular issue does not trade. Bond transactions of major corporations for fewer than 100 bonds (less than $100,000) are called "odd lots" and are typically traded on the New York Exchange. In fact, many of these trades involve ten or fewer bonds; any transaction of less than ten bonds *must* be executed on the trading floor under the Exchange's "Nine Bond Rule." Corporate bond quotations in *The Wall Street Journal* are based on NYE quotations; therefore, the *WSJ* prices are an inaccurate indication of the true price because of a lack of liquidity or because reported trades did not occur near the end of the day.

Panel B of Exhibit 2-7 provides some examples of the quotations for corporate bonds. Exhibit 2-8 gives a partial listing of the New York Exchange Bond listings. As with Treasury bonds, corporate bonds typically pay interest semiannually. Corporate bonds trade in units as small as $1000. The first number after the name of the corporation in column 1 of panel B in Exhibit 2-7 is the coupon rate for the bond; the second number represents the year of maturity. Thus, the AT&T bond has a $7\frac{1}{8}$% coupon rate of interest and matures in 2003. The second column states the current yield—that is, the interest received per year (the coupon) divided by the current price.

Column 3 in Exhibit 2-7, panel B, states the volume of bonds traded and column 4 gives the price of the last transaction for the bond. Corporate bond prices are percentages of par and are quoted in $\frac{1}{8}$-point intervals. Thus, the AT&T price of $98\frac{1}{8}$ means that the cost of a $1000 par value bond is $981.25. Column 5 states the change in price from the previous close.

EXHIBIT 2-8
Selected Corporate Bond Quotations

New York Exchange Corporation Bonds
Volume, $63,970,000

Bonds	Cur Yld	Vol	Close	Net Chg.	Bonds	Cur Yld	Vol	Close	Net Chg.
AMR 9s16	9.0	92	100	−½	ATT 7⅛03	7.3	495	98⅛	−⅜
AMR zr06	...	1	45¹/₃₂	...	ATT 8.80s05	8.5	258	103⅝	−½
ANR 10⅝95	10.4	10	102	−¼	ATT 8⅝s07	8.3	206	103⅝	+¾
AbbtL 9.2s99	8.8	16	104	+¼	ATT 8⅝26	8.4	728	103⅛	+⅛
Advst 9s08	cv	7	84½	+2	ATT 8⅝31	8.3	122	103½	...
AetnLf 8⅛07	8.1	10	100½	+½					
AlaP 9s2000	8.8	42	102¾	+¼					
AlaP 7¾s02	7.8	10	99⅜	...	Disney zr05	...	2174	53½	−⅝
AlaP 8⅞s03	8.6	20	103½	+¾	DmBk 7¾96	8.2	50	94	...
AlaP 8¼s03	8.1	22	102¼	+⅛	Dow 7.75s99	7.8	5	100	...
AlaP 9¾s04	9.4	12	103¾	−¼	Dow 8.92000	8.6	15	103⅜	−½
AlaP 10⅞05	10.3	4	106	−½	Dow 8½s05	8.4	5	101½	−½
AlaP 8¾07	8.5	10	102½	−⅛	Dow 8½s06	8.3	30	102½	+½
AlaP 9½08	9.1	10	103⅞	−1⅛	Dow 7⅞07	7.9	7	99¾	−⅛
AlskAr 6⅞14	cv	16	92	+7¾	Dow 8⅝08	8.5	35	102	...
AlskAr zr06	...	4	35¼	+¼	duPnt 8.45s04	8.2	67	103	...
AlldC zr96	...	16	75⅞	+⅜	duPnt 8½06	8.2	30	103⅛	−¼
AlldC zr2000	...	48	50	−¼	duPnt dc6S01	6.7	314	89¾	−¼
AlldC zr95	...	50	79	−¼	duPnt 8½16	8.4	54	101¾	−¼
AlldC zr97	...	80	66¾	...	duPnt zr10	cv	211	25⅛	...
AlldC zr99	...	90	55	−⅜	DukeP 7⅜01	7.4	3	100¼	+⅛
AlldC zr01	...	105	45⅝	−¼	DukeP 7⅜02	7.3	10	101¼	+1¼
AlldC zr09	...	160	22⅞	−⅛	DukeP 8⅛03	8.0	38	101	−½
Alcoa 7.45s96	7.5	20	99⅞	−⅛	DukeP 9¾04	9.3	14	104¹¹/₁₆	+³/₁₆
AAir 5¼98	6.3	6	84	...	DukeP 9½05	9.1	13	104¼	−⅛
ABrnd 9⅛16	8.5	3	107	+3½	DukeP 8⅛07	7.8	20	103¾	+¾
ACyan 8⅜06	8.3	50	101	...	DukeP 9⅜08	8.9	5	105	+⅛
AmStor 01	cv	122	98½	−½	DuqL 8¾00	8.6	5	101¼	−¾
ATT 5⅝95	5.7	71	99⅛	−⅛	DuqL 9s06	8.8	10	102½	+⅞
ATT 5½97	5.7	56	96¼	−¼	DuqL 8⅜07	8.1	6	102⅞	+3⅜
ATT 6s 00	6.5	95	92⅞	−⅛	EKod 8⅝16	8.5	885	101	+¼
ATT 5⅛01	6.0	199	85½	−¾	Ekod zr11	...	300	29⅛	+¼
ATT 7s 01	7.1	901	98⅜	−⅞	Eaton 9s16	8.8	25	102	+¼

Source: New York Bond Exchange, January 14.

Municipal Bonds

   Municipal bonds are long-term debt instruments issued by cities, counties, states, and other nonfederal government agencies. Dealers and financial institutions trade municipal bonds in a manner similar to other bonds. The benefit of holding a municipal bond is that the coupons received are not considered income for federal income tax purposes.

Most municipal bonds also are not taxed by the state or locality in which they are issued. Consequently, this tax-exempt benefit must be included in the calculation of the effective yield on a municipal bond. These bonds are quoted like corporate bonds—that is, as a percentage of par and in terms of ⅛ point.

Municipal Bond Futures

The CBT has traded the Municipal Bond Index futures contract since 1985. Municipal Bond futures are useful for dealers and hedgers and in the municipal bond market, since the interest rates on municipal debt can act differently than T-bond interest rates. The Municipal Bond Index, which substitutes for the underlying cash security, includes 40 actively traded, high-quality general obligation or revenue municipal bonds. As noted in Goodman (1987), bonds must have the following qualifications to be included in the Municipal Bond Index:

- Be rated A− or better by Standard & Poor's or A or better by Moody's.
- Be at least $50 million in size ($75 million for housing issues).
- Have a remaining maturity of at least 19 years.
- Be callable prior to maturity, with the first call date being between 7 and 16 years from the inclusion in the bond index.
- Must have been reoffered at a price ranging from 95 to 105.
- Have a fixed, semiannual coupon.

The value of the futures contract is determined by multiplying the Bond Buyer Municipal Bond Index by $1000. Five municipal bond dealers price the index daily, with the middle three quotes being used to form the index. Each bond is then divided by a conversion factor that simulates the price for a yield of 8%. The conversion factor makes each of the bonds approximately comparable in price movements. The 40 bonds are then averaged and multiplied by a coefficient that helps to maintain the continuity of the index when bonds in the index are changed (which can occur twice monthly). Some traders have criticized the calculation of the index, since the coefficient declines over time as a result of the price decline inherent in callable bonds. From 1983 to the end of 1990 the index declined from 1.0 to .8807, creating a declining volatility in the index. Hence, hedgers need to compensate for the lower index when using futures to reduce risk.

The contract expirations use the quarterly financial cycle, with the first two contracts being most active. As with other bond futures contracts, the Municipal Bond futures trade in 32nds, with ½₂ = $31.25. The eighth to last business day of the expiration month is the last day of trading. The contract settles in cash.

Other Futures Contracts

New financial futures contracts are constantly proposed and approved. Most do not survive. Examples of low-volume and dormant interest rate futures contracts are the 30-day Interest Rate futures, the Mortgage-Backed futures, and "DIFFs." At one time the exchanges proposed several macroeconomic futures contracts. For example, a

Consumer Price Index (inflation) contract traded for almost a year before volume disappeared. A prime interest rate contract was discussed for a number of years, but never traded. Wholesale price indexes, housing starts, and other similar contracts never were approved by the CFTC.

Futures contracts recently introduced, or planned for introduction, include various versions of fertilizer futures (such as diammonium phosphate), insurance futures, Clean Air futures (often dubbed acid rain or "pollution" futures), electricity futures, and S&P Midcap 400 Stock Index futures (see Taylor, 1991). One fertilizer contract has started trading and possesses reasonable support in the market. Health and property insurance futures have regulatory difficulties and skepticism from the insurance industry to overcome. The Clean Air futures will allow hedging of the pollution credits received by electricity producers. The S&P Midcap 400 futures will provide hedging opportunities for those holding midsize companies in their portfolios.

SUMMARY AND LOOKING AHEAD

This chapter covers the basic characteristics and quoting procedures for common stock indexes, cash bonds, and their related futures contracts. One must understand these characteristics and quoting procedures in order to comprehend the applications and techniques involved with futures contracts. The next chapter discusses the terminology and uses of futures markets.

BIBLIOGRAPHY

Goodman, Laurie S. (1987). "The Municipal Futures Contract," paper presented at the American Banker/Bond Buyer Conference on Futures and Options, New York, September 10–11.

Grabbe, J. Orlin (1991). *International Financial Markets,* 2d ed. New York: Elsevier.

Hamilton, Scott W. (1987). "Stock Portfolio Management with Program Trading and Futures," The First Boston Corporation, pamphlet.

Reilly, Frank K. (1989). *Investment Analysis and Portfolio Management,* 3d ed. Chicago: Dryden.

Stigum, Marcia (1981). *Money Market Calculations, Yields, Break-Evens, and Arbitrage.* Homewood, IL: Dow Jones Inc.

Stigum, Marcia (1983). *Money Markets,* 2d ed. Homewood, IL: Dow Jones, Inc.

Taylor, Jeffrey (1991). "A Boom Year for Newfangled Trading Vehicles," *The Wall Street Journal,* December 26, pp. C1, C10.

Wessel, David (1991). "Treasury and the Fed Have Long Caved in to 'Primary Dealers'," *The Wall Street Journal,* September 25, pp. A1, A12.

PROBLEMS

*Indicates more difficult problems.

2-1 Value of Stock Index Futures Contracts

The S&P 500 index, NYSE index, and MMI are given below. Determine the underlying cash value for that contract based on the closing price.

S&P 500 Index (CME) 500 Times Index

| Sept | 389.80 | 390.80 | 386.80 | 388.45 | −.50 | 396.20 | 304.00 | 136,325 |

NYSE Composite Index (NYFE) 500 Times Index

| Sept | 213.40 | 214.05 | 211.75 | 212.75 | −.30 | 194.60 | 113.00 | 6,051 |

Major Market Index (CBT) 500 Times Index

| Sept | 321.00 | 321.50 | 317.55 | 318.00 | −1.35 | 323.50 | 305.50 | 4,515 |

2-2 Speculator's Profits in T-Bond Futures

Mr. Rosenbaum is a T-bond futures trader. After a hectic day of trading, he wants to determine the day's profit/loss. Calculate his profit/loss.

Trade	Bought at	Sold at	Number of Bond Trades
1	77-25	77-28	6
2	78-12	78-13	4
3	78-05	78-03	3
4	78-16	78-17	12
5	78-22	78-23	21
6	78-05	78-07	10
7	77-25	77-23	5
8	77-27	77-26	2
9	77-31	78-02	2
10	78-01	78-02	5
11	78-00	77-30	10
12	77-15	77-17	18

2-3 Speculator's Profits in T-Bill Futures

You forecast that interest rates will rise. To speculate on your market expectations, you sell five T-bill futures contracts at 92.80 or a 7.20% interest rate.

a. How much will you gain or lose if the interest rate increases to 7.40%?

b. How much will you gain or lose if the interest rate decreases to 7.10%?

2-4 Value of T-Bond Futures Contracts

The table below lists the current prices for three T-bond futures expirations. Calculate the underlying cash *value* of each contract by using the settle price for each expiration.

	Open	High	Low	Settle
Mar	95-12	95-27	95-05	95-27
Jun	95-09	95-23	95-03	95-23
Sept	95-03	95-18	95-00	95-18

2-5 T-Bill Pricing and Bond-Equivalent Yield

Assuming a T-bill face value of $100,000, calculate the following for the 9/1 maturity if there are 114 days until it matures:

a. Price of the T-bill
b. Bond-equivalent yield
c. Discount rate

| Maturity | Discount | | Yield |
Date	Bid	Ask	
9/1	6.36	6.29	6.51
9/15	6.37	6.40	6.53
9/29	6.47	6.40	6.66

*2-6 T-Bill Maturity Date and Yield

The price of a Treasury bill is $99,260. If the discount ask rate is 5.92 and its value at maturity is $100,000, *find the maturity date* (the current date is February 20). Also, find the bond-equivalent yield.

2-7 Trading Stock Index Futures

Mr. Foreman trades stock index futures on the Chicago Mercantile Exchange. Today's transactions for the S&P 500 futures contract are listed below. Determine Mr. Foreman's profit/loss for the day. Set up a table.

Trade	Purchase Price	Sales Price	No. of Contracts
1	417.10	415.45	6
2	418.10	416.90	4
3	416.65	418.40	2
4	419.45	420.00	10
5	418.65	419.50	5
6	417.20	416.45	3
7	416.75	414.75	4
8	420.00	420.25	7
9	416.25	415.35	3
10	415.35	416.65	5

APPENDIX 2A
FOREIGN EXCHANGE MARKETS
AND THEIR FUTURES CONTRACTS

FOREIGN EXCHANGE

Foreign Exchange Markets

Foreign currency exchange (forex) is traded for most countries in the Western block that have active import/export dealings in the world market. Currencies are traded via telephone with major money center banks in large cities. The largest markets are in New York, London, and Tokyo; other major currency trades are located in Chicago,

Los Angeles, San Francisco, and Singapore. These banks typically deal in transactions of $1 million or more, although smaller orders are taken during quiet trading periods. Some regional banks take orders for less than $1 million and provide specialized services to their customers. Currently, more than $650 billion of foreign exchange is traded *daily,* making the currency markets the largest markets in the world. Most of this trading occurs in a few currencies such as the U.S. dollar, Japanese yen, German mark (Deutschemark), and British pound sterling. However, 90% of the currency trading takes place *with respect to* the U.S. dollar, causing the dollar to be what is known as a "vehicle currency." Thus, even cross-trades between two other currencies (say, the yen and mark), are quoted as a combination of two separate trades with the dollar (yen/$ and mark/$). This more complex method is done to reduce the number of quotations dealers need to make and to eliminate arbitrage possibilities if *pairs* of rates became mispriced in relation to one another.

Uses of Foreign Exchange

Banks initially provide foreign exchange trading as a service to corporations to obtain the corporation's international financing business. This service includes advice on market timing for forex trading, easy accessibility to traders, advice on the economies of the various countries, competitive currency rates, and an ability to handle a large volume of trading. Moreover, anks also employ foreign currency trading in order to achieve international branch banking asset-liability management, to limit the inventories of currencies in their trading departments, to provide liquidity for currencies traded, and to obtain international trade financing agreements. Trading by bank dealers to achieve currency balance can require dealing in a third currency to obtain the desired liquidity and risk exposure.

Finally, once dealer trading departments in banks are active, they also attempt to achieve profits by trading the foreign currencies for their own accounts. The purpose of such trading is to increase the overall return of the currency operations. These trading returns are generated from arbitrage with exchange rate differentials, commissions, and fees (including the bid-ask spread), and trading profits from taking positions in a currency.

Foreign Exchange Quotations

A currency quotation represents an exchange rate between the domestic currency and the designated foreign currency. Exhibit 2A-1 shows the foreign exchange quotations with respect to the U.S. dollar for selected countries. These quotations are labeled "Exchange Rates" in *The Wall Street Journal.* The quotations provide both the number of U.S. dollars needed to purchase one unit of the foreign currency (U.S. dollar equivalent or direct quotation) and the number of foreign currency units needed to purchase one U.S. dollar (currency per U.S. dollar or indirect quotation). Traders typically quote only the number of foreign currency units per U.S. dollar. For example, the value of the Japanese yen is stated in Exhibit 2A-1 as 126.85, which means that 126.85 yen are needed to obtain one U.S. dollar or that one dollar would by 126.85 yen. One exception to the indirect quoting of currency values by traders is the British pound, which is

EXHIBIT 2A-1
Selected Foreign Currency Rates and Currency Futures Quotations

EXCHANGE RATES
The New York foreign exchange selling rates below apply to trading among banks in amounts of $1 million and more, as quoted at 3 P.M. Eastern time by Bankers Trust Co., Telerate Systems Inc. and other sources. Retail transactions provide fewer units of foreign currency per dollar.

Country	U.S. $ Equiv.		Currency Per U.S. $	
	Tues.	Mon.	Tues.	Mon.
Argentina (Peso)	1.01	1.01	.99	.99
Australia (Dollar)...........	.7417	.7409	1.3483	1.3497
Britain (Pound)	1.7810	1.7990	.5615	.5559
30-day Forward	1.7705	1.7881	.5648	.5593
90-day Forward	1.7532	1.7704	.5704	.5648
180-day Forward	1.7280	1.7439	.5787	.5734
Canada (Dollar)	.8693	.8699	1.1503	1.1495
30-day Forward	.86667	.8675	1.1538	1.1528
90-day Forward	.8630	.8635	1.1588	1.1581
180-day Forward	.8574	.8581	1.1663	1.1653
France (Franc)	.18374	.18587	5.4425	5.3800
30-day Forward	.18279	.18486	5.0108	5.4095
90-day Forward	.18118	.18321	5.5193	5.4583
180-day Forward	.17891	.18082	5.5895	5.5305
Germany (Mark)	.6266	.6341	1.5960	1.5770
30-day Forward	.6236	.6310	1.6037	1.5849
90-day Forward	.6185	.6257	1.6169	1.5981
180-day Forward	.6111	.6180	1.6364	1.6182
Italy (Lira)	.0008306	.0008396	1204.01	1191.04
Japan (Yen).................	.007883	.007871	126.85	127.05
30-day Forward	.007875	.007863	126.98	127.18
90-day Forward	.007863	.007849	127.18	127.40
180-day Forward	.007854	.007835	127.33	127.63
Sweden (Krona)	.1720	.1738	5.8150	5.7530
Switzerland (Franc)	.7062	.7117	1.4160	1.4050
30-day Forward	.7039	.7093	1.4206	1.4098
90-day Forward	.6998	.7050	1.4290	1.4185
180-day Forward	.6940	.6989	1.4410	1.4308
SDR......................	1.40814	1.40611	.71016	.71118
ECU......................	1.29756	z	...	...

Special Drawing Rights (SDR) are based on exchange rates for the U.S., German, British, French and Japanese currencies. *Source:* International Monetary Fund.
European Currency Unit (ECU) is based on a basket of community currencies. *Source:* European Community Commission. z-Not available.

continued next page

continued

Currency Futures Quotations

	Open	High	Low	Settle	Change	Lifetime High	Lifetime Low	Open Interest
Japanese Yen (IMM) 12.5 million yen; $ per yen (.00)								
Mar	.7905	.7926	.7856	.7867	+.0013	.8114	.7000	53,749
June	.7889	.7912	.7844	.7853	+.0016	.8097	.7015	4,125
Est vol 25,243; vol Mon 16,558; Open int 62,258, +685.								
Deutschemark (IMM) 125,000 marks; $ per mark								
Mar	.6310	.6329	.6200	.6211	−.0068	.6575	.5353	54,832
June	.6227	.6244	.6120	.6134	−.0064	.6490	.5322	2,540
Est vol 63,440; vol Mon 39,923; Open int 57,886, −340.								
Canadian Dollar (IMM) 100,000 dirs.; $ per Can $								
Mar	.8668	.8682	.8636	.8646	−.0007	.8857	.8253	15,719
June	.8626	.8626	.8584	.8591	−.0007	.8820	.8330	1,864
Est vol 5,437; vol Mon 3,766; Open int 17,797, −599.								
British Pound (IMM) 62,500 pds.; $ per pound								
Mar	1.7876	1.7930	1.7600	1.7620	−.0158	1.8646	1.5560	19,885
June	1.7580	1.7650	1.7320	1.7358	−.0146	1.8346	1.6410	1,095
Est vol 18,116; vol Mon 11,293; Open int 21,078, −85.								
Swiss Franc (IMM) 125,000 francs; $ per franc								
Mar	.7119	.7137	.7006	.7022	−.0049	.7398	.6225	23,626
Est vol 24,438: vol Mon 17,152; Open int 24,354, −2,607.								
Australian Dollar (IMM) 100,000 dlrs.; $ per A.$								
Mar	.7428	.7432	.7373	.7374	+.0011	.7880	.7307	1,390
Est vol 386; vol Mon 434; Open int 1,398, +16.								
U.S. Dollar Index (FINEX) 500 times USDX								
Mar	86.76	88.08	86.55	87.96	+ .70	98.90	83.87	5,956
Est vol 3,619; vol Mon 2,583; Open int 6,154, +555.								
The index: High 86.87; Low 85.55; Close 86.81 +.63								

Source: Bank Currency Dealers and Futures Exchanges, January 14.

quoted in terms of the number of dollars needed to purchase one pound. Specifically, Exhibit 2A-1 quotes the British pound as $1.781. When a trade is executed for a currency, there is also a bid-ask spread between the sale price and the purchase price. The size of this bid-ask spread depends on the size of the market, the stability of the currency, and the desirability of the specific currency on the world currency markets.

The major currencies also have forward contracts. The 30-, 90-, and 180-day forward exchange rates listed in Exhibit 2A-1 refer to the number of days from the date of the transaction when the currency exchange will take place. Grabbe (1991) explains the intricacies of the cash and forward markets for currencies.

Figures 2A-1 and 2A-2 show the historical Japanese yen per dollar and German DM per dollar exchange rates from the mid 1970s to the early 1990s. The value of the dollar declined from 295 yen to the dollar in January 1977 to 133 yen in late 1991. More dramatically, there was a significant drop in the yen/dollar exchange rate from 295 to 180 in 1977 to 1978, and then a decline from 260 to 120 from March 1985 to December 1987. The German mark shows an even greater tendency for trends, declining from 2.60 DM/$ in 1976 to 1.70 DM/$ in 1979, then rising to 3.40 DM/$ in February 1985, before plunging to 1.60 DM/$ in December 1987. These extreme price moves provide opportunities for speculators in foreign exchange and currency futures, as well as illustrating periods where hedging is crucial for those dealing in foreign exchange markets.

Currency Futures

The International Monetary Market (IMM) of the Chicago Mercantile Exchange and the New York Cotton Exchange (CTN) trade currency futures. Currency trading began on the IMM in 1972 and therefore has the distinction of being the first financial futures contract.

IMM Contracts

The IMM of the CMEX actively trades currency futures contracts on the British pound, Canadian dollar, Japanese yen, Swiss franc, and German mark. The Australian dollar currently has minimal volume on the IMM, while the French franc and Mexican peso contracts are inactive. Each currency contract trades a specified number of units

Figure 2A-1 Exchange rate, yen per dollar. (*Source:* Rates from Tick Data, Inc.)

Figure 2A-2 Exchange rate, deutschemarks per dollar. (*Source:* Rates from Tick Data, Inc.)

of the foreign currency. For example, the futures quotations in Exhibit 2A-1 show that the British pound contract is based on 62,500 pounds, whereas the Japanese yen futures contracts are for 12.5 million yen. The number of units of the other foreign currencies used as the basis of the futures contract is listed with the futures quotations. When the seller of these futures delivers the foreign exchange, the buyer of the futures contract receives the number of units of the foreign currency at the existing futures exchange rate.

The quotes for the foreign currency futures contracts are all in dollars per foreign currency. For example, the March expiration of the Japanese yen contract has a settle price of .007867 dollar per yen, as shown in Exhibit 2A-1. Multiplying by 12.5 million yen for one contract results in a value of $98,337.50. Similarly, one can determine that a change of .000001 in the value of the contract is worth $12.50. The currency futures typically trade the next four expirations in the quarterly financial cycle, although the nearby expiration month is most active.

U.S. Dollar Index

The Cotton Exchange trades the U.S. Dollar Index. The purpose of this contract is to provide trading in an instrument based on the Federal Reserve's trade-weighted dollar index. The benefit of using the Index instead of a specific currency future is that a position is taken in the dollar, rather than taking a position solely in one other currency. The Index includes ten foreign currencies and trades as 500 times the geometric average of these currencies. The weights used in the Index for the individual currencies are

EXHIBIT 2A-2
Characteristics of Currency Futures Contracts

Futures Contracts	Trading Unit	Deliverable Instrument	Price Quotation	Minimum Price Change		Last Trading Day	Delivery Day
				Units	Dollars		
Currencies	(1)	Foreign currency	$/FC	Varies	Varies	2 trading days before 3rd Wed.	3rd Wed.
U.S. dollar	500	Cash	Index	.01	$5	3rd Wed.	3rd Wed.

(1) The number of units of the foreign currency (FC) for each specific futures contract is stated in the *WSJ.*
Note: All currency futures contracts trade on the March, June, September, and December expiration cycle (plus other months that are not active). Currencies trade from 7:20 A.M. to 2:00 P.M. Central time.
Source: Exchange pamphlets.

based on the associated countries' world trade values. The use of the geometric average shows the *percentage* change in the value of the dollar over time. Thus, a value of 87.96 for the March expiration indicates that the dollar has declined in value by 12.04% since the base period of March 1973. Each .01 of 1% change in value is worth $5. The exchange calculates a cash price of the Index each 30 seconds, based on bank trades of the dollar with the ten relevant currencies. The Reuter's Monitor network disseminates these values. Typically two expiration months have some activity. Exhibit 2A-2 provides a listing of the characteristics of the currency futures.

Cross-Rate Futures

The CMEX initiated futures in several popular cross-rates in 1991. For example, the mark-yen cross-rate represents the exchange rate ratio between the German mark and the Japanese yen. However, the cross-rate futures failed because of lack of volume. One reason for this failure had to do with the practice of settlement in dollars, which created a risk that the dollar would change in value before the appropriate currency exchange could be made. For this reason, the CMEX plans to resurrect the mark-yen cross-rate futures with settlement in yen. However, it is still uncertain whether a cross-rate futures can build sufficient volume when transactions in mark futures, yen futures, and the dollar create the equivalent position by using more liquid contracts. In addition, there is an active market in cash cross-rates by the money center banks.

BIBLIOGRAPHY FOR APPENDIX 2A

Grabbe, J. Orlin (1991). *International Financial Markets,* 2d ed. New York: Elsevier.

PROBLEMS FOR APPENDIX 2A

*Indicates more difficult problems.

2A-1 Speculator's Profits

As a foreign currency dealer you trade in Japanese yen, Swiss franc, and Deutschemark futures contracts. Below are quotes on these contracts from *The Wall Street Journal.*

Given the tick value of $12.50 for each futures contract, calculate the profit/loss for purchasing the June contracts at the open price and then selling each position at the respective close price. (*Hint:* Note the different quotation size for the yen.)

	Open	Close
Japanese yen: 12.5 million yen; $ per yen (.00)		
June	.7815	.7878
Swiss franc: 125,000 francs; $ per franc		
June	.7528	.7568
Deutschemark: 125,000 DM; $ per DM		
June	.6130	.6178

*2A-2 Currency Forward Rates

The following are the interbank selling rates for the spot and forward Deutschemark:

	U.S. $ Equiv.	Currency per U.S. $
Deutschemark	.5328	1.8768
30-day forward	.5343	1.8716
90-day forward	.5370	1.8623
180-day forward	.5410	1.8485

a. From the above table, give the total cash value price for immediate delivery (within two days) for the Deutschemark if you need 100,000 DM to pay for imports from Germany.
b. You plan to need 100,000 DM in six months. In order to insure against loss, you enter into a six-month forward contract. The forward rate on this contract is the price that you agree to pay in six months when the 100,000 DM are delivered. What is the six-month forward rate for the Deutschemark and the total cost for 100,000 DM?
c. Which is more expensive, 100,000 DM in the 180-day forward or in the cash market?

2A-3 Quoting Currency Futures

Based on the following information, determine the cash value in U.S. dollars for these futures expirations:
a. December for the Japanese yen
b. March for the German mark
c. December for the Canadian dollar
d. March for the British pound
e. December for the Swiss franc.

	Settle	Change
Japanese yen (IMM): 12.5 million yen; U.S. $ per yen (.00)		
Dec.	.7911	+.0013
Mar.	.7982	+.0013
German mark (IMM): 125,000 marks; U.S. $ per mark		
Dec.	.5583	+.0035
Mar.	.5628	+.0036

	Settle	Change
Canadian dollar (IMM): 100,000 dollars; U.S. $ per Can. $		
Dec.	.8306	−.0005
Mar.	.8278	−.005
British pound (IMM): 62,500 pounds; U.S. $ per pound		
Dec.	1.7528	+.0126
Mar.	1.7416	+.0126
Swiss franc (IMM): 125,000 francs; U.S. $ per franc		
Dec.	.6614	+.0035
Mar.	.6682	+.0035

APPENDIX 2B
METALS, ENERGY, AGRICULTURAL, AND FOREIGN FUTURES CONTRACTS

Metals and Energy Futures

Gold is the metal that receives the most attention in the cash and futures markets. Traders' interest in gold derives from its long-standing history as a store of value when currencies inflate or when there is political turmoil. Silver and platinum also are metals of worldwide interest, and each has an associated futures market. However, the depressed price of silver for the past decade has lessened the activity in that metal and its futures contract.

Gold is a particularly intersting asset since it does not earn interest or dividends; it is therefore referred to as a "pure commodity." This characteristic of gold is useful for illustrating the pricing of futures contracts, since intermediate cash flows do not complicate the calculations. For example, the difference between adjacent gold futures expirations reflects only the expected rate of interest for buying and storing gold.

The extreme fluctuation in oil prices in the past 20 years, resulting from variations in the use of oil in the industrialized world and the changing political activity in the Mideast, has created an active market for energy futures contracts. Heating oil, crude oil, and gasoline all have large volume and open interest figures. Natural gas has lower volume and open interest. These futures also help to provide a price discovery basis for cash oil prices.

Exhibit 2B-1 shows selected metal and energy futures quotations. The underlying value of each metal futures is determined by multiplying its quoted price by the number of ounces for the contract. For example, the underlying value of the January CMX gold futures contract is $35,460 (i.e., $345.60 × 100 oz). The energy futures are valued by multiplying the quoted dollar price per barrel or per gallon times the number of barrels or gallons per contract.

Agricultural and Commodity Futures

As shown in Exhibit 2B-2, agricultural products with associated futures contracts range from grains and oilseeds (such as wheat and corn) to meats (hog bellies and cattle) to other foods and fiber (e.g., cotton, coffee, and orange joice). Most agricultural products do not have centralized or telephone cash markets such as those existing

EXHIBIT 2B-1
Selected Metals and Energy Futures Quotations

Metals and Petroleum Futures

	Open	High	Low	Settle	Change	Lifetime High	Lifetime Low	Open Interest
Gold (CMX) 100 troy oz.; $ per troy oz.								
Feb	353.40	356.50	353.30	355.20	+.70	456.50	348.50	43,487
Apr	355.40	358.60	355.20	357.30	+.80	446.00	350.70	19,177
June	357.80	360.50	357.40	359.40	+.80	467.00	353.80	16,697
Aug	360.80	362.60	360.80	361.50	+.90	426.50	355.00	6,529
Est vol 27,000; vol Mon 20,393; Open int 103,972, −94.								
Silver (CMX) 5,000 troy oz.; cents per troy oz.								
Mar	403.5	412.5	403.5	410.0	+1.3	613.0	381.0	51,989
May	407.0	416.0	407.0	413.4	+1.3	589.0	384.5	15,988
July	414.0	417.0	413.5	416.7	+1.3	557.0	388.5	8,028
Sept	416.5	416.5	416.5	420.1	+1.3	483.0	395.0	1,946
Dec	420.5	428.0	420.5	425.4	+1.3	507.0	398.0	8,225
Est vol 21,000; vol Mon 11,407; Open int 94,723, −219.								
Crude Oil, Light Sweet (NYM) 1,000 bbls.; $ per bbl.								
Feb	18.62	18.90	18.45	18.47	−.32	27.00	17.50	50,322
Mar	18.75	19.00	18.59	18.61	−.29	26.75	17.25	64,606
Apr	18.88	19.04	18.70	18.70	−.28	26.50	17.50	45,393
May	18.95	19.06	18.75	18.76	−.26	24.60	17.30	22,410
June	19.04	19.16	18.82	18.82	−.24	24.50	17.70	24,765
July	19.08	19.10	18.90	18.88	−.22	22.11	17.90	12,530
Aug	19.12	19.12	18.98	18.94	−.20	21.80	17.15	9,804
Est vol 91,398; vol Mon 112,783; Open int 322,083, −62.								
Heating Oil No 2 (NYM) 92,000 gal.; $ per gal.								
Feb	.5370	.5420	.5280	.5307	−.0153	.7070	.4910	34,413
Mar	.5405	.5450	.5320	.5337	−.0148	.6700	.5010	25,531
Apr	.5315	.5350	.5245	.5246	−.0125	.6365	.5000	11,312
May	.5215	.5250	.5150	.5153	−.0108	.6160	.4825	9,176
June	.5185	.5200	.5115	.5115	−.0089	.6020	.4800	6,263
July	.5200	.5240	.5130	.5130	−.0084	.5965	.4950	11,681
Est vol 44,180, vol Mon 50,206; Open int 110,106, −2,207.								
Gasoline, Unleaded (NYM) 42,000 gal.; $ per gal.								
Feb	.5230	.5340	.5225	.5253	−.0057	.6490	.5025	24,508
Mar	.5380	.5525	.5380	.5435	−.0053	.6565	.5050	19,035
Apr	.5850	.5955	.5850	.5856	−.0070	.6960	.5500	25,746
May	.5940	.6025	.5940	.5936	−.0067	.6900	.5525	24,73S
June	.5925	.5995	.5925	.5933	−.0056	.6770	.5500	7,580
Est vol 25,688: vol Mon 25,913: Open int 124,617, −113.								

Source: Futures Exchanges, January 14.

EXHIBIT 2B-2
Agricultural and Commodity Energy Futures Quotations

	Open	High	Low	Settle	Change	Lifetime High	Lifetime Low	Open Interest
GRAINS AND OILSEEDS								
Corn (CBT) 5,000 bu.; cents per bu.								
Mar	260	261	257½	259¼	+3	277¼	228½	106,798
May	268	268	264	265½	+2¾	279½	234¾	56,506
July	270½	272½	268½	269¾	+2¼	282	239½	47,177
Est vol 55,000; vol Mon 51,982; Open int 238,526, +5,348.								
Soybeans (CBT) 5,000 bu.; cents per bu.								
Mar	567	569	557½	560½	−6¼	666	538	46,525
May	573	576¼	564¾	567¼	−6¾	668	547	20,156
July	581	585	573½	576¼	−6½	668	554	23,987
Nov	592	594	584	585¾	−6	620¾	552	10,987
Est vol 36,000; vol Mon 25,465; Open int 110,295, +1,593.								
Soybean Meal (CBT) 100 tons; $ per ton.								
Mar	175.80	176.70	171.50	172.10	−3.20	197.00	163.50	31,443
May	176.00	177.30	172.50	173.10	−2.10	194.00	164.50	13,765
July	177.40	119.30	174.30	174.80	−2.50	196.00	166.00	10,985
Est vol 19,000; vol Mon 14,271; Open int 69,669, +1,338.								
Soybean Oil (CBT) 60,000 lbs.; cents per lb.								
Mar	18.88	19.09	18.61	18.98	+.10	24.10	18.60	30,363
May	19.14	19.30	18.91	19.21	+.10	24.00	18.93	21,101
July	19.39	19.58	19.21	19.56	+.11	24.30	19.25	7,852
Est vol 17,000; vol Mon 13,736; Open int 69,563, +1,299.								
Wheat (CBT) 5,000 bu.; cents per bu.								
Mar	415	418	408¾	413	+1½	418	279	28,387
May	399	399	393	391¼	+4¼	399	280½	9,581
July	367	372	365	371¼	+8	372	279	15,104
Est vol 25,000; vol Mon 24,908; Open int 57,088, +2,388.								
LIVE STOCK AND MEATS								
Cattle-Live (CME) 40,000 lbs.; cents per lb.								
Feb	75.07	75.50	74.02	74.27	−.42	76.70	68.90	26,605
Apr	75.00	75.35	74.05	74.37	−.40	77.00	70.45	24,866
June	70.50	70.87	69.80	69.95	−.42	75.95	67.40	14,461
Aug	67.80	68.27	67.40	67.47	−.17	72.60	65.90	5,395
Est vol 29,236; vol Mon 18,275; Open int 74,617, −212.								
Hogs (CME) 40,000 lbs.; cents per lb.								
Feb	40.15	40.37	39.22	39.40	−.47	48.35	38.82	8,003
Apr	39.45	39.70	38.95	39.12	−.15	46.62	37.25	7,123
June	44.10	44.22	43.30	43.43	−.57	50.60	42.37	3,068
Est vol 6,246; vol Mon 5,613; Open int 22,221, +838.								

continued next page

continued

	Open	High	Low	Settle	Change	Lifetime High	Lifetime Low	Open Interest
Pork Bellies (CME) 40,000 lbs.; cents per lb.								
Feb	36.45	36.55	34.90	35.05	−1.20	63.15	34.65	5,992
Mar	36.85	37.00	35.47	35.62	−.97	63.05	35.20	2,746
May	38.10	38.10	36.50	36.70	−1.15	59.00	36.25	1,817

Est vol 4,088; vol Mon 2,923; Open int 12,348, +109.

FOOD AND FIBER

	Open	High	Low	Settle	Change	Lifetime High	Lifetime Low	Open Interest
Cocoa (CSCE) 10 metric tons; $ per ton								
Mar	1,197	1,200	1,186	1,193	−0	1,538	997	18,379
May	1,227	1,233	1,221	1,227	−3	1,388	1,020	12,728
July	1,200	1,207	1,258	1,263	−4	1,410	1,056	5,777

Est vol 2,725; vol Mon 1,987; Open int 53,094, +370.

	Open	High	Low	Settle	Change	Lifetime High	Lifetime Low	Open Interest
Coffee (CSCE) 37,500 lbs.; cents per lb.								
Mar	78.40	78.60	77.70	77.90	−.05	107.50	70.85	29,154
May	81.15	81.25	80.50	80.75	−.50	106.00	79.50	10,406
July	83.05	83.75	83.20	83.55	−.50	106.40	82.10	4,154

Est vol 10,503: vol Mon 3,983; Open int 45,282, −72.

	Open	High	Low	Settle	Change	Lifetime High	Lifetime Low	Open Interest
Sugar-World (CSCE) 112,000 lbs.; cents per lb.								
Mar	8.43	8.48	8.28	8.30	−.14	10.14	7.56	40,392
May	8.46	8.48	8.34	8.37	−.09	9.77	7.05	24,870
July	8.45	8.47	8.33	8.37	−.10	9.16	7.80	11,767
Oct	8.45	8.47	8.37	8.40	−.07	9.06	7.93	15,282

Est vol 17,080; vol Mon 10,006; Open int 90,253; +1,157.

	Open	High	Low	Settle	Change	Lifetime High	Lifetime Low	Open Interest
Cotton (CTN) 50,000 lbs.; cents per lb.								
Mar	56.25	57.05	56.20	56.93	+.36	77.15	56.20	13,779
May	58.10	58.70	57.97	58.50	+.27	77.30	57.97	9,590
July	59.28	59.95	59.20	59.70	+.25	77.70	59.20	8,449

Est vol 5,500; vol Mon 6,967; Open int 38,270, −542.

	Open	High	Low	Settle	Change	Lifetime High	Lifetime Low	Open Interest
Orange Juice (CTN) 15,000 lbs; cents per lb.								
Mar	159.50	159.90	155.45	156.90	−1.55	178.40	113.60	5,401
May	159.25	159.50	156.00	156.90	−2.05	177.95	115.00	2,032

Est vol 1,000; vol Mon 1,748; Open int 8,946, +127.

Source: Futures Exchanges, January 14.

for stocks and bonds. Hence, their futures markets provide an important price discovery mechanism to determine the value of these products.

Agricultural futures have expiration months that correspond to the production or harvest months of the particular commodity, plus additional months that relate to the storage of these commodities. Thus, one finds "new crop" and "old crop" expiration months that reflect expected prices from the new crop and storage prices for the old crop. Obviously, these prices can differ substantially. The underlying value of an agricultural futures is found by multiplying the price of the futures by the number of units for the futures contract.

International Futures Markets

The success of futures contracts in the United States has generated an explosion of futures markets around the world. The most important international futures markets are in London, Tokyo, and France. In fact, the Chicago Exchanges recognize that international markets are important to consider; thus, the CME trades the Japanese Nikkei 225 stock average and dually lists contracts with the Singapore Exchange to promote Far Eastern activity.[1] *The Wall Street Journal* reports some of the more important and active international futures contracts and lists them with the U.S. interest rate futures, namely the German Government Bond (or LIFFE: the London International Financial Futures Exchange), Sterling (British short-term interest rates on LIFFE), and the Long Gilt (British bonds on LIFFE); see Exhibits 2B-3 and 2B-4. In addition, the *WSJ* lists T-bond futures and Eurodollar futures traded on LIFFE. Additional contracts traded on

EXHIBIT 2B-3
International Futures Quotations

	Open	High	Low	Settle	Chg	Lifetime High	Lifetime Low	Open Interest
Nikkei 225 Stock Average (CME) $5 times NSA								
Mar	22140.	22425.	22135.	22350.	+540.0	26725.	21780.	15,914
Est vol 1,233; vol Mon 865; Open int 15,942, +85.								
Index high 22019.94; Low 21662.99; Close 21775.13 +78.27.								
German Gov't. Bond (LIFFE) 250,000 marks; $ per mark (.01)								
Mar	n.a.	n.a.	n.a.	n.a.	n.a.	87.28	85.39	112,817
June	88.53	88.67	88.53	88.74	+.24	88.75	87.25	1,049
Est vol 65,618; vol Mon 46,888; Open int 113,866, −3,139.								
Sterling (LIFFE) £500,000; pts of 100%								
Mar	89.48	89.62	89.42	89.60	+.14	90.49	86.68	73,804
June	89.81	89.93	89.77	89.90	+.11	90.46	87.45	59,604
Sept	90.07	90.19	90.03	90.17	+.11	90.41	87.46	12,938
Dec	90.27	90.29	90.23	90.29	+.06	90.43	87.55	10,122
Mr	90.37	90.41	90.33	90.40	+.02	90.52	87.50	7,355
Est vol 67,395; vol Mon 40,669; Open int 176,489, +3,920.								
Long Gilt (LIFFE) £50,000; 32nds of 100%								
Mar	96-14	97-00	96-07	96-28	+0-16	97-28	93-28	53,286
June	96-19	96-24	96-19	97-03	+0-16	97-22	96-19	179
Est vol 32,429; vol Mon 32,047; Open int 53,465, +5,515.								

Source: Futures Exchanges, January 14.

[1] The CMEX Nikkei futures contracts employ a price-weighted average of 225 large and actively traded Japanese stocks. Those who trade Japanese stocks can use the Nikkei futures to speculate or hedge their positions, without having to consider changes in the currency exchange rate. The Nikkei futures are valued as $5 times the index, with a minimum price change of $25. They are settled in cash. The CBT listed a TOPIX Japanese stock index futures and a Japanese government bond futures; however, both failed to achieve the needed liquidity.

EXHIBIT 2B-4
Characteristics of International Futures Contracts

Futures Contract	Trading Unit	Deliverable Instrument	Price Quotation	Minimum Price Change Units	Minimum Price Change $;£	Last Trading Day	Last Delivery Day
Nikkei 225	$5 × index	cash	Index	5	$25	(1)	(1)
Long Gilt	£50,000	(2)	Points and 32nds	$\frac{1}{32}$	£15.625	(3)	(5)
German government bond	DM 250,000	(4)	Points of 100	.01	DM 25	(5)	(5)
Three-month sterling deposit	£500,000	Cash	Index	.01	£12.50	(6)	Cash

(1) First business day preceding the determination of the final settlement price, usually the business day preceding the second Friday of the contract month. The contract is settled in cash.
(2) A hypothetical 9% coupon gilt bond maturing in 2003.
(3) Last trading day is the third-to-last business day of the contract month (the financial cycle). The delivery day is any business day in the contract month at the seller's choice.
(4) A hypothetical German government bond with an 8- to 10½-year remaining life and 6% coupon.
(5) The last trading day is three Frankfurt business days before delivery. The delivery date is the tenth calendar day of the contract month or the following Frankfurt business day.
(6) The last trading day is the third Wednesday of the delivery month.
Source: Exchange pamphlets.

LIFFE include short-term interest rate futures on the mark (Euromark) and Swiss franc (Euroswiss), and Italian government bond contract, and the British stock index (called the FTSE 100).

Active futures contracts traded on international exchanges, and not available on U.S. exchanges, include the German Bond futures, the *Financial Times* Stock Exchange Index futures (the British blue-chip index traded), and Eurosterling futures on LIFFE, the French Government Bond futures on the Marché à Terme International de France (Matif: Paris) Exchange, Japanese Bond futures on the Tokyo Stock Exchange, Euroyen contracts on TIFFE (Tokyo International Financial Futures Exchange), and Australian debt and stock index futures. The French Government Bond futures traded more than 20 million contracts in 1991, and LIFFE's German Bond futures traded 10 million contracts. The Euroyen futures traded 25 million contracts, and Japanese Bond futures traded more than 20 million contracts. Europe's share of the world's futures and options volume was 20% in 1991 (McAuley, 1991), while the United States kept the lead at 60% (down from 67% in 1990). However, LIFFE and Matif grew by 11% and 15%, respectively, in 1991. Other European exchanges include the Deutsche Terminborse in Germany and Telematico, the computer-based system in Italy to trade bonds and futures. The Japanese bond contract principally attracts domestic hedgers and traders. Contracts traded on international exchanges are quoted in the home country currency. The value of all such contracts is calculated in the same manner as equivalent futures contracts traded in the United States.

Risk Management Magazine annually publishes the *Mitsubishi Finance Risk Directory* (1990), which lists the characteristics of the futures and options contracts currently trading on international exchanges.[2] Although *Futures Magazine* annually includes *all* of the futures contracts listed worldwide with their contract characteristics and trading hours for each futures, it does not distinguish between highly active and marginally active contracts, and contracts that do not trade. Currently, 22 countries have futures exchanges.

Bibliography for Appendix 2B

McAuley, Tony (1991). "Europe's Futures Markets Hotly Pursue U.S. Leaders," *The Wall Street Journal,* December 27, pp. C1, C10.
Mitsubishi Finance Risk Directory 1990–91 (1990). Chicago: *Risk Management Magazine.*

PROBLEMS FOR APPENDIX 2B

*Indicates more difficult problems.

2B-1 Speculating in Gold Futures

Bart Wildman is a speculator who takes risks in order to have a chance at high returns. Bart believes that gold prices will drop substantially in response to a change in the economy. On July 9, he sells five gold futures contracts at $375.60 per troy ounce (one contract is 100 troy ounces). On September 9 Bart buys back the gold contracts at $350.20 and closes out his position so that he can buy pork belly contracts. If the brokerage house has a $2500 per contract margin on gold futures, then determine the following:

a. What is Bart's profit or loss in dollars?
b. What is Bart's return on his investment?
c. What is his annualized return?

2B-2 Speculating in Gold Futures

Susan expects the price of gold to increase in the near future. To take advantage of this expectation, Susan buys gold futures. She deposits $2000 with her broker and instructs the broker to buy one October Comex gold futures at the close on 8/27. The following are settlement prices for various days for the October gold contract (100 troy oz):

Date	Price
8/27	$356.20
8/29	352.40
9/02	349.60
9/03	349.70
9/06	350.20
9/10	350.90
9/12	345.10
9/16	345.20
9/17	347.30

Show Susan's profit/loss and current account balance for each day listed above.

[2] This annual also lists and describes software for institutional risk management, as available from vendors, and also lists financial consultants.

2B-3 Trading LONG GILT Futures

Mr. Hung is an international businessman who trades LONG GILT March futures contracts on LIFEE.

a. Calculate his profit/loss in pounds based on the following transactions.

b. Determine the dollar amount of the total profit/loss if the exchange rate is 1 British pound = $1.4360

Trade	Purchase Price	Sales Price	Contracts
1	96–14	96–21	2
2	96–01	95–22	3
3	95–10	95–23	3
4	95–24	96–02	4
5	96–04	95–12	2

CONCEPTS AND STRATEGIES FOR FUTURES MARKETS

Overview

 This chapter covers the terminology and uses of futures markets and provides a foundation for more specific discussions of pricing, hedging, and speculation issues in later chapters. Terminology must be understood before it is possible to comprehend how futures markets operate. Important terminology and concepts include margins, price limits, convergence, the importance of the clearinghouse, and delivery when futures expire. The basic strategies of how to use futures markets include speculation, hedging, spreading, and arbitrage. Examples of each strategy are presented and the key aspects of the strategies are outlined so as to provide an overview to the applications of futures contracts. This chapter concludes with historical evidence on the return and risk of trading futures contracts and the relative importance of hedgers and speculators to the futures markets.

Terminology

Arbitrage   See Chapter 1.

Asset-liability management   The activity of financial institutions whereby they manage their investments (assets) in bonds and loans, while minimizing their cost of funds (liabilities) so that the difference between these categories provides a profitable return.

*Basis The difference between the relevant cash instrument price and the futures price (i.e., $P_C - P_F$). Often used in the context of hedging the cash instrument.

Basis risk The variability over time in the basis; alternatively, the risk that remains after hedging with futures.

Clearinghouse A division of the exchange that verifies trades, guarantees the trade against default risk, and transfers margin amounts. Legally, a market participant makes a futures transaction with the clearinghouse.

*Convergence The movement of the cash asset price toward the futures price as the expiration date of the futures contract approaches.

*Cost of carry pricing Calculating the appropriate price of a futures contract by determining the costs involved in holding the asset until the futures contract expires. The time value of money is one of these costs.

Credit risk See Default risk in Chapter 1.

*Delivery See Chapter 1.

*Hedging See Chapter 1.

*Initial margin The amount of funds put on deposit by the market participants as a "good faith" guarantee against a loss from adverse market movements. A trader can deposit cash T-bills to meet the initial margin requirement.

*Maintenance margin The lower limit that the margin account can fall to before the market participant must put up more funds.

*Marking-to-market The daily adjustment of the margin balance to account for changes in the market price. If the margin account falls to or below the maintenance margin, then additional funds are needed.

Opportunity loss Forgoing a gain (or creating a smaller loss) by not taking a specific action or trade.

*Price limit The daily maximum change in price that may occur for a given futures contract. The price limit often changes over time and varies from one type of futures contract to another. If the price limit is activated, then the next day's limit increases in size.

Short hedge Hedging the value of a currently held cash instrument by selling a futures contract.

*Spread The purchase of one expiration month and the sale of a different expiration month, or the purchase of one type of futures contract and the sale of another type of contract. A spread is less risky than a pure one-sided speculative transaction.

FUTURES TERMINOLOGY AND CONCEPTS

Margins

Initial Margin.   The **initial margin** is the amount of funds placed in the account of the trader or **hedger** as a *good faith* deposit against adverse price changes that create losses for the account. This margin is used to make sure that a trader does not default when losses occur. Since futures margins are not used to buy the asset (as is the case with stock margins), no additional funds need to be borrowed from the brokerage house to trade futures. Since futures margins are a good faith deposit, the margin amount is a relatively small percentage of the underlying value of the contract.

Margins are stated as *dollar* amounts for each futures contract. These amounts change over time. The size of the good faith futures margin varies from a low of about 2% of the underlying cash value for some agricultural futures to 10% or more of the underlying cash value for stock index futures. The size of the margin relates to such factors as the recent volatility of the relevant futures market and the desire by the futures regulatory agency to keep unsophisticated individuals out of stock index futures. The initial margin for futures contracts can be made with cash Treasury bills, with the customer retaining the implicit interest on the T-bills. Consequently, using cash instead of T-bills for margin creates an **opportunity loss**, since interest is not received on any cash deposit. Whereas hedgers consistently use T-bills or letters of credit for the initial margin, small- to medium-size speculators often post cash for margin. Small speculators often use cash for margin because of their smaller accounts or out of ignorance. Most brokerage houses also allow traders to use 80% of their stock value as margin.

Marking-to-Market and Maintenance Margin.   As futures prices fluctuate over time, the customer's profits or losses in the futures account also change. These price movements necessitate **marking-to-market** rules and **maintenance margin**. Marking-to-market is the adjustment in a customer's account balance to reflect the change in value of the futures contract on a daily basis. Maintenance margin is the smallest margin balance allowed before additional funds are required in the account. Thus if the *value* of the futures position declines (i.e., the position loses money), the customer's good faith margin account balance also declines. When the margin account balance becomes less than the required maintenance margin, then the customer receives a margin call requiring the customer to put up additional margin funds to return the balance of the account to the initial margin level. If this is not accomplished by the beginning of trading on the next trading day, then the brokerage house is authorized to close out the futures position at the current market price. The maintenance margin and marking-to-market rules protect the brokerage house from sustaining losses on individual accounts. Losses would occur if the change in value exceeds the initial margin *and* the customer does not pay the brokerage house for the additional losses. Additional margin funds can be deposited in cash, Treasury bills, or letters of credit (despite the common misconception that additional margin can be made only in cash).

If the futures account generates profits from price changes, then the customer can withdraw any excess funds above the initial margin amount on a daily basis. These funds then can be deposited elsewhere to draw interest. Margins vary depending on the type of trading strategy employed. A hedging strategy involves less risk and therefore

Table 3-1 Margins and Price Limits for Stock Index Futures

	Speculative Margins		Hedging Margins	Spread Margins[a]	Price Limit[b]	Trading Hours[c]
Contract	Initial	Maintenance				
S&P 500	$22,000	$9000	9000	490	(1)	8:30 A.M.–3:15 P.M.
MMI	18,000	7400	7400	0	(2)	8:15 A.M.–3:15 P.M.
NYSE	9,000	4000	4000	200	(3)	9:30 A.M.–4:15 P.M.

[a] Across expirations. Intercommodity spreads vary according to the instruments used in the spread.

[b] The stock index futures contracts have a series of "circuit breakers" or price limits that are activiated when a given large move in the futures price occurs (in addition, see Focus 3-1 for information on trading halts).

(1) For the S&P 500 contract: If the futures *drop* by 12 points, then that price limit stays in effect for 30 minutes. After 30 minutes, a 20-point limit becomes effective. In addition, there is a 5-point up *or* down opening limit; that is, the open price can vary from the previous day's close by a maximum of 5 points.

(2) For the MMI contract: If the futures either fall or increase by 15 points, then the price limit stays in effect for 30 minutes. There also is a 10-point up *or* down opening limit.

(3) For the NYSE contract: If the futures *fall* by 7 points, then this price limit is in effect for 30 minutes. If the futures then fall by a total of 12 points, this limit exists for one hour. A drop of 18 points creates a price limit that exists for the rest of the day. An opening limit of 3 points (up or down) also exists. A price limit of 18 points exists on the up side, which stays in effect for the entire day.

[c] All times are local times.

Note: Margins change on a regular basis.

Source: Adapted from Chicago Board of Trade (1991); Chicago Mercantile Exchange (1991).

requires a smaller initial margin. **Spreading** is also a low-risk strategy whereby a trader buys one (say stock index) futures and sells another, or buys one expiration month and sells a different month. Spreading margins are extremely small and thus significant leverage effects are created.

Margin amounts change as the volatility of the futures contracts changes; that is, margins increase when the price volatility increases significantly. Hence, the exchange margins provided in Tables 3-1 and 3-2 for speculative, hedging, and spreading positions are for guidance only. The margin/volatility relationship is based on the Standard Portfolio Analysis of Risk (SPAN) margining system. The SPAN system directly associates margins with the volatility of each market, attempting to determine an "optimal" margin amount.[1] Also be aware that many brokerage houses request larger margins than the exchange listed minimums given here, especially for smaller customers. Example 3-1 shows the essential aspects of the operation of the margin process and marking-to-market.

The marking-to-market and maintenance margin rules make it imperative for the customer to stay in touch with the brokerage house concerning the status of the customer's account. A futures trader who takes a secluded vacation in the mountains often

[1] An explanation of how the SPAN system calculates margin is available from The Chicago Board of Trade by requesting their current margin document. Note that the size of the initial margin can be related to the maximum allowable daily price change; see the next section and footnote 2. SPAN also considers the risk of an entire portfolio, including the characteristics of both futures and options. SPAN allows traders to use excess margin from one contract *or* exchange to cover deficiencies in other contracts. Alternatively, a trader who does not have excess margin to withdraw can make an additional deposit to decrease the possibility of a margin call.

Table 3-2 Interest Rate Futures Margins and Price Limits

Contract	Speculative Margins		Hedging Margins	Spread Margins[a]	Price Limit	Trading Hours[b]
	Initial	Maintenance				
T-bills	540	400	400	200	None	7:20 A.M.–2 P.M.
Eurodollar	540	400	400	200	None	7:20 A.M.–2 P.M.
One-month LIBOR	540	400	400	270	None	7:20 A.M.–2 P.M.
T-bonds	2700	2000	2000	200	$96/32$	8 A.M.–2 P.M.
T-notes:						
10-yr	1300	1000	1000	200	$96/32$	8 A.M.–2 P.M.
5-yr	675	500	500	0	$96/32$	8 A.M.–2 P.M.
Municipals	1350	1000	1000	0	$96/32$	8 A.M.–2 P.M.

[a] Across expirations. Intercommodity spreads vary according to instruments employed.

[b] All times are local times. Evening hours also exist from 5–8:30 P.M. Central Standard Time or 6–9:30 P.M. Central Daylight Savings Time Sunday through Thursday for T-bonds and 10-year T-notes. Half-size contracts trade on the Mid-America Exchange; this exchange trades until 3:15 P.M.

Note: Margins change on a regular basis.

Source: Adapted from Chicago Board of Trade (1991); Chicago Mercantile Exchange (1991).

finds out later that the vacation had a disastrous effect on the trader's futures account! A major movement in the stock market for even *one* day could wipe out the trader's margin balance, with the customer being liable for any losses in excess of the margin amount placed with the brokerage house.

Price Limits

The Concept of Price Limits. **Price limits** reflect the maximum amount that a futures price can change in one day. No trading can occur outside the daily price limit, although trading can continue within the allowed daily price range. The argument for supporting price limits is that they allow time for the market to assimilate and evaluate major events without causing large market swings as the result of speculative panic. In addition, the existence of price limits allows the brokerage houses time to collect additional margin money from customers to cover losses from the large market moves. Without price limits the brokerage houses might liquidate customers' positions during the day to reduce losses, which would put additional pressure on prices. Thus, some market regulators argue that without price limits the combination of large speculative price fluctuations and high leverage would cause many market participants to be forced out of the market with huge losses, only to find that the price move had been exaggerated, with prices subsequently moving back to a more appropriate level.

Ma, Rao, and Sears (1989a, b) examine the price adjustments of futures contracts after they hit a limit. They find no significant difference between the price level before hitting the limit versus the price in the following market period of trading. Thus, Ma, Rao, and Sears conclude that *excess* demand/supply does *not* delay additional trading in the futures. This suggests that the volatility that activates price limits is related to

EXAMPLE 3-1
Margins and Marking-to-Market

The following examples illustrate how initial margins, maintenance margins, and marking-to-market interact to affect the cash flows from a futures transaction. Here we provide examples for a speculator who purchases a futures contract on stock index futures and sells a Eurodollar futures contract. A similar table is applicable for hedgers or spreaders, since margins and marking-to-market affect all transactions by those who are not at the exchange, regardless of the type of trader. Traders on the exchanges do not need to post initial margins, since their positions are marked-to-market each day. Margins listed in Tables 3-1 and 3-2 are employed in these examples. Margin balances that fall below the maintenance margin are identified within the table. In these cases a margin call occurs and the trader must restore the margin account to the initial margin level.

Long S&P 500 Stock Index Futures

Date	Settle Price	Underlying Value of the Contract	Mark-to-Market Amount (Change in Value)	Margin Account Balance
8/9	$385.65	$192,825		$22,000
8/16	376.25	188,125	−$4700	17,300
8/23	366.35	183,175	−4950	12,350
8/30	351.45	175,725	−7450	4,900[a]
9/6	340.20	170,100	−5625	16,375
9/13	336.80	168,400	−1700	14,675

[a] The margin balance falls below the maintenance margin of $9000, and therefore additional funds must be deposited to bring the balance back up to $22,000.

Short Eurodollar Futures

Date	Settle Index	Mark-to-Market Amount (Change in Value)	Margin Account Balance
8/16	93.99		$540
8/23	93.87	$300	840
8/30	93.98	−275	565
9/6	94.09	−275	290[a]
9/13	94.20	−275	265[a]
9/20	94.17	75	615
9/27	94.34	−425	190[a]

[a] The margin balance falls below the maintenance margin of $400; therefore, additional funds must be deposited to bring the balance back up to $540.

trader's *overreaction* to price movements. Consequently, they conclude that price li.
are not detrimental to the pricing function of futures markets.[2]

Limit Effects and Variable Price Limits. Even though price limit moves are relatively rare, sometimes they have been more of a difficulty for futures markets than
a benefit. For example, during the severe winter freeze of 1980–1981, the damage
to the orange groves in Florida caused orange juice concentrate futures to increase
by 70 cents per pound over a seven-day period. Although growers assessed the damage
within two days, the 10-cent daily price limit on orange juice futures ($1500 per con-
tract) kept the futures price from rising to the level where trading would resume until
seven trading days had passed. Since no one would sell orange juice futures during this
upward price adjustment period, no trading took place, forcing short traders to place
increasing amounts of funds into their margin accounts to cover their losing positions.

During the time period when price limits are affecting the futures markets, the
hedging and pricing activities associated with futures markets also are inoperative,
negating these important benefits of futures. Consequently, variable price limits reduce
the delay effect of sequential daily limits on futures price adjustments. Variable price
limits cause the size of the daily limit to increase once the futures contract has experi-
enced a normal price limit move for a given number of days. Although the variable
limit rule differs from one exchange to another, a general rule is that after a futures
contract has hit a limit move for one or two days, then the limit is expanded to 150% of
the initial price limit and then to 200% of the initial limit.[3] In addition, many futures
contracts do not have daily price limits during the month of **delivery**. Hence these futures expirations react immediately to major factors affecting the cash markets.[4]

---

[2] Brennan (1986) develops a theory of the existence of price limits. First, he argues that neither preven-
tion of excessive price changes nor daily resettlement of margins is an adequate reason for the existence
of price limits. He argues that closing a market to reduce panic and large price changes creates other
problems. Moreover, the existence of price limits for most futures markets does not explain why other
futures markets and other speculative markets do not have limits, or why an entire day has to pass before the limits are revised. (In fact, stock index futures now have price limits that change *within* the
day.) Brennan also argues that the daily settlement procedure does not completely explain the existence
of limits, since not all futures have price limits (but it would explain why certain futures have price limits but other markets do not). Brennan's theory of price limits is that limits exist as a partial substitute
for margin requirements; that is, the initial margin deposit can be reduced when price limits provide
daily resettlement before default is contemplated by traders. Thus, such limits reduce the information to
traders concerning the total potential losses, thereby reducing the likelihood of default.

[3] Although actual price limit rules change occasionally, the current rules are as follows: (1) Chicago
Board of Trade: if a financial futures contract hits a limit price for one day, then 150% of the original
price limit applies for each of the three subsequent consecutive days; this rule becomes effective only if
the futures prices hit a limit for each of three of the contract months of the current calendar year (or two
expiration months if only two are being traded). (2) Chicago Mercantile Exchange: if a futures contract
hits a limit price for two days in a row, then 150% of the original limit price applies for the third day *if*
any expiration month hits a limit price on the second day, with 200% of the original limit price applying
for the fourth day if any expiration hits a limit price on the third day; the 200% limit applies until no
expiration month hits a limit.

[4] When limits are in force, traders often move to other markets. For example, on October 19, 1987, the
T-bond futures contract hit its limit. Traders then switched to options on T-bond futures.

Breakers for Stock Index Futures

...mits existed for stock index futures when these futures started trading in
...owever, these limits were removed soon after these contracts started to
...ade. Even though stock index futures operated continuously and reasonably effectively throughout the October 1987 crash, unlike other markets, the events of the
crash caused the reintroduction of a type of price limit for these contracts. These
new price limits are called "circuit breakers." Circuit breakers take two forms. The
first involves price limits that restrict the size of the opening price change (either up
or down) as well as limiting trading beyond the price limit if the market *falls* a designated amount. If the price limits are hit after the open, then prices cannot change
more than the limit for a specified period of time (e.g., 30 minutes, one hour, or two
hours). For example, the S&P 500 contract has a series of circuit breakers, including
a 12-point circuit breaker that stays in effect for 30 minutes. Table 3-1 lists the circuit breaker price limits.

The second part of the circuit breaker system is related to NYSE rules concerning
trading halts for stocks and restrictions on program trading. If stocks stop trading,
then futures trading also is halted. The restrictions and halts are as follows:

- If the Dow increases or decreases by 50 points, then all program trades executed (index
  arbitrage trades) must help to *stabilize* prices (e.g., if stock prices are falling, then orders
  must be purchase orders). This rule is in effect for the rest of the day, unless the Dow re-
  tracts by 25 points.
- If the S&P 500 futures decline by 12 points, then a "sidecar" becomes effective: *any* program trading order entered via the computer system is held up for five minutes. In addition, there is a prohibition on new "stop" orders from institutions or "stop" orders from
  individuals for more than 200 shares.
- If the Dow declines by 250 points, then trading is halted in stocks and futures for
  one hour.
- If the Dow declines 400 points, then the markets close for two hours.

These rules, though complicated, were put into place to reduce potential adverse
effects of computer-based program trading and to reduce panic selling. Although
the effectiveness of such circuit breakers has not been proved, they are one result of
the market crash that traders must accommodate.

Basis, Basis Risk, and Convergence

Basis is the difference between the price of a cash investment and the price of the
relevant futures contract (i.e., $P_C - P_F$). **Basis risk** is the price *variability* between the
cash price and the futures price; that is, it represents the extent to which the basis
changes. The extent of this basis risk shows how effective a hedge is between the cash
security and the futures contract. For example, extensive basis risk (a poor hedge) can
occur when an over-the-counter stock portfolio is hedged with the S&P 500 futures
contract. Thus, if the relationship between the values of these two types of portfolios
change (i.e., the basis changes), then the risk reduction obtained from hedging the
over-the-counter stock position is limited.

Convergence is the movement in the price of the underlying cash security toward the futures price as the delivery or expiration date of the futures contract approaches. Until delivery, the time value of money causes the futures and cash price to differ.[5] As convergence occurs, the basis between the cost price and futures price becomes smaller. The futures and cash prices *must* converge at delivery, otherwise an **arbitrageur** could buy the lower-priced instrument (e.g., the cash security) and sell the higher-priced instrument (e.g., the futures contract), using the delivery process to obtain risk-free profits. Similarly, before expiration, the cash and futures prices differ only by the time value of money plus an amount attributable to unique factors of the futures contract. Figure 3-1 shows how the convergence of the basis occurs over time between the S&P 500 futures and the associated cash index. Since the futures price is above the cash index, the basis ($P_C - P_F$) is negative. Notice that the convergence is not smooth over time.

Exact convergence to zero when trading ceases for "cash delivery" futures exists by design. Some futures contracts such as the stock index futures, Eurodollar futures, and the municipal bond futures contracts are settled in *cash;* that is, the price of the futures contract is set equal to the cash asset price at the end of the last day of trading. An arbitrageur who holds the equivalent of the cash index therefore would experience the desired convergence to zero of the difference between the cash and futures prices. There are two benefits to cash delivery. First, cash delivery avoids problems in obtaining the exact cash asset needed to correspond to the futures contract. For example, to deliver the S&P 500 basket one would need all 500 stocks in the index *and* hold them in the exact weights these stocks appear in the index. Second, cash delivery reduces unusual

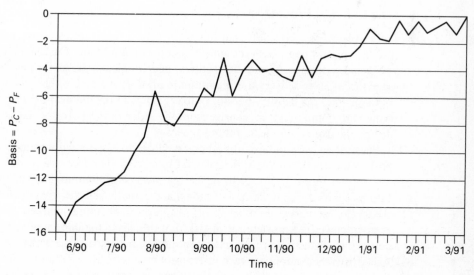

Figure 3-1 Convergance of the basis: S&P 500 futures. (*Source:* Prices from Tick Data, Inc.)

---

[5] The time value of money—or, equivalently, the cost of carrying the cash security until the futures expire—includes the interest cost of the funds used to purchase the cash security plus the storage cost for nonfinancial assets. Chapters 4, 8, and 9 cover cost of carry pricing.

supply-and-demand pressures on the cash assets near the expiration period of the futures contract. In general, cash positions having characteristics that differ from the futures contract encounter significant basis risk.

Making Trades and the Clearinghouse

Futures transactions are completed at specific physical locations known as futures exchanges. The major financial futures exchanges are The Chicago Board of Trade (CBT), The Chicago Mercantile Exchange (CMEX), The New York Futures Exchange (NYFE), The Commodity Exchange (COMEX) in New York, and The London Futures Exchange (LIFFE).[6] A completed futures transaction is legally a transaction between the market participant and the exchange **clearinghouse**. This association is made for two reasons. First, if one side of the trade defaults, then the other market participant is not adversely affected; since the transaction is legally with the exchange clearinghouse, the clearinghouse absorbs the loss on the trade, keeping intact the reputation of the exchange and eliminating the default risk for the nondefaulting market participant. Second, if one side of the open interest contract desires to close its position, then the "closing trade" is accomplished easily in the futures pit (e.g., selling if the trader originally purchased futures, and vice versa). Thus, the closing trade does *not* have to be made with the specific individual with whom the position was originally created; rather, it is executed with anyone willing to take a position. Such flexibility with futures trades is possible because the name associated with the contract is simply changed on the clearinghouse's books when the trade is accomplished. Consequently, the clearinghouse procedure solves several potentially troublesome problems.

The Delivery Procedure

Delivery is the procedure that forces the price of the futures contract to converge to the cash price when a cash settlement system is not relevant. Cash settlement exists for stock index futures, Eurodollar futures, and Municipal Bond futures contracts. The specifics of asset delivery are important to arbitrageurs and to those who carry futures positions into the delivery period. Delivery refers to the physical delivery of the underlying cash commodity or security from the seller to the buyer of the futures contract during the expiration of the futures contract.

Physical delivery of agricultural commodities to a specified location involves transportation costs (including insurance and spoilage). Therefore, many agricultural hedgers use the futures markets to hedge the *price* of a commodity, but then cover the futures contract (repurchase the futures) and actually sell their physical commodity in the local cash market. In other words, the purpose of futures markets for commodities is to enhance the transference of risk, *not* to deliver the commodity. However, some delivery mechanism (or cash settlement procedure) must exist so that the futures contract prices the appropriate cash instrument precisely. Since futures do not promote delivery, most traders believe that less than 2% of the open interest of agricultural commodity futures are actually delivered to fulfill these futures contracts. Recent

---

[6] The Mid-America Exchange (Chicago) deals in smaller futures contracts that mimic the contracts traded on the other exchanges. These minicontracts typically are half the size of the normal contracts.

research by Peck and Williams (1991, 1992) contradicts this belief. They show that sellers deliver 8% to 19% of the *maximum* open interest for wheat, corn, and soybeans, and 25% to 65% of the open interest existing on the first day of the futures expiration month for these contracts.

Delivery for interest rate futures involves an inexpensive wire transfer of securities and funds, making delivery much simpler than for commodity positions. Moreover, interest rate futures are more homogeneous in quality, especially cash T-bills that must have a maturity of either 90, 91, or 92 days. On the other hand, the user (buyer) of an agricultural futures contract may need a specific quality of that commodity for a specific purpose, which does not correspond to the quality priced by the futures contract. Finally, interest rate futures are much easier to arbitrage, with the delivery process being the culmination of the arbitrage transaction. Consequently, delivery for interest rate futures often can be 20% or more of the open interest.

Delivery occurs only during a specified period of time, which varies from one type of futures contract to another. For T-bill futures, the delivery period is three specified days in the month of expiration of the contract. For Treasury bond futures, delivery can occur any day during the expiration month of the contract, at the option of the seller of the futures. Consequently, a speculator with a long futures position must be wary of holding a contract during the delivery period unless the speculator either wants to obtain the underlying cash instrument or is confident that the speculator's position is sufficiently down the delivery lists where delivery will not immediately take place. Since the long position chosen for delivery is based on the oldest long in existence, those who hold long positions for a lengthy time possess a high probability of having the cash asset delivered into the futures contract. Delivery can occur on any day in the expiration month.

STRATEGIES FOR FUTURES MARKETS

There are four basic strategies for using the futures markets: speculation, hedging, spreading, and arbitrage. The most important distinction between these uses is their differing risk-return characteristics. Speculating in futures increases risk by undertaking a futures position with potential high returns but also with the risk of a large loss. Hedging exists when a futures position is taken to reduce the risk of a current or anticipated cash position. Spreading involves taking almost offsetting futures positions that create a net position that typically possesses significantly less risk than pure speculation, but has lower expected returns. Arbitrage provides a risk-free profit when a trader takes opposite positions in a cash asset and the associated futures contract when these respective instruments are mispriced in relation to one another.[7]

[7] Unfortunately, the distinction between these four basic uses of futures markets are not as clear-cut as suggested. Spreading is considered by some to be a form of speculating, since a spread involves only futures contracts. In addition, some hedgers determine when to take a position in futures based on their forecasts of future cash prices; this practice is also a type of speculation. Others find similarities between hedging and spreading. Moreover, hedgers who deliver the cash asset into the futures contracts are similar to arbitrageurs, and arbitrageurs often must take on some risk in order to form a position. Discussions later in this book examine these subtle differences.

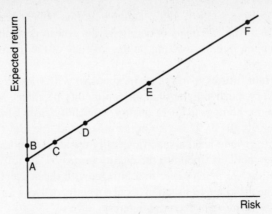

Figure 3-2 The risk-return trade-off curve and futures strategies.
  A. Risk-free rate without futures (e.g., the T-bill cash rate).
  B. Arbitrage profits from a combined futures-cash position (often arbitrage has some risk and hence B is often to the right of its present position).
  C. Hedging by using a futures contract that corresponds to the cash security held.
  D. "Spreading," a speculative position that attempts to reduce risk.
  E. An unhedged cash position.
  F. Speculating in futures (this is more risky than E due to the leverage effects).

Risk management strategies can be illustrated by a linear risk-return trade-off curve. Figure 3-2 illustrates the risk-return relationship, along with the various strategies involving futures and cash markets. A market participant chooses strategies that vary from a no-risk position at points A or B (point B is an example of arbitrage), to a hedging position at C, to a cash or speculative position at D, E, or F. Hedging with futures (point C) eliminates most, but not all, of the risk of holding a cash position. Recall that the risk of a loss increases as the *expected* return increases. Which risk-return strategy a market participant desires depends on the participant's attitude toward risk *and* return as well as the conviction that any mispricing of the instruments has been properly identified.

The following material provides the basic concepts of these important strategies for futures markets. This introductory discussion describes the relations within the futures market and how each type of market participant enhances the functioning of the market.

SPECULATION

The Futures Speculator

A speculative position can be either a long position or a short position. A long position occurs when the futures contract is purchased; one profits when prices increase. A short position occurs when the futures contract is sold (with the intention to buy the contract back at some later date); a short trader profits when prices decrease.

Speculative futures positions are very profitable for those who are able to forecast correctly both market direction and the extent of the market move. This profitability is enhanced because the speculator needs to put up only a small percentage of the value of the underlying cash instrument for margin, thereby allowing a significant degree of leverage. Of course, if a speculator forecasts incorrectly, then the mark-to-market rules cause a cash outflow as the futures position deteriorates. Consequently, a speculator needs forecasting ability and substantial knowledge of the underlying cash markets, plus sufficient funds to overcome a short-term (or permanent) loss of funds from losing trades.

Speculators include individual off-the-floor speculators and speculators on the trading floor. The off-the-floor speculator (sometimes dubbed the "dentist from Des Moines") holds a position for an average of three or four weeks, although there is a wide range of holding periods. Daigler (1993) discusses trading procedures used by speculators to help them make decisions, such as trading models and technical analysis. Chapter 5 discusses on-the-floor trading operations.

Most large brokerage houses require off-the-floor speculators to have a minimum net worth and a minimum trading account. These minimums are set to ensure that the speculator can afford any potential losses in the highly leveraged futures market. In the past, brokerage houses have encountered bad publicity as well as court suits when account executives inappropriately speculated with the small life savings of uninformed individuals. The minimum net worth figure required is often $50,000 to $60,000, with a minimum trading account value of $25,000 to $30,000.[8]

The speculator needs to establish realistic goals for trades. After reaching these goals it is best to cover the trade. If a speculator becomes emotionally involved in a position (which generates greed and fear), the ability to make realistic decisions about covering a position is impaired. Some speculators attempt to circumvent such emotional considerations by placing special trading orders with the broker so that the trader is automatically removed from a disadvantageous situation. Although such orders are useful for speculators who are not in constant contact with the market and have specific forecasts of market movements, many active traders believe that recognizing the current trend in the market and then adapting to that trend is more important than mechanical position trading.

Examples of Speculating in Futures

Example 3-2 provides two basic examples of speculative trades that show the advantages and disadvantages of speculation. Keeping in mind that these situations are extraordinary and assume perfect forecasting ability, one realizes that speculating in futures provides extremely large leverage on a small cash market deposit.

Panel A of Example 3-2 shows the effect of the market crash of October 1987 on futures prices. The potential profit of selling short the S&P 500 futures contracts before the crash and then repurchasing them after Black Monday is significant: one could have made $44,375 on each S&P 500 contract. Using the $10,000 margin in existence at that

---

[8] In addition, many brokerage houses previously had a restriction on whom the house would accept as a speculator. Specifically, women were often excluded from having their own accounts since it was claimed they were "too emotional and panic stricken" to trade futures. Significant political pressure and changing attitudes finally prevailed, and these houses have eliminated such restrictions.

EXAMPLE 3-2
Examples of Speculating in Futures

A. Stock Index Futures

		S&P 500 Futures
10/14/87	Sell	305.00
10/20/87	Purchase	216.25
	Profit	88.75
		× $500
	Dollar profit	$44,375
Margin deposit (on 10/87)		$10,000
Return on margin deposit per contract		444%

B. Eurodollar Futures

		Interest Rate	Price Index
8/26/91	Purchase	6.13	93.87
12/17/91	Sell	4.17	95.83
	Profit		196 basis points
			× $25 per basis point
	Dollar profit		$4900
Margin deposit			$ 540
Return on margin deposit per contract			741%

time, the return based on the margin deposit was 444%! Obviously, the significant leverage and profitability on such an extreme move illustrates the lure of speculation. However, a speculator who forecasted incorrectly and *purchased* stock index futures on October 14, 1987, only to sell them on October 20 would have *lost* $44,375. Moreover, such extreme moves are rare, and substantial fluctuations often mask any hoped-for clear-cut trend.

For the Eurodollar futures example in panel B, a speculator who forecasted correctly the decline in short-term interest rates from August 1991 to December 1991 (from an interest rate of 6.13% to 4.17% for the December futures) could have made 4900 *per contract* on a margin of $540. Here one could have earned a return on the margin deposit of 741%.

HEDGING: APPLICATIONS OF RISK MANAGEMENT

The Concept of Hedging

Hedging provides a method for reducing the risk of a potential price decline for those who must hold cash securities. The risk reduction from hedging is accomplished by taking the opposite position in the futures markets to the position one has in the cash market. Thus, if a portfolio manager owns the cash asset, then a **short hedged** position is created by selling the corresponding futures contracts. However, hedging also reduces the benefits of a price *increase* in the cash position by offsetting the profit obtained on the cash asset. Examples 3-3 and 3-4 provide basic short hedging examples for stock and bond portfolios. Other hedgers *buy* futures. Thus a company that uses, say, wheat

EXAMPLE 3-3
A Short Hedge for a Stock Position

In October 1987 a portfolio manager senses uneasiness in the stock market. The S&P 500 cash index has fallen from 328.08 on October 5 to 298.08 on the morning of October 16. This money manager decides to hedge the stock portfolio, which is structured to resemble the S&P 500 cash index. The following shows the effects of such a hedge only several days later. Note that a loss in the cash portfolio of more than $23 million became a net gain of almost $3 million since the futures dropped *more* than the cash index.

	Cash	**Futures**
October 16	S&P 500 cash index at 298.08; portfolio has $100 million of stock	Sells 665 December S&P 500 futures contracts at 300.50 for a value of $99,916,250 (i.e., 665 × 300.5 × 500)
October 26	S&P 500 cash index closes at 227.67, for a portfolio value of $76,378,822 ($100 million × 227.67/298.08)	Repurchases 665 December S&P 500 futures at a close of 220.50 for a value of $73,316,250 (i.e., 665 × 220.50 × 500)
Change in value:	Loss of $23,621,180	Gain of $26,600,000
	Net gain of $2,978,820	

or cattle can buy futures to lock in the price they will pay for these commodities in the future. Another example of a buy hedge is when a mutual fund or pension fund buys futures for a temporary substitute of a cash transaction that will be implemented later. Figure 3-3 compares the dollar value of an S&P 500 stock position that is not hedged to a position hedged with S&P 500 futures. Note that the volatility of the hedged position is significantly less than the volatility of the unhedged position. Moreover, the unhedged position loses approximately $15,000, but the hedged position's value remains about the same. Chapter 5 presents various hedging examples and explains the concepts related to hedging. Chapters 7 and 10 present the techniques employed to obtain the best hedge position. Chapter 17 provides applications for hedging.

Portfolio Management

A major use of futures markets for hedging is to protect the current value of a cash portfolio of stocks and bonds. A futures hedge is less costly than selling the cash security, and it avoids potential liquidity problems that occur with trades made solely in the cash market. Futures also allow greater flexibility to pension funds to determine timing, individual security selection, and reallocation of funds among assets. Dealers in bonds, stocks, and currencies also often employ futures to minimize the risk of potential adverse price changes on their inventory. Chapter 17 examines portfolio management uses of futures markets.

EXAMPLE 3-4
A Short Hedge for T-Bonds

A portfolio manager for long-term Treasury bonds is concerned that interest rates will increase over the next few months (bond prices fall); the portfolio manager wants to protect the current value of the bond portfolio without selling the bonds. The money manager holds a portfolio of $1 million of August 2000 bonds. A short hedge is implemented in September when long-term yields are at 10.0%; by December, interest rates have risen to 12.1%. The hedge offsets most of the loss on the cash bond position of $127,187, creating a reduction of more than 90% of the loss.

	Cash	Futures
September 16	Holds $1 million of August 2000 T-bonds, coupon rate 9¾%, yielding 10.0% with a price of 98⁷⁄₃₂	Sells 10 December T-bond futures with a price of 82⁷⁄₃₂ (a projected yield of 10.1%)
December 10	Price of bonds has dropped to 85¹⁶⁄₃₂ with a yield of 12.1%	Repurchases 10 December T-bond futures at a price of 70¹⁶⁄₃₂ (with a projected yield of 12.0%)
Change in value:	Loss of $127,187.50 (i.e., 12²³⁄₃₂ × $1 million)	Gain of $117,187.50 (i.e., 11²³⁄₃₂ × $100,000 × 10 or 375 × $31.25 × 10)

Net loss of $10,000

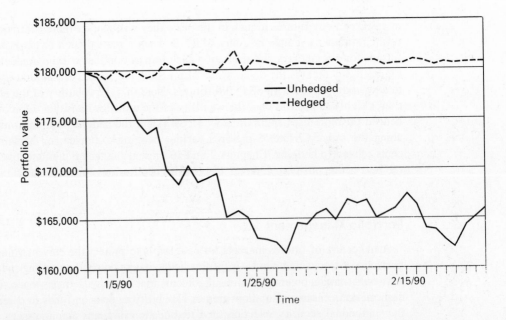

Figure 3-3 Unhedged vs. hedged S&P 500 portfolio. (*Source:* Prices from Tick Data, Inc.)

Financial Institutions

Banks and savings and loan institutions use futures markets in a myriad of ways to reduce risk. One of the most important uses of futures by financial institutions is for **asset-liability management.** Thus, earnings of financial institutions vary when the interest rates on the assets (loans given by the institutions) change at a different time than the interest rates on the liabilities (the funds obtained by the institutions). Futures reduce the variability of earnings by locking in the cost of new funds or by changing the effective characteristics of the institution's assets.

Mortgage bankers also employ futures. For example, when an institution sells a package of mortgages, a delay of several months occurs between the issuance of the mortgage and the sale of the mortgage in the open market. Futures reduce the risk of an adverse change in interest rates while these mortgages are waiting to be sold. Chapter 17 discusses the uses of futures contracts by financial institutions.

Corporate Uses of Futures

Corporations employ futures contracts for asset-liability reasons and for pension fund management. Examples of asset and liability uses are hedging inventory prices and hedging currency exposure. Futures also are employed for many types of long-term financing strategies; for example, the interest rate on a bond issuance is locked in months ahead of the sale of bonds by using futures contracts.

SPREADING

The Spread Transaction

A spread occurs when a trader buys one futures expiration month and sells another expiration month (a calendar spread), or buys one type of contract and sells a different type of futures contract (a cross spread). Some users categorize spreads simply as a speculative transaction. We treat spreads separately, since most market participants view spreads as distinct from a pure speculative position *and* because the risk-return characteristics of a spread differ from those of a pure speculative trade.

In order to profit from a spread transaction, the trader attempts to determine whether the size of the *difference* between the prices of the two contracts will increase or decrease. A spread earns a profit if the correct direction of the price difference is forecasted *and* the appropriate spread transaction is set up in conjunction with the changing price structure of the futures contract.

Spreaders must forecast the relevant factors that cause changes in the spreads. For example, changes in agricultural spreads over different crop years depend on expectations concerning the new crop, whereas changes in silver, gold, and financial futures spreads depend on the behavior of interest rates. A profitable spread creates a gain on one side of the spread that is larger than the loss on the other side of the spread. A pure speculator would make more money by taking only the profitable side of the market; however, a spread reduces the risk of a position in case the forecast is incorrect. In recognition of the reduced risk, margins on spread positions are much less than the margins on pure long or short positions, and hence the leverage for spreads is increased. Risk is reduced, since both sides of the spread usually move in the same direction, even though their prices can change by different amounts.

Spreaders previously benefited from the tax advantages of tax straddles. Tax straddles exist when taxable income can be postponed by taking the losses on one side of a spread but rolling over the gains from the spread into future years. However, the 1981 tax law eliminated this tax benefit for floor spreaders as well as for off-the-floor straddlers by taxing gains and losses on *all* positions at the end of each year, whether or not the positions had been terminated. The result from this tax law change has been to reduce significantly the liquidity of deferred contracts, since one of the economic benefits to the spreader was eliminated.

Risk and Return for Spreads

Whereas the futures expiration months for a calendar spread almost always move in the same direction, the risk for a cross spread between different types of futures contracts depends on the extent to which the contracts are influenced by the same underlying factors. Hence, the risk for a T-bill futures to Eurodollar futures spread is determined by changes in the **credit risk** relationship; on the other hand, a spread between T-bill futures and T-bond futures is even more risky because one can lose on both sides of the transaction if the relationship between short- and long-term interest rates changes. A spread between two unrelated contracts (e.g., gold and soybeans) often is more risky than one speculative position.

Figure 3-4 illustrates how the changing relationships between different futures contracts can create profitable spreading opportunities. The T-bill–Eurodollar spread (called the TED spread) has varied significantly since the Eurodollar futures inception. For each 20-basis-point change (.20 in the figure), the spread position profits or loses $500. Since the TED spread margin is $270 per contract, the percentage profit or loss on the initial margin deposit per 20 basis points is almost 200% per contract.[9] Another popular spread is the municipal bond futures versus T-bond futures spread, or the MOB spread. Over time, this spread illustrates the importance of having *different* futures contracts available to hedge differing types of risk.

Example 3-5 provides an example of a spread in which the trader expects the price difference to narrow. The subsequent actual narrowing of the spread allows the trader to make a profit of $1750 per spread, or a return of 875% on margin. Of course, if the spread had widened (the difference between the prices increased over time), the speculator would have lost money.

ARBITRAGE

Arbitrage exists when a trader is able to obtain risk-free profits by taking one position in the cash market and an exact opposite position in the futures market. The

---

[9] The Eurodollar rate is always larger than the T-bill rate in Figure 3-4, creating a positive spread for Eurodollar futures. Two factors cause this relationship. First, Eurodollar rates are money market rates, whereas T-bill rates are quoted on a discount basis. Second, Eurodollar rates include a credit risk differential, whereas T-bills are considered to be default-free.

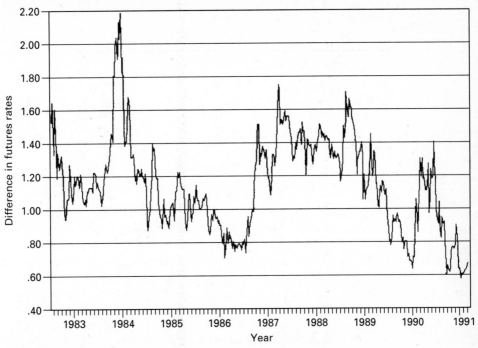

Figure 3-4 Eurodollar less T-bill rates. (*Source:* Data from Tick Data, Inc.)

EXAMPLE 3-5
A Spread Transaction

Before the market crash in 1987, a speculator expected the spread between the December and March S&P 500 futures to become smaller (less negative). To profit from this possibility, the trader purchases the lower-priced futures and sells the higher-priced futures. Profits occur when the spread narrows two weeks later.

	Nearby Futures	**Deferred Futures**	**Spread**
October 14, 1987	Buy the lower-priced December S&P 500 futures at 304.80	Sell the higher-priced March S&P 500 futures at 308.80	−4.0
October 28, 1987	Sell (cover) the December futures at 232.00	Buy back (cover) the March futures at 232.50	−.5
Change in value:	Loss of $36,400 (i.e., −72.8 × $500)	Gain of $38,150 (i.e., 76.3 × $500)	Narrowing of 3.5

Net gain: $1750
Margin deposit (for 10/87): $200
Return on margin deposit: 875%

arbitrage position is covered later by delivering the cash security into the futures position.[10] The arbitrageur can close the position prior to delivery if the profit potential has been achieved; this situation occurs principally in the stock index futures markets because of their price swings.

Arbitrage keeps the futures and cash prices in line with one another. This relationship between the cash and fair futures prices is best shown by the simple **cost of carry pricing** model:

$$P_{FAIR} = P_C(1 + i)^t \qquad (3\text{-}1)$$

where P_{FAIR} = fair futures price (also called the theoretical futures price)

$\quad P_C$ = current cash price

$\quad\quad i$ = the interest rate for financing the cash position

$\quad\quad t$ = the time until the futures contract expires (days/365)

This pricing model shows that the fair futures price is the cost of buying the cash asset now and financing this asset until delivery into the futures contract. If the current futures price is higher than the fair price dictated by the cost of carry pricing model, then arbitrage is possible by buying the cheaper instrument (the cash) and selling the more expensive instrument (the futures). Alternatively, if the current futures price is less than the fair price, then the arbitrageur purchases futures and sells the cash short. This activity forces the prices of the cash and futures instruments back into their appropriate relationship. Chapter 4 explains the cost of carry model. Chapters 8 and 9 discuss the complications and evidence relating to this model. Example 3-6 presents a simple arbitrage example that illustrates how arbitrage is profitable and how if affects the pricing process.

SPECULATION, HEDGING, AND SPREADING IN FUTURES MARKETS

Historical Returns of Speculators and Hedgers

A brief examination of the historical profit behavior of off-exchange traders provides some insights into the ability of speculators, as a group, to beat the market. A study by Hartzmark (1987) uses 1.2 million observations on the daily positions of traders over a $4\frac{1}{2}$-year period to examine the profitability of large and small speculators and hedgers. Table 3-3 shows that for nine futures markets, small speculators are big losers, large speculators are small winners, and hedgers are big winners.

Since the profits of the large speculators for the individual futures markets are small, Hartzmark concludes that speculators do *not* earn sufficient profits to compensate for the risk of trading in futures markets. Moreover, only 46% of the large speculators earn profits. Although Table 3-3 shows that small speculators profit from long positions, these profits result entirely from large gains in the T-bond futures markets.[11]

---

[10] When a futures contract settles in cash, the futures often are allowed to expire, whereas the cash portion is reversed at futures expiration.

[11] The classic studies of trader behavior are by Rockwell (1967) and Houthakker (1957). Using monthly data, these authors conclude that large speculators earn large profits, small speculators earn profits in large markets but lose in small markets, and hedgers lose money. Hartzmark (1987) shows that these studies provide inaccurate results because of the use of aggregate monthly data rather than daily data on individual traders.

EXAMPLE 3-6
A Basic Arbitrage Transaction

The following quotes exist for the S&P 500 cash and futures indexes for the day before the futures expire:

    Cash S&P 500: 452.00
    S&P 500 futures: 452.75

Total trading costs are $250 for both the cash and futures trades combined, per one futures contract.

The arbitrageur executes the trade for the following amount of dollars per one futures contract:

Sale of S&P 500 futures at 452.75	= $226,375
Purchase of cash stock in S&P 500 index	= 226,000
Gross profit per futures contract	= $ 375
Less trading costs	= − 250
Net profit per futures contract	= $ 125

Note that the financing or dividend aspects of the position are not important issues, since there is only one day until the expiration of the futures contract. If a longer time period before expiration existed, then these factors would have to be considered. Although the net profit for this example is small in dollar terms, it constitutes an annualized return of more than 30%. The dollar return would be larger for arbitrage positions with a longer time period before futures expiration.

These results raise the question of why small traders continue to trade if they consistently lose money. The following are possible reasons:

- Small speculators enjoy "playing the game"; it is exciting, dynamic, and a great conversational topic.
- Small speculators believe they can forecast; in other words, they remember their profits but forget their losses.
- Losers drop out, with their places being taken by new small speculators; meanwhile, winners become large speculators.
- The perceived utility of potential *large* gains is greater than the "disutility" of small losses, with the possibility of large losses discounted as being "unlikely" by the small speculator.

Table 3-3 Market Profits by Group (in Millions of Dollars)

	Total Profits	Net Long	Net Short
Small speculators	−854	992	−1846
Large speculators	125	−653	778
Hedgers	729	−339	1068

Source: Hartzmark (1987)

Table 3-4 Reported Speculative, Hedging, and Spreading Futures Activity, November 1991

Type of Contract	Total Open Interest	Percentage of Open Interest[a]				
		Hedging		Speculative		
		Long	Short	Long	Short	Spread
Stock indexes:						
S&P 500	159,403	69.6	52.7	4.7	22.1	.3
NYSE	5,012	23.8	14.7	26.2	22.3	1.0
Major market	8,740	84.6	75.0	6.3	11.6	.3
Long-term debt:						
T-bond	277,383	50.3	59.1	9.3	4.1	5.4
10-year note	84,992	44.5	66.0	12.5	1.6	5.9
Muni bonds	9,075	58.5	59.6	22.3	29.0	0.0
Short-term debt:						
Eurodollar	724,558	54.9	63.6	8.4	1.4	1.9
T-bills	49,757	54.8	73.1	21.5	10.1	0.0

[a] Hedging plus speculative long or short percentages do not total 200% because of nonreportable positions.
Source: Adapted from CFTC, "Reportable Positions," November 1991.

Open Interest in Futures Markets

Table 3-4 illustrates the speculative, hedging, and spreading activity for a number of financial futures contracts by showing the breakdown of open interest positions within the hedging and speculative categories. The hedging and speculative open interest figures in the table show positions for large reporting traders.

Table 3-4 shows which markets have active hedging programs, whether the hedging positions are short or long, and the relative size of the hedging speculative, and spreading positions. For the larger markets, hedging activity represents the major portion of the open interest. In fact, the long and short hedging activities are approximately balanced for most futures listed in Table 3-4. Figure 3-5 shows that the large hedging (commercial) positions in the S&P 500 futures have grown from 50% of the 200% of the total positions in 1983 to 140% by 1988. Meanwhile, the large speculative (noncommercial) positions have dropped substantially. Smaller (nonreporting) positions also have become less important. In general, the reporting speculative positions do not represent a large proportion of the open interest; that is, relatively few large speculators are active in these markets in relation to the total size of the open interest. Alternatively, a large percentage of the activity can be associated with the nonreporting positions—that is, with speculators, spreaders, hedgers, and arbitrageurs who have positions smaller than the reporting requirements.

Risk, Return, and Diversification with Futures

Bodie and Rosansky (1980) compute the historical annual return and risk (standard deviation) for a number of commodity futures contracts based on a deposit of the

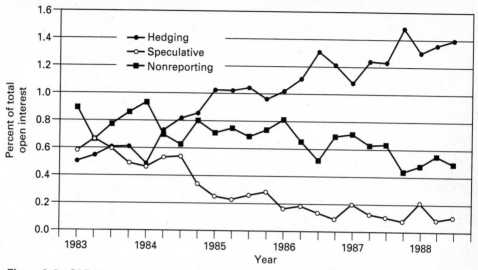

Figure 3-5 S&P 500 proportions of open interest. (*Source:* Daigler, 1990.)

entire value of the futures contract for margin purposes. Table 3-5 shows the average annual return and volatility of these contracts. The two most striking features of these results are

- The highest and lowest returns for each commodity futures would provide substantial returns, and losses, especially if the actual required margins are used.
- The large standard deviations (risk) show the inconsistency of the returns over time.

Table 3-5 Historical Commodity Futures Returns and Risks

Commodity Futures	Mean Return[a]	Standard Deviation	Highest Annual Return	Lowest Annual Return
Wheat	3.18	30.75	113.0	−40.0
Corn	2.13	26.31	101.6	−26.1
Soybeans	13.57	32.32	131.6	−40.5
Potatoes	6.91	42.11	125.0	−73.3
Cotton	8.94	36.24	163.2	−41.2
Orange juice	2.51	31.77	74.5	−32.3
Cocoa	15.71	54.63	197.5	−37.5
Propane	68.26	202.09	559.2	−48.2
Copper	19.79	47.20	130.1	−32.2
Sugar	25.40	116.22	492.0	−71.8

[a] Annual returns (percent per year), 1950–1976.
Source: Bodie and Rosansky (1980), p. 35.

The Bodie and Rosansky results also show that an equally weighted commodity futures portfolio is comparable to a portfolio of common stocks. This result illustrates the diversification potential of futures contracts; that is, the low or negative correlations between futures eliminate most of the risk inherent in the individual contracts. In fact, a portfolio of 60% stock and 40% commodity futures has a return equivalent to a stock portfolio, but it only has two-thirds of the risk of the stock portfolio.[12]

These results raise the question of the pricing of futures contracts—that is, the factors affecting the returns of futures. Chapter 4 considers three approaches:

- Return is a function of risk, especially the systematic (market) risk advocated by the Capital Asset Pricing Model.
- "Normal backwardation" occurs; that is, speculators earn a positive return on average when short hedgers dominate, since the hedgers pay speculators to take over the risk of the futures position.
- Cost of carry pricing creates a link between the cash asset and the futures, due to arbitrage, with interest rates being the dominating factor explaining the difference in price between the cash and futures contract.

SUMMARY AND LOOKING AHEAD

This chapter covers the key terminology of futures and the basic strategies used by traders. An understanding of the terminology is needed to comprehend how the markets operate, and the strategies are important to provide an overview of the rest of the book. Knowledge of how the cash and futures markets work and why they are useful can now be employed in studying pricing and arbitrage, hedging, and speculation. Chapters 4, 8, and 9 cover pricing and arbitrage for futures markets; Chapters 6, 7, and 10 examine hedging; and Chapter 17 applies hedging concepts to specific situations and discusses trading models and efficient markets.

BIBLIOGRAPHY

Bodie, Zvi, and Victor Rosansky (1980). "Risk and Return in Commodity Futures," *Financial Analysts Journal*, Vol. 36, No. 3, May–June, pp. 27–39.

Brennan, Michael J. (1986). "A Theory of Price Limits in Futures Markets," *The Journal of Financial Economics*, Vol. 16, No. 2, June, pp. 213–233.

Chicago Board of Trade (1991). "Margins," Xeroxed.

Chicago Mercantile Exchange (1991). "Minimum Performance Bond/Margin Requirements and Contract Specifications," Xeroxed.

Commodity Futures Trading Commission (1991). "Reportable Positions," November.

Daigler, Robert T. (1993). *Financial Futures Markets: Concepts, Evidence, and Applications.* New York: Harper Collins.

Daigler, Robert (1990). "The S&P Index Futures: A Hedging Contract," *CME Financial Strategy Paper*, Chicago Mercantile Exchange.

[12]Irwin and Brorsen (1985) find that portfolios of public futures funds, common stocks, and T-bills reduced portfolio risk by .6% to 3.7% compared to a stock and T-bill portfolio for the same return. Herbst and McCormack (1987) determined that including futures in a portfolio improves only the low and moderate return/risk portfolios because of the benefits of low to negative correlations, thereby suggesting that futures are beneficial for risk-adverse investors.

Hartzmark, Michael L. (1987). "Returns to Individual Traders of Futures: Aggregate Results," *Journal of Political Economy,* Vol. 95, No. 6, December, pp. 1292–1306.

Herbst, Anthony F., and Joseph P. McCormack (1987). "An Examination of the Risk/Return Characteristics of Portfolios Combining Commodity Futures Contracts with Common Stocks," *The Review of Futures Markets,* Vol. 6, No. 3, pp. 416–425.

Houthakker, Hendrik (1957). "Can Speculators Forecast Prices?" *The Review of Economics and Statistics,* Vol. 39, No. 1, May, pp. 143–151.

Irwin, S. H., and B. W. Brorsen (1985). "Public Futures Funds," *The Journal of Futures Markets,* Vol. 5, No. 3, Fall, pp. 463–485.

Ma, Christopher K., Ramesh P. Rao, and R. Stephen Sears (1989a). "Limit Moves and Price Resolution: The Case of the Treasury Bond Futures Markets," *The Journal of Futures Markets,* Vol. 9, No. 4, August, pp. 321–336.

Ma, Christopher K., Ramesh P. Rao, and R. Stephen Sears (1989b). "Volatility, Price Resolution, and the Effectiveness of Price Limits," *Journal of Financial Services Research,* Vol. 3, No. 213, December, pp. 165–200.

Peck, Anne E., and Jeffrey C. Williams (1991) "Deliveries on CBT Wheat, Corn, and Soybean Futures Contracts: 1964–65 to 1988–89" *Food Research Studies,* Vol. 22, No. 2, pp. 129–225.

Peck, Anne E., and Jeffrey C. Williams (1992). "Deliveries on Commodities Futures Contracts," *Economic Record,* forthcoming.

Rockwell, C. S. (1967). "Normal Backwardation, Forecasting, and the Returns to Speculators," *Food Research Institute Studies,* Supplement to Vol. VII, pp. 107–130.

PROBLEMS

*Indicates more difficult problems.

3-1 S&P 500 Futures and Margins

On October 27 Shaina Long purchases one March S&P 500 futures contract at a price of 341.20. Construct a table showing Ms. Long's weekly account based on the data given below. Assume that the initial margin is $12,000 per contract and the maintenance margin is $6000. Withdraw any excess profits each week.

Date:	11/6	11/13	11/20	11/27	12/4	12/11
Price:	343.70	345.90	347.05	349.50	355.90	353.55
Date:	12/18	12/26	1/2	1/8	1/15	1/22
Price:	354.15	351.05	356.35	354.60	340.95	342.20

3-2 Margins and T-Bond Futures

An investor buys one T-bond futures contract. The initial margin is $2700 and the maintenance margin is $2000. Find the missing information in the following table (labeled A to E):

Date	Price	Underlying Value of Futures	Marking-to-Market Amount	Margin Account Balance
10/20	100-8	$100,250		$2700
10/27	101-3	101,094	$844	3544
11/03	101-1	A	−63	3481
11/10	100-6	100,188	B	C
11/17	99-15	99,469	−719	D
11/24	100-14	100,438	969	E

*3-3 **Margin Table with T-Bill Futures**

A futures speculator forecasts an increase in interest rates. Therefore, he sells five T-bill futures contracts on August 15 at 94.85. The speculator covers his position on September 26 at 93.70. The weekly closing quotes for T-bill futures are as follows:

Date:	8/15	8/22	8/29	9/5	9/12	9/19	9/26
Price:	94.85	94.81	94.89	94.47	94.77	94.13	93.70

Calculate the weekly values in the margin account by setting up a margin table. Calculate the return on margin for the period. The initial margin is $540 per contract and the maintenance margin is $400. Make sure to determine the equivalent underlying value of the cash T-bill being priced by the futures. (Show how the first T-bill is calculated and the margin table.)

3-4 **Speculator's Return on Stock Index Futures**

A stock index futures speculator purchases two S&P 500 futures contracts on Monday at a price of 332.90. At the end of the week the market closes at 341.60. However, the following week the market suffers a decline in price to 328.50. Determine the profit/loss in dollars and the return on margin for each trading week and for the combined period. The initial margin is $22,000 per contract.

*3-5 **Speculator's Return on Multiple Futures Positions**

On September 17 a speculator purchases 10 T-bond futures and 50 T-bill futures, and shorts 30 Five-Year T-note futures and 2 S&P 500 futures. The traders close out all positions on September 18. Calculate the gain/loss and return on margin for these transactions.

	Treasury Bonds	T-Bills	Five-Year T-Notes	S&P 500
Sept. 17 prices	98-23	94.83	102-245	389.20
Sept. 18 prices	98-28	94.81	102-255	388.20
Initial margins	$2700	$540	$675	$22,000

3-6 **Hedging with Stock Index Futures**

The manager of the Conservative Fund foresees a decline in the stock market. He decides to hedge against the projected decline by using S&P 500 futures to offset any loss in the currently held $1 million stock portfolio that mirrors the S&P 500 cash index. On January 5 the cash index stands at 355.67, whereas the S&P futures are selling for 359.85. By January 25 the S&P cash index falls to 330.26 and the futures fall to 333.10. Set up a table showing the effects on the cash portfolio and the futures position. (Choose the number of futures contracts whose underlying value comes closest to the cash position.)

3-7 **Hedging with T-Bond Futures**

On August 1 a bond dealer holds $1 million of 20-year Treasury bonds priced at 94-26. He believes that interest rates will rise; thus the value of the portfolio will decline, as follows:

Cash Market		Futures Market	
Aug 1	Aug 31	Aug 1	Aug 31
94-26	86-16	86-28	79-26

Set up a hedge and show the results.

3-8 Spreading with S&P 500 Futures

On January 4 the March S&P 500 futures are trading for 369.05 and the June S&P 500 futures are priced at 373.20. A spreader forecasts a narrowing of the price relationship between these contracts; therefore, he purchases the nearby futures and sells the deferred futures. By February 2 the March contract is selling for 330.50 and the June contract is priced at 334.45. Set up a table showing a spread initiated on January 4 and covered on February 2.

3-9 Spreading with T-Bond Futures

On January 31 the price of the March T-bond futures is 95-02 and the June contract is 94-18. A spreader expects the price relationship between these two contracts to narrow. In fact, by February 27 the price of the March contract is 93-19 and the June contract is selling for 93-14. Set up a table showing the spread transactions and then calculate the return on margin when the spreader trades two T-bond contracts per expiration month.

3-10 Cost of Carry with Gold Futures

Walter Higginsmith is an aspiring futures trader. His first assignment by his mentor is to determine the fair value of gold futures. On September 21 the spot price of gold is $346.70. The December futures price is $350.40, with the futures expiring on the 21st day of the expiration month. Determine whether the futures price is fair if the financing rate is 5%.

3-11 Basic Arbitrage for Stock Index Futures

The price of the December S&P 500 futures contract two days before its expiration is 349.45, with the underlying cash index valued at 349.05. Is it possible for an arbitrageur to make a profit if trading costs (including holding the cash stocks for two days) equal $150? Show your calculations.

Chapter 4

THE BASICS OF FUTURES PRICING AND ARBITRAGE

Overview

Determining the fair price of financial futures is important for speculators, hedgers, spreaders, and arbitrageurs. If the actual futures price differs significantly from the fair price, then speculators and hedgers need to alter their trading strategies. Pricing differences are even more important for spreaders and arbitrageurs, since these traders focus on pricing discrepancies to obtain profits.

The three approaches to pricing futures are the Capital Asset Pricing Model, the hedging pressure theory, and the cost of carry model. Each model is examined, with the cost of carry selected as the best approach for purposes of pricing and arbitrage.

The pricing and arbitrage processes associated with the cost of carry model link the cash and futures markets via the net financing cost (the financing cost less the cash inflow). For example, the cost of carry model for stock index futures shows that the cash and futures prices should deviate only by the financing cost and the effect of dividends. If the futures are priced correctly (linked to the cash market), then speculators and hedgers can be confident that strategies based on correct cash market analysis will be successful. If futures prices deviate substantially from their fair prices, then arbitrage profits are possible.

This chapter discusses the terminology, concepts, and issues involving financial futures pricing and arbitrage, including calculating forward rates and implied financing rates. Chapters 8 and 9 delve into the specifics of pricing various financial futures contracts and implementing arbitrage strategies.

Terminology

*Cheapest-to-deliver   The cash security that provides the lowest cost (largest profit) to the arbitrage trader; the cheapest-to-deliver instrument is used to price the futures contract.

Contango   The hypothesis that futures are overpriced (short speculators will profit) because hedgers are net long.

*Conversion factor method   The procedure developed to adjust the futures delivery values for different cash T-bonds and T-notes. This adjustment is needed because the bonds (notes) that are eligible for delivery have different maturities and coupons, creating differing cash prices. This method provides a greater pool of cash instruments for delivery and therefore avoids squeezes.

*Cost of carry pricing   See Chapter 3.

Delivery   See Chapter 1.

*Delivery options   Choices provided to the seller of the T-bond futures contract concerning which bond to deliver and when to deliver it.

*Forward rate   The resulting interest rate obtained from owning a longer-term debt instrument and selling short a short-term cash instrument.

*Implied repo (financing) rate   The rate of return before financing costs implied by a transaction where a longer-term cash security is purchased and a futures contract is sold (or vice versa).

Integration of cash and futures markets   Integration occurs when these two markets possess sufficient volume such that active arbitrageurs keep the relative prices from these markets in line with one another.

Interest rate parity   The no-arbitrage relationship for currency futures that relates the price of the futures to the relative financing interest rates for the two currencies.

*Long arbitrage   Buying futures in connection with a cash market transaction in order to create risk-free profits.

*Normal backwardation   The hypothesis that futures are underpriced (long speculators will profit) because hedgers are net short.

*Pure arbitrage   Creating a risk-free profitable transaction using futures and the associated cash instrument by employing external financing (i.e., internal funds are not necessary for the transaction).

*Quasi-arbitrage   Creating a risk-free profitable transaction with futures and the associated cash instrument by employing internal funds; equivalently, a transaction providing a higher alternative return than an equivalent cash security.

*Repurchase (repo) transaction   Borrowing funds by providing a government security for collateral and promising to "repurchase" the security at the end of the agreed upon time period. The associated interest rate is the "repo rate."

*Short arbitrage   *Selling* futures in connection with cash market transactions in order to create risk-free profits.

Spread   See Chapter 3.

Variable interest rate   When the short-term interest rate changes over time, it affects the costs/returns to the margin account.

THEORIES OF FUTURES PRICING

Three models exist that attempt to explain the pricing of futures contracts:

- The Capital Asset Pricing Model (CAPM): Return is a function of market risk.
- Net hedging pressure: Returns are systematically biased against the net hedging position and in favor of the net speculative position.
- Cost of carry model: Arbitrage creates a link between the futures and cash positions, with the difference in price related to the net financing cost of holding the cash position.

The Capital Asset Pricing Model

The CAPM states that the return on a security is a function of the market (systematic) risk. The CAPM is defined by Equation (4-1), where the measure of systematic risk (beta) is the covariance of the asset return (futures price change) with the return on the market portfolio, divided by the variance of the market return; that is,

$$E(R_j) = R_f + \beta_j[E(R_m) - R_f] \qquad (4\text{-}1)$$

where $E(R_j)$ = the expected return on security j

R_f = the risk-free rate

$E(R_m)$ = the expected return on the market portfolio

$\beta_j = \text{cov}(R_j, R_m)/\sigma_m^2$ = the beta of the instrument

The CAPM is an important theory for pricing stocks and portfolios of stocks.[1] When applied to futures contracts, the CAPM states that the dollar change in the futures is directly proportional to the relationship between the futures and the "market"; that is, return is a function of the systematic risk as measured by beta. The CAPM shows that only the systematic risk should be priced (i.e., the diversifiable unsystematic risk is avoidable). The unavoidable systematic risk occurs due to the instrument's relationship with the market portfolio. The systematic/unsystematic relationship is shown by separating the instrument's return into its two components via the following regression equation:

$$R_j = \alpha_j + \beta_j R_m + e_j \qquad (4\text{-}2)$$

where β_j = the systematic risk of security j

    $\sigma(e_j)$ = the unsystematic risk of security j

Dusak (1973) and Bodie and Rosansky (1980) find that the betas of commodity futures contracts are near zero; that is, commodity futures are *not* directly related to stock market index returns. According to the CAPM, futures betas of zero mean that futures should have a return of zero—that is, that futures prices are unbiased estimates of the future cash price.[2] Dusak finds that wheat, corn, and soybeans do have returns near zero. Bodie and Rosansky find positive returns, although the variability in the returns is large from year to year. Bodie and Rosansky state that the positive returns in their study in combination with the zero betas reject the CAPM as the appropriate pricing model.

The major concern with applying the CAPM to futures prices is whether the stock market index adequately measures the undiversifiable risk of commodity futures contracts. If the stock market index does *not* adequately measure all of the undiversifiable risk for futures, then the remaining unsystematic risk possesses patterns that create an obstacle to diversification among futures contracts. When individual stocks are priced in relation to the stock market then typically no major patterns appear in the e_j values in Equation (4-2). However, patterns in commodity futures e_j values do exist in relation to the stock market index. These patterns are caused by factors such as weather conditions, which are unrelated to general stock market movements but are important determinants of agricultural futures prices. Consequently, the assumptions of the CAPM are not met.

Breeden (1979, 1980) extended the CAPM approach to consumption-based betas and the consumption-based CAPM by employing a basket of commodity goods to serve as the "market index." A logical extension to the stock CAPM for futures markets, the consumption-based CAPM includes factors that affect the general movement of commodity prices. The purpose of the consumption CAPM is to improve the measure of undiversifiable risk. Breeden found positive consumption-based betas for goods such as livestock and negative betas for grains. However, in general, the fact that

---

[1] Developed by William Sharpe (1964), the CAPM is one of the cornerstones of financial theory. Sharpe shared the Nobel Prize for Economics in 1991 for the CAPM and his other contributions to finance.

[2] Although the CAPM states that purchases of assets with betas of zero must earn the risk-free rate, purchasing futures does not require an investment. Thus, the expected return of futures under the CAPM are zero.

the explanatory power of the results was low served to cast doubt on the ability of the consumption-based CAPM to provide an important explanation for the behavior of futures prices.[3]

The Hedging Pressure Theory:
Futures as Unbiased (or Biased) Predictors of Cash Prices

One view of futures prices as a forecast of subsequent cash prices is that futures provide an unbiased prediction of the subsequent (expected) cash price; that is, prices only reflect current information. Even though new information changes prices and therefore creates errors for the predictions, this theory states that *on average* the predictions are not biased toward either a consistent positive or negative return. Alternatively, supply-and-demand factors could cause the futures to be consistently under- or overpriced relative to its true value. The hedging pressure theory of futures pricing states that if net short hedging exceeds net long speculation, then long speculators require above-average returns as compensation for purchasing additional futures contracts in order to equate supply and demand. This relationship is known as **normal backwardation**; that is, futures prices must be underpriced relative to their true value to encourage speculators to buy futures. Similarly, **contango** means that futures must be overpriced for short speculators to earn abnormal returns when net long hedging is greater than net short speculation.

Although the number of long positions *must* equal the number of short positions for trading to exist, the hedging pressure theory states that when a net short or long hedging position exists, then futures prices become a biased estimate of the subsequent expected cash price. Thus, a net hedging position forces futures prices to become underpriced or overpriced (biased) in order to encourage additional speculators to enter the market and create the needed activity to offset the hedger's activity in the market. Figure 4-1 illustrates the effect of a supply/demand imbalance of open interest on futures prices. When net short hedgers predominate (points A and B in Figure 4-1), net long speculators are needed to balance open interest. In this case of normal backwardation, the current futures price is below the expected future cash price. Conversely, when net long hedging predominates (points C and D) then net short speculation is needed and the current futures price lies above the expected future cash price.

Keynes (1930) and Hicks (1946) developed the normal backwardation and contango concepts. They stated that futures typically have net short speculators; in other words, futures prices typically create excess returns for long speculators due to the normal backwardation of futures markets. The issue of excess returns for speculators, or equivalently whether futures provide *on average* an unbiased or biased prediction of subsequent cash prices, has received substantial interest in the literature.

Two early and well-known studies of whether futures are an unbiased or biased predictor of subsequent cash prices are by Houthakker (1957) and Rockwell (1967). Although they employed similar methodologies, Houthakker concluded normal backwardation existed, whereas Rockwell's study of a larger set of data states the opposite.

---

[3] Breeden employed quarterly observations to calculate the consumption-based betas. An alternative is to employ the CRB cash index or futures contracts with a shorter time interval.

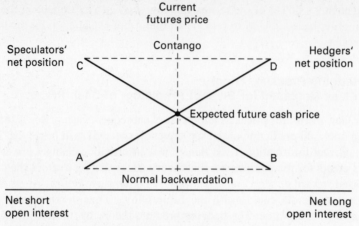

Figure 4-1 The effect of net open interest on futures prices.
(*Source:* Daigler, 1985, p. 9.)

Fama and French (1987) find weak support for normal backwardation. One of the most complete studies on normal backwardation is by Murphy and Hilliard (1989), who conclude that normal backwardation does *not* exist after 1974. Kolb (1992) uses nearly one million daily futures prices to determine that only 7 of 29 futures show evidence of normal backwardation or contango, with currencies and debt futures providing unbiased estimates of the subsequent cash prices (stock index futures are not examined). Although Bodie and Rosansky (1980) support normal backwardation by finding positive returns for 22 of 23 commodities, only 3 of these turned out to be statistically significant. The Hartzmark (1987) study outlined in Chapter 3 shows that speculators lose money overall, which is inconsistent with normal backwardation and contango. Phillips and Weiner (1991) use intraday trades in the petroleum forward markets to determine that no identifiable group of traders make significant profits using daily prices. However, using within-the-day transactions data, the Japanese trading houses with superior *information* do profit. In general, the studies noted above and other studies relating to normal backwardation are inconsistent in their conclusions. However, most of the evidence, especially the more recent evidence, rejects normal backwardation in favor of futures as an unbiased estimate of the subsequent cash price.[4]

The Accuracy of Futures Prediction

Futures can provide an unbiased prediction of subsequent cash prices *on average,* but still can cause large errors in the prediction process. In fact, even if the futures and cash markets include all current information, market participants are not able to anticipate all future economic developments accurately. Thus, the actual cash price when the futures contract expires differs from the estimated price provided by the futures contract during its trading life because of the availability of new information. The question is: how *variable* is the futures forecast of subsequent cash prices?

[4] In addition, Table 3-4 and Figure 3-5 illustrate that the reportable long and short hedging positions for financial futures contracts often have net hedging positions that are near zero. This fact negates the key assumption of the normal backwardation/contango concepts for financial futures. However, no in-depth study of the net reportable hedging positions has been undertaken for financial futures contracts.

MacDonald and Hein (1989), Hegde and McDonald (1986), and Howard (1982), among others, examine the relative ability of futures interest rates to predict accurately the subsequent cash interest rates at futures expiration. Figure 4-2 shows the results from Howard, comparing futures, no-change, and "best time series" forecasts of the subsequent cash interest rates for various weeks before futures expirations.[5] The mean absolute percentage error (MAPE) between the futures interest rate and the actual interest rate is 8.24% for a time horizon of 4 weeks and increases rapidly to 15.41% for 12 weeks. Obviously, the forecasting ability of futures is limited, especially as the time to expiration of the futures contract lengthens. However, for periods of eight weeks or longer, the futures forecasts are superior to both the no-change forecast and to the "best time series" estimate, with the superiority of the futures forecasts increasing as the time horizon increases. These results differ from earlier studies by Fama (1976) and by Hamburger and Platt (1975), who concluded that a no-change model is superior to a forward contract forecast. However, the Fama and the Hamburger and Platt studies employed data from a much less volatile interest rate period: namely the 1950s and 1960s.[6] Logically, a no-change model would be a less accurate procedure during the volatile period of the late 1970s and early 1980s, the time period employed in the aforementioned study by Howard.

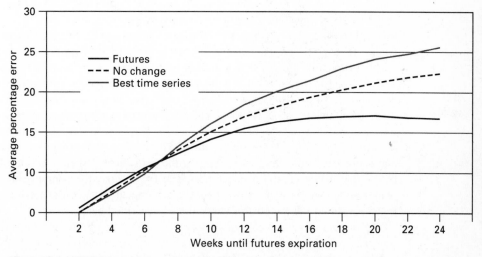

Figure 4-2 T-bill futures forecasting ability. (*Source:* Abstracted from results in Howard, 1982.)

[5] The "best time series" values are obtained by using the Box-Jenkins procedure, which finds the best-fit equation by employing both an autoregressive (time series regression) and a moving average simultaneously. Forward forecasts provide almost identical, but inferior, forecasts of the cash rate; therefore, the forward forecasts are omitted from the graph. Calculating forward rates is discussed later in this chapter. MacDonald and Hein (1989) show that the futures provides superior information to the forward rate for forecasting purposes. The Howard study is emphasized here because of its inclusion of alternative procedures for forecasting the cash interest rate.

[6] The Fama and the Hamburger and Platt studies use forward rates rather than futures. Hegde and McDonald (1986) show that the R^2 values of regressions between the futures errors and the no-change errors is relatively high for the four weeks before futures expiration, but then drops below 15%. In other words, there is a significant amount of variability around the MAPE value.

PRICING AND ARBITRAGE BASICS: THE COST OF CARRY MODEL

Pricing and Arbitrage Building Blocks

The pricing of futures contracts and arbitrage between futures and cash are closely related concepts. The fair price of a futures contract is determined by a pricing model that incorporates the value of the underlying cash asset, the time to expiration of the futures contract, the cost of financing the cash position, the cash inflows of the asset, and any special characteristics of the futures contract of expiration.[7] In perfect markets—that is, when transactions costs and tax effects are not relevant—the actual futures price equals the fair price.

Arbitrage exists when the actual futures price deviates from the fair price by more than transactions costs. When sufficiently large profits above the risk-free return exist, arbitrageurs step in and buy the lower-priced security (e.g., the cash asset) and sell the higher-priced security (e.g., the futures contract). Such actions force the futures price back toward the fair price. Without arbitrage, the futures price could deviate significantly from the fair price, causing hedgers to avoid using futures markets because of poor hedging results and the uncertainty of the pricing process.

An illustration of arbitrage will help to clarify the process. Let us use gold futures, since gold is a basic cash asset that does not have cash flows. Assume that on the futures expiration day, gold futures are priced at $350 an ounce and cash gold is trading for $345. If trading costs are minimal, an arbitrageur could buy gold in the cash market for $5 less than it is trading in the futures market. The arbitrageur eliminates any chance that the price difference will change between the two markets by having two telephones and talking to both the cash and futures traders of gold at the same time. The arbitrageur then can immediately use the cash gold to fulfill the delivery requirement of the futures contract, making a risk-free and immediate profit. Actions by many arbitrageurs to obtain these risk-free profits would cause the cash and futures prices to converge, since the demand for cash gold forces that price up and the selling of futures forces the futures price down. These actions eliminate the arbitrage profits and cause the futures and cash prices to be equivalent. When a period of time exists before the expiration and delivery period of the futures, the comparison of prices becomes more complicated. In this case the arbitrageur must consider the cost of financing the position via the cost of carry model described below.

The pricing of futures is based on one key concept: *significant deviations from the fair price should not be possible if the futures and cash markets are effectively linked.* Arbitrage strategies provide the mechanism that **integrates the cash and futures markets.** The cost of carry model determines the fair futures price in terms of the variables that influence this price.

The Cost of Carry Model

The cost of carry model explains the relationship between the cash asset price and the futures price. Simply stated, this model shows the relationship created between these markets when an arbitrageur buys the cash asset now, holds and finances the asset

---

[7] Costs for physical assets include storage and transportation costs and insurance.

with borrowed funds for the life of the futures contract, and then delivers the cash asset into the futures contract when the futures expire. Under these circumstances, Equation (4-3) determines the fair futures price:

$$P_{FAIR} = P_C(1 + i)^t \qquad (4-3)$$

where P_{FAIR} = the fair price for the futures

P_C = current price of the cash asset

i = the financing rate (interest rate)

t = the proportion of the year until the futures expire

In a perfect market, P_{FAIR} should equal the current futures price.

Using gold provides a good example of how the cost of carry relationship works. For example, an arbitrageur purchases gold (with borrowed funds) and sells gold futures. The gold is held until the futures expire, at which time the gold is delivered into the futures contract. An example of the cash flows for this relationship is given in Exhibit 4-1. This procedure of buying the cash asset and holding it until futures expiration causes the futures price to be a function of the cash price, the time until futures expiration, and the financing cost. This price relationship exists because the arbitrageur buys the lower-priced gold and sells the higher-priced futures contract so that futures prices do not deviate significantly from the fair futures price. (One also could sell gold and buy the futures.) Similarly, the cost of carry model explains pricing for agricultural futures markets. Thus, a grain merchant sells the futures contract, buys wheat with the

EXHIBIT 4-1
Cash Flows for the Cost of Carry Model

To illustrate how cash flows explain the cost of carry equation let us use the following prices and interest rates:

Price of gold	$350
Futures price of gold (expiration and delivery in 1 year)	$385
Interest rate for financing	10%

Transaction	Cash Flow at Time = 0	Cash Flow at Time = 1 Year
Borrow $350 for 1 year at 10%	+$350	−$385
Buy 1 ounce of gold at cash price	−350	
Sell futures contract at $t = 0$ ($P = 385$) for delivery of gold at $t = 1$	0	+385
Total cash flow	$ 0	$ 0

This exhibit illustrates that the cost of carry equation $P_{FAIR} = P_C(1 + i)^t$ equates the cash flows from the futures and the cash transactions.

use of borrowed money, stores the wheat until the futures expire, and then delivers the wheat into the futures contract.[8]

The cost of carry model for financial futures works in a similar manner. For example, a money manager purchases a portfolio of common stocks that is equivalent to the S&P 500 index, sells the corresponding futures contract, and then holds the position until the futures expire. The important difference in contrast to the gold and agricultural examples is that stock index futures are settled in cash; that is, the futures index is set equal to the cash index at the end of the last trading day for the futures. Thus, one must sell the cash common stocks when the futures expire rather than deliver them into the futures contract. The pricing of interest rate futures contracts is more complicated due to their delivery procedure. Chapters 8 and 9 examine these issues.

Arbitrage Concepts

Arbitrage, the existence of risk-free profits, is illustrated by the cash flow relationships presented in Exhibit 4-2. This example shows the "cash and carry" relationship given in the cost of carry model; here the cash gold is purchased, "carried" in storage, and then delivered into the short futures position. The difference between Exhibits 4-2 and 4-1 is the arbitrage profit obtained in Exhibit 4-2 resulting from $P_F > P_C(1 + i)^t$, that is, $P_F > P_{FAIR}$ (where P_F = the futures price).

Similarly, Exhibit 4-3 shows how to profit when $P_F < P_C(1 + i)^t$; that is, $P_F < P_{FAIR}$. In this case, the arbitrageur sells gold short, and the cash proceeds from the short sale

EXHIBIT 4-2
Cash and Carry Arbitrage

Price of gold	$350
Futures price of gold (expiration and delivery in 1 year)	$387
Interest rate for financing	10%

Transaction	Cash Flow at Time = 0	Cash Flow at Time = 1 year
Borrow $350 for 1 year at 10%	+$350	−$385
Buy 1 ounce of gold at cash price	−350	
Sell futures contract at $t = 0$ $(P = 387)$ for delivery of gold at $t = 1$	0	+387
Total cash flow	$ 0	$ 2

This exhibit shows how risk-free profits are obtained when the futures price is above the fair futures price.

[8] For wheat futures, the financing cost includes both the cost of borrowed funds *and* the cost of storing the wheat. If merchants who store the wheat use their own funds to finance the cash asset, then the financing cost measures the opportunity cost of funds for the merchant rather than the interest rate on borrowed funds.

FOCUS 4-1
Impediments to Pricing Futures: Squeezes and Large Trades

The cost of carry model shows that futures prices are linked to the underlying cash value, the financing rate, any cash inflows, and the time to futures expiration. However, when traders attempt to squeeze the market by obtaining a large portion of the cash asset, unusual pricing and volatility can result. Similarly, large volume also creates havoc in the markets. Several famous attempted squeezes and large volume situations are described below.

- **The Russian Wheat Deal.**   In the early 1970s the Soviets purchased massive quantities of U.S. wheat and corn by separate secret deals with U.S. grain dealers. These dealers hedged their sales in the futures market. The resulting wheat shortage in the United States caused prices to increase significantly. Farmers who had hedged their crop with forwards and futures were locked in to the agreed-upon price. Since the futures market price increased before harvest time, futures were blamed for the higher wheat prices. A similar situation occurred in the late 1980s when drought in the Midwest caused prices to rise on the futures exchanges before harvest, which encouraged stores to increase the price of wheat products *before* the harvest. These actions by the stores created yet another accusation that futures traders caused higher prices for food.

- **The Potato Default.**   Potato futures require the delivery of Maine potatoes. However, the majority of potatoes are grown in Idaho and surrounding states. In 1976, two major Idaho potato producers, J.R. Simplot and the Taggares family, sold futures contracts to deliver 50 million potatoes. They assumed that the large supply of Idaho potatoes would cause prices to fall. However, those who purchased the futures bought up most of the *Maine* potatoes, creating a short squeeze. Simplot and the Taggares chose to default rather than pay off the long futures positions. After long court battles, no one emerged as a winner.

- **Silver and the Hunts.**   The Hunt brothers purchased millions of ounces of silver, silver futures contracts, causing the price to increase substantially. Although a large amount of silver existed, only a small portion met the standards needed for delivery into a futures contract. The Hunts made millions of dollars by buying contracts and taking delivery. Feeling successful, they attempted to play the game again in 1979 and 1980. Prices rose from $8 an ounce to $50 an ounce. As prices increased, the Hunts used the profits from these positions to purchase additional contracts. This time the CFTC and the exchanges stepped in, ordering high margins and a liquidation of the Hunts' position. The selling of the cash and futures holdings in silver caused prices to fall to $5 an ounce.

- **Soybeans and the Hunts.**   The Hunts began purchasing soybeans when their advisors predicted a shortage of protein, of which soybeans are a major source. The Hunts purchased a total of 24 million bushels of soybeans. The CFTC argued the Hunts acted as one group and therefore were subject to the position limits discussed in Chapter 3— namely three million bushels. While court cases ensued, the Hunts were told merely not to collaborate again. Meanwhile, Cook Industries (a large commodities firm in Memphis) analyzed that soybeans were overpriced. While their analysis was eventually correct, Cook went bankrupt holding onto short futures positions as soybean prices rose.

are lent out to receive interest; when the long futures position expires, the gold received is used to fulfill the short sale.

The above examples are often described as "perfect arbitrage," since perfect markets without transactions costs are assumed to exist. The examples above and the cost of

EXHIBIT 4-3
Reverse Cash and Carry Arbitrage

Price of gold		$350
Futures price of gold (expiration and delivery in 1 year)		$382
Interest rate for financing		10%

Transaction	Cash Flow at Time = 0	Cash Flow at Time = 1 Year
Sell short 1 ounce of gold	+$350	
Lend proceeds from the short sale for 1 year at 10%	−350	+$385
Buy futures contract at $t = 0$ ($P = 382$) and receive delivery of gold at $t = 1$	0	−382
Use gold received at $t = 1$ to cover short sale		0
Total cash flow	$ 0	$ 3

This exhibit shows how risk-free profits are made when the futures price is below the fair futures price.

carry Equation (4-3) can be extended to include transactions costs. Thus, with transactions costs, arbitrage exists if a profit can be made by satisfying the following equation:

$$P_C(1 + i)^t + T < P_F < P_C(1 + i)^t - T \qquad (4\text{-}4)$$

where P_F = the futures price as determined by the market

T = transactions costs per unit of the cash asset

Note that if $P_C(1 + i)^t + T < P_F$, then the arbitrageur purchases the less expensive cash asset and sells short the more expensive futures. If $P_F < P_C(1 + i)^t - T$, then the less expensive futures contract is purchased and the cash asset is sold. If neither case exists (i.e., P_F lies within the inequality bounds), then no arbitrage is possible.

An arbitrageur can hold a position until the expiration of the futures contract, when either physical delivery is implemented or the cash settlement procedure forces the arbitrageur to cover the futures position. However, the arbitrageur does not have to wait until the expiration of the futures contract in order to liquidate the arbitrage transaction. If the difference between the futures price and the cost of carry forward price narrows significantly before the futures expire, then it is often beneficial to reverse the futures and cash positions and take the profits on the position. Although these profits may be less in magnitude than would be the case if the arbitrageur waited until the expiration of the futures, these funds would be available for executing other arbitrage trades. Such "temporary" arbitrage positions are often taken in the stock index futures market, where the differences between the futures and forward prices often change significantly, even within the day. In general, profitable arbitrage positions exist for only a short time period before disappearing. Such transactions also require large amounts of funds and exchange floor contacts in order to achieve effective execution of the trade.

Pure and Quasi-Arbitrage

Pure Arbitrage.   **Pure arbitrage** exists when funds are borrowed to complete the arbitrage transaction. For pure arbitrage, the transaction must consider the cost of borrowed funds, transactions costs, and the size of the difference between the futures and cash prices. This type of arbitrage is employed frequently for interest rate and currency futures markets.

The interest rate associated with the cost of financing T-bond and T-bill arbitrage is often the **repurchase (repo)** rate. The repo rate is the interest rate on short-term funds, where the funds are backed by government securities. The borrower of funds for the repo agreement provides the government securities as collateral, with the borrower promising to "repurchase" these securities at a later date and pay interest on the funds. An arbitrage transaction is profitable when the return on the pure arbitrage transaction before considering the financing costs is greater than the repo rate associated with the financing.

Quasi-Arbitrage.   **Quasi-arbitrage** exists when internal funds are employed to execute the arbitrage transaction. Quasi-arbitrage is a viable transaction when the futures-cash arbitrage provides higher returns than an equivalent cash security investment. For example, quasi-arbitrage exists when a manager obtains a higher return with a T-bill futures quasi-arbitrage than on an equivalent maturity cash T-bill investment. This strategy is also known as an alternative return strategy.

Another example of an alternative return or quasi-arbitrage strategy using futures is to buy stocks that are equivalent to the S&P 500 index and sell futures. If this strategy provides a return above a T-bill or similar risk-free rate, then the arbitrage position obtains a higher alternative return.

Trading costs and the size of the difference between the futures and cash prices are the important factors that determine whether a quasi-arbitrage transaction is preferable to a cash-only position. In reality, the implementation of quasi-arbitrage transactions is less frequent than pure arbitrage transactions for interest rate securities, since a portfolio manager holding the cash instrument must decide to include quasi-arbitrage as a viable portfolio strategy to complement strategies involving the selection and timing of the cash instruments. The lack of familiarity with futures markets by most financial institutions and some money managers is the main reason for a lack of quasi-arbitrage activity for debt instruments. The reluctance to execute quasi-arbitrage strategies, in conjunction with the widespread use of pure arbitrage, typically results in profits for those who do engage in quasi-arbitrage strategies.

On the other hand, quasi-arbitrage is the dominant strategy for stock index futures. Pension funds and other large pools of funds employ stock futures arbitrage to earn returns above the risk-free return. Brokerage houses often do not operate pure arbitrage programs because of the availability of higher-yielding alternative uses for these funds and because of pressure to avoid arbitrage transactions.

Restrictions on Arbitrage Profits

The Factors. The previous discussion on arbitrage identifies transactions costs as an impediment to profitable transactions. Let us identify the components of transactions costs and other restrictions to profitable arbitrage transactions. Such restrictions are

- **Transactions costs:** commissions to brokers, fees to the exchange, and bid-ask spreads. The bid-ask spread is the cost of buying from a dealer at the higher ask price and selling at the bid price.
- **Short selling restrictions:** when the cash asset is sold short for reverse cash-and-carry transactions, our example assumes that all of the proceeds are available to invest in an interest-bearing security. Often only part (or none) of the funds are available to the short seller. In addition, short sellers of stock must wait for an "uptick" in the stock price to execute a short sale.
- **Borrowing funds:** the cash-and-carry transactions assume that the entire cost of the asset can be borrowed. Arbitrageurs using repurchase transactions for debt futures typically obtain 90% to 100% of the asset's value. However, only 50% of stock purchases can be financed.
- **Equal borrowing and lending rates:** Equations (4-3) and (4-4) assume that the cost of borrowing funds for a cash-and-carry transaction equals the interest received on depositing funds for a reverse cash-and-carry transaction. This is often not the case.
- **Interest received or paid on marking-to-market:** Equations (4-3) and (4-4) treat futures as a forward contract; that is, no intermediate cash flows occur. The next paragraph describes the effects of marking-to-market.

Marking-to-Market and Variable Interest Rates. Cash transactions are not marked-to-market. However, futures prices are marked-to-market on a daily basis for all traders; that is, an additional deposit equal to any loss must be made, and profits can be withdrawn, both on a daily basis. If additional funds to cover losses are made in cash, then the trader must finance these funds. This financing typically is calculated at the current short-term interest rate. Similarly, profits can be withdrawn and invested at the short-term interest rate. If the *daily* interest rate is used for financing and investment purposes, then the unpredictable variability of interest rates affects the overall profitability of the futures arbitrage transaction. However, if the arbitrage uses Treasury securities to cover the margin calls, then the effect of **variable interest rates** is mitigated. See Daigler (1993) for an additional discussion of the effect of variable interest rates on futures prices.

STOCK INDEX FUTURES PRICING AND ARBITRAGE

The basic cost of carry model given in (4-3) can be amended for stock index futures to consider the dividends received from holding the stocks in the index:

$$P_{\text{FAIR}} = P_C(1 + i)^t - D \qquad (4\text{-}5)$$

where P_{FAIR} = the fair futures price for a stock index

P_C = the current value of the underlying cash stock index

i = the financing rate of interest or equivalent investment return desired, in percentage terms

D = the dollar dividend amount in index points received on the stocks in the index from now until the expiration of the futures contract[9]

t = number of days until expiration of the futures divided by 365

For example, if $P_C = 400.00$, $i = 5\%$, $t = \frac{1}{4}$ year, and $D = 3.0$ index points over the next three months, then

$$P_{\text{FAIR}} = 400(1 + .05)^{.25} - 3 = 401.91$$

Equation (4-5) illustrates both the relationship between the futures and current cash values and the net difference between the financing (or opportunity) costs and the income received. In particular, the larger the difference between interest cost and dividends, the larger the price difference between P_{FAIR} and P_C. In addition, the larger the value of t, the larger the price difference between the futures and cash prices.

Figure 4-3 illustrates the difference between the S&P 500 futures price and the fair price for five-minute intervals during February 1988. Equation (4-5) is used to calculate the fair price, with the S&P cash index being employed for P_C. The figure shows that many of the futures prices are within .5 index point of the fair price, with very few observations being more than 1.0 index point from the fair value. However, there is a tendency late in the month for the futures price to be above the fair price; that is, the

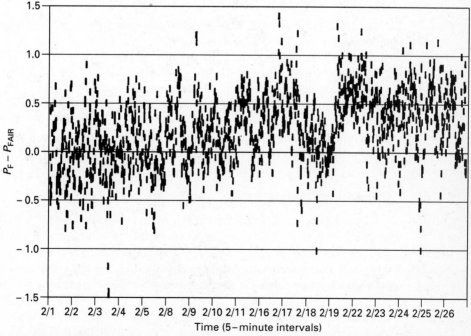

Figure 4-3 S&P 500 futures; Fair price, February 1988. (*Source:* Data from Daigler, 1991, and Tick Data, Inc.)

[9] Theoretically, the futures value of these dividends until contract expiration is appropriate here. However, the difficulty of calculating the dividends and the uncertainty of the dividends makes the present value calculation less useful in reality. Chapter 8 presents an alternative dividend yield model that considers continuously compounded values.

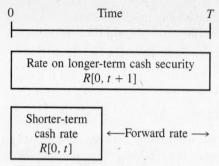

Figure 4-4   The forward rate.

points in the figure are above 0. Chapter 8 discusses stock index pricing and arbitrage issues, and helps to explain why differences from the fair price exist and whether arbitrage is possible. The chapter includes examples on stock index pricing and arbitrage. Appendix 8A derives Equation (4-5).

FORWARD AND IMPLIED FINANCING RATES: THE FOUNDATION OF DEBT ARBITRAGE

The pricing and arbitrage of interest rate futures contracts is based on the calculation of **forward rates** and the comparison of these rates with the futures interest rates. If the difference between the forward and futures rates is large enough to cover transactions costs, then arbitrage is possible. Short-term interest rate futures rely on the forward rate and similar calculations to determine the pricing accuracy of the futures and whether arbitrage exists. Long-term interest rate futures start with forward rate calculations and then consider factors unique to these futures contracts. This section illustrates how to calculate and use forward rates for pricing and arbitrage. Subsequent sections discuss specifics of short-term and long-term interest rate futures arbitrage.

Calculating Forward Rates

Forward rates are important for debt futures, especially for short-term interest rate contracts. Figure 4-4 illustrates the concept of a forward rate as the resulting interest rate obtained from owning a longer-term debt instrument and selling short a shorter-term debt instrument. Conceptually, a forward rate is the compounded "difference" between the longer-term and shorter-term rates. Thus, forward interest rates are calculated by using two cash interest rates from debt instruments with different maturities. First, the calculation of forward rates is described in terms of periods, often thought of as years. Hence, one determines a one-year forward interest rate starting one year from now, by calculating the interest rate, when compounded with an initial one-year cash rate, is equivalent to a two-year cash rate. Typically, all interest rates are annualized, regardless of the time periods employed. Equation (4-6) specifies how to find a one-period forward rate starting one period from now; that is,

$$r[1,2] = \frac{(1 + R[0,2])^2}{(1 + R[0,1])} - 1 \qquad (4\text{-}6)$$

where $r[1, 2]$ = the one-period (annualized) forward rate from time 1 to time 2 (the one-period forward rate starting at time period 1)

$R[0, 1]$ = the current one-period interest rate from time 0 (now) to time 1

$R[0, 2]$ = the current two-period interest rate from time 0 to time 2

Note that R stands for the current cash rate, whereas r represents a forward rate. Thus, the one-period forward rate $r[1, 2]$ starting at time 1 is determined from the current two-period cash rate $R[0, 2]$ and the current one-period cash rate $R[0, 1]$. Daigler (1993) derives Equations (4-6) to (4-8) and (4-10).

One can generalize the one-period forward rate in Equation (4-6) to determine a one-period forward rate starting at any time period; that is,

$$r[t, t + 1] = \frac{(1 + R[0, t + 1])^{t+1}}{(1 + R[0, t])^t} - 1 \tag{4-7}$$

where $r[t, t + 1]$ = the one-period forward rate from time t to time $t + 1$

$R[0, t]$ = the current t period interest rate from time 0 to time t

The first number in the brackets is the starting time period for the interest rate, and the second number is the ending time period. The difference between the two numbers states the number of periods employed to calculate the rate. A multiperiod forward rate is determined by further generalizing the above equations:

$$r[a, b] = \left[\frac{(1 + R[0, b])^b}{(1 + R[0, a])^a} \right]^{1/(b-a)} - 1 \tag{4-8}$$

where $r[a, b]$ = the $(b - a)$ period forward rate from time a to time b (the forward rate for $b - a$ periods starting at time period a)

Thus, for example, $r[1, 3]$ is the two-period forward rate from time 1 to time 3 (the two-period forward rate starting at time period 1). Example 4-1 shows how to determine a one-year forward rate starting one year and four years from today, and a two-year forward rate starting two years from today.

The Forward Transaction for Short-Term Debt Instruments

Figure 4-5 shows the diagram of a forward contract transaction for T-bills: a commitment entered into today to purchase a 90-day cash T-bill at time $t = 90$. The figure shows that a forward transaction can be created by buying a 180-day cash T-bill and selling short a 90-day cash T-bill, thereby leaving the net transaction for the last 90 days of the 180-day period as a long forward position. A similar transaction can be completed for Eurodollar time deposits. A dealer, say a bank, who sells a forward contract creates this instrument by instituting these long and short cash market transactions. The interest rate associated with this forward transaction is the relevant forward interest rate.

Forward Versus Futures Rates: Identifying Arbitrage Possibilities

The forward rate is employed to determine whether a **short** or a **long arbitrage** is appropriate and whether an arbitrage is profitable. A short arbitrage occurs when futures are sold, while a long arbitrage occurs when futures are purchased. The equation

EXAMPLE 4-1
Calculating Forward Rates

Equation (4-7) shows how to find a one-period forward rate, that is,

$$r[t, t + 1] = \frac{(1 + R[0, t + 1])^{t+1}}{(1 + R[0, t])^t} \tag{4-7}$$

The following calculations determine the one-period forward rates starting one year from now ($r[1, 2]$) and four years from now ($r[4, 5]$).

Years to Maturity	Actual *N*-Year Rate
1	.06
2	.065
3	.07
4	.077
5	.084

$$r[1, 2] = \frac{(1.065)^2}{(1.06)} - 1 = .0700$$

$$r[4, 5] = \frac{(1.084)^5}{(1.077)^4} - 1 = .1125$$

We can also calculate a two-year forward rate starting two years from today:

$$r[a, b] = \left[\frac{(1 + R[0, b])^b}{(1 + R[0, a])^a} \right]^{1/(b-a)} - 1 \tag{4-8}$$

$$r[2, 4] = \left[\frac{(1.077)^4}{(1.065)^2} \right]^{1/2} - 1 = .0891$$

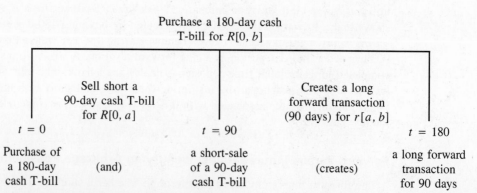

Purchase a 180-day cash
T-bill for $R[0, b]$

| $t = 0$ | | $t = 90$ | | $t = 180$ |

Sell short a
90-day cash T-bill
for $R[0, a]$

Creates a long
forward transaction
(90 days) for $r[a, b]$

Purchase of
a 180-day   (and)
cash T-bill

a short-sale
of a 90-day   (creates)
cash T-bill

a long forward
transaction
for 90 days

Figure 4-5 Diagram of a forward transaction.

to determine the forward rate when the periods are less than one year is simply an application of Equation (4-8) with a and b equaling the maturities of the shorter- and longer-term cash rates. Thus, the equation when the shorter-term cash has 90 days to maturity and the longer-term cash has 180 days to maturity, creating a 90-day forward rate starting 90 days from now, using fractions of the year, is

$$r[.25, .5] = \left[\frac{(1 + R[0, .5])^{.5}}{(1 + R[0, .25])^{.25}} \right]^{1/(.5-.25)} - 1 \qquad (4\text{-}9)$$

Exhibit 4-4 shows the relationship between the forward rate and the futures rate, as well as the type of arbitrage implied by this relationship.[10] Example 4-2 illustrates how to calculate a short-term forward rate for T-bills and compares it to the futures rate. One calculates Eurodollar time deposit forward rates in the same manner as for T-bills, except the Eurodollar money market rates do *not* have to be converted from bank discount rates to yields as is done for T-bills.

The Implied Financing Rate

The **implied repo rate** (or more generally the **implied financing rate**) is another straightforward method for deciding whether a short or long arbitrage position is appropriate. The implied financing rate represents the short-term interest rate for the near-term period where a longer-term cash security is purchased and a futures contract is sold, or vice versa. Figure 4-6 shows the implied financing rate relationship in diagram form; that is, the implied repo rate is determined by finding the rate that, when compounded with the futures rate, equals the long-term cash rate. Equation (4-10) shows how to calculate this rate.

$$\text{IFR} = \left[\frac{(1 + R[0, b])^{b}}{(1 + r^*[a, b])^{(b-a)}} \right]^{1/a} - 1 \qquad (4\text{-}10)$$

where IFR = the implied financing rate

r^* = the futures rate

EXHIBIT 4-4
Arbitrage Rules for Comparing Futures and Forward Rates

Short Arbitrage: If forward rate > futures rate,

- Then cash is underpriced relative to futures (buy cash, sell futures)

Long Arbitrage: If forward rate < futures rate

- Then cash is overpriced relative to futures (sell cash, buy futures)

---

[10] Marking the futures to market and the type of financing employed affects the final decision of whether an arbitrage is possible. Marking-to-market is a minor factor and typically is ignored. Chapter 9 discusses financing as well as other qualifications of the forward/futures comparison.

EXAMPLE 4-2
Short-Term Forward Rates and Futures Rates

On September 20, 1982, the following rates were in effect:*

	Bank Discount Rate	Yield
90-day cash T-bill	7.74%	7.99%
180-day cash T-bill	9.38%	9.97%
Dec. 82 T-bill futures index	89.62	
T-bill futures interest rate	10.38%	10.66%

Using Equation (4-9) we can determine the forward rate from the current cash yields as follows:

$$r[.25, .5] = \left[\frac{(1 + R[0, .5])^{.5}}{(1 + R[0, .25])^{.25}} \right]^{1/(.5-.25)} - 1 \qquad (4-9)$$

$$= \left[\frac{(1.0997)^{.5}}{(1.0799)^{.25}} \right]^{4} - 1$$

$$= \left[\frac{1.048666}{1.019403} \right]^{4} - 1$$

$$= 1.1199 - 1$$

Hence the forward rate = 12.00%.

Comparing the forward rate to the futures rate:

forward rate > futures rate

12.00% > 10.66%

From Exhibit 4-4 this result shows that short arbitrage is appropriate.

*The actual interest rates depicted here reflect an unusual and very volatile environment, as shown by the 71 basis point range for the T-bill futures on this day (the highest futures interest rate for the day is used in the example). Typically, such large differences between the 90-day and 180-day cash rates or between the forward rate and the futures rate do not exist. The purpose of this example is to show that arbitrage is possible during volatile time periods. Also note that the T-bill rates chosen here are for the December 16 and March 17 maturities, which differ from the simplified example of using 90- and 180-day maturities. These maturity differences only have a minor effect on the calculated results.

An implied financing rate resulting from a 180-day cash T-bill and a T-bill futures contract expiring in 90 days can be determined by applying Equation (4-10) to generate the following after converting to fractions of a year:

$$IFR = \left[\frac{(1 + R[0, .5])^{.5}}{(1 + r^*[.25, .5])^{(.5-.25)}} \right]^{1/.25} - 1 \qquad (4-11)$$

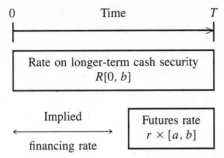

Figure 4-6 The implied financing rate.

Once calculated, the implied financing rate is compared with the actual short-term financing rate in order to determine whether a short or long arbitrage strategy provides arbitrage profits. Note that this approach typically ignores transactions costs; however, such costs need to be considered before an arbitrage is attempted. Exhibit 4-5 presents the decision rules and associated strategies using the implied financing rate. An example of calculating the implied financing rate and its comparison with the actual financing rate is given in Example 4-3.

EXECUTING SHORT-TERM INTEREST RATE ARBITRAGE

Eurodollar and T-bill futures arbitrage are similar in concept but differ in the specifics of how they are executed. Here we list the basic transactions involved in short-term interest rate futures arbitrage. Chapter 9 discusses Eurodollar and T-bill pricing and arbitrage in detail. Examples 4-2 and 4-3, show how to make the calculations and comparisons necessary for determining the possibility that arbitrage exists and the potential profits from such a transaction.

Exhibit 4-6 illustrates the transactions necessary for the execution of short and long Eurodollar and T-bill futures arbitrage. Note that transactions costs need to be considered in the analysis. Exhibit 4-6 shows that for a short arbitrage the arbitrageur borrows funds via a loan. These funds are then invested for (say) six months in a Eurodollar time deposit or cash T-bill. At the same time, the futures are sold. Since the forward

EXHIBIT 4-5
Arbitrage Rules Using the Implied Financing Rate

Short Arbitrage: If the implied financing rate $>$ short-term financing rate $=$ if forward rate $>$ futures rate,

- Then cash is underpriced relative to the futures (buy cash, sell futures)

Long Arbitrage: If the implied financing rate $<$ short-term financing rate $=$ if forward rate $<$ futures rate,

- Then cash is overpriced relative to the futures (sell cash, buy futures)

EXAMPLE 4-3
Determining the Implied Financing Rate

Using the data from Example 4-2, we can determine the implied financing rate from Equation (4-10) as follows:

$$IFR = \left[\frac{(1 + R[0, b])^b}{(1 + r^*[a, b])^{(b-a)}} \right]^{1/a} - 1$$

$$= \left[\frac{(1.0997)^{.5}}{(1.1066)^{.25}} \right]^4 - 1$$

$$= \left[\frac{1.048666}{1.025646} \right]^4 - 1$$

$$= 1.0928 - 1$$

Hence the implied financing rate is 9.28%.

Comparing the implied financing rate to the actual overnight short-term financing rate of 8.31%, we have

Implied financing rate > financing rate[†]

9.28% > 8.31%

From Exhibit 4-5 this result indicates that a short arbitrage is appropriate.

[†] Most arbitrageurs employ the overnight financing rate rather than a three-month financing rate. This practice adds an element of risk that the financing rate will change. Chapter 9 discusses the use of the overnight versus three-month financing rate.

EXHIBIT 4-6
Transactions for Executing Short-Term Interest Rate Futures Arbitrage

Short Arbitrage: If the implied repo (financing) rate > short-term financing rate = if forward rate > futures rate, then

- Obtain funds from borrowing for three months
- Invest in the six-month interest-bearing instrument
- Sell the futures contract

Long Arbitrage: If the implied repo (financing) rate < short-term financing rate = if forward rate < futures rate, then

- Obtain funds from borrowing for six months
- Invest in a three-month interest-bearing instrument
- Buy the futures contract

rate $>$ futures rate $+$ transactions costs for a short arbitrage, the above set of transactions guarantees a profit. In other words, selling the futures contract locks in an interest rate on the cash instrument starting in three months.

Three months later (at $T + 3$), the initial loan is rolled over to a new three-month loan, with the latter rate being previously locked in with the futures transaction. (The interest on the initial three-month loan must be paid.) At the end of six months, the arbitrage profits have been earned, since the cost of the loans are less than the earnings from the time deposit.

A similar (but opposite) strategy is relevant for long arbitrage. These strategies, numerical examples, and associated empirical results are covered in Chapter 9.

FACTORS AFFECTING T-BOND PRICING AND ARBITRAGE

The basic cost of carry model is relevant for T-bond futures pricing and arbitrage. For short arbitrage, a cash bond is purchased, financed by a loan or other funding method such as a repo, the bond is carried until the futures delivery month, and then the cash instrument is delivered into the short futures position.[11] The implied repo method is employed to examine the profitability of this opportunity. However, T-bond futures pricing and arbitrageurs also need to consider other factors that affect the process:

- The size of the coupon of the relevant deliverable bond in *comparison* to the financing rate is an important factor affecting the pricing and arbitrage of long-term debt futures contracts.
- The **conversion factor method (CFM)** is employed to allow delivery of *any* T-bond with at least 15 years to maturity or 15 years to the call date (if callable). This procedure significantly affects both the pricing and arbitrage of debt futures. The system was developed to calculate the delivery price for T-bonds with varying coupons and maturities. However, the CFM creates biases that affect the relative delivery pricing of bonds in comparison with their value, causing one **"cheapest-to-deliver"** bond to exist. This lowest-cost bond maximizes the arbitrageur's profits and therefore is the bond that directly controls the futures price.[12]
- **Delivery options** allow the seller of the debt futures contract several alternatives concerning which bonds to deliver and when to deliver them. These options complicate the pricing of the futures contracts just before and during the delivery month.

The complications and uncertainties created by these three major factors create pricing difficulties for T-bond futures and provide opportunities for arbitrageurs to increase their profits. These factors are discussed in Chapter 9 in an effort to examine

---

[11] Municipal bond futures contracts are settled in cash.

[12] In general, quality differences affect which cash asset is cheapest-to-deliver. For example, grains have different qualities. Although lower quality grains can be delivered only at a discount to the futures price, it may still be more profitable to deliver the lower-quality grain if the cash price difference is larger than the prespecified futures discount. For financials, lower-quality (higher-risk) bank CDs dominated the pricing of CD futures contracts, since the lower the quality, the cheaper the CD that could be delivered. In general, the cheapest-to-deliver concept is modified by one caveat: there must be sufficient liquidity in the specific cheapest-to-deliver cash instrument to allow for sufficient purchases of that instrument without adversely affecting the cash price.

their effects on the pricing process. These factors overshadow the pure versus quasi-arbitrage issue, although T-bond arbitrage is typically a pure arbitrage transaction executed by government bond dealers who finance their positions. Other long-term debt futures have pricing and arbitrage considerations similar to T-bond futures.

PRICING FUTURES CONTRACTS ACROSS MARKETS

In addition to the financing costs associated with the cost of carry model, other factors affect the pricing of financial futures contracts. The following list summarizes the effect of differing cash flow characteristics for different types of financial futures contracts and shows that futures specifications and market characteristics affect cash flows, and hence the pricing of the contracts. These characteristics are discussed in detail in Chapters 8 and 9.

- Stock index futures prices are lowered by the size of the expected dividends on the stocks in the index. The uneven payments of dividends creates difficulties in pricing stock index futures.
- The futures price tracks the *cheapest*-to-deliver cash instrument that fulfills the specifications of the futures contract.
  - (a) The effects of differing coupons and maturities for different cash T-bonds and T-notes are minimized by the conversion factor method. However, the conversion factors do create errors for pricing and in turn create a cheapest-to-deliver bond.
  - (b) Actual or perceived risk differences can exist for different deliverable cash instruments. This situation presented a major difficulty for both the bank certificate of deposit and commercial paper futures contracts (neither of which trade now), where the various deliverable cash CDs and commercial paper issues had varying risk and thus created a cheapest instrument for the riskiest asset.
  - (c) The T-bond and T-note contracts possess delivery options that provide choices to the seller concerning when and what to deliver. These options affect the pricing of the futures contract.
- Differences between the time when the cash security last traded and when the futures contract traded can *imply* that arbitrage opportunities exist when in reality such pricing differences are due to using an "old" cash price that is no longer relevant. This problem is especially relevant for stock index futures contracts.
- Cost differences between the cash and futures markets, such as commissions, margin costs, and bid-ask spread differences, affect the size of the no-arbitrage bands. As these costs change, the pricing of futures contracts in terms of the cash prices change.
- Tax and accounting treatments affect the futures and cash markets in different ways. For example, before the 1981 Tax Act, T-bill futures with expirations greater than six months were priced differently than the T-bill futures with less than six months to delivery. This difference was due to differing tax treatments between the cash and deferred futures expirations.

SUMMARY AND LOOKING AHEAD

The Capital Asset Pricing Model links the return on a futures contract to its systematic risk. The hedging pressure theory states that an imbalance of net hedging causes futures prices to be biased so as to cause additional speculators to enter the market.

The cost of carry model shows that futures prices are linked to the underlying cash price via the financing costs to arbitrageurs.

We show that futures prices are best described by the cost of carry model. This model then is adjusted for the cash flow of the asset and any delivery options. Arbitrage exists when risk-free profits are possible, which occurs when the futures and fair prices deviate by more than transactions costs. Pure arbitrage involves borrowed funds, whereas quasi-arbitrage employs assets owned by the arbitrageur. Interest rate futures pricing and arbitrage can be examined by calculating forward rates and implied repo rates. Rules are available that determine whether futures are overvalued or undervalued.

Chapters 6 and 7 examine hedging concepts and techniques for determining hedge ratios. Additional information on hedging is provided in Chapters 10 and 17.

BIBLIOGRAPHY

Bodie, Zvi, and Victor Rosansky (1980). "Risk and Return in Commodity Futures," *Financial Analysts Journal,* Vol. 36, No. 3, May–June, pp. 27–39.

Breeden, Douglas (1979). "An Intertemporal Asset Pricing Model with Stochastic Consumption and Investment Opportunities," *Journal of Financial Economics,* Vol. 7, No. 3, September, pp. 265 –296.

Breeden, Douglas (1980). "Consumption Risk in Futures Markets," *Journal of Finance,* Vol. 35, No. 2, May, pp. 503–520.

Daigler, Robert T. (1993). *Financial Futures Markets: Concepts, Evidence, and Applications.* New York, Harper Collins.

Daigler, Robert T. (1991). "Stock Index Arbitrage with Intraday Data," Working Paper, Florida International University.

Dusak, Katherine (1973). "Futures Trading and Investor Returns: An Investigation of Commodity Marketing Premiums," *Journal of Political Economy,* Vol. 81, No. 4, December, pp. 1387–1406.

Fama, Eugene (1976). "Forward Rates as Predictors of Future Spot Rates," *Journal of Financial Economics,* Vol. 3, No. 4, pp. 361–372.

Fama, Eugene F., and Kenneth French (1987). "Commodity Futures Prices: Some Evidence on Forecast Power, Premiums, and the Theory of Storage," *Journal of Business,* Vol. 60, No. 1, January, pp. 55–73.

Hamburger, Michael J., and Elliott Platt (1975). "The Expectation Hypothesis and the Efficiency of the Treasury Bill Market," *Review of Economics and Statistics,* Vol. 57, No. 2, pp. 190–199.

Hartzmark, Michael L. (1987). "Returns to Individual Traders of Futures: Aggregate Results," *Journal of Political Economy,* Vol. 95, No. 6, December, pp. 1292–1306.

Hegde, Shantaram P., and Bill McDonald (1986). "On the Informational Role of Treasury Bill Futures," *The Journal of Futures Markets,* Vol. 6, No. 4, Winter, pp. 629–644.

Hicks, J. R. (1946). *Value and Capital,* 2d ed. Oxford: Oxford University Press, Chap. 10.

Houthhakker, H. S. (1957). "Can Speculators Forecast Prices?" *The Review of Economics and Statistics,* Vol. 39, No. 1, pp. 143–151.

Howard, Charles T. (1982). "Are T-bill Futures Good Forecasters of Interest Rates?" *The Journal of Futures Markets,* Vol. 2, No. 4, Winter, pp. 305–315.

Keynes, John Maynard (1930). *Treatise on Money,* 2d ed. London: Macmillan, pp. 142–144.

Kolb, Robert W. (1992). "Is Normal Backwardation Normal?" *The Journal of Futures Markets,* Vol. 12, No. 1, February, pp. 75–91.

MacDonald, S. Scott, and Scott Hein (1989). "Future Rates and Forward Rates as Predictors of Near-Term Treasury Bill Rates," *The Journal of Futures Markets,* Vol. 9, No. 3, June, pp. 249–262.

Murphy, Austin, and Jimmy E. Hilliard (1989). "An Investigation into the Equilibrium Structure of the Commodity Futures Market Anomaly," *The Financial Review,* Vol. 24, No. 1, February, pp. 1–18.

Phillips, Gordon M., and Robert S. Weiner (1991). "Trading Performance in Forward Markets: A Microdata Test of Normal Backwardation," Center for the Study of Futures Markets Working Paper No. 217, Columbia University, July.

Rockwell, C. (1967). "Normal Backwardation, Forecasting and Returns to Commodity Futures Traders," *Food Research Institute Studies,* Vol. 7 Supplement, pp. 107–130.

Sharpe, William (1964). "Capital Asset Prices: A Theory of Market Equilibrium Under Conditions of Risk," *Journal of Finance,* Vol. 19, No. 3, September, pp. 425–442.

PROBLEMS

*Indicates more difficult problems.

4-1 Calculating Forward Rates

Based on the following data, determine the one-period forward rates starting: one year, two years, three years, and four years from now.

Years to Maturity	Actual *N*-Year Cash Rate
1	.075
2	.079
3	.085
4	.09
5	.11

4-2 Calculating Forward Rates

Based on the following information, determine the one-period forward rates starting two and three years from now.

Years to Maturity	Actual *N*-Year Cash Rate
1	.08
2	.084
3	.089
4	.096
5	.101

4-3 Multiyear Forward Rate

If the rate of return on a five-year security is 9.5% and the rate of return on a two-year security is 8.7%, then what is the expected (forward) rate of return on a three-year security starting two years from now?

4-4 Forward vs. Futures Rates

Given the following money market interest rates, determine whether there is an arbitrage opportunity.

90-day Eurodollar time deposit	7.97%
180-day Eurodollar time deposit	7.92%
Eurodollar futures (expiring in three months)	7.82%

4-5 Forward Rate and Arbitrage

Based on the following information, calculate the forward rate and state the type of arbitrage indicated.

Three-month Eurodollar time deposit	6.44%
Six-month Eurodollar time deposit	6.85%
Index of Eurodollar futures (expiring in three months)	93.10

4-6 Implied Financing Rate

Using the information given, calculate the implied financing rate and state what type of arbitrage is indicated.

Three-month Eurodollar time deposit	8.24%
Six-month Eurodollar time deposit	8.42%
Index of Eurodollar futures (expiring in three months)	91.50
Actual short-term financing rate	7.70%

*4-7 Implied Financing Rate

The interest rate on a Eurodollar time deposit with 204 days to maturity is 9.14%. The current Eurodollar futures index with 114 days until expiration is 91.01. For purposes of arbitrage, what is the implied financing rate?

*4-8 Cost of Carry for Stock Index Futures

Find the fair futures price and compare it to the futures price, given the following information:

S&P 500 cash index	386.49
T-bill rate	5.13%
Dollar dividend in index points	2.73
Futures expiration	83 days
Current S&P 500 futures index	388.90

*4-9 Cost of Carry for Stock Index Futures

The S&P 500 cash index is 345.21. Determine the fair price for an expiration in 65 days, given a 7.01% T-bill interest rate and a 3.1% dividend yield.

4-10 Cash and Carry for Gold

Set up the cash flows of the cash and carry transaction below. Is arbitrage possible?

Price of gold (cash market)	$330.00
Futures price of gold (expires in 1 year)	$342.00
Interest rate (financing)	3.50%

APPENDIX 4A
THE PRICING OF CURRENCY FUTURES CONTRACTS

Pricing a gold, stock index, or debt futures contract is based on the (net) financing cost of holding the cash asset (the cost of carry model). Currency futures and forwards represent the *relative* exchange rate between two currencies, starting at a specific time in the future. Thus, currency futures pricing reflects the *relative* interest rate/financing costs for the two currencies.

As with other futures contracts, the fair pricing of currency futures is based on a "no-arbitrage" relationship, that is, the price at which risk-free profits are not available. **Interest rate parity** is the formal name of the no-arbitrage relationship for currency futures and forward pricing. If the interest rate in the United States is greater than the interest rate for foreign currency funds (i.e., if $i_{U.S.} > i_{foreign}$), then the futures exchange rate > cash exchange rate.[1]

The following discussion develops the futures pricing equation. The notation used is

- $S(t)$ is the domestic (U.S.) currency price of cash foreign exchange at time t in terms of dollars per unit of foreign currency (American terms).
- $F[t, t + T]$ is the domestic (U.S.) currency price of a futures or forward contract in foreign exchange at time t for settlement at time $t + T$ (the time of the futures expiration).
- i is the annual interest rate on Eurocurrency deposits for the domestic (U.S.) currency.
- i^* is the annual interest rate on Eurocurrency loans for the foreign currency.
- i and i^* are money market interest rates that are quoted using a 360-day year (the British pound rates use 365 days); money market rates are *not* compounded.

The following discussion shows the transactions that create a no-arbitrage situation—that is, a fair futures price. Note that the first three steps are initiated *at the same time,* and that none of the arbitrageur's funds are employed in the transaction.

Step 1: Borrow 1 unit of the domestic currency ($1) at i at time t. Repay the loan plus interest at time $t + T$, with the loan being held for the time period T; thus, repay

$$1 + i(T/360) \qquad (4A-1)$$

---

[1] The relationships and examples in this appendix assume the currency futures contract is based in the United States and is quoted in dollars. For futures or forwards based in other countries, one substitutes "domestic" for "U.S." Also note that the relationship of the futures rate > cash exchange rate when $i_{U.S.} > i_{foreign}$ holds because futures are quoted in American terms—that is, the number of dollars per one unit of the foreign currency.

Step 2: Convert the 1 unit of the domestic currency ($1) into $1/S(t)$ units of the foreign currency. Deposit this amount at the money market interest rate i^*. At the end of time $t + T$ receive the principal plus interest:

$$[1/S(t)][1 + i^*(T/360)] \qquad (4A\text{-}2)$$

Step 3: In order to ensure that changing currency values do not create a loss, the trader locks in the domestic value by executing a futures (or forward) contract: sell the futures in the foreign exchange for expiration at time $t + T$; that is, create $F[t, t + T]$. The total domestic (U.S.) value of the futures transaction at time $t + T$ is

$$[1/S(t)][1 + i^*(T/360)] \ F[t, t + T] \qquad (4A\text{-}3)$$

Step 4: At time $t + T$,

- Receive the deposit of the foreign currency, including interest (step 2).
- Use the foreign currency to fulfill the forward contract—that is, exchange the foreign currency for the domestic currency (U.S. dollars) by executing the forward contract at the exchange rate determined at time t (step 3).
- Repay the domestic (U.S.) loan (step 1).

Since none of the arbitrageur's funds are used, the "no-arbitrage" rule states that no profits should exist. Consequently, the cost from the domestic loan should exactly offset the interest received from the deposit of the foreign currency:

$$1 + i(T/360) = [1/S(t)][1 + i^*(T/360)] \ F[t, t + T] \qquad (4A\text{-}4)$$

Solving for the futures/forward rate $F[t, t + T]$ we obtain the fair futures price for foreign exchange, as determined by the interest rate parity theorem:

$$F[t, t + T] = \frac{S(t)[1 + i(T/360)]}{1 + i^*(T/360)} \qquad (4A\text{-}5)$$

This equation shows that the fair futures price for currencies is a function of the cash exchange rate, the domestic interest rate, and the foreign interest rate. In turn, the interest rates are affected by the business conditions, money supplies, and inflation rates in the two countries. Example 4A-1 illustrates the calculations.

EXAMPLE 4A-1
Calculating a Fair Currency Futures Price

The fair currency futures price is calculated for a contract expiring in 90 days, given the following: cash yen exchange rate = 145 yen/$ (i.e., $.0068966/yen), $i_{dollar} = 8\%$, and $i^*_{yen} = 5\%$,

$$F[t, t + T] = \frac{S(t)[1 + i(T/360)]}{1 + i^*(T/360)}$$

$$F[0, 90] = \frac{\$.0068966/\text{yen} \ [1 + .08(^{90}/_{360})]}{1 + .05(^{90}/_{360})} \qquad (4A\text{-}5)$$

$$= \$.0068966/\text{yen} \ [(1.02)/(1.0125)]$$

$$= \$.0069477/\text{yen}$$

PROBLEMS FOR APPENDIX 4A

*Indicates more difficult problems.

*4A-1 Pricing Currency Futures

Find the currency futures fair price if the cash yen is 120 to the dollar, the U.S. interest rate is 5%, and the Japanese interest rate is 7%. Compare your answer to the actual futures rate of 141 yen to the dollar and calculate the dollar difference for $1 million. The futures will expire in 90 days.

*4A-2 Pricing Currency Futures

Find the fair currency futures price if the yen is 145/$, the U.S. interest rate is 9%, and the Japanese interest rate is 5.5%. The futures will expire in 90 days.

Chapter 5

THE "PITS" AND MARKET MICROSTRUCTURE

Overview

This chapter discusses traders on the exchange floor, the activity in the "pits," and intraday pricing effects. The types of floor traders are identified and profiles of their actions on the exchange floor are given, including a brief discussion of methods of trading used in the pits. Thus, the first part of this chapter describes the functioning of the futures "pits" and the motivations of the different types of traders in the "pits." The second half of the chapter discusses "market microstructure." Market microstructure includes the study of the effect of information on intraday prices, the pattern of volatility over the trading day, scalper's profits, the size of bid-ask spreads for futures contracts, the distribution of price changes from one trade to the next, and the clustering of prices around integer and half-integer intervals of prices.

Terminology

Floor broker A floor trader who, for a fixed fee, executes orders that originate off the exchange floor.

Market microstructure The study of price behavior within the day and the structure of the market trading system affecting this price behavior.

Outtrade   A mismatch in the records of two traders concerning a transaction.

*"Pits"   The location of futures trading on the exchange floor. The pit is a multileveled octagonal structure that allows contact among a maximum number of traders.

*Scalper   Floor trader who buys at the bid and sells at the ask price; this activity provides short-term market liquidity.

THE FUTURES "PITS" AND THEIR PARTICIPANTS

Layout of the Pit and Order Flow

Futures exchanges execute trades in areas called **pits.** The term "pits" exists because the trading areas are sunk into the floor of the trading area; the rumors that traders who lose their trading capital are "thrown to the lions in the pits" Roman style seem to be false.[1]

The shape of the pit is an octagon, with different levels leading down to the bottom of the pit. The nearby contract trades at the bottom of the pit; the theory is that the rapid action and multitude of trades in this expiration require that the traders be near one another. Other expirations trade on different levels and/or different areas of the pit.

"Runners" deliver orders from off the exchange to the pits or the orders are signaled to traders by hand from the phone banks that surround the trading area.[2] Telephone booths on the trading floor are used for communications by off-the-floor traders. Of course, brokerage houses with phones near a given pit have a time advantage in delivering orders to that pit, especially during hectic trading periods when the floor is crowded. These houses also have an advantage when off-the-floor customers desire information on current price trends occurring in a specific pit. The popularity of financial futures contracts and the introduction of new types of futures contracts over the past few years necessitated the building of new trading floors for the Chicago Board of Trade and the Chicago Mercantile Exchange. The Chicago Board of Trade moved its agricultural futures contracts to the new floor, while transferring the successful T-bond futures contract from the "back room" to the old soybean pit.[3] This move has allowed the T-bond pit to grow from about 200 traders to 600 traders and provided room for options on financial futures contracts.

---

[1] However, an incident on a stock exchange floor in which traders were encouraging a bankrupt colleague to jump from the second-floor railing above the trading floor provides some evidence to the contrary.

[2] A runner brings an order from the telephone banks to the broker in the futures pit. Although the runners are instructed to deliver the orders as fast as possible, exchange rules prohibit them from actually running on the floor. Most runners are college students and trainees; the CBT president started as a runner.

[3] This move provided much needed room for the T-bond traders, who were cramming 500 or more traders into a space the size of a large living room. Once a floor trader got into a position on the floor, he or she did not leave until trading ended! Some traders arrived two hours ahead of the opening bell just to secure their places. Moreover, the room for runners to maneuver on the outside of the pits was very limited, causing extremely slow movement. In fact, this room was where stock option trading began in 1972 before the CBOE obtained its own floor and achieved separate corporate designation.

Figure 5-1 shows the execution sequence for a futures order. Note that each order is time-stamped for control purposes. The entire process, from when the order reaches the floor until the confirmation of the trade by telephone, takes about three minutes during normal trading times. The trade price is disseminated worldwide on the quotation system within minutes of the trade. Pit recorders on a platform above the pit electronically record each trade price. After a trade execution, the traders communicate the price via hand signals to the pit recorder, who enters the price into the electronic system. This technique is a vast improvement over the historic days when prices were written on a blackboard and only transmitted daily to the financial press.

Brokers

The participants in the pits vary in their approach to trading, depending on their function in the markets. The types of participants are: commission merchants/**floor brokers**, position or day traders, spreaders, and **scalpers**.[4]

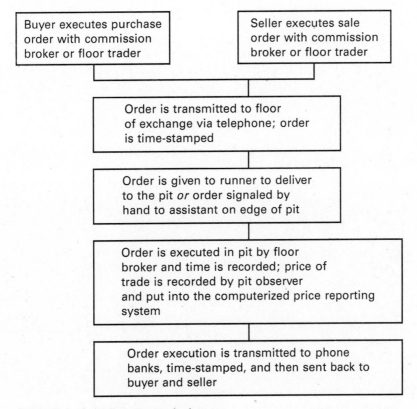

Figure 5-1 Order flow process for futures.

---

[4] Melamed (1981) describes the functioning of most of these pit traders in terms of their effect on the liquidity of the market.

Futures commission merchants are brokers who work for institutional houses, executing trades that come from off the floor. These futures commission brokers are a small percentage of the total number of traders in the pits; however, they are often the focus of attention, since most of the trades generating new open interest come from these off-the-floor trades. Floor brokers in the pits help the commission brokers handle off-the-floor orders during periods of heavy, hectic trading. The commission brokers compensate the floor brokers on a fee-per-trade basis. The commission brokers and floor brokers constitute 15% to 20% of the number of traders in the pits.

FOCUS 5-1
The Deck of a Futures Broker

Futures commission merchants and brokers keep a deck of cards showing each proposed trade, including special orders, that must be executed at a specific price or for a specific market situation. Although two key ingredients to a broker's success are an ability to fill orders at a good price and the skill to fill large orders without disrupting the market, the broker also must be able to handle a deck of cards efficiently. He or she often has several hundred special orders in the deck; traders typically place such orders because of the importance of small price moves for futures or due to the adverse effects of a volatile market. The deck is arranged in ascending and descending price order from the current price, as well as according to priority, so that the special orders are identified quickly as prices change. As new orders come into the pit, the broker must be able to arrange these orders into the proper deck sequence quickly and efficiently to guarantee proper future execution. If a trade is not properly executed, the broker is liable for the difference in price. It is not uncommon to see brokers receive orders from runners, look at the orders, and proceed to stuff them into one of several coat pockets for expediency and to create their own filing system. Another currently popular alternative is to have an assistant standing just outside the pit who receives the orders from either a runner or by hand signals from the telephone banks. The assistant passes to the broker only those orders that need to be filled immediately, keeping other orders in the assistant's deck.

The pressure of being a broker can best be seen when large price changes exist during an active market. Not only does the broker have to tend to the special orders in the deck, but a large number of new orders enter the pits that require execution or filing. The ability to handle such situations efficiently and calmly is the true test of a broker. Of course, the fact that the other traders in the pits are yelling and gesturing at the broker to make a trade with them does not help the broker's concentration or emotional stability. Understandably, there have been cases where brokers lose their composure and are unable to handle the trading activity. In one situation a broker became completely frustrated with his inability to cope with the market action, threw his entire deck of trades into the air and walked off the floor, gesturing to his assistant to put the deck back in order. After composing himself, the broker came back onto the floor 20 minutes later. His frustration had cost him $100,000 for failing to execute orders at their specified prices!

Day Traders and Position Traders

Day traders take long or short positions on one side of the market for one trading session, based on their convictions concerning daily market direction. Day traders usually even up their positions at or before the close of the market so unforeseen overnight developments do not create losses. Although day traders represent only a small percentage of the number of traders in the pits, they do increase market liquidity for large positions that originate off the floor.

Position traders take long-term positions on one side of the market and keep these positions for several days to several weeks; thus, position traders have holding periods that are similar to outside speculators. Since there is little benefit for position traders to complete their transactions on the floor, their numbers in the pits are small, typically being only 1% to 2% of the total number of pit traders. One advantage that on-the-floor

FOCUS 5-2
Illegal Trading Practices in the Pits

In the late 1980s FBI "moles" traded on futures exchanges to catch pit traders who participated in illegal activities. The FBI issued 350 subpoenas and arrested dozens of traders. The illegal activities found to occur in some pits during certain trading periods included:

- **Bagging or bucketing:** Brokers often use a two- to five-minute "rule of thumb" to execute a trade from off the floor. Meanwhile, the broker fills the order with a "bagman" who is a trader working with the broker. At the end of the two- to five-minute interval, the broker makes another trade with the bagman, with the worst of the two trades reported to the customer. The difference in price is "bagged" as a profit.

- **Front running:** A broker on the floor receives a large order that will move the market. The broker traders for his or her own account first and then fills the order, with the broker profiting from the subsequent price change. This activity is allowed by the "dual trading" rule for brokers, a practice criticized by other traders in the pits.

- **Prearranged trading:** Traders negotiate a trade outside the pit to manipulate prices or determine who receives the commissions.

- **Curb trading:** Traders buy and sell contracts after the closing bell to even out their positions before the end of the day or to reverse previous outtrades. Outtrades should be settled in cash.

The exchanges attempt to police floor traders with fines, trading suspensions, and permanent expulsion from the pits. During a six-year period in the late 1980s the four major exchanges fined floor traders almost $10 million dollars and suspended traders for 26,000 trading days (see Angrist, 1989). Exchanges also are improving the tracking of trades. In particular, the exchanges are testing hand-held electronic transaction entry devices to replace the cards and pencils currently used by traders. These hand-held systems immediately record transactions for audit purposes and reduce the costs of outtrades.

day traders and position traders have over off-the-floor traders is the low cost of executing a trade. Exchange fees for trading are only $1.50 for a round-trip trade as compared to $15 to $30 for off-the-floor traders.

Spreaders

Spreaders, whether they are on or off the floor, buy one expiration month and sell another month, or buy one type of futures contract and sell another. Spreaders attempt to profit from changes in the differential between the two sides of the trade. The risk of a spread position is typically much less than the risk for a position or day trader, but the potential profit also is smaller; however, lower margin requirements compensate the spreader for the reduced profit potential.

Spreaders in the pits also execute a transaction in order to make a market in a deferred expiration for a trader who is off the floor. The price assigned by the spreader includes a premium for the reduced liquidity in the deferred expiration. The spreader executes a trade in order to reduce the floor trader's risk until the deferred expiration position is covered by an opposite trade in the same expiration.

Spreaders must make quick decisions with accurate calculations. To reduce risk, they often even up or reduce their positions at the end of the day. When traders spread with other markets, they must have phone or visual contact with the partner(s) in the other pit. Spreaders with visual contact, as in the soybean complex, have developed hand signals to communicate their trades, prices, and positions to their partners in the other pits.

The spreader derives profits from several sources. First, a spreader attempts to profit from small discrepancies in the relationships between the nearby and deferred prices. Second, the spreader is compensated for generating trades in a less liquid market for deferred expirations via larger bid-ask differentials. Finally, the spreader creates positions based on expectations concerning shifts in the price relationship of the underlying cash instrument.

Scalpers

Scalpers are the market makers of the futures pits. Scalpers buy at the bid price and sell at the ask price, thereby creating a significant amount of liquidity for the heavily traded expirations, while generating a large number of small profitable trades for themselves. An accurate description of a scalper is a market maker who takes inventory, since a typical round-trip trade is executed in one minute or less. Scalpers earn moderate but reasonable returns, leaving the headline gains and bankruptcies to pure speculators. Scalpers even up their position at the end of the day in order to avoid the speculator's overnight risk.

The benefit of short-term liquidity provided by the scalper is a critical factor in the success and usefulness of futures markets. The extent of this liquidity is evident when one realizes that scalpers account for 40% to 60% of the volume in active expirations (they often trade among themselves). This activity reduces the size of the bid-ask spread and provides instant liquidity for any order entering the pit. However, more volatile pits often have fewer scalpers, since the short-term position risk is larger for such markets.

FOCUS 5-3
Globex: A 24-Hour Trading Innovation

Globex is the computerized night trading system developed by Reuters Holdings PLC for the Chicago futures exchanges. The object of Globex is to offer 24-hour worldwide trading capabilities without requiring scalpers' physical presence in the pits. Market makers wishing to participate in Globex will put their bids and offers into the computerized system. Those wishing to execute an order will place this order electronically. The computer matches the two prices and the trade is executed. Advantages to the system include the 24-hour trading capabilities, an on-screen listing of all limit orders, an accurate "audit trail" showing the sequence and timing of trades, and the ability to help regulators keep track of the open positions of traders.

Many pit traders are concerned that Globex could be the precursor to a totally electronic exchange trading system that would put them out of business. However, developments to date suggest that such worries have little merit. First, the initiation of Globex was promised in 1989, but the system was not started until 1992. Technical problems with the system and the lack of capacity for large-volume days kept Globex in the testing stage. Second, the computer screen cannot provide as much information as the visual and auditory clues from the traders in the pits. Third, a system without a physical location can shut down during crisis situations. For example, during the crash, bond traders simply stopped answering their telephones. On the other hand, pit traders are obligated to make a market. Finally, Bollerslev and Domowitz (1990) show via simulated trading activity that the volatility of returns create patterns over time with the Globex system, but such patterns do not occur with the open outcry system used in the pits. This time dependence in volatility is related to the change in the bid-ask spread caused by Globex when special orders are executed. Until these problems are solved, volume traders will not want to use the Globex system for trading purposes.

PIT ACTION

Trading in the Pits

Trading in the pits is by open voice outcry and by hand signals. The traders indicate whether they want to buy or sell, how many contracts they want to trade, and their price. Shouts such as "5 at 10" can effectively communicate the desire to trade 5 contracts at 10 basis points for T-bill futures or $^{10}/_{32}$ for T-bond futures, since everyone knows the integer price of the contract. Hand signals reinforce the open outcry method by showing that the traders wish to buy (palm of the hand inward toward the trader) or sell (palm outward). The positioning of the hand and the number of fingers extended indicate both the number of contracts to trade and the price desired. Figure 5-2 describes the hand action found in the pits.

The action in the pits is fascinating to see, especially during active markets and during the opening and closing periods. When the volume of off-the-floor trades is extremely heavy, such that the pit traders are having a difficult time executing new trades and keeping abreast of the associated price action, then the exchange can call a "fast

Hand signals indicate if the trader is buying or selling and the price being bid or offered. The hand is held away from the body to indicate the price. Palms inward toward the body indicate buying, palms outward indicate selling. From left to right, the first six hand diagrams with fingers extended vertically show prices from zero to five. Prices from six through ten are quoted with the fingers extended horizontally. Prices from eleven to twenty require two hands, and prices above twenty are indicated by rapid sequential hand signals using fingers and a closed fist. Quantity is indicated by the fingers when the hand is held near the head.

Figure 5-2 Hand signals in the pit. (*Source:* "A World Marketplace," Chicago Mercantile Exchange, 1985, p. 9.)

market." A fast market means that no new off-exchange trades can enter the pits until the current off-exchange trade volume can be adequately handled. This action eventually reduces the panic factor in the pits so that activity can return to normal. Often a fast market exists when trading activity is so hectic that trade prices in one part of the pit are different from prices in another part of the pit.

Opening and closing markets resemble fast markets in that a significant amount of trading occurs in a short period of time. The opening of the market constitutes a significant volume of trading since a large number of off-exchange orders have accumulated since the previous trading day's close. The close is active because a large number of off-exchange traders, hedgers, and cash market dealers wait until near the close to decide what position to take. They base their decisions on the day's price movement and how much cash inventory exists that requires hedging; pit traders also use this final trading activity to close positions accumulated over the day's trading.

Brokers who possess a large backlog of trades to fill at the open, especially large block trades, usually inform the other traders in the pit of this fact before the market opens. This practice permits the traders to determine any appropriate price adjustments from the previous day's closing price that are consistent with the required liquidity needs of the market, as well as to warn the pit traders that the broker will be an active participant at the open.[5] Of course, such statements by the broker, along with overnight

[5] Warning the pit of a large opening volume benefits the broker as well as the traders. If no warning is given, then the opening price will differ significantly from what the broker receives for a large block order, causing the broker difficulties in explaining why the order was not filled at the prevailing market price at the open.

FOCUS 5-4
The Trials and Tribulations of a Scalper

Scalpers have to endure stress, loud noises, strained vocal cords, pushes and shoves, fights, and hot close quarters for the opportunity to become either rich or poor (or more often, to earn a living wage). But how do scalpers really earn their living when the market becomes active? In other words, how does a scalper operate during active or fast markets?

The major key for a successful scalper is to be quick. The faster he or she can buy and sell, the more trades a scalper can make, and consequently the greater the potential profits. But recording one's trades can be a severe detriment to quickness, since the number of contracts, the futures expiration, the price, whether it was a purchase or sale, the time of the trade, and the other trader's three-letter ID must be recorded. Many of the financial futures scalpers circumvent the immediate need for recording all of this information by simply *remembering* it; then, when a lull in the trading occurs, the trader records the information for the last seven, eight, or nine trades.

Unfortunately, scalpers do not always have perfect memories. They forget a trade, or note the wrong price or trader's ID. When each scalper's record of the day's trades is entered into the computer, then all the mismatches between traders' records are discovered (there is always a buyer and a seller, and their records must match). These mismatches are called **outtrades**, and traders must settle each outtrade the next morning before they can continue to trade. Usually, outtrades are mistakes, since a trader would not last long in a pit if false trades are purposely recorded, since no one would continue to trade with that person. A typical mistake occurs when several traders believe they had made the same transaction with another trader across the pit, since a simple hand gesture usually closes a trade and several traders might believe the gesture was meant for them. Traders usually settle outtrades by splitting the profit or loss created by the open trade occurring from the outtrade. However, these mistakes and gestures that cause outtrades are not always minor in nature. One outtrade in a wildly changing market created a loss of $250,000 on the unfilled side of the trade! Since scalpers typically make only several basis points per trade, such large outtrades can create a significant risk for a scalper.

A pilot program at the exchanges is attempting to reduce the effect of outtrades by capturing trade information electronically as soon as traders record the information on hand-held units. Such a system can identify outtrades before devastating price changes create large losses.

information concerning these markets, often cause the opening price to differ significantly from the previous day's closing price. Correspondingly, closing activity typically brings the most exciting trading of the day, since the volume of activity, the need for floor traders to even up their positions, and the stress from a day's trading all affect the market participants. It is not unusual to see traders face-to-face, screaming at each other while they are trying to agree on a trade; in fact, on occasion two traders roll on the floor fighting when they do not readily agree on their potential trade.

Speculators and the Pits

The action in the pit is important for off-the-floor speculators as well as pit traders. By understanding the pit action, the speculator can determine how the market may react to specific situations and factors, and can place informed special orders. Similarly, other market participants can understand short-term price movements better by realizing what occurs in the pits. With this in mind, off-the-floor traders should realize that they need to develop different methods and styles than those used by floor traders. The speculator's advantage is that there is time to *think* about the behavior of prices, unaffected by the commotion created by the pit action. The speculator's disadvantage is that real-time exchange quotes are at least two minutes behind floor transactions. Thus, by the time a transaction price is communicated through the quotation system, the speculator reacts with an order to the exchange floor, and the floor broker receives the order, a *minimum* of two minutes elapses. Moreover, if the speculator does not have direct access to the exchange floor via telephone, then a much greater lag time is incurred. Thus, off-the-floor trading based solely on transaction price behavior should not be profitable, given the advantage that the pit traders possess.

Price Behavior in the Pits

The interaction among the pit traders is relevant to the speculator since it can affect price behavior; moreover, this pit interaction is interesting in its own right. One major factor affecting pit behavior and contract prices is the large block trading caused by computerized models. The price effects of a large number of block orders can be significant, and computer models often trigger many of the commodity fund orders at the same time. In other words, many of these computer models are similar, causing a sequence of block orders to hit the market within minutes of each other. Such large blocks can temporarily affect market prices for as long as 15 minutes, depending on the size of the order(s) and the type of futures contract.

These computer models initially operated relatively well. However, because of the increase in the number of commodity funds using these models, coupled with the realization by pit traders that they can artificially trigger the models, a situation is created in which the pit traders profit rather than the funds.

Trading in the pits is part strategy, part psychology. A pit trader can first start selling, even though the trader eventually wants to buy; the initial selling may start a downward trend so that the trader can generate a long position at a lower price. Such trends are common, though short-lived. When a trend or panic situation does arise, then prices can become exaggerated. Since it is difficult to "see the forest for the trees" in a pit, traders are more vulnerable to such crowd tendencies as greed and fear. In particular, when a price breaks downward, traders often panic.

MARKET MICROSTRUCTURE

Market microstructure is the study of price behavior within the day and the structure of the market trading system affecting this price behavior. Recent availability of intraday prices has increased the interest of microstructure studies in futures, options,

FOCUS 5-5
Factors Affecting the Success of Pit Traders

The methods and approaches used by pit traders differ according to the type of trader they are, which pit they are in, and by the trading technique they use. Therefore, there are almost as many different approaches to trading as there are traders. Some use fundamentals, others employ price charting methods, while still others rely on their quick reflexes and memory. Of course, position and day traders have a different viewpoint than scalpers, and they differ from spreaders and arbitrageurs. The pit brings all of these different types of traders with different approaches and expectations into a pit to settle on a consensus opinion, which is reflected in the futures price.

All of these traders have one thing in common—namely, that they must execute their trades in the pits. Without the characteristics needed to be a successful pit trader, using the best strategies still creates losses. For the active financial futures pits, the characteristics needed to be successful include stamina, a strong voice, and certain physical characteristics. The need for stamina is obvious, given the stress-filled, hectic trading period of up to six hours where floor traders are constantly on their feet, mentally and physically active. A pit trader needs a strong, unique voice to yell trades above the din of the pit crowd. If a trader's voice fails, or cannot be heard, then communication with others in the pits is limited. Hand signals usually are not sufficient to get the attention of other traders. Recently, some traders even have taken voice lessons from drama and singing coaches in order to learn how to maintain the strength of their voices throughout the day and how to be heard above the shouts of the other traders.

Finally, the physical characteristics of height, size, and strength can be very important in a crowded pit that is active and action-filled. A tall person can be seen easily in the pit; moreover, a larger and stronger trader is more likely to keep his or her position as the traders are being pushed and hit by other traders. One of the more successful traders in the financial pits is an ex-football player who is 6 feet 6 inches tall and weighs 280 pounds. On the other hand, women traders in the financial pits are unusual, since their shorter stature, lighter weight, and weaker voices create severe handicaps that are difficult to overcome. However, successful women traders exist in other, less crowded pits.

The activity in the financial pits can make for an exhausting, stress-filled day. This hectic trading pace does take its toll, and most financial traders either move to another pit or retire after three to five years, making room for more eager traders. Perhaps this is the reason the average trader in the active financial pits is only 25 years old. Although many of the traders realize the stress they are under, the excitement of the game and the promise of riches is more than enough to spur them on to another day of trading.

and stock markets. Other chapters discuss studies that use intraday data to examine pricing and arbitrage issues. Here we examine the intraday workings of the market in relation to information, volatility, returns to scalpers, bid-ask spread costs, and price clustering.

FOCUS 5-6
An Example of a Price Break

A classic story of a price break occurred at the Chicago Board of Trade just at the harvest time for wheat. The "old" CBT trading floor has three-story-high windows lining one side of the trading floor. On the afternoon in question a storm started to deluge the downtown Chicago area with heavy rain. With a prime wheat harvesting area within 50 miles of Chicago (in Peoria), pit traders started a panic buying spree of wheat futures, since heavy rains would delay the harvest and probably ruin the crop. After five minutes of a hectic market one trader walked to a bank of nearby telephones and called Peoria to find out why no off-exchange buy orders were coming from that area. The trader found a simple answer: the sun was shining in Peoria! Of course, this fact immediately started a selling panic in the wheat pit.

Although this story is amusing, except to the floor traders, it does illustrate how false assumptions or rumors can initiate a panic in the pits. Traders should realize that such unfounded price breaks can occur. Speculators should think about the possible causes of such price breaks before reacting, rather than simply joining the crowd.

Information and Intraday Price Behavior

Information changes supply and demand, which in turn changes prices. Financial economists have examined the relationships between information and prices using daily and weekly data for more than two decades. However, an examination of how quickly prices adjust to information within the day has not been possible because of data limitations. More than 200 financial economists are now investigating these issues by using transaction-by-transaction data.

The U-Shaped Volatility Curve

Examination of minute-by-minute price changes for S&P 500 futures for January and February 1988, aggregated into 15-minute volatility intervals, provides the relationship shown in Figure 5-3. This figure shows a definite U-shaped relationship in volatility over the day, with higher volatility of prices occurring at the open and close of the stock market. Volatility is measured both by the standard deviation of percentage price changes and the *number* of price changes (called ticks) in the interval. The greater volatility at the open is related to the uncertainty concerning the supply and demand. The higher volatility at the close seems to be related to institutional activity at the close of the stock market at 4 P.M. Eastern time. Notice that the volatility of the futures declines from 4 P.M. to the futures close of 4:15 P.M.[6]

---

[6] Jordan, Seale, Dinehart, and Kenyon (1988) have shown that soybean futures exhibit the same U-shaped pattern.

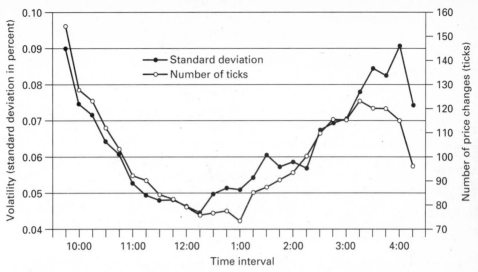

Figure 5-3 U-shaped volatility curve: S&P 500 futures. (*Source:* Prices from Tick Data, Inc.)

FOCUS 5-7
Real-Time Quotation and Trading Systems

Knight-Ridder, Reuters, and several smaller firms offer real-time quotation systems for futures and other securities such as stocks, options, foreign exchange, bonds, swaps, money market instruments, and foreign securities. These systems allow traders to know the current status of the market, the relationship between markets, and whether arbitrage trades are profitable.

For example, the "Money Center" system from Knight-Ridder provides access to more than 100 different screens of information on the markets via a satellite hookup from New York and Chicago. Trades from these financial centers appear on the Money Center screens seconds after they occur on the exchanges. In addition, cash dealer markets in bonds and foreign exchange and up-to-the-minute news items appear on the screen. Intraday or historical daily prices are often graphed for comparison purposes or built-in technical analyses are employed. A windows-type environment allows traders to organize the information they need on the trading screen at the same time.

Scalper's Profits

The actions and profitability of scalpers are typically a closely guarded secret. However, Silber (1984) reports the activities of a scalper trading the NYSE futures contract over a six-week period. The interesting results and conclusions from these records are

- Scalper's earnings are positively related to the bid-ask spread and negatively related to the length of time a position is held. Thus, the scalper is paid for providing liquidity.

- Of the scalper's trades, 48% were profitable and 22% unprofitable.
- The average per contract profit was $10.56, with an average holding time of two minutes. Trades held more than three minutes provided losses on average.

Bid-Ask Spreads

A market maker, such as a scalper in futures, buys at the bid price and sells at the ask price. This bid-ask spread represents the "commission" paid to the scalper. In turn, this spread is a cost to the off-the-floor trader. Bid-ask spreads for stocks and options are relatively easy to estimate, since these values appear on the data tapes that record all transactions in these securities. However, futures transactions data list only prices for completed transactions.

Several approaches exist to estimate the size of the bid-ask spread. The most popular method is to employ transaction data or data spaced at regular time intervals in the following equation developed by Roll (1984):

$$\text{Spread} = 2\sqrt{-\text{cov}(\Delta P_t, \Delta P_{t-1})} \tag{5-1}$$

where cov = covariance

Roll's equation is based on the assumption that no trend exists in the price series. Unfortunately, trends create a negative covariance term, which results in taking the square root of a negative number (a so-called "imaginary" number in mathematics). Although several researchers have attempted to avoid this problem, no satisfactory model is available for calculating spreads accurately.

In spite of the difficulties with obtaining an adequate model for spreads, studies on futures bid-ask spreads to date have indicated the following relationships:

- Ma, Peterson, and Sears (1989) find a U-shaped curve over the day for bid-ask spreads, although the difference from open to lowest spread for T-bond futures is only one-fifth of a tick.
- Wang, Moriarty, Michalski, and Jordan (1990) show that the 1987 crash caused bid-ask spreads to increase by a factor of seven.
- Wang, Michalski, Moriarty, and Jordan (1990) determine that once the effect of volatility is *removed* from the data, the bid-ask spread no longer has a U-shaped pattern during the day.
- Laux and Senchack (1992) calculate that deferred currency futures contracts have larger spreads than nearby futures.

Distribution of Transaction Price Changes

A high-volume, efficient market should possess transaction price changes in normal markets of 1 tick. Figure 5-4 shows the price distribution for the S&P 500 futures for January 8, 1988. This date was one of the 25 most volatile days of 1988. Approximately 80% of the price changes are only 1 tick, with over 2 ticks (.10 index point) occurring toward the end of the day. Figure 5-5 illustrates the price changes on October 19, 1987, during the stock market crash. Here .50 index point (10 ticks) and 1 index point (20 ticks) price changes from one trade to the next *were the rule of the day.*

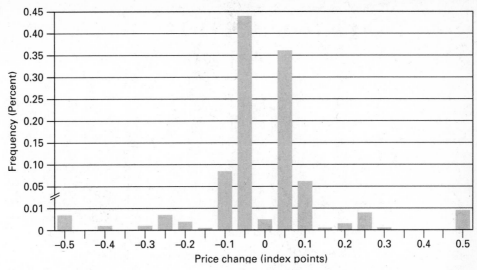

Figure 5-4 Distribution of price changes for the S&P 500 futures: 1/8/88. (*Source:* Prices from Tick Data, Inc.)

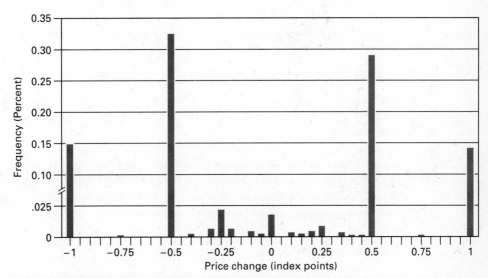

Figure 5-5 Distribution of price changes for the S&P 500 futures: 10/19/87. (*Source:* Prices from Tick Data, Inc.)

Clustering of Prices

Individual stock prices cluster at even integers, halves, quarters, and eighths, in that order. These clusterings of prices are linked to special orders such as limit orders and stop-loss orders. A large percentage of futures orders are special orders. Figure 5-6 illustrates the clustering of prices for the S&P 500 futures on January 8, 1988. This figure

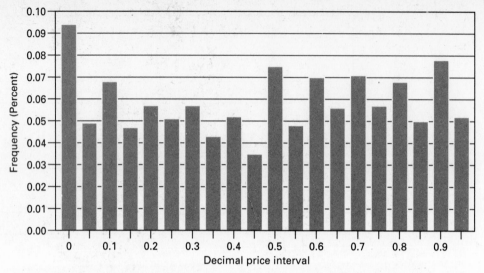

Figure 5-6 Clustering of S&P 500 futures: 1/8/88. (*Source:* Prices from Tick Data, Inc.)

shows that clustering of prices is only a minor phenomenon for stock index futures, since the distribution of prices is evenly spread out after considering a slightly higher tendency to trade at integers.[7]

SUMMARY AND LOOKING AHEAD

This chapter examines the different types of traders on the trading floor, what happens in the futures pit, and intraday price action. The behavior and motivations of each type of trader in the pit are discussed, with suggestions on how these traders influence price behavior. The study of market microstructure examines the U-shaped volatility curve over the trading day, the size of scalper's profits and bid-ask spreads, and the behavior of prices from one transaction to the next. The Focus items provide additional insights into the different types of traders in the pit, their behavior, the new Globex 24-hour trading system, and the real-time trading screens.

BIBLIOGRAPHY

Angrist, Stanley W. (1989). "Commodity Exchanges Crack the Whip," *The Wall Street Journal,* September 29, p. C1.

Bollerslev, Tim, and Ian Domowitz (1990). "Price Volatility, Spread Variability, and the Role of Alternative Market Mechanisms," *The Review of Futures Markets,* Vol. 10, No. 1, pp. 78–101.

Jordan, James V., William E. Seale, Stephen J. Dinehart, and David E. Kenyon (1988). "The Intraday Variability of Soybean Futures Prices: Information and Trading Effects," *The Review of Futures Markets,* Vol. 7, No. 1, pp. 79–109.

[7] Futures transactions data only record price *changes.* Therefore, there is a bias against recording a clustering of prices when a series of bids or a series of ask prices are hit in sequence *and* the equilibrium price of the contract does not change.

Laux, Paul A. and A. J. Senchack (1992). "Bid-Ask Spreads in Financial Futures," *The Journal of Futures Markets,* Vol. 12, No. 6, December.

Ma, K. C., R. L. Peterson, and R. S. Sears (1989). "Trading Noise, Private Information and the Intraday Bid-Ask Spreads in Futures Markets," Working Paper, Texas Tech University.

Melamed, Leo (1981). "The Futures Market: Liquidity and the Technique of Spreading," *The Journal of Futures Markets,* Vol. 1, No. 3, Fall, pp. 405–412.

Roll, Richard (1984). "A Simple Implicit Measure of the Effective Bid-Ask Spread in an Efficient Market," *Journal of Finance,* Vol. 39, No. 4, September, pp. 1127–1139.

Silber, William L. (1984). "Marketmaker Behavior in an Auction Market: An Analysis of Scalpers in Futures Markets," *Journal of Finance,* Vol. 39, No. 4, September, pp. 937–953.

Wang, George H. K., Raphael J. Michalski, Eugene J. Moriarty, and James V. Jordan (1990). "An Intraday Analysis of Liquidity and Prices for the S&P 500 Index Futures Market," Columbia Working Paper No. 203, December.

Wang, George H. K., Eugene J. Moriarty, Raphael J. Michalski, and James V. Jordan (1990). "Empirical Analysis of Liquidity of S&P 500 Index Futures Markets During the Market Break," *Advances in Futures and Options Research,* Vol. 4, Winter, pp. 191–218.

"A World Marketplace" (1985). *The Chicago Mercantile Exchange.*

Chapter 6

FUTURES HEDGING CONCEPTS

Overview

Hedging is undertaken to reduce the price risk of a cash position. The managerial goals of a hedging program are to make a hedging decision and to manage the program. In order to accomplish these goals one must comprehend the concepts, issues, and factors associated with hedging. A discussion of what hedging entails, the hedging process, and hedging strategies provides a foundation of hedging concepts. Examples of the three types of short hedges help to illustrate the concepts and issues associated with hedging. The three types of hedges are a portfolio hedge, an inventory hedge, and an asset-liability hedge. A portfolio hedge is undertaken when a money manager desires to reduce the risk of a potential price decline for a portfolio of cash assets. An inventory hedge occurs when a market maker locks in the current value of the asset held in inventory until that asset can be sold. Financial institutions execute asset-liability hedges in order to overcome the effects of differences between either the maturities or the price volatilities of the institution's assets and liabilities.

Long hedges, crosshedges, and changing the effective volatility of an asset are additional applications of futures hedging. A long hedge is undertaken in order to "lock in" a price for a cash position when the cash position will be initiated in the future. A crosshedge is implemented when the characteristics of the existing futures contracts do not match the characteristics of the cash instrument. Changing effective volatilities of assets is a common portfolio management tool.

Return is also a consideration when hedging. Returns associated with hedging are related to whether the basis gets "weaker" or "stronger." The relationship between risk and return also is examined by hedgers. Finally, the subjective advantages and disadvantages of hedging and the circumstances that would prompt a money manager to hedge are discussed. These concepts concerning hedging provide an important foundation for forthcoming chapters on quantitative techniques and procedures for using futures as a risk management tool.

Terminology

*Anticipatory hedge   See long hedge.

*Asset-liability hedge   A hedge undertaken by a financial institution in order to offset the variability in earnings caused by maturity or price volatility differences between its assets and liabilities.

Basis   See Chapter 3.

Basis risk   See Chapter 3.

Convergence   See Chapter 3.

*Crosshedge   Hedging when the characteristics of the deliverable instrument (the cash asset underlying the futures) differ from the characteristics of the cash instrument being hedged. The characteristic(s) can differ in terms of quality, maturity, or coupon. Hedging a corporate (risky) bond with a Treasury (no default risk) bond futures is an example of a crosshedge.

Hedging   See Chapter 1.

*Inventory hedge   A hedge used by a market maker in order to reduce the price risk of the market maker's inventory of assets until the assets can be sold.

*Long hedge   Buying a futures contract in order to reduce the price variability of an *anticipated* cash position; alternatively, to "lock in" the price of a cash security that will be purchased in the future. Thus, a long hedge is a tempory substitute for a future cash position.

Marking-to-market   See Chapter 3.

Negative basis   Occurs when the cash price is less than the futures price.

Opportunity loss   See Chapter 3.

*Portfolio hedge   Hedging assets in order to reduce price risk.

Positive basis   Occurs when the cash price is greater than the futures price.

Selective hedging   Deciding when to hedge based on a forecast of the direction of the cash market. This method attempts to enhance overall returns but typically causes higher risk because of imperfect forecasts.

*Short hedge   See Chapter 3.

*Stronger basis   The cash price increases more or falls less than the futures price (i.e., the difference between the cash and futures prices becomes more positive or less negative); in this case, a short hedge generates positive returns while a long hedge generates negative returns.

Systematic risk   The variability associated with general market movements; also called undiversifiable risk.

Unsystematic risk   The variability associated with the unique characteristics of the individual asset; also called diversifiable risk.

*Weaker basis   The cash price increases less or falls more than the futures price (i.e., the difference between the cash and futures prices becomes less positive or more negative), in this case, a short hedge generates negative returns while a long hedge generates positive returns.

FUTURES HEDGING CONCEPTS: AN INTRODUCTION

The Objective and Benefits of Hedging

The key to risk management is determining risk-return objectives and trade-offs. Without a clear understanding of the relevant objectives and trade-offs appropriate for the institution, futures hedging is controversial and therefore can produce unwanted results. Thus, **hedging** is only a *tool* for achieving clearly defined risk management objectives.

The primary objective of hedging is to reduce the price risk of a current or potential cash position. Those who *must* hold cash inventories, such as bond and currency dealers, routinely reduce their risk by undertaking a hedge position. Financial institutions and pension funds often determine that it is easier and more cost effective to hedge with futures than to restructure their position solely by making cash transactions. In fact, the principal reason for the existence of futures markets is to allow hedgers to transfer their price risk.[1]

The price variability in the financial markets since the mid 1970s has created a surge in volume in the related futures markets. Market participants using futures markets have realized the benefits of reducing price risk (hedgers) or trading on price variability

---

[1] In some markets speculators provide the risk capital needed for this transfer of risk; however, in the most active financial futures markets both long and short hedgers exist, and speculators provide a time bridge between trades by the long and short hedgers.

(speculators) provided by these markets. The benefits of risk reduction are so important to many money managers that they employ futures contracts to hedge even when there is no specific futures instrument directly associated with the cash instrument held in their portfolio. For example, corporate bondholders often hedge with T-bond futures in order to minimize the price risk caused by the volatility of long-term interest rates, even though a change in the yield spread between the T-bond and corporate bond yields causes adverse effects for this specific type of hedge.

Hedging benefits society as well as the individual hedger. As outlined in Chapter 1, the ability to transfer risk allows the commodity hedger a more stable estimate of the cost of a product, which translates into a lower and more stable price for the product. Also, users of commodities are able to "lock in" the future purchase price of the item they need with only a small cash margin "down payment," thereby allowing a reduction in current inventory. This reduction in inventory reduces the cost of business and improves the firm's liquidity, benefits that can be passed on to the consumer. The existence of financial futures allows pension funds to stabilize returns and reduce risk for the pension fund participants, enables financial institutions to reduce risk, and provides the means to create new products in the insurance, loan and investment arenas.

Hedging is also a tool used to offset the market (**systematic**) **risk** of stock portfolios. Previously, risk management for common stocks concentrated on diversification to eliminate **unsystematic risk**, but until futures and options contracts on stock index futures came into existence, there was no effective means for eliminating most of the systematic risk of a stock portfolio. Alternatively, futures are used to adjust the beta of the stock portfolio to the desired value.

Finally, hedging is extremely important for the proper functioning, long-term liquidity, and open interest of a futures market. Thus, viable futures contracts are linked to commercial hedging activity. Although speculative interest provides shorter-term volume, speculative activity can be wavering and uncertain, especially since many speculators hold a position for only several weeks. Market makers on the futures floor provide intraday liquidity, but without speculators and hedgers the market makers soon depart to another pit. Likewise, arbitrageurs provide only limited liquidity for the markets. Hedgers are the key to the market, as is evident when a futures contract stops trading because of a lack of trading volume.

Hedging Concepts

Price Changes and Hedging.   In order to understand the basic concepts of hedging, let us assume that we own a portfolio of assets (e.g., stocks and/or bonds). The value of the assets is defined as follows:

$$TV_C = P_C N_C \tag{6-1}$$

where TV_C = the total value of the cash position

$\qquad P_C$ = the price per unit of the cash instrument or asset

$\qquad N_C$ = the number of cash units held

Without hedging, the value of the cash position changes over time as the price of the cash asset changes; that is,

$$\Delta TV_C = \Delta P_C(N_C) \tag{6-2}$$

If a short position in futures is taken to offset partially or fully the change in the long cash position, we have

$$\Delta TV_{C-F} = \Delta P_C(N_C) + \Delta P_F(-N_F) \tag{6-3}$$

where ΔTV_{C-F} = the net change in value

ΔP_F = the change in the futures price

$-N_F$ = the short position on N units of the futures

If the purpose of the hedge is to minimize the net price change (minimize risk), then we have as our objective:

$$\Delta TV_{C-F} = 0 = \Delta P_C(N_C) + \Delta P_F(-N_F) \tag{6-4}$$

The next chapter employs this concept to determine the number of futures contracts needed to minimize risk.

Basis, Basis Risk, and Crosshedges. A method for visualizing how hedging affects risk is to examine the basis between the cash and futures position. **Basis** is the difference between the cash price of the specific instrument one is hedging and the futures price of the futures instrument employed for the hedge (i.e., $P_C - P_F$). Therefore, **basis risk** is the variability in the basis over time—that is, the variability of the net hedging position. Hedging reduces the price risk inherent in the total price variability of the cash instrument to the variability of the basis; in other words, *hedging replaces absolute price risk with basis risk.* For example, if the cash stock portfolio has a standard deviation of 20% then hedging can reduce the net ($P_C - P_F$) variability to less than 4% (a reduction of more than 80% of the total variability). This reduction in risk occurs because the futures price change offsets the effect of the cash price change. Figure 3-3 illustrates absolute risk and basis risk.

If the cash instrument possesses essentially the same characteristics as the futures contract, then the basis risk should be minimal. However, if significant differences exist between the cash and futures characteristics (i.e., if one is executing a *crosshedge* between instruments with substantially different characteristics), then the basis risk is often large. This large basis risk occurs because the futures and cash prices do not move together. In fact, the extent of the basis risk is a critical factor in determining whether a hedge is appropriate for a given situation.

Quantity Risk. Another risk affecting a hedge position is uncertainty over the quantity to hedge. For example, because of weather conditions, a grain farmer is not sure how many bushels of grain will be harvested. A financial institution has similar forecasting problems in anticipating how many certificates of deposit will be purchased by investors. Thus, the fact that N_C in Equations (6-1) to (6-3) can be an uncertain number for some types of hedges creates difficulties in estimating N_F.

Anticipated and Unanticipated Price Changes. It is essential to understand that futures prices reflect the expectations of market participants concerning changes in the cash price; that is, futures prices reflect *anticipated* changes in the cash price. In other words, futures are a forward price. Thus, even if current short-term interest rates are at 5%, the forward/futures markets could forecast that short-term rates will be at 6½% within nine months. A hedger who desires to hedge an interest rate position with a futures contract expiring nine months from now is hedging against any change *from the projected forward/futures* rate of 6½%; that is, one can hedge only against *unanticipated* changes not yet reflected in the futures market price. Another way to state this idea is that futures *cannot* protect the hedger against differences between the current interest rate and the *expected* interest rate implied by the current futures price. Note that hedging with futures is equivalent to locking in a forward rate starting, say, nine months from now; it is *not* possible to lock in the *current* interest rate to start in nine months. Similarly, prices of non-interest rate futures contracts reflect expectations concerning future cash price changes. For example, new information or changes in expectations are reflected in stock index futures prices 5 to 30 minutes before they show up in all cash stock prices because of the lower cost and greater liquidity of the futures market. However, this knowledge will *not* help a trader profit in cash stocks, since the *next* trade in the cash stocks (in 5 to 30 minutes) accounts for the change in expectations.

Risk Management. The foregoing discussion emphasizes the primary purpose of futures: the control of risk of the cash position. Risk is described in terms of price change, a change in the basis, Equation (6-2), and unanticipated price changes. Each concept reflects the same need, to control risk. Hence, the first decision is *whether* the portfolio manager or firm wishes to avoid unanticipated price changes. Hedging eliminates most of the effect of these price changes, but it also eliminates potential positive returns. The risk preferences of the potential hedger dictate whether hedging is appropriate for this situation or whether the cash asset's absolute price variability is tolerable.

Avoiding Losses: Sell or Hedge?

A typical question concerning hedging is, "Why should I hedge when I can sell the cash asset if I expect prices to decline?" In fact, selling the cash asset is preferable in some circumstances.[2] The principal rule for deciding whether to make a transaction in the cash market or to hedge in the futures market is:

> *If you can accomplish your goal effectively in the cash market, then complete your transaction in that market.*

---

[2] In fact, dealers do *not* have a choice: they *must* have an inventory of the cash asset to act as a dealer. Thus, dealers often use futures for hedging.

The key to this rule is the word "effectively." In many situations, one or more of the following factors cause difficulties if the transaction is completed in the cash market:

- **Liquidity:** The cash market for a given asset often is not liquid for large trades. Thus, the portfolio hedger who sells or buys the cash asset, or the dealer who shorts the asset, causes a significant price change in that security when liquidity does not exist. There is no liquidity problem for trades in most (near-term) financial futures contracts.
- **Cost:** The commissions and size of the bid-ask spread in the cash market often cause the cash transaction to be expensive relative to the same transaction in the futures market. For example, trades in a stock portfolio cost ten times the equivalent trade in futures.
- **Execution:** A futures transaction is initiated much quicker than a cash transaction due to liquidity.
- **Short selling:** A short sale in the cash market is typically expensive. For example, a short sale of a cash T-bill costs approximately 50 basis points per year. Moreover, the same exact T-bill maturity has to be replaced when the short is covered—often a difficult and expensive process.
- **Internal policy or government regulations:** These factors can prevent the desired cash market transaction. For example, a portfolio manager often is required to have a given minimum percentage of assets in bonds rather than in cash or short-term securities, or a financial institution may be prevented from shorting a cash security to obtain an effective cash market hedge.
- **Credit risk:** Creating a forward or short sale in the cash market often involves an implicit credit risk on the part of the participants. Futures transactions are completed with the clearinghouse, virtually eliminating the credit risk problem.

Strategies for Hedging

Hedging typically is associated with reducing risk (reducing price volatility). However, those who employ futures markets have different strategies and different goals for implementing a hedging program. Market participants practice four overlapping strategies:

- **Reduction of risk:** The primary use of futures for hedging is to reduce the price variability associated with the cash asset position. Naive, regression, and duration methods determine the appropriate number of futures contracts for a hedge position. The objective of the regression and duration methods is to minimize the risk associated with a cash position. Chapters 7 to 10 discuss these methods.
- **Selective hedging:** Hedging only during those time periods when a forecast determines that the cash position will lose money is called selective hedging. If the forecasts are correct then risk is minimized during the hedged periods; meanwhile, the asset earns positive returns during the unhedged periods. If the forecasts are incorrect, then risk is not reduced. Many institutions employ some type of market timing to decide when to use selective hedging.
- **"Speculating on the basis":** When the returns from the hedge are a consideration in whether the hedge will be undertaken, this approach is equivalent to predicting the change in the basis during the hedge period. The considerations in predicting hedge returns are discussed later in this chapter.

- **Optimal risk-return hedging:** The optimal hedge decision considers both the reduction in risk *and* the return from the combined cash-futures position. Such an optimal position is associated with portfolio analysis and is discussed in Chapter 7.

The above strategies also can be designated as passive or active. A passive strategy is independent of cash market price/interest rate expectations. Passive strategies depend on the risk attitude of the hedger and the volatility of the cash markets. Active strategies require a forecast of future cash prices/interest rates for implementation. The forecast helps the money manager decide when and how much of the cash position to hedge. Thus, an active hedging strategy readjusts the hedging position over time.

The "reduction of risk" strategy listed above is a passive strategy. "Selective hedging" and "speculating on the basis" are active strategies. The "optimal risk-return" strategy can be either passive or active, depending on whether the risk attitude of the hedger or the forecasts of the cash market determine the size of the hedge position.

The Hedging Process

The examples presented below illustrate how hedging entails taking a position in futures that "offsets" the price change in the cash asset. Hence, hedging a current long cash position consists of taking a short futures position. In order to determine whether one should sell or buy futures to initiate a hedge, a potential hedger can follow a two-step process:

1. Determine the exposure of the cash position to potential losses; that is, in what direction must cash prices change in order to create a loss? Thus, a loss occurs for a current long cash position when prices decline, whereas a loss occurs for a short cash or an *anticipated* cash position when prices increase.
2. Determine whether a short or a long futures position is needed to offset the potential loss in the cash position.

Exhibit 6-1 illustrates the possible situations. The hedging examples in the following sections show how to implement these hedges.

TYPES OF SHORT HEDGES

A **short hedge** exists when a short futures position is undertaken in order to offset adverse price changes in a long cash position. The following discussion illustrates three basic types of risk-reducing short hedges.

A Portfolio Hedge

When a money manager forecasts a decline in the price of a portfolio of financial assets *or* does not want the risk associated with those assets, the money manager can:

- Do nothing (which creates a loss if the forecast is correct).
- Sell the cash assets.
- Execute a short hedge with a futures contract or alternative hedging instrument.

EXHIBIT 6-1
Initiating Hedging Positions

Cash Position	Cash Market Loss Occurs When	Change in the Associated Futures Contract	Appropriate Hedge Position
Own (long)	P_C decreases	P_F decreases	Short futures
Short	P_C increases	P_F increases	Long futures
Anticipated long	P_C increases (opportunity loss)	P_F increases	Long futures
Anticipated short	P_C decreases (opportunity loss)	P_F decreases	Short futures

P_C = price of the cash
P_F = price of the futures

Typically, a futures hedge provides benefits over simply selling the asset, as discussed earlier in this chapter. Hedging the currently owned cash asset is called a **portfolio hedge.**

Example 6-1 presents a case in which a portfolio manager hedges $1 million of Treasury bonds when a money manager expects interest rates to increase. By selling T-bond futures short, the money manager profits on the futures side when prices decline (interest rates increase), thereby partially or totally offsetting the loss on the long cash T-bond position as its price declines. The example shows how the loss of $144,687.50 in the value of the cash bond position is reduced to a net loss of $20,312.50 when the profit from the short sale of the futures contracts is considered. Thus, the hedge reduces the loss on the cash portfolio by nearly 86%.

Many basic trade booklets and publications on futures markets present hedging examples by showing a net loss of $0—that is, a situation in which the gain on the futures position *exactly* offsets the loss on the cash position. This situation is equivalent to having a perfect negative correlation of −1.0 between the cash and futures price changes. Although such a situation would be welcome by hedgers, the reality is that such "perfect hedges" do not exist.

An Inventory Hedge

A dealer is a market maker for an asset or instrument that does not trade on an exchange. The dealer holds inventory of the asset in order to transact trades. For example, bond and currency markets are dealer markets. These dealers trade billions of dollars in government and corporate bonds and foreign currencies each day. An **inventory hedge** occurs when market makers use futures contracts to lock in the value of their inventory until the market makers can sell the inventory. On occasion, dealers also lock in the price of assets about to be obtained, especially when bond dealers bid for a new issue of government bonds. Bond and currency dealers routinely use the futures markets to control their risk exposure.

EXAMPLE 6-1
A Portfolio Short Hedge Example

A portfolio manager for long-term Treasury bonds forecasts that interest rates will increase over the next few months (bond prices are expected to fall). The money manager holds a portfolio of $1 million ($1MM) of May 2011 bonds. A short hedge is implemented in September when long-term rates are at 7.8% and lifted in February after rates rise to 9.1%.

	Cash	**Futures**
Sept. 16	Holds $1 million par of May 2011 T-bonds coupon rate 10¾%, yielding 7.8% with a price of 129¹³⁄₃₂	Sells 10 March T-bond futures with a price of 100 (a projected yield of 8.0%)
Feb. 22	Price of bonds has dropped to 114³⁰⁄₃₂ with a yield of 9.1%	Repurchases 10 March T-bond futures at a price of 87¹⁸⁄₃₂ (with a projected yield of 9.4%)
Change in value	Loss of $144,687.50 (14¹⁵⁄₃₂ × $1MM)	Gain of $124,375 (12¹⁴⁄₃₂ × $100,000 × 10 or 398 × $31.25 × 10)

Net Loss: $20,312.50 (i.e., $144,687.50 − $124,375)

Although the concept and setup for this type of a hedge is equivalent to the portfolio hedge discussed in Example 6-1, the motivation differs. Both the portfolio manager and the dealer execute a hedge in order to reduce the price variability of the assets they are holding. However, the portfolio manager could simply sell the cash asset, although the dealer *must* keep the current cash inventory in order to transact business. Hence, the money manager completes the portfolio hedge because futures provide important advantages over simply selling the cash asset, including lower transactions costs and greater liquidity; however, a dealer's futures hedge is used to avoid the problems associated with covering an inventory position in the cash market. In particular, covering an inventory position by short selling a similar cash asset can be difficult to execute, and can be very costly or impossible because of the size of the dealer's position. Alternatively, if the dealer is long on some cash assets and short on others (for example, different bond maturities), then the dealer is naturally hedged for part of the inventory. Example 6-2 shows the classic inventory hedge of the IBM sale of $1 billion of bonds during October 1979; in this case, the dealer avoided a significant loss of hedging.

An Asset-Liability Hedge

Financial institutions and the portfolios hedger have different problems. Whereas the portfolio hedger desires to reduce the price risk of a set of assets, the financial institution is concerned about the *relationship* between its assets and liabilities. Specifically, changes in the financial institution's earnings are caused by the relative effect of a

EXAMPLE 6-2
A Dealer's Inventory Hedge: The IBM Underwriting

In October 1979, IBM offered $1 billion of notes and bonds to the financial market, the largest offering in U.S. corporate history. Solomon Brothers and Merrill Lynch were comanagers of the underwriting, heading a group of 227 members. The underwriters' commission on the notes was ⅝% and the bonds provided ⅞%; the spread above the government notes and bonds was only 7 and 12 basis points, respectively. Given that the prime rate had increased five times during the previous month, the commission rate and spread were minimal given the risk being undertaken by the underwriters. The sale began on Thursday, October 4, the same day a Treasury auction took place.

On Saturday, October 6, the Fed announced its famous dictum that it was changing its policy from controlling interest rates to controlling the money supply in order to reduce the rate of inflation. That day, the Fed increased the discount rate from 11% to 12%. By October 9, the prime rate had increased one percentage point to 14.5%. By October 10, the IBM note yield had increased from 9.62% to 10.65% and the bond yield had increased from 9.41% to 10.09%.

When the underwriting syndicate was disbanded on Wednesday, October 10, approximately $650 million of the $1 billion offering had been sold, generating $5 million in fees. However, the subsequent loss on the remaining $350 million in unsold notes and bonds was $15 million.

The potential loss on the inventory of bonds from the dramatic increase in interest rates was significantly higher than the underwriting commissions on these issues. Solomon Brothers, which took $125 million of the unsold issue, had hedged its inventory position in the futures market by selling T-bond futures. This hedge undoubtedly allowed Solomon to save a significant portion of its revenues from the underwriting. Since this historic underwriting, dealers in bond issues have routinely hedged their inventory position by employing the T-bond and T-note futures markets.

change in interest rates on both the assets and liabilities of the insitution. If the cost of funds (liabilities) increases, then this cost is partially or completely offset by the additional return from higher interest on assets. Thus, the financial institution is naturally hedged for part of the balance sheet. However, many financial institutions find that it is not possible to reduce the volatility of earnings adequately from this natural asset-liability relationship, since assets often are long-term in nature while liabilities are short-term. This situation creates a "gap" in the maturity relationship, which causes changes in earnings when interest rates change. Hedging this maturity gap is called an **asset-liability hedge.**

Example 6-3 illustrates a typical asset-liability problem facing a financial institution and shows how a futures hedge can alleviate this problem. The example begins by showing the problem that occurs when asset returns are fixed for the long term, but the liability costs vary over a much shorter period. It then provides an illustration of how a simple T-bill futures hedge can significantly reduce the volatility of a financial institution's earnings by "locking in" the future cost of the liability. Chapter 17 covers the uses of futures by financial institutions.

EXAMPLE 6-3
An Asset-Liability Hedge Example

AAA Savings and Loan has assets in the form of a mortgage portfolio of $500 million, with $300 million of the portfolio having a 9½% fixed-rate with 20 years to maturity. The other $200 million in mortgages are variable-rate loans linked to the 90-day T-bill rate plus a 2% premium, adjustable quarterly. For simplicity, let us assume that the liabilities of AAA consist of $500 million of three-month certificates of deposit, where the interest rate is based on the 90-day T-bill rate plus ¾%.

Since the variable-rate mortgages are repriced at the same time and with the same instrument as the liabilities of the S&L (i.e., both are based on the T-bill rate), this portion of the asset-liability mix does not have a pricing risk. However, the fixed-rate portion of the mortgage portfolio is *not* repriced when the cost of the CDs changes in relation to changing interest rates. This creates a significant potential change in the earnings of the S&L as interest rates change.

PART A: WITHOUT A FUTURES HEDGE
The three-month T-bill rate is 7% on January 15; this rate changes to 11% by April 15. Note the change in the annualized spread between the fixed-rate portion of the mortgages and the liability interest rate from Jaunary to April, causing a significant change in earnings.

	Assets	Liabilities	Annualized Spread
Jan. 15	$200MM variable; 7% T-bill + 2% premium	$200MM 90-day CD, 7¾%	9% − 7¾% = +1¼%
	$300MM fixed, 9½%, 20-year	$300MM 90-day CD, 7¾%	9½% − 7¾% = +1¾%
April 15	$200MM variable, 11% T-bill + 2% premium	$200MM 90-day CD, 11¾%	13% − 11¾% = +1¼%
	$300MM fixed, 9½%, 20-year	$300MM 90-day CD, 11¾%	9½% − 11¾% = −2¼%

continued next page

USING LONG HEDGES

The Long Hedge Concept

A **long hedge** is initiated when a futures contract is purchased in order to reduce the price variability of an *anticipated* future long position. Equivalently, a long hedge "locks in" the interest rate or price of a cash security that will be purchased in the future, subject to a small adjustment due to the basis risk. Long hedges are sometimes considered speculative, since the hedger is attempting to offset a *projected* position rather than a current position. However, if future cash inflows can be forecasted accurately; if these funds are invested; and if interest rates are forecasted to decline (prices

continued

PART B: FUTURES HEDGE FOR FIXED-RATE MORTGAGES

T-bill futures are sold to offset the higher cost of the CDs *to be issued* during July, the CDs being the cost of funds to the S&L. Thus, the hedge is executed in order *to avoid higher costs* from the new CDs.

	Cash Liabilities	**Futures**
Jan. 15	Current cost: $300MM 90-day CDs at 7¾%	Sell to hedge cost of new CDs in April: 300 Sept. T-bill futures at 92.60, or 7.40%
April 15	CDs issued: $300MM 90-day CDs at 11¾%	Buy back futures: 300 Sept. T-bill futures at 88.90, or 11.10%
Net (three months)	($300MM) (4%) (¼ year) = − $3MM	(300 futures) (370 basis points) ($25 per basis point) = +$2.775MM
	Net loss with hedge:	$.225MM
	Net loss without hedge:	$3MM

The net loss shows the *higher cost of funding* for the financial institution. Note that the hedge given here offsets the higher CD cost for only one quarter, since the T-bill futures are 90-day instruments and a one-to-one hedge between the cash CDs and the T-bill futures is executed. Also, the hedge is not perfect: the cost on the CDs increases more than does the T-bill futures rate, creating a net loss of $.225MM on the combined net position; *however,* this loss is significantly less than the $3MM that would occur without any hedge.

expected to increase); then executing a long hedge locks in the *current* forward rate in the market. Consequently, a long hedge creates profits that offset the subsequent higher price in the cash market. A long hedge is also known as an **anticipatory hedge,** because it is effectively a substitute position for a future cash transaction.

The use of a long hedge serves as an effective *temporary* substitute for the purchase of a cash security, where the cash purchase is undertaken in the future. Thus, if interest rates do decline (prices increase) and no long hedge is executed, then the return on the invested funds will be lower than it would be if a hedge were executed. In other words, a long hedge can prevent an **opportunity loss** on future funds to be invested.[3] Example 6-4 shows how a long hedge is useful in locking in an effective yield on investment when the funds are not available until a given time in the future. The initiation of

---

[3] An alternative method to lock in a future interest rate (price) when funds will not be available until later is to buy the financial instrument now (e.g., purchase a cash T-bond), and finance that purchase with borrowed funds until money becomes available. In this way, the buyer guarantees the long-term yield on the bond. Whether the futures long hedge or the cash financing method is superior depends on the relationship of the bond yield to the financing rate, plus any difficulties in arranging financing for the cash transaction or convincing the board of directors of the firm to allow such financing.

EXAMPLE 6-4
Example of a Long Hedge

A greeting card company anticipates a large inflow of funds at the end of January when retail outlets pay for the stock of cards sold during the holiday season in December. Management intends to put $10 million of these funds into a long-term bond because of the high yields on these investments. The current date is November 1 and the financial manager of the greeting card company projects that the long-term interest rate will fall significantly by the time the firm receives the funds on February 1. Thus, unless a long hedge is initiated now, the financial manager believes that the return on investment will be significantly lower (the cost of the bonds significantly higher) than is currently available via the futures market.

Objective of the long hedge: to benefit from the high long-term interest rates, even though funds are not currently available for investment.

Date	Cash Market	Futures Market
Nov. 1	Bonds at $86^{20}/_{32}$ to yield 9.96%; 8% coupon, 12 years to maturity; $10MM to invest February 1	Buy 100 March T-bond futures at $87^{16}/_{32}$ as a long hedge (9.4% projected yield)
Feb. 1	Receive $10MM; buy $10MM of T-bonds at 100 to yield 8%	Sell futures at $100^2/_{32}$ to cover long position (yield 7.9%)
Change	Opportunity loss: $1,337,500 ($10MM $\times$ $13^{12}/_{32}$%)	Gain: $1,256,250 ($100,000 $\times$ 100 $\times$ $12^{18}/_{32}$%)

Net change: $1,256,250 − $1,337,500 = −$81,250
Net yield with futures hedge: 9.83%

The example shows that the purchase of the T-bond futures contracts creates a gain for the futures instrument and that this gain is used to offset most of the higher future cash T-bond price. To look at it another way, the gain obtained on the futures transaction increases the total yield so that the yield approaches the projected yield given by the futures market on November 1. Although the net loss of $81,250 on the long hedge shows that the hedge is not perfect, this loss is significantly less than the opportunity loss of $1,337,500 that occurs without any hedge position.

a long hedge, as in Example 6-4, is made by management either if the firm wishes to reduce risk substantially *or* if the firm has a better forecast of future interest rates than is available from the forward rate (selective hedging).

Disadvantages of a Long Hedge

Disadvantages of a long hedge are as follows:

- If the financial manager incorrectly forecasts the direction of future interest rates or prices and a long hedge is initiated, then the firm still locks in the futures yield (price) rather than fully participating in the higher returns available because of the higher interest rates or lower price.

- If prices fall, an immediate cash outflow due to margin calls occurs. This cash outflow will be offset only *over the life of a bond* via a higher yield on investment, or from a higher asset price if the asset recovers in the market and it is sold. Thus, the net investment is the same, but the timing of the accounting profits differs from the investment decision.

- If the futures market already anticipates an increase in prices similar to the increase forecasted by the financial manager, then the futures price reflects this higher price, negating any return benefit from the long hedge. Specifically, one hedges only against *unanticipated* changes that the futures market has not yet forecasted. Hence, if the eventual cash price increases only to a level *below* the current futures price, a loss occurs on the long hedge. Consequently, an increase in return from a long hedge in comparison to the future cash market investment occurs only if the financial manager is a superior forecaster of future interest rates or prices. However, the long hedge does lock in the currently available long-term futures interest rate or price (or a close approximation), thereby reducing the risk of unanticipated changes in this rate or price.

- Financial institutions are prohibited from employing long hedges, since their regulatory agencies believe that long hedges are similar to speculation, and these agencies do not want financial institutions to be tempted into affecting the institution's return with highly leveraged "speculative" futures positions.

CROSSHEDGES AND CHANGING VOLATILITIES OF AN ASSET POSITION

Crosshedges

A **crosshedge** occurs if the characteristics of the cash asset underlying the futures contract differs from the cash instrument being hedged. A number of factors affect the degree of a crosshedge for a given position. The extent of a stock portfolio crosshedge is affected by the relative stock composition and relative stock weights of the cash and futures positions; any differences in the dollar size between the cash and futures positions also affect the hedge. For a T-bond futures hedge, one must consider the effect of the coupon, the time to maturity of the cash position, whether the bond possesses default risk, and the relative size of the underlying cash position. If any of these factors differ from the characteristics of the futures contract or the cheapest-to-deliver cash bond for pricing the futures, then a crosshedge exists. The extent of a crosshedge can be measured by the size of the correlation coefficient between the changes in value of the cash and futures position. The lower the correlation coefficient, the greater the difference in the two positions. When a low correlation exists, the futures contract is not a good instrument to use for hedging purposes.

Crosshedges arising from some of these characteristics, such as coupon differences, have a minimal effect on the performance of the hedge when the cash and futures prices still move nearly in tandem. Crosshedge factors affecting the volatility of the position (e.g., the maturity of the cash bond) are dealt with by adjusting the number of futures contracts employed in the hedge (as shown in the next chapter). However, the effect of a quality difference, such as hedging corporate bonds with Treasury bond futures, depends on whether there is a major change in the perceived risk in the economy during the hedge period, which would significantly alter the basis. Consequently, the difficulty of overcoming crosshedge effects depends on the particular characteristic(s) that differ between the futures and cash positions, whether the factors remain stable over time, and the economic environment at the time of the hedge.[4,5]

In reality, most hedges involve some type of a crosshedge risk, since the cash asset typically differs from the underlying cash instrument priced by the futures contract. The greater the deviation of any of these factors from the underlying cash instrument, the greater the basis risk. For example, the effect of a large change in the shape of the term structure needs to be considered when the maturities of the cash bond and the cheapest-to-deliver bond for the futures contract differ. The creation of the T-note futures contracts with shorter maturities was undertaken in order to provide a more appropriate hedging vehicle under these circumstances. Also note that care must be taken when hedging the prime rate. Because the prime is an administered rate, it does not usually change in the same manner as market rates; in fact, the prime rate is slow to react to downward changes in interest rates. Hence, it is sometimes difficult to hedge the prime effectively, especially over the short term.

Example 6-5 shows a crosshedge between a cash portfolio mimicking the S&P 100 cash index and the S&P 500 futures contract. As shown in the example, crosshedges create net gains or losses that often vary to a greater extent than is the case when the characteristics of the futures and cash securities are nearly equivalent. Many of the hedging applications examined in Chapter 17 involve recognizing and dealing effectively with crosshedge characteristics. The hedging techniques discussed in Chapters 7 and 10 also help reduce crosshedge risk.

Adjusting Risk: Altering Effective Volatilities

An important use of futures markets is to change the *effective* volatility of a cash position. For example, selling a T-bond or stock index futures contract reduces the effective volatility of the cash position, whereas buying futures increases the effective volatility of a bond or stock portfolio. In other words, selling bond futures shortens the effective maturity of a bond. Similarly, buying bond futures increases the price sensitivity of the position to changes in interest rates, creating a position that acts like a bond with a longer maturity. A bond portfolio manager often wants to change the volatility of a bond portfolio when the interest rate forecast indicates a change in rates and the portfolio manager wishes to act on this forecast. Decreasing volatility by selling futures reduces losses when rates increase; on the other hand, increasing the effective volatility of the bond position by buying futures increases gains if interest rates decrease. Of course, these strategies also decrease and increase the risk of the bond portfolio, respectively. Correspondingly, selling stock index futures decreases the beta of a portfolio, whereas buying futures increases the portfolio's beta.

---

[4] For example, hedging one currency with the futures contract of another currency often causes significant crosshedge risk because of the differing economic conditions in the two countries.

[5] Liquidity also can be an issue in *measuring* the basis for a given security, since thinly traded issues often have reported prices that differ from their true prices, especially when the market changes but the thinly traded issue does not trade. Moreover, cash prices typically are reported in terms of bid prices and ask prices rather than transaction prices, and the newspaper prices occur at a different time of day than the close of the futures market; both of these factors affect the *apparent* stability of the basis.

EXAMPLE 6-5
Example of a Crosshedge

A major pension fund holds $50 million in stocks, with the portfolio configured to match the S&P 100 index. The fund's money manager forecasts an increase in volatility in the market, which increases the probability of a major market decline. To reduce risk the money manager sells S&P 500 futures. Although the S&P 500 futures do not match the S&P 100 price movements exactly, the money manager decides that this type of a crosshedge is the best strategy to use in this situation.

Date	Cash Market	Futures Market
Jan. 12	Stock portfolio of $50 million, with the S&P 100 = 325.09	Sell 287 June S&P 500 futures, with the S&P 500 futures = 348.20 for a value of $49,966,700
April 26	The S&P 100 declines to 315.82 for a portfolio value of $48,574,240 = $50MM × (315.82/325.09)	Buy back the S&P 500 futures at 335.25 for a value of $48,108,375
Change	Loss of $1,425,760	Gain of $1,858,325 = 287 × 500 × (348.20 − 335.25)

Net gain: $432,565

The crosshedge generates a gain of $432,565. The large deviation between the loss in the cash portfolio and the futures gain shows the relative ineffectiveness of this crosshedge.

Chapter 17 illustrates ways to determine the number of futures contracts to buy or sell in order to change the effective volatility of a bond or stock position. Chapter 17 also discusses techniques whereby futures are employed to turn a bond position into an equivalent T-bill position while providing returns higher than those available in the current T-bill position.

RETURNS, BASIS, AND CASH FLOWS

Returns and Hedging: Considering the Basis

The sole objective of a "pure" hedging model is to reduce the variability of the cash position as much as possible. This approach is consistent with the objective of minimizing risk, which is the cornerstone of many hedging techniques and examples. However, most hedgers also consider the effect of the hedge on the returns of the position.

When one considers the potential effect of the hedge on returns, it is enticing to concentrate (incorrectly) only on **convergence** and whether there is a **positive** or **negative** **basis**—that is, whether $P_C - P_F > 0$ or $P_C - P_F < 0$. If these were the only relevant factors, then a negative basis—in combination with a short hedge—would produce a positive return when the prices converged at expiration. Thus, the cash price would increase to equal the futures price at the expiration of the futures contract. Similarly, a positive basis would produce a negative return for a short hedge. These relationships are shown in Figure 6-1. However, this scenario *is guaranteed* only if the underlying cash position is the cheapest-to-deliver instrument—that is, if no type of crosshedge exists and the position is held until the expiration of the futures contract.[6]

In order to determine whether the returns from a crosshedge will be positive or negative, the hedger must examine the *direction of the change* in the basis *in conjunction with* the question of whether a positive or negative basis exists. An example of this situation is a crosshedge between a corporate bond and a T-bond futures contract. In order to simplify terminology, the effect of the direction and type of basis (positive or negative) for a crosshedge is described in terms of a **weaker** or **stronger basis.** A weaker basis occurs when the cash price increases less or falls more than the futures price. Consequently, a "weaker" basis means that the difference between the cash and futures prices becomes less positive or more negative. A weaker basis in conjunction with a short hedge generates negative returns. Thus, for a short hedge, the long cash position loses more than the short futures position gains (or the cash gains less than the futures loses). Conversely, a "stronger" basis occurs when the cash price increases more or falls less than the corresponding futures price. In this situation, the basis becomes more positive (or less negative), since the cash position gains more than the futures position loses (or loses less than the futures gains). These relationships are described in Exhibits 6-2 and 6-3 and in diagram form for a short hedge in Figure 6-2.

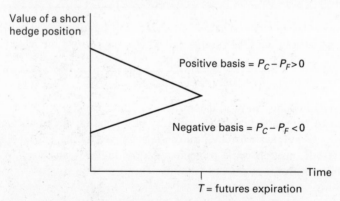

Figure 6-1 Positive and negative basis effects on return. (*Source:* Kellerman, 1990, p. 4.)

EXHIBIT 6-2
Hedge Position and Returns

Type of Hedge	Basis Weakens	Basis Strengthens
Short hedge	Returns < 0	Returns > 0
Long hedge	Returns > 0	Returns < 0

[6] This explanation also assumes that the hedger owns the cash asset. If the asset is being financed, then the basis should equal the net financing cost, as discussed in Part II.

EXHIBIT 6-3
Effect of Weakening and Strengthening of the Basis

Basis Movement		Effect			
Basis = $P_C - P_F$	Price Movements	Type of Hedge	Type of Basis	Direction of Basis	Return
"Weakens"	P_C increases less or falls more than P_F	Short	$P_C - P_F > 0$ (positive)	Narrows	Negative
			$P_C - P_F < 0$ (negative)	Widens	Negative
		Long	$P_C - P_F > 0$ (positive)	Narrows	Positive
			$P_C - P_F < 0$ (negative)	Widens	Positive
"Strengthens"	P_C increases more or falls less than P_F	Short	$P_C - P_F > 0$ (positive)	Widens	Positive
			$P_C - P_F < 0$ (negative)	Narrows	Positive
		Long	$P_C - P_F > 0$ (positive)	Widens	Negative
			$P_C - P_F < 0$ (negative)	Narrows	Negative

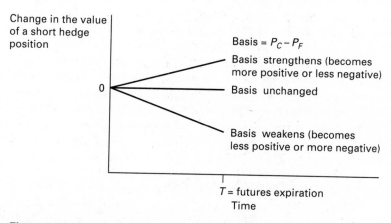

Figure 6-2 The effect of basis changes on the value of a short hedge.
(*Source:* Kellerman, 1990, p. 4.)

Since yields change in opposite directions to prices, when an upward sloping curve (i.e., a positive basis) exists, losses occur for a short hedge if the yield curve flattens out (the basis weakens). Similarly, when a downward sloping yield curve flattens out, a short hedge provides positive returns because the negative basis strengthens.[7,8]

In conclusion, some practitioners attempt to determine hedge returns by forecasting whether the basis will strengthen or weaken before entering into a hedge. The temptation to consider this type of basis trading as the *primary* factor dictating *when* to place

[7] Another reason for a change in the basis is a change in the short-term financing rate employed for arbitrage between the futures and cash positions. This change in the cost of funds to arbitrageurs is the major factor affecting the difference between the futures price and the cheapest-to-deliver cash instrument. Consequently, the basis changes as the financing rate changes.

[8] Basis movements also affect our conclusion concerning the ability of the hedge to reduce risk. Thus, when the basis changes over the life of the hedge, which is typical, the convergence of P_C and P_F creates an imperfect hedge.

the hedge must be guarded against so that the primary objective of risk reduction is implemented immediately. Management and hedge traders should realize that reduction in price risk is more important than a small improvement in return through basis changes.

Marking-to-Market and Cash Flows

The discussion of margins and **marking-to-market** in Chapter 3 shows that the futures account balance fluctuates as prices change. The change in the account balance affects the overall return of the position since earnings can be withdrawn to earn interest, while losses require additional infustion of cash to meet maintenance margin calls. The additional cash infusions cause a loss on interest on these funds, unless T-bills are used to cover the margin calls.[9] Hill, Schneeweis, and mayerson (1983) and Elton, Gruber, and Rentzler (1984) show that the net effect of interest earned/paid on margin accounts is small, approximating 2% of the entire return.

On the other hand, the cash flows resulting from marking-to-market require the liquidity management of funds. Earnings need to be invested in a timely manner. Additional funds can be deposited in the account to avoid margin calls; moreover, a line of credit may be needed to borrow funds to cover losses. A liquidity management model for margin balances can be used to maximize profits. Kolb, Gay, and Hunter (1985) show how an adaptation of a cash management model used by corporate finance managers is applicable to liquidity management for margin balances. Such a model determines the probability of a margin call, given an initial margin balance and the variability of futures prices. Alternatively, the manager can assign a desired probability of a margin call and the model shows the required margin balance and/or the length of time before additional funds are needed. Such a model would reduce criticisms of unmanaged cash outflows by the firm's directors.

If marking-to-market timing effects are considered to be an important factor affecting the hedge, then the manager can "tail" the hedge. Tailing adjusts the size of the hedge for marking-to-market effects. See Kawaller and Koch (1988) and Kawaller (1986) for examples of tailing a hedge position.

THE ADVANTAGES AND DISADVANTAGES OF HEDGING WITH FUTURES

There are a number of advantages to employing a futures hedge as a tool for risk management:

- Hedging with futures provides a risk management tool that usually reduces the price variability of a cash position significantly; if an unwanted risk exposure in the asset position exists, hedging is recommended.

- Futures provides an inexpensive and easy-to-use instrument for hedging purposes, especially in comparison with hedging in the cash market.

- Long-term hedges are possible with futures contracts, unlike transactions for most cash foward markets; for example, one can hedge out to three years with T-bond futures and four years with Eurodollar futures but less than one year by using interest rate forward contracts.

[9] Recall that T-bills or similar assets can be used to cover both initial margin and maintenance margin calls. The hedger earns the interest on the T-bills. If funds are not available to cover margin calls, then cash must be borrowed, thus creating an interest expense.

- Futures can alter the net effect of the cash position quickly; for example, financial institutions that desire to change their maturity structure can do so almost immediately with futures, while it could take many months to change the maturity structure by solely employing cash transactions. Quick executions also become important in fast-moving markets, such as during the October 1987 adjustments in the stock and bond markets. In these situations, futures markets operate and provide continuous trading, whereas making a trade in the cash markets may be difficult or impossible.

- Some hedges are possible only in the futures market (e.g., a NYSE stock index hedge).

- One can avoid an adverse cash market impact due to liquidity problems by hedging with futures when the cash security has a thin market or when there is a large cash position. For example, a dealer in bonds often has difficulty in adequately hedging the firm's inventory position using only the cash market, since the trading of moderate size cash positions often affects the price of the cash security.

Disadvantages also exist when hedging with futures:

- A cash, forward, or futures hedge offsets the cash position, *whether or not* the cash price changes in an unfavorable or a favorable direction; thus, a short hedge loses money on the futures side if the cash market rises.

- Margin calls occur if the futures market goes in the opposite direction than expected, causing a cash outflow and possibly the need for a cash line of credit. Most importantly, margin calls necessitate an understanding of the objective of the hedge by upper management.

- Accounting treatment of the hedge may differ from the tax or regulatory treatment. Thus, interim futures gains may be taxed or futures losses may appear on accounting statements, while the changes in the cash position are not considered until the sale of the asset.

SUMMARY AND LOOKING AHEAD

This chapter examines the qualitative aspects of hedging. Examples of various types of hedges are provided and risk management considerations are discussed. This material provides a foundation for using futures markets as a hedging tool. Quantitative hedging tools are examined in Chapters 7 and 10, with applications of risk management with futures covered in Chapter 17.

BIBLIOGRAPHY

Elton, E. J., M. J. Gruber, and J. Rentzler (1984). "Intra-Day Tests of the Efficiency of the Treasury-Bill Futures Market," *Review of Economics and Statistics,* February, pp. 129–137.

Hill, Joanne, Thomas Schneeweis, and Robert Mayerson (1983). "An Analysis of the Impact of Marking-to-Market in Hedging with Treasury Bond Futures," *The Review of Research in Futures Markets,* Vol. 2, No. 1, pp. 136–159.

Kawaller, Ira (1986). "Hedging with Futures Contracts: Going the Extra Mile," *Journal of Cash Management,* July–August, pp. 34–36.

Kawaller, Ira, and Timothy Koch (1988). "Managing Cash Flow Risk in Stock Index Futures: The Tail Hedge," *Journal of Portfolio Management,* Vol. 15, No. 1, Fall, pp. 41–44.

Kolb, Robert W., Gerald D. Gay, and William C. Hunter (1985). "Liquidity Requirements for Financial Futures Hedges," *Financial Analysts Journal,* Vol. 46, No. 3, May–June, pp. 60–68.

PROBLEMS

*Indicates more difficult problems.

6-1 Portfolio Hedge

You hold a portfolio of $10 million of June 2005 Treasury bonds on December 8 and you expect prices to fall over the next few months. What type of hedge, if any, would you implement and what would be the net gain/loss given the additional following information (set up the relevant table):

	Cash	Futures
December 8	T-bonds priced at 91:00	T-note futures priced at 69-2
March 15	Price of bonds drop to 79:30	Price of futures drops to 60-2

6-2 Asset-Liability Futures Hedge for Fixed-Rate Mortgages

On March 12, a 90-day $400 million CD pays 8.25%. A bank plans to issue this same amount and type of CD six months in the future, but it expects interest rates to be higher by that time. In fact, the actual rate six months later is 12%. A September T-bill futures contract is priced at 92.40 on March 12 and 88.55 six months later. Since the interest rate of a CD represents the cost of funds to the bank and the bank wants to avoid an increase in costs, determine how the bank can hedge its position. What is the result?

6-3 Anticipatory Hedge

You expect to have funds to invest starting in several months. However, you expect interest rates to decrease. Thus, you set up an anticipatory hedge on T-bonds on June 1 to purchase $1,000,000 par value of T-bonds with a current price of $91^{25}/_{32}$. The current T-bond futures price is $92^5/_{32}$. On September 1, you close out the position with the price of the T-bond being $87^2/_{32}$ and the T-bond future being $87^{16}/_{32}$. What is the net change of the hedge? (Set up the cash and futures positions in a table format.) Explain your answer.

6-4 Long Hedge

A large hotel anticipates a large inflow of funds at the end of August, when the influx of tourists is at its peak. Management wants to put $1 million into a long-term bond as of June 1, since it believes the yield on T-bonds will fall after that date. Unfortunately, the funds will not be received until September. Based on the data below, what strategy should the hotel take in order to minimize any opportunity losses? Set up in a table format.

June 1	T-bonds selling for 85:24
	T-bond futures selling at 86-30
Sept. 1	T-bonds selling at 100:6
	T-bond futures selling at 101-1

6-5 Loss on a Short Hedge When the Basis Weakens

A short hedge is initiated when the basis weakens. A long S&P 500 cash and short S&P 500 futures position is used, with the following prices being relevant:

	February 6	February 8
Cash stocks	329.66	332.96
Sept. futures	338.15	343.50
Basis	8.49	10.54

Set up the hedge in a table format.

6-6 Stronger Basis

An investor currently owns $1 million of T-bonds maturing in the year 2000, which are currently trading at $93^{24}/_{32}$. The investor is afraid that interest rates will continue to rise. The investor decides to hedge against this unfortunate possibility by selling March T-bond futures that are selling for $84^{30}/_{32}$. The hedge is initiated in November and lifted in January. The investor is happy to see that his cash bonds are trading at $88^{16}/_{32}$ and that he was able to buy the futures at $75^{10}/_{32}$. Determine the investor's profit/loss on his strategy and explain how basis affects this hedge.

Chapter 7

THE NAIVE AND PORTFOLIO/REGRESSION HEDGING TECHNIQUES

Overview

A major objective of the hedger is to determine the number of futures contracts (the hedge ratio) that obtains the best risk-return trade-off. However, the complexities in obtaining this optimal hedge ratio causes hedgers to calculate the hedge ratio that minimizes the basis risk of the position. Equations are given to show how to calculate the naive, conversion factor, and regression (portfolio) based hedge ratios to minimize risk.

The most popular technique for determining a hedge ratio is based on portfolio/regression analysis. The minimum variance hedge ratio is developed from the general portfolio model (as proved in Appendix 7A). Empirical evidence concerning this model is presented for T-bonds, corporate debt, T-bills, currencies, and stock indexes. These results show that the hedging effectiveness of futures is very high in most circumstances.

Appendix 7B examines the effects of an instability in the hedge ratio over time. In particular, if hedge ratios are highly unstable, then the hedging effectiveness measure obtained from past periods can be an incorrect estimate of the current hedging effectiveness.

Terminology

Conversion factor   See Chapter 4.

Conversion factor hedge   Creating a hedge for a long-term debt instrument by using the conversion factor as the hedge ratio.

Dollar equivalency hedge   Equating the dollar changes in the cash position with the dollar changes in the futures position in order to minimize the change in total value. This method employs the relative maturities/expirations and relative volatilities of the cash and futures instruments in order to determine the appropriate hedge ratio.

Ex-post   After the fact; the use of historical data to determine an empirical relationship.

*Hedge ratio   Determining the ratio of the futures to the cash position so as to reduce price risk.

*Hedging effectiveness   The proportion of variability in the cash position eliminated by a futures hedge.

*Minimum-variance hedge ratio   The hedge ratio of futures to cash that provides the smallest variance of price changes.

One-to-one hedge   Creating a hedge such that the total value of the futures contracts employed for the hedge equals the total value of the cash instruments being hedged.

Optimal hedge ratio   The hedge ratio of futures to cash that provides the best risk-return hedge trade-off for the combined position.

Serial correlation   A correlation in sequential price changes; it is a violation of one of the assumptions of regression analysis and results in upward biased R^2 values and unstable hedge ratios over time.

NAIVE HEDGE RATIOS

Figures in Chapter 2 show the historical volatility of various financial instruments. These price changes create risk for portfolios of cash assets. Offsetting as much of the change in the cash price as possible is the goal of quantitative techniques of **hedge ratio** management, where a hedge ratio is the ratio of the futures to the cash position that reduces risk. These techniques range from the naive method of finding the ratio of the total values of the cash portfolio to the futures contract to the more sophisticated techniques of employing portfolio/regression analysis and duration. The simpler hedge ratio techniques are discussed in this section, with the remainder of the chapter concentrating on the portfolio/regression method. Chapter 10 examines the duration method.

What Is a Minimum-Risk Hedge Ratio?

A simplified explanation of a hedge ratio is the ratio of the change in the cash price to the change in the futures price. This definition of "relative price volatility" allows the hedger to determine how many futures contracts must be employed in order to minimize the risk of the combined cash-futures position. We can develop this simplified hedge ratio by assuming that the goal is to offset *completely* the adverse price change from the cash position for any *one* time period. Consequently, the cash price change in combination with the futures price change is zero if the risk is eliminated:

$$\Delta P_C + \text{HR}\,\Delta P_F = 0 \qquad (7\text{-}1)$$

where HR = the hedge ratio between the futures and cash instruments that forms a one-period perfect hedge that eliminates risk

P_C = the cash price change per unit for the period

P_F = the futures price change per unit for the period

Solving for HR, the hedge ratio, we find the value of the ratio that causes a net change of zero for the combined cash and futures position:

$$\text{HR} = -[\Delta P_C/\Delta P_F] \qquad (7\text{-}2)$$

The purpose of determining the hedge ratio is to reduce the basis risk between the cash and futures price changes. The minus sign in Equation (7-2) refers to taking the opposite position in the futures as compared with the cash asset. For example, a futures contract is sold to offset the change in a *long* cash position, creating a short hedge. Often this minus sign is left off the equation for the hedge ratio for convenience. Consequently, in the simple world shown above, where one concentrates only on the beginning and ending price of the period *and* the ending price can be perfectly forecasted, the hedge ratio reflects a simple measure of the relative change in the price of the cash and futures instruments (the "relative volatility").

Equation (7-2) is based on the assumption that the total values of the futures and cash instruments are equal. To adjust for unequal total values we calculate the number of contracts, N_F, needed for the hedge position:

$$N_F = (\text{HR})\text{TV}_C/V_F \qquad (7\text{-}3)$$

where $\quad N_F$ = the number of futures contracts for the hedge

TV_C = the total value of the cash position

V_F = the underlying cash value of one futures contract

TV_C/V_F = the scale adjustment for the relative size of the cash and futures position

The objective of finding the appropriate hedge ratio and the resultant number of futures contracts is to obtain a futures hedge position that offsets exactly the relative price changes between the cash and futures instruments. For example, for a $300,000 cash bond position where the cash price changes by 2 points for every futures change of 1 point, the hedge ratio from Equation (7-2) is -2 and the number of short T-bond futures contracts needed to offset the cash price change is

$$N_F = -2(\$300,000/\$100,000) = -6$$

We can easily show that the cash and futures positions for this perfect hedge have equal changes in total value by comparing the cash and futures positions:

$$(\Delta P_C)(\text{TV}_C) = (\Delta P_F) N_F (V_F) \tag{7-4}$$

For our example,

$$(2)\$300,000 = (1)(6)\$100,000$$

In reality, futures hedges cannot eliminate all risk. Recall the discussion in Chapter 6 concerning basis risk. In particular, hedging allows us to substitute basis risk for the absolute price risk of the cash asset, where basis risk refers to the variability of the cash price minus the futures price. Thus, if the change in the basis is less than the change in the cash price, hedging reduces the risk of a cash-only position. In the above example, the change in the basis for the total position is zero, which creates a perfect hedge that *eliminates* risk.

Naive (Traditional) Hedging Techniques

The Naive Methods.   Several simple methods exist to determine a hedge ratio and the number of futures contracts needed for a hedge. The first naive method is used exclusively for debt instruments. The hedge ratio is found by taking the ratio of the par value of the cash instrument and dividing by the par value of the futures contract. This is the traditional **one-to-one hedge** ratio method for debt instruments:

$$\text{HR}_1 = \frac{\text{par value of each cash instrument}}{\text{par value of futures}} \tag{7-5}$$

$$N_1 = \frac{\text{total par value of cash}}{\text{par value of one cash instrument}} (\text{HR}_1) \tag{7-6}$$

where HR_1 = the hedge ratio for the first naive method
    N_1 = the number of contracts for the first naive method

For example, if the portfolio to be hedged involves $50 million of bonds, each with a $1 million par value, then 500 futures contracts are needed for the hedge [i.e., from Equation (7-5), $\text{HR}_1 = \$1,000,000/\$100,000$ par for the T-bond futures = 10, and from Equation (7-6), $N = 50 \times 10 = 500$]. This method is based on the assumption that equal dollar movements occur between the cash and futures positions for each $100,000 par value of the bond.

An adjustment to the one-to-one debt method, which also provides a naive method for stock and currency hedges, employs the current prices of the cash and futures instruments:[1]

$$HR_2 = \frac{\text{cash price per unit}}{\text{futures price per unit}} \tag{7-7}$$

$$N_2 = \frac{\text{total cash value}}{\text{underlying value of one futures contract}} (HR_2) \tag{7-8}$$

The cash and futures prices for debt instruments in Equation (7-7) are calculated as a percentage of par, and par values are used in Equation (7-8) for debt positions. This method is equivalent to taking the ratio of the total investment values of the two instruments, whereas the one-to-one debt method in Equations (7-5) and (7-6) employs the total *par* values of the instruments. If the cash and futures prices change in proportion to the level of their prices, then the investment value method is more accurate than the one-to-one debt method.

Practitioners sometimes use a naive 1-to-1 hedge ratio rather than a more sophisticated method when the cash position is nearly equivalent to the characteristics of the futures contract; more complicated hedges do require more sophisticated methods. Practitioners sometimes prefer the 1-to-1 approach because the results often are as good as the more sophisticated hedge ratio methods when simple hedges are involved. The empirical results in a later section show that more sophisticated methods create hedge ratios that are often near one when the cash and futures positions are equivalent.

Disadvantages of the Naive Methods.   Although the above naive methods are simple to use and often are reasonably accurate for cash positions with similar characteristics to a given futures contract, difficulties exist with these methods in many situations. The following difficulties are associated with situations in which the naive methods do not adequately account for changes in the basis of the cash/futures position:

- Bonds with different maturities and coupons have different relative volatilities. In such a case, the basis risk created by a naive hedge ratio method is much greater than necessary. A similar situation exists when the composition of the cash stock position differs from the futures index.

- T-bill or Eurodollar hedges for cash instruments with maturities other than 90 days need to consider the effect of the *dollar* change on the portfolio rather than just the change in interest rates or basis points. In particular, the following tabulation shows the *dollar* change for both a $1-million cash position with a varying number of days until maturity and a $1-million 90-day futures contract, given a 1% change in interest rates:

Maturity of Cash Instrument	Cash Instrument	Futures Instrument
1 year	$10,000	$2,500
6 months	5,000	2,500
3 months	2,500	2,500
1 month	833	2,500

[1] See Asay and Schirr (1983), Gay and Kolb (1983), and Gay, Kolb, and Chiang (1983).

Thus, if one hedges a six-month cash T-bill with the 90-day T-bill futures contract, then a 1% change in interest rates causes a $5000 change in value of the $1 million six-month cash T-bill, but only a $2500 change in the 90-day T-bill futures contract. Thus, equating the dollar change rather than the interest rate change between the cash and futures positions is relevant in this situation; equating dollar changes necessitates a 2-to-1 hedge ratio for this six-month cash vs. three-month futures example.

- For crosshedge situations, such as using T-bond futures to hedge a corporate bond position, the relationship between the *risky* corporate debt and the *default-free* Treasury debt is not considered by the naive methods. Similarly, hedging an over-the-counter stock portfolio with the blue-chip MMI futures index creates a significant basis risk due to the different types of market risks.

More sophisticated methods attempt to overcome the naive methods' inability to adjust for basis changes.

Dollar Equivalency Hedge Ratios

A **dollar equivalency hedge** ratio equates the dollar change in the cash instrument to the dollar change in the futures contract. The initial section on "What Is a Minimum-Risk Hedge Ratio?" demonstrates the importance of thinking about hedge ratios in terms of dollar equivalency. One can expand on this concept by determining the factors that affect the relative changes in the futures and cash prices.

The most important of these factors for debt securities are the relative maturities and the relative price volatilities of the cash and futures instruments. Thus, if a bank wishes to hedge a six-month certificate of deposit position with the 90-day Eurodollar futures, then the ratio of the relative maturities of these instruments (180 days/ 90 days = 2) and the relative volatilities of the two securities (perhaps CDs are 1.5 times as volatile as Eurodollars) are multiplied to determine that a hedge ratio of 3 is needed for this dollar equivalency hedge.[2] For longer-term instruments, the duration of the instruments are employed to consider the effect of the relative maturities and volatilities (as discussed in Chapter 10). Similarly, for stock and currency positions, the relative volatilities of the cash and futures positions are relevant.

In essence, the dollar equivalency method considers the factors needed to equate the futures price change and the cash price change. The difficulty of this method is to measure the appropriate relationships between cash and futures for the time period in question. The following methods attempt to measure these relationships.

The Conversion Factor Hedge

A **conversion factor hedge** employs the conversion factor method for long-term debt instruments to determine the appropriate hedge ratio. This method reduces the problem of maturity differences between the cash and futures instruments that exist for the

---

[2] Technically, such a hedge should involve a strip of two sequential futures expirations so that the equivalent six-month period is effectively hedged. If two T-bill or Eurodollar futures contracts with the same expiration are employed to hedge the six-month CD *and* a change in the shape of the term structure occurs (the relative forward rates for the adjacent three-month periods change), then an uncovered basis risk would exist.

naive methods. Chapter 9 describes ways to use the conversion factor method to determine the invoice value of cash T-bonds/T-notes that are delivered into these futures contracts; namely, the conversion factor method explicitly considers the coupon and maturity of the cash debt instrument in relation to the specifications of the relevant futures contract. Conversion factors also are found in tables provided by the exchanges. The conversion factor hedge is promoted in practitioner literature as being superior to the naive methods.

The conversion factor hedge ratio is determined in the following manner:

$$HR_{CF} = CF \qquad (7-9)$$

$$N_{CF} = CF\left(\frac{\text{total par value of cash}}{\text{par value of one futures}}\right) \qquad (7-10)$$

where HR_{CF} = the conversion factor hedge ratio

CF = the conversion factor

N_{CF} = the number of futures contracts needed for the CF hedge

However, this method also has problems. First, changes in the term structure of interest rates adversely affect this method. Second, a crosshedge risk exists when corporate bonds are hedged. Third, the biases from the conversion factor method, as described in Chapter 9, cause problems.[3] Using the CF method *assumes* that the factors considered by this method accurately represent the relative prices of the different bonds in relation to the futures contract, and that the various bonds have an equal percentage sensitivity to a change in interest rates. In actuality, the CF method incorporates biases and thus futures prices move in relation to the cheapest-to-deliver bond.

THE PORTFOLIO CONCEPT

Introduction

The related concepts of diversification and portfolio analysis have been applied to common stocks for decades in order to reduce risk and obtain an optimal risk-return combination, respectively. However, both diversification and portfolio analysis, when applied solely to cash assets, still leave a significant amount of risk in the portfolio. Hedging with futures allows the portfolio manager to remove most of this remaining risk.

Finding a method to determine the best hedge ratio has generated interest in both the academic and practitioner communities. In general, an **"optimal" hedge ratio** means

---

[3] Arak and Goodman (1986) show why the conversion factor method is biased: (1) the method causes low coupon, long maturity bonds to appear to be more valuable than high coupon, short maturity bonds; (2) the CF method calculates the yield on all bonds to the *call* date, which favors the low coupon bonds; in reality, lower coupon bonds trading at a discount should be valued to *maturity* since at the current level of interest rates these bonds will not be called; and (3) the CF method does not consider the fact that bonds trading at a premium trade at a lower price (have higher yields) than par bonds because investors are not willing to take a capital loss as maturity approaches. The beneficial capital gains tax treatment that existed before 1987 typically caused lower coupons to have higher prices (lower yields) than if the tax effect did not exist; however, this benefit was not significant enough to offset the other biases.

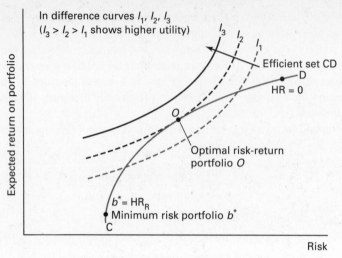

Figure 7-1 Portfolio risk-return curve.

the appropriate ratio of the futures position to the cash position that provides the best risk-return combination for the specific hedger. Figure 7-1 shows the efficient set, labeled CD, that provides the positions with the best available return at each level of risk; other nonoptimal available portfolios are below and to the right of curve CD. Curves I_1, I_2, and I_3 represent the hedger's risk-return trade-off curves; I_1, I_2, and I_3 are called the hedger's indifference curves, since each curve describes which risk-return combinations provide the same utility to the hedger. The hedger wants to be on the highest indifference curve possible, since such a curve maximizes return in relation to risk. Point O shows the optimal combined portfolio of the cash asset and the futures position that *maximizes* the total utility of the hedger, since point O is the tangency of the highest indifference curve I_2 with the efficient set.

The optimal risk-return hedge ratio concept has been refined to identify a **minimum-variance hedge ratio.** The reasons for using the minimum-variance ratio rather than an optimal ratio are that it is easier to derive, it is easier to understand because one variable (risk) rather than two variables (risk and return) is employed, it is determined empirically with minimal effort, it does not require indifference curves for the hedger, and it corresponds to the risk minimization concept often associated with hedging. Figure 7-1 denotes the minimum-variance hedge ratio as b^*. Daigler (1993) discusses a closed-form equation to obtain an optimal risk-return hedge ratio.

The Minimum-Variance Hedge Ratio

Ederington (1979) and Johnson (1960) employ portfolio theory to derive the mathematical model that defines the minimum-variance hedge ratio (HR) as the proportion of the futures to the cash position that minimizes the net price change risk. The variance of the price changes of the hedged position measures the price change risk. Although percentage price changes (rates of return) are advocated by some, most practitioners use price changes. The use of price changes, percentage price changes, or price levels is examined in a later section.

The minimum-variance hedge ratio is found by solving the following equation, as derived in Appendix 7A:

$$b^* = \text{HR}_R = \frac{\rho_{C,F}\,\sigma_C}{\sigma_F} \qquad (7\text{-}11)$$

where $\qquad b^* = \text{HR}_R =$ the minimum-risk hedge ratio

σ_C and $\sigma_F = \sigma(\Delta P_C)$ and $\sigma(\Delta P_F) =$ the standard deviations of the cash and futures price changes, respectively

$\rho_{C,F} = \rho(\Delta P_C, \Delta P_F) =$ the correlation between the cash and futures price changes

Note that the HR represented in Equation (7-11) is the product of the correlation between the cash and futures price changes *and* the relative volatility of the cash and futures instruments. These measures are determined by using all of the observations in a given period (e.g., weekly data for the last six months).

Figure 7-2 also explains the minimum-variance hedge ratio concept. This figure illustrates the regression line obtained by minimizing the sum of the squared deviations from the line; the slope of this regression line, $\Delta P_C/\Delta P_F = b^*$, is the hedge ratio. [Compare this equation to Equation (7-2).] Deviations from the regression line are called residuals, which constitute the basis risk that is not hedged.

The following section interprets the minimum-variance hedge ratio. Then empirical evidence concerning the size of the hedge ratio and the effectiveness of this ratio to reduce price change variability is examined. Finally, various factors affecting hedge ratios are discussed, including what problems to avoid when analyzing these ratios.[4]

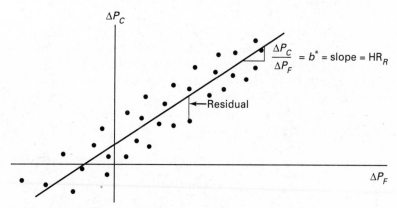

Figure 7-2 Illustrating the regression hedge ratio approach.

[4] Gay and Kolb (1983) provide a simple comparison of some of the methods discussed in this chapter, as well as discussing the factors affecting their effectiveness. Clayton and Navratil (1985) and Pitts (1985) critique the Gay and Kolb article. These criticisms note that the Gay and Kolb duration example employs perfect information, whereas the portfolio (regression) method assumes inferior information in comparison to what was available when the regression hedge ratio was determined.

Interpreting the Minimum-Variance Hedge Ratio and the Hedging Effectiveness

The Hedge Ratio. The hedge ratio defined in Equation (7-11) determines the minimum-risk hedge position. Thus, Equation (7-11) is equivalent to point $b^* = \mathrm{HR}_R$ in Figure 7-1. Alternatively, if one wishes to maximize expected return, then using $\mathrm{HR} = 0$ is appropriate, which is at the top of curve CD. The points between $\mathrm{HR} = 0$ and $\mathrm{HR}_R = b^*$ provide different risk-return combinations associated with varying degrees of risk. Here we concentrate on the minimum-risk position because of its widespread use and ease of calculation.

Equation (7-11) shows that the size of the minimum-variance hedge ratio depends on two factors: the correlation between the cash and futures price changes and the relative volatility of the cash and futures price changes. The minimum-variance hedge ratio does not have to be near one, unlike the 1-to-1 naive hedge ratio. In fact, if the standard deviations of the cash and futures price changes are nearly equivalent, then the hedge ratio is *less* than one, since the correlation is always less than one. Thus, in addition to the relative volatility of the cash and futures instruments affecting the hedge ratio, the *association* (correlation) between the cash and futures price changes is critical in formulating the appropriate minimum-variance hedge ratio.

The importance of the correlation coefficient can be shown by examining the extreme situations. At one extreme the hedger may own the same cash asset that is driving the futures price; in this case, the hedge ratio is near one. At the other extreme, if one calculates a hedge ratio for two instruments that have a low correlation, then the hedge ratio will be near zero. For example, attempting to hedge the Bolivian bolivar with Japanese yen futures produces a hedge ratio near zero, since the correlation is close to zero.

Hedging Effectiveness. Equation (7-11) is equivalent to the equation for the slope of the regression line between changes in the futures price (the independent variable) and changes in the cash price (the dependent variable). This relationship conveniently leads to a measure for the minimum-variance **hedging effectiveness** of the model, e^*, where the hedging effectiveness measures the proportion of the variability of the cash price changes that can be offset by the futures price changes. Based on our definition, hedging effectiveness is measured by the coefficient of determination, R^2, which is the measure of fit of the regression equation

$$e^* = \frac{\mathrm{var}(\Delta P_C) - \mathrm{var}(\Delta H)}{\mathrm{var}(\Delta P_C)}$$

$$= 1 - \left[\frac{\mathrm{var}(\Delta H)}{\mathrm{var}(\Delta P_C)}\right]$$

$$= 1 - \left(\frac{\text{basis risk}}{\text{cash asset risk}}\right)$$

$$= R^2 \qquad\qquad (7\text{-}12)$$

where $e*$ = the hedging effectiveness

var = variance

ΔH = change in value of the net hedged position with futures (i.e., the change in the basis)

Interpretation of R^2 is straightforward. If a regression analysis determines that $R^2 = .85$, then a futures hedge eliminates 85% of the variability in the cash price changes. Note that Equation (7-12) determines the ratio of the basis risk from the hedge to the total cash asset price risk; 1.0 minus this remaining basis risk ratio equals the hedging effectiveness.[5]

R^2 determines the **ex-post** hedging effectiveness when the minimum-variance hedge ratio, $b* = HR_R$, is employed. When the same cash and futures instrument is used, the hedging effectiveness is typically large. However, hedging effectiveness is often a low number for crosshedges with nonsimilar commodities. Thus, the minimum-variance hedge ratio can be unstable over time for crosshedges. Appendix 7B discusses this instability.

The Number of Futures Contracts.   In the initial section of this chapter we derived a general formulation for the total number of futures contracts needed for a hedge, based on the concept of wanting to offset the total change in value of the cash position with the total change in the futures short position—that is, Equations (7-2) and (7-3). We found that the number of futures contacts needed for the hedge is

$$N_F = [-\Delta P_C/\Delta P_F][TV_C/V_F] \qquad (7\text{-}13)$$

where N_F = the number of futures contracts

TV_C = total cash value being hedged (par value for debt instruments)

V_F = the underlying futures value per contract (par value for debt)

TV_C/V_F = the scale adjustment for the relative size of the cash and futures positions

Since the portfolio/regression hedge ratio finds the *average* $\Delta P_C/\Delta P_F = b = HR_R$, then

$$N_R = HR_R[TV_C/V_F] \qquad (7\text{-}14)$$

where HR_R = the hedge ratio measuring the relative volatility of the cash and futures prices

N_R = the number of futures contracts using the regression method

[5] The total dollar variance created by employing the minimum variance hedge ratio is:

$$\sigma_{b*}^2 = X_C^2 \sigma_C^2[1 - \rho_{C,F}^2]$$

where σ_{b*}^2 = total dollar variance when the minimum-variance hedge ratio is used

X_C = the total amount of the cash holdings

For hedges with a large coefficient of determination ρ^2, it is obvious that the variance of the hedged position is only a fraction of the variance of the cash position. We also can show that the hedging effectiveness can be measured by the variability of the residual errors terms (the basis risk) divided by the variability of the total cash position; that is,

$$e* = \frac{X_C^2 \sigma_C^2 - \sigma_{b*}^2}{X_C^2 \sigma_C^2} = \rho_{C,F}^2$$

Calculating the Hedge Ratio and Hedging Effectiveness from Raw Data

Since the hedge ratio is the slope of the regression line and the hedging effectiveness is the R^2 value from the regression, the standard regression technique is used to find these values when only the raw data are available. Equations (7-15) and (7-16) are the standard equations from regression analysis that are used to calculate the $b*$ and $e*$ values, based on the change in price of the cash and futures data. The $b*$ and $e*$ values can be calculated from Equations (7-15) and (7-16) with a calculator, the correlation and standard deviations can be determined from the data so that Equations (7-11) and (7-12) can be used, or a spreadsheet program can be employed to calculate $b*$ and $e*$ directly. Example 7-1 provides an example of how to employ the following equations to determine $b*$ and $e*$.

$$b* = \frac{\Sigma \, \Delta P_F \Delta P_C - (\Sigma \, \Delta P_F \, \Sigma \, \Delta P_C)/(N-1)}{\Sigma \, \Delta P_F^2 - (\Sigma \, \Delta P_F)^2/(N-1)} \tag{7-15}$$

$$e* = R^2 = \frac{[\Sigma \, \Delta P_F \Delta P_C - (\Sigma \, \Delta P_F \, \Sigma \, \Delta P_C)/(N-1)]^2}{[\Sigma \, \Delta P_F^2 - (\Sigma \, \Delta P_F)^2/(N-1)][\Sigma \, \Delta P_C^2 - (\Sigma \, \Delta P_C)^2/(N-1)]} \tag{7-16}$$

where N = the number of observations

THE EVIDENCE ON HEDGING EFFECTIVENESS AND HEDGE RATIOS

During the 1980s a significant number of articles and research reports were written to determine the hedging effectiveness and minimum-variance hedge ratios for various cash positions. Most of these studies concentrated on financial futures. These investigations examined the relative size of the hedging effectiveness value, whether the hedge ratio varied from one, how these factors changed as the size of the observation period changed or as the nearby versus deferred futures expirations were employed, and the behavior of $b*$ and $e*$ for crosshedges. The studies employed here examine specific issues of interest concerning hedge ratio determination and provide evidence for specific instruments. Other hedge ratio studies can be found in the literature.

Treasury Bonds

Hegde (1982) determines the hedging effectiveness and hedge ratios for a number of different instruments for 1979 and 1980. Table 7-1 shows Hegde's results for the T-bond and T-note hedges using T-bond futures. The hedging effectiveness values of these hedges shown in Panel A range from .59 to .97 for the T-bonds and from .36 to .82 for the T-notes. The effectiveness ratios at or above .79 show that a large percentage of the price variability can be hedged; in fact, 21 of the 24 bond positions with maturities of 15 years or greater have effectiveness values of at least .79. The worst hedging effectiveness values for these instruments are related to the change in the shape of the term structure during this period and the periodic substitution of new cash bonds. Problems with the relative timing of the cash and futures quotes also may have affected the

EXAMPLE 7-1
Hedge Ratio and Hedging Effectiveness Calculations

Date	S&P 500 Futures	S&P 100 Cash Index	ΔP_F	ΔP_C	$(\Delta P_F)^2$	$(\Delta P_C)^2$	$(\Delta P_F)(\Delta P_C)$
01/05	328.60	312.48					
01/12	348.20	325.09	19.60	12.61	384.16	159.01	247.16
01/20	336.35	319.99	−11.85	−5.10	140.42	26.01	60.44
01/27	328.60	312.48	−7.75	−7.51	60.06	56.40	58.20
02/06	334.25	308.01	5.65	−4.47	31.92	19.98	−25.26
02/13	336.45	310.58	2.20	2.57	4.84	6.60	5.65
02/21	333.30	307.45	−3.15	−3.13	9.92	9.80	9.86
02/28	336.70	312.48	3.40	5.03	11.56	25.30	17.10
03/07	340.90	316.64	4.20	4.16	17.64	17.31	17.47
03/14	341.50	317.33	.60	.69	.36	.48	.41
03/21	342.00	321.08	.50	3.75	.25	14.06	1.87
03/28	345.90	323.17	3.90	2.09	15.21	4.37	8.15
04/04	343.10	321.29	−2.80	−1.88	7.84	3.53	5.26
04/11	345.20	322.51	2.10	1.22	4.41	1.49	2.56
04/19	339.60	320.45	−5.60	−2.06	31.36	4.24	11.54
04/26	335.25	315.82	−4.35	−4.63	18.92	21.44	20.14
	Sum of column:		6.65	3.34	738.8825	370.0214	440.568
	Sum squared:		44.2225	11.1556			

$$b^* = \frac{\Sigma \Delta P_F \Delta P_C - (\Sigma \Delta P_F \, \Sigma \Delta P_C)/(N - 1)}{\Sigma \Delta P_F^2 - (\Sigma \Delta P_F)^2/(N - 1)}$$

$$b^* = \frac{440.57 - (6.62)(3.34)/14}{738.88 - 44.22/14}$$

$$= .597$$

$$R^2 = \frac{[\Sigma \Delta P_F \Delta P_C - (\Sigma \Delta P_F \, \Sigma \Delta P_C)/(N - 1)]^2}{[\Sigma \Delta P_F^2 - (\Sigma \Delta P_F)^2/(N - 1)][\Sigma \Delta P_C^2 - (\Sigma \Delta P_C)^2/(N - 1)]}$$

$$R^2 = \frac{[440.57 - (6.65)(3.34)/14]^2}{[738.88 - 44.22/14][370.02 - 11.16/14]}$$

$$= .709$$

poorer results. In addition, Table 7-1 shows that T-notes have a much higher effectiveness value for the two-week intervals than for the one-week intervals. These results are typical in that hedges with longer observation periods typically possess higher effectiveness values.

The T-bond hedge ratios shown in Panel B of Table 7-1 are below one for the first period of the analysis and above one for the second period; however, all but one of the

Table 7-1 T-Bond Hedge Results

Panel A. Hedging Effectiveness ($e^* = R^2$)

Instrument	Cash Maturity (yrs.)	Futures Expiration (mo.)	One-Week Hedge[a]		Two-Week Hedge[a]	
			I	II	I	II
T-bond	15	6–9	.735	.923	.586	.955
		21–24	.700	.878	.860	.972
T-bond	24	6–9	.832	.919	.860	.972
		21–24	.790	.893	.846	.889
T-note	5	6–9	.358	.426	.562	.820
		21–24	.315	.357	.551	.772
S&P LT govt. index	15	6–9	.829	.904	.867	.962
		21–24	.793	.881	.860	.870

Panel B. Hedge Ratios ($b^* = HR_R$)

Instrument	Cash Maturity (yrs.)	Futures Expiration (mo.)	One-Week Hedge[a]		Two-Week Hedge[a]	
			I	II	I	II
T-bond	15	6–9	.964	1.057	.943	1.199
		21–24	1.023	1.082	1.039	1.275
T-bond	24	6–9	.840	1.072	.887	1.032
		21–24	.891	1.110	.969	1.108
T-note	5	6–9	.395	.626	.466	.910
		21–24	.419	.601	.508	.965
S&P LT govt. index	15	6–9	.517	.668	.531	.652
		21–24	.551	.692	.583	.677

[a] Period I is from January to September 1979; period II is from October 1979 to June 1980.
Source: Hegde (1982).

T-bond hedge ratios are insignificantly different from one. Six of the eight T-notes ratios *are* significantly different from one, which occurs because the maturities of the T-bond futures and T-note cash instruments are substantially different.

The results in Table 7-1 also show that the hedging effectiveness values improve from period I to period II. Hegde discusses how a greater volatility of prices causes a higher volume of trading, which in turn makes the market more liquid. Greater liquidity causes gains in operational efficiency and strengthens the relationship between the cash and futures market. Since period II had a greater volatility of interest rates, larger values for hedging effectiveness should follow. The results in Table 7-1 bear out this hypothesis.

Corporate Debt

Although corporate bonds are an important security, the corporate debt futures instrument never becomes a liquid contract. Thus, one must use T-bond or T-note futures to hedge corporate debt issues. Hill and Schneeweis (1982b) employ T-bond futures to

Table 7-2 Treasury/Corporate Bond Hedging Results

Merrill Lynch Index[a] Coupon Level	8/1977–1978[b]		1979	
	$e^* = R^2$	$b^* = HR_R$	$e^* = R^2$	$b^* = HR_R$
High-Quality Corporate				
6%–7.99%	.849	1.05	.919	1.49
8%–9.99%	.829	1.01	.982	1.58
Medium-Quality Corporate				
6%–7.99%	.760	0.73	.765	1.19
8%–9.99%	.736	0.85	.975	1.64
High-Quality Utility				
4%–5.99%	.563	1.24	.904	1.53
6%–7.99%	.875	1.27	.841	1.28
8%–9.99%	.846	1.00	.824	1.25
Medium-Quality Utility				
6%–7.99%	.761	1.22	.767	1.39
8%–9.99%	.786	1.26	.675	1.28
10%–11.99%	.741	1.20	.775	1.27

[a] Merrill Lynch High-Quality includes ratings AAA and AA; Medium-Quality includes ratings A and BAA.
[b] Number of observations: 1977–1978 (20); 1979 (15).
Source: Abstracted from Hill and Schneeweis (1982b).

hedge corporate bond *indexes* in order to examine the resultant hedging effectiveness and the size of the minimum-variance hedge ratios. Table 7-2 shows their results for two-week hedges, using both the near-term futures contract and the Merrill Lynch bond indexes, with different bond coupon levels and for two time periods in the late 1970s.[6] The hedging effectiveness results shown in Table 7-2 are very high, with all but two R^2 values being above 73%. In addition, the values for the more volatile 1979 period are higher than for the earlier period.

Hill and Schneeweis (1980) examine hedging results for two-week hedges with *individual* corporate issues. These hedging effectiveness results are much worse than for the indexes of bonds reported in Table 7-2. The R^2 values for individual bond hedges range from 2% to 25%, with most of the effectiveness measures being below 12%. The major reason for these poor results seems to be the risk characteristics of the individual bonds. This type of risk *cannot* be hedged with a T-bond futures contract.[7]

Kuberek and Pefley (1983) provide additional corporate hedging results with T-bond futures by employing monthly hedges with the first six T-bond futures expirations. Figure 7-3 shows that the hedging effectiveness for these hedges is higher than for the

---

[6] The article includes results for both time periods combined into one data set, for three other futures expirations, for values for the means and standard deviations, and for mortgage futures. These results are comparable to the ones presented here.

[7] Moreover, the use of GNMA futures also seems to affect the results adversely, since a comparison of the GNMA futures hedges for the Merrill Lynch indexes in this article with the equivalent indexes for T-bond future hedges in Hill and Schneeweis (1982b) shows a decline of 25% to 30% (and sometimes much more) in the hedging effectiveness measures. In addition, timing differences between the individual corporate issues that do not trade frequently and the futures prices also would distort the results.

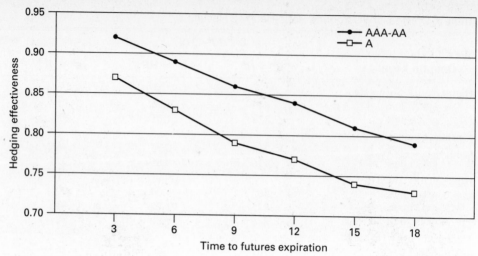

Figure 7-3 Corporate bond hedging effectiveness. (*Source:* Adapted from table in Kuberek and Pefley, 1983.)

previous studies. This figure also shows that A-rated bonds lose about 6% for the effectiveness values as compared to the AAA-AA bonds, as would be expected given their higher default risk. In addition, the hedging effectiveness decreases as one moves from the nearby contracts to the more distant deferred contracts. Kuberek and Pefley use a more general regression procedure to adjust data for differing variances, increasing the preciseness of their results.

T-Bills

Ederington's article (1979) is credited as the catalyst that initiated the use of regression studies to determine the hedge ratio and hedging effectiveness for various futures markets. After Ederington derives the hedging model from the two-asset portfolio model, he empirically analyzes the hedging results for 90-day T-bills, GNMAs, wheat, and corn. The hedging effectiveness measures for these contracts are mostly above 65% for both the two-week and four-week hedges for all the markets except T-bills; the T-bill contracts have R^2 values ranging from 27% to 14% for the two-week hedges and from 74% to 37% for the four-week hedges. Franckle (1980) discovers two problems with the T-bill hedging results determined by Ederington; namely,

- Ederington unknowingly employed a weekly index of daily values for the cash T-bill data, which smooths out the daily fluctuations for the cash T-bill data, creating a lower R^2 value than justified. Thus the use of smoothed data via the weekly averages conceals much of the variation in the cash prices. Once this error is corrected (in conjunction with one incorrect data point in the original data), the two-week nearby hedge improves from a 27% effectiveness value to a 68% value.[8]

[8] The nearby four-week hedge did not improve. Ederington's results showed an R^2 value of 74% for this hedge. This high value can be related to the variability of the cash rates for the time period, which overwhelmed the negative effect of the smoothed index numbers. The R^2 values for the deferred contract in Ederington's analysis was much smaller for the four-week hedges; however, Franckle only examines the nearby contract effects.

Table 7-3 Stock Index Hedging Results

Cash Portfolio	Unhedged	Futures	Portfolio Beta	One Day		One Week		Two Weeks	
				b*	e*	b*	e*	b*	e*
S&P 500	24.2	S&P 500	1.00	.65	.77	.85	.95	.85	.96
		NYSE	.99	.61	.78	.85	.93	.84	.95
NYSE	23.2	S&P 500	1.00	.60	.75	.80	.94	.82	.95
		NYSE	.99	.56	.75	.81	.91	.82	.95
AMEX	23.2	S&P 500	1.33	.41	.45	.69	.70	.81	.83
		NYSE	1.36	.37	.41	.68	.64	.82	.85
NASDAQ	19.6	S&P 500	.84	.29	.33	.57	.66	.57	.66
OTC		NYSE	.87	.25	.28	.57	.62	.58	.71
DOW 30	24.1	S&P 500	.85	.67	.76	.83	.92	.85	.95
		NYSE	.83	.64	.79	.84	.92	.85	.95

Source: Adapted from Figlewski (1985).

- Ederington did not adjust the hedges to consider the declining maturity of the cash T-bills. Thus, a 90-day cash T-bill becomes a 76-day T-bill after two weeks have elapsed; similarly, after four weeks a 90-day bill becomes a 62-day T-bill. Treasury bills that have a shorter maturity also have less variability in price and thus have an imperfect correlation with the 90-day futures contract. This declining maturity affects the hedging effectiveness of the results: in one of the four cases, R^2 decreases by 10% after the correct adjustment, but it decreases by less than 2% in the other cases.[9] More important, the maturity adjustment affects the size of the minimum-variance hedge ratio. Franckle finds that adjusting for the maturity effect with corrected data causes a decrease in the minimum-variance hedge ratio by a factor of 20% to 25%. Franckle derives the relationship between the minimum-variance hedge ratio for a 90-day maturity T-bill and a T-bill with n days to maturity:

$$_nb^* = [n/90]_{90}b^* \qquad (7\text{-}17)$$

where $_nb^*$ = the minimum-variance T-bill hedge ratio for maturities of n days

Stock Indexes

Figlewski (1985) shows the effectiveness of hedging stock portfolios with stock index futures. Table 7-3 shows Figlewski's results with various cash portfolios and the S&P 500 and NYSE futures contracts for observation periods of one day, one week, and two weeks. Data from the last seven months of 1982 are employed to generate the results in the table. The hedge ratios for the portfolios tend to be substantially below one, especially for the cash portfolios that are significantly different from the futures contract. The hedging effectiveness e^* generally increases as the length of the observation period lengthens. Note that Over-the-Counter and American Stock Exchange portfolios are not effectively hedged with these futures contracts for the one-day and one-week observation periods. However, the other hedge relationships do have high R^2 values.

[9] The decline in hedging effectiveness due to declining maturity must be tempered by the fact that the shorter maturity positions have less variability overall. Thus, the hedges for the T-bill positions with declining maturities had 15% to 42% less variability overall than the constant maturity positions, even though the former had somewhat lower R^2 values.

Currency Futures

Most currency futures studies employ data from the 1970s to examine hedging effectiveness. Daigler (1990, 1991) shows that the more recent volatility in currencies can be hedged with currency futures, as long as a futures contract exists in that currency's denomination. Table 7-4 provides a summary of the hedging results for the Canadian dollar, the Japanese yen, the German mark, and the British pound. Six-month periods from 1980 through 1986, with weekly observation periods, are used in the analysis. The hedge ratios are near one and the hedging effectiveness measures are 83% for the Canadian dollar and over 92% for the other currencies.

Table 7-5 shows whether other currencies can be hedged with currency futures. The same time period and weekly observation length are employed here as in Table 7-4. The British pound futures crosshedging results with other European currencies are relatively low, with all of the cross-currency hedging effectiveness values being below 50%. The results for the non-European countries are even worse, with *none* of the hedging effectiveness values above 25%. The German mark futures crosshedging results with the stronger European currencies (the Belgian franc, the French franc, the Italian lira, and the Netherlands guilder) averages above 75% for each currency. The results for Greece and Spain are less impressive, but still average above 50%. Note that these results suggest that the mark futures is an excellent hedging tool for most of the European currencies that do not have futures contracts. The crosshedging results for the non-European countries are poor, with the hedging effectiveness results below 25% and often below 10%.

Conclusions Concerning the Empirical Evidence

The preceding studies concerning the regression method for determining hedge ratios and hedging effectiveness, in conjunction with other studies on these topics, provide the following conclusions:

- When the cash asset has characteristics that are nearly identical to the cash underlying the futures contract, then $R^2 = e*$ is large (often more than 90%) and the hedge ratio is near one.
- The hedging effectiveness improves when the cash instrument is more volatile.
- Longer observation periods (e.g., when two-week periods are used) provide larger hedging effectiveness values.
- Crosshedge results (e.g., using currency futures) provide very low $R^2 = e*$ values when the characteristics of the cash and futures instruments differ.

Table 7-4 Average Biweekly Currency Hedging Results

Country	$b*$	$e*$
Canada	.892	.831
Germany	.985	.941
Japan	.940	.928
U.K.	.979	.934

Source: Daigler (1991).

Table 7-5 Average Cross-Currency Hedging Results: 1980–1986

	British Pound		German Mark	
	*b**	*e**	*b**	*e**
European countries				
Belgium	.612	.383	.890	.777
France	.665	.422	.919	.832
Greece	.500	.275	.643	.513
Italy	.575	.373	.831	.802
Netherlands	.648	.435	.945	.911
Spain	.632	.459	.714	.673
Other countries				
Australia	.223	.215	.239	.256
Argentina	−.039	.067	.000	.043
Brazil	.034	.030	.020	.025
Canada	.152	.160	.138	.185
Hong Kong	.087	.086	.153	.115
Israel	.044	.042	.126	.042
Mexico	.171	.048	.133	.032
Singapore	.202	.221	.212	.275
South Africa	.254	.219	.282	.215
Taiwan	.035	.035	.023	.025
Uruguay	−.160	.058	−.201	.075

Source: Daigler (1990).

An important consideration for all of the previous studies is that *historical* data are employed to determine the hedge ratios and hedging effectiveness measures. If these results are used to determine the appropriate hedge ratios and effectiveness for *future* time periods, then the hedger is assuming that the relationships are stable over time. Appendix 7B examines the stability of hedge ratios over time.

CONSIDERATIONS IN DETERMINING A HEDGE RATIO

This section examines application considerations when employing the minimum-variance hedge ratio concept. These considerations include the use of price changes instead of price levels, the characteristics of the hedge period and nature of the data, and problems with reported cash data. These factors are important since a correct statistical analysis is needed in order to ensure that the results of the investigation are valid.

Data Considerations

Using Price Changes, Percentage Changes, or Price Levels. Practitioners typically employ price *changes* to implement the regression procedure so as to obtain the minimum-variance hedge ratio. This is especially true when hedge ratios for long-term debt futures are determined, since long-term debt issues are priced in terms of the *percentage* of par value. Using price changes corresponds to the intention of equating the *dollar* change in the cash asset to the *dollar* change in the futures contract, as shown earlier in this chapter and in Appendix 7A. Percentage price changes are advocated by some academicians in order to reduce the effect of a nonconstant variance on the regression procedure. Such an adjustment is beneficial when large price changes occur for the data in question. However, using percentages equates the *percentage* changes between the cash and futures positions, not the dollar changes. An adjustment to the hedge ratio $b*$ must be made to convert a hedge ratio that minimizes net percentage changes to one that minimizes net dollar changes. Hill and Schneeweis (1980) find that price changes and percentage changes provide comparable R^2 values.[10]

Using price *levels* instead of changes or percentage changes incorporates **serial correlation** into the results; that is, the assumption of no correlation in sequential time series data for the regression model is violated. Serial correlation causes the R^2 value that measures the hedging effectiveness to be much larger than its true value, and the slope coefficient of the regression (the hedge ratio) to be erratic from one sample to another. For example, when Dale (1981) employed price *levels* to examine the hedge results for currency futures, he obtained R^2 values of 98% and 99%. Hill and Schneeweis (1981, 1982a) find that the true values are closer to 70% to 80%.

The Number of Observations.   Too few observations, especially if there are outliers in the data (i.e., large changes), typically cause difficulties in obtaining a true estimate of the hedge ratio. The difficulty of this data problem is that conclusions are obtained based on an inadequate sample size, and perhaps an inappropriate sample. The hedger wants to determine a hedge ratio that is valid for all time periods, not merely to fit a specific set of historical data. Theoretically, a larger number of observations reduces any inaccurate estimate of the hedge ratio. Statistically speaking, 30 observations are typically the norm used to obtain a reasonable estimate of the population hedge ratio. Although fewer observations are acceptable, a small number of observations (e.g., 10) often causes instability in the hedge ratio and a less accurate hedging effectiveness value. Appendix 7B examines the question of unstable hedge ratios over time.

The Length of the Time Intervals.   The length of the intervals for the observations in the hedge period affects the hedge ratio and the hedging effectiveness. It is generally accepted that employing a one-day interval for each observation provides relatively poor hedging effectiveness. In fact, empirical studies often avoid one-week hedge ratios for the same reason, although such hedge lengths are used by practitioners. Two- and four-week hedge intervals are common in hedging studies, although one must be careful of the effect of convergence on the results as the interval length approaches one month or longer. Moreover, these longer time intervals require the use of several futures contract expirations to obtain a sufficient number of observations for the sample period.

---

[10] Using percentage changes is equivalent to using rates of return. However, the rate-of-return terminology is seldom used with futures because of the implication that an "investment of funds" is needed for the futures position, which is not the case. One advantage to using the rate-of-return terminology is that the mean-variance efficient set used for cash-only portfolio analysis, as developed earlier in this chapter, employs rates of return.

The Normality of the Data. The regression procedure is based on the assumption that the error terms form a normal distribution. Although small deviations from normality are not critical for the regression procedure, a large number of observations beyond two and three deviations from the mean (or one very *large* deviation such as the October 19, 1987 crash value) would create serious problems for the validity of the regression hedge ratio procedure. One way to reduce the effect of larger error terms on the hedge ratio and hedging effectiveness measures is to employ absolute-value regression analysis. Although this method is not popular, it does avoid the problem created by the typical least-squares regression of squaring each deviation from the regression line.[11]

Using Historical Data

One must take care in the preparation and use of historical data for hedge ratio analysis. A major consideration is whether the *reported* cash data provides an appropriate value for the true cash price. In particular, there can be a timing difference between the closing cash price and the closing futures price. This effect is most prevalent for long-term debt instruments, currency prices, and smaller stocks.

A major factor affecting the timing of cash and futures debt issues is that the futures close at 2 P.M. Central time, while the cash market remains open the rest of the afternoon. Hence, closing cash prices can reflect information not impounded in the closing futures prices. This timing difference often adversely affects the calculation of hedging effectiveness values. For example, if one examines the cash T-bond prices in the Chicago Board of Trade Statistical Annual, one finds that cash prices often change more than futures prices, especially during significant market moves. The futures do not adjust to the cash market price until the opening on the following trade day. Thus, one must take care in using cash prices by determining the timing of the close of these prices. Some services use the 2 P.M. price of the cash market as the day's "close," whereas other services use the last trade of the day; obviously, the former price is more appropriate for hedge ratio analysis due to the timing factor. Other futures have similar problems, such as currencies futures that close between 1 P.M. and 1:30 P.M., depending on the currency.

Liquidity in the cash issue also can have a major effect on the timing of the last trade. For example, a bond that does not trade frequently can possess a reported 2 P.M. "closing" price that is not representative of its true price at the time, simply because it did not trade after interest rates changed. Alternatively, illiquid issues can trade at inappropriate prices *because* they are not liquid. For example, the corporate bond issues reprinted in *The Wall Street Journal* are for odd lots traded on the bond exchange; often these issues trade ten or fewer bonds on a given day. The major action in these corporate bonds occurs off the exchange by institutions, who trade thousands of the most liquid bonds in a day. Hence, the prices reported in *The Wall Street Journal* often are poor representations of the true closing prices for these issues.

[11] One might argue that the assumption of a normal distribution of the price changes is not a critical factor, as long as both the cash and futures prices change in a comparable manner across time. However, situations with large cash price changes also usually have the *largest* errors from the regression line, since timing problems between the cash and futures instruments and unusual price relationships for these atypical situations often exist.

Another consideration is that a reported price may not be a trade price. Specifically, Merrill Lynch provides a "matrix pricing" service for corporate bonds where bond traders input either a trade price or a "representative" price for each issue. The "representative" price is input for issues that do not trade near the time that prices are put into the matrix. If these representative prices are not accurate representations of what the true trade price would be for that bond, then the regression analysis impounds larger errors than would actually occur if trade data were available.

Finally, another critical factor when historical data are employed is whether the hedge ratios are stable over time. Authors of hedge ratio studies have assumed that the hedge ratios and hedging effectiveness are in fact stable. The use of the historical regression values implicitly assumes that other time periods would provide the same results. In fact, when fundamental conditions change, the cash/futures relationships can change; or statistical problems may exist. Appendix 7B examines the considerations for hedge ratio instability, whether such instability exists, and the potential effect of such instability on hedging effectiveness.

SUMMARY AND LOOKING AHEAD

This chapter examines the issues and techniques relating to risk reduction hedging strategies. The following hedge ratio procedures are examined: naive ratios, the conversion factor method, the dollar equivalency concept, and the minimum-risk procedure developed from regression analysis. The difference between the optimal model and the minimum-variance model is explored, empirical evidence relating to the regression method is presented, and considerations in determining the regression hedge ratio are discussed. Appendixes derive the minimum risk hedge ratio and examine the effects of unstable hedge ratios over time.

Chapter 8 discusses pricing and arbitrage of stock index futures, including various issues related to program trading and the difficulties in implementing successful trades. Chapter 9 discusses pricing and arbitrage of T-bond futures, including issues concerning the conversion factor method and the delivery options. Chapter 9 also examines short-term interest rate futures pricing. Chapter 10 explores the uses of duration for cash debt and futures hedging. The concepts and problems relating to the duration method are explored and evidence concerning this method is given.

BIBLIOGRAPHY

Arak, Marcelle, and Laurie S. Goodman (1986). "How to Calculate Better T-Bond Hedge Ratios," *Futures,* February, pp. 56–57.

Asay, Michael, and Gary Schirr (1983). "Determining a Hedge Ratio: Two Simple Approaches," *Market Perspectives: Topics on Options and Financial Futures,* Chicago Mercantile Exchange, Vol. 1, No. 2, May, pp. 1, 5–6.

Clayton, Ronnie J., and Frank J. Navratil (1985). "The Management of Interest Rate Risk: Comment," *Journal of Portfolio Management,* Vol. 11, No. 4, Summer, pp. 64–66.

Daigler, Robert T. (1990). "Cross Currency Hedging Results: Implications for EEC Unification and LDC Trade," working paper, Florida International University.

Daigler, Robert T. (1991). "Hedge Ratio Instability for Currency Futures," working paper, Florida International University.

Daigler, Robert T. (1993). *Financial Futures Markets: Concepts, Evidence, and Applications.* New York: Harper Collins.

Dale, Charles (1981). "The Hedging Effectiveness of Currency Futures Markets," *The Journal of Futures Markets,* Vol. 1, No. 1, Spring, pp. 77–88.

Ederington, L. H. (1979). "The Hedging Performance of the New Futures Markets," *Journal of Finance,* Vol. 34, No. 1, March, pp. 157–170.

Figlewski, Stephen (1985). "Hedging with Stock Index Futures: Theory and Application in a New Market," *The Journal of Futures Markets,* Vol. 5, No. 2, Summer, pp. 183–200.

Franckle, Charles T. (1980). "The Hedging Performance of the New Futures Market: Comment," *Journal of Finance,* Vol. 35, No. 5, December, pp. 1272–1279.

Gay, Gerald D., and Robert W. Kolb (1983). "The Management of Interest Rate Risk," *Journal of Portfolio Management,* Vol. 9, No. 2, Winter, pp. 65–70.

Gay, Gerald D., Robert W. Kolb, and Raymond Chiang (1983). "Interest Rate Hedging: An Empirical Test of Alternative Strategies," *Journal of Financial Research,* Vol. 6, No. 3, Fall, pp. 187–197.

Hegde, S. P. (1982). "The Impact of Interest Rate Level and Volatility on the Performance of Interest Rate Hedges," *The Journal of Futures Markets,* Vol. 2, No. 4, Winter, pp. 341–356.

Hill, Joanne, and Thomas Schneeweis (1980). "The Use of Interest Rate Futures in Corporate Financing and Corporate Security Investments," *Proceedings of the International Futures Trading Seminar,* Vol. 7, pp. 72–93.

Hill, Joanne, and Thomas Schneeweis (1981). "A Note on the Hedging Effectiveness of Foreign Currency Futures," *The Journal of Futures Markets,* Vol. 1, No. 4, Winter, pp. 659–664.

Hill, Joanne, and Thomas Schneeweis (1982a). "The Hedging Effectiveness of Foreign Currency Futures," *Journal of Financial Research,* Vol. 5, No. 1, Spring, pp. 95–104.

Hill, Joanne, and Thomas Schneeweis (1982b). "Risk Reduction Potential of Financial Futures for Corporate Bond Positions," in *Interest Rate Futures: Concepts and Issues,* edited by Gerald D. Gay and Robert W. Kolb, Robert F. Dame Inc.

Johnson, L. L. (1960). "The Theory of Hedging and Speculation in Commodity Futures," *Review of Economic Studies,* Vol. 27, No. 3, pp. 139–151.

Kuberek, Robert C., and Norman G. Pefley (1983). "Hedging Corporate Debt with U.S. Treasury Bond Futures," *The Journal of Futures Markets,* Vol. 3, No. 4, Winter, pp. 345–353.

Pitts, Mark (1985). "The Management of Interest Rate Risk: Comment," *Journal of Portfolio Management,* Vol. 11, No. 4, Summer, pp. 67–69.

PROBLEMS

*Indicates more difficult problems

7-1 Naive Hedging Techniques

Given the following information:

Cash instrument: 75 T-bonds, each at $100,000 par; price 99:0

Futures: $100,000 par per contract; price 99-24
Conversion factor: .9159

Calculate the naive hedge ratios and the conversion factor hedge ratio as well as the corresponding number of futures contracts.

7-2 Dollar Equivalency Hedge

A financial institution has a one-year T-bill that it wishes to hedge with a Eurodollar futures contract. The T-bill is 25% less volatile than the Eurodollar futures. What is the dollar equivalency hedge ratio?

7-3 Hedging Effectiveness

a. Determine the hedging effectiveness when the variance of T-note cash price changes is 12.1% and the variance of the net hedge position between cash and T-note futures is 1.6%.

b. Calculate the hedging effectiveness between a cash T-note and a T-bond futures when the variance of the cash T-note price changes is 12.1% and the variance of the net hedge position is 4.8%.

c. What can you conclude from the values you obtained for the hedging effectiveness in parts (a) and (b) respectively?

*7-4 Minimum-Variance Hedge Ratio

Calculate the minimum-variance hedge ratio and the hedging effectiveness based on the following cash bond and T-bond futures data (prices have been converted to decimals).

Futures	Cash Bond	Futures	Cash Bond
87.59	99.53	88.22	99.84
87.75	99.44	88.25	99.78
87.72	99.56	87.78	99.28
87.72	99.44	87.88	99.44
88.53	99.94	88.22	99.75
87.91	99.50	87.91	99.44
88.09	99.88	87.94	99.41
88.56	100.13		

*7-5 Minimum-Variance Hedge

Using the following weekly data for the NYSE cash and futures index, find the minimum-variance hedge ratio and the hedging effectiveness.

Futures	Cash	Futures	Cash
192.55	187.51	181.70	178.43
193.40	188.05	184.25	182.33
196.05	191.34	185.55	182.85
199.10	194.07	183.25	181.37
197.60	192.83	184.60	182.16
194.00	190.17	188.95	186.17
195.65	191.72	186.80	185.25
202.00	198.00	188.10	186.18
196.45	193.35	189.65	187.40
191.20	188.37	190.95	188.55
184.90	183.60		

APPENDIX 7A
DERIVING THE MINIMUM-VARIANCE HEDGE RATIO

Ederington (1979) and Johnson (1960) employ portfolio theory to derive the mathematical model that defines the minimum-variance hedge ratio (HR) as the proportion of the futures to the cash position that minimizes the net price change risk. Price change risk is measured by the variance of the price changes of the net hedged position.[1]

The portfolio model developed for stocks by Markowitz can be employed to derive the minimum-risk model. In the two-asset portfolio case, made up of a futures and a cash position, the expected price change on a hedged position is defined as

$$E(\Delta H) = X_C E[P_{C(t+k)} - P_{C(t)}] + X_F E[P_{F(t+k)} - P_{F(t)}] \qquad (7A-1)$$

where ΔH = expected price change on a net hedged position

X_C = the total amount X of cash holdings C (this amount is assumed to be fixed)[2]

$P_{C(t)}$ = the cash price at time t

X_F = total amount X of the futures market position F

$P_{F(t)}$ = the futures price at time t

The risk of the position can then be defined in terms of the portfolio model for the variance in the price change of a two-asset portfolio:

$$\mathrm{var}(\Delta H) = X_C^2\, \sigma_C^2 + X_F^2\, \sigma_F^2 + 2X_C\, X_F\, \sigma_{C,F} \qquad (7A-2)$$

where $\mathrm{var}(\Delta H)$ = the variance of the net price changes of the hedged position

$\sigma_C^2 = \mathrm{var}(\Delta P_C)$ = the variance of the cash price changes

$\sigma_F^2 = \mathrm{var}(\Delta P_F)$ = the variance of the futures price changes

$\sigma_{C,F}$ = the covariance between the cash and futures price changes

There are two procedures for deriving the minimum-variance hedge ratio:

1. Taking Equation (7A-2) we find the derivative of $\mathrm{var}(\Delta H)$ with respect to X_F, set the solution to that derivative equal to zero, and then solve for X_F. This approach provides the total value of the futures contract that minimizes the price change variability of the hedged position; that is,

$$X_F = -X_C(\sigma_{C,F}/\sigma_F^2) \qquad (7A-3)$$

---

[1] Johnson (1960) uses calculus in conjunction with the two-asset portfolio model to derive the minimum-risk hedge ratio for a short futures and long cash position. Stein (1961) also mentions the minimum-risk possibility, but does not derive the relationship. However, it was not until Ederington (1979) rediscovered the relationship that the procedure became well known, resulting in a number of empirical studies and the implementation of the regression procedure by hedgers.

[2] The size of both the cash and futures holdings for bonds are determined by using the par values of the holdings, since price changes are in terms of percentages of par.

Note that the minus sign designates a short position in futures to initiate a short hedge. We can then find the appropriate minimum variance hedge ratio by dividing both sides of Equation (7A-3) by $-X_C$:

$$b^* = -X_F/X_C = \sigma_{C,F}/\sigma_F^2 \qquad (7A-4)$$

$$b^* = HR_R = \rho_{C,F}\sigma_C/\sigma_F \qquad (7A-5)$$

where $\rho_{C,F}$ is the correlation between the cash and futures price changes. This result also could be derived by using proportions for X_C and X_F; that is, assume that $X_C = 1$ and X_F would be some proportion of X_C. One then would find Equation (7A-5) directly. Note that HR in Equation (7A-5) is made up of the correlation between the cash and futures price changes *and* the relative volatility of the cash and futures instruments.

2. Alternatively, we can multiply each term on the right side of Equation (7A-2) by X_C^2/X_C^2 (which is equal to one), then substitute the eventual minimum-variance hedge ratio of the amount of futures to the amount of cash $b = -X_F/X_F$ into Equation (7A-2), and rearrange, which gives

$$var(\Delta H) = X_C^2(\sigma_C^2 + b^2\sigma_F^2 - 2b\sigma_{C,F}) \qquad (7A-6)$$

Taking the partial derivative of $var(\Delta H)$ with respect to b (the desired minimum-variance hedge ratio), setting the equation equal to zero, and then solving for b, one obtains the minimum-variance hedge ratio $b^* = HR_R$ as given in Equations (7A-4) and (7A-5).[3]

BIBLIOGRAPHY FOR APPENDIX 7A

Ederington, L. H. (1979). "The Hedging Performance of the New Futures Markets," *Journal of Finance,* Vol. 34, No. 1, March, pp. 157–170.

Johnson, L. L. (1960). "The Theory of Hedging and Speculation in Commodity Futures," *Review of Economic Studies,* Vol. 27, No. 3, pp. 139–151.

Stein, Jerome (1961). "The Simultaneous Determination of Spot and Futures Prices," *American Economic Review,* Vol. 51, No. 5, pp. 1012–1025.

APPENDIX 7B
HEDGE RATIO INSTABILITY

If the relationship between the cash and futures price changes varies from one period to the next, then the hedge ratios also are unstable. Using historical data and the regression model to measure the hedge ratio and hedging effectiveness implicitly assumes that the cash/futures relationship does remain stable over time. This appendix examines the

---

[3] If we are interested in both the return *and* the variance in order to determine the *optimal risk-return* hedge ratio, then we would want to maximize return *relative* to the risk. This trade-off depends on the hedger's risk-return trade-off relationship, which we can call γ. Assuming that the hedger is risk adverse, γ is negative. We then can maximize Z with respect to HR_O, where $Z = E(\Delta H) + \gamma \, var(\Delta H)$ and HR_O = the optimal risk-return hedge ratio.

potential effect of unstable hedge ratios on both basis risk and the hedging effectiveness measure when the regression procedure is employed, and then shows the extent of unstable hedge ratios for currency data.

The Effect of Unstable Hedge Ratios on Hedging Effectiveness

Both empirical research and practitioner application of the regression model has implicitly assumed that the hedge ratio is stable over time. In this case, the hedge ratios derived by employing data from time period t are deemed to be relevant measures for hedging purposes for subsequent time periods. However, if hedge ratios are unstable over time, then additional basis risk exists that is not apparent by simply applying the regression model to ex-post data without any adjustment for the changing nature of the hedge ratio. This additional basis risk means that the R^2 value representing the traditional ex-post hedging effectiveness measure is upward biased due to the inappropriate hedge ratio.

Let us designate R_{t+1}^2 as the hedging effectiveness measure from using the hedge ratio b_{t+1} for data from $t + 1$, and R_t^2 as the hedging effectiveness measure from using the hedge ratio b_t for data from $t + 1$. Then we can determine the upward bias in the typical ex-post R_{t+1}^2 value when hedge ratios are unstable by finding $\Delta R^2 = R_{t+1}^2 - R_t^2$. These relationships are shown as follows:

Data from Period t		Data from Period ($t + 1$)
b_t	$\rightarrow$	$b_{t+1} \rightarrow R_{t+1}^2$
		R_t^2
		$\Delta R^2 = R_{t+1}^2 - R_t^2$

Daigler (1991) shows that the bias in the hedging effectiveness neasure when historical data are employed to determine the hedge ratio *and* the hedge ratio is unstable over time is determined by

$$\Delta R^2 = \Delta b_t^2 (\sigma_F^2 / \sigma_C^2) \tag{7B-1}$$

where $\Delta R^2 =$ the bias in the hedging effectiveness measure from unstable hedge ratios

$\Delta b_t^2 =$ the change in the hedge ratio from the measurement period to the subsequent period

$\sigma_F^2 / \sigma_C^2 =$ the standard deviation ratio (squared) of the futures and cash price changes

Consequently, if hedge ratios are unstable over time, then the use of the hedge ratio from the previous period results in an upwardly biased R^2 value for hedging effectiveness. Conceptually, if b_{t+1} is the minimum-variance hedge ratio during time $t + 1$, then any other hedge ratio b_t that has a different slope to the regression line has a larger sum of squared errors and thus a lower R^2 value. Hence, a bias occurs when the historical hedging effectiveness measure based on b_t is used to estimate the current hedging effectiveness.

Table 7B-1 Hedging Effectiveness Bias: Same-Currency Hedging Results

Country	Average Results per Period			
	b_{t+1}	$|\Delta b_t|$	e^*	ΔR^2
Canada	.892	.112	.831	.017
Germany	.985	.072	.941	.010
Japan	.940	.078	.928	.009
U.K.	.979	.056	.934	.005

Note: $\Delta R^2 = \Delta b_t^2 [\sigma_F^2 / \sigma_C^2]$.
Source: Daigler (1991).

Table 7B-2 Hedging Effectiveness Bias: Crosshedging Results

Country	Average Results per Period			
	b_{t+1}	$|\Delta b_t|$	e^*	ΔR^2
Japan vs.				
Australia	.315	.366	.275	.121
Belgium	.652	.313	.360	.133
Italy	.641	.399	.416	.219
Netherlands	.734	.365	.443	.175
Spain	.556	.345	.319	.281
France	.721	.389	.398	.183
Germany vs.				
Australia	.239	.215	.256	.112
Belgium	.890	.145	.777	.047
Italy	.831	.100	.802	.024
Netherlands	.945	.085	.911	.014
Spain	.714	.166	.673	.087
France	.919	.087	.832	.018
U.K. vs.				
Australia	.223	.172	.215	.060
Belgium	.612	.309	.383	.092
Italy	.575	.250	.373	.078
Netherlands	.648	.250	.435	.078
Spain	.645	.237	.458	.123
France	.665	.241	.422	.057

Note: $\Delta R^2 = \Delta b_t^2 [\sigma_F^2 / \sigma_C^2]$.
Source: Daigler (1991).

Examining Currency Hedge Ratio Instability

Daigler (1991) examines the instability of hedge ratios by employing weekly currency cash and futures prices changes for the period 1980 through 1986 in order to generate semiannual hedge ratios both for currencies that have futures contracts and for currencies without futures. Tables 7B-1 and 7B-2 show the average minimum-variance hedge ratio per period, b_{t+1}^*, the absolute value of the change in the minimum-variance hedge ratio from the previous period, $|\Delta b_t|$, the hedging effectiveness value for period $t + 1$, $e^* = R_{t+1}^{*2}$, and the bias in the hedging effectiveness that exists when the hedge ratio is unstable over time, ΔR^2.

Table 7B-1 shows that the bias in the R^2 values for hedges using the same cash and futures currencies are essentially nonexistent (namely, about 1%). However, Table 7B-2 indicates the difficulty that can arise when crosshedges are obtained. In this case, the resulting *average* bias for the hedge effectiveness measures are much larger, ranging from 12% to 28% per period for the yen futures, with individual period biases (not shown here) *often* being above 20%. Moreover, most cross-currency results possess several periods where the variability in price changes are actually *increased* by using the previous period's hedge ratio as compared to using a no-hedge strategy.

The existence of unstable hedge ratios means that the use of past hedge ratios to estimate future hedge ratios and the use of minimum-variance hedging effectiveness measures must be undertaken with greater care for crosshedging situations. Previous researchers implicitly assumed that the hedge ratios obtained from past data provide an appropriate hedge ratio for subsequent periods, and that the minimum-variance hedging effectiveness measure is an unbiased value of the true hedging effectiveness. Since unstable hedge ratios increase the basis risk of the hedge (i.e., reduce the hedging effectiveness) compared with the typical minimum-variance results, the hedger may need to reevaluate the firm's analysis procedure for hedging.

BIBLIOGRAPHY FOR APPENDIX 7B

Daigler, Robert T. (1991). "Hedge Ratio Instability for Currency Futures," working paper, Florida International University.

Chapter 8

STOCK INDEX FUTURES PRICING AND ARBITRAGE

Overview

The cost of carry model for stock index futures shows that the cash and futures prices should deviate only by the financing cost and dividends. However, the nonconstant dividend effect and the lead-lag effect arising from stocks that do not trade frequently complicate the pricing process.

Stock index arbitrage is often called program trading, although program trading is a more general term (see Focus 2-1). Program trading involves trading a basket of stocks in order to mimic the behavior of an entire cash index. Critics claim that program trading creates greater market volatility, as well as being a cause of the October 1987 crash; this chapter examines these allegations. The factors affecting arbitrage transactions are the financing cost, transactions costs, the liquidity in the cash market, restrictions on selling short cash stocks for long arbitrage, the nonconstant payment of dividends over time, and the difficulty of creating a perfect arbitrage situation for some index contracts. Empirical evidence shows that apparent profitable arbitrage exists when end-of-the-day prices are employed, but most of these profitable opportunities disappear quickly when intraday data is tested. Therefore, arbitrageurs often must take on risk or monitor the market carefully to obtain profits. However, futures do occasionally become mispriced; thus hedgers, speculators, and arbitrageurs must be able to recognize when such mispricings occur and be able to adjust for factors that affect pricing. This chapter shows how to price stock index futures and illustrates arbitrage trades for stock index contracts. In addition, the relationship between program trading, market volatility, and the market crash is discussed.

Terminology

*Designated order turnaround (DOT) system** The computerized system at the NYSE that allows traders to send buy and sell orders for stocks directly to the floor of the exchange by electronic means, speeding execution time significantly.

*Portfolio insurance** A technique that allows participants to benefit from market advances by increasing the exposure to stocks during up-markets and providing insurance from market declines by selling stocks during down-markets.

*Program trading** See Chapter 2.

*Stock index fund** See Chapter 2.

PRICING STOCK INDEX FUTURES

The price of a futures contract depends on the underlying cash value. Stock indexes are a portfolio of stocks, weighted by size or other factors. The calculation of a stock index, the trading environment for stocks, and the characteristics of stock index futures are covered in Chapter 2.

Institutional investors employ stock indexes as benchmarks for comparison purposes. In addition, a number of mutual funds attempt to match exactly the performance of the S&P 500 index. Moreover, the existence of stock index futures markets has caused many other funds to institute investment strategies based on a portfolio that mimics the S&P 500 index. This chapter examines stock index futures pricing and arbitrage with such portfolios of stocks.

Applying the Cost of Carry Model to Stock Index Futures

The fair futures price calculated by the cost of carry model for stock index futures must consider the dividends received from holding the stocks in the index; that is,

$$P_{\text{FAIR}} = P_C(1 + i)^t - D \tag{8-1}$$

where P_{FAIR} = the fair futures price for a stock index

P_C = the current value of the underlying cash index

i = the financing rate of interest or equivalent investment return desired, in percentage terms

D = the dollar dividend amount in index points received on the stocks in the index from now until the expiration of the futures contract[1]

t = number of days until expiration of the futures, divided by 365

The dollar dividends D must be recalculated whenever a stock in the index pays its quarterly dividend or a firm alters its dividend. The model shows that the effect of receiving dividends over the life of the futures contract is to *lower* the futures price. This relationship occurs because (1) the dividends received reduce the net funds needed to finance the cash position and (2) a purchase of the futures contract is an alternative to holding the cash stocks, but a long position in futures does *not* provide any income from dividend payments.[2]

The continuous time equivalent to the above cost of carry equation is used frequently, since only the dividend yield rather than the frequently changing total dollar dividends are needed for its calculation:

$$P_{FAIR} = P_C e^{(i-d)t} \tag{8-2}$$

where d = the dividend yield on the stock index

If one has only the dividend yield, then an alternative to using Equation (8-2) is to convert the yield to dollar dividends, as follows:

$$D = d P_C t \tag{8-3}$$

Note that Equation (8-1) provides the most accurate calculation of the effects of dividends and therefore is employed in many of the arbitrage computer models.

Equations (8-1) and (8-2) and Example 8-1 illustrate both the relationship between the futures and current cash index values and the net difference between the financing costs and the dividend income received. In particular, the larger the difference between i and d, the larger the price difference between P_{FAIR} and P_C. In addition, the larger the value of t, the larger the price difference between the futures and cash index values.

Example 8-1 illustrates that using Equations (8-1) and (8-2) for determining the fair futures price can provide slightly different values for P_{FAIR}. Which equation the trader employs depends on which equation the trader believes describes the cash flow process

[1] The future value of the dividends at contract expiration could be calculated. However, the difficulty of the process and the uncertainty of future dividends makes this approach undesirable in practice, especially given the small effect on P_{FAIR}. For example, if expected dividends during the 2 months before futures expiration are 1.90 index points and the interest rate is 8%, then the future value effect adds .014 index point to the calculation. This is equivalent to $7 per futures contract. Note that the dividend yield model given in Equation (8-2) does consider future values.

[2] The stock index futures pricing equation is developed in two ways. One approach is to set the returns from the arbitrage transaction equal to the risk-free interest rate. Thus one would buy stock, sell futures, and receive dividends, which would be equivalent to owning a T-bill (transactions costs are ignored in the pricing equation). The second approach is to compare the returns from holding a stock portfolio to those from a futures position plus buying T-bills. This approach is equivalent to comparing two alternative strategies that have the same amount of risk. The only difference is that the stock position receives dividends whereas the futures position does not. The equivalent equation is derived if futures are purchased and stocks sold short, since dividends must be paid in this circumstance. The cash flows for short and long stock index futures are presented later.

EXAMPLE 8-1
Determining the Fair Value of a Stock Index Futures Contract

The following values represent actual (historical) stock market values:

S&P 500 Index	319.72
T-bill yield	6.59%
Dividend yield on the Index stocks	3.02%
Days until expiration of the futures	84

Using these data, the fair price is calculated as follows:

$$P_{FAIR} = P_C e^{(i-d)t} \tag{8-2}$$

$$P_{FAIR} = 319.72 e^{(.0659-.0302)(84/365)}$$

$$= 319.72 e^{.0082159}$$

$$= 319.72(1.0082497)$$

$$= 322.36$$

One also can use Equation (8-1) to calculate the fair price if the dividend yield is first converted to total dollar dividends (or if the total dollar dividends expected over the life of the futures contract are added up separately for the individual stocks). Equation (8-3) is employed to convert dividend yields to dollar dividends:

$$D = d P_C t \tag{8-3}$$

$$D = (.0302)(319.72)(^{84}\!/_{365}) = 2.222$$

Then one is able to calculate the fair price as follows:

$$P_{FAIR} = P_C(1 + i)^t - D \tag{8-1}$$

$$P_{FAIR} = 319.72(1 + .0659)^{84/365} - 2.222$$

$$= 319.72(1.01479) - 2.222$$

$$= 322.23$$

Notice that the two calculated values for the fair futures price differ slightly. There are two reasons for this. Most important, Equation (8-1) calculates the dividend value in index points, whereas Equation (8-2) uses the dividend yield. [Compare the results for Equation (8-1) to the results when $P_{FAIR} = P_C(1 + i - d)^t$ is calculated.] Moreover, the first formulation uses discrete compounding, whereas the second employs continuous compounding.

best *and* which method is used by other traders in the market. Considerations concerning the uneven payments of dividends are covered shortly. These considerations imply that Equation (8-1) would be more useful in practice if *actual* dividends are calculated over the life of the futures contract.

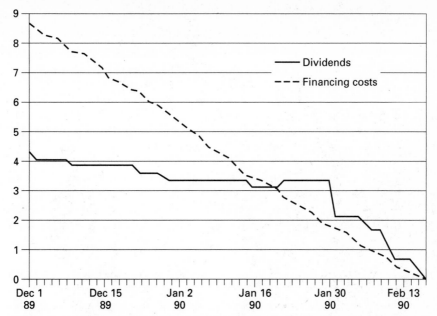

Figure 8-1 MMI futures: Financing costs versus dividends. (*Source:* Chicago Board of Trade, 1990.)

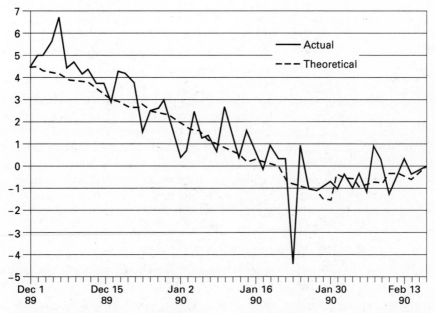

Figure 8-2 MMI futures: Actual basis vs. net financing costs. (*Source:* Chicago Board of Trade, 1990.)

Dividend Payments and the Pricing Process

Although the pricing equations for stock index futures given above, especially Equation (8-2), are employed on the basis of the assumption that total dividends are received *evenly* throughout the period, dividends are actually paid out quarterly by corporations. Moreover, many corporations pay dividends at approximately the same time in the quarter. For example, about 70% of the dividends for the MMI contract are paid in the second month of each quarter, whereas 75% of the dividends for the S&P 500 index are paid during the last seven weeks of the quarter. Figure 8-1 shows the changing relationship between financing costs and dividends over time for the MMI contract. Notice that dividends are *greater* than financing costs for the latter part of the quarter. The financing cost and the dividend income decline over time since they measure the total cost from the date in question *until the futures expires.* As the time until expiration decreases, the financing cost and dividends received decrease. Figure 8-2 relates the net financing cost (financing less dividends) to the actual futures-cash basis for the MMI futures contract to show when the futures are over- and underpriced. When $P_F - P_C >$ net financing cost, futures are overpriced, and vice versa (where P_F designates the current futures price). Figure 8-2 shows that futures can become mispriced by more than one index point when using end-of-day prices, with the mispricing fluctuating from overpricing to underpricing. If such mispricings occur within the day, then arbitrage profits are possible.

Because of the dividend effect, it is possible for stock index futures to sell at a *discount* to the cash index because of the so-called "seasonality" effect of the time at which dividends are paid. Futures sell at a discount when the dividend yield until the expiration of the futures contract exceeds the risk-free rate. Figure 8-2 shows this discount effect during the latter part of the quarter. The MMI contract is particularly affected by dividend seasonality, since the stocks composing the MMI index have high dividend yields. Thus, the dividend effects are greater for the MMI in comparison with other stock index futures for spreads over calendar months or spreads with other futures contracts. For example, a constant relationship over time does not exist between various MMI calendar spreads.

Another dividend factor affecting futures pricing is that dividends are only owed by the corporation once they are approved by the board of directors. Dividends are increased or cut, depending on the needs of the firm.[3] This situation creates uncertainty that does not exist for other futures contracts. Although some researchers believe that the dividend effects discussed here are relatively minor in most circumstances (for example, see Saunders and Mahajan, 1988), many arbitrageurs calculate total expected dividend payments on a daily basis to determine the most accurate fair futures price possible.

Evidence on Pricing Stock Index Futures

Employing the cost of carry modes, early studies using the end-of-day stock index futures prices typically conclude that mispricings are relatively large for the time periods studied. Cornell and French (1983a,b) found mispricings for the S&P 500 and NYFE contracts for the initial futures expirations, attributing the mispricings to a tax

---

[3] An unexpected dividend increase creates larger profits for a short futures arbitrage and smaller profits for a long futures arbitrage.

timing option related to obtaining capital gains for the cash stocks. However, Cornell (1985) shows empirically that tax timing did not affect the results and that the mispricings began to disappear as the contract gained volume.[4] Saunders and Mahajan (1988) adjust for several assumptions made in other studies by considering mark-to-market effects and providing a partial adjustment for nonconstant dividend payments. Employing a regression analysis on daily data for the S&P 500 and NYSE contracts from late 1982 to 1984, they conclude that the pricing process of stock index futures improved over time. However, all daily pricing studies are adversely affected by the 15-minute timing difference that exists between the futures and cash market closing times. More meaningful analysis requires intraday data.

MacKinlay and Ramaswamy (1988) perform the only cost of carry pricing study on stock index futures that involves intraday data. Using the S&P 500 contract from June 1983 to June 1987, they examine the mispricing of futures contracts from their fair value for every 15-minute interval. MacKinlay and Ramaswamy determine that a positive or negative *persistence* in mispricing exists and that these mispricings are a function of the number of days until expiration, with larger mispricings occurring farther from expiration.

Timing Differences Between the Index Futures and Cash Prices

A factor affecting *apparent* mispricings of stock index futures is timing differences between cash index values and futures prices. These timing differences cause futures price changes to lead cash index changes. The conventional wisdom is that stock index futures prices lead the cash index by 20 to 30 minutes. This timing effect is an example of the "price discovery" criteria for futures discussed in Chapter 1. Several reasons exist to explain this timing difference:

- Infrequent trading of smaller stocks
- Higher cost in the cash market
- Lower futures margins

Let us briefly explain each of these factors.

Infrequent trading for smaller stocks in the S&P 500 and NYSE cash indexes cause these indexes to be "old." Since the cash indexes reflect only the *last* trade for each stock, the futures contract is a better indicator of the current status of the overall market, whereas the cash index reflects *past* price information on the individual stocks.

Higher commissions, bid-ask spreads, and liquidity costs in the cash market make trades on a portfolio of individual stocks very costly, especially in comparison with equivalent trades in a futures index. Overall, cash trades are ten times more costly than equivalent futures transactions. Thus, market participants wishing to implement a "market basket" trade immediately can do so quicker, more effectively, and with less cost in the futures market.

Market participants with relevant information or differing expectations from the market price prefer the futures markets to the cash markets because of the lower margin

---

[4] Critics of stock index futures program trades claim that futures cause an increase in cash market volatility. These critics have called for an increase in futures margins to reduce the importance of stock index futures.

FOCUS 8-1
Stock Market Volatility and Futures Markets

Two issues of concern to market professionals are a possible increase in stock market volatility in the 1980s and the critics' claims of a relationship between the market's volatility and futures markets. Concern over the increase in market volatility in the past decade stems mostly from large daily moves in the Dow Jones Industrials during this time period. However, with the Dow ranging from 1000 to 2800 during most of the 1980s, the percentage changes in prices generally have been consistent with time periods when the Dow was below 1000.

Even though overall price volatility in the 1980s seems to be consistent with past time periods, there have been specific days and time periods where prices have changed dramatically. *Business Week* (see Laderman, 1986) chronicles these changes through early 1986 and associates them with program trading. More dramatically, on September 11, 1986, and January 23, 1987, the markets gyrated more than 100 points on an intraday basis; on January 23, 1987, more than 300 million shares were traded, the largest daily volume to date, and a 115-point drop in the Dow occurred in only 71 minutes. And then there was the market crash in October 1987, as discussed in Focus 8-2. On October 13, 1989, the Dow dropped 190 points in the last 90 minutes of trading. On a more consistent basis, there was significant market volatility at the quarterly expiration of the futures and options contracts, which became known as the "triple witching hour." On these expiration dates, the Dow Jones Index sometimes moved 100 points within the last hour of trading.

The large intraday price moves and the volatility during the triple witching hours were blamed on trading with baskets of stocks, called program trading. However, data for the S&P 500 futures contract show that the volume of program trading was not large during the declines in September 1986 and January 1987 (see Brodsky, 1987). In fact, in January and October 1987 the market moved too fast for the program traders to execute their trades.

On the other hand, the price swings associated with the last hour of trading before the expiration of the futures and options contracts logically could be related to arbitrageurs closing their positions. Recall that the stock index futures contracts are settled in cash at expiration by setting the futures price equal to the closing cash index value. Consequently, for arbitrageurs to avoid price risk, both futures and cash trades typically have to be closed at the end of trading on the expiration day. This activity often creates market imbalances for the individual stocks. In fact, the stock arbitrage positions are closed with a "market on close" order, where the brokerage house trades the stock during the last minute of trading. This concentrated activity can create conditions for wildly chaotic markets. For example, during the expiration of the December 1986 futures contract, 86 million shares were traded on the NYSE in the last *minute* of trading, using market on close orders.

Stoll and Whaley (1986, 1987) examine the relationship between expiration days and market volatility. They find that futures and option expirations contribute to both volume and price effects. In particular, volume is about twice the normal level in the last hour before futures and options expire. Moreover, S&P 500 stocks decline significantly during the last hour when futures expire. However, the price effects during this time period seem to be consistent with the effects of block trading by institutions during other time periods.

In order to reduce the effects of the triple witching hour on market volatility, the exchanges decided to stagger the expirations of the stock index futures, options on futures, and options on individual stocks. In particular, the S&P 500 futures would stop trading at the third Thursday's close but would be valued at the next day's open. These changes in the closing procedures, starting with the June 1987 contract, have reduced volatility on expiration day.

requirements for futures. The lower margins provide greater leverage for speculators and a reduced cost for arbitrageurs.[5]

Evidence of the Lead-Lag Effect

Research on the lead-lag and price discovery issues for stock index futures examines whether there is a timing difference between the futures and cash prices changes. Kawaller, Koch, and Koch (1987) examine minute-by-minute S&P 500 futures and cash data for 42 days in 1984 and 1985. They determine that the futures contract leads the cash index for as long as 20 to 45 minutes, even though equivalent price changes often occur simultaneously. Laatsch and Schwarz (1988) find simultaneous pricing for minute-by-minute data for the Major Market Index (MMI) contract. However, Finnerty and Park (1987) conclude that a significant lead-lag relationship between the futures and cash price changes exists. Herbst, McCormack, and West (1987) determine that futures lead the cash index for the S&P 500 and Value Line futures contracts, with the lead time varying from 0 to 16 minutes.

Stoll and Whaley (1990) employ correlation coefficients to examine five-minute intervals for the S&P 500 and MMI contracts. They determine that futures provide a price discovery function with a lead time of 5 minutes on average and occasionally up to 10 minutes or more *after the cash index is adjusted for nontrading and bid-ask affects.* Swinnerton, Curcio, and Bennett (1988) determine that a lead time of 5 minutes is the best predictor of the cash index, although the futures provide some predictive ability for up to 30 minutes. In summary, the research on the lead-lag effect provides consistent conclusions that futures do lead cash prices during most time periods, although equivalent price changes between the futures and cash markets often occur. Thus, pricing and arbitrage models need to consider this timing difference.

STOCK INDEX FUTURES ARBITRAGE: PROGRAM TRADING

Observations on Program Trading

Institutional funds and brokerage houses with millions of dollars invested in the market practice stock index arbitrage. Consequently, arbitrage did not interest the general public until program trading of baskets of stocks and stock index futures was blamed for creating wild swings in the stock market. Soon program trading became synonymous with stock index arbitrage. The popular press interest in program trading peaked after the stock market crash in October 1987 and the minicrash of 190 points in the last 1½ hours of trading in October 1989. Program trading was labeled as one of the

---

[5] Moreover, the Cornell and French studies assume that investors can use the entire proceeds of the short sale of stocks in order to earn interest. These funds typically are available only to dealers.

culprits of these crashes.[6] Although such accusations were challenged by many, including the various government and exchange studies on the crash, the outcry for controls on program trading caused the NYSE to place limitations on the intraday movement of the cash indexes and futures prices. These limitations are called circuit breakers. One aspect of circuit breakers is to trigger adjustments to how traders execute program trades through the **Designated Order Turnaround** or **DOT system** after a market move of at least 50 Dow Jones points. The benefit of the DOT system is that it provides major traders with a system that is computer linked to the floor of the exchange; such a system speeds up the execution of a stock index futures arbitrage transaction significantly. Additional circuit breakers place limits on price changes and stop trading in the cash and futures markets for 30 minutes or more, depending on the size of the price change. Chapter 3 provides details on circuit breakers.

Initiating Stock Index Futures Arbitrage

When the actual stock index futures price differs from the cost of carry fair price by more than transactions costs, arbitrage profits are possible. We can restate Equation (8-1) as follows to consider transactions costs to define the arbitrage opportunities for stock index futures:

$$P_C(1 + i)^t - D + T < P_F < P_C(1 + i)^t - D - T \tag{8-4}$$

or more compactly as

$$P_{FAIR} + T < P_F < P_{FAIR} - T \tag{8-5}$$

with T being the total transactions costs.

There are two possible arbitrage strategies: short and long futures arbitrage. Which strategy is relevant depends on whether $P_{FAIR} \pm T$ is less than or greater than P_F, as given in Equation (8-5). If the relationship in Equation (8-5) is not met, then no potential arbitrage exists. Short futures arbitrage (selling futures) occurs when the cost of carry fair price $P_{FAIR} + T < P_F$. In this case, the arbitrageur purchases stocks that are the equivalent of the cash index, and the futures contract is sold. The arbitrageur then typically holds the position until the futures expiration or unwinds it before expiration if it is more profitable to do so. If the position is held until futures expiration, then the arbitrageur simply arranges to sell the cash stocks at *exactly* the same time the futures stop trading via placing a "market on close" or "market on open" order, whichever is relevant. The market on close/open is effective in eliminating price risk since the futures contract price is set equal to the cash index at the end of trading for the futures contract; that is, the contract is settled in cash. This procedure guarantees a profit equal to $P_F - P_{FAIR} - T$, as long as no other factors affect the results. Of course, the arbitrageur also could close both sides of the trade before the futures expiration if it is

[6] After the market crash of 1987, many of the brokerage houses eliminated program trading *for their own accounts* for public relations purposes. The critics of program trades created an adverse public clamor, and brokerage houses did not want to alienate their individual customers. However, most houses continued to execute program trades for their institutional customers. Grossman (1988) compares 10 months of daily program trading activity with market volatility, determining that program trading is not associated with volatility.

EXHIBIT 8-1
Cash-and-Carry Arbitrage for Stock Index Futures

Transaction	At Initiation of Arbitrage (Time t)	From Initiation to Futures Expiration	At Futures Expiration (Time T)
Buy stocks at time t to mimic stock index (sell stocks at time T)*	$-P_C(t)$	$+D$	$+P_C(T)$
Borrow funds or use own funds†	$+P_C(t)$		$-P_C(1 + i)^t$
Sell stock index futures at time t‡	0		$P_F(t) - P_C(T)$
Total	0	D	$P_F(t) - P_C(1 + i)^t$

The cash flow is $P_F(t) - P_C(1 + i)^t + D$.

If the futures price at time t equals the fair price, then $P_F(t) = P_{FAIR}(t) = P_C(1 + i)^t - D$.

Alternatively, if $P_F(t) > P_C(1 + i)^t - D$, then arbitrage is possible if transactions costs are covered.

---

*Dividends should be reinvested; however, the difference in total return is marginal.
†Only 50% of the purchase price of stocks can be borrowed. The cost of borrowed funds is the financing rate, whereas the cost of the institution's own money is the opportunity cost of funds. The average cost is labeled i for this situation.
‡At time T (the futures expiration) the stock index futures price is set equal to the cash index.

profitable to do so. Exhibit 8-1 shows the cash flows for cash-and-carry stock index futures arbitrage. Example 8-2 provides numerical illustrations of short futures arbitrage opportunities for the S&P 500 and MMI futures contracts.

Long futures arbitrage (buying futures) occurs when $P_{FAIR} - T > P_F$. One way to initiate a long arbitrage transaction is to purchase the futures and sell short the equivalent of the cash index. Alternatively, if the cash stocks are already in the arbitrageur's portfolio, the arbitrageur sells the stocks and invests the resultant funds in T-bills or other short-term instruments. This technique creates a position equivalent to the original stock position (less dividends) plus an excess return resulting from the arbitrage. This position is then held until the futures expire, at which time the stocks are repurchased. Exhibit 8-2 shows the cash flows for this reverse cash-and-carry arbitrage. Example 8-3 describes a case of long futures arbitrage.[7]

[7] An arbitrageur can calculate a type of implied financing rate for stock index arbitrage; namely,

Implied financing rate = basis yield + dividend yield

where basis yield = $(P_F - P_C)/P_C$. Thus, both the basis yield and dividend yield are in percentage terms. The implied financing rate can then be compared to either the financing rate or the equivalent yield one would receive on T-bills if funds were invested in that risk-free instrument. If the implied repo rate is higher than these other rates, then short futures arbitrage can provide enhanced returns, and vice versa. Of course, transactions costs need to be considered.

EXAMPLE 8-2
Short Arbitrage and the S&P 500 Index

Using the data and results from Example 8-1 we found that the fair price for the S&P 500 contract is 322.23. The actual futures price on the same day is 323.95. Since the actual futures price of 323.95 is greater than the fair price of 322.23, one is able to profit by selling the higher-priced futures contract and purchasing the equivalent of the lower-priced index. Each of the relevant factors affecting the potential arbitrage is considered here:

Sell futures at	323.95
Buy the stocks in the S&P 500 Index at	319.72
Futures premium	4.23
Plus dividends received	+2.22
Gross profit	6.45
Less opportunity ("financing") costs (see below)	−4.85
Less transactions costs (see below)	−1.09
Projected net profit	.51
or .51(500) = $255 net profit per contract	

Annualized return above T-bill rate = $[.51/319.72] [^{365}\!/_{84}] = .0069$; that is, the return is 69 basis points higher than the yield on T-bills.

OPPORTUNITY ("FINANCING") COSTS FOR ONE FUTURES CONTRACT

The cost of holding the position is based on the arbitrageur's opportunity cost of funds, and/or the borrowing rate, whichever is relevant. Here the arbitrageur is using internal funds and therefore is simply attempting to earn a return in excess of the T-bill rate. The opportunity cost is determined as follows:

$$\text{Cost in index points} = (\text{T-bill yield}) (\text{index value}) (\text{no. days}/365)$$

$$= (.0659) (319.72) (^{84}\!/_{365}) = 4.85$$

Transaction Costs per Futures Contract	Index Points
Stock: $.08 per share round-trip × 2895 shares = $231.60	.46
Futures: $15 per contract round-trip × 1 contract = $15	.03
Market impact (bid-ask) effects =	.60
	1.09

The typical *short* arbitrage strategy involves the use of only the arbitrageur's funds to purchase stocks, although borrowing 50% of the funds is a strategy that also is employed. The typical *long* arbitrage is employed by pension funds and other institutions that sell stocks currently in the portfolio and buy the equivalent futures. This strategy is called stock replacement. Factors that affect the profitability or risk of these strategies are transactions costs, short selling risks, dividends and margin effects, tracking risk, cash index lag effects, and stock price movements. These factors are explained in detail in the next section.

EXHIBIT 8-2
Reverse Cash-and-Carry Arbitrage for Stock Index Futures

Transaction	At Initiation of Arbitrage (Time t)	At Futures Expiration (Time T)
Sell stocks currently in portfolio at time t; buy back stocks at time T*	$+P_C(t)$	$-P_C(T)$
Receive funds from sale of stocks and invest in T-bills (or equivalent)†	$-P_C(t)$	$+P_C(1 + i)^t - D$
Buy stock index futures at time t‡	0	$P_C(T) - P_F(t)$
Total	0	$P_C(1 + i)^t - D - P_F(t)$

The cash flow is $P_C(1 + i)^t - D - P_F(t)$.

If the futures price at time t equals the fair price, then $P_F(t) = P_{FAIR}(t) = P_C(1 + i)^t - D$.

Alternatively, if $P_F(t) < P_C(1 + i)^t - D$, then arbitrage is possible if transactions costs are covered.

---

*An alternative is to sell stocks short. In this case the short seller must *pay out* dividends when they are paid by the corporation.

†Dividends are subtracted from $P_C(1 + i)^t$ at time T because stock prices are adjusted *downward* when dividends are paid.

‡At time T (the futures expiration) the stock index futures price is set equal to the cash index.

Considerations for Stock Index Arbitrage

Implementing risk-free stock index arbitrage transactions is not as straightforward as the previous section may have implied. Several complications and risks must be taken into account, including the dividend and lag effects discussed earlier in relation to pricing stock index futures. The following discussion describes these considerations.

Transactions Costs. Commissions and bid-ask spread costs must be included in the profit analysis before implementing the arbitrage. Commissions for large transactions are relatively small, \$.03 to \$.06 per share each way for the stocks and \$12 to \$15 round-trip for each futures contract.[8] The bid-ask spread on stock trades is important because, everything else considered, the arbitrageur buys stocks at the specialist's ask price and sells at the bid. Often only half the bid-ask spread is relevant in arbitrage calculations, since the closing stock trades are executed at a "market on open" or "market

---

[8] Funds intending to sell a market basket of stocks *independently* of the possibility of arbitrage can profit when $P_F > P_{FAIR}$ (when short futures arbitrage exists), since their *marginal* transactions costs involve only a futures commission. However, few funds use this type of arbitrage strategy.

EXAMPLE 8-3
Long Futures Arbitrage

Profits from long futures arbitrage may exist when the actual futures price is less than the fair price. In this case an arbitrageur would buy futures and sell stocks, as long as the profits are greater than the costs. Let us use the values and costs derived in Example 8-2:

Investment interest in index points	4.85*
Transactions costs	1.09
Dividends paid or given up on stocks, in index points	2.22†

The futures price is 323.95 and the fair price now is 325.40. A pension fund holds the equivalent of the S&P 500 index, which it is willing to sell now and replace with a futures contract (the stocks are repurchased later). The objective is to hold the *equivalent* of the S&P 500 with the futures contract as well as earning a risk-free rate of return via the arbitrage. The calculations to determine whether a profit is possible are

Sell S&P 500 equivalent stocks in portfolio at	322.74
Buy futures at	323.95
Futures discount	−1.21
Plus investment yield in T-bills	+4.85
Less dividends forgone	−2.22
Gross profit	+1.42
Less transactions costs	−1.09
Projected net profit	.33

Annualized return above T-bill rate $= [.33/322.74] [^{365}\!/_{84}] = .0058$ or 58 basis points above the T-bill yield.

*For short arbitrage, this amount is a cost of funds or opportunity cost while here it represents the interest received from taking the funds received and investing in a T-bill or equivalent instrument.
†Stocks are sold (or sold short); therefore, dividends are given up (or they must be paid out on a short sale).

on close" order so as to link the stock prices to the expiring futures contract price.[9] Although current bid-and-ask values for stocks and total bids/asks for portfolios of stocks are shown on many computer screens, bids and asks are often old values that change with new trades.

[9] If an arbitrageur believes that most stocks will sell at the ask price when a short futures arbitrage is unwound, perhaps because of significant arbitrage activity, then a full bid-ask spread cost would be justified.

Short Selling Considerations for Long Futures Arbitrage.   Brokerage houses have access to the funds generated when they sell stocks short.[10] However, since other arbitrageurs often do not have access to these funds, higher financing costs are created for such transactions. Higher costs arise because needed funds must be borrowed or because the arbitrageur has an opportunity cost from lost interest on the arbitrageur's funds. Moreover, short sellers of stock are hampered by the "uptick" rule; that is, stocks can be sold short only if the most recent *change* in price was positive. This rule attempts to reduce the downward pressure on stock prices when prices are falling. When the futures price is below the cash index value and prices are falling, a pure arbitrageur would like to buy the futures contract and short the stocks; however, short sales may not be possible for all stocks because of the uptick rule. Because of these problems, most long futures arbitrage is conducted by institutions that *already own* the relevant stocks. To implement a long futures arbitrage they buy the futures and sell the stocks already in the portfolio, creating the net effect desired. The funds obtained from the stock sale are invested in T-bill or equivalent short-term instruments. Such a quasi-arbitrage transaction is often called a stock replacement strategy. Example 8-3 illustrates this strategy.

Cash Flow Effects.   Dividends are *not* a constantly decreasing function of time; that is, dividend payments occur in spikes during each quarter, as discussed in relation to the pricing process and shown earlier in Figure 8-1. Moreover, companies can change their dividend payout before the futures contract expires. The mark-to-market effect of the futures contract often creates a cash flow during the life of the arbitrage transaction, creating an uncertain amount of interest received or paid on these funds (at least if cash funds are employed for margin calls). Although these factors do not cause a major bias in the arbitrage model, many investment houses include these effects in their computer models.

Tracking Risk.   The S&P index is composed of 500 stocks, with each stock's weight in the index being determined by its market value in proportion to the market value of the total index; the NYSE index is made up of 1800 stocks, also proportionally weighted. Generating a cash portfolio that exactly matches the relevant cash index is costly, since the arbitrageur must include all 500 or 1800 stocks in the transaction *and* the weights in the portfolio must be matched to the weights in the index. Therefore, many arbitrageurs have used a portfolio of 50 to 200 stocks that closely track the activity of the S&P 500 index in order to execute a "near" arbitrage transaction. However, this procedure creates tracking errors (basis risk) between this 50- to 200-stock portfolio and the index, creating imperfect arbitrage. Such a strategy has created large losses

---

[10] Brokerage houses act as the principal pure arbitrageurs for stock index futures activity since their financing costs are lower than those of other potential pure arbitrageurs and their marginal commissions are zero for their cash trades. However, Stoll and Whaley (1987) state two reasons why brokerage house arbitrage activity is limited in this market (exclusive of the potential adverse publicity): (1) the availability of capital to institute such trades is constrained by net capital requirements; and (2) they may have more profitable uses for their borrowed funds.

in certain circumstances. Now, most S&P 500 arbitrage trades are completed by matching the cash index exactly, a practice that necessitates a minimum of $25 million.[11] Of course, the NYSE index *cannot* be effectively matched with a reasonable amount of funds. The MMI futures require only $3 million to avoid tracking risk. Although arbitrageurs would like to trade large positions in the MMI, liquidity often does not exist. For the NYFE contract, the arbitrageur compensates for the tracking error by requiring a greater difference between the futures and cash index prices before the arbitrage is undertaken. The NYSE contract also has limited liquidity for large trades.

The Lag Effect.   The lag of cash prices to futures prices examined in the pricing section also has an effect on the arbitrage process. If futures lead cash index prices by 5 to 20 minutes (or more), then using simultaneous data to calculate the potential arbitrage profits provides erroneous results. In addition, the use of end-of-day prices to infer potential arbitrage situations is hazardous, inasmuch as the futures contracts stop trading 15 minutes after the common stocks end trading. Evidence given below elaborates on this factor.[12]

Potential Stock Price Movements.   Since trades are executed by the DOT system within 2 minutes, individual stock prices typically do not change significantly (if at all) before execution. More importantly, stock prices that increase are offset by those that decrease, unless a major market move is under way. Also, the arbitrageur does not usually move the market since each individual stock in the arbitrage trade only constitutes a few hundred shares or less. Brokerage houses that institute arbitrage trades for funds provide at least two options for clients. One is a "guaranteed price" for the portfolio and a second is a "best efforts price" for the portfolio. The commission costs for the first alternative are higher than for the second.

Evidence Concerning Stock Index Arbitrage

Modest and Sundaresan (1983) completed an early study of stock index futures arbitrage by applying the cost of carry model to daily data. They calculate no-arbitrage bands based on their assumed transactions costs, finding that the daily futures versus cash relationships fall within the bands if the proceeds from short sales are not available; arbitrage *is* possible when short sale proceeds are available for reinvestment. However, the transactions costs used by Modest and Sundaresan are much higher than institutions pay. Moreover, their assumption that long futures arbitrage is unduly costly (because of the short sale rule) does not conform to the industry practice used by pension funds of initiating long futures arbitrage by selling stocks already in their portfolios.

---

[11] When the DOT system is employed, the trader can execute any odd size order in excess of 100 shares. Thus, the smallest stock must trade 100 shares but other stocks can trade 101, 102, etc. shares. Thus the arbitrageur can mimic the S&P 500 index with $25 million by buying all 500 stocks in the S&P 500 index in the exact same proportions as found in the index.

[12] Although composite bid-and-ask prices for the portfolio of stocks making up the cash index do appear on traders' screens, these bid-and-ask values also are old, since specialists update the quotes only as time permits.

MacKinlay and Ramaswamy (1988) provide limited arbitrage results in conjunction with their pricing results, examined earlier. They employ intraday data, but their choice of the size of the transactions bands seems to be arbitrary at .6% of the value of the cash index and they do not provide information on average arbitrage profits. However, MacKinlay and Ramaswamy do find that the average time that futures prices are above the upper transaction bound is 2 hours and the average time they are below the lower bound is 36 minutes (using 15-minute interval data). The large number of upper plus lower bound violations averages 234 intervals per three-month contract; the number of boundary crossings averages 41 per period. Further analysis of the arbitrage violations leads MacKinlay and Ramaswamy to conclude that the arbitrage violations are path dependent; that is, once an arbitrage boundary is crossed, it is less likely for the mispriced value to cross the opposite arbitrage boundary.

Merrick (1989) examines early unwindings and rollovers of arbitrage positions before futures expiration to determine whether such dynamic strategies affect the profits of arbitrage transactions. Although Merrick only employs daily S&P 500 data, he finds that the *effective* total transactions cost is only 73% of the original anticipated transactions cost when unwindings and rollovers are employed as part of a complete arbitrage strategy.

Daigler (1991) uses five-minute intervals to calculate arbitrage profits for the three major stock index futures contracts: the S&P 500, the Major Market Index, and the NYFE Index. Daigler employs an exact cost structure for the arbitrage transactions, examines the effect of timing lags between the futures and cash indexes on the reported arbitrage profits, and provides implicit evidence of the tracking risk on arbitrage results. Table 8-1 shows the average arbitrage profits for a $25 million portfolio for the intraday results. The early-morning results in Column 2 show the results for simultaneous prices (no lags in the cash index). These results show large apparent profits. However, the early-morning profits (not shown here) decline quickly when 5- and 15-minute cash lags are considered; that is, once most of the stocks in the index trade and their new prices are recorded in the index, the apparent arbitrage profits shown in the early morning almost disappear.

The importance of the timing effects becomes even clearer when one examines the intraday results from Table 8-1 and Figure 8-3. This table and figure show the size of the arbitrage profits when *intraday* cash and futures prices are employed. The profits for the simultaneous intraday cash and futures prices in column 3 are significantly smaller than the simultaneous early morning profits found in column 2, especially when the October–December 1987 period is eliminated from the results. In addition, even the profits shown in column 3 essentially disappear for the S&P 500 and MMI contracts when cash prices are employed with a five-minute lag, as given in column 4. (December 1987 is the exception.) Moreover, the arbitrage profits are eliminated for the NYFE contract when a 15-minute lag is employed (exclusive of December 1987). Thus, the lag effect due to "old" prices in the cash index explains average arbitrage profits, except for unusual periods such as October to December 1987, although the NYFE contract takes a longer time (15 minutes) for the lag effect to manifest itself. Although it is not shown here, all three contracts have a large number of *apparent* arbitrage possibilities per three-month period; that is, prices *temporarily* deviate outside the transactions bounds, but these deviations are due to the lag effect of the cash index. Figure 8-3 dramatically illustrates the effect of lags on the average results (the December 1989 quarter is excluded).

Table 8-1 Average Arbitrage Profits per $25 Million Portfolio: Intraday Results (Profits in Thousands)

Expiration (1)	Early-Morning Profits No Lag (2)	Intraday Results		
		No Lag (3)	5-Minute Lag (4)	15-Minute Lag (5)
A. S&P 500				
Mar 87	36.1	21.3	−2.5	−10.7
Jun 87	98.4	24.8	6.9	−2.3
Sep 87	29.2	11.5	−7.3	−16.1
Dec 87	333.3	194.0	167.6	146.5
Mar 88	91.9	24.1	−1.8	−13.8
Jun 88	56.2	26.4	13.0	.9
B. MMI				
Mar 87	40.7	18.8	3.3	−6.4
Jun 87	74.2	17.7	−1.3	−11.0
Sep 87	29.1	18.9	8.8	1.2
Dec 87	363.2	250.2	225.8	205.0
Mar 88	87.9	24.8	5.8	−4.0
Jun 88	53.9	17.2	.5	−8.8
C. NYFE				
Mar 87	50.1	35.1	6.1	−3.7
Jun 87	110.7	38.0	21.3	7.5
Sep 87	37.0	13.1	−12.7	−23.9
Dec 87	329.7	138.3	116.7	94.6
Mar 88	119.9	42.2	22.5	8.2
Jun 88	59.6	31.0	19.2	7.6
D. Averages				
S&P 500				
with Dec 87	107.5	50.4	29.3	17.8
w/o Dec 87	62.4	21.6	1.7	−7.9
MMI				
with Dec 87	108.2	57.9	40.5	31.5
w/o Dec 87	57.2	19.5	3.4	−3.2
NYFE				
with Dec 87	117.8	49.6	28.9	15.7
w/o Dec 87	75.5	31.9	11.3	−.1

Source: Daigler (1991).

Chung (1991) calculates the value of the cash index by using actual subsequent *trades* on each of the stocks making up the MMI index *after* the arbitrage opportunity appears. Using data from 1984 to 1986, Chung finds that the size and the frequency of arbitrage profits are significantly smaller than indicated in the *daily* studies referenced above, especially for transactions costs of .75% and 1%. In fact, only the .5% transactions costs are consistently profitable when actual trades are employed. He also finds that the existence of arbitrage profits has declined over time.

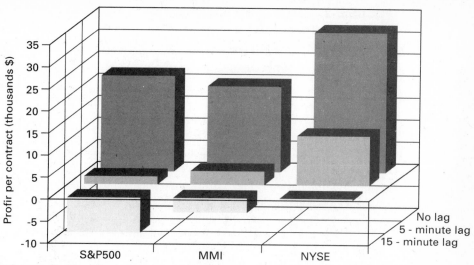

Figure 8-3 The effect of lags on arbitrage profits. (*Source:* Adapted from Daigler, 1991.)

Several important conclusions are derived from these studies on stock index arbitrage. First, the use of closing or early-morning prices to examine the pricing and arbitrage aspects of stock index futures markets causes difficulties in determining the actual potential for arbitrage as a result of the nonsimultaneous nature of end-of-the-day prices and the cash index lag effects. Second, assumptions concerning the cost structure for the marginal arbitrageur are critical in determining the existence of arbitrage profits. Third, apparent intraday arbitrage profits are mostly illusionary because of the lag effect of the cash index prices. Finally, the cost of carry model apparently does a good job of describing stock index futures prices once the factors noted above are considered, although additional evidence is needed concerning the relationship between these factors and futures pricing.

FUTURES AND THE MARKET CRASH

Although many critics blame stock index futures for the stock market crash of 1987, financial economists explain that futures reflected market sentiment during that time period. Why should we care about this historical event? First, the behavior of futures prices calls into question the pricing mechanism of futures markets. Second, we want to know whether it is important to find ways of protecting stock portfolios from another potential crash. Third, the crash actually did result in regulatory changes for the market. In particular, exchanges placed circuit breakers (price limits) on stock index futures to reduce volatility during market panics and to avoid criticism concerning the crash.

What did happen on "Black Monday" and how was the market behavior affected by futures? Here we examine the explanations and criticisms as related to futures markets. Figure 8-4 shows the extent of the crash on an intraday basis and the resultant volatility on the next day. This figure shows the almost straight decline in the S&P 500 futures

FOCUS 8-2
The Market Crash and Program Trading

On "Black Monday" (October 19, 1987) the Dow Jones Industrial Index fell 508 points or 22.6%, in comparison with the 12.8% one-day drop in 1929. Panic reigned on Wall Street and in other financial capitals. How did program trading relate to this devastating market crash? How did the market function on that day? What can we learn from this catastrophic event?

A number of commentaries on the market crash were written. In fact, several government agencies conducted hearings and issued special reports on the events of the crash. Two of the more interesting commentaries are by Joanne Hill (1987) and Scott Hamilton (1987); these commentaries were written soon after the crash and form the basis of the following discussion.

Early warnings of a problem in the stock market began on October 6 when the Dow Jones Industrials declined 91 points in one day. During the following week the market declined more than 90 points each day on Wednesday and Friday, October 14 and 16, and 57 points on Thursday the 15th. The market was down a total of 10% on these three days and 15% over the two-week period. Volatilities in the stock, futures, and options markets were up 25% to 30% before the crash. The merchandise trade deficit news was discouraging, and interest rates were increasing. On the weekend before Black Monday, news programs focused on the market's problems, on Treasury Secretary Baker's remarks concerning prospects for further declines in the dollar, on technical indicators turning bearish, and on the problems in the Mideast.

On Monday morning the Tokyo and London markets fell sharply. Both the U.S. futures and stock markets had amassed heavy sell orders by the open. The futures market opened down 7% on the S&P 500. Many of the large issues on the stock exchange did not open until after 11 A.M., and thus comparison of the futures and cash index prices was impossible. The Dow Jones Industrial Average was down 190 points by 11 A.M. The DOT system for program trades and for many of the retail stock orders was overburdened, and most program trading desks stopped taking orders. In fact, program trading never really effectively operated on Monday, October 19, because most of the major stocks in the S&P 500 were not open in the morning, the futures prices were too volatile, the cash bid-ask spreads too wide to assure reasonable execution, and prices moved downward by several points at a time. The link between the stock market and futures was severed. Stock traders saw their orders delayed and executed at lower prices than existed when the orders were entered. Futures traders could execute their orders, but there was no way to determine the true value of the underlying cash index; by the afternoon, futures prices were trading at large discounts to the cash index. Although theoretical models showed that large arbitrage profits were available, based on the last reported trade values of stocks, the markets were in turmoil. Brokers were not willing to risk their own capital to assure clients of a specified price for the trades, especially given the poor executions and unfilled orders that existed.

Trading in the S&P 500 futures was 162,000 contracts, which represented 1.5 times the previous week's daily average. Cash stocks traded 604 million shares, three times the previous week's average. Futures volume declined as the week progressed, representing only one-third of its typical ratio to cash market activity. For the week, the S&P 500 index was down 12.2%, the Dow Industrials 13.2%, and the OTC market 19.2%, including the partial recovery from Monday's decline. Stock indexes were down 26% to 30% from their highs at the end of August. Markets around the world fell significantly.

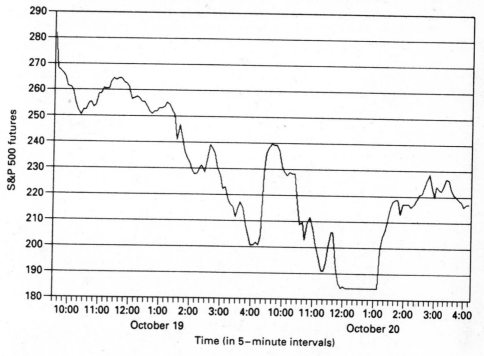

Figure 8-4 Stock index futures: October 19 and 20, 1987. (*Source:* Prices from Tick Data, Inc.)

on the 19th. The index then opened up higher on the 20th before retreating again until the market closed in midday. Focus 8-2 provides a background for our discussion by explaining the events of the crash.

Program Trading and the Crash

Although futures markets and program trading did not serve their typical market adjustment and arbitrage roles on October 19 (because of the breakdown of the system, as described in Focus 8-2), neither did they *cause* the market decline. In fact, stock index arbitrage was very difficult to execute on Monday: bid-ask spreads for futures were 1 point and for stocks (when the latter were trading) were 1% or more of the price of the stock. Moreover, traders were not confident about the execution price of their orders once the orders came to the floor of the exchange. In addition, most of the pension funds and institutions that typically executed program trades were at their trading limit, since they had initiated trades the previous week and did not have funds for additional trades. Statistics reveal that only 9% of the volume on the 19th and 2% on the 20th was index arbitrage.

Portfolio Insurance as a Factor

The effect of **portfolio insurance** on the market decline is harder to measure. Portfolio insurance is a technique that allows participants to benefit from market advances by increasing the exposure to stocks during up-markets and providing insurance from market declines by selling stocks during down-markets. The declines occurring before October 19 should have triggered portfolio insurance sell programs, but futures open interest figures suggest that such selling was only about 15% of total stock market volume on the 19th and 20% on the 20th; however, it does account for nearly 40% of the *sales* of futures contracts. Moreover, portfolio insurers often use futures only to execute trades quickly and at low cost; eventually, they cover the futures positions and sell the stocks. Hence, at worst, futures were used only for convenience by the portfolio insurers; in fact, the discounts on the futures were so large that many portfolio insurers simply traded solely in the cash market and/or waited until later in the week to trade. Of course, the *potential* for portfolio insurers selling on Monday may have panicked other money managers into selling at the open on October 19. In fact, Jacklin, Kleidon, and Pfleiderer (1992) develop a model that associates uncertain portfolio insurance positions with the potential for a market crash. Overall, the technique of portfolio insurance did not work well in the market collapse.

The Cash-Futures Basis During the Crash

Figure 8-5 shows the basis between the S&P 500 index and the S&P 500 futures during the crash period. The substantial futures discount and the widening of the basis from midday on the 19th through the 20th shows the lack of arbitrage activity in the market.[13] However, this widening of the basis also creates a mystery: *Why* did the futures fall *faster* than the cash index? Was it solely due to a lack of index arbitrage? Three explanations help to solve this mystery.

- Harris (1989) shows that the cash index fell slower than futures before 11 A.M. on the 19th because many of the major stocks did not open until 10:30 to 11 A.M. Thus, the cash index was "old" because it reflected the *last* price of each stock in the index, which in this case was Friday's close on the 16th for stocks that had not yet opened on Monday, as well as old prices for smaller stocks in the index that do not trade often.
- Blume, MacKinlay, and Terker (1989) found that the S&P 500 stocks fell 7 percentage points more than non-S&P stocks on the 19th. By the morning of the 20th, the difference had disappeared. They also found that the decline in the S&P 500 stocks was related to order imbalances. Thus, Blume, MacKinlay, and Terker suggest that activity related to the S&P 500 futures caused these aberrations in the cash market.
- Kleidon (1990) determines that on the afternoon of the 19th and on the 20th the cash-futures basis did not close due to mechanical reasons on the NYSE. In particular, buy-limit orders arrived on the exchange floor up to 45 minutes after traders placed them because of printer delays and breakdowns. These buy-limit orders kept cash prices at a higher level than dictated by supply-and-demand forces; that is, the limit orders created "stale" prices. Since the crash, the NYSE has upgraded its order-taking system.

[13] Notice the behavior of the MMI futures contract during midday on the 20th. Manipulation of the MMI contract was suspected during this period, but no proof was forthcoming from the investigations of the crash period.

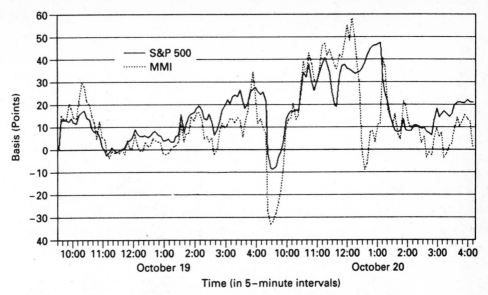

Figure 8-5 Cash-futures basis during the crash. (*Source:* Prices from Tick Data, Inc.)

Conclusions on the Crash and Futures Markets

Program trading and futures were blamed for the market catastrophe. The above argument maintains that this blame was generally misplaced. Moreover, other world stock markets did not have significant program trading or portfolio insurance programs, and their decline was comparable to the fall in the U.S. markets. The studies of "Black Monday" also stated that futures markets were not the culprit in the market crash. Scott Hamilton (1987) described the situation best when he commented on those placing the blame: "Monday's market was somewhat analogous to a group of individuals finding themselves in a smoke-filled room. Those with foresight and preplanning used futures and options to find the exit quickly. Others, without the benefit of these instruments, were left to slower and less efficient means of departure. It's not unusual for those who find themselves at the back of the line to complain that those in front had an 'unfair' advantage."

SUMMARY AND LOOKING AHEAD

This chapter examines the concepts and applications of pricing and arbitrage for stock index futures. Understanding stock index futures pricing and arbitrage concepts is important not only to those who execute program trades but to anyone who deals with futures markets, since pricing is a key component in the appropriate implementation of most trading and hedging strategies. This chapter shows that a number of factors affect futures pricing and whether a stock index arbitrage is profitable. Consequently, such a trade is not the straightforward undertaking implied by the mass media. In particular, the lag effect created by stale cash index prices creates a particular problem for evaluating pricing models and arbitrage trades. The next chapter examines pricing and arbitrage for interest rate futures contracts.

BIBLIOGRAPHY

Blume, M., A. MacKinlay, and B. Terker (1989). "Order Imbalances and Stock Price Movements on October 19 and 20, 1987," *Journal of Finance,* Vol. 44, No. 4, September, pp. 827–848.

Brodsky, William J. (1987). "Demystifying Stock Index Products, " *Market Perspectives,* Vol. 5, No. 7, September, pp. 1–5.

Chicago Board of Trade (1990). "Dividends Payouts and the MMI," *Financial Futures Professional,* Vol. 14, No. 4, April, p. 4.

Chung, Y. Peter (1991). "A Transactions Data Test of Stock Index Futures Market Efficiency and Index Arbitrage Profitability," *Journal of Finance,* Vol. 46, No. 5, December, pp. 1791–1809.

Cornell, B. (1985). "Taxes and the Pricing of Stock Index Futures: Empirical Results," *The Journal of Futures Markets,* Vol. 5, No. 1, Spring, pp. 89–101.

Cornell, B., and K. French (1983a). "The Pricing of Stock Index Futures," *The Journal of Futures Markets,* Vol. 3, No. 1, Spring, pp. 1–14.

Cornell, B., and K. French (1983b). "Taxes and the Pricing of Stock Index Futures," *Journal of Finance,* Vol. 38, No. 2, June, pp. 675–694.

Daigler, Robert T. (1991). "Stock Index Arbitrage with Intraday Data," working paper, Florida International University.

Finnerty, J. E., and H. Y. Park (1987). "Stock Index Futures: Does the Tail Wag the Dog?" *Financial Analysts Journal,* Vol. 43, No. 2, March–April, pp. 57–61.

Grossman, Sanford J. (1988). "Program Trading and Market Volatility," *Financial Analysts Journal,* Vol. 44, No. 4, July–August, pp. 18–28.

Hamilton, Scott W. (1987). "Did Program Trading Cause the Crash?" Equity Research Report SF2873, The First Boston Corporation, October 23.

Harris, Lawrence (1989). "The October 1987 S&P 500 Stock-Futures Basis," *Journal of Finance,* Vol. 44, No. 1, March, pp. 77–99.

Herbst, A. F., J. P. McCormack, and E. N. West (1987). "Investigation of a Lead-Lag Relationship Between Spot Stock Indices and Their Futures Contracts," *The Journal of Futures Markets,* Vol. 7, No. 4, pp. 373–381.

Hill, Joanne (1987). "Massive Selling Strains Worldwide Equity and Index Derivative Markets," *Stock Index Weekly Report,* Kidder, Peabody and Co., October 23.

Jacklin, Charles J., Allen W. Kleidon, and Paul Pfleiderer (1992). "Underestimation of Portfolio Insurance and the Crash of October 1987," *Review of Financial Studies,* Vol. 5, No. 1, Spring, pp. 35–64.

Kawaller, Ira, Paul Koch, and Timothy Koch (1987). "The Temporal Relationship Between S&P Futures and the S&P 500 Index," *Journal of Finance,* Vol. 42, No. 5, December, pp. 1309–1329.

Kleidon, Allan W. (1990). "Arbitrage, Nontrading, and Stale Prices: October 1987," Research Paper No. 1091, Standord University, May.

Laatsch, Francis E., and Thomas V. Schwarz (1988). "Price Discovery and Risk Transfer in Stock Index Cash and Futures Markets," *The Review of Futures Markets,* Vol. 7, No. 2, pp. 272–289.

Laderman, Jeffrey M. (1986). "Those Big Swings on Wall Street," *Business Week,* April 7, pp. 32–36.

MacKinlay, C., and K. Ramaswamy (1988). "Index-Futures Arbitrage and the Behavior of Stock Index Futures Prices," *Review of Financial Studies,* Vol. 1, No. 2, Summer, pp. 137–158.

Merrick, John, Jr. (1989). "Early Unwindings and Rollovers of Stock Index Futures Arbitrage Programs: Analysis and Implications for Predicting Expiration Day Effects," *The Journal of Futures Markets,* Vol. 9, No. 2, April, pp. 101–112.

Modest, David M., and Mahadevan Sundaresan (1983). "The Relationship Between Spot and Futures Prices in Stock Index Futures Markets: Some Preliminary Evidence," *The Journal of Futures Markets,* Vol. 3, No. 1, Spring, pp. 15–41.

Saunders, Edward M., Jr., and Arvind Mahajan (1988). "An Empirical Examination of Composite Stock Index Futures Pricing," *The Journal of Futures Markets,* Vol. 8, No. 2, April pp. 211–228.

Stoll, Hans, and Robert Whaley (1990). "The Dynamics of Stock Index and Stock Index Futures Returns," *Journal of Financial and Quantitative Analysis,* Vol. 25, No. 4, December, pp. 441–468.

Stoll Hans, and Robert Whaley (1986). "Expiration Day Effects of Index Options and Futures," Series in Finance and Economics, Monograph 1986-3, Solomon Brothers Center for the Study of Financial Institutions.

Stoll, Hans, and Robert Whaley (1987). "Program Trading and Expiration-Day Effects," *Financial Analysts Journal,* Vol. 43, No. 2, March–April, pp. 16–23.

Swinnerton, Eugene, Richard J. Curcio, and Richard E. Bennett (1988). "Index Arbitrage Program Trading and the Prediction of Intraday Stock Price Change," *The Review of Futures Markets,* Vol. 7, No. 2, pp. 300–323.

PROBLEMS

*Indicates more difficult problems

8-1 Cost of Carry Model for Stock Index Futures

Given the following information, determine the equilibrium or fair price for a stock index contract using both the discrete and continuous form equations:

Underlying cash index = 325.00
Financing rate = 10%
Annual dividend rate = 3.5%
The futures contract expires in 79 days.

8-2 Cost of Carry Model for Stock Index Futures

S&P 500 futures are selling at 342.90 with 72 days left until expiration. On the same day, the S&P 500 index is 339.75 and the T-bill yield is 8.3%. If the dividend yield on the index stocks is 3.84%, what should the dollar dividend in index points be? What is the fair price of the index based on this information? What does this fair price tell you about the futures price, and what could you do with this knowledge?

8-3 Futures Price for Stock Index Futures Arbitrage

On March 5, the following data are relevant:

S&P 500 Index	335.54
T-bill yield	7.76%
Days until futures expiration	101
Projected dividends on the index stocks	3%

An arbitrageur detemines that a profit of $300 per contract would be required to justify her risk. What would the S&P 500 futures price have to be for this arbitrageur to execute a short arbitrage? Assume that the transactions costs are 1.09 points. (Use the discrete equation in your calculations.)

8-4 Stock Index Arbitrage

Given the following information:

S&P 500 Stock Index	340.27
T-bill yield (internal)	7.87%
Cost of external financing	10.50%
Dividend yield on index stocks	3.25%
Days until futures expiration	98
Stock index futures price	344.50
Futures commission per contract	$12
Market impact costs per contract	$300
Costs per round-trip for stocks (2895 shares needed)	$.06 per share

a. Find the fair price and determine the type of arbitrage that is possible.
b. Determine whether arbitrage would be profitable if 50% of the funds were borrowed and the rest generated internally.
c. Determine whether the arbitrage would be profitable if all of the funds were internal.

Chapter 9

INTEREST RATE FUTURES PRICING AND ARBITRAGE

Overview

T-bond and Eurodollar futures are very active and important contracts. The complexities of the pricing of the T-bond futures contract create numerous opportunities for profit for short arbitrageurs *and* short hedgers, as well as difficulties in determining the fair price of the contract. Because of the pricing difficulties, unsophisticated traders can lose without even realizing why a loss has occurred. Short hedgers holding a position into the delivery month should take advantage of the opportunities available with the delivery process in order to benefit fully from a short position in futures.

T-bond futures pricing and arbitrage are affected by the net financing cost (financing cost less interest received), the conversion factor method, and the delivery options associated with the futures contract. The conversion factor determines the cheapest-to-deliver cash instrument that is priced by the futures contract; proper consideration of this factor increases profits from an arbitrage. The four delivery options are the quality option (which is related to the conversion factor), the timing option (when during the expiration month to deliver), the wild card option, and the end-of-the-month option.

One method for determining whether arbitrage exists is to calculate the implied repo (financing) rate; this chapter examines the factors that affect the calculation of this rate. We then show how to use the delivery options. In fact, whether T-bond arbitrage transactions are profitable often is directly associated with the price and proper use of these delivery options.

The type of financing arrangement is the important consideration affecting short-term interest rate futures pricing. Market participants execute both pure and quasi-arbitrage. Pure arbitrage employs outside financing to obtain risk-free profits, whereas quasi-arbitrage occurs when a security currently in the portfolio is sold and replaced with an identical security for a lower cost. These strategies are important for low-cost traders in the cash markets (money center banks for Eurodollars and dealers for T-bills who execute pure arbitrage) and for those who hold Eurodollar time deposits or T-bills in their portfolios (quasi-arbitrage). However, comparisons of futures and forward rates to determine whether arbitrage exists must be made with care.

Terminology

*Accrued interest option   The right of the seller to choose when during the delivery month to deliver the T-bond into the futures contract. This choice is affected by the net financing cost.

Basis point   See Chapter 2.

*Cheapest-to-deliver   See Chapter 4.

*Conversion factor   See Chapter 4.

Delivery options   See Chapter 4.

*End-of-the-month option   The right of the seller of the futures to announce delivery on any business day of the delivery month after the market stops trading futures, namely the eight business days before the end of the delivery month. The price of the transaction is based on the last day of the futures trade.

Eurodollars   See Chapter 2.

*"Implied put option"   The end-of-the-month delivery option for T-bond futures is equivalent to providing the seller with a put option—that is, the choice of *when* to sell the T-bond at a predetermined price. The holder of the put option profits if the cash T-bond price declines during the end-of-the-month period.

*Implied repo (financing) rate   See Chapter 4.

*Invoice amount   The delivery price the buyer of the bond pays the seller at delivery.

*Quality option   The right of the seller of the futures to deliver *any* cash T-bond (T-note) that meets the specifications of the contract.

Repurchase (repo) transaction   See Chapter 4.

Squeeze   See Chapter 1.

*Wild card option   The right of the seller of the futures to announce delivery up to 8 P.M. on any business day during the delivery month, with the price based on the 2 P.M. futures close.

T-BOND FUTURES PRICING: THE COST OF CARRY FACTOR

The contract specifications, price history, and importance of the T-bond futures contract are presented in Chapter 2. This material is necessary for a complete understanding of the material on pricing T-bond futures. Although this section concentrates on T-bond pricing and arbitrage, the same factors affect T-note pricing and arbitrage.

The Cost of Carry Model for Debt Futures

The basic cost of carry model presented in Chapter 4 is amended for the income received from the coupons of the bond as follows:

$$P_{FAIR} = P_C(1 + i - r)^t \tag{9-1}$$

or, equivalently, for continuously compounded rates,

$$P_{FAIR} = P_C e^{(i-r)t} \tag{9-2}$$

where P_{FAIR} = the fair futures price determined by the cost of carry model

P_C = the adjusted cash bond price

i = the annual financing rate

r = the coupon yield received on the cash bond

t = the number of days until the futures expiration, divided by 365

For the cash bond price to be comparable to the futures price one of these two prices must be adjusted to consider maturity and coupon between the instruments. The conversion factor method, discussed shortly, makes this adjustment. For Equations (9-1) and (9-2), it is sufficient to realize that the cash price used, P_C, has already been adjusted to be comparable to the futures price.[1]

Unlike other futures contracts, T-bond and T-note futures prices are affected by factors other than the basic cost of carry variables; that is, the **conversion factor** method and the **delivery options** also are important factors. However, the cost of carry model represents a reasonable first approximation to the fair futures price.

[1] Technically, the cash bond used must be the "cheapest" cash bond, as shown later in the chapter.

The Financing Versus Income Relationship

The Relationship.   The financing versus income (or *net* cost of carry) relationship is the most important factor affecting the pricing of T-bond futures contracts. Thus, let us use the cost of carry model to compare the theoretical price difference between the futures and cash markets to the actual price difference between these markets.[2]

The net cost of carry model in Equations (9-1) and (9-2) shows that the greater the income received on the bond, the lower the futures price. This relationship occurs for two reasons: (1) the larger the income, the smaller the *net* cost of financing the position; and (2) the purchase of the futures contract is an alternative to holding the cash bond, and a long position in futures does *not* receive coupon payments. The timing of the coupon income received also affects the futures price, since cash income received earlier in the period creates greater reinvestment returns. Thus, the payment schedule of one T-bond versus another affects the net financing cost.

The net cost of carry relationship from Equation (9-1) is altered and rearranged slightly to show the relevance of the income versus financing relationship in comparison to the futures versus cash price:

$$\frac{P_F - P_C}{P_C} = (i - r)t \tag{9-3}$$

where P_F = the futures price. Note that the left side of Equation (9-3) is simply the percentage difference between the futures and cash prices, while the right side of the equation is the time-adjusted percentage difference between the financing rate and the income rate. Using time simply adjusts for the effect of convergence as the time until futures expiration shortens.

Equation (9-3) shows that when the financing rate is *less* than the income received (that is, when the yield curve is upward sloping for cash T-bonds), then the futures price must be less than the cash price and the deferred futures prices must be less than the nearby futures price. Conversely, when the financing cost is above the income received on the bond, the futures price must be greater than the cash price and the deferred futures price must be greater than the nearby futures price. This relationship exists for T-bond futures when there is a downward sloping yield curve for cash T-bonds. Exhibit 9-1 shows examples of these price structures.

One can justify the relationship between the cash and futures prices in Equation (9-3), as well as the structure of futures prices in Exhibit 9-1, by determining the net cash flow to an arbitrageur who buys the cash bond and sells the futures contract. For an upward sloping yield curve (the left set of numbers in Exhibit 9-1), the arbitrageur earns more money from holding the cash bond than is paid out due to the financing cost. Thus, the arbitrageur is willing to accept a *loss* from buying cash at a price above the sales price of the futures [thus $P_C > P_F$ on the left side of Equation (9-3)], as long

---

[2] This approach and example ignore the complications for pricing caused by the conversion factor method. In reality, one should determine the cheapest-to-deliver bond by employing the conversion factor method, and then employ *that* bond for the price spread analysis between the futures and cash markets shown in this section. This example arbitrarily picks one bond. Also, the financing rate for the arbitrageur, usually the overnight repo rate, is more appropriate than the T-bill rate employed here. A more detailed analysis of the cheapest-to-deliver bond is provided later in this chapter.

EXHIBIT 9-1

The Effect of the Net Financing Rate on T-Bond Futures Prices

$i - r < 0$ or $r > i$ Upward Sloping Yield Curve (Normal Curve)		$i - r > 0$ or $i > r$ Downward Sloping Yield Curve (Inverted Curve)	
March	103-10	March	62-04
June	102-09	June	62-14
September	101-09	September	62-28
December	100-12	December	63-04
March	99-18	March	63-15

where i = the financing rate

r = the rate of income on the T-bond

as this loss is equal to or smaller than the difference between the income received from the bond and the financing cost [as given on the right side of Equation (9-3)]. Similarly, for a downward sloping yield curve (the right set of numbers in Exhibit 9-1), the arbitrageur loses money from the net cash flow because the financing cost is greater than the income received from owning the asset. Consequently, the arbitrageur wants a larger difference $P_F - P_C$ [on the left side of Equation (9-3)] as the time until futures expiration increases in order to offset the loss from the net financing cost [on the right side of Equation (9-3)].

An Example.   To examine the pricing relationship for T-bond futures let us assume that $i = 8\%$, $r = 7\%$ (an inverted curve relationship), and there are six months until the expiration of the futures contract. Equation (9-3) provides the appropriate financing/income relationship:

$$(i - r)t = (8\% - 7\%)^{182}/_{365} = \tfrac{1}{2}\%$$

Thus, the financing cost is greater than the income received. Consequently, the actual percentage price difference $(P_F - P_C)/P_C$ from the left side of Equation (9-3) also should be approximately $\frac{1}{2}\%$. For a bond priced near 100, if $P_F - P_C > {}^{16}/_{32}$, then the profit from delivering the bond would be *greater* than the extra financing cost from the bond's financing rate being above the coupon yield.[3] Conversely, a price difference $P_F - P_C$ that is *less* than ${}^{16}/_{32}$ would create an overall loss for the arbitrageur, since the loss generated from the financing rate, being greater than the coupon yield, would be larger than the gain obtained from the $P_F - P_C$ price spread.

Table 9-1 provides an example of the cost of carry and actual price differences (on one particular day) for a positively sloped yield curve environment—that is, a declining price structure for the futures prices. The most important result shown in this table

---

[3] The profit arising from $P_F - P_C$ occurs since the arbitrageur buys the cash bond at P_C, while *receiving* a price of P_F from the sale of the futures contract. This price difference becomes a profit when the cash bond is delivered into the futures contract.

Table 9-1 Bond Cost of Carry Versus Actual Cash/Futures Differences

(1) Contract Expiration	(2) Months to Expiration	(3) Futures Price	(4) Financing Rate[a]	(5) Percentage Difference Cost of Carry Difference[b]	(6) Actual Difference[c]	(7) Error (5) − (6)
March	2	97-14	6.87	− .22	− .19	−.03
June	5	97-03	6.87	− .55	− .55	0
September	8	96-28	7.18	− .68	− .77	+.09
December	11	96-24	7.25	− .87	− .90	+.03
March	14	96-20	7.30	−1.05	−1.03	−.02
June	17	96-15	7.35	−1.20	−1.19	−.01

[a] The financing rate is obtained from the Treasury yield curve based on the relevant number of months until maturity.
[b] The cost of carry difference is based on the right side of Equation (9-3) in the text, using a coupon yield of 8.2% for the cash bond.
[c] The actual price difference is calculated by taking the percentage difference between the futures price and the cash bond price—that is, the left side of Equation (9-3). The cash bond price is 97-20 in January for the hypothetical 8% coupon bond due in 17 years. Using an 8% coupon simplifies the calculations by avoiding an adjustment for the conversion factor.

is that the actual price differences (column 6) are almost identical to the theoretical cost of carry differences (column 5) for all futures expirations. Thus, the prices for the T-bond futures are justifiable, and the futures and cash markets are linked.

T-BOND FUTURES PRICING: CONVERSION FACTORS AND DELIVERY OPTIONS

The Conversion Factor Method

The Chicago Board of Trade developed the conversion factor method (CFM) so that traders, hedgers, and arbitrageurs could deliver a wide range of cash T-bonds into the T-bond futures contract. Although previous promotional literature from the exchange stated that the T-bond contract "prices" a hypothetical long-term cash T-bond with an 8% coupon, no such cash bond exists. Therefore, the CBT allows *any* T-bond with at least 15 years left to maturity (or 15 years to the first call date, if the bond is callable) to be used as a deliverable bond. Since each cash bond possesses different coupon and maturity characteristics, and therefore different prices, a method is needed to adjust the futures price for the delivery of different cash bonds. The conversion factor is a factor multiple that adjusts the futures price in order to obtain a fair cash bond price for delivery purposes.

The advantage of the conversion factor method is that it allows futures shorts to deliver a wide range of T-bonds, thereby guaranteeing a sufficient number of cash bonds to avoid a **squeeze** or other delivery problems. The disadvantage of the CFM is that it creates several biases that determine the "best" bond to deliver and thus affects the pricing of the futures contract. Because of these biases, the CFM creates *one* and *only one* **cheapest-to-deliver** bond at any given time. Consequently, the futures market uses this cheapest-to-deliver instrument to price the T-bond and T-note futures contracts.

The delivery price and conversion factor for T-bonds is specified as follows: the **invoice amount** (the delivery price the buyer pays the seller) when a T-bond is used for delivery is

$$\text{IA} = (\text{SP})\,(\$100{,}000 \text{ face amount})\,(\text{CF}) + \text{AI} \qquad (9\text{-}4)$$

where IA = the invoice amount (i.e., the value the buyer pays the seller)

    SP = the futures settlement price as a percentage of par, based on the closing price of the futures contract on the day that the delivery notice is given

    CF = the conversion factor, which is the multiple given to the particular T-bond being delivered and is based on the maturity and coupon of the bond

    AI = accrued interest on the cash bond being delivered

The conversion factor is determined as follows:

1. One must find the time until maturity (or to the call date) for the appropriate bond, as measured in *complete* three-month quarters of a year. Parts of a quarter are ignored in the maturity calculation; that is, the maturity calculation is rounded *down* to the nearest quarter. The first day of the delivery month for the futures contract is employed to begin the calculation for the time to maturity of the bond.

2. The bond's term to maturity and coupon rate are used in conjunction with Equation (9-5) to determine the conversion factor. Tables also are available.

The following equation calculates the conversion factor for an even number of quarters:

$$\text{CF}_E = \sum_{t=1}^{N} \frac{C_t/(1 + .08/2)^t}{100{,}000} \qquad (9\text{-}5)$$

where CF_E = the conversion factor for a bond with an even number of quarters before maturity or call date

    t = the time period, measured semiannually[4]

    N = the number of semiannual periods

    C_t = the cash flows for the bond (the coupons and principal received during time t). *The annual coupon is divided by two to obtain C_t,* since coupons are paid semiannually. This equation uses a face value of \$100,000, although one can use any par value as long as the denominator is adjusted accordingly.

If the number of quarters is odd, then the following adjustment is made to determine the conversion factor:

$$\text{CF}_O = [\text{CF}_E + C_t/100{,}000]/(1 + .08/2)^{.5} - (C_t/2)/100{,}000 \qquad (9\text{-}6)$$

with C_t = semiannual coupon

    CF_O = conversion factor for a bond with an odd number of quarters

The CF procedure given in Equations (9-5) and (9-6) uses the hypothetical 8% coupon of the futures contract as the discount rate, and divides by 100,000 in order to obtain a conversion factor per \$1 of the face value of the bond. In other words, the conversion factor represents the price of the bond *if the yield was 8%,* divided by

---

[4] The time variable, t, is measured in semiannual periods for compounding purposes when coupons are paid semiannually. Thus, the 8% discount rate is divided by two in order to equate the compounding periods to one-half of the year.

the par value of the bond. For example, a $100,000 par value bond with a maturity of 17½ years and a coupon of 10% would have a price of $118,660 if the yield was 8%; thus, the conversion factor for this bond would be 118,660/100,000 or 1.1866. Example 9-1 shows how to find the conversion factor and invoice amount for a T-bond.

One basic use of the conversion factor is to compare the cash bond and futures prices. Equation (9-7) shows how to obtain the adjusted cash price used earlier in Equations (9-1) and (9-2):

$$\text{Adjusted } P_C = \text{actual } P_C/\text{CF} \tag{9-7}$$

Similarly, the futures price is converted into an adjusted futures price to compare to the cash price; that is,

$$\text{Adjusted } P_F = P_F \cdot \text{CF} \tag{9-8}$$

These comparisons are important when one wants to find the cash bond priced by the futures contract.

EXAMPLE 9-1
Example of Calculating Conversion Factors and Invoice Amounts

BOND CHARACTERISTICS

February 15, 2015, bond with a coupon of 7⅝%

Delivery for June 11, 1993

Futures settlement price on position day of 83-16, or 83.50 as a percent of par

CONVERSION FACTOR (EVEN NUMBER OF QUARTERS)
As of June 1, 1993, the bond in question is callable in 21 years, 8 months, and 14 days; rounding down to the nearest quarter we obtain 21 years and 2 quarters (43 semiannual periods). Using Equation (9-5) we calculate a conversion factor value stated in terms of a per dollar of par value figure (the conversion factor is determined as a ratio of the par value). Present value calculations are used to obtain 20.37079 (the present value of an annuity for 43 periods and 4%) and .18517 (the present value of a single amount for 43 periods and 4%).

$$\text{CF} = \frac{\sum_{t=1}^{n} [C_t/(1 + .08/2)^t]}{100,000} \tag{9-5}$$

$$\text{CF} = \frac{\sum_{t=1}^{43} [(^{7625}\!/_2)/(1.04)^t + 100,000/(1.04)^{43}]}{100,000}$$

$$\text{CF} = \frac{3812.5(20.37079) + 100,000(.18517)}{100,000}$$

$$= \frac{77,663.66 + 18,516.82}{100,000}$$

$$= .96180$$

continued next page

continued

INVOICE AMOUNT

Accrued interest is determined based on the number of days since the last coupon payment, which was February 15. Thus, interest accrues from February 15, but is not paid until August 15. There are 116 days from (but not including) February 15 to and including June 11. The semiannual coupon is $3812.50 for a $100,000 face bond (i.e., $7\frac{5}{8}\% \times \$100,000/2$). To determine the amount of accrued interest we multiply the daily interest amount by the number of days of accrued interest, as follows:

$$\text{Daily interest} = \frac{\text{semiannual coupon amount}}{\text{number of days between coupons}}$$

$$\text{Daily interest} = \frac{3812.50}{181} = \$21.06354$$

$$\text{Accrued interest} = \$21.06354 \times 116 \text{ days} = \$2443.37$$

Thus, the invoice amount is

$$\text{Invoice amount} = (\text{futures settlement price} \times \$100,000)$$
$$\times \text{ conversion factor} + \text{accrued interest} \quad (9\text{-}4)$$

$$\text{Invoice amount} = (.835 \times \$100,000) \times .9618 + \$2443.37$$

$$= \$82,753.67$$

CALCULATION OF CONVERSION FACTORS
FOR AN ODD NUMBER OF QUARTERS

To illustrate how Equation (9-6) is implemented to determine the conversion factor for an odd number of quarters, let us use the above results, with the one exception of having the bond mature in 21 years and 3 quarters. Employing Equation (9-6) we find

$$\text{CF}_o = [\text{CF}_E + C_t/100,000]/(1 + .08/2)^{.5} - (C_t/2)/100,000 \quad (9\text{-}6)$$

$$\text{CF}_O = [.96180 + (^{7625}\!/_2)/100,000]/(1 + .08/2)^{.5} - (3812.50/2)/100,000$$

$$= [(.96181 + .038125)/(1.04)^{.5}] - .0190625$$

$$= .999925/1.01980 - .0190625$$

$$= .961445$$

Table 9-2 provides conversion factors for various futures expiration dates for those T-bonds that are eligible for delivery. Note that bonds with coupons below 8% have conversion factors below one, and bonds with coupons above 8% have conversion factors above one. Also, after adjusting for coupon effects, longer-term bonds have higher conversion factors than shorter-term bonds. The conversion factor tables are available quarterly from the Chicago Board of Trade.

Table 9-2 T-Bond Conversion Factors for Specific Bonds

T-Bonds, Eligible for Delivery February, 1993

	Coupon	Maturity	Amount ($ Bins.)	Mar 93	Jun 93	Sep 93	Dec 93	Mar 94	Jun 94
1)	7⅛ᵃ	Feb 15, 2023	9.30	0.9011	0.9014	0.9015	0.9019	0.9019	0.9023
2)	7¼	May 15, 2016	18.82	0.9217	0.9218	0.9223	0.9224	0.9229	0.9231
3)	7¼	Aug 15, 2022	10.01	0.9155	0.9159	0.9159	0.9163	0.9163	0.9167
4)	7½	Nov 15, 2016	18.86	0.9474	0.9474	0.9478	0.9478	0.9482	0.9482
5)	7⅝	Nov 15, 2022	10.30	0.9578	0.9577	0.9579	0.9579	0.9581	0.9580
6)	7⅞	Feb 15, 2021	11.01	0.9860	0.9862	0.9860	0.9863	0.9861	0.9863
7)	8	Nov 15, 2021	32.33	1.0000	0.9998	1.0000	0.9998	1.0000	0.9998
8)	8⅛	May 15, 2021	11.75	1.0139	1.0137	1.0138	1.0136	1.0137	1.0135
9)	8⅛	Aug 15, 2021	12.01	1.0137	1.0139	1.0137	1.0138	1.0136	1.0137
10)	8⅛	Aug 15, 2019	20.01	1.0134	1.0136	1.0134	1.0135	1.0133	1.0134
11)	8½	Feb 15, 2020	10.06	1.0546	1.0547	1.0543	1.0544	1.0540	1.0540
12)	8¾	May 15, 2017	18.19	1.0795	1.0790	1.0789	1.0784	1.0783	1.0778
13)	8¾	May 15, 2020	10.01	1.0825	1.0820	1.0820	1.0816	1.0816	1.0811
14)	8¾	Aug 15, 2020	21.01	1.0825	1.0825	1.0820	1.0820	1.0816	1.0816
15)	8⅞	Aug 15, 2017	14.02	1.0928	1.0927	1.0922	1.0921	1.0915	1.0914
16)	8⅞	Feb 15, 2019	19.25	1.0946	1.0946	1.0941	1.0940	1.0935	1.0934
17)	9	Nov 15, 2018	9.03	1.1081	1.1075	1.1074	1.1068	1.1067	1.1061
18)	9⅛	May 15, 2018	8.71	1.1208	1.1202	1.1200	1.1194	1.1192	1.1186
19)	9¼	Feb 15, 2016	7.27	1.1298	1.1295	1.1287	1.1284	1.1277	1.1273
20)	9⅞	Nov 15, 2015	6.90	1.1943	1.1932	1.1926	1.1916	1.1910	1.1899
21)	10⅝	Aug 15, 2015	7.15	1.2706	1.2697	1.2683	1.2674	1.2659	1.2649
22)	11¼	Feb 15, 2015	12.67	1.3322	1.3310	1.3293	1.3280	1.3262	1.3249
23)	11¾	Nov 15, 2009-14	6.01	1.3403	1.3374	1.3351	1.3322	1.3298	1.3267
24)	12	Aug 15, 2008-13	14.76	1.3485	1.3458	—	—	—	—
25)	12½	Aug 15, 2009-14	5.13	1.405	1.4022	1.3987	1.3957	1.3921	1.3891
26)	13¼	May 15, 2009-14	5.01	1.4692	1.4652	1.4617	1.4575	1.4539	—

ᵃ Most recently auctioned 30-year Treasury bond eligible for delivery.

(*Source:* Chicago Board of Trade.)

Biases Caused by the Conversion Factor Method and the Cash Market

The Issues. The CF uses only whole quarters when it is calculated. Rounding down the time to maturity of the bond to the nearest quarter, in conjunction with using the 8% hypothetical yield as the discount rate, cause biases in calculating the exact value of the bond for delivery purposes. In addition, biases relating to how the cash market values certain bonds causes such bonds to be preferred for delivery at certain times. These two effects create what is known as the "cheapest-to-deliver" cash T-bond. An approximation method to determine the cheapest bond based on the CFM is the one with the *lowest* cash price/conversion factor ratio, or more accurately the lowest (cash price + accrued interest)/conversion factor ratio. In symbolic terms we have

$$CTD = MIN_B[(P_0 + AI)/CF] \tag{9-9}$$

where CTD = cheapest-to-deliver

MIN_B = the minimum ratio for all deliverable bonds

P_0 = the current price

Conversion Factor Biases.   The objective of the conversion factor method is to adjust the futures price in order to conform to the maturity and coupon differences of the individual cash bonds available for delivery. The CF is the price of the bond *if* the yield is 8%, divided by its par value. Theoretically, this conversion is intended to *equate* the relative value of all bonds by finding the value of the cash bond *relative* to the futures benchmark 8% bond such that the *invoice amount per dollar of investment is the same for all deliverable bonds.* Unfortunately, the CF adjustment creates biases in the relative conversion factors among the bonds available for delivery such that there is a difference between the calculated conversion factors and the fair conversion values of the bond. Daigler (1993) details the causes and effects of these conversion factor biases as well as the cash market biases created by the preferences of market participants for certain bonds.

The most important of these biases often occurs when rates are above 8%, since the use of an 8% discount rate overvalues distant cash flows. Since low coupon bonds have much of their cash inflow in the principal repayment, these bonds possess conversion factors that are larger than warranted. Similarly, long maturity bonds tend to be overvalued by the conversion factor method. Consequently, the long position would pay more for these low coupon bonds than they are worth, since the conversion factor method sets the payment price for delivery purposes.

Cheapest-to-Deliver Bond

The biases created by the conversion factor method and the cash market preferences, plus the effect of differing ratios of financing costs to coupon returns for different bonds, cause some bonds to provide a higher rate of return for arbitrage positions than other bonds. In fact, typically there is only *one* bond that is best for an arbitrageur for a given market yield. This bond is called the cheapest-to-deliver bond and is used by the futures market for pricing purposes.[5] Thus, in order to maximize profits, arbitrageurs choose this cheapest-to-deliver bond (if it has sufficient liquidity) when exercising their arbitrage strategy. As previously shown in Equation (9-9), an approximation method for finding the cheapest-to-deliver bond is to determine the bond with the lowest $(P_0 + AI)/CF$. This procedure considers all of the biases, but it does not consider the importance of the size of the coupon in relation to the financing cost.

The cheapest-to-deliver bond often changes as interest rates change, since the relative arbitrage profits for the different bonds change. These profits change because (1) the ratios and rankings of the prices of the bonds to the conversion factors are affected as the rate of interest changes, due to the biases discussed previously, and (2) the ratio of the financing rate to the coupon rate affects the net profit of the arbitrage position over the term of the holding period.

Delivery Options

The delivery options[6] for the T-bond and T-note futures contracts affect the pricing of these contracts and the size of the arbitrage profits for these futures, especially during the month of delivery. These options provide choices to the seller of the futures concerning when and what to deliver. For T-bond and T-note futures the seller can deliver on *any* day during the delivery month that the exchange is open. The delivery options are a benefit to the futures seller who is instituting arbitrage, since these options increase profits on the transaction. If arbitrageurs fully employ these options, then the corresponding futures contracts should sell at a lower price than they would if no such options existed.

The delivery options for T-bond and T-note futures are as follows:

- The **quality option:** The futures seller is given the option to deliver *any* of the cash T-bonds that meet the specifications of the contract—that is, any T-bonds having at least 15 years to delivery or 15 years to the first call date. The quality option makes it difficult to undertake "long arbitrage" (i.e., selling cash bonds and buying futures) since the arbitrageur does not know which T-bond will be delivered into the long futures contract that is being held.[7] However, the quality option is very beneficial to the short arbitrageur because it allows the arbitrageur to choose the "cheapest-to-deliver" T-bond that fulfills the delivery specifications of the futures contract. The quality option is the result of the conversion factor and cash market biases discussed previously.

- The **accrued interest** (or "timing") **option:** The seller has the option of choosing *when* to deliver the cash bond during the futures expiration month. If the costs of financing exceed the current income from the coupon (the accrued interest), then this option provides an incentive to deliver early in the month. Similarly, if the financing costs are less than the accrued interest, then it is profitable (all other timing options being ignored) to deliver toward

---

[5] Often the "best bond for delivery" is described as the only bond providing a *positive* return for a given market yield. In fact, because of the delivery options described below, even the best bond typically does not have a positive return before consideration of the value of the delivery options.

[6] Gay and Manaster (1984, 1986) examine the concepts covered in this section in detail.

[7] A long arbitrage spread strategy may be profitable. Thus, the arbitrageur would buy the nearby futures and sell the deferred futures. After receiving delivery of the bond from the nearby futures, the arbitrageur would hold the bond for three months and then deliver it into the deferred contract.

the end of the delivery month. This accrued interest option is typically used in conjunction with the other delivery options to provide the seller with opportunities during the delivery month to execute the quality and "wild card" options.

- The **wild card option:** The seller can announce delivery up to 8 P.M. Central time on any trading day during the delivery month. If delivery is undertaken, then the 2 P.M. futures closing price is employed to calculate the invoice price. If the cash price drops significantly after the futures close the arbitrageur can (a) use the cash market to obtain any needed cash bonds at a lower price in order to complete the arbitrage position, or (b) substitute the new cheapest-to-deliver bond for the bond currently being held by the arbitrageur.

- The **end-of-the-month option:** The final invoice price for delivery is set based on the closing price on the final trading day of the futures contract (eight business days before the end of the month). However, the seller has an additional seven business days after this date to announce delivery. Consequently, with the "end-of-the-month option" the seller can wait to determine what happens in the final cash trading days of the delivery month in order to obtain the best price to buy any needed cash bonds, or to obtain a cheaper-to-deliver bond in order to complete the arbitrage position.

The importance of the quality option is associated with the cheapest bond, as determined from the biases of the conversion factor method. The benefits of the accrued interest option are based on whether the net financing cost is positive or negative, as well as providing the arbitrageur a choice as to when to execute the other delivery options. Strategies for how to employ the "wild card" and "end-of-the-month" options, and their importance, are discussed below.

IMPLEMENTATION OF T-BOND ARBITRAGE STRATEGIES

The logical arbitrage strategy of buying the less expensive instrument and selling the more expensive one is applicable for T-bond futures arbitrage. Short futures arbitrage is implemented with the following transactions:

- The cheapest long-term cash T-bond is purchased.
- The T-bond futures contract is sold.
- Funds are borrowed to finance the holding of the cash bond until the delivery date.
- At the optimum time during the delivery month the cash bond is delivered into the futures contract.

For optimum arbitrage results, the cheapest-to-deliver bond must be determined by considering the biases created by the conversion factor method and the delivery options must be used wisely to maximize the profits from the arbitrage transaction. The cash flows of this cash-and-carry trade result in Equation (9-1) and are equivalent to the examples given in Chapters 4 and 8, with the exception of the bond coupons representing the cash inflows during the arbitrage.

Pure Arbitrage Transactions

Government bond dealers are the primary pure arbitrageurs in the T-bond futures market. Bond dealers keep a significant amount of cash T-bonds in inventory, are not affected by cash transactions costs, and finance 99% of their inventory. In fact, a large percentage of the open interest in T-bond futures is attributable to the activity of these dealers in arbitraging *and* hedging their inventory. These arbitrage positions are financed via the repo market, as discussed below.

In general, major arbitrageurs take a cash position in the most recent T-bond issue, which is also the most liquid. They then switch to the cheapest bond at a later date; one reason for initially buying the bellwether bond is that less liquid bond prices are affected if an institution decides to take a large position in a particular bond. While certain cash T-bonds are sometimes in short supply near futures expiration, which would adversely affect the liquidity of the bond if it was the cheapest-to-deliver, *dealers* typically do not have a significant problem obtaining any particular bond.[8]

Long pure arbitrage involves difficulties not present in short T-bond arbitrage. Namely, the short side of the futures transaction determines *which* T-bond is delivered via the quality delivery option. Someone transacting a long arbitrage situation (i.e., buying the futures and shorting the cash security) does not know which cash bond will be delivered. Thus, the arbitrage transaction would not be perfect. The only alternatives for the long arbitrageur are (1) to sell the T-bond delivered and purchase the appropriate bond to cover the original short sale, an expensive and risky undertaking; (2) to forecast which T-bond will be delivered in order to determine the correct bond and number to sell so as to equate the futures and cash dollar price changes, also a risky undertaking; or (3) buy the nearby futures and sell a deferred futures, thereby allowing redelivery of the bond originally received, although the potential profits of such a strategy are uncertain. These costs and uncertainty reduce the attractiveness of generating a long pure arbitrage with T-bond futures.[9]

Financing via Repo Transactions

To finance a T-bond arbitrage dealers use a **repurchase (repo) transaction.** A repo agreement allows the arbitrageur to sell *temporarily* a cash T-bond to receive funds, with the agreement that the T-bond will be repurchased after a stipulated time period. Thus, the interest rate associated with borrowing the funds received from the repo (with the T-bond acting as collateral) is the appropriate financing rate. However, the arbitrageur still receives the coupon income from the bond.

A term repo is a repurchase agreement for a specific period of time—for example, the length of the arbitrage. In view of the illiquidity of the term repo market and the inflexibility associated with longer-term financing, most dealers use the overnight repo market for financing. The overnight repo market is extremely liquid. The rates on overnight repo transactions are slightly less than the federal funds rate. Consequently, a series of overnight repos are employed to obtain funds for the arbitrage. Since overnight repo rates can change daily, this financing procedure creates uncertainty concerning the total financing cost.

---

[8] See Nancy Johnson's discussion of the paper by Resnick and Hennigar (1983) for comments on how institutional factors affect arbitrage trades.

[9] Nancy Johnson (see the discussion to Resnick and Hennigar, 1983), who is a trader in the T-bond pit, states that "when a contract expires—there is this heavy trading going on during the last 60 seconds because the long wants it to close one way and the short wants it to close another to give the advantage to their arbitrage."

FOCUS 9-1
When Arbitrage Is Risky: The Salomon Squeeze

In May 1991, Salomon Brothers, in conjunction with several large hedge funds, controlled more than 90% of the $12.26 billion two-year T-note auction, even though Treasury rules stipulate a single dealer can hold only 35% of any praticular issue via the auction. Salomon benefited from cornering this issue by squeezing the other players in the market. The following events are based on reports by Mitchell (1991a, 1991b). A particular issue starts trading in the "when-issued" or preissue market one week before the issue is sold by the Treasury. Historically, new two-year issues start increasing in price before the auction as the result of demand and then fall after the issue is sold. Many players on Wall Street arbitrage this predictable price change in the cash market by selling short the two-year new issue before the auction and buying another equivalent cash position or buying futures contracts. For this auction, traders had shorted $5 billion of the two-year issue. However, in May of 1991, Salomon owned such a large part of the T-notes that those who shorted the issue had to either buy it back or borrow the issue from Salomon at an expensive price. In fact, one week after the auction the T-notes at $100\,^{5}\!/_{32}$, which was an increase from the auction price of $99\,^{29}\!/_{32}$. The $^{8}\!/_{32}$ price difference caused a price appreciation of $30.6 million on the original issue. The unusually high price persisted for more than a month after the auction. Salomon subsequently paid a fine and payments of $290 million. Salomon also slipped from No. 5 in the underwritings to No. 10.

This squeeze created losses of more than $100 million for many large and small bond players across the United States. In fact, since the squeeze, many bond traders have lost their jobs and funds playing the new issue game have gone bankrupt, exited the market, or scaled down operations. Continental Bank even gave up its role as a primary dealer after losing money in the May auction. This perception of a lack of fairness in the markets concerns regulators because investors could decide to avoid the U.S. bond market, causing interest rates on government debt to increase. When new Salomon officers and the government investigated this squeeze, they found other situations where Salomon and other investment houses attempted to control government bond and note issues. Moreover, dealers have shared information about their bids on Treasury issues for the past decade. This cooperation prompted the Treasury to change the auction rules to allow a wider group of players into the auction process.

Determining the Cheapest Bond

A more accurate approach to determine the cheapest-to-deliver T-bond than the approximation method of Equation (9-9) is to determine the implied repo rate or the annualized rate of return on the arbitrage position. Specifically, one calculates the implied repo rate for *each* deliverable bond; the bond with the *highest* **implied repo rate** is the cheapest. The implied repo rate is preferable to the approximation methods noted above, since arbitrageurs desire accurate values for transactions involving tens of millions of dollars. The calculations to determine the implied repo rates consider the following factors:[10]

- The cost to purchase the cash instrument.
- The amount received when the cash T-bond is delivered into the T-bond futures contract.
- The net cost of carry, that is, the cost of financing the cash position held less the value of the accrued interest and reinvestment income from coupons received.

Table 9-3 shows the important variables needed to determine an implied repo rate and an annualized return. These calculations determine the cheapest bond for delivery and for arbitrage transactions. The bond with the highest annualized rate of return (column 8), or equivalently the highest implied repo rate (column 10), is the cheapest-to-deliver bond. Note that no bond in column 8 of Table 9-3 has an implied repo rate above the financing rate (alternatively, no bond has a positive annual rate of return) based solely on the cost of carry formulation. Thus, column 8 shows that the delivery options have value that is not captured by the cost of carry model. Hence, the delivery options affect the pricing of the futures contract.

The basic idea of the process shown in Table 9-3 is to compare the invoice price for futures delivery with the cash market price of the bond (adjusted for the net financing cost); the cash T-bond with the most advantageous difference is the cheapest-to-deliver bond. Each of the relevant variables affecting the arbitrage returns are expressly considered in Table 9-3, with the relevant equations listed below the column titles.[11] Note the significant differences in net returns in column 8 for bonds with different coupons and maturity dates. Thus, the conversion factor and cash market biases have major effects on the potential arbitrage returns for the deliverable Treasury issues.

As interest rates change, the relative rates of return for the bonds in Table 9-3 also change, since

- The prices of the cash bonds are affected in different degrees as the rate of interest changes.
- The conversion factor biases affect the deliverable bonds differently as interest rates change.
- The ratio of the financing rate to the coupon rate affects the net profit of the arbitrage position over the holding period.

Consequently, the cheapest-to-deliver bond often *changes* as the interest rates change. A computer program can determine at what point another bond becomes the new cheapest-to-deliver. This change in the cheapest bond can have significant effects on the arbitrageur's profits; hence, arbitrageurs often sell a bond if it is no longer the cheapest-to-deliver and buy the new cheapest bond. Such transactions must consider the effect of transactions costs. Moreover, arbitrageurs use the delivery options to maximize their profits when interest rates change and a new cheapest-to-deliver bond comes into existence.

---

[10] See Arak, Goodman, and Ross (1986) for two equations and their associated procedures to determine the implied repo rate for T-bond arbitrage situations.

[11] The effects of some of the delivery options are considered shortly.

Table 9-3 Bond Implied Repo Rates

(1)	(2)	(3)	(4)	(5)	(6)	(7)	(8)	(9)	(10)
		Cash Prices	Conversion Factor	Adjusted Futures Price[a]	$P_F^* - P_c$	Net Cost of Carry[b]	Annualized Rate of Return[c]	Coupon (points)	Implied Repo Rate
Coupon	Maturity			$P_F(4) = P_F^*$	$(5) - (3)$	$(3) \times [i - (1)/(3)] \times t$	$\{[(6) - (7)]/(3)\}\{1/t\}$	$(1) \times t$	$\{[(6) + (9)]/(3)\}\{1/t\}$
7.25	2016	81.7188	.9171	81.4786	-.2401	-.0274	-.0211	.8938	.0649
7.5	2016	84.2188	.9444	83.9040	-.3147	-.0317	-.0273	.9247	.0587
9.25	2016	101.6875	1.1375	101.0598	-.6277	-.0622	-.0451	1.1404	.0409
8.75	2017	96.9063	1.0833	96.2444	-.6618	-.0513	-.0511	1.0788	.0349
9.875	2015	107.8750	1.2054	107.0923	-.7827	-.0737	-.0533	1.2175	.0327
8.875	2017	98.2188	1.0977	97.5238	-.6950	-.0528	-.0530	1.0942	.330
10.625	2015	115.4063	1.2871	114.3508	-1.0555	-.0863	-.0681	1.3099	.0179
10.375	2012	110.2500	1.2284	109.1357	-1.1143	-.1102	-.0739	1.2791	.0121
9.125	2018	101.0938	1.1262	100.0558	-1.0379	-.0531	-.0790	1.1250	.0070
12.5	2014	130.2500	1.4498	128.8057	-1.4443	-.1601	-.0800	1.5411	.0060
11.25	2015	121.5938	1.3534	120.2411	-1.3526	-.0978	-.0837	1.3870	.0023
12	2013	125.1250	1.3917	123.6438	-1.4812	-.1528	-.0861	1.4795	-.0001
11.75	2014	124.3438	1.3764	122.2845	-2.0592	-.1302	-.1258	1.4486	-.0398

Numbers in parentheses refer to the relevant columns.

[a] The futures price P_F is 88–27.

[b] A negative value indicates that the coupon income is greater than the financing cost; i is the financing rate = 8.60% annually; t is the proportion of the year the position is held, where $t = {}^{45}/_{365}$ in this example. One could employ compounded rates such as in Equations (9-1) and (9-2) instead of simple rates of return.

[c] An arbitrageur considers the cost of financing the accrued interest paid when the bond is purchased and the reinvestment returns from coupons received during the holding period. However, these technicalities only complicate the example and do not significantly change the results. See Schneeweis, Hill, and Philipp (1983) for consideration of these variables.

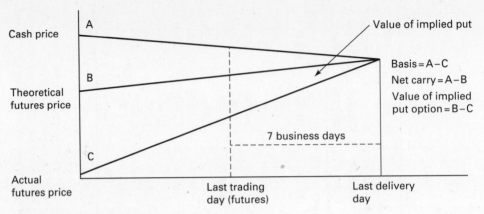

Figure 9-1 The implied put option.

Using the Delivery Options

The "wild card" and "end-of-the-month" delivery options increase the arbitrageur's profits by providing an opportunity to obtain deliverable bonds at prices below the futures invoice price. These options allow the futures short to announce delivery of cash bonds either hours or days *after* the futures delivery price is set. Consequently, any advantageous changes in the cash bond prices after the futures price is set are used by an arbitrageur to increase profits. These two delivery options create an option for the seller concerning *when* the cash bond can be delivered; this option is called an **implied put option,** and is illustrated in Figure 9-1. These delivery options can be separated into the "tail" of the arbitrage and changes in the cheapest bond.

The "Tail" of the Arbitrage. The wild card and end-of-the month options are beneficial to arbitrageurs since they purchase only $100,000/CF par value of the current cheapest cash bond per one short futures contract. This ratio equates the dollar change in the cash position with the dollar change in the futures position, since the futures price follows the cheapest cash price. However, $100,000 par value of cash must be delivered into the futures contract; the arbitrageur still needs $100,000(1 − 1/CF) par value of a deliverable bond (if the conversion factor is greater than one). This remaining $100,000(1 − 1/CF) par value per futures contract is called the "tail" of the arbitrage; that is,

$$\text{Tail} = 100,000(1 - 1/CF) \qquad (9\text{-}10)$$

The wild card and end-of-the-month options are used to determine *when* the remaining tail of the cash bonds for the arbitrage is purchased to maximize profits. If cash prices decline after the 2 P.M. futures market closing time (or after trading ceases) during the delivery month, the arbitrageur can purchase the deliverable cash bonds at a cheaper price than the invoice price calculated from the futures price, increasing the profits of the arbitrage.[12] However, if the cheapest bond has a conversion factor near one, the tail

---

[12] The existence of these delivery options causes the futures price to sell at a discount to P_C/CF, at least in the month of delivery. For additional discussion of the delivery options, see Meisner and Labuszewski (1984); Arak, Goodman, and Ross (1986); and Daigler (1993).

EXAMPLE 9-2
Use of the Tail of the Arbitrage

> If the cheapest-to-deliver bond has a conversion factor of 1.21, then the amount of additional par value of bonds needed to deliver into the futures when 10 futures contracts are short is
>
> $$\text{Tail} = \$100,000(1 - 1/CF)(\text{number of futures contracts})$$
>
> $$= \$100,000(1 - 1/1.21)(10)$$
>
> $$= \$100,000(1 - .82645)(10)$$
>
> $$= \$173,550$$
>
> If the price of the cheapest bond declines 2 points between 2 and 8 P.M. on a delivery day (the wild card option) or after trading ceases at the end of the month (the end-of-the-month option), then the futures seller profits by
>
> $$\$173,550(.02) = \$3471$$

of the arbitrage is negligible and this portion of the wild card and end-of-the-month options is near zero. Example 9-2 illustrates this use of the tail of the arbitrage.

Changes in the Cheapest Bond. Another application of both the wild card and end-of-the-month options is to react to a change in interest rates that *changes* the *cheapest* bond after the futures market closes by selling the entire amount of the cash bond currently being held and buying the new cheapest bond to be purchased. The wild card option then is used to deliver cash bonds that have an invoice amount above their cost; the end-of-the-month option is used for the same purpose during the last seven days of the month when futures no longer trade.[13] Although transactions costs do have to be considered before implementing such a switch, such substitutions are often made by arbitrageurs, as shown by Arak, Goodman, and Ross (1986). Finally, it is important to note that the potential profit associated with changes in the cheapest bond and the wild card and end-of-the-month delivery options is greatest for bonds with the largest conversion factors; that is, the value of these options is an increasing function of the conversion factor. Daigler (1993) discusses the empirical analysis of the value of the delivery options.

Quasi-Arbitrage as an Alternative to a Short-Term Investment

T-bond futures quasi-arbitrage is equivalent to creating a synthetic short-term cash instrument. Thus, the purchase of a long-term cash T-bond and the sale of a T-bond futures contract should theoretically provide a return similar to a cash T-bill. If the return on this synthetic instrument is greater than the return on a short-term T-bill, then

---

[13] To use the end-of-the-month option, the arbitrageur equates the par value of the cash and the futures on the last futures trading day. This strategy allows the arbitrageur to take advantage of either price increases or price decreases in the cash market without incurring any risk. See Arak and Goodman (1987) for a description of the process.

executing the quasi-arbitrage is beneficial. However, the discussion above shows that the delivery options on the T-bond futures contract are valuable to the seller of the futures contract. Consequently, anyone who institutes a quasi-arbitrage transaction must also employ these delivery options in order to receive the full value from the short futures position. Since the futures price is lower due to these delivery options, calculating the synthetic short-term interest rate without including the option values typically shows the quasi-arbitrage strategy to be inferior to the short-term instrument.

MUNICIPAL BOND FUTURES PRICING

The pricing of Municipal Bond Index (MBI) futures is based on the basic cost of carry model, although the muni futures are settled in cash and an index is employed as the equivalent "cash security." The composition of the Index used to value the futures contract is explained in Chapter 2. The process to value the bonds is completed as follows: Each bond in the Index is priced daily by five municipal bond brokers between 1:45 P.M. and 2 P.M. (Chicago time), and also between 10:45 A.M. and 11 A.M. during the futures expiration month. The highest and lowest prices for each bond are dropped, and the remaining three prices are averaged as an appraisal value. This value is divided by a conversion factor in order to standardize each bond for coupon and maturity differences. Thus, the Index is composed of hypothetical 8%, 20-year bonds. These standardizations reduce potential problems when the composition of the Index changes. Changes in the Index are considered on the 15th and the last day of the month; changes occur when bond ratings change and when bonds are inactive. The MBI portfolio changes *entirely* about every three months. This situation complicates the pricing and arbitrage of the futures contract.

The use of a conversion factor creates the same type of biases as exist for the T-bond and T-note futures, except that these biases are less important for pricing purposes because no cash bonds are delivered. On the other hand, it creates difficulties for arbitrageurs because the futures contract is settled in cash but the arbitrage must be arranged based on actual bonds. The influence of the tax rate on the effective municipal bond yields also complicates the valuation process.

Hamilton, Hein, and Koch (1994) develop a cost of carry model for MBI futures and explain the influence of the factors that affect the pricing of these futures. Their empirical tests show that the prices of these futures contracts do not consider transactions costs on all of the bonds in the index. Thus, arbitrageurs may be using cash portfolios that are smaller than the 40-bond futures specifications *or* arbitrageurs may not be revising their portfolios as the composition of the index changes. Kochin and Parks (1988) found that the pricing of MBI futures when it started trading in 1985 traded at large discounts to fair values, creating profits for long futures arbitrage. Before transactions costs, profitable opportunities switched several times from long to short futures arbitrage through 1986.[14] After transactions costs, quasi-arbitrageurs in a 25% tax bracket typically gained $1500 to $4500 per contract through the September 1986 futures expiration.

---

[14] The authors did not investigate 1987 and later because of a change in the proposed tax code.

PRICING AND ARBITRAGE FOR SHORT-TERM INTEREST RATE CONTRACTS

The Cost of Carry Model

There are three methods for determining the pricing of **Eurodollar** and T-bill futures contracts, all of which employ the cost of carry formulation. The first is directly applying the cost of carry equation by using prices of the instruments; this approach is most feasible for T-bill futures. The second is comparing the forward rate to the futures rate. The third is comparing the implied repo (financing) rate to the actual financing rate.[15] Chapter 4 presents the latter two methods. Although each method is based on the same model, convenience of data availability or industry practice often dictates the use of one method over another.

Using the cost of carry model for short-term interest rate futures contracts provides more exact pricing, and therefore lower profit opportunities, than other futures contracts. This is because there are fewer difficulties with exact matching of cash instruments with futures delivery requirements (essentially no tracking risk), transactions costs are minimal, and all cash inflow effects are known and occur at the end of the period.

The basic cost of carry concept is applicable for Eurodollar and T-bill futures pricing without adjustment, since there are no intermediate cash flows and a *specific* cash instrument is priced by the futures contract. "Delivery" for Eurodollar and T-bill futures is limited to a two-day period and the interest received is adjusted depending on which day is employed, eliminating any uncertainty concerning the deliverable instrument.[16] However, the exact specification of the cost of carry concept does differ slightly between T-bill and Eurodollar futures pricing because of the method of interest payment and pricing on the instrument.

Using Forward and Implied Financing Rates

A number of market participants, as well as empirical pricing and arbitrage studies, use either the forward rate or implied repo (financing) rate for pricing and arbitrage decisions. The forward rate determined from the term structure of interest rates is compared to the interest rate implied from the futures price in order to determine whether a significant difference exists between the cash and futures prices. Alternatively, the implied financing rate is compared to the actual financing rate to determine whether the futures pricing is fair or arbitrage exists. Chapter 4 illustrates how to calculate the forward and implied financing rates.

[15] Technically, the implied repo rate is relevant for T-bill and T-bond futures only, since repurchase agreements are used for financing these contracts. However, the equivalent concept of the implied financing rate is applicable for Eurodollar future pricing via term loans.

[16] Recall that Eurodollar futures are settled in cash. Starting with the June 1983 contract, the expiration date of the T-bill futures is set based on the maturity of the one-year cash T-bill. In addition, 180-day and/or 90-day T-bills are also deliverable into the futures contract. Typically, the specific cash T-bill maturity that can be delivered into the futures contract is uniquely priced in relation to the other cash T-bills with similar maturities (maturities within 2 weeks of the deliverable cash bill). In other words, the additional demand for the deliverable T-bill often drives down its yield in relation to the nearby maturities. Although one can hypothesize that this pricing discrepancy should not occur in *perfect* markets, the evidence shows that futures market activity may have an important effect on this specific T-bill maturity.

Exhibit 9-2 states the circumstances when short or long futures arbitrage is appropriate, *and* the type of transactions needed to implement the arbitrage.[17] For example, a short futures arbitrage is appropriate when the forward rate is greater than the futures rate (i.e., the forward *price* is less than the futures price); thus, the arbitrageur sells the more expensive futures and invests in a longer-term cash instrument. How funds are obtained for financing arbitrage transactions is examined below.

Arbitrage Issues

Arbitrage for short-term interest rate futures is often transacted by pure arbitrageurs; that is, the transaction is executed via borrowed funds. Quasi-arbitrage strategies to obtain higher alternative returns also are employed—for example, when a financial institution already owns the short-term instrument.

Pure arbitrageurs often borrow funds at the overnight financing rate and roll over the overnight loan for as long as the arbitrage transaction is kept in place, rather than obtaining a loan for the entire period. This financing method is particularly relevant for T-bill futures arbitrage. Of course, this procedure creates a risk that the financing rate will change over the term of the arbitrage, causing the transaction to no longer be "risk-free." This practice sometimes is referred to as speculating on changes in the overnight interest rate. Consequently, the method of financing becomes an important consideration for short-term interest rate futures arbitrage.

Quasi-arbitrage occurs when risk-free profits exist for a combination of cash and futures transactions for which the arbitrageur already owns an equivalent cash security. For example, assume that a financial institution owns three-month cash T-bills. If the institution can obtain an additional profit by (1) selling the currently owned three-month T-bills and (2) creating a synthetic three-month T-bill using futures contracts and longer maturity cash T-bills, then a quasi-arbitrage opportunity exists. Alternatively, one can think of quasi-arbitrage in terms of returns: A financial institution should choose the transaction that provides the largest risk-free return over the period in question, either the cash T-bill or the synthetic cash-futures T-bill.

Quasi-arbitrage is essentially equivalent to pure arbitrage except for one major factor: The quasi-arbitrageur does *not* have to finance the cash position since the cash T-bill is already being held in the portfolio. Hence, the relevant comparison becomes the alternative rate of return with the currently held cash instrument, rather than the cost of borrowed funds.

EURODOLLAR FUTURES PRICING AND ARBITRAGE

Eurodollar Futures Pricing

The concepts of Eurodollar time deposit futures pricing and T-bill futures pricing are very similar because both contracts are based on cash assets with 90 days to maturity and both have a two-day window for delivery/settlement. Differences that exist relate to the characteristics of the two futures and cash markets. In particular, Eurodollar time deposit futures settle in cash rather than in delivery of a cash instrument. Hence, there is a small risk that the futures contract will have a different interest rate than a

---

[17] Exhibit 9-2 is a combination of exhibits originally presented in Chapter 4.

EXHIBIT 9-2
**Decision Rules and Strategies for Using the Implied Repo Rate
and the Forward Rate**

Chapter 4 discusses and develops the following rules to implement arbitrage strategies. These transactions are examined in the "Strategies" discussed in this chapter.

**If the implied repo (financing) rate > short-term financing rate* (i.e., if the for-
ward rate > futures rate), then for**

- Short pure arbitrage:

    Obtain funds from borrowing for three months.
    Invest in the six-month interest-bearing instrument.
    Sell the futures contract.

- Short quasi-arbitrage (as an alternative to buying or holding for three months):

    Invest in the six-month interest-bearing instrument from existing funds.
    Sell the futures contract.

**If the implied repo (financing) rate < short-term financing rate* (i.e., if the for-
ward rate < futures rate), then for**

- Long pure arbitrage:

    Obtain funds from borrowing for six months.
    Invest in a three-month interest-bearing instrument.
    Buy the futures contract.

- Long quasi-arbitrage (as an alternative to buying or holding for six months):

    Invest in a three-month interest-bearing instrument from existing funds.
    Buy the futures contract.

*For quasi-arbitrage, the relevant risk-free rate is substituted for the financing rate.

selected bank Eurodollar time deposit, since the cash settlement price for futures is
based on an average rate from eight banks. (Twelve banks are contacted for quotes, but
the two highest and two lowest quotes are dropped.) However, the competition for dollar transactions in London is so intense that any difference is only a few **basis points.**
Eurodollar cash loans and time deposits quote London Interbank Offer Rates
(LIBOR), with Eurobanks dominating the cash activity in Eurodollars. The spread between the bid rate (the rate the London bank pays for deposits) and the ask rate (the rate
the bank earns on funds loaned out) is small, typically 12½ basis points. This spread
is consistent regardless of the maturity, as shown by Grabbe (1986, p. 224). Rates are
money market rates. Of course, the loan rate depends on the perceived risk of the borrower. If the borrower is a U.S. money center bank that is conducting arbitrage, then
the risk is considered to be unimportant. Rates to corporations are higher. The Eurodollar futures are based on the bid LIBOR rate, since the futures reflect the *time deposit*
rate. Also recall that the Eurodollar futures are based on a $1 million time deposit,
whereas T-bill futures track a $1 million *face* value T-bill that sells at a discount.

Eurodollar Futures Arbitrage Strategies

Eurodollar futures arbitrage is transacted simply by borrowing from or lending to a Eurobank in London. Being able to obtain or lend funds in large amounts at small spreads simplifies the arbitrage strategies significantly.

Pure Arbitrage Strategies. Strategy 9-1 illustrates a pure short arbitrage for Eurodollar time deposit futures. Execution of the pure long strategy is shown in Strategy 9-2. Note that these strategies can be implemented by using different dates than those employed here; for example, for the pure short strategy one could initially borrow for one month and lend for four months to correspond to a futures contract expiring in one month. Notice that no funds from the arbitrageur are needed to implement the pure short arbitrage. Hence, a profitable pure arbitrage transaction can be repeated many times until the arbitrage profits disappear when the prices readjust or until no additional financing is available to the arbitrageur. Example 9-3 illustrates how to calculate potential profits from a short pure Eurodollar arbitrage.

Quasi-Arbitrage Strategies. Quasi-arbitrage strategies are implemented by Eurobanks that deal in Eurodollars. For example, let us assume that banks are borrowing longer-term and lending shorter-term, which is typically the case if they expect interest rates to increase. If futures are expensive (futures rates < forward rates), then a short quasi-arbitrage with futures provides a higher return than the cash market alternative. Similarly, if banks are lending longer-term and borrowing shorter-term in anticipation of lower interest rates, then when futures are cheap (futures rates > forward rates) buying futures provides a higher return than the cash transactions.

Forward/Futures Considerations

There are several considerations that affect the profitability of the Eurodollar arbitrage calculation, especially if it is based on a forward/futures comparison; namely,

- The effect of the financing procedure must be considered. It is possible that overnight financing using LIBOR rates can be employed for arbitrage. Since the forward/futures comparison implicitly employs a term financing rate, the effect of overnight financing would have to be considered in the analysis.
- The timing of the cash and futures quotes is critical. London time is 6 hours ahead of Chicago time; hence closing quotes for time deposits are closer in time to the opening of the Chicago Eurodollar futures than to its close.
- Calculation of forward rates when an irregular number of days is employed provides a distorted forward price, since odd-day time deposits are not often quoted. Consequently, Eurodollar rates for *monthly* intervals are typically employed to determine the forward rates, even if this is an approximation of the actual length of the time period in question.[18]

---

[18] For example, as noted by Kawaller (1988), if today is February 13 and the March Eurodollar futures stops trading on March 18, then the time span from value date to value date is 34 days. One could then calculate a forward rate for 91 days based on cash quotes of 34 and 125 (34 + 91) days. However, using one- and four-month time deposit rates would provide more accurate results because of the liquidity in these rates.

STRATEGY 9-1
A Pure Short Eurodollar Arbitrage

The diagrams of the strategies illustrated in this chapter show the *source of the funds received* and *how the funds are invested*. These strategies are executed only if there is a relative mispricing between the futures and cash instruments, creating an arbitrage opportunity. *When* these transactions are initiated is stated in the specific strategies listed below the diagrams.

The situation is as follows: futures rate < forward rate (futures price > forward price).

A + B create a *long* forward position for time $T + 3$ to $T + 6$.

C is a *short* futures position expiring at $T + 3$.

A: Invest in Eurodollar time deposits for six months

B: Borrow funds for three months with a Eurodollar loan at LIBOR	C: Borrow funds for three months as of $T = 3$ with a Eurodollar loan (rate locked-in with a sale of futures at $T = 0$)

| 0 | Three months | Six months |
| T | $T + 3$ | $T + 6$ |

At time T (now):

Borrow funds for three months with a Eurodollar loan at LIBOR.

Invest for six months by placing funds in a Eurodollar time deposit.

Sell a futures contract now to *lock-in a cheap interest rate (high price)* for Eurodollar time deposits starting in three months.

At time $T + 3$:

Futures contract expires; daily marking-to-market means one has collected or paid the difference between the original futures rate and the cash maturity rate.

Original three-month loan comes due; pay interest on three-month loan (partially or fully offset by interest earned but not yet collected on six-month time deposit).

Take out new three-month loan at LIBOR (rate locked in from original futures sale).

Consequence: if interest rates rise from T to $T + 3$, then the higher cost of a new loan is offset from profits on the short sale of a futures contract (and vice versa).

At time $T + 6$:

Collect interest on six-month time deposit.

Pay interest on second three-month loan.

- Only certain arbitrageurs have access to Eurodollar borrowings at 12½ basis points above the investment rate, namely financial institutions with good credit risks. Others must pay higher rates, and therefore the likelihood of obtaining arbitrage profits is reduced.[19]
- There could be marking-to-market of the futures, although this is minor in most situations.

[19] The full bid-ask spread must be included in the numerical analysis, since one borrows funds at the higher rate and invests (lends) them at the lower rate; see Kawaller (1988).

STRATEGY 9-2
A Pure Long Eurodollar Arbitrage

This situation is as follows: futures rate > forward rate (futures price < forward price).

A + B create a *short* forward position for time $T + 3$ to $T + 6$.

C is a *long* futures position expiring at $T + 3$.

A: Borrow funds for six months with Eurodollar loan at LIBOR

B: Invest in three-month Eurodollar time deposit	C: Invest in three-month Eurodollar time deposit starting at $T + 3$ (rate locked in with a purchase of futures at $T = 0$)

0	Three months	Six months
T	$T + 3$	$T + 6$

At time T (now):

Borrow funds for six months with a Eurodollar loan at LIBOR.

Invest for three months by placing funds in a Eurodollar time deposit.

Buy a futures contract now to *lock in a high interest rate (cheap price)* for Eurodollar time deposits starting in three months.

At time $T + 3$:

Futures contract expires; daily marking-to-market means one has collected or paid the difference between the original futures rate and the cash maturity rate.

Original three-month time deposit comes due; collect interest on deposit.

Take out new time deposit for three months (rate locked in from original futures purchase).

Consequence: If interest rates rise from T to $T + 3$, then the loss on the long futures position is offset by higher interest on a three-month time deposit starting at $T + 3$.

At time $T + 6$:

Collect interest on second three-month time deposit.

Pay interest on six-month loan (partially or fully offset by the interest earned on time deposits).

T-BILL FUTURES PRICING AND ARBITRAGE

The concepts of pricing T-bill futures are adequately explained in the earlier section on short-term interest rate futures pricing. Since T-bills are deliverable into the futures contract, no pricing risk exists for arbitrage transactions. T-bill futures arbitrage transactions are equivalent to Eurodollar futures arbitrage except that T-bills and repurchase agreements are used.

EXAMPLE 9-3
A Pure Eurodollar Short Arbitrage

The following rates are quoted for Eurodollar time deposits (bid) and loans (ask):

Three-month Eurodollars	8.475–8.60
Six-month Eurodollars	8.575–8.70
Eurodollar futures	91.75

Pure arbitrage transactions:

At time T: borrow funds for three months at 8.60%; invest for six months by placing funds in Eurodollar time deposit at 8.575%; sell a futures contract now to lock in low interest rate for Eurodollar loan starting in three months (loan rate is 12 ½ basis points above time deposit rate of 8.25%—that is, 8.25% + .125% = 8.375%).

At time $T + 3$: pay interest on original three-month loan that comes due; take out new three-month loan with an interest rate locked in with expiring futures.

At time $T + 6$: collect interest on six-month time deposit; pay interest on second three-month loan.

Interest income on six-month time deposit:

$$\$1,000,000(.08575)\,(^{180}\!/_{360}) = \$42,875$$

Interest paid on first three-month loan:

$$\$1,000,000(.0860)\,(^{90}\!/_{360}) = \$21,500$$

Interest on second three-month loan:

$$\$1,021,500(.08375)\,(^{90}\!/_{360}) = \$21,387$$

Net profit: $\$42,875 - \$21,500 - \$21,387 = -\$12$

A loss is created because of the 12 ½ basis point difference in the time deposit and loan rates.

Short Arbitrage with Repurchase Agreements

The strategy typically employed to obtain funds for a short T-bill futures arbitrage is to use repurchase agreements. A repo agreement allows the arbitrageur to sell a cash T-bill *temporarily* in order to receive funds, with the agreement that the T-bill is repurchased after a given period of time. The arbitrageur pays interest on the repo for the time the borrowed funds are in use, whereas the T-bill is used as collateral to guarantee that the funds are repaid. All transactions are completed simultaneously. Although interest is paid on the funds received from the repurchase agreement, the arbitrageur receives interest on the cash T-bill purchased. Hence, the difference between the T-bill and repo interest rates is a critical factor for this type of arbitrage. Of course, the relationship between the rates of the cash T-bill and the T-bill futures contract is also an important factor in determining if an arbitrage should be initiated, as well as determining the size of the arbitrage profits.

Implementing T-Bill Futures Arbitrage with Repos

T-bill futures arbitrage typically is initiated by using repo agreements. Since the repo market is an active and liquid market, it is easy to initiate an agreement for standard maturity dates. Funds for the arbitrage are obtained from executing either a term repo or a series of overnight repos. The term repo is a loan for the entire arbitrage period, in our example a loan for three months. The interest rate paid on the repo agreement is known before the arbitrage transaction is initiated.

Alternatively, a series of overnight repos is executed when daily loans are obtained, with the cash T-bill being used as collateral. The interest rate paid on the overnight repos can change daily. Hence, this type of arbitrage is *not* risk-free, but rather depends on the behavior of interest rates over the period of the arbitrage. Hence, the use of overnight repos is essentially speculating on the short-term interest rate. An advantage of using a series of overnight repos is that the arbitrageur can close the arbitrage whenever conditions warrant—for example, when prices change to such an extent that most of the profit potential on the arbitrage transaction is realized. Moreover, overnight repos are a very liquid market and represent the majority of the arbitrage transactions. The overnight repo market is the key financing market because primary fixed-income dealers use this market to finance their holdings of T-bills and T-bonds. The rates on overnight repo transactions are slightly less than the Fed funds rate.

Comparing forward and futures rates for T-bill arbitrage has problems equivalent to those discussed for Eurodollar futures. The most important factor affecting the forward/futures comparison is the financing rate. In fact, if we carefully compare the pure arbitrage, quasi-arbitrage, and futures/forward procedures, we find that the interest rates and prices for the instruments used in the arbitrage transactions are basically the same. Only the implied financing rate differs. Another difference between the procedures is that the forward rate model concentrates on the second period of the transaction, whereas the pure and quasi-arbitrage transactions concentrate on the first period of the transaction (the first three months in the examples). Traders emphasize the first period, since the first period is their holding period. In general, all of the approaches examine the same type of transaction, but the empirical evidence shows that the different assumptions concerning financing costs can be critical in determining whether arbitrage profits exist and how futures contracts are priced.

An Example of Short Pure Arbitrage

Example 9-4 provides a basic numerical example of a pure short arbitrage with T-bill futures. The data is taken from late 1982, a time when interest rates were volatile and expectations concerning inflation differed significantly for the three-month versus six-month time periods. The overnight repo rate is employed as the appropriate financing rate for funds. Since this rate is used in our example as the financing rate for the entire three-month period, we are implicitly assuming that the *repo rate does not change*. The example shows that an arbitrage profit of $3071 was possible before transactions costs by using the overnight repo rate; this profit is due to two factors:

1. The major differences in interest rates between the futures and the six-month T-bill, and between the six-month T-bill and the repo rate.
2. The use of the overnight repo rate of 8.25% instead of the term repo rate of 9.7%; use of the term repo eliminates this profit.

EXAMPLE 9-4
An Example of a Pure Short T-Bill Arbitrage

On September 20, 1982, the following rates were in effect:

90-day cash T-bill bid	7.74%
180-day cash T-bill bid	9.42%
Dec 82 T-bill futures price	90.25
Repo rates: overnight	8.25%; three-month, 9.70%.

Prices for the T-bill cash and futures positions and the cost of the repo are calculated as follows:*

$$\text{T-bill price} = \text{face value} - \frac{(\text{discount rate})(\text{face value})(\text{days to maturity})}{360}$$

Interest cost on repo = (principal)(repo rate)(days/360)

Price of the 180-day T-bill = $1MM − (.0942)($1MM)(180)/360 = $952,900

Price of the 90-day T-bill = $1MM − (.0774)(1MM)(90)/360 = $980,650

Value of the futures = $1MM − (.0975)($1MM)(90)/360 = $975,625

Interest cost on repo = ($952,900)(.0825)($^{90}/_{360}$) = $19,654

A pure arbitrage transaction is initiated as follows:

At time T: buy six-month cash T-bill; fund purchase with three-month repo transaction; sell futures contract.
At time $T + 3$: deliver original six-month T-bill into futures contract.

Return on six-month T-bill held for three months (interest received + gain from price difference between cash and futures rates):

Futures price − cost of six-month T-bill = $975,625 − $952,900 =		$22,725
Interest cost on repo transaction	=	−$19,654
Net profit per $1,000,000 transaction (before transactions costs)	=	$3,071

Note: Using the overnight repo makes the implicit assumption that interest rates will remain constant. Moreover, since technically this would be a series of overnight repo transactions, the correct interest is found by determining $P_t e^{it} − P_t$ or $952,900e^{.0825(90/360)} − 925,900 = \$19,858$. Using the term three-month repo rate creates interest of $23,108.
*$1MM = $1 million.

Short Quasi-Arbitrage

A short quasi-arbitrage transaction involves buying a long-term cash T-bill and a short futures contract to create a synthetic three-month T-bill that is equivalent to the three-month cash T-bill originally held in the portfolio. Thus, the new position is equivalent to the old cash position, except that a higher return is earned on the synthetic position.

The factors affecting the existence and size of the quasi-arbitrage profits are the rates on the three- and six-month cash T-bills and the price of the futures contract. Transactions costs are typically insignificant, although the initial sale of the three-month cash T-bill originally held in the portfolio does create an extra set of costs in comparison with the pure arbitrage transactions. Alternatively, the financial institution could decide whether the cash-only strategy or the synthetic strategy is better *before* any security is purchased for the portfolio. This alternative return approach reduces transactions costs.

As hinted at above, which alternative return strategy provides a superior return can be determined by comparing the cash three-month rate with the synthetic three-month rate. In general, whether quasi- or pure arbitrage strategies are profitable can be determined by comparing forward and futures rates, or by determining the implied repo rate, as discussed in Chapter 4.

Example 9-5 provides a basic numerical example of a short quasi-arbitrage transaction. The appropriate quasi-arbitrage trades in this example guarantee a return that is $3375 higher than the cash-only transaction. Note that this profit is *not* affected by the overnight versus term repo financing assumptions since the financial institution is choosing between alternative strategies and no funds are borrowed to finance the transaction.

SUMMARY AND LOOKING AHEAD

This chapter examines long-term and short-term futures pricing and arbitrage. The cost of carry model links the futures to the underlying cash prices. This pricing link provides justification to use futures as a hedging mechanism. The conversion factor method creates *one* cheapest-to-deliver bond for T-bond futures arbitrage purposes.

EXAMPLE 9-5
An Example of a Short T-Bill Quasi-Arbitrage

See Example 9-4 for data, equations, and prices of cash and futures T-bills.
  Quasi-arbitrage transactions:

  At time T: sell three-month cash T-bill currently in portfolio; purchase six-month cash T-bill; sell T-bill futures contract for delivery in three months.
  At time $T + 3$: deliver original six-month cash T-bill into futures contract.

Opportunity loss on original three-month T-bill:

$$\text{Face value} - \text{cost} = \$1,000,000 - \$980,650 = -\$19,350$$

Return on six-month T-bill held for three months (interest received + gain from price difference between cash and futures):

$$\text{Futures price} - \text{cost of six-month T-bill} = \$975,625 - \$925,900 = \underline{\$22,725}$$
$$\text{Net gain from arbitrage (alternative return strategy)} = \$ \ 3,375$$

However, the pricing and arbitrage of these contracts are complicated by the biases that arise from the conversion factor method and cash market preferences and by valuing the delivery options. Overall, short T-bond arbitrage provides substantial profitable opportunities. Others also need to consider the factors that influence pricing since (1) speculators need to know the fair price of the futures, and (2) hedgers can use the delivery options if they carry a short futures position into the delivery month, short-term interest rate pricing, and arbitrage.

Pure and quasi-arbitrage procedures for short-term interest rate contracts are discussed at length, with specific short and long arbitrage strategies illustrated for Eurodollar and T-bill futures contracts. In general, the type of financing used to create these arbitrage transactions is critical. The following chapter examines duration and immunization.

BIBLIOGRAPHY

Arak, Marcelle, and Laurie S. Goodman (1987). "Treasury Bond Futures: Valuing the Delivery Options," *The Journal of Futures Markets,* Vol. 7, No. 3, pp. 269–286.

Arak, Marcelle, Laurie S. Goodman, and Susan Ross (1986). "The Cheapest to Deliver Bond on the Treasury Bond Futures Contract," *Advances in Futures and Options Research,* Vol. 1, Part B, pp. 49–74.

Daigler, Robert T. (1993). *Financial Futures Markets: Concepts, Evidence, and Applications.* New York: Harper Collins.

Gay, Gerald, and Steven Manaster (1984). "The Quality Option Implicit in Futures Contracts," *Journal of Financial Economics,* Vol. 13, No. 3, September, pp. 353–370.

Gay, Gerald, and Steven Manaster (1986). "Implicit Delivery Options and Optimal Delivery Strategies for Financial Futures Contracts," *Journal of Financial Economics,* Vol. 16, No. 1, May, pp. 41–72.

Grabbe, J. Orlin (1986). *International Financial Markets.* New York: Elsevier.

Hamilton, Thomas R., Scott E. Hein, and Timothy W. Koch (1994). "The Pricing of Municipal Bond Index Futures," The Journal of Futures Markets, Vol. 14, No. 5, August.

Kawaller, Ira (1988). "Determining the Fair Value for Eurodollar Futures," *Market Perspectives,* Vol. 6, No. 3, April, pp. 1, 3.

Kochin, Levis A., and Richard W. Parks (1988). "Was the Tax-Exempt Bond Market Inefficient or Were Future Expected Tax Rates Negative?" *Journal of Finance,* Vol. 43, No. 4, September, pp. 913–931.

Meisner, James F., and John W. Labuszewski (1984). "Treasury Bond Futures Delivery Bias," *The Journal of Futures Markets,* Vol. 4, No. 4, Winter, pp. 569–577.

Mitchell, Constance (1991a). "Critical Issue: Did Salomon Seek to Control 2-Year Sale?" *The Wall Street Journal,* August 19, p. A4.

Mitchell, Constance (1991b). "Salomon's 'Squeeze' in May Auction Left Many Players Reeling," *The Wall Street Journal,* October 31, pp. A1, A6.

Resnick, Bruce G., and Elizabeth Hennigar (1983). "The Relationship Between Futures and Cash Prices for U.S. Treasury Bonds," *The Review of Research in Futures Markets,* Vol. 2, No. 3, pp. 282–299. "Discussion," pp. 300–313.

Schneeweis, Thomas R., Joanne M. Hill, and Michael B. Philipp (1983). "Hedge Ratio Determination Based on Bond Yield Forecasts," *The Review of Research in Futures Markets,* Vol. 2, No. 3, pp. 338–349.

PROBLEMS

*Indicates more difficult problems.

9-1 Financing vs. Income Relationship

In order to improve your understanding of the financing and income relationship and its effects on the linkages between the cash and futures markets, you are given the following information:

Futures price	93-24
Cash bond price	99:25
Days until futures expiration	90
Financing rate	7.0%
Income rate	7.25%

Determine the percentage difference for the net financing cost, as well as between the cash and futures price. Also, determine whether the investor gains or loses money; also, interpret the equation.

9-2 Cost of Carry Relationship

Determine from the following information whether the cost of carry method for pricing T-bond futures provides accurate results. Assume the June 1990 futures contract expires in 2 months. Also assume a coupon yield of 8.4% for the cash bond, with the cash price on the hypothetical 8% coupon bond being 93:26. Hint: Use Equation (9-3) and Table 9-1.

T-Bond Futures Expiration	Settle Price	Financing Rate
June 90	93-19	7.00%
Sept.	93-14	7.23%
Dec.	93-09	7.42%
Mar. 91	93-04	7.51%
June	92-31	7.66%
Sept.	92-26	7.68%
Dec.	92-21	7.69%

9-3 Calculating the Conversion Factor

Find the conversion factor for a 7 1/8% coupon bond (paying coupons semiannually) with a $100,000 face value, maturing in 24 years 6 months, that is deliverable into a futures contract expiring in 4 months.

9-4 Calculating the Invoice Amount for a T-bond

A T-bond matures April 12, 2008–2013 with a coupon of 10%. The current futures settlement price is 79-00. Compute the invoice amount when the bond is delivered into the futures on September 15, 1991. Assume a conversion factor of 1.212. The last interest payment was made on April 12.

9-5   Conversion Factor and Invoice Amount

A 7⅜% T-note has a $100,000 par value and 8½ years until maturity. Its semiannual coupon was paid today, the current settlement price is 91:10, and we are within the futures expiration month.

a. Calculate the futures invoice amount of this note. (*Hint:* You need to calculate the conversion factor.)

b. What is the invoice amount if the note has two months until the next coupon, and all the other variables are the same?

9-6   Conversion Factor for an Odd Number of Quarters

Find the conversion factor for an 8¾% coupon bond (paying coupons semiannually) with a $100,000 face value, maturing in 15 years 8 months that is deliverable into the futures contract expiring in 4 months.

9-7   Cheapest-to-Deliver Bond Using the Approximation Method

Find the cheapest-to-deliver bond deliverable into the December T-bond futures as of October 14, using the approximation method of $(P_C + \text{AI})/\text{CF}$. Interest is paid on the 15th of the relevant month for each bond. Use Table 9-2 in the text to find the conversion factors. (Use 182 days for the half year.)

T-Bond	Coupon	Price
May 2016	7.25%	92:11
Nov. 2016	7.5%	94:29
Aug. 2019	8.125%	101:22
Feb. 2020	8.5%	105:30
Feb. 2021	7.875%	99:8
May 2021	8.125%	102:8

*9-8   Cheapest-to-Deliver Bond

Use the implied repo rate method to find the cheapest-to-deliver bond when the financing rate is 8.0%, the position is held 93 days, and the September futures price is 95-14.

Bond	Coupon	Maturity	Decimal Cash Price	Conversion Factor
A	7¼%	May 15, 2016	88.9375	.9200
B	7½%	Nov 15, 2016	91.4375	.9463
C	7⅞%	Feb 15, 2021	95.9375	.9858
D	8⅛%	May 15, 2021	98.9688	1.0141

*9-9   Accrued Interest Option

Show how an arbitrageur's profits are affected by the timing option (accrued interest option), given the following data. Assume that a position is taken on March 15. Calculate the net financing cost from the initiation of the position until June 1, 11, and 25. Assume a 7⅝% T-bond with a maturity date of February 15, 2010, a price of 100:00 and a financing rate of 9%.

*9-10 Wild Card Option

At 2:00 P.M. the futures invoice amount is established and the cheapest-to-deliver T-bond is a 7.5% coupon T-bond with 20 years to maturity, with a calculated CF = .9505. Today is the coupon payment date. If yields increase from 8.2% to 8.25% between 2 P.M. and when the cash market closes, how much does one's profit increase if one waits until after yields change to deliver? (For simplicity, assume that the bond held at 2 P.M. is sold at that time, with the new bond purchased after the yield changes.)

9-11 Tail of the Delivery Option

An arbitrageur has sold short 20 T-bond futures contracts. The par value of the bonds originally purchased to equate the dollar value of bonds to the dollar value of futures is therefore $100,000/CF times the number of futures contracts sold.

a. If the conversion factor of the cheapest-to-deliver bond is 1.18, what is the dollar amount of additional bonds needed to be purchased to be delivered into the futures contract at the delivery date?

b. How can an arbitrageur increase his or her profits by using the tail of the position in conjunction with the delivery options?

9-12 Eurodollar Short Arbitrage

A bank interested in an arbitrage opportunity learns that the following rates/prices are current:

Today's three-month Eurodollar loan rate	8.48%
Price of a three-month ED futures contract	91.52
Six-month Eurodollar time deposit	8.55%

Is profitable arbitrage possible? Explain the strategy you would use, and show the net profit (loss) based on a $1 million transaction. Show the timing for each transaction, as shown in the chapter.

9-13 Eurodollar Futures Short Arbitrage

Given the following data at time T:

Three-month Eurodollar rates	8.4375–8.5625
Six-month Eurodollar rates	8.530–8.655
Eurodollar futures price	91.81

Set up a short Eurodollar arbitrage. State the transactions for the strategy you would implement and calculate the size of any net profit.

9-14 Long Eurodollar Arbitrage

An arbitrageur sees an opportunity to make a risk-free profit based on a discrepancy between the Eurodollar cash market and its related futures market. From the following data, verify that a long arbitrage strategy is appropriate and state the necessary transactions and profits for the investor to take advantage of this opportunity. The bid-ask spread for the cash market is 15 basis points. Today's date is March 15.

Money rates (time deposit rate):	Eurodollar	8.5625%	(three-month)
	Eurodollar	8.75%	(six-month)

Eurodollar futures rate: June, 90.87.
Trading cost per futures contract is $50.

9-15 Pure Short Arbitrage

State the transactions for a short arbitrage with repo financing and determine the net profit for the following data:

	Rate/Index
90-day cash T-bill	9.15
180-day cash T-bill	9.30
T-bill futures expiring in 90 days	90.75
Repo rate	9.02%

9-16 Pure Short Arbitrage

Based on the information provided, state the appropriate arbitrage transactions and determine the total profit.

Price of three-month cash T-bill	$971,600
Price of six-month cash T-bill	$939,200
Price of three-month cash based on T-bill futures	$965,400
Repo rate	6.95%

9-17 Short Quasi-Arbitrage

You currently own a three-month cash T-bill. Based on the information provided, devise a short quasi-arbitrage strategy and calculate the gain from such a strategy.

Price of three-month cash T-bill	$979,600
Price of six-month cash T-bill	$959,200
Price of three-month cash based on T-bill futures	$979,900
Repo rate	7.80%

*9-18 Synthetic Short-Term Securities

On December 10 a money manager is looking for alternative ways to invest funds short-term. He can either: (1) purchase a shorter-term T-bill and hold it until maturity, or (2) purchase a longer-term T-bill and sell the March T-bill futures, creating a synthetic three-month T-bill. The money manager has nearly $1 million sitting idle that will not be needed for 100 days. Current T-bill cash and futures quotes are as follows:

T-bill maturing 3/20, yield 8.11% (100 days)
T-bill maturing 6/19, yield 8.27% (191 days)
March T-bill futures: 91.79 (91 days)

Assuming the March T-bill futures expire on the 20th, and that commissions on a futures contract are $60, what strategy yields the highest return? Calculate the profit in dollars for both strategies.

Chapter 10

DURATION, IMMUNIZATION, AND DURATION HEDGING

Overview

Duration and the related risk-reduction technique of immunization are popular methods that provide the user with information concerning the volatility of bonds and ways to hedge the cash bond portfolio, either with or *without* the use of futures contracts. Moreover, duration provides a means for determining the price change of a bond for a given change in interest rates.

Duration combines all of the factors affecting a bond price into one number. Specifically, duration considers the effects of time until maturity, coupon rate, and the yield to maturity on the price change of a bond, given a change in the market interest rate. Duration also measures the relative price sensitivity of bonds to changes in interest rates. Thus, the longer the duration, the greater the price change of the bond to a given change in interest rates. Consequently, bonds with longer durations are more volatile.

Immunization uses duration to guarantee a minimum target rate of return on the bond portfolio if the assumptions of the duration procedure are met. A consideration in determining the final portfolio value, either with or without immunization, is the role of the reinvestment rates on the cash flows received from the bond's coupon and principal payments. The role of these reinvestment rates is examined to show their effects.

Using duration to determine the appropriate futures hedge ratio is an alternative to the regression-based method for fixed-income investments. The duration-based hedge ratio considers the relative volatilities of the cash and futures instruments by computing the durations of these instruments. Here we develop the duration-based hedge ratio and then compare and contrast this approach to the regression methodology.

Terminology

Anticipatory hedge   See Chapter 6.

*Convexity   The curvature in the bond price-yield relationship; convexity creates errors when duration is employed for bond management.

Derivative   The calculus procedure that determines the small change in one variable given a small change in another variable. The value of the derivative of a curve at a given point is the slope of the line that is tangent to the curve at that point.

Dollar duration   Modified duration times the price of the bond; dollar duration is used to determine the dollar price change in a bond for a given change in yield.

*Duration   A measure of the relative volatility of a bond; it is an approximation of the price change of a bond for a given change in the interest rate. Duration is measured in units of time. It includes the effects of time until maturity, cash flows, and the yield to maturity.

*Duration-based hedge   A futures hedge used to minimize the net price change of a position, where the hedge ratio is determined on the basis of the relative durations of the cash and futures positions.

*Immunization   A bond portfolio management technique that "guarantees" a predetermined total value for the portfolio at the end of the investment period regardless of how interest rates change. Thus, immunization provides a stated target annual rate of return for the investment.

Modified duration   The duration of the bond divided by $(1 + i)$; modified duration is used to determine the approximate percentage change in the price of a bond for a given change in the yield.

*Reinvestment risk   Variability in the interest rate when coupons received are reinvested.

DURATION: THE CONCEPTS

Duration is a risk management tool for fixed-income securities. Duration identifies the risk of a bond, provides a tool for changing the risk of a bond portfolio, and through immunization, provides a means for eliminating most risk. Duration also is used with futures later in this chapter to control the risk of a bond portfolio.

Factors Affecting Interest Rates

For a given change in interest rates:

1. Longer-term bonds change more in price than shorter-term bonds; that is, bond price volatility is *directly* related to the time to maturity.
2. Higher coupon bonds change less in percentage terms than lower coupon bonds; that is, bond price volatility is *inversely* related to the coupon.

Consequently, the price change of a bond is affected by *both* the maturity and coupon of the bond. Moreover, when longer-term bonds have higher coupons, then the coupon effect on the price partially offsets the maturity effect. This combined maturity-coupon effect creates difficulties in determining *which* bonds are more volatile; in other words, maturity is an outdated method for measuring the relative volatility of bonds. In addition, the timing of the cash flows, the size of the coupon, and the realized reinvestment rates are also determinants of relative volatility. **Duration** overcomes the limitations of using only maturity as the relevant factor affecting volatility and price change by incorporating all of the above factors to determine the relative volatility of a bond.

Duration and Its Uses

Duration quantifies the relative volatility of a fixed-income instrument, incorporating the timing of the cash flows, the size of the payments, and reinvestment effects. Duration has become a popular technique for bond professionals because it is easy to use and it has a multitude of applications. Duration is employed to

- Approximate quickly the price change of a bond or bond portfolio for *any* given change in interest rates.
- Summarize in one value the cash flow characteristics of bonds (i.e., the coupon, maturity, and yield effects), thereby providing a measure of the relative volatility of bonds.
- Achieve specific bond portfolio objectives, such as immunizing the portfolio against adverse interest rate effects.

Spreadsheets can be employed to accomplish the same objectives without using duration measures. However, duration has become popular among professionals because it is used without relying on more sophisticated computer programs and because this easily understood relative measure of volatility allows quick decision making. Leibowitz (1983) states that bond portfolio managers turned to duration starting in the late 1970s because of a number of factors:

- Higher interest rates and a broader range of coupons made average maturity a less satisfactory measure of average life.
- There was a greater volatility in interest rates, which made a comparative measure of volatility necessary.
- An intermediate-term corporate bond market was developing.
- The increased focus on short-term rate-of-return and performance measures required new decision-making tools.
- Greater flexibility in the management of maturity necessitated better measures of volatility.
- Use of computer tools for bond portfolio management became standards in the industry.

Calculating Duration

Macaulay Duration. Macaulay developed the most popular measurement of duration, which is calculated by determining the ratio of the sum of the *time-weighted* present values of the cash flows to the total present value of the cash flows. Mathematically this concept is presented as follows:

$$D = \frac{\sum \text{time-weighted present values}}{\text{total present value}}$$

$$D = \frac{\sum\limits_{t=1}^{M} t\,PV_t}{\sum\limits_{t=1}^{M} PV_t} \qquad (10\text{-}1)$$

where
D = the duration of the instrument or portfolio

t = the unit of time, typically measured in years

M = the maturity of the bond, in terms of the number of periods

PV_t = the present value of the cash flows received at time t

A more descriptive definition of the Macaulay duration given in Equation (10-1) is the weighted *average time* to each bond payment (coupon and principal), where the weights are the size of the present values of each of the payments as a percentage of the total present value of all the payments. This definition is shown mathematically as

$$D = \frac{\sum\limits_{t=1}^{M} t\, C_t/(1 + i)^t}{\sum\limits_{t=1}^{M} C_t(1 + i)^t} = \frac{\sum\limits_{t=1}^{M} t\, C_t/(1 + i)^t}{PV_B} \qquad (10\text{-}2)$$

or equivalently as

$$D = \sum_{t=1}^{M} tw_t$$

such that

$$w_t = \frac{C_t/(1 + i)^t}{\sum\limits_{t=1}^{M} C_t/(1 + i)^t} = \frac{PV_t}{\sum\limits_{t=1}^{M} PV_t} = \frac{PV_t}{PV_B}$$

where
C_t = coupon amount per period, with C_M being the coupon plus principal

i = yield to maturity (interest rate in the economy for similar risk bonds)

w_i = the weights, as defined by the size of the present values of each of the payments as a percentage of the total present value of all the payments

PV_B = the present value of the bond based on the yield i

Describing the Duration Process. The denominators of Equations (10-1) and (10-2) are simply the present value of the bond. The numerator is the sum of the individual present values for each coupon payment multiplied by the associated time until payment. Thus, duration is measured in units of time, typically years. In fact, duration is the point in time at which the total present values of the cash flows of the bond before the duration value equal the total present values of the cash flows after the duration value. Figure 10-1 illustrates this point, with the dark areas of the cash flows representing the respective present values.

The key aspect of Equation (10-2) is the time factor t. The multiplication of t by the associated present values in the numerator of the duration equation causes t to be *the* critical variable affecting the duration value, as shown in Example 10-1. The procedure to calculate duration, as given by Equation (10-2) and illustrated in Example 10-1, is as follows:

1. Find the present value of each cash payment—that is, the coupons and principal.
2. Time weight the present values by multiplying each present value by the time period. This procedure associates each cash flow value to time.
3. Calculate the duration by taking the ratio of the time-weighted present values to the total present value of the cash flows of the bond.

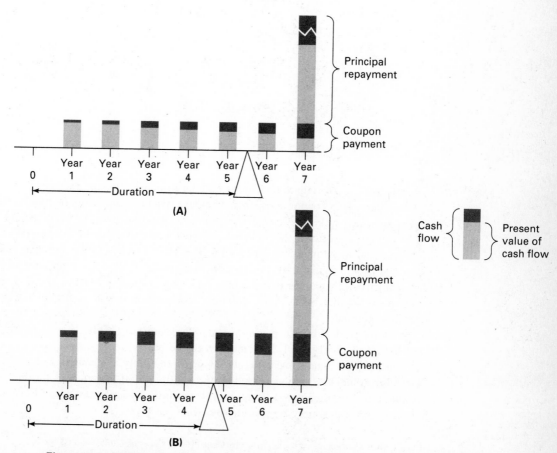

Figure 10-1 Duration: Equating present values. (A) Seven-year 7% bond. (B) Seven-year 14% bond.

EXAMPLE 10-1
Calculating Duration

A bond has a 10% coupon that is paid annually, the bond matures in five years, and the yield to maturity for an equivalent bond is 14%. The following table uses Equation (10-2) to calculate duration for the bond in question. Each term in the equation is specified in the table.

(1) Time Period t	(2) Cash Payment C_t	(3) PV Factor $1/(1 + i)^t$	(4) Present Value (2) × (3) $PV = C_t/(1 + i)^t$	(5) Time-Weighted Present Value (4) × (1) $(t)PV_t$
1	100	.87719	87.72	87.72
2	100	.76946	76.95	153.89
3	100	.67497	67.50	202.49
4	100	.59208	59.20	236.83
5	100	.51936	51.94	259.68
5	1000	.51936	519.36	2596.80
Total			862.67	3537.41

$$D = \frac{\sum \text{time-weighted present value}}{\text{total present value}}$$

$$= 3537.41/862.67$$

$$= 4.10 \text{ years}$$

Recall that a zero-coupon bond pays a given principal amount at the maturity date, with no intervening coupon payments. The advantage of a zero-coupon bond is that no reinvestment rate risk exists; thus, the promised yield to maturity is the actual compound yield to maturity if the bond is kept until it matures. A zero-coupon bond has a duration equal to its maturity, since all of the weights (cash flows) are zero until the face value is paid at maturity. A bond with a duration D *acts like* a zero-coupon bond with maturity M. Moreover, the duration of a coupon-paying bond is always less than the maturity of that bond. Also, duration decreases as the frequency of the coupon payments increases.

The duration for bonds paying coupons semiannually also is calculated from Equation (10-2), with $t = 1, 2, \ldots$ measuring the half-year periods (i.e., $t = 1$ equals six months, $t = 2$ equals one year, etc.). Correspondingly, the coupon and yield values used in Equation (10-2) are measured semiannually as half the annual value. The resultant durations are calculated in six-month periods. Typically, this duration value is converted to years simply by dividing by two.[1]

---

[1] Closed-form duration measures are given by Chua (1984), Babcock (1985), and Caks, Lane, Greenleaf, and Joules (1985). Moser and Lindley (1989) extend the concept to coupons paid within the period.

Related Duration Measures

Two related terms often used in conjunction with the Macaulay duration given by Equation (10-2) are **modified duration** and **dollar duration**.

$$\text{Modified duration} = \frac{D}{1 + i} \tag{10-3}$$

Modified duration is used to calculate the percentage change in price of a bond for a given change in yield, as shown below. Dollar duration is employed to determine the dollar price change in a bond when yields change, where dollar duration is defined as

$$\text{Dollar duration} = \text{modified duration } (P_B) \tag{10-4}$$

where P_B is the current price of the bond. Dollar duration is important because the *dollar* price change is the relevant value for hedging purposes.

Implementing Duration

The longer the duration of a bond, the greater the price sensitivity of that bond to a given change in interest rates. The effect of a change in interest rates on the price of the bond is found by the simple relationship:

$$\Delta P_B = -D\, P_B\, \Delta i \tag{10-5}$$

where ΔP_B = change in the price of the bond

$\quad\quad D$ = (Macaulay) duration of the bond

$\quad\quad P_B$ = current price of the bond

$\quad\quad \Delta i$ = forecasted change in the interest rate

Interest rates and bond prices are inversely related, which is the reason for the negative sign in front of duration in this equation. Although Equation (10-5) is the relationship often given to determine the price change of a bond, in reality it is a simplification, and it becomes less accurate for higher interest rates. A more accurate equation is as follows:[2]

$$\Delta P_B = \frac{-D\, P_B\, \Delta i}{1 + i} = -\text{modified duration } (P_B)\,(\Delta i) \tag{10-6}$$

An equivalent expression to Equation (10-6) for the dollar price change of a bond is determined by using dollar duration:

$$\Delta P_B = -(\text{dollar duration})\, \Delta i \tag{10-7}$$

---

[2] One can see how Equation (10-5) is only an approximation by realizing how the equation is developed. The effect of a change in interest rates on bond prices is determined by taking the derivative of the price of the bond with respect to the interest rate (i.e., dP_B/di). This results in the equation $dP_B/P_B = -D(di)/(1 + i)$, or when changes are used and the equation rearranged, $\Delta P_B = -DP_B\Delta i/(1 + i)$. Obviously, the level of interest rates affects relative values given by Equations (10-5) and (10-6). In addition, *both* equations are approximations when large changes in the interest rate occur, since the derivative finds the slope of the line that is *tangent* to the *nonlinear* bond price relationship, resulting in the instantaneous change in price rather than the average change in price. Hence, the larger the change in interest rates, the larger the error in the duration measure. This relationship is explored later in this chapter.

The *percentage* change in price of a bond is found as follows:

$$\%\Delta P_B = \frac{\Delta P_B}{P_B} = \frac{-D\Delta i}{1 + i} = -\text{modified duration } (\Delta i) \qquad (10\text{-}8)$$

If the bond has semiannual coupons (cash flows are determined semiannually to determine duration), then $(1 + i)$ in Equations (10-6) and (10-8) must reflect a semiannual yield, *regardless* of whether or not the duration value is converted to years. Similarly, if the cash flows are paid every three months then $(1 + i)$ would reflect this payment schedule by the adjustment $i = \text{annual yield}/4$.

The simplicity of Equations (10-5) to (10-7) allows a user to *approximate* quickly the effect on the price of a bond for numerous potential changes in interest rates. These equations also show why duration is considered a relative measure of volatility among a number of bonds, since a larger duration value translates into a larger change in price. Example (10-2) shows the effect of a potential change in interest rates on the bond price.

Duration Relationships

Duration is superior to time until maturity as a price sensitivity measure, since duration considers both time to maturity *and* coupon payments. The relationships between duration and the factors influencing it are as follows:
Duration is longer

- for bonds with a longer time to maturity
- for bonds with a lower coupon[3]
- as the yield to maturity decreases[4]

Table 10-1 and Figure 10-2 show how duration varies as the coupon rate and years to maturity change. As can be seen, for a specific maturity an increase in the coupon rate causes a decrease in the duration, although the decline is not dramatic. For example, in Table 10-1 duration drops from 10.74 to 8.89 for the 20-year bond. For a specific coupon rate, an increase in the time until maturity increases the duration measure significantly. For example, a 5% coupon bond increases duration from 1.95 years to 10.74 years as the maturity increases from 2 to 20 years. The largest durations occur with the combination of the longest maturities and the lowest coupons.

Another beneficial characteristic of duration is that the duration of a portfolio of fixed-income securities is calculated easily from the durations of the individual securities. Thus:

$$D_p = \sum_{i=1}^{n} w_i D_i \qquad (10\text{-}9)$$

---

[3] Smaller coupons cause the more distant time periods to be relatively more important (in comparison with the distant time periods for larger coupons) both as a percentage of the total present value of the cash flows of the bond and the total time-weighted value. This situation occurs because of the discounting effect.

[4] The yield is important since the discount rate determines the compounding effect. As the discount rate increases, the more distant payments become less important, causing the duration value to fall, and vice versa.

EXAMPLE 10-2
Determining the Price Change with Duration

Using the information from Example 10-1, we have a bond with a duration of 4.1 years, a current price of $862.67, and a yield of 14%. If we forecast an immediate drop in interest rates of 30 basis points, then the forecasted change in the bond price is as follows:

$$\Delta P_B = -D\, P_B\, \Delta i$$

$$= -4.1(\$862.67)(-.0030) \qquad (10\text{-}5)$$

$$= \$10.61$$

Equation (10-6) gives a more accurate result:

$$\Delta P_B = \frac{-D\, P_B\, \Delta i}{(1 + i)} \qquad (10\text{-}6)$$

$$= \frac{-4.1(\$862.67)(-.0030)}{1.14}$$

$$= \$9.31$$

The *percentage* change in price is determined as follows:

$$\%\Delta P_B = \frac{-D\, \Delta i}{(1 + i)} \qquad (10\text{-}8)$$

$$= \frac{-4.1(-.0030)}{1.14}$$

$$= .0108 = 1.08\%$$

These equations show that bonds with longer durations are affected to a greater extent by a given change in interest rates. Thus, duration is used as a ranking device to determine which bonds change the most in price when interest rates change.

where D_p = the duration of the portfolio of securities

w_i = the weight (proportion) of funds in security i

D_i = the duration of security i

This linear association between individual securities and the portfolio of securities simplifies calculations and promotes the implementation of bond strategies involving interest rate forecasts.

A simple strategy using duration is to buy bonds with long durations when interest rates are expected to decline (prices increase), since these bonds would increase *more* in price than bonds with shorter durations. Similarly, when rates are expected to increase, then one can switch to shorter-duration bonds. Moreover, the use of duration allows the money manager to realize that duration provides more information than simply using

Table 10-1   Bond Duration Values for a 7% Yield

Years to Maturity	Coupon Rates				
	.05	.08	.10	.12	.14
2	1.950	1.925	1.909	1.895	1.881
5	4.488	4.281	4.170	4.074	3.991
10	7.661	7.044	6.759	6.536	6.358
15	9.648	8.741	8.367	8.091	7.880
20	10.741	9.746	9.365	9.095	8.893

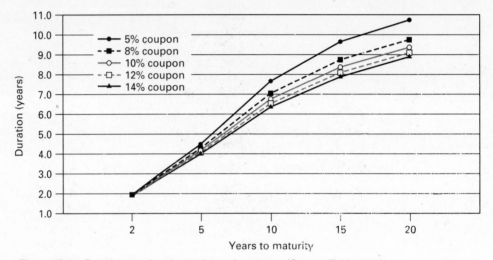

Figure 10-2   Durations vs. bond maturity and coupons. (*Source:* Table 10-1.)

maturity; for example, a shorter-term low coupon bond can actually have a larger price change than a longer-term high coupon bond. A money manager concentrating on maturity effects alone could not be as precise.[5]

Convexity and Duration Assumptions

Duration is based on the concept of *small* changes in interest rates. Consequently, an important factor affecting the usefulness of duration is **convexity**. Convexity is the effect of the curvature of the graph representing the relationship between the bond price and interest rates, as shown by curve *BB'* in Figure 10-3. Duration is interpreted as the

[5] The portfolio concept of maximizing returns relative to the risks also can be applied to durations: One can maximize yields relative to the duration of the portfolio. Duration is used in the mortgage-backed security field as well as with traditional bonds. However, owners of mortgages often prepay their loans, causing complications in using duration to measure adequately the relationship between changes in interest rates and changes in the mortgage-backed security value. Another application of duration is matching the durations of assets versus the duration of liabilities, rather than matching the cash flows of assets and liabilities. The assumptions of duration, as examined shortly, show that duration and cash flows may not provide equivalent answers.

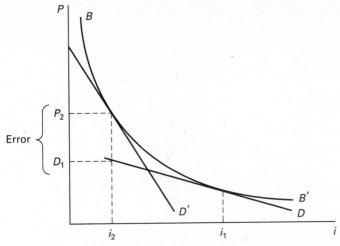

Figure 10-3 Convexity. As the interest rate changes from i_1 to i_2, the duration (which is approximated by the slope of the line tangent to BB') changes from D to D'. $P_2 - D_1$ represents the error if D is used to calculate the change in price when D' is the appropriate value.

(approximate) slope of the line that is tangent to this bond price curve BB' at the current interest rate. This slope is designated as D in Figure 10-3; that is, D is the line tangent to BB' at interest rate i_1. In this context, duration is defined mathematically by Equation (10-10) for small changes in P_B and i:

$$D = \frac{-\Delta P_B / P_B}{\Delta i / i} \tag{10-10}$$

More precisely, we could use derivatives to show

$$D = \frac{d(P_B)/P_B}{d(1 + i)/(1 + i)} \tag{10-11}$$

where $d(\cdot)$ is the **derivative**.

Thus, duration is defined in economic terms as the elasticity of price changes to yield changes—that is, the effect of a percentage change of yields on the percentage change in price.[6]

The importance of convexity is that only very small (infinitesimal) changes in the interest rate are appropriate when the slope is used to approximate the price change of the bond. More specifically, Figure 10-3 illustrates that as the interest rate changes from i_1 to i_2, then the slope to the nonlinear bond price curve changes. Thus, as interest rates change, duration changes, since duration is represented by the changing slope of the line tangent to the bond price curve. If the interest rate changes significantly, then the duration also changes significantly. Consequently, using the original duration D creates an error in the estimated price change because of the *change in the slope* of the

---

[6] The elasticity approach to duration helps to explain the concept and difficulties of duration. However, calculating duration by elasticities is difficult and often inaccurate.

tangent line; the size of the error is shown to be $P_2 - D_1$ in Figure 10-3. In this situation it is obvious that the portfolio manager *must constantly recalculate duration* in order to determine the price volatility, as well as to *rebalance the bond portfolio* to achieve the desired duration. Table 10-2 shows how convexity distorts the estimate of the size of the price change of the bond when large interest rate changes occur and duration is not recalculated.

Whereas duration is defined in Equation (10-11) by means of the derivative of P_B in terms of i, convexity is explained in terms of the second derivative. Thus, the slope of curve BB' in Figure 10-3 is the first derivative of the nonlinear price–interest rate relationship, whereas the second derivative (convexity) represents the *rate of change in the slope*. The existence of convexity means that higher-order derivatives are needed to account for the change in price, especially when the change in interest rate is large—that is, when one cannot rebalance the portfolio of bonds quickly enough to overcome the effect of the change in duration.

Another problem for the Macaulay duration measure exists when the *shape* of the term structure curve changes, since the Macaulay duration is based on the assumption of a flat term structure curve that undergoes only parallel shifts. Violations of these assumptions, or a *large* change in interest rates, in combination with the convexity effect, cause difficulties for the Macaulay duration measure. Daigler (1993) shows how (Macaulay) duration-convexity hedges are employed to mitigate the problems created by convexity and term structure curve shifts.

IMMUNIZATION

The Concept

An important goal of any large pension or insurance fund is to guarantee now what the value of a portfolio will be at a given future time period, with that value occurring *regardless* of how interest rates change. Equivalently, the fund wants to obtain a *predetermined* annual rate of return on funds invested (which is typically a rate equal to the current yield to maturity). **Immunization** achieves these objectives. Immunization exists if the total value of the portfolio at the end of the investment period equals the ending value expected at the time of purchase. If a portfolio is immunized, then changes in interest rates will *not* affect the ending value of the portfolio. In other words, immunization eliminates the risk of a change in bond portfolio value due to a change in interest rates. Therefore, the funds needed to pay off a future liability will be available from the assets, regardless of the behavior of future interest rates.[7]

Immunization is straightforward when the fund owns zero-coupon bonds. In this case, the ending value of the bonds is known with certainty (if the bonds do not have default risk), since there are no coupons to reinvest. However, only a limited number of originally issued zero-coupon bonds exists. Moreover, those created by brokerage houses include an extra cost that makes their yield to maturity too low to be used by funds.

Immunization for coupon-paying bonds is based on the natural trade-off between the price change in the value of the bonds and the reinvestment rate effect of the cash flows

[7] The discussion of immunization assumes the use of Treasury bonds, since the potential default risk of corporate bonds is not considered.

Table 10-2 Effect of Convexity on Bond Price Changes[a]

Change in Interest Rate, Basis Points	Price	Percent Change in Value	Percent Change Estimated by Duration	Error Due to Duration
+300	80.26	−19.7%	−24.3%	−4.6%
+250	83.02	−17.0	−20.2	−3.2
+200	85.96	−14.0	−16.2	−2.2
+150	89.11	−10.9	−12.2	−1.2
+100	92.48	−7.5	−8.1	−.6
+50	96.11	−3.9	−4.0	−.1
No change	100.00	NC	NC	0.0
−50	104.20	4.2	4.0	.2
−100	108.72	8.7	8.1	.6
−150	113.62	13.6	12.1	1.5
−200	118.93	18.9	16.2	2.7
−250	124.69	24.7	20.2	4.5
−300	130.96	31.0	24.3	6.7

[a] Calculations are based on a 30-year bond with a current yield of 12%.

when a given change in the interest rate occurs. Specifically, if the portfolio manager adjusts the structure of the portfolio so that any *potential adverse changes* in the bond value are offset with beneficial changes in the reinvestment rate (and vice versa), then the *portfolio is immunized*. The variability in the reinvestment rate is known as **reinvestment risk**. Duration is employed to help determine the appropriate structure of the portfolio in order to immunize its value. The concept of duration also is used by financial institutions to equate the duration of their assets to the duration of their liabilities, creating a matched or immunized balance sheet.

The Reinvestment Rate Effect

In order to immunize a portfolio, the money manager must deal with the dual problems of a loss in the value of the portfolio if interest rates increase and with the reinvestment rate problem of having unknown and inconsistent rates of return when investing the proceeds from bond coupons and principal payments. This trade-off between bond value and reinvestment returns is the key to immunization.

The reinvestment rate over time has a significant effect on both the ending value and the realized compound yield to maturity (RCYTM) for a portfolio. Table 10-3 provides an example of the effect of the reinvestment rate on the final portfolio value and on the RCYTM when different interest rates and investment horizons are considered for a ten-year, 10% coupon bond. The effects of the change in interest rates given in Table 10-3 are shown in Figure 10-4.

Figure 10-4 shows the dollar change in the price of the bond and the dollar change in reinvestment returns for an increase and decrease in interest rates. The time t the position is held, in conjunction with the change in interest rates, determines the net profit or loss on the bond position. The same results are shown in Table 10-3. The top panel of

Table 10-3 Investment in Ten-Year 10% Coupon Bond Priced at Par of $1000

	Future Reinvestment Rate		
	8%	10%	12%
10-year horizon:			
Coupon receipts	$1000	$1000	$1000
Accumulation from coupon reinvestment	489	653	839
Total value of coupons	$1489	$1653	$1839
Repayment at maturity	1000	1000	1000
Total terminal value	$2489	$2653	$2839
Terminal value ratio[a]	2.489	2.653	2.839
Realized compound YTM	9.33%	10.00%	10.71%
15-year horizon:			
Value of bond at maturity			
(See "10-year horizon" terminal value)	$2489	$2653	$2839
Accumulation from reinvestment of bond proceeds for 5 years	1195	1669	2246
Total terminal value	$3684	$4322	$5085
Terminal value ratio[a]	3.684	4.322	5.085
Realized compound YTM	8.89%	10.00%	11.14%
5-year horizon:			
Coupon receipts	$ 500	$ 500	$ 500
Accumulation from coupon reinvestment	100	129	159
Total value of coupons	$ 600	$ 629	$ 659
Price of bond	1081	1000	927
Total terminal value	$1681	$1629	$1586
Terminal value ratio[a]	1.681	1.629	1.586
Realized compound YTM	10.67%	10.00%	9.43%

[a] The realized compound yield is found from the equation

$$RCYTM = (\text{terminal value ratio})^{1/N} - 1$$

for N periods (using semiannual compounding).
Note: All calculations are based on semiannual coupons and yields to maturity.
Source: McEnally (1980, p. 60).

Table 10-3 has the fund's investment horizon of ten years equal to the maturity of the bond. The middle column of this top panel states that the future interest rate associated with the reinvestment returns of the coupons will equal the original yield to maturity of the bond; that is, the future reinvestment rate equals 10%. This situation causes the *RCYTM to equal the initial return on investment of 10%.* However, when the future reinvestment rate immediately falls to 8% (the left column of the table), the rate of return obtained from reinvesting the coupons is *less* than the original YTM of 10%. This coupon reinvestment effect causes the terminal value from the total investment to be less than the return initially expected (i.e., less than the original YTM), causing the actual RCYTM to fall to 9.33%. An increase in the reinvestment rate to 12% after the bond is purchased (the right column of the table) results in higher reinvestment returns

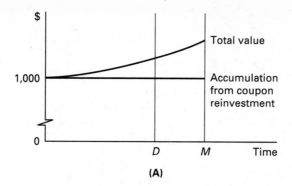

(A)

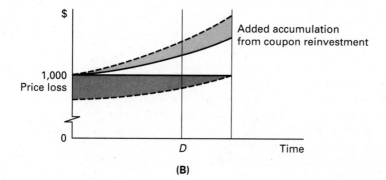

(B)

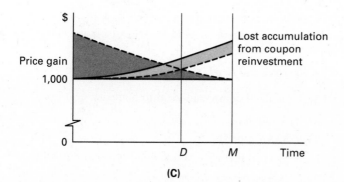

(C)

M is the maturity of the bond, while *t* indicates the holding period of the bond.

The solid line equals the total value of the bond returns plus the reinvestment returns *before* a change in interest rates. The dotted lines and hatched areas show the effects of a change in interest rates on bond price and reinvestment returns.

D is the duration of the bond. When the duration equals the holding period then change in the bond price equals the change in reinvestment returns, that is, the bond returns are immunized. At time periods other than *D* the price change does *not* equal the change in reinvestment returns.

Figure 10-4   Reinvestment rate effect. (A) Unchanged reinvestment rate. (B) Increase in reinvestment rate. (C) Decrease in reinvestment rate. *Source:* McEnally (1980).

for the coupons than expected, creating a RCYTM of 10.71%. The variability in the final RCYTM values and the terminal value ratios in Table 10-3, which range from 9.33% to 10.71% as the reinvestment rate assumptions change, can cause a wide range of total dollar amounts for pension funds that deal in hundreds of millions of dollars.

The other panels of Table 10-3 show situations in which the investment horizon is not equal to the maturity of the bond. When the investment horizon is 15 years, then the principal of the bond must be reinvested after 10 years, as well as continually reinvesting the coupon payments. The middle panel of Table 10-3 shows the compounding effect of reinvesting proceeds at various interest rates for the 15-year time horizon. For an interest rate of 8% the RCYTM for the 15-year horizon falls to 8.89%, which compares unfavorably with the 9.33% RCYTM for the ten-year, 8% reinvestment rate horizon and with the original expected 10% YTM. On the other hand, a subsequent interest rate of 12% increases the RCYTM for the 15-year horizon to 11.14%.

The five-year horizon in the final panel of the table shows a reversed picture from the 15-year horizon, with an 8% interest rate providing lower reinvestment returns on the coupons, but with this adverse effect being more than offset by the capital gains from the higher bond value obtained after five years as the result of the lower interest rate. Likewise, the higher 12% interest rate provides larger reinvestment returns but generates a capital loss when the bond is sold. These examples show that the relationship between the investment horizon and the maturity (duration) of the bond must be considered *in conjunction with* the reinvestment rate in order to determine the RCYTM and the relevant investment strategy.

RCYTM and Immunization

The effect of the reinvestment rate, the horizon (holding period) of the fund, and the duration on the realized compound yield to maturity is conveniently summarized by Babcock (1984) as follows:

$$\text{RCYTM} = (D/H)(\text{YTM}) + (1 - D/H)(\text{ARR}) \tag{10-12}$$

where RCYTM = realized compound yield to maturity

D = duration

H = horizon period

YTM = yield to maturity on the bond or bond portfolio

ARR = average reinvestment rate

This equation shows that the RCYTM is a weighted average of the YTM and the reinvestment rate, with the weights being determined by the relationship between the duration and the horizon period. Moreover, when the *duration equals the horizon, then the RCYTM equals the YTM.* In this case, the portfolio is *immunized.*

Equation (10-12) shows that an immunized portfolio is possible for a properly chosen duration and horizon. For example, Table 10-4 gives the terminal value and RCYTM for the bond used in Table 10-3, with the additional knowledge that the horizon period equals the duration of the bond at 6½ years. Both the terminal values and the RCYTM for the various assumed reinvestment rates in Table 10-4 show that the effect of changing the reinvestment rate is exactly offset by the change in the value of the bond. Thus,

Table 10-4 Reinvestment Rates and Immunization with a Ten-Year 10% Coupon Bond Priced at Par of $1000

	Future Reinvestment Rates		
	8%	**10%**	**12%**
$6\frac{1}{2}$-year horizon:			
Coupon receipts	$ 650	$ 650	$ 650
Accumulation from coupon reinvestment	181	236	294
Total value of coupons	$ 831	$ 886	$ 944
Price of bond	1060	1000	945
Total terminal value	$1891	$1886	$1889
Terminal value ratio	1.892	1.886	1.889
Realized compound YTM	10.04%	10.00%	10.02%

Note: All calculations are based on semiannual coupons and yields to maturity.
Source: McEnally (1980).

setting the horizon period equal to the duration immunizes the portfolio.[8] This relationship is also shown in Figure 10-4, where part B shows graphically how the additional funds received from a higher reinvestment rate offset the loss from the decline in the value of the bond; part C shows the same effect when the loss from a lower reinvestment rate is offset by the gain in the value of the bond. However, one does need to rebalance the bond portfolio if there is a change in the time to maturity, a major change in interest rates, or a change in the shape of the term structure curve.

APPLYING DURATION CONCEPTS TO FUTURES HEDGING

Introduction

Duration provides an alternative technique to regression in order to determine an appropriate hedge ratio for fixed-income investments. Based on the duration concept, one can find the hedge ratio that minimizes the net price change from the combined futures/cash position, given that the assumptions of the duration model are met. Recall that duration includes time until maturity, coupon, and the level of interest rates to determine the effect of a change in interest rates on the price of the relevant fixed-income instrument. Thus, the relative durations of the cash and futures instruments are the key elements in the **duration-based hedge** model.

A difficulty with the use of cash immunization for hedging covered previously is that changes in interest rates, time, or the shape of the term structure often force the portfolio manager to rebalance the portfolio. Rebalancing adjusts for changing durations in order to benefit fully from immunization. This rebalancing of the portfolio to keep the desired duration often creates large transaction costs and/or is difficult to implement when there are thin cash markets. The use of futures contracts to adjust durations significantly reduces these costs and liquidity problems.

---

[8] The RCYTM in Table 10-4 differs from 10% by several basis points because the actual duration is 6.545 years rather than 6.5 years, and because of the effect of convexity.

The Development of the Duration Model for Hedging

In Chapter 11, we state that the basic objective of hedging is to find a hedge ratio that offsets the price change in the cash instrument with the price change in the futures position; that is,

$$\Delta P_C + (\text{HR})\Delta P_F = 0 \tag{10-13}$$

where ΔP_C = the price change of the cash instrument

$\quad \Delta P_F$ = the price change of the futures instrument

$\quad \text{HR}$ = the futures hedge ratio

or, equivalently, that the appropriate hedge ratio to eliminate or minimize the net change in the combined cash/futures value is

$$\text{HR} = -\Delta P_C/\Delta P_F \tag{10-14}$$

where the minus sign stands for a futures position that is opposite the cash position. Thus, a manager who owns the cash asset would short futures.

The regression model finds the "appropriate hedge ratio" illustrated in Equation (10-14) by determining the "*average* relationship between the ΔP_C and the ΔP_F" via the slope of the regression line such that the variance of the errors around the regression line is minimized. The duration-based hedge method determines the hedge ratio by minimizing the *net change in wealth* of the hedger. Expressed another way, regression inputs historical price changes in order to minimize the variability of the net hedge position over the period of the hedge, whereas the duration method employs the relative volatilities of the cash and futures instruments as measured by duration in order to minimize the net price change between the initiation and termination of the hedge.[9]

The price change equation developed earlier in this chapter describes the effect of a change in interest rates on the price of a debt instrument when duration is used to measure volatility:

$$\Delta P_C = -D\,P_C\,\Delta i/(1 + i) \tag{10-15}$$

We can then develop the duration-based hedging model in terms of instantaneous changes by using derivatives and Equation (10-15):[10]

$$dP_C = -D_C P_C\, di_C/(1 + i_C) \tag{10-16}$$

$$dP_F = -D_F P_F\, di_F(1 + i_F) \tag{10-17}$$

where $d(\cdot)$ stands for the derivative of the associated variable. Thus dP_C, dP_F, and di represent ΔP_C, ΔP_F, and Δi, respectively, from Equations (10-14) and (10-15). In addition,

D_C, D_F = the durations of the cash and futures instruments

$\quad P_C, P_F$ = the prices of the cash and futures instruments

$\quad\quad i_C, i_F$ = the interest rates (yields) associated with the cash and futures positions

[9] Toevs and Jacob (1986) show that the regression and duration models are equivalent when the horizon of the hedge is instantaneous and when regression uses forecasted values.

[10] The small parallel changes in the yield curve as an assumption of duration, relate to the use of calculus for the derivation of the duration and duration-based hedge ratio equations.

If we assume that the change in the cash and futures interest rates di_C and di_F are equally sensitive to a change in the risk-free interest rate (i.e., $di_C/di_F = 1$), then we can take the ratio $dP_C/dP_F = \Delta P_C/\Delta P_F = \text{HR}$ stated in Equation (10-14) to derive the duration-based hedge ratio, resulting in

$$\text{HR}_D = \frac{D_C P_C (1 + i_F)}{D_F P_F (1 + i_C)} \qquad (10\text{-}18)$$

The number of contracts needed for a hedge follows the format for the previous hedge ratio method as follows:

$$N_D = \text{HR}_D \frac{\text{total par value of cash}}{\text{par value of one futures contract}} \qquad (10\text{-}19)$$

Some formulations of Equation (10-18) include a minus sign to indicate a futures position that is opposite the cash position. The duration of the futures contract is determined by finding the duration of the cheapest-to-deliver bond. In addition, recall from our previous discussions of duration that i_F and i_C are measured in terms of *six-month yields* for bonds issuing coupons semiannually.

Incorporating Relative Sensitivities

Equation (10-18) is the most common formulation of the duration hedge ratio. However, if we wish to incorporate unequal sensitivities of the cash and futures interest rates to a change in the risk-free rate, then we must determine the sensitivity of Equations (10-16) and (10-17) to a small change in the risk-free interest rate i_{RF}. We then substitute these results into Equation (10-14) in order to obtain the duration formulation for the hedge ratio. The result is a refined hedge ratio, as follows:

$$\text{HR}_{D2} = \frac{D_C P_C (1 + i_F)}{D_F P_F (1 + i_C)} \text{RS} \qquad (10\text{-}20)$$

where RS is the relative sensitivity of the cash market yield to the futures market yield, given a change in the risk-free rate; that is,

$$\text{RS} = \frac{di_C/di_{RF}}{di_F/di_{RF}}$$

In most cases, the interest rate relative sensitivity is obtained from a historical analysis of the instruments in question. Such an analysis reduces the advantage of the duration method over the regression method, since Equation (10-18) does not employ historical data.[11]

The interest rate relative sensitivity to the risk-free rate can be important when the default risk between the cash and futures instruments differs, when the term structure curve is not flat, or when the term structure has a nonparallel shift in conjunction with significantly different durations for the futures and cash instruments. However, since the calculation of the relative sensitivity is complicated and typically not determined in practice, Equation (10-18) is usually employed for duration-based hedging, even though

[11] A more involved derivation of the duration hedge model is found in Kolb and Chiang (1981, 1982), who call the model the "price sensitivity" approach to hedging.

HR_D would include some bias. Moreover, the assumptions of a flat term structure curve and nonparallel shifts impounded in the calculation of the duration values in Equations (10-18) and (10-20) can cause inaccurate hedge ratio results in any case.

Example of a Duration Hedge

Example 10-3 shows how to use Equations (10-18) and (10-19) to calculate the hedge ratio and the number of contracts needed for a short hedge. Since both the cash and futures are based on T-bonds, we assume that RS in Equation (10-20) is equal to one; that is, the relative sensitivity of the cash and futures yields to a change in interest rates

EXAMPLE 10-3
Determining a Duration Hedge Ratio

Current portfolio value	$10,000,000
Cash instrument to be hedged	T-bonds: 12% of May 05
	YTM: 10.4%
	Price: 113:24
	Duration: 7.75
Number of bonds at current price	
($1000 face value)	8791
T-bond futures*	Price: 81:8
	YTM:10.8%
	Duration: 8.36

The duration hedge ratio is as follows:

$$HR_D = \frac{D_C P_C (1 + i_F)}{D_F P_F (1 + i_C)} \qquad (10\text{-}18)$$

$$= \frac{(7.75)(113.8)(1.054)}{(8.36)(81.25)(1.052)}$$

$$= \frac{929.58}{714.57}$$

$$= 1.300$$

For this example, $(1 + i_F) = 1.054$ and $(1 + i_C) = 1.052$, since the bonds have semiannual coupons.

$$N_D = HR_D \text{(total par value of cash/par value of futures)}$$

$$= 1.3000 \ (\$8,791,000/\$100,000)$$

$$= 114.28$$

$$= 114 \text{ contracts}$$

*The cheapest-to-deliver cash bond is assumed to be a 14% bond due in 20 years with a conversion factor of 1.5875. The futures price is determined by finding the present value of the bond for the relevant time to maturity and then dividing by the conversion factor.

is the same. Example 10-4 shows the effect of the duration hedge when cash and futures prices decline—namely, that the hedge eliminates more than 96% of the loss in the cash bonds.

Considerations in Implementing the Duration Model

Two considerations in implementing the duration hedge model are the effect of unstable input values on the hedge ratio and whether current or expected input values should be employed in the model. Instability in the input values over time can cause a change in the hedge ratio, thereby necessitating a change in the number of futures contracts employed for the hedge.

If the cash instrument is a close substitute for the cheapest-to-deliver futures instrument, then the input ratios of P_C/P_F and $(1 + i_F)/(1 + i_C)$ in the model will not change significantly over time. If the cash instrument is not the cheapest, then volatile values for P_C/P_F and $(1 + i_F)/(1 + i_C)$ can occur. The stability of D_C/D_F depends on the characteristics of the instruments, the size of the change in interest rates, the length of time until the termination of the hedge, and the extent of violations of the assumptions of a flat yield curve and nonparallel shifts in the yield curve. Thus, the stability of the durations is related to the effects of convexity.

Kolb and Chiang (1981) indicate that the application of the duration-based hedge ratio given in Equations (10-18) and (10-20) requires future *expected* values for the input variables as of the *termination* date of the hedge. Toevs and Jacob (1984) qualify this statement by maintaining that **anticipatory hedges** should use expected values, whereas a short hedge for a currently held asset should use the current values for the cash instrument and the expected values for the duration of the futures instrument based on the (expected) delivery date. The use of expected values in the duration model is associated with the *cash flows* of the relevant instrument when the cash instrument is actually held, and thus the effect of convergence on the results is eliminated. *However,* forecasting the value of these variables can be difficult. Consequently, in practice, hedgers often use the current values of the input variables. The effect of using current values in place of expected values for anticipatory hedges is related to the same factors

EXAMPLE 10-4
Results of a Duration Hedge

	Cash Market	Futures Market
March:	Portfolio value: $10 million Current cash T-bond price: 113:24 Total bonds of $1000 par value: 8791	Sell 114 T-bond futures contracts at 81-8 Value of futures: $9,262,500
June:	Price per bond: 102:16 Value of bonds: $9,010,775	Buy back 114 futures contracts at a price of 72:23 Value: $8,311,312
Gain/loss:	($989,225)	$951,188
	Net loss: ($38,037)	
	Percentage of loss offset: 96.2%	

noted above for unstable hedge ratios over time; that is, major differences occur only when the cash and cheapest-to-deliver instrument have significantly different characteristics.

EXAMINING THE DURATION-BASED HEDGING MODEL

Comparing the Duration and Regression Models

The duration hedging model differs from the regression model in two fundamental ways:

1. How relative volatilities are determined:

   - The duration model uses the *duration values* of the cash and futures instruments to determine the relative volatilities of these instruments, which in turn are employed to obtain the relevant hedge ratio for *minimizing the net price change* of the combined futures/cash position.
   - The regression model uses *historical price changes* for the futures and cash instruments to determine their relative volatility such that the hedge ratio *minimizes the variance* of the net futures/cash position.

2. Assumptions concerning the data:

   - The duration model assumes that the expected future input values for the duration, price, and yield variables for an anticipatory hedge are correct, and that interest rate behavior is described by a flat yield curve with small parallel shifts in the term structure.
   - Regression assumes that the hedge ratios based on historical data are good estimates of the hedge ratios over the hedge period—that is, that the associations between the futures and cash price changes remain stable.[12]

Advantages and Disadvantages of the Duration Method

The duration method possesses advantages and disadvantages in comparison with other hedge ratio methods. The advantages of the duration method are:

1. It is superior to naive hedge ratio methods because duration provides a logical procedure to minimize the net change in price over the period of the hedge. In particular, the duration method considers the relative volatilities of the futures and cash instruments, whereas the naive methods ignore this valuable information.

2. The duration procedure can provide near-perfect hedge results if the violations of the assumptions of duration are minimal or if the hedge ratio is periodically recalculated and the hedge rebalanced. By comparison, the regression method requires stable hedge ratios over time and no violations of the assumptions of the regression model in order to minimize the variance of the price changes of the hedged position.[13] Stable hedge ratios for the regression method are less likely for crosshedges.

---

[12]Geske and Pieptea (1987) present a combined regression/duration method for hedging. The futures implied interest rate is regressed with the cash rate to identify the interdependency between the futures and cash position. This information then is used in combination with the sensitivity of the fixed-income portfolio to interest rate changes as measured by duration to obtain the hedge ratio.

[13]The regression method can use *forecasts* of the inputs to determine the hedge ratio rather than historical data, although this approach is not typically used.

3. The duration model typically is employed when there is no history of price changes, since the regression procedure employs historical data. For example, when new bond issues are sold that have maturity, coupon, and/or default risk characteristics differing from existing issues, then historical data cannot be used to model a regression procedure, but duration can provide accurate results.

4. The duration method is a more convenient method to use when the analyst wishes to adjust the model; for example, when call provisions affect the volatility of the bond or when the analyst wants to model the basis.[14]

The disadvantages of the duration method are

1. Major deviations from the assumptions of duration cause large net hedging errors, at least if frequent rebalancing is not undertaken.

2. Forecasting the inputs to the model as of the termination of the hedge is recommended for anticipatory hedges. Accurate forecasts often are difficult to achieve.

SUMMARY AND LOOKING AHEAD

This chapter discusses the bond management techniques of duration, immunization, and duration-hedging. Duration provides a method for measuring the relative volatility of a bond as well as the effect of a change in interest rates on the price of a bond. Immunization allows the portfolio manager to lock in a final portfolio value. Those who wish to use futures markets to hedge can use the duration model to determine the optimal number of contracts to employ to hedge a portfolio. Part III examines options markets.

BIBLIOGRAPHY

Babcock, Guilford C. (1984). "Duration as a Link Between Yield and Value," *Journal of Portfolio Management,* Vol. 10, No. 4, Summer, pp. 58–65.

Babcock, Guilford C. (1985). "Duration as a Weighted Average of Two Factors," *Financial Analysts Journal,* Vol. 41, No. 2, March-April, pp. 75–76.

Caks, John, William R. Lane, Robert W. Greenleaf, and Reginald G. Joules (1985). "A Simple Formula for Duration," *Journal of Financial Research,* Vol. 8, No. 3, Fall, pp. 245–249.

Chua, Jess H. (1984). "A Closed-Form Formula for Calculating Bond Duration," *Financial Analysts Journal,* Vol. 40, No. 3, May–June, pp. 76–78.

Daigler, Robert T. (1993). *Financial Futures Markets: Concepts, Evidence, and Applications.* New York, Harper Collins.

Geske, Robert L., and Dan R. Pieptea (1987). "Controlling Interest Rate Risk and Return with Futures," *The Review of Futures Markets,* Vol. 6, No. 1, pp. 64–86.

Kolb, Robert, and Raymond Chiang (1981). "Improving Hedging Performance Using Interest Rate Futures," *Financial Management,* Vol. 10, No. 4, Autumn, pp. 72–79.

Kolb, Robert, and Raymond Chiang (1982). "Duration, Immunization, and Hedging with Interest Rate Futures," *Journal of Financial Research,* Vol. 5, No. 2, Summer, pp. 161–170.

Leibowitz, Martin L. (1983). "How Financial Theory Evolves into the Real World—or Not: The Case of Duration and Immunization," *Financial Review,* Vol. 18, No. 4, November, pp. 271–280.

McEnally, Richard (1980). "How to Neutralize Reinvestment Rate Risk," *Journal of Portfolio Management,* Vol. 6, No. 3, Spring, pp. 59–63.

---

[14]See Toevs and Jacob (1986) for their views on the superiority of the duration methodology.

Moser, James T., and James T. Lindley (1989). "A Simple Formula for Duration: An Extension," *Financial Review,* Vol. 24, No. 4, November, pp. 611–615.

Toevs, Alden L., and David P. Jacob (1984). "Interest Rate Futures: A Comparison of Alternative Hedge Ratio Methodologies," Morgan Stanley Research Report, June.

Toevs, Alden L., and David P. Jacob (1986). "Futures and Alternative Hedge Ratio Methodologies," *Journal of Portfolio Management,* Vol. 12, No. 3, Spring, pp. 60–70.

PROBLEMS

*Indicates more difficult problems.

*10-1   Duration and Alternative Investments

Use duration as a tool for selecting between alternative investments. As an investor, you have forecasted an unanticipated decrease in interest rates of 1% during the next quarter. Determine durations based on the table format, select the bond with the greatest potential for price appreciation, and discuss the factors affecting the results. Find the potential change in price for each bond.

	Alternative	
	A	**B**
Face amount	$1000	$1000
Coupon rate	8%	10%
Coupon amount	$80	$100
Time to maturity	7 years	5 years

Assume a market rate of interest of 9% and annual coupons.

*10-2   Duration

a. Calculate the Macaulay duration by means of the table format, given that a bond has a 12% coupon (paid annually), a current yield of 15%, and will mature in ten years. Assume a $1000 par value.

b. Given a bond with the above duration, present value, and interest rate, calculate the projected change in the bond price assuming that the interest rate drops from 15% to 12.5%.

10-3   Finding the Change in Interest Rates

Our investment portfolio includes a bond with a duration of 3.9 years, a current price of $976.50, and a current interest rate of 8%. If the price goes to $1082.28, what is the change in the interest rate?

*10-4   Immunization

Given the following information for a bond portfolio:

Duration = 6.95 years	Average reinvestment rate = 6.92%
Yield to maturity = 7.5%	Realized compound yield to maturity = 7.3%

a. Calculate the investment horizon needed in order to immunize the portfolio.

b. What would the realized compound yield to maturity be if the horizon is set to 6.95 years?

*10-5 Recalculating Duration for a Large Change in Rates

A bond with a maturity of ten years has a coupon of 8.5%, paid annually, and a current YTM of 8.54%. Use the table method to determine the durations asked for in the question.

a. Calculate the duration of the bond.

b. If interest rates increase to 10.5%, what would be the new duration?

c. Calculate duration if interest rates increase to 14%.

d. From the results in parts (a) to (c) state your conclusion concerning the relationship between interest rates and duration.

e. Compare the change in bond price using the original duration from (a) and the approximation equation versus the actual change in the bond price.

10-6 Duration of a Portfolio

As a financial advisor you are asked how to determine whether the duration of the bond portfolio listed below is similar to another portfolio that has a duration of 5½ years. All of the bonds have a face value of $1000 and the YTM is 8.5%. All coupons are paid annually.

Percentage of Holdings	Coupon	Duration
50	10%	4.2
25	9%	5.8
25	11%	6.8

*10-7 Immunization

Given a ten-year $1000 par value bond with an 8% annual coupon, paid annually, calculate the realized compound yield to maturity when interest rates are 6%, 8%, and 10% for a 10-year, 15-year, and 5-year holding period. The current yield is 8%. Also, immunize the portfolio against changes in the current interest rate and show your justification of this immunization.

10-8 Duration Hedge Ratio

Expected cash flow in March 1991	$20,000,000
Cash instrument to be hedged	T-note: maturing April 1997
Current YTM (December 1990)	9.65%
Current price	97:05
Current number of bonds (Dec. 1990, $1000 par)	20,585
T-bond futures price	85:0

	Expected Values for Cash Instrument in March 1991	Expected Position in T-Bond Futures in March 1991
Expected YTM	8.32	8.57
Expected price	103:4	97:19
Duration at expected YTM	4.91	10.35

Find the duration hedge ratio and the corresponding number of contracts needed for an anticipatory hedge. Assume annual coupons.

10-9   **Duration Hedge Ratio**

Use duration hedge techniques to find the hedge ratio and the number of futures contracts for an expected $8 million June cash inflow to be invested in cash T-bonds. The bonds have semiannual coupon payments.

Cash T-bonds as of March:	
Current price	98:07
Yield	8.75%
Number of bonds at current price	8145 ($1000 face)
Expected values in June:	
Price	103:16
Yield	8.05%
Duration at expected yield	4.72 years
June T-bond futures:	
Expected price	89:24
Expected YTM	8.45%
Duration at expected YTM	9.63 years

*10-10   **Duration Hedge Ratio with Unequal Sensitivities**

Expected cash inflow (July 199X)	$8,000,000
Cash instrument to be hedged (Feb. 199X)	T-notes with annual coupons
	Current YTM: 8.90%
	Current price: 116:16
Number of T-notes to be purchased	8,000,000/(1000)(1.1650)
Face value: $1000	= 6866 bonds
Expected value of cash instrument	Expected YTM: 8.61%
(July 199X)	Expected price: 121:18
	Duration at expected YTM: 2.952
Feb. 199X T-note futures price	Price: 88:08
Expected position in T-note futures	Expected YTM: 8.95%
(July, 199X)	Expected price: 92:16
	Duration at expected YTM: 3.485

Relative sensitivity (RS) of cash market yield to futures market (given a change in the risk-free rate of return) is .9895.

a. Using the information above, determine the duration-based hedge ratio with unequal sensitivities incorporated (HR_{D2}) for an anticipatory hedge. Also determine the number of futures contracts to be employed in the hedge.

b. Show the hedge setup. What percentage of the opportunity loss is offset with the hedge?

Chapter 11

QUOTATIONS AND CHARACTERISTICS OF STOCK OPTIONS

Overview

Options possess characteristics that are beneficial to many speculators and hedgers. A major advantage of options is that they alter the risk-return characteristics of a portfolio. Thus, speculators who buy options obtain substantial leverage with a minimal cash investment while having a maximum potential loss equal to the cost of the option. Hedgers can reduce the risk of owning a cash instrument by using options, or they can increase their total portfolio returns by selling options. In general, options provide profit distributions different from those obtained by either owning stocks or trading in futures contracts.

A call option gives the buyer the *right* to purchase a stock at a fixed price for a specific period of time. Speculators who purchase call options typically expect that the price of the underlying stock will increase. A put option gives the buyer the right to *sell* the stock at a fixed price for a specific period of time. The buyer of the put typically expects that the stock price will decline.

The profits or losses a speculator obtains from buying and holding an option until it expires depend on the fixed ("exercise") price of the option, the stock price, and the cost of the option. Payoff diagrams help illustrate the relationships among these variables.

Another form of a stock option is a stock index option, which is an option on a popular portfolio of stocks, such as the S&P 100 Index. Index options are equivalent to individual stock options, except that index options are settled in cash at the expiration date, while stock options are settled by delivering the stock.

Terminology

Arbitrage   See Chapter 1.

*At-the-money   An option that has its stock price equal to the strike price.

*Call option   Gives the buyer the right to purchase the stock (or asset) at a fixed price for a specific period of time. The "fixed price" is called the strike price. Since the buyer has the right, *but not the obligation* to purchase the asset, the buyer exercises this right only if the stock price is greater than the strike price at option expiration.

*Cash settlement   The buyer receives from the seller the difference between the index value and the strike price of the option. Index options settle in cash at option expiration.

Deferred options   Options that expire after the nearby option.

Derivative asset   A contract whose payoff at expiration is determined by the price of the underlying asset.

Exercise price   See "strike price."

*Expiration (date)   When the option stops trading. After this date the option is worthless, since it cannot be exercised.

*In-the-money   A call option having its stock price greater than the strike price; or a put option having its stock price less than the strike price.

*Index option   An option on a stock index, with the index representing a portfolio of individual stocks.

*Intrinsic value   The difference between the stock price and the strike price, or zero, whichever is greater. A call option has a positive intrinsic value if the stock price is greater than the strike price. A put option has a positive intrinsic value if the stock price is less than the strike price.

LEAPS   Long-term options expiring up to three years in the future. LEAPS stands for "Long-term Equity Anticipation Securities."

Leverage   The percentage change for the option price is greater than the percentage change for the underlying stock price. Thus, leverage magnifies the rate of return (or loss) on the option in comparison to the return on the stock.

Liquidity   The trader's ability to buy or sell an instrument quickly, without significantly affecting the instrument's price.

*Near-the-money   The stock price is approximately the same as the strike price of the option.

Nearby option   The next option expiration month.

*Open interest   The number of contracts that have both a long and a short position.

Option class   The designation for all of the options on the same stock.

Option cycle   The expiration months for options on a particular stock depend on its "cycle." All stock options have expirations in the current and next month. In addition, the January cycle trades the next two option months with expirations in January, April, July, and October; similarly, the February and March cycles are separated by three-month intervals.

Option series   An option with a specific strike price and expiration date.

*Out-of-the-money   A call option having its stock price less than the strike price of the option; or a put option having its stock price greater than the strike price of the option.

*Put option   Gives the buyer the right to *sell* the stock (or asset) at a fixed price for a specific period of time. A large decline in the price of the stock is profitable for a put buyer.

Short sale   Selling a stock now, with the promise to buy the stock back later. A short sale profits from a decline in the stock price.

Stock split/dividend   An increase in the number of shares issued to each shareholder by the corporation. A 2-1 stock split means that an owner of 100 shares of a particular stock will have 200 shares after the split, with the stock price being cut in half. A stock dividend occurs when the additional stock received is less than a 25% increase in the number of shares currently owned.

*Strike price   The "fixed price" at which the option buyer can execute the option. The buyer of the option can purchase the stock (call option) or sell the stock (put option) at this fixed price, *regardless* of the current price of the stock in the market.

Systematic risk   The risk associated with market movements. This risk cannot be reduced by diversification.

Time to expiration factor   As the time until the expiration of the option becomes shorter, the price and time value of the option become smaller (everything else held constant); this relationship is called "time decay."

*Time value   The difference between the option price and the intrinsic value. The size of this difference depends on the time until option expiration, the difference between the stock price and the strike price, and the volatility of the stock.

Unsystematic risk   The risk associated with the individual stock and industry factors. This risk is reduced substantially by diversifying the portfolio with the purchase of additional stocks of other companies.

*Writer   The seller of an option.

OPTIONS MARKETS AND CONTRACTS

Why Do Options Markets Exist?

Option contracts exist because they provide unique risk-return choices for speculators and hedgers. In particular, options markets are employed:

- To adjust the risk and return of a position at a minimum cost.
- To hedge both price and quantity risk—that is, options are preferable to futures markets when the quantity one wishes to hedge is uncertain.

Speculators often prefer options to other speculative instruments because options provide large returns when the forecast of asset movements is correct, while limiting the loss to the cost of the option when the forecast is incorrect. In addition, the cost of "playing the game" is often only a few hundred dollars. Hedgers like options because the cost of the hedge is known when the hedge is initiated, and no additional funds are needed throughout the hedge.

The consequence of having an options market is that speculators accept risk for the chance for a large profit, while hedgers reduce their risk to obtain a more stable return on assets. This *risk transfer* has made options markets popular for both individuals and financial institutions. In addition, the options markets provide *price discovery* for the underlying asset, since the liquidity and low cost of many options cause traders to enter the options market before trading in the underlying asset.[1] Unlike futures markets, options also provide price discovery for *volatility*. Options include a time value in their cost that reflects the volatility of the asset. Thus, when expectations concerning a change in volatility occur, the price of the option changes. All of these factors make options an important and interesting market.

History of Options Markets

Option trading can be traced back to the 1600s, when the Dutch traded options on tulips. Tulip bulbs were traded as a speculative commodity by many of the Dutch, with prices reaching 1,000 times their true value. Tulip growers sold options which allowed the buyers to profit if prices declined. When prices did fall, the growers went bankrupt without fulfilling the option contracts, giving options a bad name. In the 1900s, overseas trades reintroduced put and call options, but they manipulated their prices based on placing rumors. Trading in options was banned in England, especially in the 1930s

---

[1] Options on the S&P 100 Index and other indexes provide price discovery, because some of the stocks in the index may not have traded recently, making the index "old." Options do not have this problem.

and from World War II until 1956. In the United States, options traded in the streets of Chicago on an illegal basis. In 1934, the Options Dealers Association was established, although trading volume was thin and options cost 30% more than their fair value.

Modern Options Markets

Stock options, as we know them today, started to trade in April 1973 on the Chicago Board Options Exchange (CBOE). Prior to that time, options were created by option dealers. These pre-1973 "Over-the-Counter" (OTC) options were very expensive, almost impossible to resell before they expired, and usually structured to take advantage of the six-month capital gains tax laws. CBOE−traded options possess several important advantages over the OTC options. In particular,

- The CBOE options have *standardized* characteristics regarding their **expiration** date (when the option stops trading) and **exercise price** (the purchase price of the stock or asset).
- The standardized characteristics cause like options to be *interchangeable*—that is, they can be traded before the option expires.
- The tradeability of the options provides significant **liquidity** for these options, which in turn creates lower option prices and lower commissions.
- The existence of the options exchanges provides traders with added safeguards against trading abuses.

The CBOE traded 16 stocks when the exchange opened in 1973. In 1975–1976 the American, Philadelphia, and Pacific Exchanges began to trade stock options. Later, the New York Exchange added options. By the early 1980s the volume on the options exchanges exceeded the stock volume on the New York and American stock exchanges. After the 1987 stock market crash, option volume decreased substantially. Current option volume is over 1 million contracts per day (each for 100 shares of stock), while NYSE stock volume is typically 200 to 300 million shares per day. Currently, options on over 700 stocks trade on the options exchanges.

Options on stock indexes started trading in 1983, and by 1985 these indexes made up over 30% of total option volume. Current index option volume is approximately 350,000 contracts per day, which is about 25% of total stock option volume. Exchange-traded options on foreign exchange (currencies) and options on futures contracts also exist. Furthermore, most specialized options on various assets and interest rate securities trade on an over-the-counter basis. Here we concentrate on the popular stock options. Later we examine the other option contracts.

Calls and Puts

The two basic types of options are **call options** and **put options.** A call option for a stock gives the buyer the *right* to purchase the stock at a fixed price for a specific period of time. The term "option" reflects the concept that the call buyer has the right, *but not the obligation*, to purchase the stock. This means that the maximum amount of money the buyer can lose is the initial cost of the option. If the stock price *increases* sufficiently, the call buyer profits. A put option for a stock gives the buyer the right to

EXHIBIT 11-1
Option Decisions for Buyers and Sellers

Buying options:

- **Call:** can *purchase* the stock at the strike price.
- **Put:** can *sell* the stock at the strike price.

Selling options:

- **Call:** obligated to *sell* the stock at the strike price (the buyer chooses if and when to exercise the option).
- **Put:** obligated to *buy* the stock at the strike price (the buyer chooses if and when to exercise the option).

sell the stock at a fixed price for a specific period of time. The put buyer has the right, *but not the obligation,* to sell the stock. If the stock price *declines* sufficiently, the put buyer profits.

The seller of an option is often called the **writer** of the option. Buyers of call options are typically speculators, while the buyers of puts and the writers of call and put options can be either speculators or hedgers, depending on the strategy involved. Strategies for call and put options are discussed in Chapters 15 and 16. Options are often called **derivative assets,** since the dollar payoffs of an option are completely determined by the price of the underlying asset of the option.[2]

The "fixed price" of an option is typically called the **strike price** or exercise price. The strike price for a call option is the price the buyer pays for the stock, if and when the right to purchase the stock is exercised. The put strike price is the price the buyer *sells* the stock for, if and when the put option is exercised. The "specific period of time" until the expiration of the option states the amount of time remaining before the option ceases to exist. Once the option expires the buyer *no longer* has the right to buy/sell the stock at the exercise price. An "American" option can be exercised any trading day on or *before* the expiration date. A "European" option can be exercised *only at* its expiration. Stock options traded in the United States are American-type options. Exhibit 11-1 summarizes what buyers of options *can* do and what sellers are *obligated* to do.

STOCK CALL OPTION QUOTATIONS AND PRICING RELATIONSHIPS

The price of the option is negotiated between the buyer and the seller. Each option on an individual stock is for 100 shares of the stock, although the option quotations illustrate the option price per *one* share of the stock. Therefore, one must multiply the option price by 100 in order to obtain the total dollar price for an option contract representing 100 shares of stock.

---

[2] A "contingent claim" is a class of assets whose payoffs are completely determined by a predefined set of underlying variables. For example, an inflation futures contract whose payoff depends on the Consumer Price Index (CPI) is a contingent claim but not a derivative asset, since the CPI is not an asset. Contingent claims include derivative assets such as stock options.

Call Option Quotations

The vast majority of the option quotations encountered in the newspaper are for individual stocks. Each line in Exhibit 11-2 shows a different option. Options differ in terms of the underlying stock, whether they are a call or a put option, their strike price,

EXHIBIT 11-2
Stock Option Quotations

Option/Strike			Vol	Exch	Last	Net Chg	Stock Close	Open Int
Most Active Contracts								
G M	May	40		5,090	CB	$1\frac{1}{2}$	$+^{13}\!/_{16}$	$40\frac{1}{2}$	9,713
I B M	May	50		3,152	CB	$^{11}\!/_{16}$	$-\frac{1}{8}$	$47\frac{3}{4}$	21,264
Intel	May	105		2,961	AM	$^{13}\!/_{16}$	$-\frac{1}{2}$	$92\frac{3}{4}$	7,876
Marriot	May	$22\frac{1}{2}$	p	2,925	PB	$\frac{1}{16}$	$+\frac{1}{16}$	$25\frac{1}{8}$	. . .
Chryslr	May	40		2,471	CB	$1\frac{1}{2}$	$+^{5}\!/_{16}$	$39\frac{5}{8}$	9,489
Intel	May	100		2,467	AM	$1^{11}\!/_{16}$	$-^{15}\!/_{16}$	$92\frac{3}{4}$	8,059
Intel	May	95		2,444	AM	$3\frac{3}{8}$	$-1\frac{1}{2}$	$92\frac{3}{4}$	979
Amgen	Jul	45		2,304	AM	$1\frac{3}{4}$	$+\frac{1}{8}$	$39\frac{3}{4}$	2,912
A S A	May	40		2,186	AM	$3\frac{1}{8}$	$+1\frac{1}{8}$	$43\frac{1}{8}$	4,477
G M	May	35		2,143	CB	$5\frac{5}{8}$	$+1\frac{3}{8}$	$40\frac{1}{2}$	2,741
Intel	May	90	p	2,025	AM	$3\frac{1}{8}$	$+1\frac{3}{8}$	$92\frac{3}{4}$	2,234
Marriot	May	25	p	1,980	PB	$\frac{5}{8}$	$-\frac{1}{8}$	$25\frac{1}{8}$	5,936
Mobil	May	70		1,951	CB	$\frac{3}{8}$	$-\frac{1}{8}$	$68\frac{1}{4}$	12,116
TelMex	May	55		1,941	CB	$\frac{3}{4}$	$-^{7}\!/_{16}$	$52\frac{3}{4}$	21,847
Motrla	Jul	45	p	1,800	AM	$\frac{1}{8}$	. . .	$70\frac{5}{8}$	3,127
Amgen	May	40		1,714	AM	$1\frac{7}{8}$	$-\frac{1}{4}$	$39\frac{3}{4}$	7,229
Homstk	May	15		1,670	CB	$1^{1}\!/_{16}$	$+\frac{3}{4}$	16	2,467
Alza	Jun	25		1,567	PC	$4\frac{3}{8}$	$+4\frac{3}{8}$	$29\frac{1}{4}$	. . .
Micsft	May	80	p	1,517	PC	$2\frac{1}{4}$	$+\frac{1}{2}$	$81\frac{3}{8}$	1,811
BankAm	Jun	45	p	1,513	CB	$1\frac{3}{8}$	$+1\frac{3}{8}$	$47\frac{1}{8}$	60
DellCpt s	May	30		1,454	PB	$1\frac{3}{8}$	$-1^{1}\!/_{16}$	28	2,390
A M D	May	30	p	1,446	PC	$1\frac{3}{8}$	$+\frac{1}{8}$	$30\frac{1}{2}$	1,475
Micsft	May	85		1,388	PC	$1^{11}\!/_{16}$	$-^{11}\!/_{16}$	$81\frac{3}{8}$	2,033
Synopt	May	95	p	1,347	CB	$1\frac{1}{4}$	$+^{3}\!/_{16}$	$106\frac{3}{4}$	159
A M D	May	30		1,312	PC	$1\frac{7}{8}$	$-\frac{1}{2}$	$30\frac{1}{2}$	2,484
Equity Options **-A-B-C-**								
A Hess	May	50		160	PB	$2^{15}\!/_{16}$	$-^{13}\!/_{16}$	53	634
A Hess	Jun	55		53	PB	$1\frac{1}{8}$	$-\frac{1}{16}$	53	42
A M D	May	20		60	PC	$10\frac{1}{2}$	$+\frac{3}{8}$	$30\frac{1}{2}$	89
A M D	Jul	20		98	PC	$10\frac{5}{8}$	$-\frac{5}{8}$	$30\frac{1}{2}$	1,303
A M D	Oct	20	p	162	PC	$\frac{5}{8}$	$+\frac{1}{8}$	$30\frac{1}{2}$	633
A M D	Jul	$22\frac{1}{2}$		168	PC	9	$+\frac{3}{4}$	$30\frac{1}{2}$	2,483
A M D	May	25		1,111	PC	$5\frac{1}{2}$	$-\frac{5}{8}$	$30\frac{1}{2}$	3,223

continued next page

continued

Option/Strike				Vol	Exch	Last	Net Chg	Stock Close	Open Int
A M D	May	25		917	PC	¼	+¹⁄₁₆	30½	1,115
A M D	Jun	25	p	115	PC	⅝	+¹⁄₁₆	30½	466
A M D	Jul	25		115	PC	6¼	−½	30½	2,546
A M D	Jul	25	p	251	PC	¾	. . .	30½	829
A M D	May	30		1,312	PC	1⅞	−½	30½	2,484
A M D	May	30	p	1,446	PC	1⅜	+⅛	30½	1,475
A M D	Jun	30		216	PC	2⅝	−⅜	30½	1,061
A M D	Jun	30	p	262	PC	2⅛	+⅛	30½	443
A M D	Jul	30		635	PC	3⅛	−⅜	30½	1,942
A M D	Jul	30	p	67	PC	2¹³⁄₁₆	+ ⅝	30½	289
A M D	Oct	30		830	PC	4½	. . .	30½	1,290
A M D	Oct	30	p	153	PC	3½	. . .	30½	396
A M R	May	65		321	AM	4⅞	−1⅝	69⅜	6,642
A M R	May	65	p	171	AM	¹¹⁄₁₆	+⁵⁄₁₆	69⅜	3,563
A M R	May	70		76	AM	1⅞	−⅝	69⅜	2,563
A M R	May	70	p	456	AM	2⅛	+¹⁄₁₆	69⅜	2,092
A M R	Jun	70		81	AM	2¹³⁄₁₆	−¹³⁄₁₆	69⅜	353
A M R	May	75		127	AM	⁷⁄₁₆	−¼	69⅜	1,168
A M R	Jun	75		186	AM	1	−⅜	69⅜	243
A M R	Aug	75		80	AM	2⅛	−½	69⅜	2,672
A S A	May	35		98	AM	8	+1⅝	43⅛	1,373
A S A	May	35	p	463	AM	¹⁄₁₆	−⅛	43⅛	1,032
A S A	Aug	35		63	AM	8¼	+1¾	43⅛	531
A S A	Aug	35	p	213	AM	⅜	−½	43⅛	1,041
A S A	Nov	35	p	300	AM	⅞	−⅝	43⅛	281
A S A	May	40		2,186	AM	3⅛	+1⅛	43⅛	4,477
A S A	May	40	p	178	AM	⁷⁄₁₆	−1¹⁄₁₆	43⅛	1,625
A S A	Aug	40		69	AM	4⅜	+1⅛	43⅛	1,659
A S A	May	45		427	AM	¹¹⁄₁₆	+⁷⁄₁₆	43⅛	1,759
A S A	May	45	p	67	AM	3¼	−2½	43⅛	201
A S A	Jun	45		68	AM	1³⁄₁₆	+⅝	43⅛	76
A S A	Jun	45	p	130	AM	3½	+3½	43⅛	. . .
A S A	Aug	45		219	AM	2¹⁄₁₆	+¹¹⁄₁₆	43⅛	853
A S A	Aug	45	p	147	AM	4¼	−2¼	43⅛	61
AT&T	May	55		306	CB	2¼	−¾	56	1,323
AT&T	May	55	p	1,005	CB	¾	+¼	56	5,224
AT&T	Jun	55		642	CB	1¼	+⁵⁄₁₆	56	355
AT&T	May	60		159	CB	⁷⁄₁₆	−¹⁄₁₆	56	2,102
AT&T	May	60	p	60	CB	3⅝	+⅞	56	366
AT&T	Jun	60		103	CB	⅝	−⅜	56	348
AT&T	Jul	60		404	CB	¹⁵⁄₁₆	−⁵⁄₁₆	56	7,324
AT&T	Oct	60		418	CB	1⅞	−⅛	56	2,847
Abbt L	May	25		53	PB	1½	. . .	25¾	3,453
Abbt L	May	25	p	64	PB	⁹⁄₁₆	−¹⁄₁₆	25¾	2,737
Abbt L	Jun	25		255	PB	2	. . .	25¾	324

continued next page

continued

Option/Strike				Vol	Exch	Last	Net Chg	Stock Close	Open Int
Abbt L	Jun	25	p	160	PB	$^{15}/_{16}$	. . .	$25^3/_4$	174
Am Exp	Jul	$22^1/_2$		60	AM	$6^7/_8$	$+^7/_8$	$29^1/_4$	954
Am Exp	May	25		85	AM	$4^1/_4$	$+^7/_8$	$29^1/_4$	1,112
Am Exp	May	25	p	70	AM	$^1/_{16}$	$-^1/_8$	$29^1/_4$	1,814
Am Exp	Jul	25	p	150	AM	$^3/_8$	$-^1/_{16}$	$29^1/_4$	2,653
Am Exp	May	30		642	AM	$^1/_2$	$+^3/_{16}$	$29^1/_4$	3,133
Am Exp	May	30	p	109	AM	$1^3/_8$	$-^3/_4$	$29^1/_4$	291
Am Exp	Jun	30		99	AM	1	$+^3/_8$	$29^1/_4$	319
Am Exp	Jun	30	p	456	AM	$1^5/_8$	$-^3/_4$	$29^1/_4$	227
Am Exp	Jul	30		97	AM	$1^3/_{16}$	$+^7/_{16}$	$29^1/_4$	10,727
Am Exp	Oct	30		74	AM	$1^3/_4$	$+^5/_{16}$	$29^1/_4$	1,912
AmBrnd	May	30		71	AM	$2^1/_4$	$+^1/_4$	32	529
AmBrnd	Sep	30		100	AM	$3^1/_8$	$+^1/_8$	32	301
AmBrnd	Sep	35		102	AM	$^7/_8$	$+^1/_8$	32	496
Amdahl	Nov	$7^1/_2$		105	CB	$^5/_8$	$-^1/_{16}$	$5^3/_4$	98
Amgen	May	35		311	AM	$5^3/_8$	$+^1/_2$	$39^3/_4$	2,094
Amgen	May	35	p	958	AM	$^1/_2$	$-^1/_2$	$39^3/_4$	4,541
Amgen	Jul	35	p	79	AM	$1^9/_{16}$	$-^3/_{16}$	$39^3/_4$	2,336
Amgen	May	40		1,714	AM	$1^7/_8$	$-^1/_4$	$39^3/_4$	7,229
Amgen	May	40	p	493	AM	$1^7/_8$	-1	$39^3/_4$	5,299
Amgen	Jun	40		251	AM	$2^7/_8$	$-^1/_8$	$39^3/_4$	526
Amgen	Jul	40		133	AM	$3^3/_4$	$+^1/_8$	$39^3/_4$	6,029
Amgen	Jul	40	p	69	AM	$3^1/_8$	$-^7/_8$	$39^3/_4$	1,016
Amgen	Oct	40	p	60	AM	$4^1/_2$	$+^1/_8$	$39^3/_4$	447
Amgen	May	45		436	AM	$^1/_2$	. . .	$39^3/_4$	1,641
Amgen	Jun	45		166	AM	$1^1/_8$	. . .	$39^3/_4$	253
Amgen	Jul	45		2,304	AM	$1^3/_4$	$+^1/_8$	$39^3/_4$	2,912
Amgen	Oct	45		59	AM	3	. . .	$39^3/_4$	906
Amgen	Oct	50		226	AM	$1^7/_8$	$+^1/_4$	$39^3/_4$	1,578

c = call
p = put
CB = Chicago Board Options Exchange
AM = American Stock Exchange
PB = Philadelphia Stock Exchange
PC = Pacific Stock Exchange
NY = New York Stock Exchange

Source: Options Exchanges, April 23.

and/or the expiration date. Financial newspapers such as *The Wall Street Journal* provide a full page showing the 1400 most active individual stock options. The volume shows the number of option contracts traded, with each contract representing 100 stock shares. The **open interest** is the number of contracts outstanding with both a long and short position. Current stock option open interest exceeds 15 million contracts,

EXHIBIT 11-3
Call Option Quotations

Company	Stock Price	Strike Price	Calls		
			Jan	Feb	March
ABC	100	90	10 ⅛	11	11 ¾
	100	95	5 ½	7	8
	100	100	2 ⅛	4	5
	100	105	½	2	3
	100	110	¹⁄₁₆	⅞	1 ⅝

Current date: January 1
Expiration dates: January 16; February 20; March 20
Volatility = 25%
Interest rate = 4%
Dividend = $0.00

representing 1.5 billion shares of stock, while stock index options add another 2 million contracts to open interest. Exhibit 11-3 presents selected call option quotations for a hypothetical stock called ABC Corporation. These call prices are listed in table format in order to better compare option prices with different characteristics.

The quotes in Exhibit 11-3 illustrate the meaning of call option quotations and describe various concepts relating to options. The hypothetical ABC stock price on the day in question closed at 100 per share. The strike prices listed for ABC in the exhibit range from 90 to 110.[3] The ABC options listed here expire during the third week of the expiration month in January, February, and March; other expiration months also exist. The next option to expire is called the **nearby option.** Later expirations are called **deferred options.**[4]

Notation. Symbols and equations will be simplified wherever possible. P_S is the price of the stock and P_C is the price of the call option. Many books use the symbol $P_C(P_S, t, K, \sigma, E)$, or something similar, to refer to the call price. The symbols within the parentheses are the factors affecting the call (P_S = the stock price; t = the time until the option expires; K = the strike price; σ = the volatility of the stock; and E = a European option). American options are designated by A. For simplicity, we will place these factors in parentheses only when it is necessary to distinguish between options with different strike prices or other variables.

In-the-Money and Out-of-the-Money Call Options. Let us first examine the prices of the ABC call options with a strike price of 95. For example, the Feb 95 call price is 7, or $700.00 for a 100-share call option. The ABC 95 call options are **in-the-money** calls—that is, the stock price is greater than the strike price. In-the-money call options have *positive* **intrinsic values,** with the Feb 95 call having an intrinsic value of 5: the 100 stock price less the 95 strike price. In general, the intrinsic value is described by Pricing Relationship #1 and Equation (11-1).

---

[3] Other strike prices often exist for a given stock option. However, limited trading occurs for options when the strike price varies substantially from the current stock price

[4] Option expiration dates and the option expiration cycle are discussed later in this chapter.

Pricing Relationship #1: The intrinsic value of a call option is either the stock price less the strike price, or zero, whichever is greater.

$$IV_C = \text{Max}[P_S - K, 0] \qquad (11\text{-}1)$$

where IV_C = intrinsic value of the call option C

$\qquad P_S$ = the price of the stock

$\qquad K$ = the strike price of the option

The value of the call option when the option *expires* is the call's intrinsic value at that time.

The ABC 100 call options are known as **near-the-money** or **at-the-money** options. For "near-the-money" options, the current stock price and the strike price are approximately the same. An "at-the-money" option exists when the stock price equals the strike price. The February 100 at-the-money option sells for 4, or \$400. The ABC February 105 call is an **out-of-the-money** option. An "out-of-the-money" call option exists when the stock price is less than the strike price. The February 105 option trades for 2, or \$200, for a 100-share option on ABC stock. Since the stock price is less than the strike price, we say that the intrinsic value for this option is equal to zero. At option expiration there is no reason to exercise an out-of-the-money option to purchase ABC stock at 105, since one can buy the stock in the open market for 100. The stock must increase in value (above 105) before an out-of-the-money option is worth exercising.

The Effect of Time.   Exhibit 11-3 shows that the prices of the March calls are greater than the February call prices. For example, the March 95 sells for 8, while the February 95 sells for 7. Comparing the other expiration dates (of equivalent strike prices) shows that the price of the option increases as the time until expiration increases. This **time to expiration factor** means that the buyer of the call option must pay in order to "purchase" more time for the stock price to increase. Conversely, as the time to expiration declines, the option price decreases (if all other factors remain constant).

The difference between the option *price* for the February 95 call of 7 and the *intrinsic value* of 5 for this option is called the **time value.** The size of this time value is determined by the time until option expiration, the difference between the stock price and strike price, and the volatility of the stock. The time value is defined as:

$$TV_C = P_C - IV_C \qquad (11\text{-}2)$$

where TV_C = the time value for the call

$\qquad P_C$ = the current price of the call option

Equations (11-1) and (11-2) provide us with our second pricing relationship:[5]

Pricing Relationship #2: An option before expiration sells for at least its intrinsic value; that is:

$$P_C \geq \text{Max}[P_S - K, 0] \qquad (11\text{-}3)$$

---

[5] Jarrow and Rudd (1983) prove these pricing relationships. Merton (1973) provides an extensive discussion of, and is the original source for, these option pricing relationships. Since these pricing relationships are intuitive, they do not need to be proved here.

Equation (11-3) is known as a boundary condition; that is, the lower bound for the price of a call option cannot be less than the "boundary" represented by whichever is the maximum: $P_S - K$ or zero. If a boundary condition is violated, risk-free profits (**arbitrage**) are possible.[6] Exhibit 11-4 provides a summary of the above relationships.

Strike Price Relationships. Exhibit 11-3 shows that the option prices constantly decrease (for the same expiration month) moving from the 90 strikes to the 110 strikes. Thus, in-the-money options are worth more than out-of-the-money options (when they have the same time to expiration). For example, the March 90 strike price has a call value of $11\frac{3}{4}$, while the higher 105 strike only has a value of 3. This pattern for the call option prices is due to the combination of the intrinsic value and time value relationships given in Equations (11-1) and (11-2). This can be formalized into the following pricing relationship:

Pricing Relationship #3: Call options with a lower exercise price are worth at least as much as call options with a higher exercise price—that is:

$$P_C(K_1) \geq P_C(K_2) \tag{11-4}$$

where $K_1 < K_2$

Profits at Call Option Expiration and Payoff Diagrams

Figure 11-1 illustrates the payoff diagram for purchasing and keeping a call option until its expiration. The call buyer has a maximum loss equal to the cost of the option. The loss on the option is reduced if the stock price at option expiration trades between

EXHIBIT 11-4
Call Option Relationships

The price of a call can be broken down into two basic components:

Price		Intrinsic Value	+	Time Value
P_C	=	$\text{Max}[P_S - K, 0]$	+	$P_C - \text{Max}[P_S - K, 0]$

If:	The Call Is:
$P_S > K$	In-the-money
$P_S = K$	At-the-money
$P_S < K$	Out-of-the-money

[6] More formally, the lower bound of a call is $P_C(E) \geq \text{Max}[P_S - K(1 + r)^{-t}, 0]$, where r is the risk-free interest rate. Due to the possibility of early exercise for an American call (when dividends exist), $P_C(A) \geq P_C(E)$. The upper bound on a call is $P_C \leq P_S$.

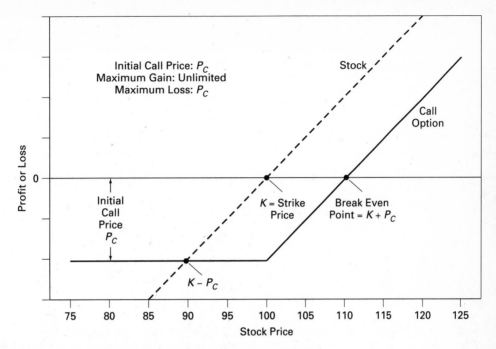

Figure 11-1 Payoff diagram at expiration for buying call options.

the strike price and the break-even point. Above the break-even point, the speculator profits from buying the call option. The stock price break-even point for the purchase of a call option is calculated by:

$$BE_C = K + P_C \tag{11-5}$$

where BE_C = the break-even point for the call option (the stock price at which the original cost of the call option is recovered)

The dashed line in the graph represents the profit/loss from a stock-only position. The stock position provides a profit/loss in dollars that is superior to the option profit/loss as long as the stock price is greater than the strike price minus the cost of the option—that is, when $P_S > K - P_C$. When the stock price is below $K - P_C$, the option position generates a smaller dollar loss than the stock position. On the other hand, options provide *larger percentage* changes than the stock position. Hence, the stock position can generate larger dollar profits, but the option provides greater **leverage** plus a limited loss feature.[7]

Figure 11-2 illustrates the payoff diagrams at option expiration for buying the Feb 95 and Feb 100 ABC call options. The profit (loss) from these option positions depends on

[7] Here we assume the initial stock price equals the strike price, but differing initial stock prices are easily implemented into the graph. Unless otherwise noted, the graphs and strategies ignore dividends, taxes, transactions costs, and the time value of money. Dividends are easily added but serve only to unnecessarily complicate the graphs and strategies. Taxes and transactions costs increase the cost of the position, but do not add to the analysis.

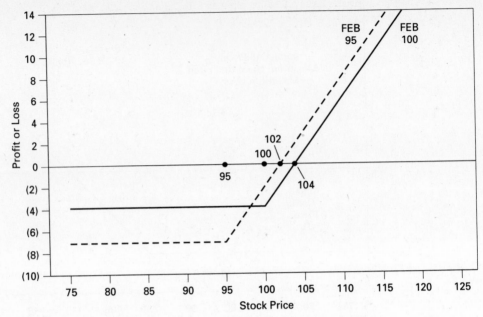

Figure 11-2 Payoff diagrams for ABC Feb 95 and 100 call option purchases.

the option purchase price and the stock price at option expiration. The figure shows that if the stock is priced below 100 when the Feb 100 option expires, then the entire $400 cost of the option is lost. In other words, there is no reason to exercise the right to purchase the stock at 100, since the stock price is below the exercise price. If the stock trades above 104 when the Feb 100 option expires, then the option buyer makes money, since a stock price above 104 means that the cost of the Feb 100 option is recovered and a profit is received. For example, if the stock trades at 110 at option expiration, then a net profit of 6 points is obtained: the 10-point intrinsic value profit from exercising the option (110 − 100) less the original option cost (4 points). Notice that the size of the profit depends solely on the price of the ABC stock being above 104.[8] The profit (or loss) relationship at the expiration of the option is stated in Equation (11-6):

$$\text{Profit} = \text{Max}[P_S - K, 0] - P_C = IV_C - P_C \qquad (11\text{-}6)$$

where IV_C = the intrinsic value at option expiration

P_C = the original cost of the call option

Thus, the profit on a call option position that is kept until the expiration of the option is the price of the stock less the strike price less the original option price. If the call option at expiration has an intrinsic value of zero, then the loss is limited to the original cost of the option. Example 11-1 illustrates important concepts concerning buying a call option: the potential profitability, the leverage, the small initial amount of funds needed, the limited loss feature, and the effect of the time value on the results.

[8] Pricing relationships among the stock price, strike price, and option price as well as speculative strategies for options, are examined in later chapters.

EXAMPLE 11-1
Buying a Call Stock Option

Motorola stock sold for 65½ in early April. During the following 10 days Motorola stock increased, based on a strong earnings report and the anticipated announcement of a new computer chip to rival Intel's Pentium chip. The stock and options prices on April 5 and April 16 (the expiration date of the options) are:

	April 5	April 16
Motorola stock	65½	73
April 65 call	2⅛	8
April 70 call	⁷⁄₁₆	3

The profits on these positions are:

Option profit $= IV_C - P_C$
April 65 profit $= 8 - 2⅛ = 5⅞$ or \$587.50 per contract
April 70 profit $= 3 - ⁷⁄₁₆ = 2⁹⁄₁₆$ or \$256.25 per contract
Motorola stock $= 73 - 65½ = 7½$ or \$750 per 100 shares

The rates of return on the options and stock are:

April 65 $=$ \$578.50/\$212.50 $= 276.5\%$
April 70 $=$ \$256.25/\$43.75 $= 585.7\%$
Motorola stock $=$ \$750/\$6500 $= 11.5\%$

A correct forecast of Motorola's price increase translates into a large percentage gain on the options (leverage). The April 65 originally near-the-money option has a greater dollar profit, but the out-of-the-money April 70 option has a larger percentage return (given its low initial price and smaller time value). While the stock has a larger dollar profit, the options possess significantly greater leverage.

If the ABC stock closes between 100 and 104, the buyer of the Feb 100 option will still exercise the option. In this case, the option buyer loses money, but the size of the loss is reduced by exercising the option. For example, if ABC closes at 102, then the intrinsic value of the Feb 100 option is 2 points (the 102 stock price less the 100 strike price). The cost of the option was 4, creating a net loss of 2 points, or \$200 per option of 100 shares. However, if the option is *not* exercised, then the loss would equal the original cost of the option: \$400, or 4 points. Consequently, exercising the option is beneficial as long as the stock price is above the strike price when the option expires.

The Feb 95 call diagrammed in Figure 11-2 is an in-the-money option; consequently, the original cost of the option is higher—specifically, 7 points. If the stock falls below 95 when the option expires, the call option is worthless and the call buyer loses the original cost of \$700. If the option is exercised when the stock trades between 95 and 102 (the strike price plus the option price), then the option buyer's losses are reduced. Above 102⅜ the option buyer profits, since the original cost of the option is covered.

Figure 11-2 also shows the *relationship* between the payoffs of the two options. The 95 in-the-money option is profitable at a lower stock price than the 100 option, but it costs more and hence loses more if the stock price declines below 98. The 100 at-the-money call is less profitable than the 95 option at any stock price above 98 (the difference in the option prices of 7 − 4 plus the 95 strike price), but it costs less.

STOCK PUT OPTION QUOTATIONS AND PRICING RELATIONSHIPS

Put Option Quotations

Exhibit 11-5 provides sample hypothetical quotations for puts. Previously, Exhibit 11-2 showed the newpaper presentation of put options. A put option provides the buyer with the right, but not the obligation, to *sell* the stock at a fixed price for a specific period of time. Thus, a put buyer profits when the price of the stock *declines* sufficiently. Put options are often considered mirror images of call options. The prices for the ABC put options in Exhibit 11-5 illustrate the "mirror-image" concept: put option prices are higher for larger strike prices, while call option prices are lower for smaller strike prices.

Out-of-the-Money and In-the-Money Put Options. Out-of-the-money put options exist when the stock price is *above* the strike price (since no put option buyer would want to *sell* stock at the strike price when it is possible to sell at a higher price in the open market). Therefore, the $1\frac{1}{2}$ price for the Feb 95 out-of-the-money put is entirely a time value. Only if the stock falls to below the strike price of 95 will the put option have a positive intrinsic value. In-the-money puts occur when the stock price is *below* the strike price. The price of $6\frac{3}{8}$ for the Feb 105 in-the-money put includes an intrinsic value of 5 and a time value of $1\frac{3}{8}$ points. The intrinsic value of 5 exists because the buyer of the put option can *sell* the stock at the strike price of 105, while simultaneously

EXHIBIT 11-5
Put Option Quotations

Company	Stock Price	Strike Price	Puts		
			Jan	Feb	March
ABC	100	90	0	$\frac{1}{2}$	$^{15}/_{16}$
	100	95	$\frac{3}{8}$	$1\frac{1}{2}$	$2\frac{1}{8}$
	100	100	2	$3\frac{3}{8}$	$4\frac{1}{8}$
	100	105	$5\frac{7}{8}$	$6\frac{3}{8}$	7
	100	110	10	$10\frac{1}{4}$	$10\frac{5}{8}$

Current date: January 1
Expiration dates: January 16; February 20; March 20
Volatility = 25%
Interest rate = 4%
Dividend = $0.00

EXHIBIT 11-6
Put Option Relationships

The price of a put can be broken down into two basic components:

Price		Intrinsic Value	+	Time Value
P_P	$=$	$\text{Max}[K - P_S, 0]$	$+$	$P_P - \text{Max}[K - P_S, 0]$

If:	The Call Is:
$P_S > K$	Out-of-the-money
$P_S = K$	At-the-money
$P_S < K$	In-the-money

buying the stock in the open market at 100. An additional one point is the difference between the option price and the intrinsic value. In general, the put intrinsic value is described by Pricing Relationship #4 and Equation (11-7). The put time value is defined by Equation (11-8).

Pricing Relationship #4: The intrinsic value of a put option is either the strike price less the stock price or zero, whichever is greater.

$$IV_P = \text{Max}[K - P_S, 0] \tag{11-7}$$

and

$$TV_P = P_P - IV_P \tag{11-8}$$

where IV_P = the intrinsic value of the put

P_P = the current price of the put

TV_P = the time value for the put

The price of the put at option expiration is the put's intrinsic value. Exhibit 11-6 provides a summary of the relationships given above. As with a call, the lower boundary condition for a put option before expiration is that a put sells for at least its intrinsic value.[9]

Time and Strike Price Relationships. The time factor relationships for put options parallel those for call options. Put options with a longer time to expiration are worth more, although Exhibits 11-3 and 11-5 show that the differences in put prices from one expiration to another (for equivalent strike prices) are smaller than they are for the associated call options. As with call options, relative put option prices are directly related to strike prices for equivalent expiration months. Exhibit 11-5 shows that put

---

[9] More formally, the lower bound for an American put is $P_P(E) \geq \text{Max}[K(1 + r)^{-t} - P_S, 0]$. The lower bound for a European put is $P_P(E) = \text{Max}[K - P_S, 0]$. Also, $P_P(A) \geq P_P(E)$ due to the possibility of early exercise for the American put. The upper boundary condition is $P_P(E) \leq K(1 + r)^{-t}$. Also, $P_P \leq K$.

option prices are higher for larger strike prices. This pattern is based on a combination of the intrinsic value and time value relationships in Equations (11-7) and (11-8). These patterns and boundary conditions are formalized as follows:

> *Pricing Relationship #5:* Put options with a higher strike price are worth at least as much as put options with a lower strike price; that is:

$$P_P(K_2) \geq P_P(K_1) \qquad (11\text{-}9)$$

Profits at Put Option Expiration and Payoff Diagrams

Figure 11-3 illustrates the payoff diagram at option expiration for purchasing a put option. A put buyer purchases the right to *sell* the stock at the relevant strike price. If the stock price is above the put strike price at option expiration, then the buyer of the put loses the original cost of the put (the maximum loss). Any gain from buying a put depends on how much the stock price declines. The break-even point is the strike price less the cost of the put:

$$BE_P = K - P_P \qquad (11\text{-}10)$$

where BE_P = break-even point for the put option (the stock price at which the original cost of the put option is recovered)

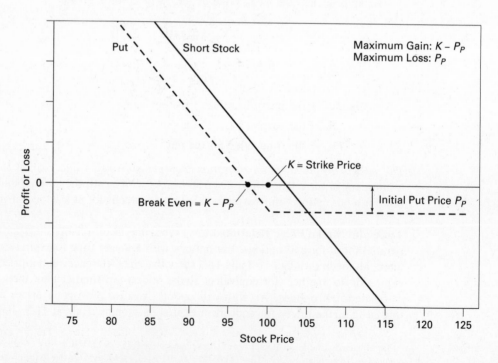

Figure 11-3 Payoff diagram at expiration for buying a put option.

If the stock price declines to a point significantly below the strike price, the put option buyer obtains a large profit on a small initial investment. The dashed line in the figure represents a **short sale** on the underlying stock. A short sale produces a larger profit than the put option when the stock price is below the strike price, but the maximum loss on the put is limited to the cost of the put. In addition, the put has more leverage than a short sale.

Figure 11-4 shows the payoff diagrams for the Feb 95 and Feb 100 put options at option expiration (see Exhibit 11-5 for the original cost information for the puts). The figure illustrates that if the stock is priced at or above 95 when the 95 put option expires, there is no reason to exercise the right to sell the stock at 95. In this case, the buyer of the put option loses the original cost of the option of $150 (1½ points). The break-even point for the Feb 95 put is 93½; that is, the strike price of 95 less the original cost of 1½ = 93½. If the stock trades below 124¼ when the put option expires, the buyer of the put profits. For example, if ABC stock closes at 90 on the expiration day, a trader could buy the stock in the open market at 90 and then exercise the put option to sell the stock at the strike price of 95. This transaction would generate a gross profit (intrinsic value) of 5 points. After considering the original cost of the put option of 1½, the trader would net a profit of 3½ points, or $350, for a 100-share option. The lower the price of the stock at option expiration, the larger the profits for the put buyer. The net profit (loss) for the buyer of a put option when the option is exercised *at expiration* is determined as follows:

$$\text{Profit} = \text{Max}[K - P_S, 0] - P_P = IV_P - P_P \qquad (11\text{-}11)$$

where IV_P = the intrinsic value of the put at option expiration

P_P = the original cost of the put option

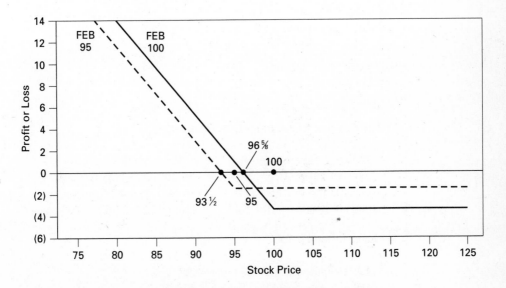

Figure 11-4 Payoff diagram for ABC Feb 95 and 100 put option purchases.

Thus, the profit on a put option position that is kept until the expiration of the option is the strike price less the stock price less the original cost of the put. The put buyer exercises the put option as long as the stock trades below 95 at the expiration of the option. Between 95 and 93½, the put buyer loses money; however, exercising the option reduces the size of the loss. If the put option has an intrinsic value of zero at expiration, then the maximum loss on the put is the cost of the option. (Example 11-2 shows how a speculator would profit if he or she purchased a put option on Intel before adverse news was made public.)

The Feb 100 put option is an at-the-money option. The 100 put provides a net profit as long as the stock trades below 96 at the expiration of the option—that is, the strike price of 100 less the cost of 3⅜. If the stock trades above 100, the put expires worthless. Comparing the 95 and 100 puts shows that the 100 option is profitable below 96⅝. However, the 100 put costs more and therefore loses more money if the stock price trades above the 100 strike price. The 100 put is a better choice than the 95 put as long as the stock trades below 98½ (the strike price of 100 less the difference in the option prices of 3⅜ − 1½).

EXAMPLE 11-2
Buying a Put Stock Option

As the premier PC chip maker, Intel's sales and profits rose dramatically due to the 386 and 486 PC chips. Over a period of one year, the stock price rose from 46 to over 121. However, the loss of a court case which allowed rival Advanced Micro Devices to sell a competing chip caused Intel's stock to drop 12¼ points in one day on volume of over 17 million shares. Over a period of one week, the stock fell 17¼ points on nearly 45 million shares traded. The following Monday, Intel dropped another 5⅜ on news from Motorola that it was going to sell a chip to compete with Intel's Pentium (a "586" chip). A speculator who bought a put on Intel before the major decline started and kept the put until expiration profited as follows:

	April 16	May 14
Intel stock	110	87⅜
May 115 put	7⅜	27⅝
May 105 put	2⅞	17⅝

The profits on the put and short sale positions are:

$$Option\ profit = IV_P - P_P$$
May 115 put profit = 27⅝ − 7⅜ = 20¼ or $2025 per contract
May 105 put profit = 17⅝ − 2⅞ = 14¾ or $1475 per contract
Intel short sale = 110 − 87⅜ = 22⅝ or $2262.50 per 100 shares

The rates of return are:

May 115 put = $2025/$737.50 = 274.6%
May 105 put = $1475/$287.50 = 513.0%
Intel short sale = $2262.50/$11,000 = 20.6%

CHARACTERISTICS OF STOCK OPTIONS

Option Classes and Expiration Dates

An **option class** is a designation for all of the options on the same stock. Thus, all of the calls and puts (all strikes and expiration dates) on IBM represent an option class. An **option series** is a particular option with a specific strike price and expiration date.

Stock option expirations follow one of the January, February, or March **option cycles.** The January cycle consists of the option expiration months of January, April, July, and October. Similarly, the February and March cycles vary by three-month intervals (thus, the February cycle is February, May, August, and November). Before 1987, only the next three expiration months in the stock option cycle were traded. As of 1987, almost all of the options follow the procedure that the current calendar month, the next calendar month, and the next two monthly expirations in the option cycle of the stock are traded. Thus, a stock in the January cycle would trade the following options on February 1: February, March, April, and July. On March 1, a January cycle stock would trade March, April, July, and October. *The Wall Street Journal* lists only the most active options on a particular stock. Quotes for other expirations are available from a broker.[10]

Options expire on the Saturday following the third Friday of the expiration month. The last day of trading for the option is the third Friday of the expiration month; delivery is on the following Monday. The next relevant option expiration is listed on the option exchange the Monday following the expiration of the previously traded option.

Strike Prices, Stock Splits, and Position Limits

Strike prices are typically spaced at intervals of $2.50 when the underlying stock is priced below $25; at $5 when the stock is between $50 and $200; and at $10 when the stock is over $200. When a new option expiration month starts to trade, the two strike prices nearest the stock price are activated for trading purposes. A *new* option strike price is created when the stock price closes two days in a row closer to the potential new option strike price than to the currently traded strike prices. For example, if a stock option has strike prices of 35 and 40, and the stock closes above $42.50 for two days in a row, then a 45 strike price starts to trade.

The strike price of an option remains the same unless a **stock split** or **stock dividend** occurs for the stock. The strike price adjustment for a stock split or stock dividend reflects the relative change in the stock price resulting from the split or dividend.[11] Cash dividends paid by the corporation do *not* affect strike prices.

Position limits refer to the maximum number of option contracts a trader can hold at one time. An option trader can hold only 3,000 to 8,000 option contracts, with the size of the limit depending on the stock's volume and number of shares outstanding.

---

[10] Newspapers listing quotations in the table format given in Exhibit 11-3 show options that do not trade on a particular day with the notation "r." The symbol "s" means that this particular option has never traded.

[11] When the stock split is an integer multiple such as a 2-1 split, then the strike price is divided by the integer split; thus a $60 strike price would be reduced to $30 for a 2-1 stock split and a second option contract would be issued. For a non-integer split, both the strike price and the number of shares are adjusted. Hence, for a 3-2 or, equivalently, a 1.5-1 split, the strike price is divided by 1.5 and the number of shares for an option is multiplied by 1.5. A stock dividend of 10% means that an option is based on 110 shares and the strike price is adjusted to $1/1.10 = .90909$ (rounded to the nearest $\frac{1}{8}$) of its former price.

LEAPS

LEAPS are long-term options that expire up to three years in the future. Except for the expiration date difference, they have equivalent characteristics to other stock options. However, the market for LEAPS is less active than for shorter-term options, creating the possibility that these options will be mispriced relative to their value and that liquidity problems will occur.

STOCK INDEX OPTIONS

Characteristics of Index Options

A stock **index option** is an option on an idex of common stocks, with the index representing a portfolio of stocks weighted by price or by total market value. Chapter 2 briefly outlines the characteristics of common stock indexes and the meaning of these indexes.

The S&P 100 Index option, also known as the OEX, began to trade in March of 1983. The S&P 100 was the first stock index option and has been the most popular. This index is based on the largest 100 companies in terms of the Standard & Poor's criteria. Other active index options are the S&P 500, the S&P Midcap Index, Russell 2000, the Major Market Index (MMI), the Institutional Index, and the Japan Index.[12]

Delivery of all of the stocks represented in a stock index when an index option expires would be very difficult, especially since each stock has a different weight in the index. Consequently, index options are settled "in cash" at option expiration. **Cash settlement** means that when the option buyer exercises the option at expiration, the buyer receives from the seller the difference between the stock index value and the strike price of the option (multiplied by the size of the option contract). Most options, such as the S&P 100 options, are American options. The S&P 500 options are European options. The expiration of most index options occurs on the Saturday after the third Friday of the expiration month.[13] Many of the index options have expirations for the current month and the next three consecutive months. Other index options possess expirations during the current month and the following month, plus the next one or two expirations in one of the January, February, or March option cycles. The position limits for the S&P 100 and S&P 500 index options are 25,000 and 5000 contracts, respectively.

---

[12] The S&P Midcap Index is an index of midsize companies that are smaller than S&P 500 firms. Options on the NYSE, Value Line, utility, Japan, and gold/silver indexes also exist, although the volume for these industry index options is relatively small. Options on the S&P 500 Index, the Institutional Index, and the Financial News Composite Index are European options. The other options are American. The NSX option also differs from the S&P 500 option in that the former's final settlement price is based on the *opening* price of these stocks in the index on the third Friday rather than on the closing price, thereby escaping any volatility created by the expirations of stock options, index options, and futures contracts.

[13] Starting with the June 1987 contract, *some* option indexes are valued on the *open* of this third Friday, with trading in the option ceasing on the previous day. The S&P 100 option, the most popular stock index option, still expires on the close of the third Friday of the expiration month. The change in expiration dates for some index options was initiated because the concurrent expirations of individual stock options, index options, and futures contracts on stock indexes sometimes created volatile markets due to unusual supply and demand factors. The simultaneous expiration of these contracts became known as the "triple witching hour."

Flex options also are available for S&P 100 and S&P 500 options. These "flexible options" allow institutional investors to design their own positions by customizing options. Flex options allow customers to choose the strike prices, expiration date, type of exercise (e.g. American or European), and type of settlement procedure of the index options. The minimum face value of these flexible options is $10 million. So far, over $6 billion of face value of exchange traded flex options has traded; over-the-counter flex option total over $50 billion per year. A major benefit of exchange-traded flex options compared to the over-the-counter version is that exchange-traded options eliminate the credit risk problem. In addition, these trades become public, providing price information to the market. Because of the success of these flex options plans exist to trade flex options on the Russell 2000 small stock index, mid-size stock index, and a Japanese stock index.

The popularity of index options is based on two factors: (1) the cash settlement feature avoids the necessity of delivery, and (2) options on "the market" provide trading and hedging opportunities not available with individual stock options. Specifically, index options allow a trader or hedger to concentrate on the risk of the market (**systematic risk**), ignoring the effects of company risk (**unsystematic risk**).[14,15]

Quoting Index Options

Exhibit 11-7 provides the quotes for the most popular index options. The S&P 100 options are by far the most active, with call and put volume totaling 300,000 contracts. The S&P 100 options also have a large open interest of 600,000 contracts. The S&P 500 options trade 70,000 contracts per day but possess a larger open interest than the S&P 100, with over 800,000 in total open interest. Total volume and open interest for stock index options are less than what existed before the stock market crash of October 1987.

The option prices for stock index options are on a per-unit basis. The total cost of the option is the per-unit price times the option's multiple. For example, the S&P 100 and S&P 500 Index options are multiplied by 100 to obtain the total cost. Similarly, the value of the option *at expiration* is determined by multiplying the difference between the value of the appropriate cash index and the strike price by $100. Thus, if the S&P 100 Index settles on the expiration day at 414, then a call option with a 400 strike price settles for $14 \times \$100$ (with $414 - 400 = 14$). The minimum price change for the

---

[14] One problem does exist with the cash-settlement feature of index options that are valued at the next day's open after the last trading day. This problem is called "exercise risk." If an option buyer exercises an in-the-money option early on the final trading day, only to have that option become an *out*-of-the-money option when the next day's opening price is used for pricing purposes, then the *buyer* of the option must *pay* the seller the difference between the index value and the option strike price. Thus, a trader should wait as long as possible on the final trading day before exercising an index option that is valued on the next day's open.

[15] Other problems exist for those who *sell* index options. If the option seller is using the sale of options to hedge a portfolio of stocks, two difficulties arise. First, the stock portfolio typically does not exactly match the index represented by the option. This is called "basis risk." Second, if the stocks are sold to pay off the option, a "timing risk" can exist—that is, if the sale of the stocks is made at a different time from the opening of the option on expiration day, then pricing differences exist.

EXHIBIT 11-7
Popular Stock Index Options

S&P 100 INDEX (OEX)

Strike		Vol.	Close	Net Chg.	Open Int.
May	360c	3	44 3/4	−5 1/4	4
May	360p	512	5/16	+1/8	4,038
Jun	360p	1,788	3/4	+1/4	1,459
May	365p	309	3/8	+3/16	2,068
Jun	365p	445	1	+5/16	988
May	370p	1,429	1/2	+1/8	4,042
Jun	370p	1,481	1 5/16	+5/16	3,264
May	375p	1,589	11/16	+1/8	6,276
Jun	375p	196	1 3/4	+1/2	1,571
May	380c	6	26 1/8	−4 3/8	53
May	380p	2,868	15/16	+1/4	14,009
Jun	380p	1,418	2 1/8	+15/16	4,895
Jul	380p	356	3 3/8	+1/2	1,425
Aug	380c	10	29 1/2	. . .	. . .
Aug	380p	1,405	5	+1 1/2	180
May	385p	5,551	1 1/4	+1/16	11,836
Jun	385p	290	2 13/16	+1/2	1,436
Jul	385p	67	4 1/4	+1/2	238
May	390c	491	16 1/4	−4 1/4	2,386
May	390p	15,177	1 3/4	+1/8	24,736
Jun	390c	132	18 1/2	−4 3/4	706
Jun	390p	2,195	3 3/4	+5/8	7,046
Jul	390p	28	5 1/4	+3/4	1,558
Aug	390c	15	21 1/4	−4 5/8	10
Aug	390p	831	7	+7/8	2,151
May	395c	487	12 1/2	−2 1/2	1,386
May	395p	20,526	2 11/16	+5/16	29,472
Jun	395c	20	14 3/4	−4 7/8	27
Jun	395p	1,383	4 7/8	+1 1/8	5,462
Jul	395p	41	6 3/4	+2	2,241
May	400c	6,933	8 1/2	−1/2	14,263
May	400p	22,017	3 3/4	+1/4	36,390
Jun	400c	12	10 7/8	−1 3/4	2,367
Jun	400p	2,470	6 1/2	+3/4	11,957
Jul	400c	1,585	13	−3	215
Jul	400p	199	8 3/8	+1 1/8	1,609
Aug	400c	30	14 1/4	−5	134
Aug	400p	149	10	+2 1/2	1,261
May	405c	16,627	5 3/8	−1/2	12,705
May	405p	29,040	5 3/4	+1/2	29,549
Jun	405c	1,031	7 7/8	−7/8	692
Jun	405p	2,823	8 3/8	+3/4	4,894
Jul	405c	129	10	−2 3/4	36
Jul	405p	115	10 1/4	+2 7/8	553
May	410c	33,597	3 1/8	−1/4	39,100
May	410p	18,726	8 1/2	+3/4	39,185
Jun	410c	1,435	5 3/8	−5/8	9,317
Jun	410p	983	10 7/8	+3/4	8,729
Jul	410c	140	7 1/8	−7/8	2,057
Jul	410p	17	12 1/4	+1	1,897
Aug	410c	45	9 1/4	−3	879
Aug	410p	23	13 3/4	+3/4	481
May	415c	27,124	1 1/2	−3/16	45,578
May	415p	5,708	11 7/8	+1/2	27,131
Jun	415c	2,251	3 3/8	−3/8	4,130
Jun	415p	535	14 1/8	+3/4	1,861
Jul	415c	67	5	−2	74
Jul	415p	19	15 1/8	+1 7/8	74
May	420c	10,505	5/8	−1/16	36,285
May	420p	821	16 1/4	+1	5,414
Jun	420c	2,963	2	−5/16	7,964
Jun	420p	140	18	+2 1/8	1,079
Jul	420c	929	3 3/8	−7/8	1,286
Jul	420p	16	18 1/2	+3 1/4	263
Aug	420c	265	4 3/4	−1 3/4	601
Aug	420p	15	19 1/2	+2 3/4	62
May	425c	4,572	1/4	. . .	27,278
May	425p	33	20 1/2	+2	423
Jun	425c	1,586	1 1/16	−1/4	3,788
Jun	425p	3	22 1/2	+7 1/2	74
Jul	425c	428	2 1/8	−3/8	1,580
Jul	425p	5	23 1/2	+6	5
May	430c	588	1/8	. . .	25,050
Jun	430c	652	9/16	−1/16	12,224
Jun	430p	6	25 1/4	+5 1/4	94
Jul	430c	4,100	1 3/16	−5/16	6,536
Aug	430c	2,694	2 1/4	−7/16	5,458
Aug	430p	14	28	+4 3/4	21
May	435c	358	1/16	. . .	21,112
Jun	435c	287	5/16	−1/8	9,094
May	440c	10	1/16	. . .	16,484
Jun	440c	9	3/16	. . .	1,882
Jul	440c	25	1/2	. . .	1,349
Jul	440p	1	35 1/2	+5	5

Call vol . . . . .122,141 Open Int 315,423

Put vol . . . . .143,763 Open Int 303,616

continued next page

continued

Strike		Vol.	Close	Net Chg.	Open Int.	Strike		Vol.	Close	Net Chg.	Open Int.
S&P 500 INDEX-AM (SPX)											
May	330p	16	$\frac{1}{16}$	. . .	1,465	Jun	440p	2,989	10$\frac{1}{8}$	+1$\frac{1}{8}$	5,841
Jun	375p	1,020	$\frac{3}{8}$	+$\frac{1}{8}$	9,033	Jul	440c	78	9$\frac{1}{2}$	. . .	. . .
Jun	390p	45	$\frac{7}{8}$	+$\frac{3}{8}$	15,754	Jul	440p	155	12	+3$\frac{7}{8}$	382
May	400p	10	$\frac{7}{16}$	+$\frac{3}{16}$	214	May	445c	4,168	2$\frac{1}{4}$	−$\frac{1}{2}$	12,399
Jun	400p	1,232	1$\frac{3}{8}$	+$\frac{1}{2}$	19,970	May	445p	1,576	10$\frac{1}{4}$	+1$\frac{1}{4}$	10,186
Jun	405p	210	1$\frac{3}{4}$	+$\frac{3}{8}$	5,625	Jun	445c	564	4$\frac{3}{4}$	−1$\frac{1}{8}$	8,252
May	410p	263	$\frac{3}{4}$	+$\frac{1}{8}$	719	Jun	445p	713	12$\frac{1}{2}$	+1$\frac{1}{2}$	7,258
Jun	410p	350	2	+$\frac{5}{16}$	6,634	May	450c	1,806	1	−$\frac{1}{2}$	13,719
May	415p	62	1$\frac{1}{8}$	+$\frac{1}{2}$	3,907	May	450p	3,318	14$\frac{3}{8}$	+1$\frac{5}{8}$	14,258
Jun	415p	475	2$\frac{7}{8}$	+$\frac{7}{8}$	4,957	Jun	450c	3,055	3	−$\frac{1}{2}$	30,580
May	420c	17	18$\frac{1}{2}$	−1$\frac{1}{8}$	4,727	Jun	450p	305	16	+2	22,739
May	420p	717	1$\frac{3}{4}$	+$\frac{1}{2}$	7,741	Jul	450c	250	4$\frac{3}{4}$	−2	3,000
Jun	420p	4,801	3$\frac{5}{8}$	+$\frac{7}{8}$	12,032	Jul	450p	50	16$\frac{1}{2}$	+4$\frac{3}{8}$	53
May	425c	19	14	−6$\frac{1}{2}$	2,537	May	455c	447	$\frac{1}{2}$	−$\frac{1}{4}$	7,513
May	425p	406	2$\frac{7}{16}$	+$\frac{7}{16}$	8,536	May	455p	97	18$\frac{1}{2}$	+3	1,060
Jun	425c	25	17$\frac{1}{8}$	−9$\frac{7}{8}$	7,364	Jun	455c	735	1$\frac{13}{16}$	−$\frac{7}{16}$	3,468
Jun	425p	1,596	4$\frac{7}{8}$	+1$\frac{1}{8}$	28,828	Jun	455p	42	19$\frac{3}{4}$	+5$\frac{5}{8}$	818
Jul	425p	530	6$\frac{3}{8}$	+1$\frac{3}{8}$	3,900	Jul	455c	13	3$\frac{1}{4}$	−$\frac{1}{4}$	1,375
May	430c	31	10	−2$\frac{1}{4}$	3,125	May	460c	4,425	$\frac{1}{4}$	. . .	12,091
May	430p	6,048	3$\frac{3}{8}$	+$\frac{3}{8}$	12,680	Jun	460c	2,831	1$\frac{3}{16}$	−$\frac{1}{8}$	15,148
Jun	430c	1,543	13$\frac{1}{8}$	−1$\frac{1}{8}$	2,866	Jun	460p	3	23	+6	186
Jun	430p	644	6$\frac{1}{4}$	+1	8,592	Jul	460p	3	24	+3$\frac{3}{4}$	7
May	435c	1,604	6$\frac{1}{2}$	−1$\frac{1}{2}$	1,810	May	465c	1,732	$\frac{1}{8}$	. . .	13,621
May	435p	2,171	5$\frac{1}{8}$	+$\frac{3}{4}$	14,331	May	465p	5	27$\frac{5}{8}$	+3$\frac{5}{8}$	36
Jun	435c	310	10$\frac{1}{8}$	−2$\frac{5}{8}$	5,314	Jul	465c	4	1$\frac{1}{8}$	−1	425
Jun	435p	644	8	+1$\frac{3}{8}$	11,146	May	470c	71	$\frac{1}{16}$	. . .	12,669
Jul	435c	25	11$\frac{5}{8}$	. . .	. . .	Jun	470p	2	32$\frac{1}{2}$	+4$\frac{1}{2}$	6,702
Jul	435p	188	9$\frac{5}{8}$	+3$\frac{1}{8}$	297	May	475c	40	$\frac{1}{16}$	−$\frac{1}{16}$	5,644
May	440c	3,089	4$\frac{1}{8}$	−$\frac{3}{4}$	9,643	Jun	475c	300	$\frac{1}{8}$	−$\frac{1}{8}$	5,530
May	440p	1,688	7$\frac{3}{8}$	+1$\frac{1}{4}$	8,144	Jun	475p	300	36$\frac{7}{8}$	+2$\frac{3}{8}$	1,076
Jun	440c	196	6$\frac{7}{8}$	−$\frac{3}{4}$	6,578						
Call vol 29,791						Open Int. 328,938					
Put vol 38,891						Open Int. 417,889					

c = call
p = put

Source: Options exchanges, April 23.

stock index options is $\frac{1}{8}$th for options priced above \$3 and $\frac{1}{16}$th for options below \$3. Strike prices for the index options vary by units of five. Otherwise, the concepts for index options are identical to those described for individual stock options.[16]

[16] Newspapers listing option quotations in the table format show " . . . " for index options that did not trade on the day in question. *The Wall Street Journal* also provides a listing of the most active index options.

LEAPS also exist on index options. The Amex has LT-20s, which are $\frac{1}{20}$th of the MMI index. The CBOE has OEX leaps, which are $\frac{1}{10}$th of the S&P 100 stock index. The total cost/value of each LEAP is $100 times the option price. Volume on these leaps tends to be low, but the open interest is relatively large.

Cash Settlement Versus Asset Settlement

Stock index options are settled in cash. Individual stock options are settled by exchanging the underlying asset (the stock).

The advantages of cash settlement relative to asset settlement are:

- Sellers of call or put options are not forced to sell the asset (for calls) or buy the asset (for puts).
- There is a potential reduction in transactions costs, since assets do not change hands.

The relative disadvantages of cash-settled options are:

- Cash-settled assets such as stock indexes are difficult to hedge, not because of cash settlement per se but because of the nature of the asset.
- There is a risk of becoming temporarily unhedged when the option is exercised because the option is transformed into cash based on the closing price, which removes the hedge until the seller learns of the exercise the next business day. Conversely, traders of asset-settled options exchange the asset, keeping the hedge in place.
- A wildcard characteristic exists in index option exercise, since the option is priced at 4:00 P.M. (Eastern time) but can be exercised until 4:10 P.M., providing a timing benefit to the option buyer. The seller does not learn of the exercise until the next business day.[17]

The disadvantages of cash-settled stock index options have not adversely affected trader interest. Approximately one-third of total stock option volume is typically in index options.

MARKET ORGANIZATION

The Clearing Corporation

Options trades *appear to be* between the buyer and seller. However, technically each trade is with the Options Clearing Corporation. This arrangement is beneficial in two ways. First, when either the buyer or the seller wants to close his or her option position, this can be done on the exchange with *any willing trader,* rather than being restricted to

---

[17] While an option buyer does not officially have to provide notification of exercise until 4:10 P.M., some brokerage houses require notification by 12 P.M. Option writers who are not notified until late the next day lose their hedge position since they end up selling their stocks one day after the option is officially exercised.

the party who took the other side of the trade. Second, if a trader defaults, the clearing mechanism comes into play to guarantee the other side of the option contract.[18]

When an option buyer exercises an option, the Options Clearing Corporation randomly selects a member firm to be the deliverer of the stock. Member firms then execute their own policy concerning who gets exercised. At the brokerage house level, the individual customer with the oldest short option position is often chosen as the designated seller of the stock. The Clearing Corporation automatically exercises stock options owned by individuals if the option is in-the-money by more than ¾ point at expiration. Index options are exercised if they are ¼ point in-the-money. Options owned by institutions are automatically exercised if a stock is in-the-money by ¼ point or an index is ¹⁄₁₀₀ th in-the-money.

Costs of Trading

Three types of costs exist when trading options:

- Commissions for trading the options.
- Stock commissions if the option is exercised and a stock is received or delivered.
- The bid-ask spread when the option is traded on the floor of the options exchange. For example, if the bid-ask spread is 3 to 3¼, then an individual buying an option pays the higher ask price of 3¼, while the bid price of 3 is received when selling an option.

Table 11-1 shows a representative commission schedule from a discount broker. Commissions from full-service brokers are higher.

Table 11-1 Commission Schedule for a Discount Broker

Dollar Amount of Trade	Commission*
< $2500	$20 + .02 of the dollar amount
$2500 to $10,000	$45 + .01 of the dollar amount
> $10,000	$120 + .0025 of the dollar amount

*The maximum commission is $30 per contract for the first five contracts plus $20 per contract for each additional contract. Minimum commission is $30 per contract for the first contract plus $2 per contract for each additional contract.

Regulation

The regulation of options is split between two government agencies. Options on stocks, indexes, and foreign exchange are regulated by the Securities and Exchange Commission. Options on futures contracts are regulated by the Commodity Futures Trading Commission. These agencies monitor trading activity, make sure that all traders abide by exchange rules and trading laws, and make sure that no illegal insider trading occurs.

---

[18] During the 1987 stock market crash, the Clearing Corporation did have a default. When a trader defaults, the brokerage firm must pay; if the brokerage house goes bankrupt, the clearing member of the exchange must pay. If the clearing member goes bankrupt, the Clearing Corporation covers the default.

Rutz (1988) gives a thorough overview of the clearance, payment, and settlement systems of options and futures exchanges.

SUMMARY AND LOOKING AHEAD

This chapter provides an overview of the quotations, basic concepts, and basic pricing relationships for individual stock options and index options. Call and put options are defined and the characteristics associated with these options are explained. Chapters 12 and 13 discuss the pricing of options. The Black-Scholes option pricing model is the focus of this discussion, but other approaches to pricing are relevant as well, such as put-call parity and the binomial model. The inputs and outputs of the pricing models are discussed in order to determine how such models can help an option trader to determine whether an option is under- or overpriced.

BIBLIOGRAPHY

Jarrow, Robert A., and Andrew Rudd (1983). *Option Pricing.* Homewood, Il: Irwin.

Merton, Robert C. (1973). "The Theory of Rational Option Pricing," *Bell Journal of Economics and Management Science,* Spring, Vol. 4, No. 1, pp. 141–183.

Ritchken, Peter (1987). *Options: Theory, Strategy, and Applications.* Glenview, IL: Scott, Foresman.

Rutz, Roger (1988). "Clearance, Payment, and Settlement Systems in the Futures, Options, and Stock Markets," *Review of Futures Markets,* Vol. 7, No. 3, pp. 346–370.

PROBLEMS

*Indicates more difficult problems.

Below are closing prices for options on a stock when the stock price is 66¼. Use this information to answer questions 11-1 through 11-4.

	Call Prices			Put Prices		
Strike Price	May	June	July	May	June	July
60	6¾	7	7¼	¹⁄₁₆	⁵⁄₁₆	⅞
65	1⅜	2⅝	3¾	⅛	1½	2⅜
70	¹⁄₁₆	¾	1¾	3⅞	4¼	4¾

11-1 Intrinsic Value

What is the intrinsic value of the May 60 call?

11-2 Break-even

If the June 65 call is purchased, how much must the stock price increase in order for the option holder to break even?

11-3 Loss on a Speculative Position

A May 70 put is purchased and the stock price subsequently climbs to 69⅜ at option expiration. What will be the loss to the put holder?

11-4 Speculative Profit

If a July 60 put is purchased, determine the stock price at option expiration in order for the put buyer to generate a profit of 1¾.

11-5 Speculative Profit

A call option on XYZ stock is currently selling for 6¼. Its exercise price is 40. How much must the stock be selling for at expiration in order for the holder of the call to earn a 2¼ point profit?

11-6 Intrinsic Value and Time Value for Puts

A put option with a 420 strike price on the S&P 500 Index is currently priced at 11¾. The S&P 500 Index is at $411.79. Find the intrinsic value and the time value of this option.

11-7 Put Break-even and Profit

Determine the break-even point and profit for the following put options if the stock is at 62 at option expiration.

Stock	Strike	August
65⅛	60	1.00
65⅛	65	2.75
65⅛	70	6.00

Chapter 12

PRINCIPLES OF OPTION PRICING AND THE BINOMIAL MODEL

Overview

The change in the option price before option expiration is a more complicated issue than the value of an option at expiration. Factors such as the change in the stock price, how close the stock price is to the exercise price, the time before option expiration, the volatility of the stock, and the level of interest rates all affect option price changes. The "Pricing Relationships" discussed in this chapter help to define how the option price changes as these factors change. Additional boundary conditions for option prices also are developed.

From our general discussion of pricing relationships, we can proceed to a more concrete relationship between option prices. Specifically, put-call parity shows that a call option plus a risk-free instrument must equal a put option plus the underlying stock. If one combination is priced lower than the other, then arbitrage profits are possible. Thus, put-call parity is our first model of option prices.

The simple two-event binomial option model then is used as a conceptual tool to help explain the important aspects of an option pricing model. In particular, the binomial model shows how to construct a hedge between the option and the stock in order to eliminate risk. In fact, if the option is mispriced, such a hedge will earn a return in excess of the risk-free rate. When a large number of time periods are employed, the binomial model is equivalent to the Black-Scholes model discussed in chapter 13. Binomial models are also useful in valuing certain types of options discussed in later chapters.

Appendix 12A shows how a proper combination of options is equivalent to a futures contract. Appendix 12B examines the binomial model for n states of nature.

Terminology

*Binomial option pricing model   A model that determines the fair value for an option based on a limited number of discrete changes for the stock price.

*Hedge ratio   The number of shares of the asset (for example, stock) as a proportion of the number of shares of the option such that a risk-free combination is produced for a (small) change in the asset price.

*Put-call parity   The relationship between a call option, a put option, the underlying stock, and the cost of financing that equates the value of a call plus risk-free instrument to the value of a put plus the underlying stock.

Reverse hedge   When the stock is sold short and the option purchased.

*Volatility factor   The greater the volatility of the underlying stock, the larger the time value and, therefore, the greater the option price.

CALL OPTION PRICE CHANGES BEFORE EXPIRATION

Boundary Conditions

Boundary conditions were introduced in chapter 11. Boundary conditions provide specific quantitative relationships for option prices, specifying the upper and lower limits that options can trade without violating an arbitrage boundary. This chapter provides more specific boundary conditions in relation to time and the difference between strike prices via equations. Recall the symbols for our equations: t = the time until option expiration; K = the strike price (with K_1 representing a lower strike price); E = a European option; and A = an American option. Commission costs and taxes are ignored in these relationships. The discussion in this chapter examines the behavior of option prices before expiration. After discussing option relationships and boundary conditions, we will examine a relative pricing relationship between calls, puts, and the stock. This will be followed by exact option pricing models. Table 12-1 summarizes the boundary conditions from this and the previous chapter.

Trading Options and Pricing Factors

Unlike the over-the-counter options exclusively traded before 1973, exchange-traded options can be bought or sold at any time prior to option expiration. This liquidity allows traders to take their profits or cut their losses at any time. Trading options eliminates the disadvantages of exercising the option, including paying for and taking

Table 12-1 Summary of the Option Boundary Conditions

	European Calls	American Calls	European Puts	American Puts
Lower bound				
Approximation	$\text{Max}[P_S - K, 0]$	$\text{Max}[P_S - K, 0]$	$\text{Max}[K - P_S, 0]$	$\text{Max}[K - P_S, 0]$
Exact	$\text{Max}[P_S - K(1 + r)^{-t}, 0]$	$\text{Max}[P_S - K(1 + r)^{-t}, 0]$	$\text{Max}[K(1 + r)^{-t} - P_S, 0]$	$\text{Max}[K - P_S, 0]$
Upper bound	P_S	P_S	$K(1 + r)^{-t}$	K
Effect of time	$P_C(t_2) \geq P_C(t_1)$	$P_C(t_2) \geq P_P(t_1)$	$P_P(t_2) \geq P_P(t_1)$	$P_P(t_2) \geq P_P(t_1)$
Effect of strike	$P_C(K_1) \geq P_C(K_2)$	$P_C(K_1) \geq P_C(K_2)$	$P_P(K_2) \geq P_P(K_1)$	$P_P(K_2) \geq P_P(K_1)$
Maximum difference between strikes	$(K_2 - K_1)(1 + r)^{-t}$	$K_2 - K_1$	$(K_2 - K_1)(1 + r)^{-t}$	$K_2 - K_1$
Other relationships				
American vs. European		$P_C(A) \geq P_C(E)$		$P_P(A) \geq P_P(E)$

$K_2 > K_1$; $t_2 > t_1$; r = risk-free interest rate.

possession of the common stock when a call option is exercised. Trading options before expiration also increases the benefits of accurate forecasting and timing, since the trader can cover the option position before the entire time value is eliminated. Since option prices before expiration typically include a time value, it is usually unwise to *exercise* options much before the expiration date.

The option profit obtainable from advantageous changes in the stock price is the most important reason most naive speculators purchase options. Therefore, a naive speculator's decision to purchase an option depends on the speculator's forecast concerning the stock price, even though the *actual price of an option* does *not* depend on the *expected* future stock price change (this is discussed in detail later).

Well-informed speculators also consider other factors that affect the option price and time value—namely, the time to expiration of the option, the volatility of the underlying stock price, the level of interest rates, and the difference between the stock and strike price. Thus, a speculator must determine if the price of the option in the market is fair, given the characteristics of the stock and the option. The relationships between these factors and option prices are examined next.[1]

Pricing Relationships

A rule of thumb is that at-the-money options change in price by about 50% of the change of the underlying stock price.[2] Deep in-the-money options (where the stock price is substantially above the strike price) change in price almost point for point with the stock price change. On the other hand, deep out-of-the-money options change very little as the stock price changes since the probability that this strike price will become an in-the-money option is minimal.[3]

> *Pricing Relationship #6:* Options change less in absolute price than the associated stock price does.
> *Pricing Relationship #7:* The percentage price change for options is greater than the percentage price change for the underlying stock.
> *Pricing Relationship #8:* Near-the-money options change less in price than in-the-money options for a given stock price change, but near-the-money options have greater leverage (the %Δ in price is greater for near-the-money options).
> *Pricing Relationship #9:* The absolute price change for deep in-the-money options is almost as large as the associated stock price change.
> *Pricing Relationship #10:* The price of deep out-of-the-money options changes only minimally as the associated stock price changes.

[1] This section is discussed in terms of a speculator to promote simplicity and ease of exposition. Determination of a fair option price is also important to hedgers and arbitrageurs, as discussed later. The discussion of the pricing aspects of options later in this chapter and in Chapters 13 and 14 specifically describes how a "fair price" is determined for options and how various factors affect the pricing of an option. This chapter also provides an intuitive understanding of how call option prices change.

[2] This relationship is based on option pricing models discussed in this and the following chapter.

[3] At times, the prices listed for deep in-the-money and deep out-of-the-money options seem to violate logic (the intrinsic value appears to be larger than the option price). These circumstances arise because deep out-of-the-money options do not trade often. Thus, the listed option could have traded hours before the close, causing the apparent mispricing, when in fact the stock price changes later in the day without an option trade.

Boundary conditions for strike prices can also be obtained. For call options, the relevant boundary condition is:

$$K_2 - K_1 \geq P_C(K_1) - P_C(K_2) \tag{12-1}$$

Call Prices Before Expiration

Figure 12-1 illustrates the effect of changing stock prices on the value of an option *before* the option expires. The line labeled T(0) in Figure 12-1 has the same shape as our original option valuation graph at expiration, as given in Figure 11-1. T(1) illustrates how the option price varies *before* expiration, as the stock price changes.

Another way to view pricing relationships is to examine the intrinsic values and time values for the call options (as originally defined in Equations (11-1) and (11-2)). Each statement below is illustrated by using Figure 12-1:

- The intrinsic value of a call option decreases as the stock price declines (assuming the call option is in-the-money; thus an in-the-money call option declines in value as stock prices decline).
- The time value decreases as the stock price moves away from the strike price.
- As the intrinsic value increases, the time value decreases.
- The option buyer typically avoids purchasing options with a large amount of intrinsic value, because the cost is high and there is less leverage.
- As the underlying stock price moves toward the strike price, the time value for an out-of-the-money option increases.

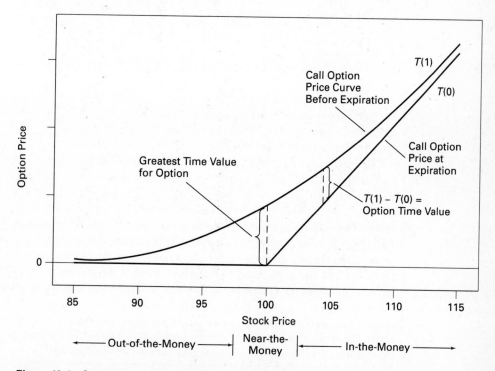

Figure 12-1 Option prices before expiration: buying calls.

Example 12-1 illustrates the profit, return, and leverage for an option before expiration.

EXAMPLE 12-1
Buying a Call Index Option

The following states the values for the Dow Jones Industrials, the S&P 500 Index, and the values of the call options on the S&P 500 for October 15 and December 10. The profitability of buying the December 410 and 425 call options on the S&P 500 is then determined.

	October 15	December 10
Dow Jones Industrials	3174.68	3323.81
S&P 500 Index	409.61	435.65
December 410 call (near-the-money)	10⅞	27
December 425 call (out-of-the-money)	3¾	10¾

Profit from buying the call options on October 15 and selling them on December 10:

December 410 option profit = (27 − 10⅞)100 = $1612.50
December 425 option profit = (10¾ − 3¾)100 = $700.00

The rates of return for the options and the S&P 500 are:

Return on December 410 option = $1612.50/$1087.50 = 103.4%
Return on December 425 option = $700.00/$375.00 = 186.7%
Return on S&P 500 = 26.04/409.61 = 6.4%

One could even annualize the returns to obtain 674% and 1217%! (The annualized rate of return is obtained by multiplying the return by 365/56. However, annualizing the return would by very unrealistic, since this would assume the same return for each 56-day period of the year.)

The most interesting aspect of buying call options is the leverage obtained: a return of 103.4% and 186.7% in 56 days on the options, as compared to a 6.4% return if the trader purchases the equivalent of the stock index. However, the option profits are only $1612.50 and $700.00, while a comparative value for the index is a $2604 profit. The difference in dollar profits occurs because the time value declines from 10⅞ and 3¾, respectively, to 1.35 and .10. The reduction in the time values occurs because the options go from out-of-the-money to in-the-money, reducing the leverage effect and hence the time value. Also note that the December 410 option earns more money than the December 425 option, but the latter earns a larger percentage return based on the original cost. A critical factor in this example is that the call buyer forecasted the direction of the market *and* the timing of the market move correctly. Such perfect forecasting can be exploited by the use of options; however, less than perfect forecasting provides smaller profits, or even losses.

The Time to Expiration

Time to expiration is an important factor affecting the price of the option. The shorter the time to expiration, the smaller the option price and the smaller the time value. This relationship between time and option price is related to the *probability* of the option buyer obtaining profits (or increasing profits) from a change in the stock price. The less time remaining, the smaller the probability of profiting from holding an option.

Time values across option months can be illustrated by finding the *differences* between option prices for the same strike price but different expiration months. The differences between the Feb and March ABC call option prices in Exhibit 11-3 are 1 for the 95, 100, and 105 strike prices, and ¾ for the 90 and 110 strikes. The differences between the January and February call prices range from ¹³⁄₁₆ to 1⅞. These differences illustrate the effect of time on the option price. If the stock price remains stable, then option prices will decrease as the time to expiration decreases. Consequently, one can say that purchasers of call options buy time—time for the stock price to increase so that the call option will be profitable. If the stock price does not increase, then the call option buyer forfeits the time value. On the other hand, part of this time value is retained if the option is sold before expiration.

> *Pricing Relationship #11:* An option with a longer time to expiration is worth at least as much as an option with a shorter time to expiration (if the options have the same strike price).

This boundary condition in equation terms is:

$$P_C(t_2) \geq P_C(t_1) \tag{12-2}$$

> *Pricing Relationship #12:* Time values decrease as the time to expiration decreases (when other factors are kept constant).
>
> *Pricing Relationship #13:* A call option is worth more "alive" than "dead"—that is, it is better to sell a call option before the expiration date than to exercise it.[4]

Figure 12-2 compares various times to option expiration, with T(1) having a shorter time to expiration than T(2), and so on. The differences in the option values for T(1), T(2), and T(3) are due to the change in the time value over time. Figure 12-2 shows that the largest time values occur near the exercise price for any given time to expiration, with the size of the premiums decreasing for deep in- and deep out-of-the-money options. Pricing Relationships #11 and #13 are also verified by Figure 12-2.

Since the time to expiration of an option is an important factor affecting the price of the option, a speculator must determine whether a particular option expiration month

---

[4] This statement refers to an American option since European options can be exercised only at expiration. Moreover, this pricing relationship was developed for non–dividend-paying stocks. Ritchken (1987) proves that call options on dividend-paying stocks should sometimes be exercised early, and that an American call option on a dividend-paying stock can be worth more than a corresponding European option on the same stock.

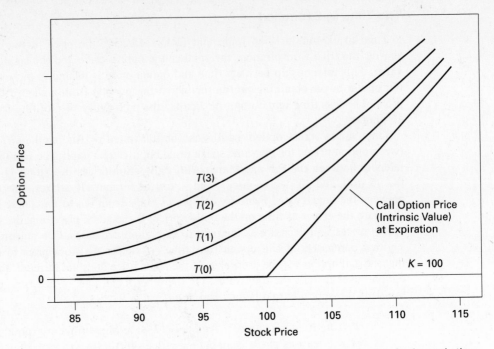

Figure 12-2 Call option prices before expiration: multiple dates to expiration. As the expiration date draws closer, $T(1)$ approaches $T(0)$.

provides sufficient time for the stock price to change substantially. Moreover, since an option is a "wasting asset"—that is, its value decreases over time (after stock price movements have been taken into account)—a speculator must determine whether the price paid for "time" is appropriate when compared to the estimated probability of making money from the forecasted stock price change.

The relationship between time to expiration and price is curvilinear, since a greater proportion of the time value is lost during the last few weeks of an option's life. This curvilinear relationship is shown in Figure 12-3. The curvilinear association is more difficult to recognize when option prices are examined on a daily or weekly basis since changes in the stock price also alter the size of the time value.

Leverage, Volatility, and Interest Rates

Stock price changes have immediate and significant effects on the prices of the associated call options. As the price of the stock increases, the prices of the call options increase. Similarly, as the stock price decreases, the call options prices decrease. Just as important, the option price changes *less* than the stock price, but the percentage change in the option price is *greater* than the percentage change in the stock price. This relationship is called the leverage factor. The leverage factor means that the rate of return on the original cost is greater for options, but the absolute price change is greater for the underlying stock. Examples in this and the previous chapter show that options possess much greater leverage than the underlying stock.

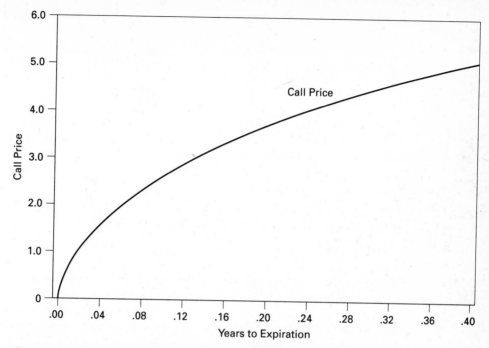

Figure 12-3 The relationship between time to expiration and option prices. (*Source:* Created from The Options and Futures Trading Simulator by Mark Rubinstein and Gerard Gennotte, 1992.)

A third factor affecting the price of an option is the **volatility factor** for the under-lying stock. The greater the volatility of the stock, the larger the option price and the time value. Exhibit 11-2 (the stock option quotes) shows that some stocks have options which possess larger time values than others. These larger premiums are due to greater stock volatilities. Because a stock that is more volatile has a greater chance of increas-ing significantly in price, and thereby creating a larger profit, option traders incorpo-rate this factor into the pricing of an option. Consequently, an option on a more stable stock such as ATT has a lower time value than an option on IBM. However, the ATT option has a lower probability of obtaining a *large* profit.

Pricing Relationship #14: Both the option price and the time value in-crease as the volatility of the stock price increases.

The level of interest rates is the final factor affecting option prices and time values. The higher the interest rate, the larger the option price and the time value. The relative importance of this factor is determined by the alternative investment opportunities available and the costs for those who trade options. Thus, one can view a call option as an alternative to buying the stock, at least in terms of obtaining future gains as a stock price increases. As interest rates increase, the cost of financing a stock purchase increases, and hence the call option becomes a more favorable purchase than the stock.

Therefore, the option price increases when interest rates increase to reflect this benefit. However, the effect of a change of interest rates on option prices is small.

> *Pricing Relationship #15:* The price of a call option increases with an increase in the interest rate.

In summary, four factors affect the size of the time value: the time to expiration factor, the leverage factor (stock versus strike price), the stock volatility, and the level of interest rates. Although this chapter describes these factors as if they affected the time value as independent forces, in reality they act on an interrelated basis to determine the time value and the option price. These relationships are considered in the pricing equations for options given in Chapter 13.

PUT OPTION PRICE CHANGES BEFORE EXPIRATION

In a manner essentially equivalent to call options, put options change price as stock prices change. However, put options change in the *opposite* direction of the stock price. As stock prices decline, put prices increase, and vice versa. As with calls, in-the-money put options can be exercised before expiration in order to obtain the intrinsic value of the option. However, since options sell for a price above their intrinsic value prior to expiration, put options are typically exercised prior to expiration only in specific situations. Thus, options are usually worth more "alive than dead." The associated boundary condition relating to time to expiration for puts is:

$$P_P(t_2, A) \geq P_P(t_1, A) \tag{12-3}$$

The time to expiration boundary condition for European puts is more complex, as two competing factors affect the price of the put. Buying a put is like deferring selling the stock at the strike price K. Thus, (1) to gain a longer time until expiration, one has to wait longer until receiving the sales price K (it is worth less now due to present value consideration); and (2) a longer time can generate greater profits if prices fall. The second factor tends to dominate in most cases. The boundary condition for the difference in two strike prices is as follows:

$$K_2 - K_1 \geq P_P(K_2) - P_P(K_1) \tag{12-4}$$

Example 12-2 illustrates the profit, return, and leverage factors for a put option before expiration.

Leverage

Put option prices change by a smaller dollar amount than the change in the stock price, while the percentage change in put prices is greater than the percentage change in stock prices, as is the case for call options. Thus, put options possess leverage. In general, the effect of the leverage factor and the associated pricing relationships for puts are equivalent to those previously discussed for call options. The statements concerning the intrinsic value of a call option and the call time value are also relevant for put options, with the exception of the first intrinsic value relationship for call options:

- The intrinsic value of a put decreases as stock prices increase (assuming the put is in-the-money).

EXAMPLE 12-2
Example of Buying a Put Option: The Market Crash of 1987

How did speculators who were lucky enough to hold a put option when the market crashed fare? On Thursday, October 13, 1987, the Dow Jones Industrials dropped over 90 points. On the following day, the market fell more than 100 points. On Monday, October 19, 1987, the Dow Jones Index took a free-fall of over 500 points!

The following illustrates the profits available to a speculator who purchased a put on Tuesday, October 13, and sold it at the end of the day on October 19. The S&P 100 put options are used for this example.

	Tuesday October 13	Monday October 19*
S&P 100 Index	307.36	216.31
S&P 100 Nov 305 put	7⅛	118

Option profit = (118 − 7⅛)100 = $11,087.50
Return on option = $11,087.50/$712.50 = 1557%
Return on short sale of index = 91.05/307.36 = 29.6%

The profit on the put option was $11,087.50 per contract, for a period of one week. This created a return on the put of 1557%, while the cash index declined by 29.6%. In fact, the time value *increased* on the put, causing a *larger* dollar change in the option than in the cash index. This increase was due to the significant increase in market volatility.

*The index and option prices for October 19 may not be end-of-the-day prices since *The Wall Street Journal* had incomplete data for that day.

Time to Expiration, Volatility, and Interest Rates

The other factors affecting put option prices and their associated pricing relationships are similar to the equivalent factors for call options.[5] In particular,

- **The time to expiration factor:** The longer the time to expiration, the larger the put option price and the put time value. As with calls, the time value decreases as the option approaches the expiration date.
- **The volatility factor:** The more volatile the underlying stock, the larger the put option price and the time value.
- **The interest rate:** The higher the interest rate, the *smaller* the put option price and the time value. This relationship is opposite that discussed for call options, since a put effectively mimics the profitability of a short sale when the stock price declines below the strike price.[6]

---

[5] However, there are circumstances in which a put option is exercised prior to the expiration of the option, as discussed in Chapter 13. Also notice that the differences in prices between the two expirations are smaller for puts than for calls. These differences also relate to the pricing process.

[6] The trader who sells a put option can hedge this position with a short sale on the stock. The large short seller can receive the funds at the time of the short sale. If interest rates increase, the interest proceeds from investing these funds increase as well; therefore, put time values decrease.

Pricing Relationship #16: The price of a put option decreases with an increase in the interest rate.

Exhibit 12-1 provides a summary of the effects of the various factors on option prices/time values.

DYNAMICALLY REPLICATING OPTIONS

The payoffs from an option contract can be *duplicated* simply by changing the number of shares of stock owned. A trader would increase the number of shares when stock prices increase and decrease the number of shares when stock prices decrease. A *replicating portfolio* changes the stock position on a dynamic basis as the stock price changes. Owning the proper number of shares at all times (plus cash) creates the same payoff diagram as buying a call option. The number of shares needed is determined by the "hedge ratio" obtained from an option pricing model such as the one developed below or the model examined in Chapter 13. Option pricing models find and use hedge ratios, also called deltas (δ). The replicating portfolio determines the call value as: call value = $P_S \delta$ − borrowing. Figure 12-4 illustrates the initial setup of a replicating portfolio.

An alternative way to look at traded options in relation to dynamically replicated option portfolios is to realize that traded options are equivalent to a *prepackaged* dynamic strategy. Thus, the option trader does not need to constantly change the stock/cash portfolio to obtain the option payoff. Moreover, traded options adequately reflect jumps in stock prices, while a replicating portfolio cannot adjust the number of shares quickly enough. The best-known application of replicating portfolios is a strategy called "portfolio insurance," which is discussed in a later chapter.

A dynamic replicating portfolio also is useful to Wall Street for other reasons. When options do not exist, Wall Street firms can "create" options by dynamically trading the asset and cash (or bonds). The firms can then sell these new options to customers.

EXHIBIT 12-1
Effects of Changes in Factors on Option Prices

Factor	Effects of Increase in Factors	
	Call Prices	**Put Prices**
Stock price	Increase	Decrease
Strike price	Decrease	Increase
Time to expiration	Increase	Increase
Volatility of stock	Increase	Increase
Interest rates	Increase	Decrease
Cash dividends on stock	Decrease	Increase

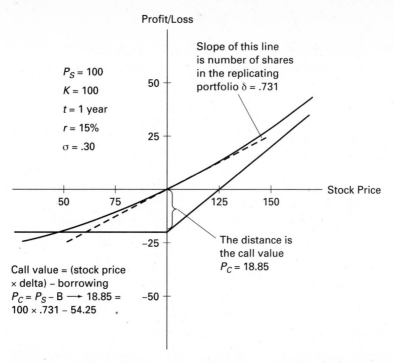

$P_S = 100$
$K = 100$
$t = 1$ year
$r = 15\%$
$\sigma = .30$

Slope of this line is number of shares in the replicating portfolio $\delta = .731$

The distance is the call value $P_C = 18.85$

Call value = (stock price × delta) − borrowing
$P_C = P_S - B \longrightarrow 18.85 = 100 \times .731 - 54.25$

Figure 12-4   Call versus stock-cash replicating portfolio. (*Source:* Rubinstein, 1991.)

PUT-CALL PARITY

Put-call parity equates buying a call (plus placing the present value of the strike price into a risk-free instrument) to buying a put and buying the stock. Figure 12-5(A) illustrates the payoff diagrams of buying a call, investing in a risk-free instrument, and their combination. Figure 12-5(B) shows the payoff diagrams of buying a put, buying stock, and their combination. Comparing Figures 12-5(A) and 12-5(B) shows that these two strategies are equivalent. Alternatively, Exhibit 12-2 uses cash flows to show how these two strategies are equivalent, as well as proving Equation (12-5):[7]

$$P_C + Ke^{-rt} = P_P + P_S \qquad (12\text{-}5)$$

where r = risk-free interest rate

The initial significance of put-call parity is that it represents an arbitrage relationship between calls, puts, and the underlying asset. If either the call or the put price becomes mispriced relative to the other instruments (by more than the transactions costs),

---

[7] Alternative approaches achieving the same result:

- Buying a call is equivalent to a portfolio of buying a put, buying stock, and borrowing the present value of the strike price.

- Buying a put is equivalent to a portfolio of buying a call, selling the stock short, and investing the present value of the strike price (investing proceeds of the short sale).

Technically, put-call parity does not *strictly* hold when early exercise of the options is possible.

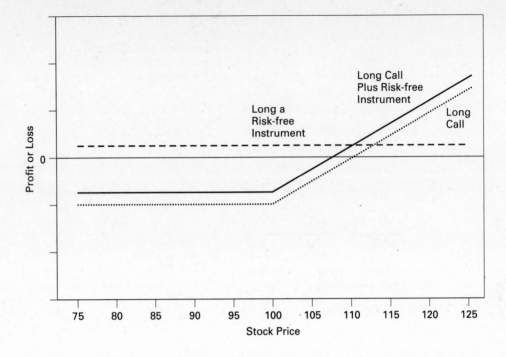

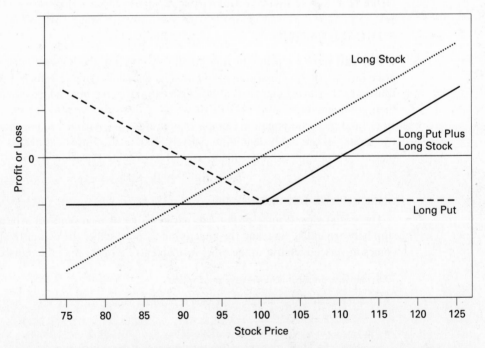

Figure 12-5 The put-call parity relationship. (A) Long call plus risk-free instrument. (B) Long put plus long stock.

EXHIBIT 12-2
Justifying the Put-Call Parity Relationship

Justifying the validity of the put-call parity relationship is straightforward. We examine two equivalent alternatives for investing funds in stocks, while protecting against downward movements in the stock price. Then we set the two alternatives equal to each other and solve for the put-call parity equation.

1. Buy a call option at P_C and invest the present value of the strike price (Ke^{-rt}) in a risk-free instrument.
2. Buy a put option at P_P and buy the stock at P_S, with the put providing downside protection against losses in the stock.

The payoff table below shows how these alternatives are equivalent at option expiration if the put and call have the same strike price and the same expiration date. Equating the two alternatives generates Equation (12-5):

$$P_C + Ke^{-rt} = P_P + P_S \qquad (12\text{-}5)$$

	Cash Flows		
	Current Date	At Expiration	
Strategy		$P_S \leq K$	$P_S > K$
(1) Buy call	$-P_C$	0	$P_{S,E} - K$
Invest present value of the strike price	$-Ke^{-rt}$	K	K
Total of (1)	$-(P_C + Ke^{-rt})$	K	$P_{S,E}$
(2) Buy put	$-P_P$	$K - P_{S,E}$	0
Buy stock	$-P_S$	$P_{S,E}$	$P_{S,E}$
Total of (2)	$-(P_P + P_S)$	K	$P_{S,E}$

$P_{S,E}$ = the stock price at option expiration

an arbitrageur can profit by buying the lower-priced combination and selling the higher-priced combination. Hence, put-call parity is a pricing and arbitrage relationship.

THE BINOMIAL OPTION PRICING MODEL

While the discussion and graphs above provide insights as to the effect of stock prices, time, volatility, and interest rates on the option price, a model is needed that considers all of these factors simultaneously. The Black-Scholes option model, covered in Chapter 13, considers all four of the input factors listed above to determine a fair price for a call option. Before turning to the Black-Scholes model, we examine what is known as the **binomial option pricing model,** developed by Cox, Ross, and Rubinstein (1979). The binomial model determines the fair value for an option based on *discrete* changes for the stock price. While the binomial model is not typically used to calculate stock option prices, it is a simple and intuitive model that illustrates the concept of a **hedge ratio.** A hedge ratio is the proportion of asset shares to option shares that creates a risk-free combination when the asset changes in price. Therefore, understanding the binomial model provides a foundation for a better understanding of the Black-Scholes pricing model. In addition, the binomial model is used to price debt options and other types of options.

Two States of Nature

The binomial option pricing model involves two possible outcomes, or "states of nature." Restricting the number of outcomes to two allows us to examine how a basic call option pricing model works before discussing the more complicated Black-Scholes model. The two stock prices associated with the two states of nature are designated as P_S^+ and P_S^-. These two possibilities are an increase (+) and a decrease (−) from the current stock price to the hypothetical stock price at the expiration of the option. Both price changes occur one time period from now. Similarly, the corresponding option prices for these two states of nature are designated as P_C^+ and P_C^-. Note the two simplifications from reality: (1) only two ending prices are possible, and (2) there is only one time period in which a price change can occur. Our example is based on the

FOCUS 12-1
OptionVue: What Is It?

OptionVue is a commercial PC program providing option pricing models (such as the binomial model and models found in Chapter 13) and trading selection screens to help traders best implement their strategies in the options market. The base Option-Vue package sells for less than $900; additional modules for record keeping and real-time quotations cost $300 and $500, respectively. (Call 800-733-6610 for more information; a trial package is available for under $50.)

The following provides an overview to the functions and uses of OptionVue. Various tables, exhibits, and graphs throughout the options chapters are created using OptionVue, as indicated in the source notes to the tables, exhibits, and figures.

- The fair values of options on stock, stock indexes, futures, and currency are determined based on the binomial, Black-Scholes (see Chapter 13), or a proprietary model. Values of the option "sensitivities" are also calculated (see Chapter 14).

- Option strategies discussed in this chapter and in Chapters 15 and 16 can be evaluated in terms of risk and return using current option prices. Various criteria can be chosen to evaluate the options in relation to the goals of the trader. The program even ranks the best option positions according to the criteria given. Graphs can be produced showing the potential profitability based on expected asset movements.

- A monthly database can be purchased that provides stock tickers, dividend information, current strike prices, and historical volatilities of all stocks and other assets that have exchange listed options.

- A record keeping function provides a summary of portfolio activity, including information on commissions, cash available, and margins.

- OptionVue can be hooked up to on-line quotations feeds in order to input up-to-the-minute option prices for analysis of the best options to trade.

assumption that the current stock price is $100 and the two possible outcomes are a stock price of either $95 or $105 at the expiration of the option, which is one time period from now. The strike price of the call option is $100, and the risk-free interest rate for invested funds over the time period in question is .5%—that is, ½ of 1% per month or 6% per year.

Given the above information, we can determine the value of the current option price that is consistent with the two possible future stock prices. We begin by finding the option value expiration under each state of nature. Thus, if the stock price decreases to $95 when the strike price is $100, then the option is out-of-the-money and expires worthless. If the stock price increases to $105, then the option is worth $5. These relationships are shown in Figure 12-6(A). Figure 12-6 (B) plots these two states of nature,

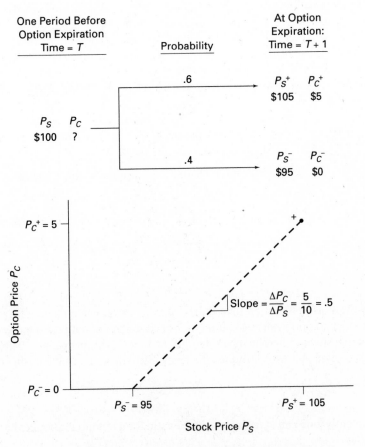

Figure 12-6 The binomial option pricing concept. (A) Stock and option prices with two states of nature. (B) Plotting the stock and option prices at option expiration.
Note: Only two states of nature exist, namely a (+) to a stock price of 105 and a (−) to a stock price of 95. Other stock prices are not relevant for this example. The slope between these two points is drawn simply to illustrate the hedge ratio.

with the stock price being on the X-axis and the option price plotted on the Y-axis. Joining the two points representing the two possible outcomes for the stock and option prices at option expiration generates the straight line shown in Figure 12-6(B). The slope of a line is simply $\Delta Y/\Delta X$, or in this case a difference of $5 for the two possible option prices divided by a difference of $10 for the two stock prices. The resultant slope of this line is .5. The slope of this option/stock price line is called a hedge ratio; we will use this value to eliminate (hedge) the risk of the position.

Eliminating Risk: The Hedge Ratio

In order to eliminate all of the risk of a position by option hedging, one must obtain a combination of call options and stock that results in identical ending values for the two states of nature. The hedge ratio for this example is .5; this means that the appropriate combination of the stock shares and option shares is a ratio of 1 to 2, or .5. For each share of stock, the hedger needs to *sell* two shares of the option—an opposite position is taken in the option to offset the stock price change. This hedge ratio is determined by the relationship between the option price difference of $5 between the two states of nature and the stock price difference of $10, as shown previously in Figure 12-6.

How does one use the knowledge of the hedge ratio to guarantee a perfect hedge? Multiplying the stock and option price changes by the number of stock and option shares determined by the hedge ratio results in the following:

$$\text{Total stock price change} = \text{Total option price change}$$

$$\Delta P_S N_S = \Delta P_C N_C \tag{12-6}$$

where ΔP_S, ΔP_C = the change in prices for the stock and the call option

N_S, N_C = the number of shares for the stock and the call option

For our example, we show that a 2 to 1 hedge ratio creates a perfect hedge:

$$(\$10)(1) = (\$5)(2)$$

Thus, the stock and option total dollar changes offset each other.[8] Therefore, the ratio of the stock to option shares is directly linked to the ratio of price changes between the option and stock. Alternatively, solving Equation (12-6) for the ratio between the stock and the option shares determines the hedge ratio in terms of the changes in price:

$$\frac{N_S}{N_C} = \frac{\Delta P_C}{\Delta P_S} \tag{12-7}$$

Equivalently, one can calculate the hedge ratio for a binomial model from the following formula:

$$h = \frac{P_C{}^+ - P_C{}^-}{P_S{}^+ - P_S{}^-} \tag{12-8}$$

---

[8] The concept of having a hedge ratio that eliminates risk is similar to having a correlation of -1 between two assets in portfolio analysis: The price change in one asset exactly offsets the change in the other asset.

Exhibit 12-3(A) also shows that the ending portfolio value is the same ($95), regardless of which state of nature occurs. As above, this example sells two options per share of stock purchased, designated as $P_S - 2P_C$ in Exhibit 12-3(A). Only one additional step remains to complete our discussion of the binomial model: to obtain a value for the call option one period before option expiration.[9]

The Value of the Option

Recall that the risk-free interest rate over the time period in question is .5% per month. Since our hedge procedure creates a risk-free situation—that is, the ending value of the stock/option position is known with certainty—the return earned on this stock/option position should equal the risk-free rate. Therefore, the original invest- ment, compounded at the risk-free rate, must equal the ending stock/option position value ($95 in this case):

$$I(1 + R_f) = V \qquad (12\text{-}9)$$

where I = the original *net* investment one period before option expiration

$\quad R_f$ = the non-annualized per period risk-free interest rate

$\quad V$ = the value of the combined stock/option position at option expiration

Moreover, the original net investment, I, is based on the cost of the stock *less* the amount received from selling the call options:

$$I = N_S P_S - N_C P_C \qquad (12\text{-}10)$$

Example 12-3 shows how these equations are employed for the case at hand.

Mispriced Binomial Options

Example 12-3 determines the fair value of the option one period before expiration, when two possible states of nature exist for the stock price. What if the price of the option differs from its fair value? For example, what if the option sells for either $2.85 or $2.60—that is, it sells for ⅛ of a point higher or lower than its fair value?

If the option is overpriced—that is, it is selling for $2.85 one period before expira- tion—then the hedger receives more than the fair value of the option. This reduces the

---

[9] The general equation for the hedge ratio for a two-state option model given in Equation (12-8) is devel- oped from what is known about the stock and option prices at option expiration. Thus, the value, V, of the combined stock/option position at option expiration is defined as follows, with $(+)$ indicating an in- crease in the stock price and $(-)$ indicating a decrease:

$$V^+ = N_S P_S{}^+ - N_C P_C{}^+$$
$$V^- = N_S P_S{}^- - N_C P_C{}^-$$

We want to determine the hedge ratio $h = N_S/N_C$ such that the position is riskfree—that is, where $V^+ = V^-$. Thus, we set these two equations equal to each other and substitute $h = N_S/N_C$:

$$hP_S{}^+ - P_C{}^+ = h P_S{}^- - P_C{}^-$$

Solving for h, we obtain Equation (12-8).

EXHIBIT 12-3
Hedge Ratios and Option Prices

One Period Before Option Expiration	State (1): Stock Price Increase	State (2): Stock Price Decrease
(A) $\quad P_S = \$100$ $\quad\quad P_C = ?$	$P_S^+ = \$105$ $P_C^+ = \$5$ $\overline{P_S^+ - 2P_C^+ = \$95}$	$P_S^- = \$95$ $P_C^- = \$0$ $\overline{P_S^- - 2P_C^- = \$95}$
(B) $\quad P_S = \$100$ $\quad\quad P_C = \$2.736$ (from Example 12-3)		
$\quad\quad$ Investment:	$P_S - 2P_C = \$94.528$	$P_S - 2P_C = \$94.528$
$\quad\quad$ Ending Value:	$P_S^+ - 2P_C^+ = \$95.00$	$P_S^- - 2P_C^- = \$95.00$
$\quad\quad$ Rate of Return:	($\$95.00 - \$94.528$)/$\$94.528$ $\$.472/\$94.528 = .5\%$	($\$95.00 - \$94.528$)/$\$94.528$ $\$.472/\$94.528 = .5\%$
(C) Option Overpriced $\quad\quad P_S = \$100$ $\quad\quad P_C = \$2.85$		
$\quad\quad$ Investment:	$P_S - 2P_C = \$94.30$	$P_S - 2P_C = \$94.30$
$\quad\quad$ Ending Value:	$P_S^+ - 2P_C^+ = \$95.00$	$P_S^- - 2P_C^- = \$95.00$
$\quad\quad$ Rate of Return:	($\$95.00 - \$94.30$)/$\$94.30$ $\$.70/\$94.30 = .74\%$	($\$95.00 - \$94.30$)/$\$94.30$ $\$.70/\$94.30 = .74\%$
(D) Option Underpriced: Naive Hedger $\quad\quad P_S = \$100$ $\quad\quad P_C = \$2.60$		
$\quad\quad$ Investment:	$P_S - 2P_C = \$94.80$	$P_S - 2P_C = \$94.80$
$\quad\quad$ Ending Value:	$P_S^+ - 2P_C^+ = \$95.00$	$P_S^- - 2P_C^- = \$95.00$
$\quad\quad$ Rate of Return:	($\$95.00 - \$94.80$)/$\$94.80$ $\$.20/\$94.80 = .21\%$	($\$95.00 - \$94.80$)/$\$94.80$ $\$.20/\$94.80 = .21\%$

(E) Option Underpriced: Reverse Hedge (short stock and receive funds, buy options, invest funds from short sale)*

$\quad\quad P_S = \$100$
$\quad\quad P_C = \$2.60$

Investment:	$+2P_C = \$5.20$	$+2P_C = \$5.20$
Ending Value:	$-P_S^+ + 2P_C^+ + P_S(1 + R_f) =$ $-\$105 + 2(\$5) + \$100(1.005) =$ $\$5.50$	$-P_S^- + 2P_C^- + P_S(1 + R_f) =$ $-\$95 + 2(\$0) + \$100(1.005) =$ $\$5.50$
Rate of Return:	($\$5.50 - \$5.20$)/$\$5.20$ $\$.30/\$5.20 = 5.8\%$	($\$5.50 - \$5.20$)/$\$5.20$ $\$.30/\$5.20 = 5.8\%$

*(E) assumes the short seller has access to all of the funds generated from the short sale. Actually, active option traders receive only 85% or less of these funds, while individuals often must put up additional funds to cover a short sale.

net investment needed and increases the rate of return to .74%, which is above the .5% return available from other risk-free investments. This situation is illustrated in Exhibit 12-3(C). When traders realize that a higher (risk-free) return is available by hedging in options rather than by investing in other risk-free investments, they will construct the stock/option hedge with the appropriate hedge ratio of .5. This activity of selling the options drives down the option price until the return on the hedge equals the risk-free rate of .5% available from other investments.

EXAMPLE 12-3
Solving for the Binomial Option Value

Using the data from Exhibit 12-3 plus Equation (12-10), we have:

$$I = N_S P_S - N_C P_C \qquad (12\text{-}10)$$

$$I = (1)(\$100) - 2P_C$$

Substituting I from equation (12-10) and (12-9) and using our values for $R_f = .005$ and $V = \$95$, we have:

$$I(1 + R_f) = V \qquad (12\text{-}9)$$

$$(\$100 - 2P_C)(1 + .005) = \$95$$

Solving for the value of the option one period before expiration, P_C, we find:

$$-2P_C = (\$95/1.005) - \$100 = -\$5.47$$

$$P_C = \$2.736$$

Thus, the fair value of the call option one period prior to expiration is \$2.736. This is verified by the following:

a. The original investment of buying the stock and selling two call options (where the hedge receives the price of these options) is:

$$I = \$100 - 2(\$2.736) = \$94.528$$

b. Investing this original amount at .5% equals the final value of the stock/option position:

$$\$94.528(1.005) = \$95.00$$

These relationships are summarized in Exhibit 12-2(B).

If the option is underpriced—that is, it is selling for \$2.60—then two situations could occur. One possibility is that naive hedgers who are unaware of the fair value of the option would execute the same type of hedge as shown above: for each share of stock purchased, the hedger sells two option shares. Exhibit 12-3(D) shows that selling the underpriced option results in a return on investment of .21%, which is *less* than can be obtained by putting the equivalent funds in other risk-free investments earning .5%.

A second possibility is that a sophisticated hedger realizes that a higher return can be obtained by *buying* the option and *selling* the stock short. This strategy is called a **reverse hedge**. In this case, the hedger sells the stock short, deposits the \$100 received from the short sale into an interest-bearing account, sells the stock short, and buys the option. Exhibit 12-3(E) shows that this alternative provides a return of 5.8% on the hedger's funds, which is much higher than the return available from other risk-free investments.

The above examples show that if an option is mispriced, an arbitrageur can step in and buy the underpriced and/or sell the overpriced instrument to earn a higher return than is available from other risk-free investments. These actions cause the price of the option to revert to its appropriate fair price. An alternative approach for potential arbitrage situations with mispriced options is to borrow funds at the risk-free interest rate in order to cover the cost of the investment. Thus, an arbitrageur would buy stock, sell options, and finance the net cost with borrowed funds. When an option is mispriced, the profit earned on the arbitrage is greater than the interest on the borrowed funds. Therefore, risk-free profits are obtained without any net investment on the part of the arbitrageur.

Call Prices and a Binomial Example

The procedure developed above shows how a hedge ratio and a call option price are determined based on a two-state model of stock prices for one period in the future. The equation for the value of a call option in a two-state world is:

$$P_C = \frac{P_S(1 + R_f)(P_C{}^+ - P_C{}^-) - P_S{}^- P_C{}^+ + P_S{}^+ P_C{}^-}{(P_S{}^+ - P_S{}^-)(1 + R_f)} \tag{12-11}$$

Example 12-4 demonstrates how to find the hedge ratio and the value of the call option for a two-state situation.

EXAMPLE 12-4
The Binomial Option Model: An Example

The current stock price is 50, with the two possible outcomes for the stock price one period from now being 56 and 46. The risk-free rate for the next period is 1%. Thus, $P_S = 50$, $P_S{}^+ = 56$, $P_S{}^- = 46$, and $R_f = .01$. To determine the appropriate hedge ratio and the current value for a call option with a strike price of 50, employ the following equation:

$$h = \frac{P_C{}^+ - P_C{}^-}{P_S{}^+ - P_S{}^-} = \frac{\Delta P_C}{\Delta P_S} \tag{12-8}$$

$$= (6 - 0)/(56 - 46)$$

$$= 6/10 = .6$$

The hedge ratio of .6 means that the appropriate ratio of shares of stock to option shares is .6 or $N_S/N_C = .6$. In other words, for every 6 shares of stock, the hedger needs 10 option shares. The equation for determining the value of the call option one period before expiration is:

$$P_C = \frac{P_S(1 + R_f)(P_C{}^+ - P_C{}^-) - P_S{}^- P_C{}^+ + P_S{}^+ P_C{}^-}{(P_S{}^+ - P_S{}^-)(1 + R_f)} \tag{12-11}$$

$$= \frac{50(1.01)(6 - 0) - 46(6) + 56(0)}{(56 - 46)(1.01)}$$

$$= 2.673$$

The call option is worth $2.673.

Extending the Model and a Summary

The above discussion of the binomial model is restrictive in that only two possible states of nature and one time period are examined. However, this simple binomial model is important for understanding the concepts of option pricing and introducing the option models discussed below. The binomial model also can be extended to a number of time periods and states of nature. For example, Figure 12-7 shows a three-state, two-period model extension of our original example. In this situation, the stock price increases or decreases 5% each period in relation to the previous period's binomial value. The value of the call option and the associated hedge ratio can be determined for each step in the binomial process. In particular, note that the hedge ratio *changes* from period T to period $T + 1$. Thus, when multiple periods are used in the binomial model, the hedge ratio must be dynamically altered for each time period. This binomial process can be extended to a large number of periods and to smaller stock price changes. When a large number of time periods are used, the resultant call values are equivalent to the prices obtained from the Black-Scholes model developed later. Table 12-2 shows the call option values derived from the binomial model with 5, 25, and 150 time periods. As the number of periods increases, the accuracy of the model increases. Appendix 12B extends the binomial model to n periods. For a rigorous derivation of the binomial approach for many time periods, see Ritchken (1987, ch. 9) or Jarrow and Rudd (1983, ch. 13).

The binomial option model provides several insights into the pricing of call options. Recall that a hedge ratio is calculated based on knowledge of the two possible values of the stock price one period in the future, at option expiration. A properly constructed hedge ratio eliminates all risk—that is, the value of the combined stock and option position one period later will be the same, *regardless of* whether the stock price increases or decreases. The fair return on such a risk-free stock/option position is the risk-free

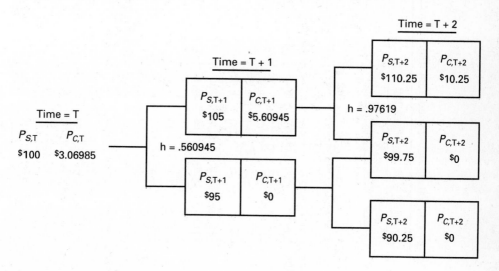

Figure 12-7 A three-period binomial tree.

Table 12-2 Call Values Determined from the Binomial Method

		$P_s = 100$					$r = .10$						
		n = 5				n = 25				n = 150			
σ	K	1	3	6	12	1	3	6	12	1	3	6	12
						Months-to-Expiration							
.2	85	15.67	17.10	19.38	23.64	15.67	17.11	19.35	23.57	15.67	17.11	19.34	23.54
	90	10.76	12.61	15.19	19.54	10.76	12.55	15.14	19.68	10.76	12.55	15.12	19.68
	95	6.25	8.41	11.29	16.23	6.20	8.51	11.38	16.12	6.20	8.50	11.34	16.15
	100	2.82	5.41	8.37	13.25	2.73	5.27	8.19	13.04	2.71	5.22	8.13	12.98
	105	.89	2.73	5.46	10.27	.84	2.92	5.62	10.23	.83	2.89	5.58	10.27
	110	.15	1.53	3.67	7.48	.17	1.42	3.65	7.99	.17	1.44	3.65	7.95
	115	.00	.46	2.38	6.07	.02	.60	2.22	6.06	.02	.65	2.28	6.07
.3	85	15.74	17.78	20.70	25.40	15.74	17.70	20.60	25.56	15.75	17.70	20.57	25.57
	90	11.06	13.70	16.68	22.17	11.09	13.64	16.92	22.31	11.08	13.64	16.88	22.24
	95	6.97	10.06	13.79	19.57	6.96	10.13	13.59	19.17	6.99	10.08	13.63	19.21
	100	4.02	7.45	11.17	16.97	3.88	7.22	10.86	16.59	3.84	7.15	10.77	16.47
	105	1.77	4.83	8.55	14.38	1.81	4.91	8.35	14.01	1.83	4.86	8.41	14.04
	110	.78	3.19	5.94	11.78	.74	3.15	6.49	11.98	.74	3.18	6.43	11.91
	115	.22	2.15	4.88	9.38	.26	1.99	4.82	10.12	.26	2.00	4.83	10.05
.4	85	15.91	18.89	22.23	27.83	15.98	18.76	22.27	28.29	16.00	18.71	22.33	28.20
	90	11.76	14.89	18.87	25.48	11.66	15.06	19.10	25.24	11.66	15.05	19.03	25.27
	95	7.73	11.97	16.43	23.13	7.96	11.82	16.01	22.58	7.93	11.84	16.07	22.56
	100	5.22	9.49	13.99	20.78	5.04	9.18	13.57	20.23	4.98	9.09	13.45	20.07
	105	2.72	7.01	11.55	18.43	2.95	6.84	11.13	17.89	2.91	6.88	11.18	17.88
	110	1.68	4.73	9.12	16.08	1.59	5.12	9.32	15.78	1.56	5.07	9.23	15.87
	115	.74	3.79	7.13	13.74	.79	3.90	7.63	14.15	.78	3.69	7.56	14.03

Source: Rubinstein (1991)

interest rate. Knowledge of this risk-free interest rate on other instruments allows us to determine the appropriate value of the call option one period before expiration of the option. If the option is mispriced, returns above the risk-free rate are available.

Finally, note that nowhere in our calculation of the hedge ratio or the value of the binomial option do the probabilities relating to the stock price change affect the results. While these probabilities would affect any calculations of the stock value, they do *not* affect the option value or the hedge ratio. This allows for the development of an option pricing model that is independent of the unknown stock price expectations. Since the option model does not need a forecast of the stock price, the resulting option equation is a very useful and powerful financial tool.

EMPIRICAL EVIDENCE

Empirical studies have examined whether option prices violate the boundary conditions or put-call parity. Such studies on past data provide evidence on whether the options markets are priced properly or whether arbitrage opportunities exist.

Option Boundary Tests

Bhattacharya (1983) employs transaction data for 10 months on 58 stocks to test for violations of the option pricing relationships. The first test examines whether option prices trade below the intrinsic value of the option. He finds that only 1.3% of over 86,000 transactions violate this pricing relationship, with the average size of these violations being $12 per contract. For 29% of the violations, this opportunity is eliminated by the next trade. A test on the lower bound for the option price finds violations 7.5% of the time, with an average value of $7.

Put-Call Parity Tests

Klemkosky and Resnick (1979, 1980) employ transactions data to examine 600 put-call positions by using one trade day per month for one year in order to test the put-call parity relationship and the pricing of options. Possibilities of early exercise are removed from the data set since the put-call parity relationship assumes that no premium for early exercise is impounded into the put option price.

Violations of the put-call parity relationship are exploited by setting up a hedge between the put, call, and stock such that the underpriced option is purchased and the overpriced option is sold. Based on the put-call relationship, an arbitrageur can buy a put and sell the call (when the put is deemed to be underpriced relative to the call) by executing the following transactions: buy the stock, buy a put, sell a Treasury bill, and sell the call option. A similar position is initiated when the put is overpriced relative to the call option.

Klemkosky and Resnick determine that 27% of put underpricing situations are profitable after transactions costs, with most of these situations occurring soon after puts started to trade on the exchanges. Only 7% of the call underpricing situations are profitable. Klemkosky and Resnick then examine the effect of the delay time between recognizing the mispricing and acting on it. They determine that delay times of 5 to

15 minutes do not eliminate the mispricings; however, the bid-ask spread cost is not factored into their results. Klemkosky and Resnick state that this bid-ask cost would tend to eliminate most of these excess profits.

SUMMARY AND LOOKING AHEAD

This chapter explores basic pricing relationships for the call and put options before option expirations and the factors affecting option prices. The put-call parity and binomial pricing models are also examined. The binomial model provides an introduction to option pricing models. The next chapter discusses the Black-Scholes option pricing model.

BIBLIOGRAPHY

Bhattacharya, Mihir (1983). "Transactions Data Tests of Efficiency of the Chicago Board Options Exchange," *Journal of Financial Economics,* Vol. 12, No. 2, August, pp. 161–185.

Cox, John C., Stephen A. Ross, and Mark Rubinstein (1979). "Option Pricing: A Simplified Approach," *Journal of Financial Economics,* Vol. 7, No. 3, September, pp. 229–264.

Jarrow, Robert A., and Andrew Rudd (1983). *Option Pricing.* Homewood, IL: Irwin.

Klemkosky, Robert C., and Bruce G. Resnick (1980). "An Ex-Ante Analysis of Put-Call Parity," *Journal of Financial Economics,* Vol. 8, No. 4, December, pp. 363–378.

Klemkosky, Robert C., and Bruce G. Resnick (1979). "Put-Call Parity and Market Efficiency," *Journal of Finance,* Vol. 34, No. 5, December, pp. 1141–1156.

Ritchken, Peter (1987). *Options: Theory, Strategy, and Applications.* Glenview, IL: Scott, Foresman.

Rubinstein, Mark (1991). "Classnotes," The University of California at Berkeley.

Rubinstein, Mark, and Gerard Gennotte (1992). *Options and Futures Trading Simulator,* Version 2.0.

PROBLEMS

*Indicates more difficult problems.

12-1 Leverage Factor

Using the following data, compute the absolute price change and percentage change of price for both the options and the stock.

Strike	Calls on June 2	Calls on July 1
90	3⅜	7
95	1¼	2⁹⁄₁₆
Stock	90⅝	96⅞

12-2 Pricing Relationships

July 3:		Calls		Puts	
Stock	**Strike**	**Jul**	**Aug**	**Jul**	**Aug**
66.875	60	*r*	*r*	*r*	0.625
66.875	65	2.875	4.75	0.75	2.00
66.875	70	0.625	2.00	3.625	5.00

July 6:		Calls		Puts	
Stock	**Strike**	**Jul**	**Aug**	**Jul**	**Aug**
65.125	60	6.125	6.25	0.1875	1.00
65.125	65	1.50	4.00	1.13125	2.75
65.125	70	0.25	1.50	5.00	6.00

Given the above prices, answer the following questions dealing with pricing relationships.

a. What pricing relationship justifies the fact that although the stock price fell by 2.6%, the July call fell by 47.8%?

b. What pricing relationship justifies the fact that the Aug 65 call fell more than the Aug 70 call?

c. What pricing relationship explains why the 60 July put is worth less than the July 65 put?

d. What pricing relationship explains why, while the stock fell by 1.75, the Aug 65 call fell by only 0.75?

12-3 Buying Call Options

The HW August 65 call option is trading at 4¾ on July 2, while the stock is trading at 66⅞. On July 8, the option is trading at 3⅜, while the stock is at 65⅛. Calculate your profit or loss and the annualized yield from buying the call as compared to buying the stock.

12-4 Put Option Profit

On July 2, Joe Investor bought 10 GM put options with a strike price of 45 for 4¾. On July 9 he sold the puts at 5¼. What was his profit?

*12-5 Binomial Hedge Ratio

The current stock price for EKD is 58. The stock prices associated with the two states of nature (one period from now) are 62 and 52. Determine the appropriate binomial hedge ratio *and* the ending value of the stock/option position in each state of nature, given an option with a strike price of 58. (*Hint:* Remember that the ending portfolio value is the same, regardless of which state of nature occurs.)

12-6 Binomial Option Price

Using the information from the above question, and given a risk-free interest rate of .5% (that is, $R_f = 0.005$), determine the current value of a call option one period before expiration by using the binomial option model.

APPENDIX 12A
COMPARING OPTIONS TO FORWARD AND
FUTURES CONTRACTS

The discussion of option contracts in this chapter emphasizes the payoffs of options and their risk and return characteristics. However, recognizing that a proper combination of options contracts is equivalent to a forward contract helps one understand the relationships between options and forward/futures contracts. Exhibit 12A-1 shows the funds flow and profits for buying a forward contract in comparison to buying a call and simultaneously selling a put option. (Selling a put means the option trader is obligated to receive stock at the stock price *if and when* the owner of the put exercises the option to sell the stock.) The first column of the payoff table shows the cash outlay at the present date (when the option and forward transactions are initiated). At the present date the forward contract does not require an investment, while buying a call and selling a put requires a cash outlay of $P_P - P_C$. The second column shows the value of the two positions when the forward contract and options expire. At option expiration, the forward contract and the option strategy provide the *same* payoff, regardless of whether the stock price is above or below the strike price at that time. Since the two positions provide the same ending value, buying a forward contract is equivalent to buying a call and selling a put. This relationship shows that options can be valued in relation to other contracts.

EXHIBIT 12A-1
Payoff Table for Options versus Forward Contracts

	Present Date	Expiration Date $P_{S,E} \leq K$	Expiration Date $K < P_{S,E}$
Buy Forward Contract:			
Based on an Asset Price of K	0	$P_{S,E} - K$	$P_{S,E} - K$
Buy Call (Strike Price = K)	$-P_C$	0	$P_{S,E} - K$
Sell Put (Strike Price = K)	P_P	$P_{S,E} - K$	0
Total Option Value	$P_P - P_C$	$P_{S,E} - K$	$P_{S,E} - K$

K = The strike price and the forward contract asset price.
P_C = Price of a call option
P_P = Price of a put option
A forward contract is equivalent to a portfolio consisting of one purchased call option on the underlying asset and one written put option on the underlying asset, both with a common expiration date equal to the delivery date, and both with a common striking price equal to the forward price.

Source: Rubinstein (1991).

APPENDIX 12B
THE MULTIPERIOD BINOMIAL MODEL

The chapter discusses the binomial model for the one-period and two-period cases, which is useful as an introduction to option pricing models. However, the binomial model can also be employed to obtain a fair value for options. This is especially useful for situations in which the option can be exercised early, or for options on assets for which the Black-Scholes model is inappropriate—for example, options on debt instruments. Since the binomial model is explained for n periods below, the symbols are changed for ease of use. In particular, here u and d stand for an increase and decrease of the underlying asset price.

The value of an option using the Cox-Ross-Rubinstein binomial model for a large number of periods is determined as follows:

$$P_C = \frac{1}{(1 + R_f)^n} \left[\sum_{i=0}^{n} \frac{n!}{i!(n-i)!} p^i (1-p)^{n-i} \text{Max}[0, P_{su} u^i d^{n-i} - K] \right] \qquad \text{(12B-1)}$$

$$P_P = \frac{1}{(1 + R_f)^n} \left[\sum_{i=0}^{n} \frac{n!}{i!(n-i)!} p^i (1-p)^{n-i} \text{Max}[0, K - P_{su} u^i d^{n-i}] \right] \qquad \text{(12B-2)}$$

where R_f = non-annualized per-period risk-free interest rate

n = the number of binomial periods

p = the subjective probability of an increase in the asset price

u = 1 plus the asset rate of return if the asset increases (up)

d = 1 plus the asset rate of return if the asset decreases (down)

where u and d are determined by:

$u = e^{\sigma_s \sqrt{t/n}}$

$d = 1/u = e^{-\sigma_s \sqrt{t/n}}$

To prevent simple arbitrage: $u > R_f > d$

For an option on a stock:

$$p = \frac{(1 + R_f)^n - d}{u - d} \qquad \text{(12B-3)}$$

For an option on futures (see Chapter 18 for a discussion of futures options):

$$p = \frac{1 - d}{u - d} \qquad \text{(12B-4)}$$

While the binomial equations seem complicated, they simply find the value of an option as an average of all the possible call values at period n. Of course, those situations in which the option expires worthless are set equal to 0 (as designated in the equation). The factorial designation determines the number of paths generating the same ending value, so that each equivalent ending call value does not have to be calculated separately.

If the intermediate call values in the binomial tree are desired, then one must first find the ending call values for the individual cells for the ending time period. These are determined by finding the value of the option at that time by using the equation:

$$\text{call: } \text{Max}[0, P_S u^j d^{n-j} - K] \qquad \text{put: } \text{Max}[0, K - P_S u^j d^{n-j}] \qquad (12\text{B-}5)$$

where j = the number of periods the stock increased for the path in question

Then the recursive formula to calculate the call prices for individual cells at time period $T - 1$ is used:

$$P_{C,T-1} = [pP_{C,T}(u) + (1 - p)P_{C,T}(d)]/(1 + R_f) \qquad (12\text{B-}6)$$

where $P_{C,T}(u)$ = the up value of the call for period T

$P_{C,T}(d)$ = the down value of the call for period T

Example 12B-1 provides a multiperiod binomial tree with the individual call option values.

EXAMPLE 12B-1
A Multiperiod Binomial Example

A. INPUT VALUES
$P_S = 100$
$K = 100$
$\sigma_S = .30$
$t = .25$
Annual r $= 10\%$
$n = 5$
Per period $R_f = (1 + r)^{t/n} - 1 = .00478$
$u \equiv e^{\sigma_S \sqrt{t/n}} = 1.06938$
$d \equiv e^{-\sigma_S \sqrt{t/n}} = .935118$
$p = .518814$
$1 - p = .481186$

B. UNDERLYING ASSET BINOMIAL TREE

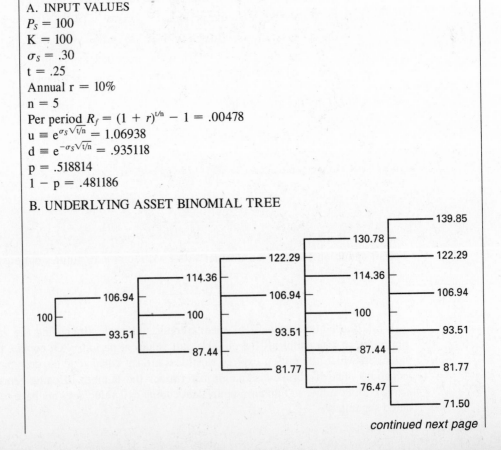

continued next page

continued

C. STANDARD EUROPEAN CALL BINOMIAL TREE

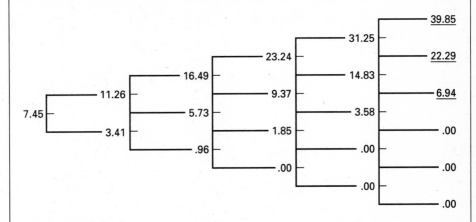

Note: Underlined option values should be exercised. Cells where the value of the call expires worthless are shown as .00. Ending values for the last time period are determined by $\text{Max}[0, P_S u^j d^{n-j} - K]$.

The recursive rule is:

$$P_{C,T-1} = [pP_{C,T}(u) + (1 - p)P_{C,T}(d)]/(1 + R_f)^{t/n}$$

Source: Rubinstein (1991).

Chapter 13

PRICING STOCK OPTIONS

Overview

This chapter examines the Black-Scholes option pricing model. The strength of the Black-Scholes model is that it provides both a theoretically sound and relatively simple equation for valuing options.

The Black-Scholes model provides both a value for the option and the appropriate hedge ratio between the stock and option positions. A simple adjustment adds dividends. The calculation of each input to the Black-Scholes model is also explained. Alternatively, one can solve the option model to determine the implied volatility of the stock returns based on the current option price. Comparing this implied volatility to the past stock volatility provides information on the consensus of the market concerning future stock variability. Put options are priced by using either the Black-Scholes model or the put-call parity relationship. Call options paying dividends and put options have the potential of early exercise.

Floor traders use the models and strategies developed here to profit from mispricings in options. These traders use the option models, put-call parity, and combinations of options and stocks to initiate arbitrage transactions. The operations of the trading floor are also explained. The chapter concludes by examining how option prices behave within the trading day.

Appendix 13A presents the assumptions of the Black-Scholes model. Each assumption is discussed in terms of its validity and how violations of the assumption can affect the option pricing results. Violations of the assumptions of the model may be the reason mispricings exist. Appendix 13B derives the Black-Scholes model.

Terminology

*Black-Scholes option model   An equation that determines the fair value for a call option in terms of the current stock price, the option exercise price, the time to expiration of the option, the volatility of the stock, and the current risk-free interest rate.

Box spread   A combination of two calls with different strike prices and two puts with strike prices equivalent to the calls. All options have the same expiration date.

*Conversion   Buying an underpriced put and selling an overpriced synthetic put, with the synthetic put being a short call and long stock position.

*Delta   The change in the option price for each $1 change in the stock price. Delta is an instantaneous hedge ratio.

*Fair value   A fair value for an option occurs when the option price provides an *expected* profit of zero to both the buyer and seller of the option.

*Hedge ratio   See Chapter 12 and see *delta*.

*Implied volatility   The estimated future volatility of the underlying stock, determined by solving the Black-Scholes option model by using the current call option price.

Instantaneous   A change that occurs immediately. Such a change is a "very small change" when associated with a derivative.

Market microstructure   The study of price behavior within the day and the structure of the market trading system affecting this price behavior.

*Put-call parity   See Chapter 12.

Ratio spread   Buying one option and selling another option on the same stock, where the number of shares traded for each option is based on an option pricing model hedge ratio. The purpose of this spread is to benefit from the relative mispricings of the two options.

*Reverse conversion   Buying an underpriced call and selling an overpriced synthetic call, with the synthetic call being a short put and a short stock position.

Scalper   A floor trader who buys at the bid and sells at the ask price.

Synthetic call   A combination of instruments that acts like a call option.

Synthetic put   A combination of instruments that acts like a put option.

BASIC PROPERTIES OF OPTION PRICING

Use of Option Models

The pricing of options is a cornerstone of finance. Early models for option pricing in the 1960s became the building blocks for the **Black-Scholes option pricing model** of the early 1970s (1972, 1973).[1] The Black-Scholes model coincided with the initiation of exchange-traded options on the CBOE in 1973. Since then, the Black-Scholes model has become an important part of both financial theory and practice. The importance of this model lies in the fact that it is both conceptually sound *and* useful for practitioners.

Since its inception, the Black-Scholes model and similar models have been extended to price many types of option-like contracts, including options embedded in other financial instruments—for example, the delivery options for Treasury bond futures contracts. Option models have even been employed to value corporations. While many recent applications of option pricing involve complicated mathematics, the beauty of the basic Black-Scholes stock option pricing model is that it is solvable with a programmable calculator. In fact, many option traders on the floor of the exchange use calculators with a version of the Black-Scholes option model to determine the appropriate value of a given stock option.

The Fair Value of an Option

The purpose of an option model is to provide an estimate of the **fair value** of an option based on the inputs to the model. A fair value for an option exists when the option price provides an *expected* profit of zero to both the buyer and seller of the option. Chapter 11 concentrates on the value of an option at its expiration, which simply determines the intrinsic value of the option. Chapter 12 examines option prices before expiration in terms of the factors that affect the fair value of an option:

- The stock price in relation to the strike price (which affects the leverage of the option).
- The time until the expiration of the option.
- The volatility of the stock returns.
- The level of interest rates.[2]

Finally, Chapters 11 and 12 present a number of "Pricing Relationships" that state how the above factors individually affect the price of an option. However, these pricing relationships do *not* integrate all of the individual factors, nor do they provide a precise value for an option. This chapter shows how the Black-Scholes option pricing model achieves these objectives.

[1] Black and Scholes (1972, 1973) derive their option pricing model in the 1973 article and test the model on over-the-counter options in their 1972 article.
[2] The current option price is *independent* of the expected future stock price.

BLACK-SCHOLES OPTION PRICING

An Overview of the Model

The binomial option pricing model can be extended to a large number of periods, as shown by Cox, Ross, and Rubinstein (1979). For an infinite number of periods, the binomial model is equivalent to the Black-Scholes model for European options. The derivation of the Black-Scholes model (1973) is considered to be one of the most important developments in finance. This derivation uses a branch of mathematics called "stochastic calculus" rather than the binomial model. A simplified derivation of the Black-Scholes model is given in Appendix 13B.

The foundation of the Black-Scholes option model is that arbitrage profits are *not* possible when the appropriate **hedge ratio** is generated between the stock and associated option. Thus, a long stock position and a short option position (as well as a short stock and a long option position) will earn the risk-free rate when the appropriate hedge ratio of stock to options is undertaken *and* the option has a fair price. If the option is either underpriced or overpriced, a return in excess of the risk-free rate is available to the arbitrageur. Arbitrageurs exploit any excess returns that exist, forcing the option back to its fair value.

One important aspect of the Black-Scholes formulation is that it does *not* depend on either the expected future stock price or investors' attitudes toward risk. Consequently, in addition to having a solid theoretical foundation, the Black-Scholes option model is calculated easily. The inputs to the model are the *current* stock price, the option exercise price, the time to expiration of the option, the volatility of the underlying stock, and the risk-free interest rate. Adjustments to the model, such as adding dividends, are considered later in this chapter.

Valuing a Call Option: The Black-Scholes Equation

The Black-Scholes option pricing model for valuing a European call option is:

$$P_C = P_S N(d_1) - Ke^{-rt} N(d_2) \tag{13-1}$$

where

$$d_1 = \frac{\ln(P_S/K) + [r + .5\sigma_S^2]t}{\sigma_S\sqrt{t}} \tag{13-2}$$

$$d_2 = d_1 - \sigma_S\sqrt{t} \tag{13-3}$$

$N(d_1), N(d_2)$ = cumulative normal probabilities: the probability that the observation is to the left of "d," based on a normal distribution with a mean of zero and a standard deviation of one.

ln = the natural logarithm[3] (of P_S/K)

P_C = the current fair value of the option

P_S = the current price of the stock

K = the exercise (strike) price of the option

[3] The natural logarithm is used for two purposes: first, it improves the computational properties of the stock distribution, and second, the value is converted to a continuously compounded return.

e = 2.71828

r = the risk-free rate of interest (continuously compounded)

t = the time remaining before option expiration, as a proportion of a year

σ_S = the annualized standard deviation of the continuously compounded stock return

Appendix A (at the end of the book) provides values for the normal distribution $N(d)$ to use in calculating the value of options. The value e^{-rt} stands for the continuous discounting function of the risk-free rate over time t; in other words, e^{-rt} calculates the interest factor for the present-value calculation needed in the Black-Scholes equation. Appendix B (at the end of the book) provides values of the natural logarithm ln. One must take care that the natural logarithm of P_S/K is calculated rather than log to the base 10. Using $\log_{10}$ will result in incorrect answers. Example 13-1 uses the Black-Scholes model given in Equation (13-1) and the values from Appendices A and B to calculate the value of a call option.

Finding the Value of the Normal Distribution Function

To calculate the Black-Scholes value of a call option, one must determine the value of the normal distribution function for $N(d_1)$ and $N(d_2)$. One method for finding $N(d)$ is to use a normal distribution table, as found in Appendix A. In this case, one must interpolate if the exact value of $N(d)$ is not in the table. Example 13-2 illustrates how to interpolate from a table.

An alternative method for determining the value of $N(d)$, especially if one wishes to use a programmable calculator or a spreadsheet, is to obtain an accurate estimate of $N(d)$ by an approximation equation. Exhibit 13-1 shows how to approximate the normal distribution function. Example 13-3 shows how to use this approximation formula.

The Black-Scholes equation uses the natural logarithm (P_S/K) in d_1. Combined with the normal distribution of d_1, $N(d_1)$, we have the lognormal distribution for stock prices. Using the lognormal distribution is equivalent to assuming that the *continuously compounded* rate of return on the stock is normally distributed. The significance of the lognormal distribution compared to the normal distribution is that the lognormal cannot have a return less than -100% (unlike the normal), and the lognormal is more skewed to the right to allow for larger positive returns. Thus, the lognormal is a more realistic distribution. Other distributions are possible, but they require other option models. Figure 13-1 compares the normal and lognormal distributions.

Interpreting the Black-Scholes Model

A close examination of Equation (13-1) provides some insights into the value of a call option:

- If the exercise of the call option is certain, then both d_1 and d_2 approach infinity and $N(d_1) = N(d_2) = 1$. Thus, $P_C = P_S - Ke^{-rt}$.
- If it is certain that exercise of the option will *not* take place, then d_1 and d_2 approach negative infinity and $N(d_1) = N(d_2) = 0$. Thus, $P_C = 0$.

EXAMPLE 13-1
Black-Scholes Call Option Value

Equation (13-1) presents the Black-Scholes option pricing model. In this formula, Equations (13-2) and (13-3) define d_1 and d_2.

$$P_C = P_S N(d_1) - Ke^{-rt}N(d_2) \tag{13-1}$$

where

$$d_1 = \frac{\ln(P_S/K) + [r + .5\sigma_S^2]t}{\sigma_S\sqrt{t}} \tag{13-2}$$

$$d_2 = d_1 - \sigma_S\sqrt{t} \tag{13-3}$$

Based on the following information, we calculate the fair value for the call option:

P_S = \$98 (the current stock price)

K = \$100 (the strike price)

r = .05 (the continuously compounded annual risk-free rate)

t = .25 (one-quarter of a year)

σ_S^2 = .25 (the continuously compounded variance of the stock returns)

σ_S = .5 (the standard deviation of the stock returns)

The values of d_1 and d_2 for the data given above are:

$$d_1 = \frac{\ln(98/100) + [.05 + .5(.25)].25}{.5\sqrt{.25}}$$

$$= \frac{-.02020 + [.175].25}{.5(.5)}$$

$$= +.02355/.25 = .0942$$

$$d_2 = .0942 - (.5)\sqrt{.25}$$

$$= -.1558$$

The value of the natural logarithm $\ln(98/100)$ is found by using the table in Appendix B. The normal probabilities associated with d_1 and d_2, as determined from the interpolation shown in Example 13-2, are:

$$N(d_1) = N(+.0942) = .5375$$

$$N(d_2) = N(-.1558) = .4381$$

The value of the option is:

$$P_C = 98(.5375) - 100\,e^{-.05(.25)}(.4381)$$

Note that $e^{-.05(.25)} = 1/e^{.05(.25)} = 1/e^{.0125}$. Since e = 2.71828, $e^{.0125} = 1.0126$ and $1/1.0126 = .9876$. Thus,

$$P_C = 98(.5375) - 100(.9876)(.4381)$$

$$= 52.675 - 43.267$$

$$= \$9.41$$

EXAMPLE 13-2
Interpolating from a Table

The values of $N(d_1)$ and $N(d_2)$ from Example 13-1 are:

$$N(d_1) = N(+.0942)$$

$$N(d_2) = N(-.1558)$$

The normal distribution table in Appendix A provides only two decimal places for d: the integer and first decimal are in the left column and the second decimal is in the top row—with the resultant value of $N(d)$ appearing within the table. To obtain the resultant value of $N(d)$ to four decimal places, as recommended for accurate Black-Scholes calculations, one must interpolate.

From Appendix A:

$$N(.09) = .5359$$

$$N(.10) = .5398$$

Since $N(.0942)$ is 42/100 between $N(.09)$ and $N(.10)$, we calculate the following:

$$N(.0942) = N(.09) + (42/100)[N(.10) - N(.09)]$$

$$= .5359 + (42/100)(.5398 - .5359)$$

$$= .5359 + (42/100)(.0039)$$

$$= .5359 + .0016$$

$$= .5375$$

Similarly, since $N(-d) = 1 - N(d) = 1 - N(.1558)$:

$$N(.15) = .5596$$

$$N(.16) = .5636$$

$$N(.1558) = N(.15) + (58/100)[N(.16) - N(.15)]$$

$$= .5596 + (58/100)(.5636 - .5596)$$

$$= .5596 + (58/100)(.0040)$$

$$= .5596 + .0023$$

$$= .5619$$

$$1 - N(.1558) = 1 - .5619 = .4381$$

- The current value of a call option is the *weighted* difference of the present value of its potential benefit (P_S) and the present value of its potential costs (Ke^{-rt}), where the weights $N(d_1)$ and $N(d_2)$ are between zero and one.
- The call price can also be interpreted as follows:

$$P_C = P_S N(d_1) + \text{Borrowing} \tag{13-4}$$

where $N(d_1)$ = the hedge ratio

    Borrowing = $-Ke^{-rt}N(d_2)$

EXHIBIT 13-1
The Approximation Formula for a Normal Distribution

To approximate the value of the normal distribution function N(d) at a specific value $d > 0$, one can use the following formula:

$$N(d) = 1 - N'(d)[b_1 k + b_2 k^2 + b_3 k^3 + b_4 k^4 + b_5 k^5 + \ldots]$$

where $N'(d) = (1/\sqrt{2\pi})e^{-d^2/2}$

$\quad k = 1/(1 + \alpha d)$

To achieve an accuracy within .00002, use three terms in the approximation equation, with:

$\alpha = .33267$

$b_1 = .4361836$

$b_2 = -.1201676$

$b_3 = .9372980$

To achieve an accuracy within .00000015, use five terms in the approximation equation, with:

$\alpha = .2316419$

$b_1 = .319381530$

$b_2 = -.356563782$

$b_3 = 1.781477937$

$b_4 = -1.821255978$

$b_5 = 1.330274429$

In addition:
If $d = 0$ then N(d) = .50
If $d < 0$ then find N($|-d|$), and calculate N(d) = 1 - N($|-d|$)

Source: M. Abramowitz and I. Stegen (1970). *Handbook of Mathematical Functions*. Washington DC: United States Department of Commerce, p. 932.

The hedge ratio is an important element of the Black-Scholes pricing model. It is discussed below and used both here and in Chapter 14.

The Hedge Ratio

The Concept. The basic concept of a hedge ratio for the Black-Scholes option model is equivalent to a hedge ratio for the binomial model: The hedge ratio is the ratio of stock shares to option shares that keeps the combined portfolio value the same for a given small change in the stock price. The hedge ratio does *not* keep the portfolio value the same for larger stock price changes unless the hedge ratio is altered accordingly. Equations (12-2) and (12-3) show the relevance of a hedge ratio.

EXAMPLE 13-3
Using the Approximation Formula for the Normal Distribution

In order to find the Black-Scholes option value, one must calculate $N(d_1)$ and $N(d_2)$. Example 13-2 shows how to use the normal distribution table and interpolate. An alternative method, which is useful for computers, is the approximation method.

From Example 13-1 we have $N(d_1) = N(.0942)$. Based on the formula in Exhibit 13-1, we have:

$$N(d) = 1 - N'(d)[b_1 k + b_2 k^2 + b_3 k^3 + b_4 k^4 + b_5 k^5 + \ldots]$$

where $N'(d) = (1/\sqrt{2\pi})e^{-d^2/2}$

$\qquad k = 1/(1 + \alpha d)$

For our example,

$$N'(d_1) = (1/\sqrt{2\pi})\, e^{-(.0942)^2/2}$$

$$= [1/\sqrt{2(3.14159)}]\, e^{-.044368}$$

$$= (.398942)(.995573)$$

$$= .397176$$

$$k = 1/[1 + (.33267)(.0942)]$$

$$= 1/1.031338 = .969614$$

$$N(d) = 1 - (.397176)[(.4361836)(.969614) - .1201676(.969614)^2$$
$$+ .9372980(.969614)^3]$$

$$= 1 - (.397176)[.4229297 - .1129757 + .8544257]$$

$$= 1 - (.397176)[1.1643797]$$

$$= 1 - .46246$$

$$= .5375$$

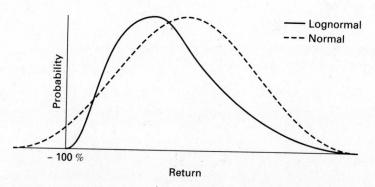

Figure 13-1 Comparing the normal distribution to the lognormal distribution.

FOCUS 13-1
The Option Simulator: What Is It?

The Options and Futures Simulator is a unique and useful PC computer program that allows the user to practice trading options and futures by using actual intraday historical prices. The program also determines the option value and other factors affecting call and put pricing (we will examine these factors in Chapter 14). Option prices can be determined for many types of options, as well as for different option pricing models. Moreover, all of the three-dimensional graphs presented later in this book were developed using the Simulator, as well as many of the two-dimensional options graphs.

A brief look at the Option Simulator shows some of its power.

- The PC trader can buy and/or sell any combination of S&P 500 calls and puts, the S&P 500 Index, and index futures to create a portfolio. Prices used by the program are actual five-minute prices for these securities. Prices are updated either by the user or automatically to show the wisdom of the trader's choices. The status and history of the trader's account is one of the alternative choices in the program. News events for the period show at the bottom of the screen and historical news summaries can be accessed.

- The values of the various options and the "sensitivities" of the options (see Chapter 14) are available, as calculated by the Black-Scholes, binomial, jump process, and constant elasticity option pricing models. The extended binomial trees can be shown on the screen. The values of alternative options (see Chapter 20) are also available in either table or graph form.

- Two-dimensional graphs on the payoffs of current or anticipated positions are available, as well as graphs on the option "sensitivities." Three-dimensional graphs (two inputs and one output) are available for the different option pricing models and the alternative options discussed in Chapter 20 (and their sensitivities), for a total of 32 different models/options. Graphs and actual Monte Carlo simulations on various dynamic replication strategies are also available.

- Tables on the option models and types of options noted above can also be generated (for an example, see Table 13-1). All tables and graphs provide alternatives that allow the user to change the value of the inputs.

- Historical data on 5- and 30-minute and one- and two-day volatilities are available in table form. Daily historical data on stock index, futures, and options, in addition to monthly data on bonds, are available for a number of years. Tables and graphs on implied volatility can be generated as well.

The Simulator is a very powerful and interesting program. It will be useful to provide hands-on experience to current and future traders, as well as knowledge of what affects option prices. There is also potential for research into how option prices react in certain circumstances. The Options and Futures Simulator's anticipated availability is late 1994, with an expected price for a site license of $5,000 to universities. Prices and availability for commercial use have not yet been determined.

The initial market screen of the Options Simulator is shown below. The market screen provides price quotations, time of the quotations, last trade price, and time of the trade. This screen also shows several hypothetical trades.

							Volume	

Market Screen

4/07/86 11:05

Sn	Security	Bid	Ask	QTime	Trade	TTime	Volume Held	Open
1	SP500 Index	227.73	227.73	11:05	227.73	11:05		
2	F/ /Jun86				228.20	11:05		
3	F/ /Sep86		230.85	11:05	231.10	11:05		
4	F/ /Dec86		234.10	11:05	234.00	8:35		
5	F/ /Mar87		236.90	11:05	239.00	4/04		
9	C/230/Apr86	2.06	2.25	11:00	2.63	4/04	5	
10	C/235/Apr86	0.88	1.00	11:00	1.13	4/04	20	
11	C/240/Apr86	0.31	0.38	10:55	0.44	10:20	10	
12	C/245/Apr86	0.13	0.19	9:30	0.19	10:25	50	
18	C/245/May86	1.19	1.31	11:00				
109	P/235/Apr86	8.38	8.63	11:05				

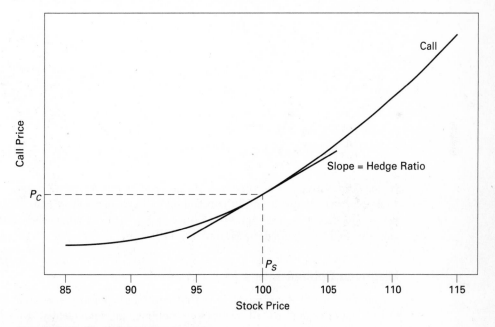

Figure 13-2 Black-Scholes hedge ratio.

Figure 13-2 shows the relationship between the option value and stock prices before the expiration of the option. The *slope* of the option value line *at the current stock price* represents the Black-Scholes hedge ratio. This hedge ratio is conceptually equivalent to Figure 12-2 for the binomial model, where the slope of the line for the two possible stock prices in the binomial case equals the hedge ratio. However, the Black-Scholes model allows a continuous stock price distribution to occur, not just the two stock prices used in the one-period binomial model. Therefore, one interprets the Black-Scholes hedge ratio in terms of a small **instantaneous** (immediate) price change for the stock.[4]

Defining Delta as the Hedge Ratio. The hedge ratio in the Black-Scholes model is equivalent to $N(d_1)$. This value is often called the option's **delta.** The option's delta states the (expected) change in the option price for a given change in the stock price:

$$\text{Delta} = \Delta P_C / \Delta P_S = N(d_1) \tag{13-5}$$

A rule of thumb is that an at-the-money option has a delta of .5—that is, for a change of \$1 in the stock price the option changes by \$.50. The delta ranges from 0 to 1, which confirms the statement in Chapter 12 that option prices move less than stock prices. Chapter 14 examines how to use an option's delta.

For the Black-Scholes model, the slope of the line at the current stock price *differs* from the slope at a different stock price. This is the reason for referring to the hedge ratio as relevant for a "small instantaneous price change." In other words, the hedge ratio (delta) *changes* as the stock price changes. In addition, the hedge ratio changes as the time to option expiration changes, although small changes in time do not affect the hedge ratio.

Black-Scholes Call Values

Table 13-1 presents Black-Scholes call values for a stock priced at 100. The table shows how the option value changes in relation to the following variables:

- The strike price (K in the left column).
- The standard deviation of the stock (σ in the left column).
- The risk-free interest rate (r in the second row).
- The number of months to option expiration (the third row).

Besides illustrating the sensitivity of the call price to the variables listed, the results in Table 13-1, when compared to the binomial call values given in Table 12-2, show that the two models value call options within one cent of each other when 150 time intervals are used to calculate the binomial model.

Mispriced Options

One objective of floor traders is to find mispriced options—that is, is to buy under-priced options and to sell overpriced options, or equivalently, to *avoid* buying overpriced options or selling underpriced options. If the Black-Scholes model correctly prices options, and if a particular option is mispriced, then a ratio between the stock and option shares can be created in order to exploit the mispricing. Such a transaction would earn a return that is greater than the risk-free interest rate. In fact, arbitrageurs on the floor of the option exchange execute such transactions daily. They find risk-free

---

[4] The slope to a curvilinear line at a particular point is the derivative of the line at that point. The concept of an instantaneous change is directly related to the derivative.

Table 13-1 Call Values Using the Black-Scholes Model

$P_s = 100$

		r = .05				r = .10				r = .15			
		Months to Expiration											
σ	K	1	3	6	12	1	3	6	12	1	3	6	12
.2	85	15.35	16.18	17.61	20.39	15.67	17.11	19.34	23.54	15.99	18.00	21.00	26.58
	90	10.43	11.65	13.46	16.62	10.76	12.55	15.12	19.67	11.09	13.43	16.74	22.68
	95	5.89	7.69	9.83	13.27	6.20	8.50	11.34	16.14	6.49	9.29	12.86	19.03
	100	2.51	4.60	6.86	10.39	2.71	5.23	8.14	12.99	2.92	5.87	9.47	15.71
	105	.74	2.47	4.56	7.97	.83	2.90	5.58	10.27	.92	3.36	6.68	12.74
	110	.15	1.18	2.89	5.99	.17	1.44	3.66	7.97	.20	1.73	4.51	10.16
	115	.02	.51	1.75	4.43	.02	.65	2.29	6.07	.03	.80	2.92	7.97
.3	85	15.43	16.86	19.05	22.85	15.75	17.70	20.57	25.56	16.05	18.51	22.04	28.19
	90	10.77	12.84	15.45	19.63	11.08	13.63	16.89	22.24	11.38	14.40	18.30	24.81
	95	6.72	9.38	12.29	16.74	6.99	10.09	13.62	19.22	7.25	10.78	14.93	21.69
	100	3.65	6.57	9.61	14.17	3.85	7.16	10.78	16.49	4.04	7.75	11.97	18.84
	105	1.71	4.41	7.37	11.92	1.83	4.87	8.40	14.06	1.95	5.35	9.44	16.27
	110	.68	2.84	5.57	9.97	.74	3.18	6.43	11.92	.80	3.54	7.33	13.97
	115	.23	1.75	4.14	8.29	.26	2.00	4.85	10.05	.28	2.26	5.60	11.92
.4	85	15.70	17.96	20.96	25.79	16.00	18.72	22.32	28.18	16.29	19.46	23.63	30.50
	90	11.37	14.33	17.73	22.93	11.65	15.04	19.02	25.25	11.93	15.74	20.28	27.52
	95	7.68	11.18	14.86	20.32	7.92	11.83	16.07	22.56	8.16	12.46	17.26	24.76
	100	4.80	8.54	12.36	17.97	4.99	9.10	13.47	20.10	5.18	9.66	14.57	22.22
	105	2.77	6.39	10.19	15.85	2.91	6.86	11.20	17.87	3.04	7.34	12.20	19.90
	110	1.48	4.68	8.35	13.96	1.56	5.08	9.24	15.85	1.65	5.47	10.15	17.78
	115	.73	3.37	6.79	12.27	.78	3.68	7.58	14.04	.83	4.00	8.39	15.85

Source: Rubinstein (1991).

arbitrage situations in which they can sell overpriced call options (buying the stock and selling options in the proportion dictated by the relevant hedge ratio) or they can buy underpriced options (selling stock and buying options in relation to the appropriate hedge ratio). Similar transactions can be executed for put options. As discussed below, these arbitrageurs must adjust their hedge ratios as conditions warrant, and such trades must be virtually free of commission charges.

Option traders off the exchange floor can also use the Black-Scholes model for mispricings, although such traders execute different strategies from those of arbitrageurs. Brokerage houses and other services create lists of the "most underpriced" and "most overpriced" options on a daily basis. However, care must be taken in using such lists, since timing differences between the stock price and option price can account for specific options making this mispricing list. The traders on the floor of the exchange also generate such lists; consequently, these mispricing opportunities often disappear early on the following trading day because of transactions made by these floor traders as soon as the option exchanges open. Chapter 15 discusses strategies for off-the-floor traders to benefit from mispricings of options.

A more general approach to using an option model and benefiting from any potential mispricing of the options is to employ the pricing sensitivities to determine the appropriate option strategy. The pricing sensitivities are the hedge ratio, time to expiration, volatility, the option leverage, and the change in the hedge ratio. Chapter 14 examines how to use these sensitivities to determine appropriate trading strategies.

Basic Assumptions of the Black-Scholes Model

Hedge ratios can be examined by comparing the binomial model to the Black-Scholes model. The hedge ratio for the one-period binomial model shown in Figure 12-7 is relevant for the *two* possible future stock prices, which in turn creates a position with no risk. Consequently, the return from the hedge between the option and the stock with a binomial model earns the risk-free rate. Figure 12-7 shows how the hedge ratio *changes* from time period T to $T + 1$ if the upper stock price of $105 occurs at $T + 1$. Similarly, as the stock price or time to expiration changes, the hedge ratio for the Black-Scholes model also changes. Hence, both the binomial and Black-Scholes models are based on the assumption that arbitrageurs periodically adjust their hedge positions as the hedge ratio changes. If the hedge position is not adjusted, then the stock/option position is no longer risk-free. The conclusion that arbitrageurs can adjust their hedge position and that the hedge ratio provides a risk-free position is based on the following assumptions:

- There are no transactions costs. Thus, an arbitrageur can adjust the hedge ratio almost continuously without cost.
- Only small changes in the stock price occur within a short time period. Therefore, the arbitrageur has sufficient time to alter the hedge ratio before a large stock price change occurs.

The first assumption is true for arbitrageurs on the floor of the options exchange, but not for others who have to pay commissions each time they trade. This means that off-the-floor traders must rely on arbitrageurs who are on the floor of the exchange to keep the prices of options "fair." Consequently, only floor arbitrageurs have the opportunity to profit when option prices differ from their fair value. Moreover, to profit from arbitrage opportunities, the floor trader must take a position with the appropriate hedge ratio and be able to change this hedge ratio as stock prices change.

The second assumption, which relates to the existence of small price changes, is typically valid in normal markets. However, when a chaotic market exists (such as the October 1987 market crash), or when a takeover bid for a stock is announced, prices "jump." When prices do *not* change smoothly, arbitrageurs cannot adjust their hedge ratios quickly enough. In these circumstances, floor traders often go bankrupt. This "jump" factor is also used as a justification for pricing call options higher than the value calculated by the Black-Scholes model—that is, the unpredictable risk from jumps may create an additional premium in the call price.[5]

The Black-Scholes model is *not* a good model for valuing long-term options since Black-Scholes assumes that volatility increases *exponentially* as time increases. Therefore, LEAPS and other long-term options need a more realistic volatility process. One such process is a mean reverting volatility assumption.

While the above discussion suggests that an option pricing model that is superior to the Black-Scholes model may exist (in fact, researchers have developed more sophisticated models), the Black-Scholes model is still considered the most important model for option traders for two reasons. First, actual option prices tend toward the Black-Scholes price because of arbitrage, since jumps in price are infrequent and unpredictable. Second, major brokerage houses and many traders use some form of the Black-Scholes or binomial models to generate their estimates of a fair option price. Further discussion of the assumptions of the Black-Scholes model and alternative models is presented in Appendix 13A.

CALCULATING THE INPUTS

The inputs to Equation (13-1) are the current stock price, the strike price, the time to expiration of the option, the risk-free interest rate, and the volatility of the stock returns. The strike price of the option is a known value that does not have to be calculated. The other variables need some explanation.

Current Stock Price

If the stock has traded within the last few minutes, then the last stock price is a valid value for the current stock price. However, if the stock has not traded for hours, then the last trade may be an inappropriate value to use in the Black-Scholes model. In addition, stock index options suffer from the fact that stocks trade at different times, causing the index to be "old." There is no widely accepted method for dealing with old prices in the option model.

---

[5]Any pricing model is based on certain assumptions that are used to derive the final result of the model (in this case, the option price). For example, one criticism concerning the input factors of the Black-Scholes model is that stock price changes do *not* follow a normal distribution (which includes possible jumps in prices). If the actual option price in the market deviates from the price estimated by the model, either the actual option price is mispriced (providing profit opportunities), the assumptions of the model are incorrect, or the model is missing one or more important input factors. Chapter 14 investigates how well the Black-Scholes model estimates the true market option prices. While some deviations do exist, overall the Black-Scholes model provides very accurate estimates of actual option prices.

Time to Expiration

The time until option expiration in Equation (13-1) is input as a fraction of a year. Hence, an option with 90 days left until expiration has a value of $t = 90/365 = .2466$. The number of decimal places employed for the calculation depends on the accuracy desired. Four decimal places provide sufficient accuracy to obtain a call value that is accurate to within one cent. Traders using the Black-Scholes model use the actual number of days until expiration when trading within the day. However, near the end of the day these traders start to use the *following* trading day's time to expiration in order to price the option. Thus, near the end of a Friday session, traders use the value of t for the following Monday in the Black-Scholes calculations.

The number of trading days appears in the option pricing equation in two places. The first place is in the discounting function for the exercise price—that is, e^{-rt} in Equation (13-1). Here the number of days used should equal the actual number of days until option expiration, since interest is earned/paid on a calendar-day basis. The second place time appears is in adjusting the variability of the stock price in Equations (13-2) and (13-3). For this situation some researchers argue that t needs to be adjusted to reflect the nonconstant variability of stock prices over time. In particular, stock prices vary less over the nontrading time periods of weekends as compared to when the market is open during the week. A rule of thumb is to equate three nontrading days to one actual trading day in order to make the variability more consistent. However, in our examples we will assume constant variability across time for simplicity.

The Risk-Free Rate

Typically, the Treasury bill interest rate is employed to calculate the risk-free rate. T-bills do not have default risk and are very liquid. Chapter 2 discusses the quotation of T-bills and their characteristics. The average of the bid and ask discount interest rates is often employed to obtain a *simple* T-bill risk-free discount interest rate. The next step is to determine the risk-free discount price as a percentage of the par value:

$$P_{RF} = 100 - i_d(M/360) \tag{13-6}$$

where P_{RF} = the risk-free discount price as a percentage of the par value

$\quad\quad i_d$ = the T-bill discount interest rate, typically as an average of the bid and ask discount rates

$\quad\quad M$ = the number of *days* until maturity of the T-bill (the maturity matches the option expiration)

Note that M in Equation (13-6) refers to a number of days, while t in Equations (13-1) through (13-3) refers to a portion of the year. Also, the discount price in (13-6) is based on a 360-day year, which is based on historical convention. The simple *yield* for this risk-free instrument is determined by:

$$R_f = [100/P_{RF}]^{365/M} - 1 \tag{13-7}$$

The Black-Scholes model uses the continuously compounded risk-free interest rate to determine the value of a call option. The simple rate calculated above employs *annual* compounding. An interest rate that is *continuously* compounded uses the exponential function "e" to calculate the effect of compounding (see Equation (13-1)). A simple interest rate is converted to a continuously compounded rate by using the natural logarithmic function, which is the inverse of the exponential function:[6]

$$r = \ln(1 + R_F)$$ (13-8)

where r = the continuously compounded risk-free interest rate

$\ln$ = the natural logarithm

R_F = the simple risk-free interest rate

An example of how to implement the above equations is given later in this chapter.[7]

Volatility

The Black-Scholes option model employs the volatility of the underlying stock returns as part of the option valuation equation. Volatility is an important variable, since option prices are sensitive to small changes in volatility. Volatility typically is determined by calculating the historical variance of the returns—that is, the standard deviation of the returns, squared.[8] Both the variance and the standard deviation of returns are used in Equations (13-2) and (13-3) to calculate the option value. Daily, weekly, bimonthly, monthly, or similar data can be employed to determine the historical volatility.[9] As with the risk-free rate, the variance of the returns is defined in terms of continuously compounded returns. Thus, the return for each period used to calculate the variance needs to be converted to a continuous return. Per-period returns below .05 are not affected significantly by the conversion from simple returns to continuously compounded returns. Therefore, the difference between simple and continuous returns is noticeable only in the third decimal place. However, returns above .05 are affected more noticeably by the conversion.

---

[6] R_F and $r = \ln(1 + R_F)$ create the same ending value for $1 invested for a particular length of time. However, the continuous compounding nature of r allows this ending value to occur with a value of r, which is less than the corresponding value for R_F.

[7] Chapter 12 states that a change in the risk-free interest rate does not significantly affect the value of the call option. Therefore, one might be tempted to use the simple R_F rate rather than calculate the continuously compounded rate r. Whether a trader employs such a substitution depends on the accuracy desired for the analysis. The use of R_F determines a value for the call option that is about .2% too high. Similarly, the use of an interest rate that does not exactly correspond to the actual expiration of the option has only a minor effect on the calculated value of the option.

Some traders and researchers state that the Certificate of Deposit rate or the broker call rate (the rate of interest charged to investors for loans on margin accounts) is more appropriate than the T-bill rate. Their reasoning is that the T-bill rate is below the borrowing rate for funds. The T-bill rate is still justifiable if marginal investors obtain funds from their cash management account, which is invested in T-bills. Moreover, the call price is not very sensitive to varying interest rates.

[8] An alternative to using the historical volatility is for the analyst to devise a probability distribution of *expected* outcomes, determining the variance of that probability distribution.

[9] The reliability of the historical volatility estimate can be improved by using the open, high, low, and close of whatever measurement interval is chosen. For example, if daily data are employed, then the daily open, high, low, and close prices can be used to improve the estimate of volatility by a factor of eight. See Garman and Klass (1980).

A full-function calculator or a spreadsheet easily and automatically makes the conversion from simple returns to continuously compounded returns. Determining the variance of returns is a four-step process:

1. Calculate the rate of return for each time period:

$$R_{S,T} = (P_{S,T} - P_{S,T-1})/P_{S,T-1} \qquad (13\text{-}9)$$

where $R_{S,T}$ = the simple rate of return for the stock during time period T

$P_{S,T}$ = the price of the stock at time T

2. Convert the simple returns to continuously compounded returns:

$$r_{S,T} = \ln(1 + R_{S,T}) \qquad (13\text{-}10)$$

where $r_{S,T}$ = the continuously compounded return on the stock during time period T

3. Determine the variance of the continuously compounded returns:

$$\sigma_{S,T}^2 = \frac{\sum\limits_{t=1}^{N} (r_{S,T} - \bar{r}_S)^2}{N - 1} \qquad (13\text{-}11)$$

where $\sigma_{S,T}^2$ = the variance on the stock returns using daily, weekly, monthly, etc. intervals

$\bar{r}_S$ = the average return on the stock over the period in question

N = the number of observations used in the calculation

4. Annualize the variance (the variance calculated in Equation (13-11) is based on the time intervals used. For example, weekly time periods provide a weekly variance):

$$\sigma_S^2 = \sigma_{S,T}^2 N_T \qquad (13\text{-}12)$$

where σ_S^2 = the annualized continuously compounded variance for the stock

N_T = the number of time intervals in a year; for example, for weekly time intervals $N_T = 52$; for monthly intervals $N_T = 12$

The standard deviation, σ_S, is then computed by taking the square root of the annualized variance.[10]

The volatility value determined by the above calculations is based on historical information. The appropriate value for the variance in the Black-Scholes option model is the volatility *during* the time period when the option is being traded. The difference between the historical volatility and the market's estimate of future volatility is examined shortly.

---

[10] The calculation of the variance in Equation (13-10) involves dividing by $N-1$. Subtracting one from N is required when a sample is used for the calculation, as in this case. If a spreadsheet is used to determine the relevant volatility values, an adjustment must often be made for the variance, since most spreadsheets use N in the divisor. The relevant adjustment is to multiply the results by $N/(N-1)$.

Dividends on Stocks

The Black-Scholes option model as discussed so far ignores the effects of dividends—that is, the model is based on a non–dividend-paying stock. However, dividends are added to the model with a relatively minor adjustment. Cash dividends tend to reduce the value of a call option, since the strike price is *not* adjusted for cash dividends but the stock price does decline when a stock goes ex-dividend. The adjustment procedure used here quantifies the appropriate reduction in the price of the call option, given the size and timing of the cash dividends on the stock.

The most popular adjustment for dividends is to subtract the present value of the cash dividends from the stock price, using the resultant adjusted stock price in the Black-Scholes model. Using the continuously discounted interest rate for the present value adjustments, we have:

$$P'_S = P_S - D_T e^{-r\tau} \tag{13-13}$$

where P'_S = the stock price adjusted for dividends (this value then is used in the Black-Scholes model)

D_T = the dollar dividend paid at time T

$e^{-r\tau}$ = the continuously discounted risk-free rate r, discounted over time period τ

τ = the proportion of the year from the present time until the *ex-dividend date* for the stock

Note that τ differs from t, where t is the expiration of the option. P'_S must adjust for *each* cash dividend expected before option expiration.[11]

Call options are sometimes exercised early in order to obtain the cash dividends on a stock about to go ex-dividend. If there is a short time before option expiration, this is a rational strategy, since the stock prices are adjusted downward on the ex-dividend day by the size of the dividend, while strike prices are *not* adjusted. At times, call options are exercised a significant time before the expiration date. However, such exercises are generally irrational decisions on the part of the call option buyer, since the call option could be sold for a greater profit than generated from exercising the option.[12] Other things being equal, the optimal early exercise of an American call is more appropriate the higher the stock price, the lower the strike price, the shorter the time to option expiration, and the higher the cash dividends yet to be paid. Table 13-2 shows the effect of different dividend payments on call option values.

Since the existence of dividends creates the possibility of early exercise for an American call option, one can now recognize the difference between American and European options. While the dividend adjustment to the European Black-Scholes model provides a credible adjusted call option value, some traders prefer using the binomial model that directly shows each cell when the call should be exercised.

---

[11] The stock owner does not receive the dividends until four to six weeks after the ex-dividend date. However, the ex-dividend date is when the stock price is adjusted downward and therefore when the call option price is adversely affected.

[12] Exercising an option entails a commission on the stock, even though the stock is not purchased on the exchange. Thus, an option exercise does not avoid this cost.

Table 13-2 Call Values for Different Dividend Payments

$P_s = 100$ $r = .10$

		d = .05				d = .10				d = .15			
		\multicolumn{12}{c}{Months to Expiration}
σ	K	1	3	6	12	1	3	6	12	1	3	6	12
.2	85	15.27	15.94	17.10	19.27	14.89	14.84	15.07	15.60	14.52	13.82	13.24	12.49
	90	10.37	11.46	13.05	15.69	9.99	10.46	11.22	12.35	9.64	9.54	9.61	9.60
	95	5.85	7.56	9.53	12.51	5.53	6.73	7.96	9.56	5.24	5.98	6.63	7.20
	100	2.49	4.51	6.63	9.78	2.28	3.89	5.37	7.24	2.10	3.36	4.33	5.28
	105	.73	2.42	4.40	7.49	.65	2.02	3.45	5.37	.58	1.68	2.69	3.79
	110	.15	1.16	2.78	5.62	.12	.93	2.11	3.90	.11	.75	1.59	2.66
	115	.02	.50	1.68	4.15	.02	.39	1.23	2.78	.01	.30	.89	1.84
.3	85	15.35	16.61	18.52	21.64	14.97	15.60	16.67	18.27	14.62	14.66	15.01	15.37
	90	10.71	12.64	15.01	18.58	10.36	11.74	13.34	15.47	10.04	10.91	11.85	12.84
	95	6.68	9.23	11.94	15.83	6.39	8.46	10.46	12.99	6.12	7.76	9.17	10.63
	100	3.63	6.46	9.32	13.39	3.43	5.84	8.05	10.84	3.24	5.28	6.96	8.74
	105	1.69	4.33	7.15	11.26	1.57	3.86	6.09	8.98	1.47	3.44	5.19	7.14
	110	.68	2.79	5.39	9.41	.62	2.44	4.52	7.40	.57	2.14	3.80	5.80
	115	.23	1.72	4.00	7.82	.21	1.49	3.31	6.06	.19	1.28	2.74	4.69
.4	85	15.62	17.70	20.39	24.45	15.26	16.76	18.65	21.22	14.92	15.88	17.08	18.41
	90	11.31	14.12	17.24	21.73	10.99	13.27	15.65	18.70	10.68	12.49	14.22	16.10
	95	7.63	11.01	14.45	19.25	7.37	10.27	13.01	16.44	7.11	9.59	11.73	14.04
	100	4.77	8.41	12.01	17.02	4.57	7.78	10.72	14.41	4.38	7.21	9.59	12.21
	105	2.75	6.29	9.90	15.01	2.61	5.77	8.77	12.61	2.48	5.30	7.78	10.59
	110	1.47	4.61	8.10	13.21	1.38	4.19	7.12	11.01	1.30	3.82	6.27	9.18
	115	.72	3.31	6.59	11.60	.67	2.99	5.74	9.60	.63	2.70	5.02	7.94

d = dividends as a percentage of asset price.
Source: Rubinstein (1991).

Dividends on an Index

The above procedure is based on a discrete dividend payment made at a specific time. Such a procedure is very cumbersome to use for index options, since a large number of dividends are paid on the individual stocks that make up the index. An alternative procedure is to use the dividend yield for the stock index. Such yields for the major stock indexes are found in *Value Line Options*. The appropriate adjustment to the stock index price is:

$$P'_S = P_S e^{-d\tau} \tag{13-14}$$

where d = the dividend yield on the index

This procedure is based on the assumption that dividends are paid continuously. While this assumption is not strictly true for an index of stocks, it creates only a minor adverse effect on the estimate of the fair price of the option. More important, the continuous dividend adjustment reduces the complexity of calculating the effect of individual dividends on the index option. Equation (13-14) can also be employed for individual stocks, but the resultant call option value is too large.[13]

Calculating Inputs

Examples 13-4 and 13-5 illustrate how to calculate the inputs to the Black-Scholes option model. The calculations for the volatility of the stock shown in Example 13-5 typically are completed with a spreadsheet in order to reduce calculation time and avoid errors.

VOLATILITY AND OPTIONS

Implied Volatility

The only input to the Black-Scholes option model that is not known with certainty when one calculates the value of a call option is the volatility of the underlying stock. This is because σ_S and σ_S^2 in Equations (13-2) and (13-3) represent the volatility of the stock *over the life of the option*. Since no one knows with certainty what this *future* volatility will be, traders typically use historical variance as an appropriate estimate of future volatility. Some traders then adjust the historical volatility based on their forecast of the relevant current factors affecting this stock or index.

The price of the option includes the consensus opinion of the market participants concerning the future volatility of the stock. This estimate of the future volatility is determined by solving the Black-Scholes option equation for the **implied volatility**— that is, the volatility implied by the current option price. Thus, Equations (13-1) to (13-3)

---

[13] Using a continuously accrued dividend yield avoids potential problems relating to known discrete dividends. A dividend yield is a known percentage of the index value or stock price. As stock price levels change, the *dollar* value of the dividends changes under the procedure of a constant *yield*. This assumption is more realistic than taking a specific known dollar dividend, especially for stock indexes. An in-depth development and proof of the various dividend adjustments to the option model is found in Jarrow and Rudd (1983, ch. 9).

EXAMPLE 13-4
Calculating the Inputs to the Black-Scholes Model

A. Basic Information

Stock: J Enterprises $\quad P_S = 127.375 \quad K = 125 \quad$ Annual Dividend $= \$4.40$

Current date $=$ July 23 $\quad$ Dividend date $=$ August 4

B. Time Until Option Expiration

time until expiration: 90 days $= M$ (October 21)

$t = 90/365 = .2466$

C. The Risk-Free Interest Rate

$$P_{RF} = 100 - i_d(M/360)$$

$$i_d = 8.50$$

$$P_{RF} = 100 - 8.5(90/360)$$

$$P_{RF} = 97.875$$

$$R_F = [100/P_{RF}]^{365/M} - 1$$

$$R_F = [100/97.875]^{365/90} - 1$$

$$R_F = .091$$

$$r = \ln(1 + R_F)$$

$$r = \ln(1 + .091)$$

$$r = .087$$

D. Dividend Effect

$$P'_S = P_S - D_T e^{-rr}$$

$$P'_S = 127.375 - 1.10e^{-(.087)(11/365)}$$

$$P'_S = 126.28$$

E. Option Price

Using the inputs calculated above and in Example 13-5, and the Black-Scholes Equations (13-1), (13-2), and (13-3), the value of the call option for the October 125 strike price is 7⅞.

are solved for the standard deviation of the stock returns, with the current call option price as an input to the equation. In other words, the implied volatility is the standard deviation and variance in Equations (13-2) and (13-3), which makes the call option price from the Black-Scholes *model* equal to the current *market* price for the call option. Since volatility appears in several places in Equations (13-2) and (13-3), solving for volatility is not a simple undertaking; in fact, it requires a computer. Typically, as shown initially by Latané and Rendleman (1976), implied volatility is obtained by a trial-and-error procedure in which various values of the standard deviation and associated variance are input into Equations (13-2) and (13-3) until the market and model option

EXAMPLE 13-5
Calculating the Volatility of a Stock

Date		Close	$R_{S,T}$	$r_{S,T}$	$(r_{S,T} - \bar{r}_S)^2$
JAN	8	114.875			
	15	119.000	0.0359	0.0353	0.0010
	22	110.500	−0.0714	−0.0741	0.0061
	29	112.375	0.0170	0.0168	0.0002
FEB	5	108.000	−0.0389	−0.0397	0.0019
	12	112.000	0.0370	0.0364	0.0010
	19	113.375	0.0123	0.0122	0.0001
	26	115.750	0.0209	0.0207	0.0003
MAR	4	116.875	0.0097	0.0097	0.0000
	11	115.500	−0.0118	−0.0118	0.0003
	18	114.250	−0.0108	−0.0109	0.0002
	25	107.000	−0.0635	−0.0656	0.0049
	31	107.625	0.0058	0.0058	0.0000
APR	8	111.625	0.0372	0.0365	0.0010
	15	114.125	0.0224	0.0221	0.0003
	22	113.750	−0.0033	−0.0033	0.0001
	29	113.375	−0.0033	−0.0033	0.0001
MAY	6	110.500	−0.0254	−0.0257	0.0009
	13	110.375	−0.0011	−0.0011	0.0000
	20	109.375	−0.0091	−0.0091	0.0002
	27	108.000	−0.0126	−0.0127	0.0003
JUN	3	113.250	0.0486	0.0475	0.0019
	10	116.000	0.0243	0.0240	0.0004
	17	117.500	0.0129	0.0128	0.0001
	24	125.125	0.0649	0.0629	0.0035
	30	127.375	0.0180	0.0178	0.0002
TOTALS				0.1033	0.0248

$\bar{r}_S = .1033/25 = 0.0041$
$\sigma^2 = .0248/24 = 0.0010$
Annualized $\sigma^2 = .001(52) = 0.0520$
Annualized $\sigma = \sqrt{.052} = 0.2280$

prices are equal. For example, if the stock price and strike price are 40, $t = .333$, the risk-free interest rate is 5%, and the market call price is 3.07, one calculates an implied volatility of .3.[14]

Implied volatility is an important concept for option pricing. It determines the market's estimate of the future volatility of the stock. This estimate is then compared to the stock's historical volatility to determine the market's opinion on the potential change

[14] While finding implied volatility is a trial-and-error procedure, the Newton-Raphson search technique is a rapid procedure for finding the implied volatility. However, the difficulty of the technique and the speed of modern PCs make such a search process less important. Alternatively, one can use the approximation equation for the normal distribution given in Exhibit 13-1 to solve the option equation for volatility by trial and error.

in volatility. A difference between the option value calculated from historical data and the market call option price is typically due to the difference between the implied and historical volatility values.

If the Black-Scholes model is a perfect model, then options on the same stock that have the *same maturity* should have the same implied volatility. In practice, different options on the same stock have different implied volatilities. Table 13-3 shows the implied volatilities for IBM.

While many traders use the near-to-the-money option's implied volatility, one can also calculate an average implied volatility estimate by using most of the traded options that have the same maturity by:[15]

$$\sigma^* = \Sigma\,(w_j/\Sigma\,w_j)\sigma_j^* \tag{13-15}$$

where σ^* = the estimate of the implied volatility of the stock

w_j = the weight for the jth option's implied volatility

σ_j^* = the implied volatility for the jth option

The weights are determined by the trader, with the largest weight typically being assigned to the near-to-the-money option.[16] In addition, Brenner and Subrahmanyam (1988) determined that an at-the-money call price can be approximated by the equation:

$$P_c \approx .398\,P_S\,\sigma_S\sqrt{t} \tag{13-16}$$

Thus, solving for the implied volatility, we have:

$$\sigma_S = P_C/.398\,P_S\sqrt{t} \tag{13-17}$$

Large differences in implied volatilities should be investigated to determine whether mispricing exists. Such an investigation should include whether all of the different option strikes traded at the same time of the day, since consistency in the use of the correct stock-option combination is critical in determining whether mispricing exists.

Beckers (1981) compares the implied volatility calculated from the Black-Scholes option model to the historical volatility from the stock in order to determine which measure provides a superior prediction of the actual future volatility. Beckers finds that

Table 13-3 IBM Implied Volatilities

Strike Price	Time to Expiration			
	1 Month	2 Months	3 Months	6 Months
50	31.9%	31.3%	35.2%	34.7%
55	35.1%	33.9%	34.9%	33.6%
60	NA	NA	33.9%	33.8%

Source: Calculated using IBM option prices with OptionVue IV.

[15] Typically, deep-in- and deep-out-of-the-money options are not considered when calculating the weighted implied volatility, since small changes in the option price have significant effects on the implied volatility, *and* because these options are often mispriced or have not traded recently.

[16] Technically, the largest weight should be the call with the largest $\partial c_j/\partial\sigma_j^*$, which is usually the near-to-the-money call.

the implied volatility is the superior predictor. Moreover, the implied volatility for the near-to-the-money strike price is a better predictor of future volatility than the average of the implied volatilities for all of the strike prices of the option, perhaps because the nearby option trades more frequently. Harvey and Whaley (1992) find that S&P 100 options transactions prices can forecast future market volatility. However, a trading model cannot provide excess returns based on this information.

Later we examine how a trader's volatility estimates that differ from the market's estimate of future volatility are used to create trading strategies. In other words, a trader can determine that an option is under- or overpriced based on comparing these two values for the volatility of the stock, and then exploit this mispricing. Figure 13-3 shows the historical and implied volatilities for Eastman Kodak. Figure 13-4 illustrates the volatilities for the S&P 100 Index. These figures show that historical and implied volatilities often differ and that both measures of volatility change over time. In fact, the assumption that volatility remains constant usually is not valid.

Forecasting Volatility and GARCH

Since the future volatility of the stock is the only unknown variable in the option pricing equation, an accurate forecast of volatility is a critical factor in trading options. In fact, many option traders concentrate on volatility to make their speculative decisions. Moreover, traders predict that options whose prices are quoted in terms of volatility will trade within five years.

Methods of forecasting volatility include economic, fundamental, and technical procedures. One statistical method that has received attention in the financial community is called GARCH. GARCH stands for *generalized autoregressive conditional heteroscedasticity*. Basically the GARCH methodology uses past data to find patterns in changing volatility over time. These patterns are expressed in equation form so that an

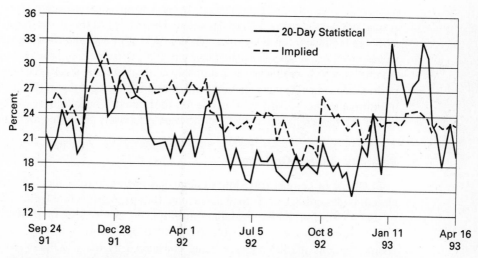

Figure 13-3 Eastman Kodak implied versus historical volatility. (*Source:* OptionVue IV.)

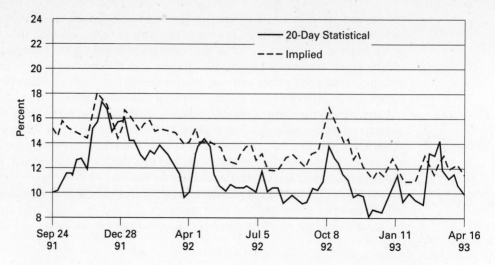

Figure 13-4 S&P 500 Index implied versus historical volatilities. (*Source:* OptionVue IV.)

estimate of future volatility can be made based on the changing structure of the most recent volatility and past patterns. Of course, this procedure is based on the assumption that future volatility can be forecasted from past changes in volatility. Recent work on different financial time series shows that volatility has a significant predictable component. In fact, O'Conner Associates, a large options trading firm, successfully uses GARCH models to trade options.

Volatility and Stock Indexes

Using the standard deviation with historical data creates a downward bias for the measure of volatility for stock indexes. In other words, the measured standard deviation is smaller than the true standard deviation. The reason for this is the illiquidity of some stocks in the index. Since all stocks do not trade at or near the close, using daily index values creates a smaller volatility measure than if true closing prices were available. Another way to state this price relationship is to realize that stock index changes have a positive and significant correlation from one day to the next that reflects the movement of information and volatility from one day to the next. This bias needs to be eliminated before the Black-Scholes model can be used effectively to value stock index options.

Volatility Quoted Options

GLOBEX (a computer trading system that operates when the U.S. exchanges are closed) trades options on T-bond and T-note futures in terms of *volatility*. Thus, instead of the price being quoted in dollars, it is quoted in terms of the (implied) volatility of the underlying asset. Such volatility quoted options are common on the over-the-counter options market and are being considered by the CBOE for potential future

FOCUS 13-2
OptionVue and Volatilities

One of the interesting features of the OptionVue historical database is that it provides information on the short-term and long-term statistical volatilities (S.V.), as well as the corresponding implied volatilities (I.V.). As an example, the following shows the S.V. and I.V. values for the most recent time and the long term for stock index options, ranked by option volume. One also can rank the results by other variables, such as volatilities or the ratio of I.V. to S.V. The ranking feature is even more useful for stock options, given the large number of stocks that trade options. Of course, one benefit of the ranking feature is the ability to determine which options have the highest/lowest volatility (if the trader has a belief about the direction of the market) or which options possess the largest difference between implied and historical volatility. The term R.D.V.O. in the table stands for the "relative dollar volume of options trading."

OPTIONVUE IV DATA BASE SURVEY
Report based on data as of: Apr 16 1993 listing the best 10 indexes in terms of options trading volume.

	Symbol	Type	R. D.V.O.	Current		Historical	
				S.V.	I.V.	S.V.	I.V.
1.	OEX	Index	35970	9.8%	11.2%	11.4%	13.5%
2.	NSX	Index	5965	8.9%	10.6%	10.0%	11.2%
3.	SPX	Index	5965	8.8%	10.8%	10.6%	13.1%
4.	SP	Index	4344	8.9%	10.7%	11.7%	13.3%
5.	XMI	Index	400	10.8%	11.0%	12.1%	13.3%
6.	MID	Index	326	9.4%	12.3%	10.2%	14.8%
7.	JPN	Index	205	15.5%	24.2%	12.9%	28.4%
8.	VLE	Index	166	6.0%	10.9%	7.1%	10.8%
9.	XOC	Index	103	16.5%	18.3%	18.1%	19.6%
10.	XII	Index	92	11.0%	10.3%	11.9%	13.2%

The symbols stand for the following indexes: OEX = S&P 100; NSX = New York Stock Exchange; SPX = S&P 500 (cash); SP = S&P 500 (futures); XMI = Major Market; MID = S&P Midcap; JPN = Japan; VLE = Value Line; XOC = National OTC; XII = Institutional.

listing. Volatility-quoted options are purchased when an increase in volatility is anticipated, while options are sold when a decrease in volatility is expected. An exchange option model converts the volatility quote to a price paid by the option buyer. The interest rate for the model is determined by the nearby Eurodollar futures rate. In addition, the trade is set up on GLOBEX to create a delta-neutral position by trading both the option and the underlying futures contract at the same time. Volatility-quoted options could become a major trading vehicle within the next few years.

PUT OPTION PRICING

Black-Scholes and Put-Call Parity Put Pricing

Black and Scholes (1973) also present a model to value puts:

$$P_P = -P_S N(-d_1) + Ke^{-rt}N(-d_2) \qquad (13\text{-}18)$$

where d_1 and d_2 are defined in Equations (13-2) and (13-3) in conjunction with the call option formula, and the symbols here are equivalent to those of the call formula of Equation (13-1). Note the similarity between this put formula and the formula to value call options. In addition, put prices can be adjusted for dividends in the same manner as call options. Example (13-6) shows how to calculate the Black-Scholes put value.

An alternative method often used to calculate the value of a put option is known as **put-call parity,** as explained in Chapter 12. Put-call parity creates the equivalent of a put option with a call option, stock, and invested funds. Such a transaction is called a **synthetic put.** The resultant put price based on put-call parity is given in Equation (13-19), which is simply a rearrangement of Equation (12-5):

$$P_P = P_C - P_S + Ke^{-rt} \qquad (13\text{-}19)$$

EXAMPLE 13-6
Black-Scholes Put Value

Equation (13-18) defines the Black-Scholes put option value as:

$$P_P = -P_S N(-d_1) + Ke^{-rt}N(-d_2) \qquad (13\text{-}18)$$

where d_1 and d_2 are defined in conjunction with call options (see Equations (13-2) and (13-3)).

Using the same input information as in Example 13-1, we have:

$$d_1 = .0942$$

$$d_2 = -.1558$$

Then (from Appendix A and interpolating):

$$N(-d_1) = N(-.0942) = 1 - N(.0942) = 1 - .5375 = .4625$$

$$N(-d_2) = N(+.1558) = .5619$$

Since $e^{-.05(.25)} = .9876$

$$P_P = -98(.4625) + 100(.9876)(.5619)$$

$$= -45.325 + 55.493$$

$$= \$10.17$$

The value of the put is larger than the call value in Example 13-1 because the put is in-the-money while the call is out-of-the-money.

The put priced in (13-19) must have the same strike price and expiration as the call option. If we substitute the Black-Scholes value for a call option from Equation (13-1) into Equation (13-19), we obtain the Black-Scholes put equation given in (13-18).[17] Example 13-7 shows how to determine a put value based on the put-call parity equation.

Dividends are added to the put valuation equation without creating any significant problems. A put for a stock that pays dividends is valued as follows:

$$P_P = P_C - P_S + Ke^{-rt} + De^{-r\tau} \tag{13-20}$$

where $\tau =$ the time period until the ex-dividend date for the stock

Early Put Exercise and the Resultant Put Models

The Black-Scholes formulation for the value of a put is based on a European-style option in that the exercise can only occur at the expiration of the option. However, the American-style put stock options that trade in the United States are often exercised early (unless large dividends are yet to be paid), while American *call* options are exercised early only if a dividend occurs near the expiration date. An early exercise for a put option on a non–dividend-paying stock occurs when a large stock price decrease makes it more profitable to exercise the put than to wait until its expiration date. This situation occurs if the price of the American put loses all of its time value.

An extreme example shows why puts are exercised early. Suppose a trader purchases a put with a strike price of $100 when the associated stock is selling for $100. Subsequently, the stock declines to $5, causing the put to have an intrinsic value of $95. If the put option still has one year before expiration, and the current interest rate is 10%, then it is more profitable to exercise the put and invest the profits from the put at 10% than to keep the put for a maximum additional gain of $5. Similarly, when a put loses

EXAMPLE 13-7
Put Prices in Terms of Put-Call Parity

The value of a put based on the put-call parity relationship is:

$$P_P = P_C - P_S + Ke^{-rt} \tag{13-19}$$

Based on the information in Example 13-1, we have:

$$P_P = 9.41 - 98 + 100e^{-.05(.25)}$$

$$= 9.41 - 98 + 100(.9876)$$

$$= \$10.17$$

This is equivalent to the put value found with the Black-Scholes formula in Example 13-6.

[17]Jarrow and Rudd (1983) prove a number of relationships associated with different forms of the put-call parity theorem.

all of its time value, exercising the put and investing the funds in a risk-free instrument provides a higher risk-adjusted return than the expected value of holding the put option.

The effect of stock dividends on puts is to decrease the probability of early exercise. Thus, the early exercise feature of American puts is worth less when the stock pays dividends, especially when ex-dividend dates exist near the expiration of the option. The put should be exercised only after the dividend is paid and the stock price is adjusted downward. Other things being equal, early exercise for an American put is more appropriate the lower the stock price, the higher the strike price, the shorter the time to expiration, and the lower the cash dividends yet to be paid.

Unfortunately, including the likelihood of early exercise in the put valuation equation creates complex problems. In fact, the resulting pricing models are not closed-form equations; they generally cannot be solved by a calculator. Several American put models have been developed; some are approximation methods, while others are exact pricing models. The approximation methods are simpler and typically only vary from the true value by several cents. The most popular methods for pricing puts with early exercise are by Parkinson (1977); Brennan and Schwartz (1977); Cox, Ross, and Rubinstein (1979); and Geske and Johnson (1984). The exact models involve complex computer calculations. Binomial models can also be used to solve for the American put value.

TRADING ON THE OPTION FLOOR

The Trading Floor

Traders on the floor of the options exchanges must know the last price of the stock underlying the option being traded, as well as the bid, ask, and most recent trades for the various strike prices and expirations of the associated options. All of this information appears on the large screens in front of the trading area, as illustrated in Exhibit 13-2. The floor trader buys options at the lower bid price and sells at the ask price. Floor traders use hand signals and shout their bid and ask quotes to show their willingness to trade a specific option (hand signals are not officially recognized by the exchange for trading purposes). Only large stocks, such as IBM and General Motors, have options that trade frequently; most of the trading areas have options on ten to fifteen stocks.

Exhibit 13-3 illustrates how trading on the option floor is conducted. Two aspects of the trading procedure are particularly important. First, note that options start trading *after* the initial stock trade on that option. Subsequently, each option on that stock is opened sequentially to find the equilibrium price for trading that option. This procedure is called the option rotation. Second, orders to buy/sell options are offered to the option floor for bids/asks. On the day of the market crash in 1987, it took two hours to go through the entire option rotation. Due to this extensive delay the exchange then went through *another* rotation. No wonder traders lost substantial amounts of money given such a delay!

EXHIBIT 13-2
Computer Screen on the Options Floor

POLAR		CLOSE	LAST	B-BID A-ASK		SIZE	MKT-QUOTE	
A	JAN 30	$8\frac{1}{2}$	$7\frac{5}{8}$	$7\frac{3}{8}$ –	$7\frac{3}{4}$	2×5	$7\frac{1}{2}$	– $7\frac{3}{4}$
B	JAN 35	$3\frac{3}{4}$	$2\frac{13}{16}$	$2\frac{3}{4}$ –	3	1×2	$2\frac{13}{16}$	– $2\frac{15}{16}$
C	JAN 40	$\frac{11}{16}$	$\frac{7}{16}$	$\frac{3}{8}$ –	$\frac{1}{2}$	3×2	$\frac{3}{8}$	– $\frac{1}{2}$
D	JAN 45	$\frac{1}{16}$		–	$\frac{3}{16}$	$\times 2$		– $\frac{1}{16}$
E	APR 35	$5\frac{1}{2}$	$4\frac{3}{4}$	$4\frac{1}{2}$ –	5	3×6	$4\frac{5}{8}$	– $4\frac{3}{4}$
F	APR 40	$2\frac{11}{16}$	$2\frac{1}{4}$	$2\frac{1}{8}$ –	$2\frac{7}{16}$	2×1	$2\frac{5}{16}$	– $2\frac{5}{16}$
G	APR 45	$1\frac{1}{8}$	$\frac{3}{4}$	$\frac{1}{2}$ –	$1\frac{11}{16}$	3×2	$\frac{3}{4}$	– $\frac{7}{8}$
H	JUL 35	$6\frac{1}{2}$	$5\frac{7}{8}$	$5\frac{1}{4}$ –	6	1×1	$5\frac{5}{8}$	– $5\frac{7}{8}$
I	JUL 40	4	$3\frac{1}{4}$	3 –	$3\frac{5}{8}$	2×2	$3\frac{1}{4}$	– $3\frac{3}{8}$
J								
K								
L								
M								
N								
O								
P								
PRD	$37\frac{1}{2}$-1	B $37\frac{3}{8}$	A $37\frac{5}{8}$	O $38\frac{3}{8}$	H $38\frac{1}{2}$	L $37\frac{1}{2}$	V 96,000 AT 1:12	
				PRD $37\frac{5}{8}$	PRD 2s $37\frac{1}{2}$		PRD 800s $37\frac{1}{2}$	

Note: Bid and ask prices are the best prices in the limit order book. "Size" (2×5) is the number to buy
    (2) and the number to sell (5) in the limit order book.
Source: Rubinstein (1991).

Trades are made by the floor broker or market maker. A floor broker executes trades that come from the public "at the best possible price," earning a fee for each trade. Market makers trade for their own accounts, profiting from their trading skills. Market maker strategies are discussed shortly.[18] A third type of floor trader at the CBOE is the Order Book Official (OBO), who puts unfilled limit orders into the computer and later executes the orders if the prices specified are reached. Limit orders have priority over all other orders at the specific price of the limit order. Orders for 10 contracts or less on the S&P 100 option (OEX) are executed via the automatic execution system called "RAYS." The cost of a seat on an exchange that allows one to trade on the floor is typically over $200,000. Two-thirds of the floor traders make over $75,000 per year.

[18] The CBOE and Pacific Exchanges use competing market makers. The American and Philadelphia Exchanges use one specialist per option, with the specialist being responsible for "making a market to the public." The American and Philadelphia Exchanges also have Registered Option Traders who buy and sell options for their own account. The CBOE does use a "designated market maker" for new stocks. The designated market makers act like specialists in that they are allowed to see the *entire* limit order book rather than only the best bid and ask limit orders. This special designation is intended to provide liquidity for new issues.

EXHIBIT 13-3
Trading Options on the Floor

7:00 A.M.*	Exchange floor quiet.
7:00	Members and trade checkers arrive to rectify clerical errors and outtrades from the previous day.**
8:25	Floor is crowded with hundreds of market makers, floor brokers, order book officials, and employees of the exchange and member firms.
8:30	New York and American Stock Exchanges open. Options trading at each post await the first print of the underlying stock.
8:35	Stock prints. Officer opens each associated option series, one at a time, calls before puts, by calling for bid and ask quotes from the trading crowd.
. . .	
2:09 P.M.	A *limit* order to sell 5 PRD/JUL/40 calls at 3⅜, initiated off the floor, reaches one of the communication booths lining the perimeter of the floor. Order is imprinted by a teletype machine on an order card.
2:10	Runner delivers order to a floor broker standing at the Polaroid post. The book bid-ask is 3–3⅝. The floor broker calls for a market and is quoted 3¼–3⅜ by the trading crowd. To afford his customer priority, he "books" the order.
2:12	A *market* order to sell 5 PRD/JUL/40 calls is delivered to the floor broker and he calls for a market. He is again quoted 3¼–3⅜ by the trading crowd—"¼–½" by one market maker and "⅛–⅜" by another. He offers to sell at ⅜ but the crowd shows no interest. He then turns to the market maker quoting "¼–½" and says, "Sold at ¼; I have five." The market maker says "Done."
2:13	The floor broker fills out a sell ticket and the market maker fills out a buy ticket. The floor broker time stamps the sell ticket and places it on a conveyer belt in front of the post.
2:14	The sell ticket is automatically conveyed to a small bin at one end of the post. The PRTO key punches the trade information into the exchange computer system. The price and volume of the trade appear in brokerage houses across the country.
. . .	
3:00	New York and American Stock Exchanges close.
3:10	Chicago Board Options Exchange closes.

* All times are Central Time.
** Outtrades occur when only one side of a trade is reported.
Source: Rubinstein (1991).

Floor Trading

The methods employed by option floor traders to profit from trading in options and their associated stocks are listed here. Subsequent sections discuss these methods in more detail. The trading methods are as follows:

- Heavily traded options are bought at the bid and sold at the ask, generating a bid-ask profit for the market maker.

- Black-Scholes hedge ratios between the stock and option are created when options are mispriced.
- **Ratio spreads** between two options for the same stock are also initiated when option mispricing exists. Ratio spreads use Black-Scholes hedge ratios to determine the number of options to trade and which option should be purchased/sold.
- Traders execute **box spreads,** consisting of two call options with different strike prices and two put options with strike prices equivalent to the calls.[19] Box spreads are executed when the options become mispriced on a *relative* basis.
- Put-call parity identifies mispriced relationships between the call, put, and stock. If the call is overpriced relative to the put, then the put is purchased and a **synthetic put,** made up of a short call and long stock, is sold (this strategy is called a **conversion**).[20] If the call is underpriced relative to the put, then the call is purchased and a **synthetic call,** made up of a short put and short stock, is sold (called a **reverse conversion**).

Except for the market maker's bid-ask spread, the other strategies given above are arbitrage transactions. However, strategies based on the Black-Scholes model require dynamic changes in the hedge ratio as the input variables change. Consequently, the possible existence of jumps in the asset price creates a risk for the floor trader using Black-Scholes strategies. The other strategies do not require dynamic adjustments and therefore are truly risk-free strategies.

The Market Maker as Scalper

When a market maker buys at the bid and sells at the ask price, he/she is called a **scalper.** Market makers can trade the same option on a bid-ask basis when sufficient liquidity exists, which typically occurs for nearby, near-the-money options. Exchange-imposed limits exist for the bid-ask spread, as shown below:

Bid Price	Maximum Bid-Ask Spread
<2	¼
≥ 2 and ≤5	⅜
> 5 and ≤10	½
>10 and ≤20	¾
>20	1

Using Black-Scholes and Ratio Spread Strategies

Both the Black-Scholes and ratio hedge strategies require an accurate estimate of the option's fair price. Hence, traders using these methods carry hand-held programmable calculators to determine the option's fair value. The option valuation equation is programmed into the calculator; then the trader inputs the current stock price, the option's

---

[19] This combination is called a box spread because the options traded form the four corners of a box when the call and put option prices from Exhibits 11-3 and 11-5 are placed next to each other.

[20] Exchanges could not list puts during the mid 1970s. Market makers and others sold "a put" to those institutions wanting to hedge with a long put. The "short put" on the market makers books was offset by a synthetic long put, created by buying a call and selling short stock.

time to expiration, and the strike price are input (interest rates and stock volatility are input in the morning since these factors do not change frequently). Traders previously employed some version of the Black-Scholes model in their calculators. More recently, the binomial model has become the popular option valuation model.

Ratio spreads are employed by floor traders in order to profit from options mispriced on a relative basis. The number of option contracts traded is based on their relative hedge ratios from the Black-Scholes model. Thus, if option A is underpriced and has a Black-Scholes hedge ratio of .25, and option B for the same stock is overpriced and has a hedge ratio of .5, then the trader would initiate a ratio spread where A is purchased and B is sold in the combination of .5/.25 = 2.0 to 1.0 of the A to B options. The relationship between the number of option contracts is as follows:

$$\frac{\text{Purchase A shares}}{\text{Sell B shares}} = \frac{\text{HR}_B}{\text{HR}_A} \tag{13-21}$$

The ratio spreader profits when the option mispricing corrects itself, while avoiding the risk from option price changes caused by stock price changes (since these option price changes offset each other). For our example, the hedge ratio of .25 for A means that stock A will change by $.25 for a $1 change in the asset. Consequently, purchasing 50 shares in A and selling 25 shares of B (as determined by Equation (13-21)) results in the following situation when the stock changes by $1:

$$\text{Buy A}(\Delta P_A) = \text{Sell B}(\Delta P_B)$$

$$50(\$.25) = 25(\$.50) \tag{13-22}$$

$$\$12.50 = \$12.50$$

Thus, the risk caused by small stock price changes is eliminated, while the eventual realignment of the mispriced option prices will generate a profit.

Floor traders prefer ratio spreads to regular Black-Scholes stock/option hedges, since the amount of investment is substantially less and the options are traded by the floor trader directly, without going to the stock exchange to buy or sell stocks. However, as with Black-Scholes hedges, using ratio spreads does require dynamic management of the ratio spread position. Since the Black-Scholes hedge changes as the stock price and other input variables change, the ratio between the option hedge ratios often changes as well. Consequently, large stock price jumps could create difficulties for managing the ratio spread. Moreover, off-the-floor traders cannot use ratio spreads effectively in most circumstances because of the costs of managing the position and the need to change the ratio on short notice.

Box Spreads and Conversions

Box spreads and conversions do not require the dynamic management of the hedge ratios needed for Black-Scholes hedges and ratio spreads. Thus, box spreads and conversions are a less risky form of option arbitrage.

The advantage of box spreads over conversions is that only options are involved—the option floor trader does not need to go to the NYSE to trade stocks as part of the arbitrage strategy. In addition, all of the options in a box spread should have the same implied volatility—and hence the same price response to a change in the stock price— since all the options have the same expiration date. In other words, the price risk of the call spread is offset by the opposite position in the put spread, leaving only the profit from mispricings of the options. However, the profit opportunities for a box spread are available only to floor traders who instantly recognize the relative mispricing among the options. Delays in executing a box spread result in other floor traders implementing the same strategy, which causes prices to realign to their relative fair values.[21]

Conversions and reverse conversions involve calls, puts, and the underlying stock. Exhibit 12-2 showed that buying a call plus investing the present value of the strike price was equivalent to buying a put and buying stock. Using the same logic, we find that:

- If a trader can *buy* an underpriced put and *sell* an overpriced or fairly priced synthetic put (a short call and long stock position), then a profit is achieved from this conversion because *net cash flows* are positive:

$$-P_P + P_C + (K - P_S) - (P_S + P_P - P_C)(e^{-rt} - 1) > 0 \qquad (13\text{-}22)$$

The positive signs before a position show a positive cash flow, while negative signs show a negative cash flow. For a conversion, funds must be borrowed to finance the purchase of the stock so that the trader does not need to use his or her own funds for the conversion. The last term in Equation (13-22) calculates the interest paid on the net borrowings. Notice that $K - P_S$ is relevant whether stock prices decline and the long put is executed at K, or stock prices increase and the stock is called away via the short call at K.

- If a trader can buy an underpriced call and *sell* an overpriced or fairly priced synthetic call (a short put and short stock), then a profit is achieved from a reverse conversion because of the positive *cash flows*:

$$-P_C + P_P + (P_S - K) + (P_S + P_P - P_C)(e^{-rt} - 1) > 0 \qquad (13\text{-}23)$$

For a reverse conversion, the funds *received* from selling short the stock are placed in a risk-free investment that earns interest. The last term in Equation (13-23) calculates this interest received. The value of $P_S - K$ occurs whether the call is executed to buy stock at K, or the stock is put to the trader at K via the execution of the short put. Again, the trader's funds are not needed for this reverse conversion. One difficulty in executing reverse conversions is that the trader typically does not receive all of the funds from a short sale.

Conversions and reverse conversions are pure, risk-free transactions since the price change on the option purchased is offset from the sale of the synthetic option (the payoff diagrams are equivalent). Consequently, only the option mispricing should affect the transaction's profits.

The most profitable transactions for market makers are trading deep-in-the-money calls and puts, since these trades create large bid-ask spreads. For example, if an individual wants to sell a deep-in-the-money call with a bid-ask spread of 8½ to 9 (due to the lack of liquidity on these options), then the market maker creates a reverse conversion with a short synthetic call to offset the call purchased by the market maker. While a trade of 8⅞ could be a fair price, the market maker buys the call for 8½ and locks in a ⅜ profit by creating a short synthetic call at the 8⅞ fair price. Of course, this assumes

---

[21] Box spreads are very sensitive to any transactions costs. In addition, box spread profits often rely on buying at the bid and selling at the ask price.

the put is fairly priced. Moreover, risks do exist for this trade. First, the stock price could change in the following one or two minutes, before the stock trade is executed. Second, the short uptick rule on stocks could keep the market maker from shorting the stock at the needed price. Example 13-8 shows that the above reverse conversion generates a profit. However, if the market maker receives only 85% of the proceeds from the short stock sale, these profits disappear at current interest rate levels. In this case, the broker keeps the remaining 15% of the short sale funds, often called a "haircut."

A total of four synthetic positions are possible with calls and puts:

Conversion positions:

- short synthetic put (equals a short call and long stock), which offsets a long put
- long synthetic call (equals a long put and long stock), which offsets a short call

Reverse conversion positions:

- short synthetic call (equals a short put and short stock), which offsets a long call
- long synthetic put (equals a long call and short stock), which offsets a short put.

While the two new synthetic positions listed here are simply rearrangements of the previously discussed synthetic positions, they provide important opportunities for market makers. Since most individuals want to buy call and put options, market makers

EXAMPLE 13-8
Reverse Conversion

The premise of a reverse conversion is that the market maker can buy an underpriced call and sell a synthetic call (a short put and short stock). The cash flows on a reverse conversion are:

$$-P_C + P_P + (P_S - K) + (P_S + P_P - P_C)(e^{rt} - 1) > 0 \qquad (13\text{-}24)$$

The following prices exist in the market:

$$P_C = 8\frac{1}{2} \qquad P_C(\text{fair}) = 8\frac{7}{8} \qquad P_S = 100 \qquad t = .5 \text{ year} \qquad r = .05$$

Therefore, based on Equation (13-24):

$$-8.50 + 6.375 + (100 - 100) + (100 + 6.375 - 8.50)(e^{(.05)(.5)} - 1)$$

$$= -2.125 + 97.875(1.025315 - 1)$$

$$= -2.125 + 2.478$$

$$= \$.35$$

Thus, the trader makes $.35 per share on the reverse conversion (with no funds invested). If the current price of the call is 8¾, the profit declines to $.096. If the market maker has access to only 85% of the short sale funds (with a call price of 8½), then a *loss* of $.03 would occur. Thus, the amount of funds available, the level of interest rates, and the difference between the market and fair option prices are all important factors for a profitable reverse conversion.

typically take a short position in these options—at least until someone else wants a short call or short put. Consequently, the market maker can generate a long synthetic call or long synthetic put to offset selling calls or puts to individuals. Market makers profit from these transactions when they earn the bid-ask spread or when demand causes call and/or put prices to rise above their fair values.

MARKET MICROSTRUCTURE IN THE OPTIONS MARKET

Intraday Options Pricing Behavior

Market microstructure is the study of price behavior within the day. Interest in intraday pricing has increased substantially since transactions price data on stock, futures, and options markets have become available in the past few years. Such intraday data is particularly important for studying options markets, since the pricing of options relies critically on the price of the underlying asset. Using end-of-day options and stock prices creates problems due to timing differences between when the options and stocks last traded. In Chapter 14 we will examine studies of the Black-Scholes and alternative option pricing models, many of which use intraday data. Here we look at the price behavior of option prices within the day.

Stephan and Whaley (1990) show that stock prices and volume *lead* individual option price movements and volume by 15 to 20 minutes, which contradicts previous studies showing that the options markets lead the stock market. Stephan and Whaley also show that option trading activity is at a maximum 45 minutes into the day, while the maximum stock activity occurs at the open and the close.

Abnormal Pricing Behavior and Bid-Ask Spreads

Kumar, Sarin, and Shastri (1992) show that options exhibit abnormal price behavior starting 30 minutes before a block trade is executed and ending 1 hour after the block trade. In comparison, the stock itself has abnormal pricing behavior for 15 minutes *after* the trade and *no* abnormal behavior before the blocks when the stock increases in price; stocks that decrease after the block trade have abnormal behavior both 15 minutes before and 15 minutes after the block trade. The authors attribute the more extensive option abnormal price behavior to traders using the options market before the stock market in what is known as "frontrunning."

Jameson and Wilhelm (1992) determine that option market makers have unique risks in managing their option inventory. In particular, the risks involved in the discrete rebalancing of their option position and the uncertainty of the stock's future volatility account for an important part of the option's bid-ask spreads. However, Dawson and Gemmill (1990) claim that these risks do not adversely affect the market maker's profit. In particular, they find that market makers on the London index option market could average over $700,000 per year, based on the authors' trading strategy and actual transactions prices.

The existence of options also affects the bid-ask spreads on the underlying stock. Fedenia and Grammatikos (1992) show that after the initial listing of options contracts on a stock, the spread decreases for less liquid stocks but *increases* for highly liquid stocks.

SUMMARY AND LOOKING AHEAD

This chapter examines option pricing using the Black-Scholes option pricing model. Both the Black-Scholes option model itself and calculating the inputs to the model are important concepts for understanding what influences option prices. The inputs to and output from the model are also discussed, including the importance of implied volatility. Put pricing follows directly from call option pricing. Finally, how option trading is executed on the floor of the exchange is discussed. The following chapter examines option pricing in greater detail, including the option sensitivities and empirical evidence concerning option models.

BIBLIOGRAPHY

Beckers, S. (1981). "Standard Deviations Implied in Option Prices as Predictors of Future Stock Price Variability," *Journal of Banking and Finance,* Vol. 5, No. 3, September, pp. 363–382.

Black, Fisher, and Myron Scholes (1972). "The Valuation of Option Contracts and a Test of Market Efficiency," *Journal of Finance,* Vol. 27, No. 2, May, pp. 399–418.

Black, Fisher, and Myron Scholes (1973). "The Pricing of Options and Corporate Liabilities," *Journal of Political Economy,* Vol. 81, No. 3, May/June, pp. 637–654.

Brennan, Michael J., and Eduardo S. Schwartz (1977). "The Valuation of American Put Options," *Journal of Finance,* Vol. 32, No. 2, May, pp. 449–462.

Brenner, Menachem, and Marti G. Subrahmanyam (1988). "A Simple Formula to Compute the Implied Volatility," *Financial Analysts Journal,* Vol. 45, No. 5, September–October, pp. 80–83.

Cox, John C., Stephen A. Ross, and Mark Rubinstein (1979). "Options Pricing: A Simplified Approach," *Journal of Financial Economics,* Vol. 7, No. 3, September, pp. 229–264.

Dawson, Paul, and Gordon Gemmill (1990). "Returns to Market Making on the London Traded Options Market," *Review of Futures Markets,* Vol. 9, No. 3, pp. 666–680.

Fedenia, Mark, and Theoharry Grammatikos (1992). "Options Trading and the Bid-Ask Spread of the Underlying Stocks," *Journal of Business,* Vol. 65, No. 3, July, pp. 335–351.

Garman, Mark B., and Michael J. Klass (1980). "On the Estimation of Security Price Volatilities from Historical Data," *Journal of Business,* Vol. 53, No. 1, January, pp. 67–78.

Geske, Robert, and H. E. Johnson (1984). "The American Put Option Valued Analytically," *Journal of Finance,* Vol. 39, No. 5, December, pp. 1511–1524.

Harvey, Campbell R., and Robert E. Whaley (1992). "Market Volatility Prediction and the Efficiency of the S&P 100 Index Option Market," *Journal of Financial Economics,* Vol. 31, No. 1, February, pp. 43–74.

Kumar, Ramon, Atulya Sarin, and Kuldeep Shastri (1992). "The Behavior of Option Price Around Large Block Transactions in the Underlying Security," *Journal of Finance,* Vol. 47, No. 3, July, pp. 879–889.

Jameson, Mel, and William Wilhelm (1992). "Market Making in the Options Markets and the Costs of Discrete Hedge Rebalancing," *Journal of Finance,* Vol. 47, No. 2, June, pp. 765–779.

Jarrow, Robert A., and Andrew Rudd (1983). *Option Pricing.* Homewood, IL: Irwin.

Latané, Henry, and Richard Rendleman (1976). "Standard Deviations of Stock Price Ratios Implied in Option Prices," *Journal of Finance,* Vol. 31, No. 2, May, pp. 369–381.

Parkinson, Michael (1977). "Option Pricing: The American Put," *Journal of Business,* Vol. 50, No. 1, January, pp. 21–36.

Rubenstein, Mark (1991). "Classnotes," The University of California at Berkeley.

Stephan, Jens A., and Robert E. Whaley (1990). "Intraday Price Change and Trading Volume Relations in the Stock and Options Markets," *Journal of Finance,* Vol. 45, No. 1, March, pp. 191–220.

PROBLEMS

*Indicates more difficult problems.

*13-1 Pricing a Call Option

Based on the following information, determine the fair value for a call option by using the Black-Scholes option model.

P_S = 42 (current stock price)

K = 36 (strike price)

r = 0.10 (continuously compounded annual risk-free rate)

t = 0.25 (one-quarter of a year)

σ_S^2 = 0.30 (continuously compounded variance of the stock returns)

*13-2 Pricing a Call Option

The current stock price of DP is 112.75. The near-the-money strike price for this stock is 110 and the nearby option has 60 days left until expiration. DP stock is risky, having a variance of 0.30. The continuously compounded annual risk-free interest rate is 6.49%. Based on these inputs, calculate the fair value for the call option using the Black-Scholes option model.

13-3 Calculating Black-Scholes Inputs

In order to use the Black-Scholes pricing model to value a call option, one must first calculate the inputs to the model. Given the discount T-bill interest rate of 7.0% and a maturity of the T-bill in 60 days, find:
a. the time to maturity (M);
b. the continuously compounded risk-free interest rate (r).

13-4 Dividend Effect on Stock Price

Chem Corp. has a stock price of 89.00 and it pays annual dividends of $3.60 per share. Today is July 17 and the next dividend date is August 4. The continuously compounded interest rate is .0714 and the nearby option has 60 days until expiration. Determine the stock price adjusted for dividends that is used in the Black-Scholes model. (*Hint:* Recall that cash dividends tend to reduce the stock price.)

13-5 Stock Index Adjustment

An equity stock index is at 66.0 and the stocks in the index pay a dividend yield of 4.5% per year. The time to expiration of the option is 90 days. Determine the appropriate adjustment to the stock index price for the Black-Scholes model.

*13-6   Black-Scholes Put Price

Based on the following variables, calculate the value of the put option by using the Black-Scholes model.

$P_S = 17\frac{7}{8}$ (current stock price of Wicker)

$K = 17$ (exercise price)

$r = 0.07$

$t = 0.5$ (one-half of a year)

$\sigma_S^2 = 0.25$

13-7   Put Pricing Using Put-Call Parity

On May 10 the stock price and relevant strike price of AE Corp. is $34\frac{3}{8}$ and 30, respectively. The associated call option is 6, and the stock pays a dividend of $0.84 annually, with the next dividend date being June 2. Given the time to expiration of 100 days for the option and a risk-free interest rate of 8.3% (compounded continuously), calculate the value of a put option using the put-call parity relationship.

APPENDIX 13A
ASSUMPTIONS OF THE BLACK-SCHOLES OPTION MODEL

The Black-Scholes option model is based on several assumptions concerning the input data. All financial models are based on assumptions, with the validity of the assumptions being a major factor in determining whether a particular model is useful in explaining the financial variable of interest. The assumptions associated with the Black-Scholes model are given below, along with a discussion concerning their importance for the accurate pricing of options. These assumptions are as follows:

- The variance of the stock returns is constant over the life of the option.
- The interest rate is constant over the life of the option.
- A continuous stock price occurs—that is, no "jumps" in price exist.
- Stock returns are described by a lognormal distribution.
- No transactions costs exist.
- No dividends are paid on the stock, and the option can be exercised only at expiration.

Constant Variance and Interest Rates

Perhaps the most important assumption of the Black-Scholes model is that the stock variance is constant. A major problem with nonconstant variance is that the hedge ratio breaks down—that is, the hedge ratio does *not* provide a risk-free hedge. However, this problem is not severe for short time periods when the hedge is constantly revised. Also, if the variance changes in a predictable pattern, then the *average variance* over the remaining life of the option can be used in the Black-Scholes model as an estimate for the variance, since the spirit of the model remains the same. An exact option model cannot be obtained for a nonconstant variance which does *not* have a predictable pattern over time, although the value for such an option can be estimated with computerized numerical techniques. In practice, this assumption of constant variance may seem unimportant, since no one knows ahead of time the true future variance of the stock over the life of the option. However, a nonconstant variance reduces the accuracy of the pricing model even *if* the true *average* future variance is known. Cox (1975) developed a "constant elasticity of variance diffusion" option model in which the variance of the stock increases as the stock price falls. Jarrow and Rudd (1983) derive this model. MacBeth and Merville (1980) and Rubinstein (1985) test the model against the Black-Scholes model. MacBeth and Merville find the Cox model to provide somewhat better estimates of actual option prices than the Black-Scholes model, but Rubinstein does not find this dominance.

The effect of an unknown and nonconstant interest rate over the life of the option is similar to a nonconstant variance, except that changing interest rates have less of an effect on the hedge ratio and the option price. To incorporate predictable nonconstant interest rates into the model, one replaces the interest rate in the formula with the product of the interest rates over each remaining subperiod before option expiration. In general, the effect of different levels of interest rates is shown in Chapter 14. Those results illustrate the relatively minor effect of interest rates on option prices. One important effect of using nonconstant, but predictable, variances and interest rates is that options with different maturities can/should use different volatilities and interest rates for their inputs into the model.

Continuous Stock Price and Lognormal Distribution

A continuous stock price is needed so that hedgers can adjust their hedge ratios whenever stock prices change in order to keep a risk-free hedge. Large jumps in stock prices make this needed revision in the hedge ratio impossible to achieve. While Merton (1976) and Cox and Ross (1976) develop a model to consider such jumps, the lack of data makes such a model difficult to test. Jarrow and Rudd (1983) develop Merton's model mathematically. Some researchers believe that the existence of jumps in stock prices is one reason for some mispricings by the Black-Scholes model, since jumps are equivalent to saying that the true distribution of returns has fatter tails than assumed by the lognormal distribution.[1]

Using the variance of the continuously discounted stock returns means that the distribution of these returns must follow a lognormal distribution. However, a significant amount of empirical evidence on stock returns suggests that there are more large price changes than warranted by a lognormal distribution. In essence, this means that the true variability of the stock is not measured accurately by the variance of the returns, creating a bias in the model. This bias is more severe as the stock price moves away from the strike price.[2]

[1] Both the Black-Scholes model and the Cox-Ross jump model can be derived from the binomial model. Differing definitions of the binomial terms generate the two option models.

[2] Ritchken (1987, ch. 6) discusses the distribution of returns in more detail. Cox and Rubinstein (1985) have an excellent bibliography on research articles concerned with stock return distributions.

Transactions Costs, Dividends, and Exercise

The assumption of no transactions costs is needed to insure that a hedge ratio can be revised often in order to keep the position risk-free. The existence of transactions costs for off-the-floor traders means that such traders are precluded from initiating an arbitrage transaction. While floor traders do have small transactions costs, these costs do not severely hamper the traders' ability to perform arbitrage, although the existence of these costs probably does reduce the accuracy of the pure Black-Scholes model slightly.

The dividend and exercise assumptions were discussed previously. Dividends are added to the model with a simple adjustment. The effect of early exercise on call options is typically minimal, except when a dividend occurs near expiration. The effect of early exercise on puts is more severe, but American models that consider this early exercise feature generally do not perform any better than the European Black-Scholes model. Tables 13A-1 and 13A-2 compare American and European call and put option values for various strike prices, volatilities, and months-to-expiration.

Table 13A-1 European Versus American Call Option Values

| | | \multicolumn{4}{c}{$P_S = 100 \quad r = .10 \quad d = .15$} | | | |
| | | European | | | | American ($n = 500$) | | | |
σ	K	1	3	6	12	1	3	6	12
	85	14.52	13.82	13.24	12.49	<u>15.00</u>	<u>15.00</u>	<u>15.00</u>	15.19
	90	9.64	9.54	9.61	9.60	<u>10.00</u>	10.16	10.60	11.31
	95	5.24	5.98	6.63	7.20	5.36	6.26	7.16	8.27
.2	100	2.10	3.36	4.33	5.28	2.13	3.48	4.61	5.94
	105	.58	1.68	2.69	3.79	.58	1.73	2.83	4.20
	110	.11	.75	1.59	2.66	.11	.77	1.66	2.91
	115	.01	.30	.89	1.84	.01	.30	.93	1.99
	85	14.62	14.66	15.01	15.37	<u>15.00</u>	15.33	16.09	17.33
	90	10.04	10.91	11.85	12.84	10.22	11.30	12.58	14.27
	95	6.12	7.76	9.17	10.63	6.20	7.99	9.65	11.68
.3	100	3.24	5.28	6.96	8.74	3.27	5.41	7.27	9.51
	105	1.47	3.44	5.19	7.14	1.48	3.51	5.39	7.71
	110	.57	2.14	3.80	5.80	.57	2.18	3.93	6.23
	115	.19	1.28	2.74	4.69	.19	1.30	2.83	5.00
	85	14.92	15.88	17.08	18.41	15.16	16.36	17.96	20.18
	90	10.68	12.49	14.22	16.10	10.81	12.81	14.86	17.50
	95	7.11	9.59	11.73	14.04	7.18	9.80	12.20	15.15
.4	100	4.38	7.21	9.59	12.21	4.41	7.34	9.93	13.09
	105	2.48	5.30	7.78	10.59	2.50	5.39	8.03	11.31
	110	1.38	3.82	6.27	9.18	1.31	3.88	6.45	9.76
	115	.63	2.70	5.02	7.94	.63	2.74	5.15	8.40

Note: *American options with underlined values should be exercised immediately.*
d = dividends as a percentage of asset price
Source: Rubinstein (1991).

Table 13A-2 European Versus American Put Option Values

		$P_s = 100$			$r = .10$	$d = .05$		
		European				American ($n = 500$)		
σ	K	1	3	6	12	1	3	6	12
---	---	---	---	---	---	---	---	---	---
	85	.00	.15	.56	1.31	.00	.15	.57	1.39
	90	.06	.56	1.28	2.27	.06	.57	1.33	2.45
	95	.51	1.54	2.52	3.64	.51	1.58	2.64	3.98
.2	100	2.10	3.37	4.39	5.45	2.13	3.48	4.64	6.03
	105	5.31	6.16	6.92	7.70	5.43	6.42	7.42	8.66
	110	9.68	9.78	10.08	10.39	10.00	10.32	10.94	11.88
	115	14.52	14.00	13.74	13.46	15.00	15.00	15.17	15.69
	85	.08	.82	1.97	3.67	.08	.83	2.03	3.86
	90	.40	1.74	3.23	5.16	.41	1.76	3.33	5.45
	95	1.33	3.21	4.93	6.96	1.34	3.27	5.09	7.40
.3	100	3.24	5.32	7.08	9.07	3.27	5.43	7.34	9.70
	105	6.27	8.07	9.67	11.48	6.35	8.28	10.09	12.37
	110	10.21	11.41	12.68	14.17	10.37	11.75	13.30	15.40
	115	14.73	15.23	16.06	17.13	15.03	15.76	16.95	18.75
	85	.35	1.91	3.84	6.48	.36	1.93	3.93	6.77
	90	1.00	3.21	5.46	8.31	1.01	3.25	5.59	8.70
	95	2.29	4.99	7.44	10.38	2.30	5.06	7.63	10.92
.4	100	4.39	7.27	9.76	12.69	4.41	7.38	10.04	13.39
	105	7.33	10.03	12.42	15.22	7.39	10.21	12.82	16.14
	110	11.00	13.23	15.40	17.97	11.11	13.51	15.94	19.13
	115	15.22	16.82	18.65	20.91	15.41	17.21	19.37	22.35

Note: *American options with underlined values should be exercised immediately.*
d = dividends as a percentage of asset price
Source: Rubinstein (1991).

Index Options and Assumptions of the Model

Combining stocks into a portfolio could create price effects for the resultant cash index that differ from the behavior of individual stocks. In addition, other characteristics of the cash index and index options should be investigated for their effect on pricing. The following lists these factors.

• **Index lognormality**

Stock indexes are closer to lognormality than individual stocks. Therefore, this factor does not adversely affect the model. Moreover, stock indexes have greater stability of volatility and fewer effects due to jumps in prices than individual stocks.

• **Wildcard option on cash-settled options**

Index options are settled in cash. The option buyer can exercise up until 4:10 P.M., with the index value based on a 4:00 P.M. stock market close. This causes index options to be worth more than their Black-Scholes values.

- **Artificial serial correlation of the cash index**

    Serial correlation is prevalent in the cash index due to the nontrading of smaller stocks making up the index. Thus, the actual volatility in the index is higher than the observed volatility.[3]

- **Dividends are paid daily with seasonal spikes**

    Dividends with spikes are not adequately treated in the Black-Scholes model.

In addition, arbitrageurs typically use stock index *futures* rather than cash stocks when executing put-call parity trades, even for the S&P 100 Index options. Therefore, the options may seem to be mispriced if the *cash index* is used in the put-call parity equation, but not when the futures price index is employed. If the futures are mispriced relative to the options, then an arbitrage trade is executed.

BIBLIOGRAPHY FOR APPENDIX 13A

Cox, John (1975). "Notes on Option Pricing I: Constant Elasticity of Variance Diffusions." Working Paper, Stanford University.

Cox, John C., and Stephen A. Ross (1976). "The Valuation of Options for Alternative Stochastic Processes," *Journal of Financial Economics,* Vol. 3, No. 1/2, January–March, pp. 145–166.

Cox, John C., and Mark Rubinstein (1985). *Options Markets.* Englewood Cliffs, NJ: Prentice-Hall.

Jarrow, Robert A., and Andrew Rudd (1983). *Option Pricing.* Homewood, IL: Irwin.

MacBeth, James, D., and Larry J. Merville (1980). "Tests of the Black-Scholes and Cox Call Option Valuation Models," *Journal of Finance,* Vol. 35, No. 2, May, pp. 285–300.

Merton, Robert (1976). "Option Pricing When Underlying Stock Returns Are Discontinuous," *Journal of Financial Economics,* Vol. 3, No. 1/2, January–March, pp. 125–144.

Ritchken, Peter (1987). *Options: Theory, Strategy, and Applications.* Glenview, IL: Scott, Foresman.

Rubinstein, Mark (1985). "Nonparametric Tests of Alternative Option Pricing Models Using All Reported Trades and Quotes on the 30 Most Active CBOE Option Classes from August 23, 1976 Through August 31, 1978," *Journal of Finance,* Vol. 40, No. 2, June, pp. 455–480.

Rubinstein, Mark (1991). "Classnotes," The University of California at Berkeley.

APPENDIX 13B
DERIVATION OF THE BLACK-SCHOLES MODEL

To obtain the Black-Scholes option pricing model, one must first make an assumption concerning the stochastic process dictating the movement of asset prices. The typical process employed is known as an Ito process, which has an instantaneous expected

---

[3] Rubinstein (1991) estimates the daily serial correlation of the S&P 500 Index at .168 and the NYSE Composite Index at .218.

mean rerun of $\mu_S P_S$ and an instantaneous variance rate of $\sigma_S^2 P_S^2$. Thus, in derivative terms, the change in the asset price is:

$$dP_S = \mu_S P_S \, dt + \sigma_S P_S \, dz \tag{13B-1}$$

In discrete terms $dt = \Delta t$, which refers to the change in time and $dz = \epsilon \sqrt{\Delta t}$ (where ϵ is a random drawing from a standard normal distribution).

A call or put option must be a function of P_S and t. Using Ito's lemma on (13B-1) provides:

$$dP_C = \left[\frac{\partial P_C}{\partial P_S} \mu_S P_S + \frac{\partial P_C}{\partial t} + \frac{1}{2} \frac{\partial^2 P_C}{\partial P_S^2} \sigma_S^2 P_S^2 \right] dt + \frac{\partial P_C}{\partial P_S} \sigma_S P_S \, dz \tag{13B-2}$$

Note that a put can be represented in Equation (13B-2) by substituting P_P for P_C. Later we will distinguish a call equation from a put equation.

The objective of the Black-Scholes model is to eliminate risk with an appropriate combination of long $\partial P_C / \partial P_S$ shares of stock and short one option. Defining V as the value of the portfolio:

$$V = -P_C + \frac{\partial P_C}{\partial P_S} P_S \tag{13B-3}$$

The change in the value becomes:

$$dV = -dP_C + \frac{\partial P_C}{\partial P_S} \, dP_S \tag{13B-4}$$

Substituting (13B-1) and (13B-2) into (13B-4) and simplifying, one obtains:

$$dV = \left[-\frac{\partial P_C}{\partial t} - \frac{1}{2} \frac{\partial^2 P_C}{\partial P_S^2} \sigma_S^2 P_S^2 \right] dt \tag{13B-5}$$

Equation (13B-5) does not include dz; thus it is risk-free over dt. Since the portfolio represented by V is risk-free:

$$dV = rV \, dt \tag{13B-6}$$

with r = risk-free interest rate

Substituting the term in parentheses from Equation (13B-5) for dV/dt in (13B-6), and Equation (13B-3) for V on the right side of (13B-6), and multiplying both sides by -1, we have:

$$\left[\frac{\partial P_C}{\partial t} + \frac{1}{2} \frac{\partial^2 P_C}{\partial P_S^2} \sigma_S^2 P_S^2 \right] = r \left[P_C - \frac{\partial P_C}{\partial P_S} P_S \right] \tag{13B-7}$$

Rearranging:

$$\frac{\partial P_C}{\partial t} + rP_S \frac{\partial P_C}{\partial P_S} + \frac{1}{2} \sigma_S^2 P_S^2 \frac{\partial^2 P_C}{\partial P_S^2} = rP_C \tag{13B-8}$$

Equation (13B-8) is called the Black-Scholes differential equation. The final equation to evaluate P_C is found by using the boundary condition at option expiration for the asset in question.

$$\text{For calls: } P_C = \text{Max}[P_S - K, 0]$$
$$\text{For puts: } P_P = \text{Max}[K - P_S, 0]$$

$(13B-9)$

Recall that the hedge ratio changes as P_S or t changes. This is why calculus is used to derive the equation. See Jarrow and Rudd (1983), Kutner (1988), and Ritchken (1987) for additional details related to this proof.

BIBLIOGRAPHY FOR APPENDIX 13B

Jarrow, Robert A., and Andrew Rudd (1983). *Option Pricing.* Homewood, IL: Irwin.

Kutner, George W. (1988). "Black-Scholes Revisited: Some Important Details," *Financial Review,* Vol. 23, No. 1, February, pp. 95–104.

Ritchken, Peter (1987). *Options: Theory, Strategy, and Applications.* Glenview, IL: Scott, Foresman.

Chapter 14

OPTION PRICING
SENSITIVITIES AND
PRICING EVIDENCE

Overview

$\mathbf{T}$his chapter examines option pricing sensitivities derived from the option formula and discusses the evidence concerning option pricing formulas. The pricing sensitivities are the derivatives of the option pricing equation. These sensitivities are the hedge ratio (the change in the option price for a given change in the stock price), the sensitivity of the hedge ratio (the change in the hedge ratio for a given change in the stock price), leverage (the percentage change in the option price for a given percentage change in the stock price), the time factor (the change in the option price for a given change in the time to option expiration), and the volatility (the change in the option price for a given change in the stock volatility). These sensitivities are examined quantitatively, graphically, and descriptively.

The empirical evidence concerning the Black-Scholes model provides two basic conclusions: First, in general, this model generates very accurate estimates of actual option prices; second, the model has certain systematic biases. These biases relate to high- and low-volatility stocks and to away-from-the-money options. However, more sophisticated option models do not seem to provide substantially better results than the Black-Scholes model, at least on a consistent basis. Another finding of the empirical studies is that actual market-generated option prices tend to be slightly mispriced. Floor traders can capitalize on these mispricings by using ratio hedges to obtain returns above the risk-free interest rate.

Terminology

*Delta   See Chapter 13.

Derivative   A procedure from calculus that determines the change in one variable given a very small change in the other variable.

Elasticity   See lambda.

*Gamma   The change in the delta (hedge ratio) for a given change in the stock price; relates to the volatility of the stock.

Instantaneous   See Chapter 13.

*Lambda   The percentage change in the option price for a given percentage change in the stock price. Also known as leverage.

Leverage   See Chapter 11.

Pricing sensitivities   The important relationships between the characteristics of the option and the option price. The pricing sensitivities are designated as delta, lambda, theta, vega, and rho.

*Rho   The change in the option price for a given change in the risk-free interest rate.

*Theta   The change in the option price for a given change in the time until expiration of the option.

*Vega   The change in the option price for a given change in the volatility of the stock. (Also known as kappa.)

THE PRICING SENSITIVITIES

What Are Pricing Sensitivities?

Pricing sensitivities represent the key relationships between the individual characteristics of the option and the option price. These sensitivities are the change in the stock price, the change in the hedge ratio, a change due to leverage, changes in the time until the expiration of the option, and changes in the volatility of the stock. The purpose of examining the effect of these sensitivities on option prices is twofold: First, it helps us to understand what causes option prices to change, and second, it provides insights for specific option strategies.

The pricing sensitivities are **derivatives** of the option price in relation to each of the individual factors. The derivative calculates the change in the option price in relation to the change in the factor. For example, Chapter 13 defines delta as the hedge ratio: the change in the option price for a given change in the stock price. A delta of .5 indicates that the option price changes by $.50 for a change of $1 in the stock price. The Greek names for the pricing sensitivities and the relationships measured by these sensitivities are:

- **Delta:** the change in the option price for a given change in the stock price—that is, the hedge ratio.
- **Lambda** or leverage: the percentage change in the option price for a given percentage change in the stock price.
- **Gamma:** the change in the delta for a given change in the stock price.
- **Theta:** the change in the option price given a change in the time until option expiration.
- **Vega:** the change in the option price for a given change in the volatility of the stock. (Also known as kappa.)
- **Rho:** the change in the option price for a given change in the risk-free interest rate.

The risk exposure of any option position is explained via the sensitivities defined above. For example, arbitrageurs on the option trading floor are particularly concerned about their risk exposure; consequently, they monitor each of the above sensitivities carefully. Other option traders can also better understand the types and extent of their risk exposure from a particular option strategy by computing the values of the pricing sensitivities. The discussion in this chapter of the pricing sensitivities and the associated equations emphasizes call options; however, these pricing sensitivities also are relevent for put options and other strategies covered in later chapters. Appendix 14A provides the partial derivatives of the Black-Scholes option model, which are the pricing sensitivities when derivatives are employed. Option sensitivities for puts are obtained by substituting P_P for P_C in all of the sensitivity equations given below. These call and put pricing sensitivities are important measures of options that are applied in certain circumstances to the option trading and hedging strategies covered in the following chapters.

Delta

The Concept. Delta represents the hedge ratio for the option model, which is also the ratio of the change in the option price for a given change in the stock price:

$$\text{Delta} = \delta = \frac{d(\text{option price})}{d(\text{stock price})} = \frac{\Delta P_C}{\Delta P_S} \qquad (14\text{-}1)$$

where $d(\cdot)$ = the (partial) derivative, which is the (**instantaneous**) small change in the variable; $d(\cdot) = \Delta$ when discrete (interval) changes are used

Graphically, the hedge ratio is represented as the slope of the option pricing line at the current stock price, as shown previously in Figure 13-2. The instantaneous hedge ratio also can be found by solving the Black-Scholes option formula. The deltas for different option and stock positions are:

Long Position	Delta	Short Position	Delta
Long call	0 to +1	Short call	−1 to 0
Long put	−1 to 0	Short put	0 to +1
Long stock	+1	Short stock	−1

Long put options possess negative deltas, because the put price declines as the stock price increases. Similarly, short positions have deltas that are opposite long positions, as the value of long and short positions go in opposite directions.

Delta measures the option price's sensitivity to changes in the stock price. A near-the-money call option typically has a delta near .5—that is, the option price changes by ½ of the stock price change. In fact, notice that a slight rearrangement of Equation (14-1) provides the *expected* change in the option price for a given stock price change:

$$\Delta P_C = \delta \Delta P_S \qquad (14\text{-}2)$$

Delta and Pricing Relationships.   Delta is associated with the pricing relationships discussed in Chapter 12. One function of these relationships is to indicate how option prices change for in-the-money and out-of-the-money options. For example, delta increases as the option goes in-the-money, showing the increased price appreciation as the stock price increases. Deep-in-the-money options change almost point for point with the stock price change (the delta is near one). Delta declines as the option goes out-of-the-money, which shows the decreased exposure of the option price to stock price declines. Delta quantifies these pricing relationships between the stock and option prices, as shown in Equation (14-2). Figure 14-1 shows how both the call price and delta change as the stock price changes, with delta measuring the slope to the call price line at the relevant stock price. Table 14-1 provides call deltas for a stock price of 100 and volatilities of 15% and 25%. Figure 14-2 illustrates how delta changes in terms of the stock price for three different volatilities. Figure 14-3 shows delta as a function of both the stock value and the strike price.

Risk Exposure and Position Delta.   Intuitively, a trader who buys one call option position with a $\delta = .6$, and *sells* a different call option position with a $\delta = .4$, has a net $\delta = .6 - .4 = .2$. Thus, a \$1 change in the stock price creates a \$+.20 increase in the combined option position. Similarly, if a hedger is long stock ($\delta = 1$) and short one call option with a $\delta = .55$, then the delta of the combined position is $1 - .55 = .45$. However, a method is needed to evaluate more complicated portfolios of several option/stock positions or portfolios with an unequal number of shares among the different positions. Besides showing how the option price reacts to stock price changes, delta is used to find the net dollar exposure of combined positions to stock price changes. The position delta measures the risk of a portfolio of option-stock positions:

$$\text{Position delta} = \Sigma n_i \, \delta_i \qquad (14\text{-}3)$$

where n_i = the number of option or stock shares in a position

δ_i = the delta of the position

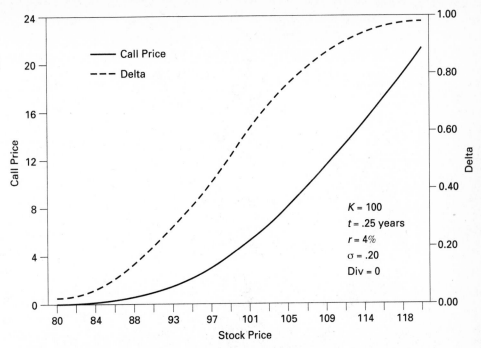

Figure 14-1 Delta: how the hedge ratio changes. (*Source:* Created from the Options and Futures Trading Simulator by Mark Rubinstein and Gerard Gennotte (1992).)

Table 14-1 Call Deltas

$P_S = 100.00$
$r = 5\%$

Panel A: Volatility = 15%

Strike:	90	95	100	105	110
Time remaining:					
1 day	1.00	1.00	.51	.00	.00
1 week	1.00	.99	.52	.01	.00
1 month	.99	.90	.55	.16	.02
3 months	.95	.81	.58	.33	.14
6 months	.90	.78	.61	.43	.27

Panel B: Volatility = 25%

Strike:	90	95	100	105	110
Time remaining:					
1 day	1.00	1.00	.51	.01	.00
1 week	1.00	.94	.52	.07	.04
1 month	.94	.79	.54	.28	.11
3 months	.84	.72	.56	.41	.27
6 months	.80	.70	.59	.48	.38

Source: Created using OptionVue IV.

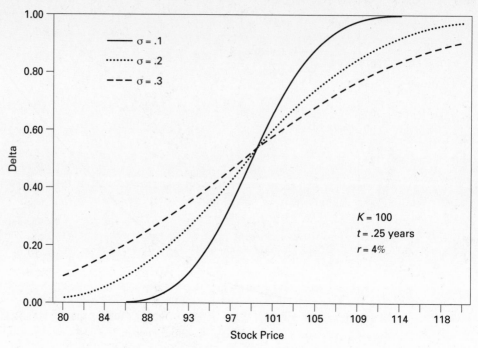

Figure 14-2 Deltas for different volatilities. (*Source:* Created from The Options and Futures Trading Simulator by Mark Rubinstein and Gerard Gennotte (1992).)

Recall that each option is equivalent to 100 shares. One interprets the position delta in terms of the dollar change in the position per a $1 change in the stock price. Therefore, a position delta of 45 means that the value of the position will change by $45 for a $1 per share stock price change. Example 14-1 provides an example of position delta.[1]

Position delta measures both the direction and extent of the risk exposure of the multiple option or the option-stock position when the stock price changes. The direction is associated with the positive or negative sign of the position delta:

Position Delta	Profitable Stock Direction
Positive	Bullish (price increases beneficial)
Zero	Neutral
Negative	Bearish (price decreases beneficial)

The extent of the risk exposure is measured by the size of the position delta. The position delta approach works equally well for individual options, combinations of stock and options, or for a combination of calls and puts. However, recall that δ *changes* as the stock price, time to expiration, or volatility of the stock changes; hence, the same value of delta is not valid for the entire life of the option.

[1]Others refer to position delta as the "net share exposure." Hence, a position delta of 45 is equivalent to owning 45 shares of the underlying stock.

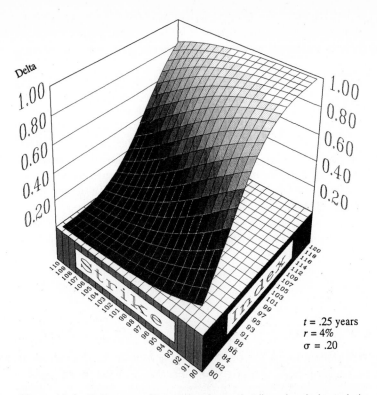

Figure 14-3 Delta versus the stock value and strike price. Index = index
value or stock price. (*Source:* Created from The Options
and Futures Trading Simulator by Mark Rubinstein and
Gerard Gennotte (1992).)

EXAMPLE 14-1
Position Delta

An option trader buys a near-the-money call option with a $\delta = .55$ and buys two
out-of-the-money puts with each put having a $\delta = -.35$. Later, the trader's account
executive convinces the trader to sell two out-of-the-money calls, each with a
$\delta = .30$ (selling an option is recorded as a minus number of shares). The position
delta for the combined position is:

$$\text{Position delta} = n_1 \delta_1 + n_2 \delta_2 + n_3 \delta_3 \qquad (14\text{-}3)$$

$$= 100(.55) + 200(-.35) - 200(.30)$$

$$= 55 - 70 - 60$$

$$= -75$$

For a $1 *increase* in the stock price, this combined option position *declines* $75.
Thus, the trader has a net *short* position.

Hedgers and Delta. If a trader wants a position delta of zero when using two stock-option positions, then setting Equation (14-3) equal to zero and solving for δ_2/δ_1 provides the ratio of shares needed in terms of the given deltas of positions 1 and 2 in order to obtain a delta of zero:

$$n_1 \delta_1 + n_2 \delta_2 = 0 \leftrightarrow n_1/n_2 = \delta_2/\delta_1 \qquad (14\text{-}4)$$

A trader who uses the hedge ratio (delta) to set up a risk-free hedge when the delta is zero creates a combined stock-option position that does *not* change in value as the stock price changes (at least for small changes in the stock price). In other words, the delta for a risk-free hedge is zero. When a delta of zero is created for a stock-option position (or with multiple option positions), *and* a return above the risk-free rate is guaranteed, then the trader has generated an arbitrage transaction. Example 14-2 illustrates Equation (14-4).

The above discussion shows that delta is useful in determining a net measure of risk (the position delta). In fact, hedgers often use delta to measure the net risk of a position. Even margins on options often are set in terms of the delta of an option position. Consequently, delta is the most significant option factor used in connection with option positions.

Elasticity (Lambda)

Elasticity refers to the leverage of the option position. Elasticity measures the percentage change in the option price for a 1% change in the stock price:

$$\text{Elasticity} = \text{lambda} = \lambda = \frac{\% \, \Delta P_C}{\% \, \Delta P_S} \qquad (14\text{-}5)$$

EXAMPLE 14-2
Delta and Risk-free Hedges

A floor trader is short 20 call options with a $\delta = .6$. To set up a risk-free hedge with the underlying stock, the trader uses Equation (14-4) as follows:

$$n_1/n_2 = \delta_2/\delta_1 \qquad (14\text{-}4)$$

Defining the call option delta as δ_1, we have:

$$2000/n_2 = 1/-.6$$

$$n_2 = 2000(-.6)$$

$$n_2 = -1200 \text{ stock shares (short)}$$

An increase in the stock price causes the delta to increase to .7. To keep the risk-free hedge the stock position now changes to:

$$n_2 = 2000(-.7)$$

$$n_2 = -1400 \text{ stock shares (short)}$$

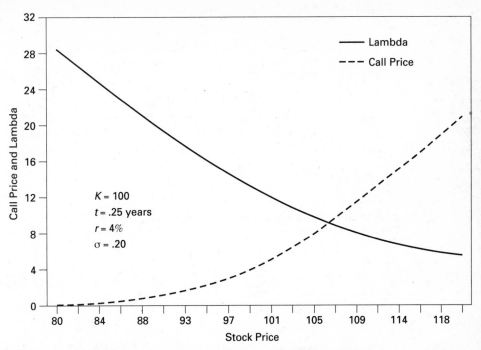

Figure 14-4 Lambda: the effect of leverage. (*Source:* Created from The Options and Futures Trading Simulator by Mark Rubinstein and Gerard Gennotte (1992).)

A lambda of 8 means that a 1% increase in the price of the stock causes an 8% increase in the price of the option. Typical elasticity values are 8 to 10. Leverage is an important characteristic of options that attracts speculators. Also note that Equation (14-5) is equivalent to the following:[2]

$$\lambda = \delta(P_S/P_C) \qquad (14\text{-}6)$$

Figure 14-4 illustrates how lambda changes as the stock price changes. This graph shows that the leverage is very high when the option is deep out-of-the-money and relatively low when the option is deep-in-the-money. While the *delta* of an option decreases significantly when the option goes out-of-the-money (Figure 14-1), the lambda increases for out-of-the-money options. Consequently, many speculators prefer buying out-of-the-money options.

A more encompassing illustration of leverage is shown by Table 14-2. The effect of leverage is shown by comparing the call option prices when the stock is at 100 and 105. While the stock price change from 100 to 105 is not a major one, Table 14-2 shows that leverage has a major effect on the associated option prices. For example, the one-month 95 call increases from $6\frac{1}{4}$ to $10\frac{5}{8}$, a 70% increase. The corresponding stock increased by only 5%. Similarly, the one-month 105 option increased 170% and the other options also obtained large percentage increases.

[2]Since $\%\Delta P_C/\%\Delta P_S = [\Delta P_C/P_C]/[\Delta P_S/P_S]$, a simple rearrangement creates $[\Delta P_C/\Delta P_S]\ [P_S/P_C] = \delta(P_S/P_C)$.

Table 14-2 The Leverage Factor for Calls

$P_S = 100$		$\sigma_S = .25$		Risk-free rate = 5%		No dividends
			Call Prices			
Strike Price	**Stock = 100**			**Stock = 105**		
	1 Month	**2 Months**	**3 Months**	**1 Month**	**2 Months**	**3 Months**
95	6¼	7⅜	8½	10⅝	11½	12⅜
100	3⅛	4⅜	5⅝	6½	7⅝	8¾
105	1¼	2⅜	3⅜	3¼	4⅝	5⅞

Source: Developed using OptionVue IV.

Table 14-3 The Leverage Factor for Puts

$P_S = 100$		$\sigma_S = .25$		Risk-free rate = 5%		No dividends
			Put Prices			
Strike Price	**Stock = 100**			**Stock = 95**		
	1 Month	**3 Months**	**6 Months**	**1 Month**	**3 Months**	**6 Months**
95	¹⁵⁄₁₆	1⅝	2⅜	2½	3⅜	4⅛
100	2¾	3⅝	4⅜	5⅝	6⅜	6⅞
105	5¾	6½	7⅛	10	10⅛	10½

Source: Developed using OptionVue IV.

A similar leverage effect exists for puts. Table 14-3 shows that the decline in the price for the stock creates large percentage changes for the put options. For example, the one-month in-the-money put increases from 5¾ to 10 as the stock price declines, a 74% increase in value, while the stock itself changes by only 5%.

Gamma

The Concept. Gamma measures the change in the delta for a given change in the stock price:

$$\text{Gamma} = \gamma = \frac{d(\text{delta})}{d(\text{stock price})} = \frac{\Delta\delta}{\Delta P_S} \tag{14-7}$$

The gamma shows the *risk* inherent in delta—that is, the change in delta as caused by a change in the stock price. If gamma is small, delta is not sensitive to changes in the stock price. If gamma is large, delta *is* sensitive to stock price changes.[3] Gamma measures the amount of *curvature* in the call price curve. Thus, while delta measures the slope of the line at a particular point on the call price curve, gamma measures the

---

[3] For stock-option hedgers, the absolute value of the gamma measures the extent to which a change in the stock price will force a revision in the hedge ratio.

FOCUS 14-1
The Behind-the-Scenes Story on the Black-Scholes Model

The Black-Scholes option pricing model is widely known in finance circles because it has an elegant proof, it is easy to use, and it provides an answer to an important question (the value of an option). When Fischer Black went to Japan to give a talk on the Black-Scholes model, over 10,000 people showed up. (They were surprised to find out that his name was Fischer Black rather than Black-Scholes—they thought only one person developed the model.)

The Black-Scholes model did not come about by accident. Myron Scholes met Fischer Black when Scholes was teaching at MIT and Black was a consultant at Arthur D. Little in Boston. Black was interested in the interrelationships between security prices and risk, the structure and combination of assets, and substituting one security for another (which we call arbitrage). Scholes was interested in empirical research and how new ideas related to the financial literature.

While Scholes was a "pure academic" who had recently received a Ph.D. from the University of Chicago (a university that produced many of the initial wave of financial theorists), Black had wandered among many fields before settling on Finance. Black went to Harvard mainly because of its glee club. At various times he majored in French, psychology, social relations, anthropology, mathematics, chemistry, and physics (the latter being his undergraduate major). In graduate school he started in physics and then switched to applied mathematics (computers).

Black and Scholes started by writing papers on the relationships between risk and return. They began to talk about options and warrants in the spring of 1969 (remember, there was no formal options exchange at the time). They then started working on the pricing of options, including ideas related to arbitrage. The basic approach was to determine a formula that included all the factors affecting a change in the option price, while at the same time determining how many options would have the same total price change as the underlying stock. Thus, in today's terms they wanted to create an arbitrage or hedged position. Since the hedged position would essentially be risk-free, the return on the position should be the risk-free interest rate. The Capital Asset Pricing Model was applied to every moment in an option's life (how the discount rate for the option varies with time and the stock price). This resulted in a specific differential equation known as the "heat equation."

Robert Merton (also known for his work on options), Black, and Scholes had long discussions about how to best show the relationships between the stock and the option. They had difficulty obtaining a solution at first, but when they found the result they wanted, Black and Scholes tried to have the paper published. An early version of the paper was submitted in the summer of 1970, but both the *Journal of Political Economy* and the *Review of Economics and Statistics* rejected the paper—perhaps because the ideas were so new and/or because Black was not an academic. After revising the approach and receiving encouragement from University of Chicago professors Merton Miller and Eugene Fama, an article testing the model empirically was published in 1972 in *The Journal of Finance*. The proof of the model was published in 1973 in the *Journal of Political Economy* (published by The University of Chicago). In 1972, the Chicago Board Options Exchange started to trade options.

continued next page

continued

The Black and Scholes model was put into use immediately by market makers on the floor of the CBOE and investment houses in New York, which surprised both Black and Scholes. Since then, the model has become a staple of finance courses and is used to price almost all types of securities. It led to the development of the binomial option model, which is used to price securities not well-fitted for the Black-Scholes model. And it is directly related to the development of dynamic trading strategies, such as portfolio insurance (and therefore indirectly associated with events such as the market crash in October 1987). The only thing left now is the Nobel prize.

Source: This focus is based on information in Szala (1988) and Black (1989).

change in the delta (i.e., when the stock price changes, the slope measured by delta changes). Equivalently, gamma is the slope of the *delta* curve at a particular point: When the *slope of the delta line* is the greatest, the gamma is the largest; when the slope of the delta is small, the gamma is near zero.[4] These relationships are shown in Figure 14-5.

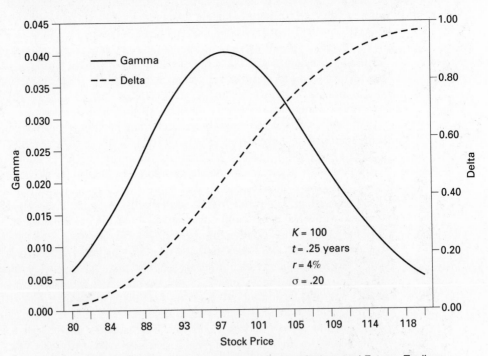

Figure 14-5 Delta and gamma. (*Source:* Created from The Options and Futures Trading Simulator by Mark Rubinstein and Gerard Gennotte (1992).)

[4] Since gamma is the derivative (slope) of the delta at each stock price, this explanation simply describes the calculation of the derivative.

Both long call and long put positions have positive gammas; a stock has a $\gamma = 0$. Gamma is one measure of the effect of instability on the option position. The other measure is volatility (vega). Gamma is interpreted as follows:

γ (gamma)	P_S	δ
> 0	increases	increases
	decreases	decreases
< 0	increases	decreases
	decreases	increases

In other words, if γ is positive, delta changes in the *same* direction as the stock price. If γ is negative, delta changes in the *opposite* direction of the stock price. If gamma is .10 and the current delta is 0, then an increase in the stock price of \$1 causes the delta to increase from 0 to .10. The new delta of .10 means that an increase in the stock price of \$1 will now increase the option price by \$.10. If the trader wants a delta neutral position ($\delta = 0$), the number of stock shares will need to be rebalanced, as noted in the discussion of delta. Figure 14-6 shows how gamma changes as the stock price changes, by illustrating gammas for three different standard deviations (volatilities).

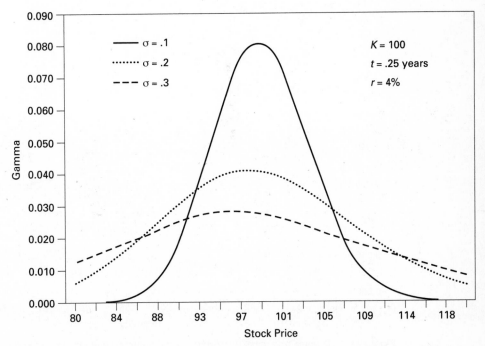

Figure 14-6 Gammas for different volatilities. (*Source:* Created from The Options and Futures Trading Simulator by Mark Rubinstein and Gerard Gennotte (1992).)

In terms of volatility, gamma shows the sensitivity of the option to changes in the underlying stock's volatility:

Gamma	Volatility
Positive	Bullish (volatility increases beneficial)
Zero	Neutral
Negative	Bearish (volatility decreases beneficial)

Hence, a positive gamma means a position will benefit from an increase in volatility, while a negative gamma will benefit from a decrease in volatility. Figure 14-7 illustrates how gamma changes as the volatility changes.

Position Gamma.   Position gamma allows the trader to determine the effect of a $1 change in stock price on the position delta. Position gamma is calculated by:

$$\text{Position gamma} = \Sigma\, n_i \gamma_i \qquad\qquad (14\text{-}8)$$

where $\gamma_i =$ the gamma of position i

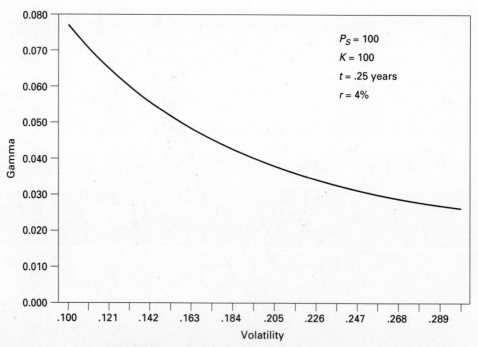

Figure 14-7   Gamma and volatility. (*Source:* Created from The Options and Futures Trading Simulator by Mark Rubinstein and Gerard Gennotte (1992).)

The absolute size of the position gamma, when calculated at the target delta, shows how quickly changes in the stock price will force the trader to revise the position delta to keep it constant. Example 14-3 illustrates the position gamma.[5]

Revising the position delta, and therefore gamma, is important for arbitrageurs who set up risk-free hedges. In particular, arbitrageurs want to know the price effect of a *change in the hedge ratio* (δ) or position delta on the net stock/option position *as the stock price changes*. If the position delta is continuously revised to minimize risk, then the maximum profit for the arbitrage is achieved. If the delta is not revised, then the size of the profit decreases as the stock price moves away from the initial stock price. In addition, the *size* of the position gamma shows the arbitrageur how sensitive the hedge is to changes in the stock price, which also suggests how frequently the hedge ratio needs to be revised.[6]

Changing Gammas. Another characteristic of a positive gamma is that profits are larger than losses; thus, a profitable change in the value of the position is greater than a loss in the position for equal (but opposite) size changes in the stock price. This relationship is shown in Figure 14-8, which illustrates both the gamma and the call price. The positive gamma at $P_S = 100$ indicates that an increase in the stock price to 110 is

EXAMPLE 14-3
Position Gamma

The position held in Example 14-1 possesses the following gammas:

Position	δ	γ
long 1 call	.55	.052
long 2 puts	−.35	.0455
short 2 calls	.30	.045

The position gamma for this portfolio is:

$$\text{Position gamma} = \Sigma n_i \gamma_i \tag{14-8}$$

$$= 100(.052) + 200(.0455) - 200(.045)$$

$$= 5.2 + 9.1 - 9 = 5.3$$

For a \$1 increase in the stock price, the *position delta* of this position will increase by 5.3.

---

[5] The position gamma can be used to indicate how sensitive the position is to changes in the stock's volatility when all of the options have the same expiration. For call options:

$$\Delta P_C/\Delta \sigma_C = \gamma P_S^2 t \sigma_S$$

[6] Since a two-asset zero delta position has $n_1\delta_1 + n_2\delta_2 = 0$, the position gamma for a *zero* delta position is:

$$\text{position gamma} = n_1 \Delta_1[(\gamma_1/\Delta_1) - (\gamma_2/\Delta_2)]$$

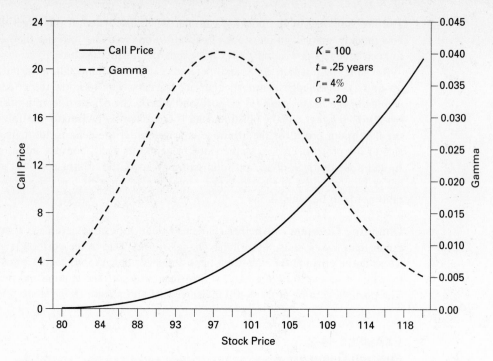

Figure 14-8 Gamma and call option prices. (*Source:* Created from The Options and Futures Trading Simulator by Mark Rubinstein and Gerard Gennotte (1992).)

more profitable than the losses incurred from a decrease in the stock to 90. Figure 14-8 also shows how the gamma changes as the stock and option prices change. The largest gamma occurs for an at-the-money option. As the option becomes deep-in-the-money or deep-out-of-the-money, the gamma declines to near zero. In addition, notice how the gamma reflects the amount of curvature of the call option price line. When the curvature of the call price is the greatest, for the at-the-money position of $P_S = 100$, the gamma has its largest value. When the option price line is straight, for deep-in-the-money and deep-out-of-the-money options, the gamma is near zero.

Theta

Interpreting Theta. Theta measures the change in the option value as the time until the expiration of the option declines:

$$\text{Theta} = \theta = \frac{d(\text{option price})}{d(\text{time to expiration})} = \frac{\Delta P_C}{\Delta t} \tag{14-9}$$

where θ is a negative number

  t = the time to option expiration (in fractions of a year)

The greater the absolute value of theta, the larger the per-day *loss* in option value from holding a long option position due to the time decay of the option position. Equation (14-9) calculates an annualized theta value. However, many computer models treat theta as a per-day amount, rather than an annualized value. The negative theta illustrates the fact that option buyers lose money as the time value declines over time. Both call and put thetas are negative. Sellers of an option generate profits from a positive theta as a result of this time decay. Example 14-4 provides an example of calculating theta.

Figure 14-9 illustrates the time decay for an at-the-money call. As the option nears the expiration date, the theta declines rapidly (the absolute size of the theta increases rapidly during the last 30 days before expiration). This figure also shows the effect of

EXAMPLE 14-4
The Value of Theta

When stock price and stock volatility are held constant, one determines that a long call price declines by ⅜ of a point over 17 calendar days:

$$\theta = \frac{-.375}{(17/365)} = -8.051$$

The annualized theta can be converted to a per-day value of:

$$\text{Per-day loss} = -8.051/365 = \$-.022$$

or a three-month loss of:

$$\$-.022 \times 91 = \$1.99 \text{ per option share}$$

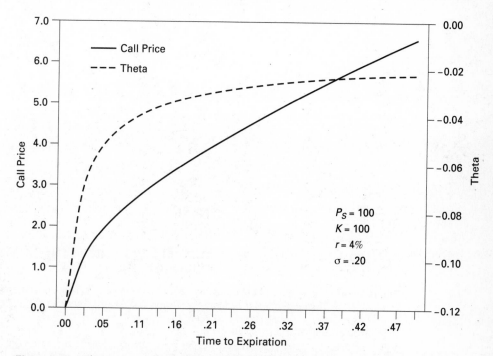

Figure 14-9 Theta as a function of time. (*Source:* Created from The Options and Futures Trading Simulator by Mark Rubinstein and Gerard Gennotte (1992).)

theta on the call price. Figure 14-10 illustrates how changes in the stock price affect theta. The largest negative theta occurs when the stock is at-the-money. As an option becomes more in-the-money or more out-of-the-money—that is, as the time value declines—the theta tends toward zero. Figure 14-11 shows how theta varies in relation to the stock price for three different times to option expiration.

Table 14-4 keeps the other sensitivities constant so that the effect of time can be analyzed. The table shows that the option price differences from one expiration month to another are larger for the nearby months as compared to the more distant months.[7] In addition, the call option price differences are larger than the put differences.

Position Theta.   The position theta measures how much a position decreases in value as the time to expiration decreases (when the stock price remains unchanged).

$$\text{Position theta} = \Sigma n_i \theta_i \qquad (14\text{-}10)$$

where θ_i = the theta of position i

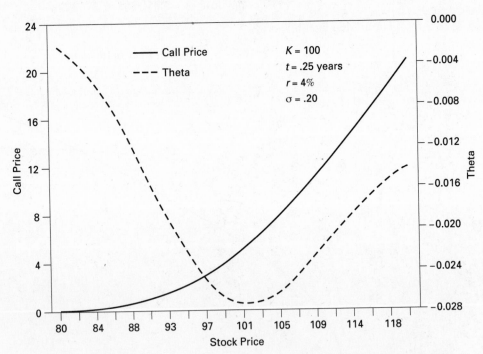

Figure 14-10   Theta and call option prices. (*Source:* Created from The Options and Futures Trading Simulator by Mark Rubinstein and Gerard Gennotte (1992).)

---

[7] The fact that some later expiration months for the in-the-money calls and one out-of-the-money put possess larger differences than the nearby expiration is due to rounding of the option prices.

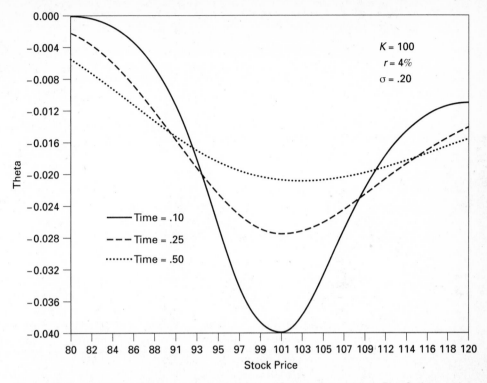

Figure 14-11   Thetas for different times to expiration. (*Source:* Created from The Options and Futures Trading Simulator by Mark Rubinstein and Gerard Gennotte (1992).)

The effects of position theta values are:

Position theta	Effect
Positive	Profits from positive time decay
Zero	Neutral time effect
Negative	Losses from negative time decay

Example 14-5 shows how to calculate and interpret the position theta.

Theta and Gamma.   The relationship between theta and gamma is also important. Theta and gamma generate tradeoffs: When theta is at its lowest point, gamma is at its highest, and vice versa. This tradeoff between the time factor and price variability is shown in Figure 14-12 on page 430. A positive gamma strategy benefits from a large change in the stock price, while the associated negative theta shows that the longer it takes to generate such a large price change, the greater the loss of the time value. A trader must be aware of this tradeoff when initiating and maintaining a position. Conversely, a writer of such a strategy benefits from the time decay, while the writer loses

Table 14-4 Time to Option Expiration and Option Prices

$P_S = 100$	$\sigma_S = .25$		Risk-free rate = 5%		No dividends	
	Option Prices			**Price Difference from Previous Month**		
	Call option strikes:			Call option strikes:		
	95	100	105	95	100	105
Expiration month	**In-the-money**	**At-the-money**	**Out-of-the-money**	**In-the-money**	**At-the-money**	**Out-of-the-money**
1	6¼	3⅛	1¼			
2	7⅜	4⅜	2⅜	1¼	1¼	1¼
3	8½	5⅝	3⅜	1⅛	1¼	1
4	9⅜	6½	4⅜	⅞	⅞	1
5	10¼	7½	5¼	⅞	1	⅞
6	11	8¼	6	¾	¾	¾
7	11⅞	9	6¾	⅞	¾	¾
8	12½	9¾	7½	⅝	¾	¾
9	13¼	10½	8⅛	¾	¾	⅝
	Put option strikes:			Put option strikes:		
	95	100	105	95	100	105
Expiration month	**Out-of-the-money**	**At-the-money**	**In-the-money**	**Out-of-the-money**	**At-the-money**	**In-the-money**
1	¹⁵⁄₁₆	2¾	5¾			
2	1⅝	3⅝	6½	¹¹⁄₁₆	⅞	¾
3	2⅜	4⅜	7⅛	¾	¾	⅝
4	2⅞	4⅞	7⅝	¾	¾	½
5	3⅜	5⅜	8	½	½	⅜
6	3¾	5¾	8⅜	⅜	⅜	⅜
7	4⅛	6⅛	8¾	⅜	⅜	⅜
8	4⅜	6½	9	¼	⅜	¼
9	4¾	6¾	9¼	⅜	¼	¼

Source: Developed using OptionVue IV.

when the stock price changes significantly. Consequently, the key consideration for a theta-gamma tradeoff strategy is whether the tradeoff is favorable to the trader. In fact, the relationships between gamma, theta, and the underlying stock price can be very complicated when dealing with multiple option positions. For example, Figure 14-13 shows the gamma for a portfolio of 10 options for varying times to expiration and stock prices.

Vega

Traders often attempt to determine which options are cheap or expensive in terms of volatility—that is, options whose implied volatility is less than or greater than what the trader believes is appropriate for the given stock. Moreover, recall the importance

EXAMPLE 14-5
Position Theta

Extending the position delta and position gamma examples to position theta, we have:

Position	δ	γ	Per day θ
long 1 call	.55	.052	−.17
long 2 puts	−.35	.0455	−.125
short 2 calls	.30	.045	−.14

Technically, the theta of the short 2 calls position is positive (one earns time value by selling calls). However, we will keep our previous convention of placing a negative in front of the number of shares of a short position, while reporting a negative theta for all calls and puts.

The position theta is:

$$\text{Position theta} = \Sigma\, n_i \theta_i \qquad (14\text{-}10)$$

$$= 100(-.17) + 200(-.125) - 200(-.14)$$

$$= -17 - 25 + 28$$

$$= -14$$

The option portfolio will *lose* $14 for each day it is held (the change in the option value for a one-day change in time).

of volatility for option pricing, including the fact that option prices are usually sensitive to relatively small changes in volatility. Table 14-5 on page 432 shows how a change in volatility affects option prices. In particular, a relatively small change in the annual standard deviation of returns causes a relatively large change in the option price, especially for the longer-term options. Volatility is the only input factor that is not directly observable when it is used in an option pricing model—that is, the market utilizes *estimates* of future volatility to value options. Therefore, changes in implied volatility have a major effect on option prices.

Vega measures the change in the option price per unit of change in the volatility of the stock:

$$\text{Vega} = v = \frac{d(\text{option price})}{d(\text{volatility})} = \frac{\Delta P_C}{\Delta \sigma_S} \qquad (14\text{-}11)$$

where σ_S = the annualized standard deviation (volatility) of the stock.

Thus, if $v = .08$, then an increase in the annual standard deviation of the stock of 1% causes the option price to increase by $.08(1) = \$.08$.

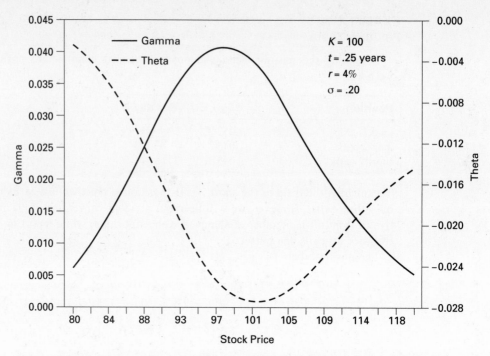

Figure 14-12 Gamma and theta. (*Source:* Created from The Options and Futures Trading Simulator by Mark Rubinstein and Gerard Gennotte (1992).)

Vega is shown in Figure 14-14 on page 433. Notice that vega has the same shape as gamma, although the specific values of vega differ from gamma. As with gamma, vega is largest for at-the-money options, and drops as the option becomes more in- or more out-of-the-money. Thus, deep-in-the-money or deep-out-of-the-money options

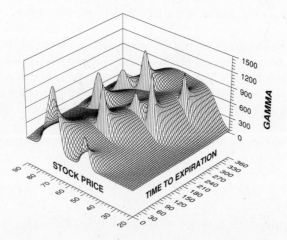

Figure 14-13 Gamma risk for multiple option positions.
(*Source:* Haug (1993).)

FOCUS 14-2
OptionVue: The Matrix of Prices and Sensitivities

An important screen in the OptionVue program is the "matrix" of prices and option sensitivities. This matrix is illustrated below using the OEX (S&P 100) options. The "Options" section of the matrix provides theoretical option prices, the percentage each option is over- or underpriced from the current option price, and a choice of 27 other possible variables. Here we have the implied volatility of each option, the delta, and the gamma. The position of each variable is defined below the matrix. The data represented here are actual OEX prices. The volatility input into the model prices is 11.4%, the long-term statistical volatility of the OEX. Therefore, the apparent "mispricing" of the options should be related to a change in the volatility.

The "Summary" section of the matrix provides the position delta, position gamma, position vega (discussed later), and per-day dollar theta. These values represent the portfolio of the following option positions (not shown in the matrix): long May and June 390 calls and short May and June 395 calls (note that the most overpriced options are sold and the least overpriced options are purchased). Thus, OptionVue provides the net portfolio position sensitivities for any (complicated) portfolio.

S&P 100 INDEX, FRI APR 23

Actuals

OEX Inx	
404.40	−1.89

Futures

	May-(29)			Jun-(57)			Jul-(85)		
CALLS	16¼	15	+8%	18½	16⅜	+13%	....	17⅞	
390	16.0%	.869	.0164	15.7%	.795	.0157		.759	.0141
CALLS	12½	10⅞	+15%	14¾	12¾	+16%	....	14⅜	
395	16.0%	.766	.0237	15.1%	.706	.0190		.681	.0162
CALLS	8½	7½	+13%	10⅞	9½	+14%	13	11⅜	+14%
400	13.8%	.631	.0291	13.6%	.603	.0213	13.6%	.596	.0175
CALLS	5⅜	4¾	+13%	7⅞	6⅞	+15%	10	8¾	+14%
405	12.8%	.479	.0308	12.9%	.494	.0220	13.1%	.506	.0181
CALLS	3⅛	2¹³⁄₁₆	+11%	5⅜	4¾	+13%	7⅛	6½	+10%
410	12.2%	.332	.0280	12.3%	.387	.0211	12.2%	.418	.0177

SUMMARY

Orig.Rqmt:	(unknown)	Commis:_____	Delta:	+19.23	AvgMIV:	13.8%
Maint.Reqmt:	(unknown)		Gamma:	−1.06	Calls:	13.8%
Cash Flow:	(unknown)	Theta: +$2.48/day	Vega:	−20.2	Puts:	_____

continued next page

continued

The "Actuals" section numbers are:

1. last index price   **2.** change in price

The "Options" section numbers are:

1. last option price   **2.** model price   **3.** % over/underpriced
4. implied volatility   **5.** delta   **6.** gamma

Source: Developed using OptionVue IV.

Table 14-5   Volatility and Call Option Prices

$P_S = 100$ K = 100 Risk-free rate = 5% No dividends			
	At-the-Money Call Option		
Annual Standard Deviation	**1 Month**	**3 Months**	**6 Months**
.10	$1\frac{3}{8}$	$2\frac{5}{8}$	$4\frac{1}{8}$
.15	2	$3\frac{5}{8}$	$5\frac{1}{2}$
.20	$2\frac{1}{2}$	$4\frac{5}{8}$	$6\frac{7}{8}$
.25	$3\frac{1}{8}$	$5\frac{5}{8}$	$8\frac{1}{4}$
.30	$3\frac{3}{4}$	$6\frac{1}{2}$	$9\frac{5}{8}$
.35	$4\frac{1}{4}$	$7\frac{1}{2}$	11
.40	$4\frac{7}{8}$	$8\frac{1}{2}$	$12\frac{1}{2}$

Source: Developed using OptionVue.

have less dollar sensitivity to changes in volatility than near-the-money options. While vega is significantly reduced by stock price movements away from the strike price, vega is also affected by a declining time to option expiration.

Buying options creates a positive vega and a positive gamma, while selling options creates a negative vega and a negative gamma. Strategies with a positive vega are "long volatility"; thus, these strategies profit when volatility increases (assuming prices keep the same expected value). Strategies with a negative vega are "short volatility" and profit when volatility is stable. Hedgers who want to protect against volatility need to take a net position that creates a small vega.

Vega indicates the sensitivity of a given strategy or position to a change in the implied volatility of the stock, whether this change occurs because of a change in the traders' forecasts or because of a change in the volatility of the stock itself. On the other hand, gamma indicates the effect of the *current* level of volatility on the option price as the stock price changes.

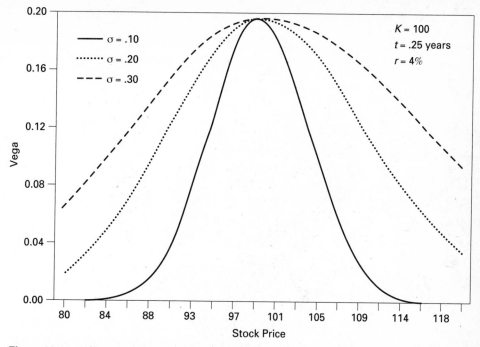

Figure 14-14 Vegas for different volatilities. (*Source:* Created from The Options and Futures Trading Simulator by Mark Rubinstein and Gerard Gennotte (1992).)

Rho

Rho measures the change in the option price for a given change in the risk-free interest rate:

$$\text{Rho} = \frac{d(\text{option price})}{d(\text{interest rate})} = \frac{\Delta P_C}{\Delta r} \qquad (14\text{-}12)$$

Table 14-6 shows that moderate changes in interest rates have only a minimal effect on the value of an option. The three-month call option in Table 14-6 changes by only ¼ of a point for a 2% change in interest rates, while the one-month option changes by ⅛ of a point or less for each 2% change in interest rates. Out-of-the-money and in-the-money options have price changes that are similar to the at-the-money options presented in Table 14-6. Therefore, option traders have only a minor interest in rho during normal times.

Interactions and a Summary of the Pricing Sensitivities

The discussion of the pricing sensitivities shows the complexity of examining the characteristics of option strategies: The sensitivities are interrelated, and the relationships between the sensitivities and the option price are nonlinear as the stock price changes. Table 14-7 shows how the option sensitivities interact.

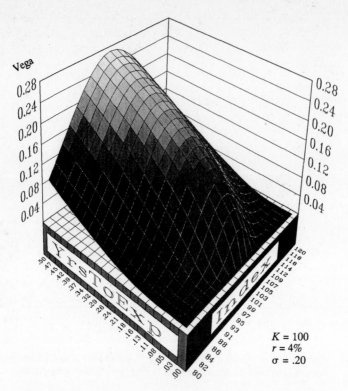

Figure 14-15 Vega in terms of stock prices and time to expiration. Yrs to Exp = years (or time) to expiration; Index = index value or stock price. (*Source:* Created from The Options and Futures Trading Simulator by Mark Rubinstein and Gerard Gennotte (1992).)

Table 14-6 Interest Rates and Fair Call Option Prices

$P_S = 100$	$K = 100$	$\sigma(\text{returns}) = .25$	No dividends
Risk-Free Interest Rate	**At-the-Money Call Options**		
	1 Month	**3 Months**	**6 Months**
4%	3⅛	5½	8
6%	3⅛	5¾	8½
8%	3¼	6	9
10%	3⅜	6¼	9½
12%	3⅜	6½	10⅛

Source: Developed using OptionVue IV.

Considering the interactions of the pricing sensitivities can be complicated. Tables such as Table 14-7 created either from OptionVue or the Option Similutor can provide a basis for analysis. In addition, three-dimensional graphs from the Option Simulator can provide a visual aid to understanding these interactions. Equation 14-13 provides another approach. Here gamma, theta, the change in the stock price, and the change in

Table 14-7 Option Sensitivity Values for Varying Strike Prices

$P_S = 100$		$\sigma_S = .25$	Risk-free rate = 5%			No dividends			$t = \frac{1}{4}$ year	
	Call Option						**Put Option**			
K	P_C	δ	γ	θ	υ	**K**	P_P	δ	γ	θ	υ
90	12⅛	.84	.019	−.026	.120	90	1⅛	−.16	.019	−.014	.120
95	8½	.72	.027	−.032	.169	95	2⅜	−.28	.027	−.019	.169
100	5⅜	.56	.032	−.034	.197	100	4⅜	−.44	.032	−.021	.197
105	3⅜	.41	.031	−.032	.194	105	7⅛	−.59	.031	−.018	.194
110	2	.27	.027	−.027	.166	110	10⅝	−.73	.027	−.012	.166

Similar results are obtained if the strike price remains the same and the stock price varies.
Source: Developed using OptionVue IV.

time are combined to estimate the change in the value of the portfolio for a position where $\delta = 0$:

$$\Delta\pi = \theta\Delta t + \gamma\,\Delta P_S^2/2 \tag{14-13}$$

where $\Delta\pi$ = the change in price of the portfolio

The interactions of δ, γ, θ, and the current interest rate are shown via Equations (14-14) and (14-15):

For $\delta = 0$:
$$P_C = [\theta + .5\sigma_S^2 P_S^2\gamma]/r \tag{14-14}$$

For $\delta \neq 0$ and a continuous dividend d is paid:

$$P_C = [\theta + (r - d)P_S\,\delta + .5\sigma_S^2 P_S^2\gamma]/r \tag{14-15}$$

Based on these equations one can determine that when θ is large and negative, γ tends to be large and positive, and vice-versa. Thus, tradeoffs exist among the sensitivities.

The pricing sensitivities are summarized in Table 14-8. This table lists each sensitivity, its function, and under what circumstances a positive or negative sign to the sensitivity is beneficial. Table 14-9 lists the basic strategies discussed so far, stating the delta, gamma, and theta of these strategies. The strategies in this table can also be reversed—for example, the signs for the sensitivities when selling a call option are opposite the signs for buying a call.

EVIDENCE ON OPTION PRICING

Empirical studies have examined how accurately the Black-Scholes model prices options and whether any systematic biases exist for the option pricing model. Violations of the pricing models provide possible arbitrage opportunities; if few violations exist, the option market is fairly priced.

The Black-Scholes Model

The Over-the-Counter Market. Black and Scholes (1972) test their call option pricing model on daily over-the-counter option prices. Since exchange-traded stock options only began trading in 1973, only over-the-counter prices were available for this initial

Table 14-8 Summarizing the Effect of the Pricing Sensitivities

Sensitivity	Function of Sensitivity	Sign of the Sensitivity*	
		Positive	Negative
$\delta = \Delta P_C / \Delta P_S$	Hedge ratio; exposure to directional price change	Position benefits from price increase	Position benefits from price decrease
$\lambda = \% \Delta P_C / \% \Delta P_S$	Leverage; elasticity	Position benefits from price increase	Position benefits from price decrease
$\gamma = \Delta \delta / \Delta P_S$	Price instability	Position benefits from price instability	Position benefits from price stability
$\theta = \Delta P_C / \Delta T$	Effect of time decay	Position benefits from passage of time	Position declines in value with passage of time
$v = \Delta P_C / \Delta \sigma_S$	Effect of change in volatility	Position benefits from volatility increase	Position benefits from volatility decrease
rho $= \Delta P_C / \Delta r$	Effect of change in interest rates	Position benefits from an increase in interest rates	Position benefits from a decrease in interest rates

* A zero value for a given pricing sensitivity means that the value of the position is not affected by a small change in the sensitivity. Puts have equivalent interpretations of their sensitivities.

Table 14-9 The Relationship Between Pricing Sensitivities and Basic Option Strategies

Strategy	Delta	Gamma	Theta
Buy a call	+	+	−
Buy a put	−	+	−
Put-call parity: buy stock, sell call, buy put	0	0	0

test of the Black-Scholes model. For this test, data on 545 different stocks with 2,039 different call options and 3,052 call plus put contracts are tested. The volatility of the stock is estimated based on the daily returns over the previous year. Call options are priced by the Black-Scholes model as well as by market prices generated by actual trades. The availability of arbitrage profits using the option model hedge ratio to generate stock/option positions is tested; alternatively, the article tests the ability of the model to price over-the-counter market options correctly.

The conclusions of the Black-Scholes study are:

- On *average,* the model calculates prices that are neither too high nor too low when compared to market prices, although subperiods show mispricing.
- For 8 of the 10 subperiods, option sellers received too high a price (when the appropriate hedge ratios are employed); thus, option buyers paid too high a price for calls.
- When the model price is compared to the market price, significant positive excess returns are obtained when options that are underpriced via the model are purchased and overpriced options are sold. These transactions are initiated using the hedge ratio of the underlying stock to the option in order to generate a risk-free hedge.

- Profit opportunities exist for buying options on low-variance stocks and selling options on high-variance stocks using historical variance and the appropriate hedge ratio to create a risk-free hedge.[8]
- When the actual variance over the life of the option is employed, the model works well in pricing the options.

CBOE Tests. Galai (1977) performs tests similar to the Black and Scholes study, except the Galai data are for exchange-traded options. Galai examines daily prices for 152 trading days for 245 options on 32 stocks. The study uses T-bill and commercial paper interest rates and three estimates of the volatility of the stock to institute option/stock hedges based on the Black-Scholes option model. The conclusions from this study are:

- The model does a good job in differentiating between overpriced and underpriced options (an arbitrageur can profit even when hedge ratios are *not* readjusted).
- Adjusting the hedge ratios daily creates significantly higher profits than not adjusting the ratios, with an adjusted strategy earning an average return of $10 per contract per day, with $\frac{1}{3}$ of the positions earning returns *significantly* greater than the risk-free interest rate.
- Different interest rates and volatility measures do not affect the conclusions of the tests.
- Including dividends increases the profits from $10 per contract to $15 per contract per day.
- When dividends are considered, low-dividend stocks provide superior profits relative to high-dividend stocks.
- When the profitable opportunities are delayed a day before a trade is executed, the majority of the profits disappear (note that a full day elapsed rather than using the next day's open).

Overall, Galai concludes that using the Black-Scholes model provides superior results relative to using the market option prices.

Biases in the Model. MacBeth and Merville (1979, 1980) examine possible systematic biases in the Black-Scholes option model. In their 1979 article, MacBeth and Merville employ the implied volatilities of the options for six actively traded stocks. They employ the average implied volatility calculated from the Black-Scholes model to price the options, using the assumption that at-the-money options with at least 90 days to expiration are priced correctly. Overall, the results show that the Black-Scholes model has a tendency to underprice in-the-money call options and to overprice out-of-the-money call options. Except for short-term out-of-the-money options, the extent of these mispricings increases when the options are deeper in-the-money or deeper out-of-the-money.[9] Moreover, on average, the mispricings increase as the time until expiration increases.

The extensive results by MacBeth and Merville do contradict (unsubstantiated) observations by others. Black (1975) states that deep in-the-money options are overpriced by the Black-Scholes model, while deep out-of-the-money options are underpriced by the model. Merton (1976) states that practitioners observe the Black-Scholes

---

[8] Using historical stock data to estimate the stock variance causes the model to overprice options on high-variance stocks and underprice options on low-variance stocks. On the other hand, using market option prices to estimate the variance creates underpriced options on high-variance stocks and overpriced options on low-variance stocks.

[9] The biases found by MacBeth and Merville are opposite those determined by Black and Scholes (1972).

model underpricing both deep-in-the-money and deep-out-of-the-money options. In conclusion, it seems that the Black-Scholes model works better in some time periods and for some situations (at-the-money options) than for others. Moreover, the biases that do exist may change over time, causing the conflicting statements noted above. Alternatively, the Black-Scholes model may be incomplete; if this is the case, then a more sophisticated option pricing model should provide superior estimates for the option prices. Other models are briefly examined in the next section.

Market Efficiency Tests.   Chiras and Manaster (1978) examine whether the Black-Scholes model is inaccurate or the option market is inefficient by buying options with low implied volatilities and selling options with high implied volatilities. This strategy obtained a profit of 10% per month, which suggests that the option market is inefficient and the Black-Scholes model is valid.

Index Options.   Evnine and Rudd (1985) show that index options were substantially mispriced after one year of trading. Not only did mispricings exist relative to the binomial model, but option boundaries and put-call parity were also violated based on transactions data. Cootner and Horrell (1989) use daily closing prices to show that the Black-Scholes model overprices calls, especially when historical rather than implied variance is used. This overpricing becomes larger as the time to expiration increases.

Sheikh (1991) uses transactions data on S&P 100 Index options to find that the market prices differ systematically from the Black-Scholes model prices. The biases created by the model are significant on both a statistical and an economic basis and are related to the changing volatility of the index. However, all of these efforts may be affected by the "old" cash index value and the difficulty in arbitraging an option on a portfolio of stocks. Moreover, Harvey and Whaley (1992) show that using a constant proportional dividend rate rather than the true discrete dividends for index options causes large pricing errors.

French and Maberly (1992) find that 28% of S&P 100 call index options are exercised early. They find this early exercise to be linked to the "wildcard" option that allows exercise until 4:10 P.M. Such early exercise near expiration could be associated with news after the 4:00 P.M. stock close or nontrading of some stocks in combination with a decline in the market.

Tests on Other Models

American Models.   The Black-Scholes model is a European option model—that is, the option cannot be exercised until its expiration. An American option can be exercised at any time. Roll (1977), Geske (1979), Geske and Johnson (1984), and Whaley (1981) all develop similar option models based on an American call option. Barone-Adesi and Whaley (1987) develop a method to efficiently approximate the price of an American option. Whaley (1982) and Sterk (1982, 1983a, 1983b) use daily data to compare the European and American versions of the call option models. They determine that the American call model is empirically superior to the European model. On the other hand, Blomeyer and Klemkosky (1983) use transaction prices to determine that the two models provide similar results. Blomeyer and Johnson (1988) examine the

Geske-Johnson model for valuing puts, using transaction data. They find that the Geske-Johnson model is significantly closer to market prices than the Black-Scholes model, although both undervalue put options relative to market prices.

Other Alternative Models.   Rubinstein (1985) compares the prices of several different option pricing models to actual market prices using transactions data and bid-ask quotes over a two-year period. He examines relationships and biases by determining the implied volatility on pairs of options differing by the strike price or time to expiration. Rubinstein concludes:

- Out-of-the-money options with a short time until expiration are relatively overpriced.
- Biases exist that relate to in-the-money and out-of-the-money options, but the direction of the bias changes with the time period.
- No model is consistently superior to the Black-Scholes model.

These results are consistent with the MacBeth and Merville study for the first period studied, but obtain results opposite to MacBeth and Merville for the second period. Rubinstein suggests that the strike price biases are related to macroeconomic factors such as the volatility of the market, interest rates, and the level of stock market prices.

A Summary of the Empirical Results

The empirical results emphasize one important fact: The Black-Scholes option model works extremely well, especially when pricing near-the-money options. In fact, the model does a good job of identifying mispriced options, although the mispricings are not large enough to be exploited by those who are off the exchange floor and, therefore, must pay commissions. However, delta arbitrageurs on the floor of the exchange can make returns above the risk-free rate by using the model to identify and then buy underpriced options and sell overpriced options, hedging their position in the underlying stock or in another option expiration or strike price. These hedges must be adjusted as the stock price or the time to expiration changes.

The Black-Scholes model often is less accurate when pricing stocks with very high or very low variances, when dividends are not properly considered in the model, and for deep-in-the-money and deep-out-of-the-money options. Specifically, the model tends to underprice in-the-money and overprice out-of-the-money options, with the extent of the mispricing increasing as the option becomes deeper in-the-money or deeper out-of-the-money and as the option has a longer time to expiration. However, the stability of these biases over different time periods has been questioned. The mispricing of in-the-money and out-of-the-money options could also be due to differences between the lognormal distribution used by Black-Scholes and the true empirical distribution. Other option models have characteristics that suggest they are superior to the Black-Scholes model, but empirical results to date show that none of the alternative models are consistently superior to the Black-Scholes model.

When examining empirical tests of pricing relationships for options, the following cautions must be observed:

- The option must have traded at the same time as the stock traded.
- The effect of the bid-ask spread needs to be considered.

- The procedure for estimating the future volatility of the stock must not impound biases into the results.
- Any test of options models is a joint test of both the validity of the model *and* whether the options markets are efficient. It is often difficult to determine whether the model is incorrect or the options are truly mispriced.

SUMMARY AND LOOKING AHEAD

This chapter examines the pricing sensitivities related to the option model and the empirical evidence concerning pricing models. The pricing sensitivities allow the option trader to determine the characteristics and risk of a particular strategy. The empirical evidence shows that the Black-Scholes model does an accurate job of predicting the market option price in general, although certain biases and mispricings do occur. The following chapter examines specific speculative strategies for options, while using the option sensitivities to enhance our knowledge of the characteristics of these strategies.

BIBLIOGRAPHY

Barone-Adesi, G., and Robert Whaley (1987). "Efficient Analytic Approximation of American Option Values," *Journal of Finance,* Vol. 42, No. 2, June, pp. 301–320.

Black, Fischer (1975). "Fact and Fantasy in the Use of Options," *Financial Analysts Journal,* Vol. 31, No. 4, July–August 1975, pp. 36–41 and 61–72.

Black, Fischer (1989). "How We Came Up with the Option Formula," *Journal of Portfolio Management,* Vol. 15, No. 2, Winter, pp. 4–8.

Black, Fischer, and Myron Scholes (1972). "The Valuation of Option Contracts and a Test of Market Efficiency," *Journal of Finance,* Vol. 27, No. 2, May, pp. 399–418.

Blomeyer, Edward C., and Herb Johnson (1988). "An Empirical Examination of the Pricing of American Put Options," *Journal of Financial and Quantitative Analysis,* Vol. 23, No. 1, March, pp. 13–22.

Blomeyer, Edward C., and Robert C. Klemkosky (1983). "Tests of Market Efficiency of American Call Options," in *Option Pricing,* ed. Menachem Brenner. Lexington, MA: Heath.

Chiras, Donald P., and Steven Manaster (1978). "The Information Content of Option Prices and a Test of Market Efficiency," *Journal of Financial Economics,* Vol. 6, No. 2/3, June–September, pp. 213–234.

Cootner, John S., and James F. Horrell (1989). "An Analysis of Index Option Pricing," *Journal of Futures Markets,* Vol. 9, No. 5, October, pp. 449–459.

Evnine, Jeremy, and Andrew Rudd (1985). "Index Options: The Early Evidence," *Journal of Finance,* Vol. 40, No. 3, July, pp. 743–756.

French, Dan W., and Edwin D. Maberly (1992). "Early Exercise of American Index Options," *Journal of Financial Research,* Vol. 15, No. 2, Summer, pp. 127–137.

Galai, Dan (1977). "Tests of Market Efficiency on the Chicago Board Options Exchange," *The Journal of Business,* Vol. 50, No. 2, April, pp. 167–195.

Geske, Robert (1979). "A Note on an Analytic Formula for Unprotected American Call Options on Stocks with Known Dividends," *Journal of Financial Economics,* Vol. 7, No. 4, December, pp. 375–380.

Geske, Robert, and Herb Johnson (1984). "The American Put Option Valued Analytically," *Journal of Finance,* Vol. 39, No. 5, December, pp. 1511–1524.

Harvey, Campbell R., and Robert E. Whaley (1992). "Dividends and S&P 100 Index Option Valuation," *Journal of Futures Markets,* Vol. 12, No. 2, April, pp. 123–137.

Huag, Espen Gaarder (1993). "Opportunities and Perils of Using Option Sensitivities," *Journal of Financial Engineering,* Vol. 2, No. 2, September.

MacBeth, James D., and Larry J. Merville (1979). "An Empirical Examination of the Black-Scholes Call Option Pricing Model," *Journal of Finance,* Vol. 34, No. 5, December, pp. 1173–1186.

MacBeth, James D., and Larry J. Merville (1980). "Tests of the Black-Scholes and Cox Call Option Valuation Models," *Journal of Finance,* Vol. 35, No. 2, May, pp. 285–300.

Merton, Robert (1976). "Option Pricing When Underlying Stock Returns Are Discontinuous," *Journal of Financial Economics,* Vol. 3, No. 1/2, January-March, pp. 125–144.

Roll, Richard (1977). "An Analytic Valuation Formula for Unprotected American Call Options on Stocks with Known Dividends," *Journal of Financial Economics,* Vol. 5, No. 2, November, pp. 251–258.

Rubinstein, Mark (1985). "Nonparametric Tests of Alternative Option Pricing Models Using All Reported Trades and Quotes on the 30 Most Active CBOE Option Classes from August 23, 1976 Through August 31, 1978," *Journal of Finance,* Vol. 40, No. 2, June, pp. 455–480.

Rubinstein, Mark, and Gerard Gennotte (1992). *Options and Futures Trading Simulator,* Version 2.0.

Sheikh, Aamir M. (1991). "Transaction Data Tests of S&P 100 Call Option Pricing," *Journal of Financial and Quantitative Analysis,* Vol. 26, No. 4, December, pp. 459–475.

Sterk, William (1983a). "Comparative Performance of the Black-Scholes and Roll-Geske-Whaley Option Pricing Models," *Journal of Financial and Quantitative Analysis,* Vol. 18, No. 3, September, pp. 345–354.

Sterk, William (1983b). "Option Pricing and the In- and Out-of-the-Money Bias," *Financial Management,* Vol. 12, No. 4, Winter, pp. 47–53.

Sterk, William (1982). "Tests of Two Models for Valuing Call Options on Stocks with Dividends," *Journal of Finance,* Vol. 37, No. 5, December, pp. 88–99.

Szala, Ginger (1988). "Fischer Black, Myron Scholes," *Futures,* pp. 8–9.

Whaley, Robert E. (1981). "On the Valuation of American Call Options on Stocks with Known Dividends," *Journal of Financial Economics,* Vol. 9, No. 2, June, pp. 207–211.

Whaley, Robert E. (1982). "Valuation of American Call Options on Dividend Paying Stocks: Empirical Tests," *Journal of Financial Economics,* Vol. 10, No. 1, March, pp. 29–58.

PROBLEMS

*Indicates more difficult problems.

14-1 Delta and Lambda

A stock has a current stock price of 54 and a strike price of 50. This in-the-money option has a price of 6⅜ with 90 days left until expiration. If the stock price increases to 55 and the option price increases to 7⅛, determine the delta and the lambda and explain the meaning of the answers.

14-2 Gamma

Assume a stock price increase from 37 to 41 and an increase in the delta for an associated option from .4 to .85. Determine the gamma and explain the meaning of the answer.

14-3 Vega

A stock has a current price of 45. If the associated at-the-money option changes from $1\frac{5}{8}$ to $2\frac{15}{16}$ and the volatility of the stock changes from 15% to 30%, calculate the vega and explain the meaning of the answer.

14-4 Theta

As the time to expiration of an option decays from 85 days to 22 days, an in-the-money option changes from $4\frac{1}{4}$ to $3\frac{1}{4}$ Determine the theta and explain the meaning of the answer.

14-5 Delta and Lambda

ABC stock is selling for 26 and the associated six-month out-of-the-money option with a 30 strike price is selling for $1\frac{3}{4}$. If the stock and option prices increase to 28 and $2\frac{5}{8}$, respectively, determine the delta and lambda of the option and explain the meaning of the answers.

14-6 Gamma

If the stock price changes from 26 to 28 and the delta of the associated six-month out-of-the-money option changes from .39 to .50, calculate the gamma and give the meaning of the answer.

14-7 Vega

The six-month out-of-the-money option for XYZ stock sells for $1\frac{1}{16}$. XYZ stock has a volatility of 30%. When the volatility of the stock increases to 40% then the option price increases by \$.6875. Determine the option's vega and explain the meaning of the answer.

14-8 Theta

An at-the-money option changes in price from $3\frac{1}{8}$ to $2\frac{1}{4}$, while its time to expiration decreases from 176 days to 85 days. Calculate the theta and explain the meaning of the answer (assume the stock price has not changed).

APPENDIX 14A
DERIVATIVES OF OPTION INPUTS:
OPTION VALUE SENSITIVITIES

The partial derivatives (∂) for each of the stock option sensitivities are given below. These derivatives use the Black-Scholes formulas for a call (P_C) and a put (P_P) developed in Chapter 13:

$$P_C = P_S \, N(d_1) - Ke^{-rt} N(d_2) \tag{13-1}$$

where

$$d_1 = \frac{\ln(P_S/K) + [r + .5\sigma_S^2]t}{\sigma_S \sqrt{t}} \tag{13-2}$$

$$d_2 = d_1 - \sigma_S \sqrt{t} \tag{13-3}$$

In addition:

$$N(d_i) = \text{the cumulative normal distribution for } d_i$$

$$N'(d_i) = \partial N(d_i)/\partial d_i = \text{the normal density function}$$

$$= e^{-d_i^2/2}/\sqrt{2\pi}$$

Delta (δ)

$$\text{call} \quad \partial P_C/\partial P_S = N(d_1) > 0 \tag{14A-1}$$

$$\text{put} \quad \partial P_P/\partial P_S = N(d_1) - 1 < 0 \tag{14A-2}$$

$$\text{call on stock index} = e^{-dt}N(d_1) > 0 \tag{14A-3}$$

$$\text{put on stock index} = e^{-dt}[N(d_1) - 1] < 0 \tag{14A-4}$$
$$\text{for a continuous dividend } d$$

Gamma (γ)

$$\text{call} \quad \partial \text{ delta}/\partial P_S = \partial^2 P_C/\partial^2 P_S = N'(d_1)/P_S \sigma_S \sqrt{t} > 0 \tag{14A-5}$$

$$\text{put} \quad \delta \text{ delta}/\partial P_S = \partial^2 P_P/\partial^2 P_S = N'(d_1)/P_S \sigma_S \sqrt{t} > 0 \tag{14A-6}$$

Elasticity (leverage) (γ)

$$\text{call} = (P_S/P_C) N(d_1) \tag{14A-7}$$

$$\text{put} = (P_S/P_P) [N(d - 1)] \tag{14A-8}$$

Theta (θ)

$$\text{call} \quad \partial P_C/\partial t = -P_S \sigma_S N'(d_1)/2\sqrt{t}) - rKe^{-rt}N(d_2) < 0 \tag{14A-9}$$

$$\text{put} \quad \partial P_P/\partial t = -P_S \sigma_S N'(d_1)/2\sqrt{t} + rKe^{-rt}N(-d_2) < 0 \tag{14A-10}$$

Vega (v) (also called kappa)

$$\text{call} \quad \partial P_C/\partial \sigma_S = P_S\sqrt{t} \, N'(d_1) > 0 \tag{14A-11}$$

$$\text{put} \quad \partial P_P/\partial \sigma_S = P_S\sqrt{t} \, N'(d_1) > 0 \tag{14A-12}$$

Rho

$$\text{call} \quad \partial P_C/\partial r = tKe^{-rt}N(d_2) > 0 \tag{14A-13}$$

$$\text{put} \quad \partial P_P/\partial r = tKe^{-rt}N(-d_2) > 0 \tag{14A-14}$$

Strike price (relates to in-the-money versus out-of-the-money options)

$$\text{call} \quad \partial P_C/\partial K = -e^{-rt}N(d_2) < 0 \tag{14A-15}$$

$$\text{put} \quad \partial P_P/K = e^{-rt}[1 - N(d_2)] > 0 \tag{14A-16}$$

Chapter 15

OPTION STRATEGIES: SPECULATING AND SPREADING

Overview

This chapter and Chapter 16 examine the uses of option instruments. The three basic uses of options are speculating, spreading, and hedging. Each of these applications involves the management of risk, with each strategy changing risk in a different way. Speculators take on additional risk by trading options in order to obtain leverage. Spreaders want an option position that is less risky than a pure long or short option position. Hedgers reduce risk by offsetting some or most of the downside risk of their cash asset position with an option position. This chapter examines the strategies associated with speculating and spreading. The following chapter examines hedging.

The strategies examined in these chapters are illustrated with payoff diagrams and pricing sensitivity graphs. The payoff diagrams illustrate the relationship between the stock price and the profit for each strategy at the *expiration* of the related option. The payoff diagrams also provide basic information on the risk and return characteristics of the option position and the break-even point of the strategy. The sensitivity graphs show the relevant deltas, gammas, etc., so that informed decisions concerning risk and profitability characteristics can be made.

Speculative strategies include buying and selling call and put options. Buying an option creates large profits if the stock price changes significantly in the direction forecasted by the speculator. Otherwise, the speculator's loss is limited to the cost of the option. Selling options that are "uncovered" provides limited profits but potentially large losses.

Traders who use spreads and straddles want to reduce the risk of a pure option position. Spreaders buy one option and sell a different option in order to reduce risk. Straddles involve the purchase (or sale) of both a call and a put option.

Spreading strategies are segregated into calendar spreads, strike price spreads, and other spreads. A calendar spread occurs when an option with one expiration is purchased and another option expiration is sold. A strike price spread occurs when an option with one strike price is purchased while another strike price is sold. These strategies reduce the risk of a pure speculative position, but they also reduce the potential gain. In addition, commissions and mispricing often are important factors affecting the profitability of a spread strategy. Straddles offer other risk-return combinations not available when only a call (or a put) is used.

Terminology

*Bear spread A strike price spread in which the lower strike price option is sold and the higher strike price option is purchased. A significant decrease in the stock price creates a profit for this type of spread.

*Bull spread A strike price spread in which the trader purchases the lower strike price option and sells the higher strike price option. A significant increase in the stock price creates a profit for this type of spread.

Butterfly spread A combination of a bull and a bear spread—that is, the trader buys the low and high strike price options and sells two of the intermediate strike prices. This spread is similar to a straddle, but it possesses a limited loss.

*Calendar (time) spread The sale of a nearby option and the purchase of a deferred option. The objective of this strategy is to profit from the faster decay of the time value for the nearby option. The profitability of this strategy also depends on a relatively small change in the stock price, since large price changes create losses.

Delta See Chapter 13.

Gamma See Chapter 14.

Naked call (selling a) The sale of a call option *without* owning the underlying stock. A naked call creates large losses for the seller if the stock price increases. If the stock price trades above the strike price at option expiration, then the naked seller must purchase the stock in the open market at that time in order to deliver the stock into the call option. Consequently, this strategy is considered very risky.

*Spread   A combination of option trades that reduces risk in comparison to a purely speculative position, but also reduces the potential gain. Examples of a spread are: buying both a call and a put option (also known as a straddle); buying one strike price and selling a different strike price; and buying one expiration month and selling a different expiration month.

*Straddle   The purchase (or sale) of both a call and a put option. Buying a straddle is profitable when the stock price changes significantly.

*Strike (price) spread   The purchase of an option with one strike price and the sale of a different strike price. Which option is purchased/sold depends on whether the spreader is bullish or bearish.

Theta   See Chapter 14.

RISK MANAGEMENT WITH OPTIONS

Risk and Options

The principal benefit of options is that the user can employ them to alter the risk of a portfolio. The resulting amount of risk differs from the risk associated with other instruments, such as stocks or futures contracts. For example, as shown in Chapter 11, a speculator who purchases calls or puts benefits from an increase (call) or decrease (put) in the price of the underlying asset, while the potential loss from buying the option is limited to the cost of the option. Consequently, the typical view of risk used in finance needs revision for option strategies. Risk is typically defined in terms of variability (standard deviation) for stock and bond portfolios. This proper use of the standard deviation is based on the assumption that a normal distribution exists. Option strategies alter the resulting profit distribution such that the distribution is no longer normal. For example, a speculator who purchases a call option has potential gains that are limited only by the price change of the stock, but the potential losses on the option are limited to the cost of the option. Thus, the speculator's potential distribution of profits and losses is truncated on the negative side of the distribution, as shown in Figure 15-1. Hence, a speculator in options should think of risk in terms of the *probability* and size of a loss, rather than the standard deviation of the profits.

Another way for a speculator to consider options is in terms of leverage and time. The leverage associated with the option allows the speculator to benefit from correctly forecasted stock price changes, with only a small cash investment in the option. The resultant *returns* from buying call options vary from a negative 100% (if the option expires worthless) to a positive return of several hundred percent (depending on the stock price change relative to the cost of the option and the strike price). The option also provides the buyer with *time* for the stock price to change before the option expires. In

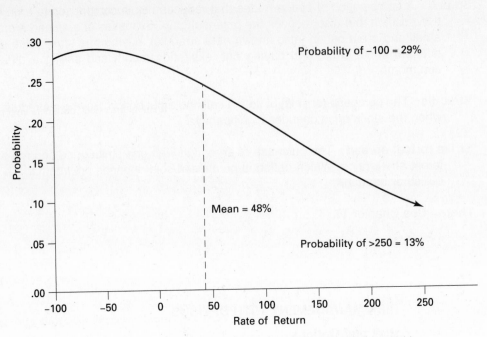

Figure 15-1 Profit distribution for buying a call option. (*Source:* Rubinstein, (1991).)

conclusion, the risks and rewards associated with option strategies must be examined in terms of the characteristics of these strategies, including the pricing sensitivities, rather than by the typical procedure of simply measuring the variability of their returns.

Strategies with Options

The success of speculative option strategies is based on appropriate forecasts of the direction, magnitude, and/or distribution of price changes of the underlying asset, since a change in the asset price is the most important factor affecting the option price. Fundamental analysis and technical pricing forecasts are typical procedures used to determine whether and when to purchase or sell a particular option. Using option strategies assumes that such an analysis has already been completed. While such analyses are far from perfect, the evidence concerning speculating with options (discussed later) shows that the alternative of buying options at random often provides inferior results to simply investing in a Treasury bill.

The appropriate price for a particular option is another factor to consider for those who execute option strategies—that is, determining whether an option is over- or underpriced compared to its fair value. Pure speculative strategies are not dependent on the small deviations from an option's fair value that typically occur. However, strategies using combinations of options, discussed later in this chapter, often are sensitive to mispricings.

The Advantages and Disadvantages of Speculating with Options

Options possess characteristics that differ from other financial instruments. These characteristics provide the option buyer with certain advantages and disadvantages. The advantages of options for speculators are:

- **Leverage:** The percentage change in the option price is greater than the percentage change in the underlying stock. Thus, the rate of return on "invested" dollars is larger with options.
- **Small investment:** The cost of an option on 100 shares of stock is much less than the cost of the stock itself. This relatively small cost of an option is another aspect of leverage, but it is also a separate consideration for small speculators who are unwilling to risk large amounts of money.
- **Limited loss:** The maximum loss a speculator will endure is equal to the cost of the option.

Disadvantages of options for speculators are:

- **Time constraint:** An option is a wasting asset—that is, the price declines as the expiration date approaches. A speculator may forecast the direction of the underlying stock price correctly but misjudge the timing of the move, creating a loss in the option position due to the timing factor.
- **Time value:** The buyer of the option pays for "time" and "volatility." The cost of buying the time value can be larger than any beneficial change in the option price resulting from changes in the stock price.

SPECULATING WITH CALL OPTIONS

Buying Calls

The payoff diagrams and profits of buying a call option are examined in Chapters 11 and 12. Here we enhance the discussion of speculating with calls and then examine the pricing sensitivities of this strategy.

Those who purchase call options typically buy *slightly* out-of-the-money calls having a relatively short time remaining before expiration. These calls maximize the buyer's leverage and minimize the size of the time value. Call buyers are often small speculators who believe they can forecast the direction of the underlying stock or market. Thus, such speculators typically do *not* use option pricing models to determine whether a fair price exists for the option. In any case, these speculators are willing to pay an extra $\frac{1}{8}$ or $\frac{1}{4}$ of a point above the fair value, due to their convictions concerning the direction of the stock price and the potential profitability of the option position.

The conventional wisdom on Wall Street is that 70% of those who buy options lose money. While this percentage seems large to an optimistic trader, the option buyer must overcome both the time value and the commission charges before obtaining a profit. Although the 70% value has not been verified by empirical results for an entire market cycle, Gombola, Roenfeldt, and Cooley (1978) use three years of data to show that over 60% of individual long call positions held for the three months before expiration lost money. During the up market period of the study, 49% of the positions lost money, while 91% had negative returns during the down market period. The average return

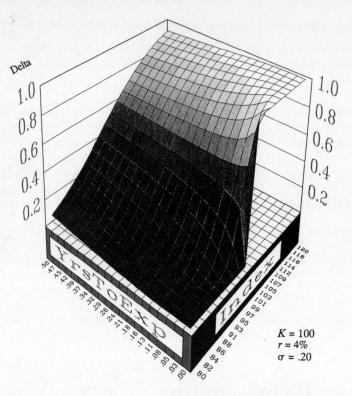

$K = 100$
$r = 4\%$
$\sigma = .20$

Figure 15-2 Delta, time to expiration, and stock price. Yrs To Exp = years (or time) to expiration; Index = index value or stock price. (Source: Created from The Options and Futures Trading Simulator by Mark Rubinstein and Gerard Gennotte (1992).)

before commissions during this time period was −.4%, with an average return of 29.5% during the up market period and a −74% return during the down market period.[1]

Figure 15-2 shows the interrelationships between time to maturity and the asset value on the **delta** of buying a call. The delta decreases as the asset value and the time to expiration decrease. The figure shows the interaction of these factors on delta. The associated **gamma** is shown in Figure 15-3. The gamma is largest when the asset value is near the strike price *and* the time to expiration is short.

[1] In fact, the large average positive returns during the up market period were influenced by some very large gains for the profitable trades, with 12% of the positions having a return in excess of 100%. Commissions reduced the average returns by 4% to 6%. The results from this study seem to be sensitive to the time period studied, since Roenfeldt, Cooley, and Gombola (1979) use the same procedure with six months' less data to determine an average return from buying options of −11%. The up and down market average returns were 50.1% and −67.6% before commissions and taxes. After commissions and taxes, the average returns were −18.1%, 12.0%, and −45.6 percent for the overall, up, and down market periods.

Trennepohl and Dukes (1979) employ weekly prices for a similar time period, showing that purchasing call options with three months to expiration results in an average loss of 7% per week and 48% per option contract. In fact, Trennepohl and Dukes find that even in *bull* markets, three-month call options lose 20% of their annualized purchase value. Of course, such a loss occurs because the decay in the time value of the option is greater than the gain from any stock price increase.

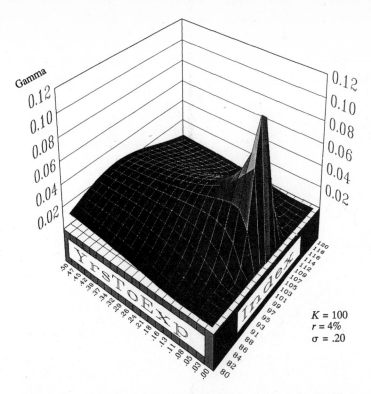

Figure 15-3 Gamma, time to expiration, and stock price. Yrs To Exp = years (or time) to expiration; Index = index value or stock price. (Source: Created from The Options and Futures Trading Simulator by Mark Rubinstein and Gerard Gennotte (1992).)

$K = 100$
$r = 4\%$
$\sigma = .20$

Figure 15-4 shows theta as a function of the strike price and asset value. In general, high and low asset values (for the same strike price) have smaller negative **thetas** (thetas nearer zero). Deep-in-the-money and deep-out-of-the-money options have the smallest negative theta. Figure 15-5 shows vega as a function of the asset value and volatility. Asset values near the strike price have the largest vega.

Buying Calls Plus Investing in T-Bills

An alternative strategy to buying only a call is to buy the call *and* invest funds in a T-bill (or an alternative risk-free debt instrument). This alternative involves using the funds that one would have employed to purchase the stock. The purpose of this strategy is to benefit from upside gains in the stock while receiving downside protection from the limited loss feature of the call option. In addition, the interest from the debt instrument reduces the cost of buying the option. The resultant call plus T-bill strategy has the same payoff diagram as buying a call, but with a lower cost. Such a strategy is advocated by some for leaps (long-term options), since the trader gains if the stock increases, while allowing the trader to purchase the stock at a lower cost if the stock declines significantly over the life of the option.

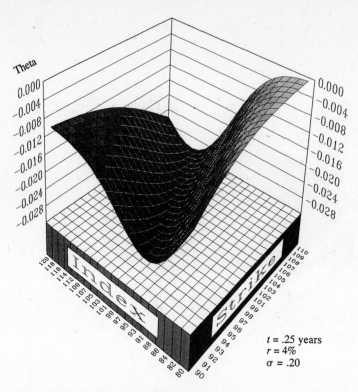

Figure 15-4 Theta, strike price and stock price. Index = index value or stock price; Strike = strike price. (Source: Created from The Options and Futures Trading Simulator by Mark Rubinstein and Gerard Gennotte (1992).)

Merton, Scholes, and Gladstein (1978) simulate the profitability of placing 10% of the total funds available into call options, while the remaining 90% of the funds are invested in commercial paper earning the market rate of interest. In-the-money, out-of-the-money, and at-the-money options are created by Merton et al. in order to compare these different approaches to buying calls. Results are determined for both the Dow Jones Industrial stocks and a stock portfolio of 136 stocks. Return and risk measures are calculated for six-month option positions for a period of 12½ years, with the call option price determined by calculating the Black-Scholes fair option price.[2]

Table 15-1 summarizes the results of the Merton et al. investigation. Specifically, Merton et al. find that buying call options and investing the remainder of the funds in commercial paper provides a superior (lower) risk/return ratio to investing in a stock-only portfolio. While this result suggests that speculating in options is profitable on average, Merton et al. correctly state that the results are sensitive to the time period studied. However, while the Merton et al. study is the most comprehensive examination of several important option strategies, criticisms of their results relating to the option

---

[2] The volatility input to the option pricing model is determined by calculating the volatility over the previous six months.

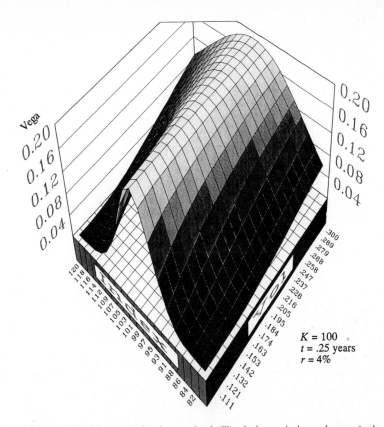

Vega

0.20
0.16
0.12
0.08
0.04

0.20
0.16
0.12
0.08
0.04

.300
.289
.279
.268
.258
.247
.237
.226
.216
.205
.195
.184
.174
.163
.153
.142
.132
.121
.111

120 118 116 114 112 109 107 105 103 101 99 97 95 93 91 88 86 84 82

$K = 100$
$t = .25$ years
$r = 4\%$

Figure 15-5 Vega, stock price, and volatility. Index = index value or stock price; Vol = volatility. (Source: Created from The Options and Futures Trading Simulator by Mark Rubinstein and Gerard Gennotte (1992).)

Table 15-1 Simulated Results for a Call Option/Commercial Paper Strategy

	10% In-the-money	At-the-money	10% Out-of-the-money	20% Out-of-the-money	Stock
136 Stock Portfolio					
Average rate of return (%)	6.3	8.2	11.1	16.2	7.9
Standard deviation (%)	7.8	10.6	15.7	27.2	16.6
Growth of $1,000 ($)	4370.	6372.	11,178.	25,670.	5043.
Standard deviation/return	1.23	1.29	1.41	1.70	2.10
Dow Jones Stocks					
Average rate of return (%)	4.2	5.1	7.2	10.6	4.1
Standard deviation (%)	7.3	10.1	14.6	25.7	13.7
Growth of $1,000 ($)	2627.	3138.	4597.	7287.	2226.
Standard deviation/return	1.74	1.98	2.03	2.42	3.34

Source: Abstracted from Merton, Scholes, and Gladstein (1978), p. 219.

pricing model cast doubt on the conclusion that the call option/commercial paper strategy will be profitable for traders.[3]

Selling Calls

Figure 15-6 shows the profit diagram for a speculator who *sells* a **naked call** option—that is, when a call is sold without holding the stock for protection against price increases. Selling a call option means that the seller is obligated to *deliver* 100 shares of the stock at the strike price to the buyer of the option (if the option is held to expiration). The option seller receives the original price of the option as compensation for the risk undertaken. Since selling a call "naked" means that the seller of the call does *not* own the stock, an in-the-money call at expiration forces the speculator to buy the stock in the open market and then deliver the stock to the option buyer, who pays the strike price. On the other hand, if the stock price is below the strike price at option expiration, the seller of the naked call keeps the entire original call option price.

Selling a naked call is the mirror image of buying a call option (the payoff diagrams are flipped vertically). The break-even point for selling a call naked is the strike price plus the cost of the option. The maximum gain is the price of the option, while the maximum loss is unlimited. For example, if a call option with a strike price of 100 is sold naked for 4 points when the stock price is 100, then the maximum profit is 4, but the possible loss depends only on how much the stock price increases. If the stock increases to 115, then the loss is 11 points (the stock price of 115 less the strike price of 100 less the option price received of 4).

The potential loss for selling a call naked is significantly greater than the potential maximum profit, as shown in the payoff diagram. The dashed line in the figure shows the payoff for a short sale of the stock. The short sale has a greater profit potential than selling a call naked, although more capital is required to initiate a short position. Since the potential loss on the sale of a naked call is much greater than the amount received from the option price, options exchanges and brokerage houses require the seller to put up additional funds to guarantee the fulfillment of the option contract. The margin for selling naked calls is the option price plus 20% of the stock value. If the call is out-of-the-money, the margin is reduced by the extent to which the call is out-of-the-money. The minimum margin is 10% of the stock value. For example, if a speculator sells a

---

[3] Gastineau (1979) and Gastineau and Madansky (1979) claim that other factors besides the time period cause these results, and state the following criticisms of the Merton et al. study:

- The option prices used in the study are 20% to 28% too low because of the model employed to calculate the price, which causes the returns for buying call options to be too high.

- The interest rates used in the model are too low, affecting the return by about two percentage points.

- The volatility value used in the model is too low. Since volatility increased over the period in question, this caused the option price to be too low, as the historical volatility would be less than the implied volatility.

- The method of creating the portfolios generates a bias toward higher-volatility stocks for in-the-money options and lower-volatility stocks for at-the-money and out-of-the-money options. This procedure significantly improves the performance of these strategies, since the time period and an increase in volatility are beneficial. Gastineau states that this criticism is the most important factor affecting the Merton et al. results.

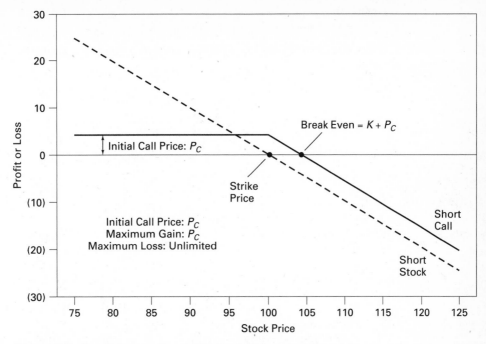

Figure 15-6 Payoff diagram at expiration for selling a call option naked.

naked call option for $3 when the stock price is $27 and the strike price is $25, then the margin is .20 ($2700) + $300 = $840. If the stock price is $23 and the option price is $1, then the margin is .20 ($2300) + $100 − $200 = $360.

Those who do sell naked calls typically sell slightly in-the-money calls, since this maximizes the leverage of the position. However, if a speculator forecasts a significant drop in the stock price, then a sale of a deep-in-the-money option maximizes the total profits on the sale of the naked call, although this strategy also loses more money if the stock price increases (due to the small time value received).

SPECULATING WITH PUT OPTIONS

Buying Puts

Buying puts is covered in Chapters 11 and 12. The pricing sensitivities are equivalent or very similar to those presented for calls earlier in the chapter. Therefore, we will concentrate here on the strategy of selling puts. First, however, Exhibit 15-1 shows the "Analysis" screen of the Option Simulator. This illustrates how one can obtain comparative option pricing sensitivities for different options to determine the best option for a given strategy. The exhibit shows the sensitivities for puts on the futures stock index. The "Analysis" screen also allows users to examine the pricing sensitivities for any combination of options and/or the underlying asset. Two-dimensional graphs of these sensitivities can then be obtained for any chosen combination for any holding period.

EXHIBIT 15-1
Analysis Screen of the Option Simulator for Puts

Sn	Security	NPrice	Value	Delta	Gamma	Theta	Vega	Rho
1	SP500 Index	237.73	237.73	1.00				
2	F/ /Jun86	238.50	239.22	1.01		0.04		0.41
3	F/ /Sep86	241.31	241.45	1.03		0.04		0.98
4	F/ /Dec86	244.08	243.47	1.04		0.04		1.56
113	P/225/May86	1.14	0.85	−0.13	0.017	−0.04	0.15	−0.16
114	P/230/May86	2.28	1.82	−0.24	0.024	−0.05	0.22	−0.14
115	P/235/May86	4.00	3.44	−0.38	0.030	−0.06	0.27	−0.12
116	P/240/May86	6.37	5.82	−0.53	0.031	−0.06	0.28	−0.09
117	P/245/May86	9.56	8.95	−0.68	0.028	−0.05	0.25	−0.06
118	P/250/May86	13.43	12.73	−0.80	0.022	−0.03	0.20	−0.04
122	P/235/Jun86	5.79	5.52	−0.40	0.021	−0.04	0.39	−0.23
123	P/240/Jun86	8.22	7.89	−0.50	0.021	−0.04	0.40	−0.19
124	P/245/Jun86	11.21	10.77	−0.60	0.021	−0.04	0.39	−0.15
125	P/250/Jun86	14.59	14.13	−0.70	0.019	−0.03	0.35	−0.12
148	P/235/Sep86	8.67	8.70	−0.39	0.013	−0.03	0.59	−0.52
149	P/240/Sep86	11.22	10.99	−0.46	0.013	−0.02	0.61	−0.47
150	P/245/Sep86	13.54	13.62	−0.52	0.014	−0.02	0.62	−0.42
151	P/250/Sep86	16.45	16.55	−0.59	0.013	−0.02	0.60	−0.36
176	P/235/Dec86	10.18	11.16	−0.38	0.010	−0.02	0.74	−0.80
177	P/240/Dec86	12.22	13.42	−0.43	0.010	−0.02	0.76	−0.74
178	P/245/Dec86	14.26	15.92	−0.48	0.010	−0.02	0.77	−0.68

Source: Developed using The Options and Futures Trading Simulator by Mark Rubinstein and Gerard Gennotte (1992).

Exhibit 15-2 shows how the "Value Sheet" function in OptionVue can be used to provide the theoretical option prices and pricing sensitivities for puts for different stock prices. The appropriate put (or other option or combination) can then be chosen from this list. Exhibit 15-3 shows the "Selection" function in OptionVue. This function provides recommended trades and expected profits (puts in this case), based on price targets or ranges.

Selling Puts

Figure 15-7 shows the payoff diagram for selling a put option. The seller of the put *receives* the option price in exchange for the obligation to *accept* 100 shares of the stock at the strike price of the option, if and when the buyer of the put exercises the option to sell the stock. A profitable put sale provides a limited maximum gain equal to the put price. For example, if a put with a strike price of 100 is sold for 3, then the maximum gain is 3. The potential loss depends on the extent to which the stock price declines below the strike price. In our example, if the stock price falls to 93, the loss on the option equals 4 (the strike price of 100 less the stock price of 93 less the option price received of 3). The break-even point for the put is the strike price less the put option price. The break-even point is 97 for our example—that is, the strike price of 100 less

EXHIBIT 15-2
Value Sheet Function from OptionVue

SYMBOL:	ABC	STRATEGY:	Single Options		
PR INTVALS:	5	CALL VLTY:	25.0	EX-DIV:	n/a
		PUT VLTY:	25.0	INTRST:	5.0%

	FEB (31)					APR (90)				
	Call Th. Pr.	Put Th. Pr.	Put Delta	Put Theta	Put Vega	Call Th. Pr.	Put Th. Pr.	Put Delta	Put Theta	Put Vega
ABC = 95										
90	6¼	13/16	(.20)	2.9	{ 7.8}	8¼	2⅛	(.28)	1.8	{15.9}
95	3	2½	(.46)	3.8	{11.0}	5¼	4⅛	(.44)	2.0	{18.7}
100	1⅛	5⅛	(.73)	2.7	{ 9.2}	3⅛	6⅞	(.60)	1.7	{18.4}
105	5/16	10	(1.00)	0.0	{ 0.0}	1¾	10½	(.74)	1.0	{15.4}
110	1/16	15	(1.00)	0.0	{ 0.0}	⅞	15	(1.00)	0.0	{ 0.0}
ABC = 100										
90	10⅝	3/16	(.06)	1.3	{ 3.6}	12⅛	1⅛	(.16)	1.4	{12.0}
95	6¼	15/16	(.21)	3.1	{ 8.5}	8½	2⅜	(.28)	1.9	{16.9}
100	3⅛	2¾	(.46)	4.0	{11.6}	5⅝	4⅜	(.44)	2.1	{19.7}
105	1¼	5¾	(.72)	2.9	{ 9.9}	3⅜	7⅛	(.59)	1.8	{19.4}
110	⅜	10	(1.00)	0.0	{ 0.0}	2	10⅝	(.73)	1.2	{16.6}
ABC = 105										
90	15⅜	1/16	(.01)	0.4	{ 1.1}	16⅝	½	(.08)	1.0	{ 7.8}
95	10⅝	¼	(.07)	1.6	{ 4.2}	12⅜	1¼	(.17)	1.6	{13.1}
100	6½	1	(.22)	3.4	{ 9.1}	8¾	2½	(.29)	2.0	{18.0}
105	3¼	2⅞	(.46)	4.2	{12.2}	5⅞	4½	(.44)	2.2	{20.7}
110	1⅜	5⅞	(.71)	3.2	{10.6}	3⅝	7⅜	(.58)	1.9	{20.5}

Source: Developed using OptionVue IV.

EXHIBIT 15-3
Selection Function of OptionVue for Buying Puts

SYMBOL: ABC   TODAY'S DATE: JAN 01   VALUATION DATE: JAN 01
CAPITAL: $1,000   PRICE: 100   CALL VLTY: 25.0
STRATEGY: Buy Puts   PUT VLTY: 25.0
TG. PRICE: Range from 94 to 102   INTREST: 5.0%
RANKING BASIS: 50% Exp.Ret. / 50% 1st St.Dev.Downside Exp.Ret.

		Recommended Trade		Exp. Ret.	St. Dev.
1.	B	5 Apr95p	@1⅝	+606	404
2.	B	3 Feb100p	@2⅞	+216	414
3.	B	1 Feb105p	@5¾	+106	197
4.	B	8 Apr90p	@1⅛	+145	390
5.	B	1 Apr105p	@7⅛	+69	156
6.	B	8 Feb95p	@1⅛	+195	594
7.	B	2 Apr100p	@4¾	+50	237

Source: Developed using OptionVue IV.

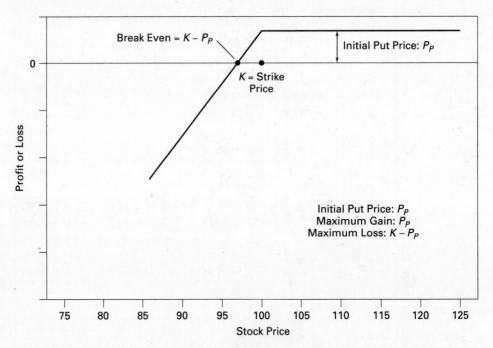

Figure 15-7 Payoff diagram at expiration for selling a put option.

the option price received of 3. The *maximum* loss occurs if the stock falls to zero, which equals the strike price less the price of the put option received. The margin rules for selling naked puts are equivalent to those for naked calls.

Those who sell puts often do so when they are willing to receive the stock at a price equal to the strike price less the option price received. Thus, those who sell puts often believe that the stock is a good buy at the strike price. On the other hand, some speculators sell out-of-the-money puts with the expectation that the put will *not* be exercised. In this case, the speculator earns the put price as the profit on the transaction. Of course, such a transaction is risky.[4]

SPREADS AND STRADDLES

What Is a Spread?

Spreads and **straddles** (which are defined below) are combinations of option positions that are less risky than a single option position, but they also reduce the potential gain. In order to have less risk, the two (or more) option positions must be partially offsetting. The offsetting nature of the options also reduces the potential dollar profit when compared to a single option position. Thus, the different types of spreads generate payoff diagrams with varying return and risk characteristics. The most popular types of combination transactions are:

> **A calendar or time spread:** the purchase of an option with one expiration month and the sale of another option with a different expiration month. This type of spread benefits from the faster decay in the time value for the nearby option.
> **A strike or price spread:** the purchase of an option with one strike price and the sale of another option with a different strike price. The profit on this strategy relates to the forecast accuracy of the trader in predicting the direction in the market.
> **A straddle:** the purchase (or sale) of both a call option and a put option. Purchasing a straddle is profitable if the stock *either* increases or decreases significantly in price. If the stock remains near the price that existed when the options were purchased, then a loss occurs. A sale of a straddle is profitable if the stock price is stable.

Many other types of combinations are possible. It has been estimated that strategies involving combinations of calls and puts, spreading over different strike prices, spreading over expiration months, and various combinations involving individual options, index options, and options on futures, total over one million different strategies! This diversity offers the trader a multitude of opportunities to generate a position with an acceptable risk-return combination, as well as opportunities to find combinations with superior returns if the relationships between the options are mispriced.[5]

---

[4] If the put seller wishes to execute a "covered" position to offset a potential price decline below the strike price, then the put seller must sell the stock short. The effect of generating a covered position becomes more evident when hedging with options is examined.

[5] The payoff diagrams for the strategies presented in this chapter show the resultant relationships between the stock price and the profit on the option spread position. Each spread is a combination of two option positions. Thus, one can develop the payoff diagram for any spread position simply by drawing the payoff diagram for the two separate option positions and combining these graphs. The individual option positions are not shown on these payoff diagrams in order to simplify the graphs and to concentrate on the characteristics of the spread transaction.

Since the spread and straddle option positions are partially offsetting, the net profits from these transactions often are critically dependent on trading costs. If trading costs are a large percentage of the net cost of the spread transaction, then strategies that continually and solely use this strategy are usually unprofitable. Trading costs include commissions, bid-ask spread costs, and costs relating to poor executions. For example, the high commission costs of a full-service brokerage house for trading a small number of option contracts often adversely affect the profitability of the strategy. A trader can either use a discount broker and/or trade a large volume of options in order to reduce commissions. However, discount brokers often have a poorer execution record for trades at the desired price level, which also reduces the profitability of the spreading or straddle strategy. A rule of thumb to reduce commission effects is to execute a spread strategy with at least 10 contracts on each side of the spread or straddle. Bid-ask spreads for trades can also greatly affect the return of certain strategies, especially when the strategy is executed in volume. Care must be taken to issue an order that stipulates the maximum net price difference between the two sides of the strategy in order to minimize bid-ask effects and to lock in that price difference; otherwise, the trade could become very costly.[6]

Straddles

Purchasing a Straddle. The purchase of a straddle involves buying a call option and buying a put option, both with the same strike price and the same expiration month. Figure 15-8(a) illustrates the profit graph for buying a straddle. Figure 15-8(b) shows the components of the straddle, as well as the combination of the call and put. These graphs show that large increases *or* decreases in the price of the underlying stock result in a profit for the straddle purchase. However, if the stock price at the option expiration date changes *less* than the total cost of the call plus the put option, then the straddle loses money. Thus, the upper and lower break-even points for a straddle are the strike price plus/minus the total cost of the two options.

$$\text{BE}_{\text{STR}} = K + P_C + P_P$$

$$\text{and} \quad K - P_C - P_P \tag{15-1}$$

where BE_{STR} = the break-even points for buying a straddle

At expiration either the call or the put will be exercised, depending on which one is in-the-money at the time. Neither option is exercised when the ending stock price equals the strike price, which corresponds to the maximum loss for the straddle:

$$\text{Max Loss}_{\text{STR}} = P_C + P_P \tag{15-2}$$

To determine the profit on a straddle one finds:

$$\text{Profit}_{\text{STR}} = |P_S - K| - P_C - P_P \tag{15-3}$$

where $|P_S - K|$ is the absolute value of $P_S - K$

Example 15-1 illustrates these concepts.

[6] Alternatively, a trader can "leg-in" or "leg-out" of a spread; this simply means a trader executes one side of a spread at one time and the other side at a later time. This procedure increases the risk of the spread. The spreader must also be aware of the potential early exercise of one side of the spread.

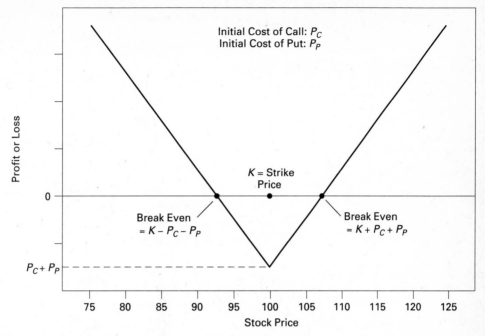

a.

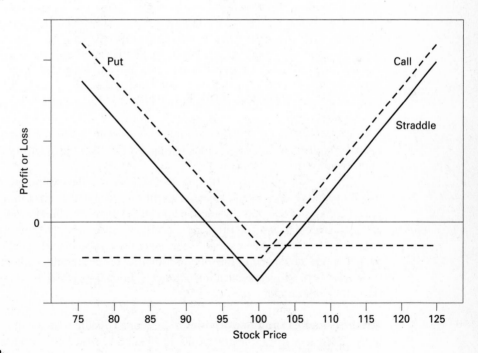

b.

Figure 15-8 Payoff diagram at expiration for the purchase of a straddle.
a. Payoff diagram.
b. Components of the payoff diagram.

EXAMPLE 15-1
Buying a Straddle

The following calculates the break-even, maximum loss, and profit on purchasing a straddle, given:

$P_C = 3$ $\qquad$ $P_P = 2\frac{1}{2}$ $\qquad$ $K = 100$ $\qquad$ P_S (at option expiration) = 103

Break-even:

$$BE_{STR} = K + P_C + P_P$$

$$\text{and} \quad K - P_C - P_P \qquad \qquad (15\text{-}1)$$

$$= 100 + 3 + 2\frac{1}{2} = 105\frac{1}{2}$$

$$\text{and} \quad = 100 - 3 - 2\frac{1}{2} = 94\frac{1}{2}$$

Maximum loss:

$$\text{Max Loss}_{STR} = P_C + P_P = 3 + 2\frac{1}{2} = 5\frac{1}{2} \qquad (15\text{-}2)$$

Profit:

$$\text{Profit}_{STR} = |P_S - K| - P_C - P_P = |103 - 100| - 3 - 2\frac{1}{2} = -2\frac{1}{2}$$

$$(15\text{-}3)$$

Using Straddles. Traders purchase a straddle under one of two circumstances. The first circumstance exists when a large change in the stock price is expected, but the direction of the change is unknown. Examples include an upcoming announcement of earnings, uncertain takeover or merger speculation, a court case for damages, a new product announcement, or an uncertain economic announcement such as inflation figures or a change in the prime interest rate. Ideally, the trader should understand the importance of such an announcement better than the market, otherwise the option price should reflect the increase in the potential volatility of the stock/market. The second circumstance in which straddles are purchased occurs when the trader estimates that the true future volatility of the stock will be greater than the volatility that is currently impounded in the option price.

A conservative approach to trading a straddle *before* the expiration of the options is to sell one of the options *if* it creates a profit for the straddle. For example, if the stock price increases to the point where the straddle is above the break-even point, then the call option could be sold. In this case, a profit is assured *and* the trader would own a put option that is essentially costless. If the stock price subsequently declines sufficiently, the put option would add to the total profitability of the straddle without any risk to the trader. Of course, this approach forgoes any additional increases in the stock price after the call option is sold.[7]

Straddles and Pricing Sensitivities. Buying a straddle with a call $\delta = .5$ and a put $\delta = -.5$ creates a delta neutral position. Either an immediate increase *or* decrease in the stock price creates a profit for the straddle, as shown in Figure 15-9. Thus, if the

---

[7] A similar, but alternative, approach is to sell part of the total position when multiple contracts are held. This strategy reduces the potential total loss, while still allowing gains when a stock price either increases or decreases.

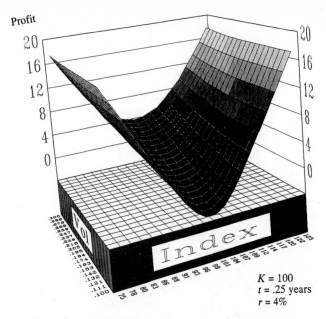

Profit

Figure 15-9 Straddle profits. Vol = volatility; Index = index value or stock price. (Source: Created from The Options and Futures Trading Simulator by Mark Rubinstein and Gerard Gennotte (1992).)

stock price increases, both the call and put deltas increase (the put delta becomes less negative), creating a $\delta > 0$. Positive deltas signify a profit for increasing stock prices. Similarly, if the stock price decreases, then both the call and put deltas decrease: $\delta < 0$ creates a profit for decreasing stock prices.[8] The disadvantage to buying the straddle is the negative theta due to the time decay: The option prices decline as time passes. Figure 15-9 also shows that a long straddle benefits from an increase in the volatility of the stock from the initial $\sigma = .2$ (an increasing gamma), since *both* the call and put prices would increase without the need for a change in the stock price.

Selling a Straddle. The sale of both a call option and a put option equals the sale of a straddle. The seller of the straddle keeps the total value of the call and put option prices, but is *obligated* to *sell* the stock (call) or *accept* the stock (put), depending on the value of the stock price at the expiration of the options. Figure 15-10 shows the pay-off diagram for selling a straddle naked—that is, when the seller of the straddle has no current long or short position in the underlying stock. The figure shows that a sale of a straddle is profitable as long as the difference between the stock price and the strike price at option expiration is less than the total of the call and put option prices received. Thus, the seller of the straddle must take care in evaluating the magnitude of the option prices before undertaking this strategy. Even so, this strategy is risky, since the potential loss can be substantial.

---

[8] Another way of describing this strategy is a positive gamma with a $\delta = 0$. *However,* a strategy with a positive gamma and a non-zero delta would *not* be profitable for *any* stock price change.

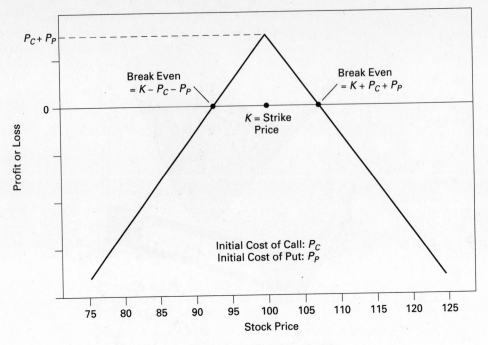

Figure 15-10 Payoff diagram at expiration for the sale of a straddle.

Selling a straddle is the reverse of buying a straddle. From Example 15-1 we find that a short straddle is profitable as long as the stock price is *between* the break-even points of 34½ and 45½. Thus, selling a straddle has the same break-even points as buying a straddle. The profit from selling a straddle is determined by finding:

$$\text{Profit}_{\text{SSTR}} = P_C + P_P - |P_S - K| \tag{15-4}$$

where SSTR = selling a straddle

The maximum gain on selling a straddle is:

$$\text{Max Profit}_{\text{SSTR}} = P_C + P_P \tag{15-5}$$

Selling a straddle is initiated under opposite conditions from purchasing a straddle. Thus, straddle sellers expect that a large price change will *not* occur, since no news is forthcoming. Also, straddles are sold when the spreader's estimate of the true future volatility of the stock is *less* than the volatility currently impounded in the option price.

CALENDAR AND STRIKE PRICE SPREADS

Calendar Spreads

Definitions and Concepts. A calendar spread exists when a call (or put) option with a deferred expiration is purchased while a nearby call (or put) option with the same strike price is sold. For example, one executes a calendar spread by buying a June 100 strike price and selling a March 100 strike price. Calendar spreads also are known as time spreads and horizontal spreads. The name "horizontal spread" is derived from the fact that different option expirations are represented horizontally in the newspaper.

The objective of a calendar spread is to profit from the faster decay of the time value on the nearby option in comparison to the deferred option. Since both options have the same strike price, they will have the same intrinsic values at the expiration of the nearby option. Thus, the price difference between the options occurs because of their different expiration dates.

Profits and Losses. The call calendar spread shown in Figure 15-11 illustrates the payoff diagrams for three time periods prior to and at the expiration of the nearby option, with the dotted line representing the value of the spread when the nearby option expires. The figure shows that the spreader obtains the maximum profit when the stock price equals the strike price and the position is held until the nearby option expires. If the stock price moves away from the strike price, the profitability of this strategy decreases or even becomes a loss. This is because the time values for *both* option expirations decrease significantly as the options become deeper in-the-money or out-of-the-money. Thus, the maximum loss on a calendar spread position is the difference between the two option prices when purchased:

$$\text{Max loss}_{CS} = P_{C,D} - P_{C,N} \qquad (15\text{-}6)$$

where Max loss$_{CS}$ = the maximum loss on a calendar spread

$P_{C,D}$ = the price of a deferred call option

$P_{C,N}$ = the price of a nearby call option

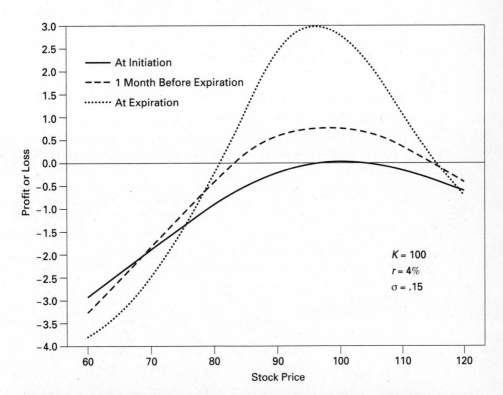

Figure 15-11 Payoff diagram for a calendar spread. (Source: Created from The Options and Futures Trading Simulator by Mark Rubinstein and Gerard Gennotte (1992).)

The break-even point for a calendar spread relates to the *relative* change in the time values. These changes are due to the effects of both the stock price change *and* the time decay. Thus, no simple equation illustrates the break-even point. The profit for a calendar spread is the difference in the change in prices of the two positions:

$$\text{Profit}_{CS} = \Delta P_{C,D} - \Delta P_{C,N} \tag{15-7}$$

where $\Delta P = P_T - P_{T-1}$

Example 15-2 illustrates the maximum loss and profit for a call calendar spread.

Calendar Spreads, Time Decay, and Deltas.   Figure 15-11 above shows that the profitability of the calendar spread changes with time. When the spread is initiated (the solid line in the figure), no profit is possible, but losses occur if the stock price changes. As time passes (the dashed and dotted lines in the figure), a profit from the spread appears as a range around the strike price, which relates to the faster time value decay on the nearby option expiration. The effect of the differing decay rates of the time values of the options is shown more clearly in Figure 15-12. Here, the nearby short option is represented by the dotted line on the lower part of the figure, while the deferred long option is represented by the solid line at the top of the figure. The dashed line in the middle shows how the spread acts over time as the time values of the two options change. Most important, notice that a major part of the spread change occurs near the expiration of the nearby option. Thus, a calendar spread has a positive theta. The rapid decline in theta near expiration shows how a calendar spread can be profitable: The positive theta from selling the nearby option increases faster than the negative theta from buying the deferred option decreases. However, the relationship shown in Figure 15-12 assumes that the stock price does not change. A change in the stock price

EXAMPLE 15-2
Trading a Call Calendar Spread

A trader executes a calendar spread to attempt to capture the time value. The current stock price is 100. A profit is obtained if the stock price stays near the strike price.

	When Initiated	At Nearby Expiration
P_S (March)		102
Nearby = March 100 (sell)	$P_{C,N} = 4$	2*
Deferred = June 100 (buy)	$P_{C,D} = 6\frac{1}{2}$	5

*$P_S - K$

Maximum loss:

$$\text{Max loss}_{CS} = P_{C,D} - P_{C,N} = 6\frac{1}{2} - 4 = 2\frac{1}{2} \tag{15-6}$$

$$\text{Profit}_{CS} = \Delta P_{C,D} - \Delta P_{C,N} = -1\frac{1}{2} - (-2) = \frac{1}{2} \tag{15-7}$$

The profit is due to the greater reduction in the time value for the nearby option (which was sold) in comparison to the deferred option (which was purchased).

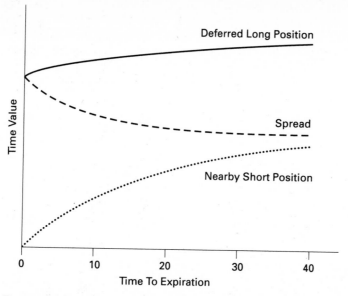

Figure 15-12   The effect of time decay for a calendar spread.

alters these time value relationships.[9] Figure 15-13 shows the delta for a calendar spread for a constant time to option expiration. Figure 15-13 shows the effect of changing stock prices on the hedge ratio (sensitivity of the option price to changes in the stock price). The calendar spread is most sensitive to stock price changes near 95 for our example, and not sensitive when the options become deep-out-of- or deep-in-the-money. This is opposite a long call position, which has a large delta for deep-in-the-money positions. A negative delta for the spread occurs near 105, since this stock price creates losses for the calendar spread. Position delta is also relevant for spreads. Thus, if a spread has a $\delta = .2$, then each option spread has a $20 change in the spread position value for each $1 change in the stock price.

In summary, the profitability of a calendar spread depends on both the different decay times for the time values and the extent of the underlying stock price change. Before the spread is initiated, the spreader must analyze the effect of the potential change in the stock price by comparing the market's estimate of the future volatility of the stock with the spreader's estimate of the volatility. This comparison is a key factor in determining whether the calendar spread will be profitable.

Reverse Calendar Spread.   A reverse calendar spread is achieved if the nearby expiration is *purchased* and the deferred option is *sold*. In this case, the spreader is forecasting that the stock *will* change significantly in price. A large change in price creates a profit, while small changes create losses (the spreader pays for the faster decaying time value on the nearby option). This strategy is used less frequently than the typical calendar spread, since a large price change is needed to obtain a limited profit while a loss

[9] Calendar spreads are also created with a combination of put options. In general, put calendar spreads are equivalent to call spreads, but differences can occur due to either a slight mispricing or early exercise of the puts.

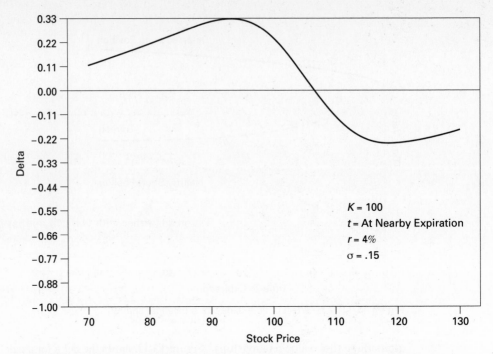

Figure 15-13 Delta for a calendar spread at nearby expiration. (Source: Created from The Options and Futures Trading Simulator by Mark Rubinstein and Gerard Gennotte (1992).)

is guaranteed if the stock price changes only to a small extent. Those who do implement this strategy cover the position several weeks before the nearby option expires so that they avoid the largest decay in the time value—that is, they resell the nearby option and buy back the deferred option.

Evidence. Gombola, Roenfeldt, and Cooley (1978) examine calendar spreads. They find average returns of 26.7% before commissions, although only 53% of the positions made money. After commissions the calendar spreads generated a −22.5% return. However, these results are based on the old fixed-commission schedule, which charged larger commissions than today's discount brokerage houses. In addition, the variability in the results was quite high, with a standard deviation of 89% for the after-commission results. The returns for the calendar spreads were inferior to simply buying call options, at least for the period covered by this study.[10]

Galai (1977) examines the profitable opportunities for calendar spreads. He finds that when the Black-Scholes model is used to determine an appropriate hedge ratio for

[10] This study employed the pre-1975 fixed commission schedule to determine the commission rates. Current discount brokerage house commissions and/or reduced rates from volume transactions can be more beneficial to the spreader than the pre-1975 rates. On the other hand, option prices in the early years of the CBOE often were mispriced, and the use of end-of-day quotes often caused timing problems. These factors make the profitability of studies using such data biased upward. A more accurate method to determine potential profits would be to use bid-ask quotes.

the calendar spread, and this hedge ratio is kept for the length of the spread, then the shorter expiration options are *not* overpriced relative to the longer expiration options. However, when the hedge ratio is revised daily, the spreads are consistently profitable. These profits are cut in half when one day elapses between when the hedge ratios are calculated and when the trades are executed, although the results still show a significant level of profitability. Overall, the results for using the Black-Scholes model with option spreads are similar to using the same model with a hedge ratio between the option and the stock.

Strike Price Spreads

Bull Spread.   A **bull spread** occurs when the strike price for the purchased option is *lower* than the strike price of the option sold. A bull spread is one type of strike price spread. Spreaders execute strike price spreads either with two call options or with two put options (in either case the trader buys the lower strike and sells the higher strike). The two options have the same expiration and the same underlying stock. An example of a bullish call spread is when a trader purchases a call option with a strike price of 100 and sells a call with a strike price of 110. Strike spreads also are known as money spreads or vertical spreads. The name "vertical spread" derives from the vertical placement of the different strike prices in the newspaper.

The shape of the payoff diagram for a bull spread in Figure 15-14 shows how it received the name bull spread: If the stock price increases, then the spread is profitable, while if the stock price decreases, the spread loses money. Typically, the purchased option is a near-the-money option. This provides the spreader with the opportunity to profit if the stock price increases sufficiently and reduces the loss (compared to an in-the-money option) if the stock price declines.

Figure 15-14 shows that if the stock price at option expiration is equal to or greater than the higher strike price—that is, when the higher strike price is at- or in-the-money—then the maximum profit of the spread is achieved. This maximum profit is due to an increase in the stock price. The size of the maximum profit for a bull spread is:

$$\text{For calls:} \quad \text{Max profit}_{BUS} = (K_H - K_L) - (P_{C,L} - P_{C,H}) \quad (15\text{-}8)$$

$$\text{For puts:} \quad = P_{P,H} - P_{P,L}$$

where Max profit$_{BUS}$ = the maximum profit of a bull spread

K_H = the higher strike price

K_L = the lower strike price

$P_{C,L}$ = the initial call price for the lower strike price option

$P_{C,H}$ = the initial call price for the higher strike price option

$P_{P,H}$ = the initial put price for the higher strike

$P_{P,L}$ = the initial put price for the lower strike

Example 15-3 illustrates a call bull spread.[11]

---

[11] Alternatively, the maximum profit (if it exists) for a call bull spread is simply the difference between the two intrinsic values of the options at expiration minus the difference in the costs.

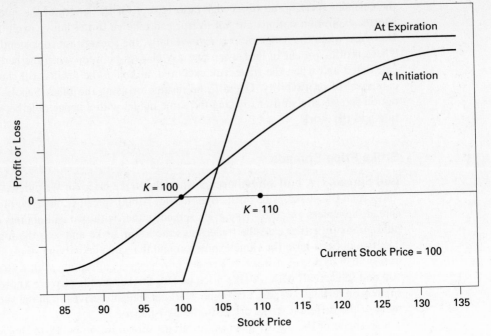

a.

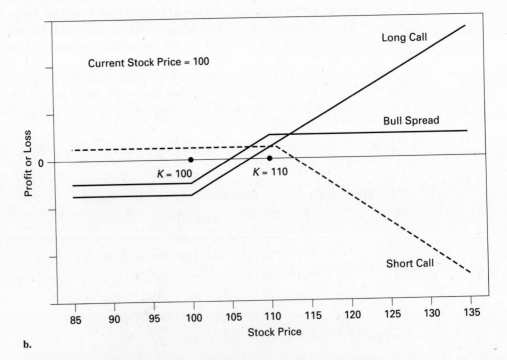

b.

Figure 15-14 Payoff diagram at expiration for a bull strike price spread.
   a. Payoff at initiation and expiration.
   b. Components of a bull spread.

EXAMPLE 15-3
Call Bull Spread

The maximum profit, maximum loss, and profit for a bull spread using calls are found, given a current stock price of 100 and the following information:

For K = 100 $\quad P_{C,L} = 5\frac{1}{2}$

$\quad$ K = 110 $\quad P_{C,H} = 2$

P_S (at option expiration) = 107

Maximum profit:

$$\text{Max profit}_{BUS} = (K_H - K_L) - (P_{C,L} - P_{C,H}) \qquad (15\text{-}8)$$

$$= (110 - 100) - (5\frac{1}{2} - 2) = 6\frac{1}{2}$$

Maximum loss:

$$\text{Max loss}_{BUS} = P_{C,L} - P_{C,H} \qquad (15\text{-}9)$$

$$= 5\frac{1}{2} - 2 = 3\frac{1}{2}$$

Profit:

$$\text{Profit}_{BUS} = (P_S - K_L) - (P_{C,L} - P_{C,H}) \qquad (15\text{-}10)$$

$$= (107 - 100) - (5\frac{1}{2} - 2) = 3\frac{1}{2}$$

If the stock price at option expiration is equal to or less than the lower strike price (the lower strike being at- or out-of-the-money), then the bull spread generates the maximum loss possible. The equation that calculates the maximum loss is:

For calls: $\quad$ $\text{Max loss}_{BUS} = P_{C,L} - P_{C,H}$ $\qquad\qquad$ (15-9)

For puts: $\qquad\qquad\qquad = (K_H - K_L) - (P_{P,H} - P_{P,L})$

Thus, for a call bull spread the maximum loss is the difference between the cost of the two options.

When the *stock price trades between the two strike prices* at option expiration, the spreader obtains either a gain or a loss, depending on the price of the stock.

For calls: $\quad$ $\text{Profit}_{BUS} = (P_S - K_L) - (P_{C,L} - P_{C,H})$ $\qquad$ (15-10)

For puts: $\qquad\qquad\qquad = (P_{P,H} - P_{P,L}) - (K_H - P_S)$

Thus, the profit or loss for a call bull spread (when the ending $P_S > K_L$ and $P_S < K_H$) is equal to the stock price less the lower strike price less the difference between the option prices.

Exhibit 15-4 illustrates the type of information available from the OptionVue Selection function when spreads are chosen. Thus, the best spreads and expected profits are given based on the input criteria. The "selection" function can also be used for the other strategies given in this chapter.

Bear Spread. A **bear spread** occurs when the strike price for the option purchased is higher than the strike price for the option sold. (This relationship holds for both calls and for puts.) Figure 15-15 shows that a bear spread is profitable when the stock price

EXHIBIT 15-4
Selection Function from OptionVue for Bull Strike Price Spreads

SYMBOL: ABC TODAY'S DATE: JAN 01 VALUATION DATE: JAN 01
CAPITAL: $10,000 PRICE: 100 CALL VLTY: 23.0
STRATEGY: Vertical Debit Spreads PUT VLTY: 23.0
TG.PRICE: Bell curve centered around 104 INTRST: 5.0%
RANKING BASIS: 70% Exp.Ret. / 30% 1st St.Dev.Downside Exp.Ret.

	Recommended Trade				Exp. Ret.	St. Dev.
1.	B 31 Feb100c	@3½,	S 31 Feb110c	@ 7⁄16	+3,061	0
2.	B 15 Feb95c	@6⅝,	S 15 Feb110c	@ 7⁄16	+2,981	0
3.	B 109 Feb105c	@1¼,	S 109 Feb110c	@ 7⁄16	+2,589	0
4.	B 9 Feb90c	@10⅞,	S 9 Feb110c	@ 7⁄16	+2,295	0
5.	B 17 Feb95c	@6⅝,	S 17 Feb105c	@1	+1,572	0
6.	B 9 Apr90c	@12¼,	S 9 Apr110c	@1⅞	+1,507	0
7.	B 10 Feb90c	@10⅞,	S 10 Feb105c	@1	+1,425	0
8.	B 14 Apr95c	@8¾,	S 14 Apr110c	@1⅞	+1,295	0
9.	B 10 Apr90c	@12¼,	S 10 Apr105c	@3¼	+925	0
10.	B 9 Jul90c	@14¾,	S 9 Jul110c	@4	+607	0
11.	B 12 Feb90c	@10⅞,	S 12 Feb100c	@3⅛	+510	0
12.	B 14 Apr90c	@12¼,	S 14 Apr100c	@5½	+420	0

Source: Developed using OptionVue IV.

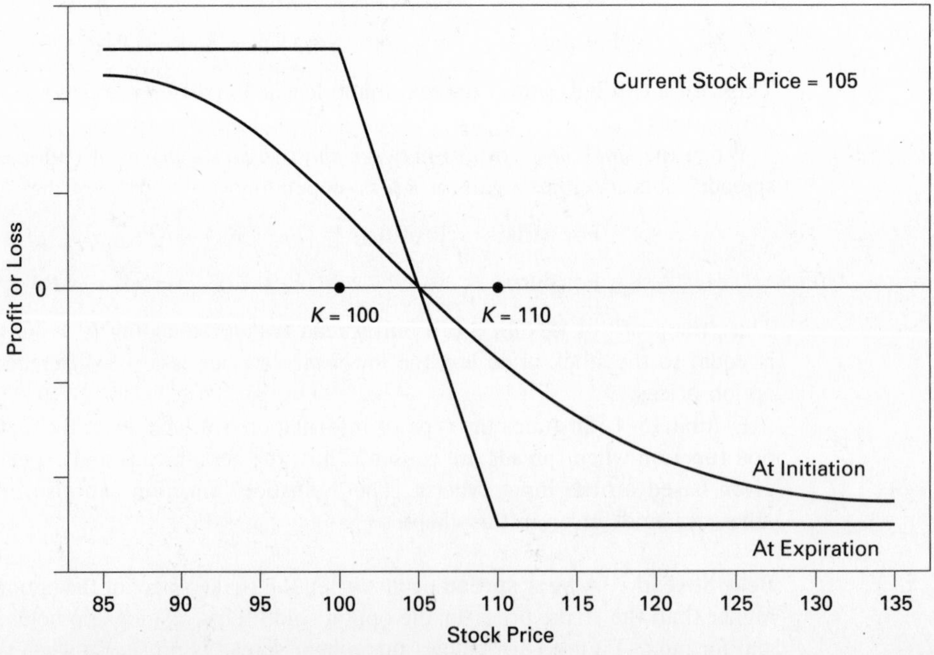

Figure 15-15 Payoff diagram for a bear strike price spread.

declines sufficiently, and creates a loss when the stock price increases. If the stock price at option expiration is less than or equal to the lower strike price (the lower strike price is out-of- or at-the-money), then the maximum profit is obtained. In other words, the bear spreader's maximum profits occur when both options expire out-of-the-money. The size of the maximum profit is:

For calls: $\quad$ Max profit$_{BES} = P_{C,L} - P_{C,H}$ $\hfill$ (15-11)

For puts: $\quad\quad\quad\quad\quad = (K_H - K_L) - (P_{P,H} - P_{P,L})$

where BES = bear spread

The profit on a call bear spread occurs when the stock price declines sufficiently, because $P_{C,L} > P_{C,H}$ and $P_{C,L}$ is *sold* while $P_{C,H}$ is *purchased*. Comparing Equation (15-11) to Equation (15-9) shows that the maximum profit for a bear spread equals the maximum *loss* for a bull spread. Example 15-4 illustrates a bear put spread.

The maximum loss on a bear spread occurs when the stock price is greater than the higher strike price at option expiration. The size of this maximum loss is:

For calls: $\quad$ Max loss$_{BES} = (K_H - K_L) - (P_{C,L} - P_{C,H})$ $\hfill$ (15-12)

For puts: $\quad\quad\quad\quad\quad = P_{P,H} - P_{P,L}$

This equation is equivalent to the maximum profit equation for a bull spread. The profit for a bear spread when the *stock price trades between the two strike prices* at option expiration is:

For calls: $\quad$ Profit$_{BES} = (P_{C,L} - P_{C,H}) - (P_S - K_L)$ $\hfill$ (15-13)

For puts: $\quad\quad\quad\quad\quad = (K_H - P_S) - (P_{P,H} - P_{P,L})$

EXAMPLE 15-4
Bear Put Spread

The maximum profit, maximum loss, and profit for a bear spread using puts (when the current stock price is 105) are as follows, given:

For K = 100 $\quad P_{P,L} = 3\frac{1}{2}$
$\quad$ K = 110 $\quad P_{P,H} = 8\frac{1}{2}$
P_S (at option expiration) = 108

Maximum profit:

$$\text{Maximum profit} = (K_H - K_L) - (P_{P,H} - P_{P,L}) \quad (15\text{-}11)$$
$$= (110 - 100) - (8\frac{1}{2} - 3\frac{1}{2}) = 5$$

Maximum loss:

$$\text{Maximum loss} = P_{P,H} - P_{P,L} \quad (15\text{-}12)$$
$$= 8\frac{1}{2} - 3\frac{1}{2} = 5$$

Profit:

$$\text{Profit} = (K_H - P_S) - (P_{P,H} - P_{P,L}) \quad (15\text{-}13)$$
$$= (110 - 108) - (8\frac{1}{2} - 3\frac{1}{2}) = -3$$

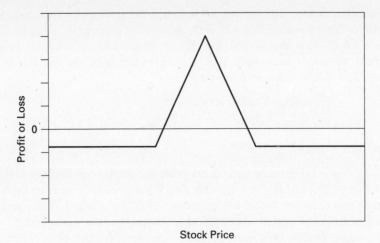

Figure 15-16 Payoff diagram at expiration for a butterfly strike price spread. Buy options at strike prices = 90 and 100; sell two options at strike price = 100.

Butterfly Spreads. A **butterfly spread** is a combination of a bull spread and a bear spread that involves three strike prices. To create a butterfly spread, a trader purchases an option with a low strike price and an option with a high strike price and sells two options with intermediate strike prices. Equivalently, one creates a butterfly spread with a bull spread and a bear spread, and netting out the difference.[12] Figure 15-16 illustrates a butterfly spread. The shape of this graph is similar to the calendar spread shown in Figure 15-11. It is also similar to the shape of a straddle, except that a butterfly spread has a limited loss feature.[13]

Pricing Sensitivities of Strike Price Spreads. Figure 15-17 shows the delta for a bull strike price spread in relation to the stock price and volatility values. The greatest option price sensitivity occurs near the higher strike price, with delta moving toward zero for deep-in-the-money and deep-out-of-the-money options. Figure 15-18 illustrates the gamma of a strike price spread in relation to the stock price and volatility values. This figure shows that delta has the largest positive change near the lower strike price and the largest negative change near the higher strike price.

Evidence. Gombola, Roenfeldt, and Cooley (1978) find that bullish strike price spreads earned average rates of return of 6.5%, 22.5%, and 44% before commissions for three-, six-, and nine-month spread positions. In general, the percentage losses for

[12] In order to create a bull spread, one buys a call with the lower strike price and sells a call with a middle strike price. A bear spread is created by buying a call with a high strike price and selling a call with a middle strike price. One can now analyze the profit situation for the butterfly spread by examining each separate spread and combining the results.

[13] The terminology varies. Some authors call this option combination a sandwich spread. A butterfly spread then becomes the *sale* of the high and low strike price options and the *purchase* of the two options with intermediate strike prices. The payoff diagram for this latter description is the mirror image of Figure 15-14—the graph is "flipped over," with the point of the graph showing the maximum loss possible.

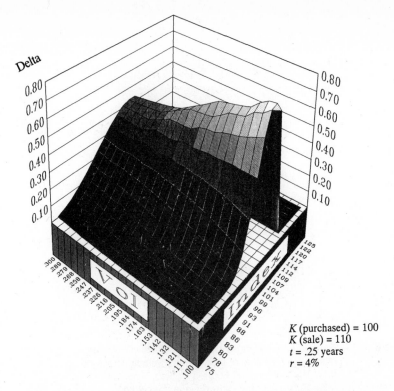

Figure 15-17 Delta for a bull strike price spread. Vol = volatility; Index = index value or stock price. (Source: Created from The Options and Futures Trading Simulator by Mark Rubinstein and Gerard Gennotte (1992).)

the bull spreads during market declines were larger than the profits earned when the market increased, but a larger number of bull spread opportunities created the net positive profits. During market declines, 85% to 100% of the bull spreads lost money, while during market advances, only 23% to 28% of the spreads generated negative returns. After commissions, the returns from the bull spreads fell to −10.2%, 3.3%, and 23.5% for the three-, six-, and nine-month strategies. The superior nine-month results in this study may be linked to the bull market during the time period in question.

Before commissions, the bull spread returns were significantly higher than the returns for simply buying calls, but the bull spreads no longer dominated buying call options after commissions. In addition, the bull spread strategy had large standard deviations—115%, 126%, and 108% after commissions. The bear spread results were much worse than the bull spreads because of the dominant upward market during the time period analyzed.

Pricing Spreads

Pricing spreads is an important topic for off-the-floor traders. Since spread profits are sensitive to relatively small mispricings of the relevant options, some spreaders decide on which option transactions to initiate based on mispricings alone. When examining potential mispricings of spreads, traders must take care to evaluate *both* sides of

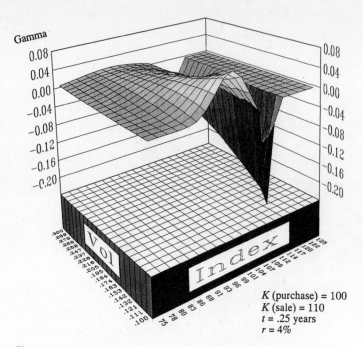

K (purchase) = 100
K (sale) = 110
t = .25 years
r = 4%

Figure 15-18 Gamma for a bull strike price spread. Vol = volatility;
Index = index value or stock price. (Source: Created
from The Options and Futures Trading Simulator by
Mark Rubinstein and Gerard Gennotte (1992).)

the spread. On many occasions, if one option is mispriced, other options on the same stock have similar "mispricings." In effect, these "mispricings" simply show that the implied volatility measures for these options differ from the estimate of the volatility used in the option model. In order to make a meaningful comparison of option prices using implied volatility, keep in mind that:

- Options with different *expirations* can have different annualized implied volatilities.
- The near-the-money, nearby option typically has the best estimate of the actual future stock volatility.
- Differences in the timing of the last trade for different options create different implied volatilities for the various options.

Calendar spreads are particularly sensitive to a mispricing of the nearby option. Unfortunately, in this case it is difficult to compare the implied volatilities of the two options, since they possess different expirations. Other option spread combinations can be profitable when the trader believes the market is using an inappropriate volatility value in the option pricing formula. Thus, inappropriate implied volatilities are also a possible cause of a mispriced option, although this type of mispricing is more difficult to determine with certainty. For example, a calendar spread is initiated when a trader believes the stock price will be stable over the time period of the spread, which is equivalent to saying that the option market is overestimating the volatility of the stock in pricing the option.

A SUMMARY AND OTHER COMBINATIONS

Summarizing Spread Combinations

Exhibit 15-5 summarizes the information on straddles and spreads discussed in this chapter. This exhibit shows which options are purchased/sold to create a given straddle/ spread, and under what circumstances each position generates a profit or loss. This exhibit, in conjunction with the payoff diagrams for each spread combination, provides the basic information needed to understand the characteristics of the most widely used straddle and spread positions. Exhibit 15-6 summarizes the pricing sensitivities for these options transactions, with the sensitivities of a call and put given for comparison purposes.

EXHIBIT 15-5
Summary of Spread Strategies

		Call		Put	
	Strike	**Jan**	**Feb**	**Jan**	**Feb**
Stock A ($P = 100$)	95	B	C	D	E
	100	F	G	H	I
	105	J	K	L	M

Name of Strategy	**Combination of Options Needed***	**Profit**	**Loss**
Straddle purchase	Buy F and H	Large increases or decreases in A	Small changes in A
Straddle sale	Sell F and H	Small changes in A	Large changes in A
Calendar spread	Sell F and buy G (or sell H and buy I)	Small changes in A; profit due to faster time decay for F	Large or moderate change in A
Reverse calendar spread	Buy F and sell G	Large change in A (profit limited)	Small change in A
Bull strike price spread	Buy F and sell J (or buy H and sell L)	A increases moderately	A decreases or remains same
Bear strike price spread	Buy F and sell B (or buy H and sell D)	A declines moderately	A increases or remains same
Butterfly spread	Buy B and J, sell 2 F	Small changes in A	Large changes in A (but limited loss)

*Often many different combinations are relevant. Only one combination is given here.

EXHIBIT 15-6
The Relationship Between Pricing Sensitivities and Option Strategies

Strategy	At Initiation		
	Delta	Gamma	Theta
Buy a call	+	+	−
Buy a put	−	+	−
Straddle purchase: buy both a call and a put	0	+	−
Straddle sale: sell both a call and a put	0	−	+
Calendar spread: sell shorter expiration, buy longer expiration	0	−	+
Reverse calendar spread: buy shorter expiration, sell longer expiration	0	+	−
Bull strike price spread: buy higher strike, sell lower strike	+	0	0
Bear strike price spread: buy lower strike, sell higher strike	−	0	0
Butterfly spread: sell two near-the-money calls, buy one in-the-money call and one out-of-the-money call	0	−	+

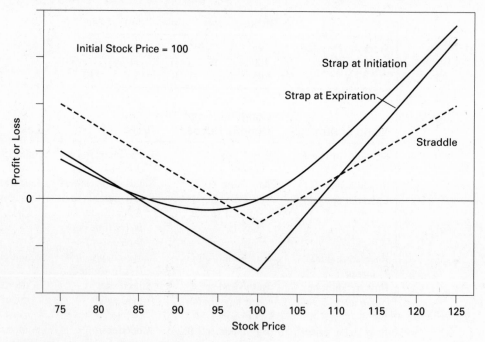

Figure 15-19 Strap versus a straddle.

Other Spreads and Option Combinations

Exhibit 15-7 provides summary information on spreads that are used less frequently by traders. These option positions are given in summary form because they are less

EXHIBIT 15-7
Summary of Other Option Strategies

Stock A (P = 100)	Strike	Call Jan	Call Feb	Put Jan	Put Feb
	95	B	C	D	E
	100	F	G	H	I
	105	J	K	L	M

Name of Strategy	Combination of Options Needed*	Profit	Loss
Strap	Buy 2 F and 1 H	Greater upside leverage than a straddle	Greater cost than a straddle (greater loss if A declines)
Strip	Buy 1 F and 2 H	Greater downside leverage than a straddle	Greater cost than a straddle (greater loss if A increases)
Diagonal bull spread	Buy G and sell J	If A increases moderately, preferably changing later	A declines or remains the same
Box spread	Buy F and sell J Buy L and sell H	When options are mispriced	If commissions are too high
Option hedge	Buy A, sell 2 F	Like selling a straddle	Large change in A
Reverse option hedge	Sell A, buy 2 F	Like buying a straddle	Small change in A

*Often many different combinations are relevant. Only one combination is given here.

popular than the other strategies and/or they provide payoff diagrams that are equivalent to the combinations discussed above.

Perhaps the most interesting strategies given in Exhibit 15-7 are the strap and the strip. These spread combinations provide greater leverage than other option positions, since more options are bought than sold, or vice versa. Figure 15-19 shows a strap before and at option expiration, and a straddle at expiration. The figure shows that the strap is similar to a straddle, except that the strap has greater upside leverage and loses more than a straddle if the stock declines in price. Both of these features of a strap are due to the fact that the trader buys two call options and one put option. On the other hand, the strip combination involves buying one call option and two puts. Thus, a strip is more profitable than a straddle when stock prices decline, while the upside performance of a strip is inferior to a straddle.

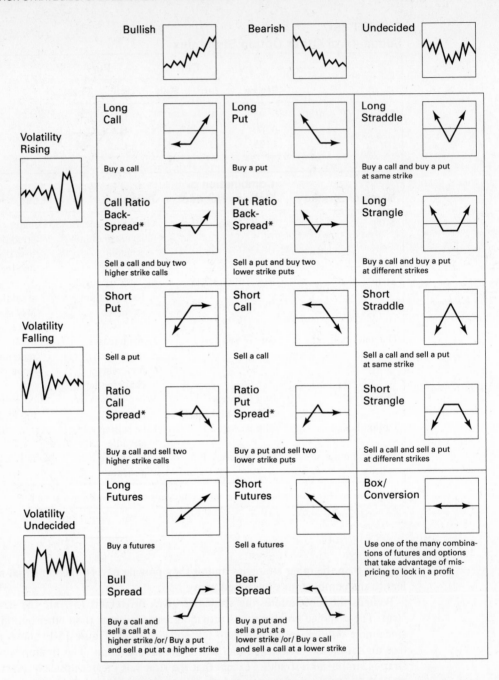

Exhibit 15-8 Initiating a market position with options. *All ratio spreads and ratio backspreads need more analysis. These strategies do not fit neatly into any of the nine market scenarios. Define your market expectation more closely and work out examples with different market scenarios before choosing these strategies. Also, ratio strategies are sometimes done at ratios other than one by two. (Source: Chicago Mercantile Exchange, *Futures and Options Strategy Guide*, p. 1.)

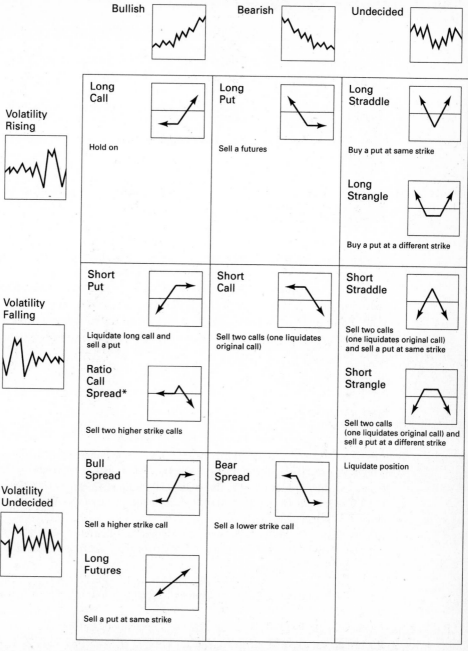

Exhibit 15-9 Follow-up strategies to buying a call option. *All ratio spreads and ratio backspreads need more analysis. These strategies do not fit neatly into any of the nine market scenarios. Define your market expectation more closely and work out examples with different market scenarios before choosing these strategies. Also, ratio strategies are sometimes done at ratios other than one by two. (Source: Chicago Mercantile Exchange, *Futures and Options Strategy Guide*, p. 11.)

Choosing a Strategy and Follow-Up Strategies

The initial option strategy employed by a speculator depends on the speculator's forecast of the direction of the market and any change in volatility. Exhibit 15-8 shows the appropriate strategies for each combination of market direction and volatility.

Once a strategy is implemented, a change in the forecast of market direction or volatility requires a change in the option position. For example, if a call is originally purchased, then Exhibit 15-9 shows how to change the position based on market direction and volatility. *Futures and Options Strategy Guide* by the CMEX provides such exhibits for the other speculative and spreading positions.

SUMMARY AND LOOKING AHEAD

This chapter discusses speculating and spreading with options. Buying options provides speculators with leverage, as well as limiting the loss on the position to the cost of the option. However, option speculators lose money the majority of the time. This chapter also discusses the strategies related to spreading. Spreading allows the trader to reduce the risk and net cost of the position by taking partially offsetting option positions, but it also limits the upside potential. In addition, spread results adversely suffer from large commission charges. The following chapter examines hedging with options.

BIBLIOGRAPHY

Gastineau, Gary L. (1979). *The Stock Options Manual,* 2d ed. New York: McGraw-Hill.

Gastineau, Gary L., and Albert Madansky (1979). "Why Simulations Are an Unreliable Test of Option Strategies," *Financial Analysts Journal,* Vol. 35, No. 5, September–October, pp. 61–76.

Gombola, Michael J., Rodney L. Roenfeldt, and Philip L. Cooley (1978). "Spreading Strategies in CBOE Options: Evidence on Market Performance," *Journal of Financial Research,* Vol. 1, No. 1, Winter, pp. 35–44.

Merton, Robert C., Myron S. Scholes, and Mathew L. Gladstein (1978). "The Returns and Risk of Alternative Option Portfolio Investment Strategies," *Journal of Business,* Vol. 51, No. 2, April, pp. 183–242.

Roenfeldt, Rodney L., Philip L. Cooley, and Michael J. Gombola (1979). "Market Performance of Options on the Chicago Board Options Exchange," *Journal of Business Research,* Vol. 7, pp. 95–107.

Rubinstein, Mark (1991). "Classnotes," The University of California at Berkeley.

Rubinstein, Mark, and Gerard Gennotte (1992). *Options and Futures Trading Simulator,* Version 2.0.

Trennepohl, Gary L., and William P. Dukes (1979). "Return and Risk from Listed Option Investments," *Journal of Financial Research,* Spring, Vol. 2, No. 1, pp. 37–49.

PROBLEMS

*Indicates more difficult problems.

Below is a partial listing of option prices for Atlas Signal stock. Use this information to answer questions 15-1 through 15-5.

Stock Price	Strike Price	Call Prices			Put Prices		
		May	June	July	May	June	July
97⅛	90	7⅛	7¾	10	r	⅜	1⅛
97⅛	95	2¼	4⅜	6¼	1⁄16	1½	2¹¹⁄₁₆
97⅛	100	1⁄16	2	3½	2⅞	4	r
97⅛	105	1⁄16	¾	1⅞	8¼	8	r

15-1 Straddle Purchase

If a speculator purchases a straddle at the June 95 strike prices, determine what stock prices (at option expiration) will allow him or her to break even. (Use the data above.)

15-2 Straddle Sale

Assuming a July 90 straddle is sold, and the stock price at option expiration rises to 100¼, determine the total profit earned by the speculator. (Use the data above.)

15-3 Bull Spread

Assume that a bullish spread is initiated using the June 95 and 100 calls. If the stock price at expiration rises to 101, calculate the total profit earned. (Use the data above.)

15-4 Bear Spread

If a bearish spread using the July 95 and 100 calls is initiated and the stock price subsequently falls to 96¼ at option expiration, determine the speculator's profit. (Use the data above.)

*15-5 Butterfly Spread

Assume that a speculator initiates a butterfly spread using the June 90, 95, and 100 calls. Calculate the profit, assuming the stock price at expiration is 96. (Use the data above.)

15-6 Selling a Call

A speculator sells a July 95 call option for 1¼. If the stock price at option expiration is 96⅞, determine the profit or loss to the speculator.

15-7 Call Calendar Spread

Find the profit and the maximum loss for the following call calendar spread: On June 1, sell 100 contracts of the July 20 calls at 1¹⁄₁₆ and buy 100 August 20 calls at 1⅝. On July 10, the July 20 call trades at 3 and the August 20 call is at 3¼.

*15-8   Put Calendar Spread

On June 9, Mr. Cox believes that the price of UL stock will remain stable for the next month. He then initiates 20 put calendar spreads. Determine the possible maximum loss and the eventual profit/loss on July 9, given:

Date	Stock	Strike	June Put	July Put
June 9	117⅞	110	1⅜	2½
July 9	114½	110	½	2½

*15-9   Call Calendar Spread

Date	Stock Price	Strike Price	July Call	August Call
June 9	44⅛	40	4⅝	5⅝
July 9	38	40	0	⅝

Today is June 9 and above are today's prices for Boeing stock and options. Ms. Jackson has predicted the prices for July 9 as given above. Should she initiate a call calendar spread or a reverse call calendar spread to profit from her predictions? Show your reasoning.

*15-10   Bull Put Spread

PM trades at 78½. Determine the profit, maximum loss, and maximum profit for a bull put spread when the 75 put sells for ¾ and the 80 put sells for 2¾.

*15-11   Diagonal Bull Spread

Ms. Myers anticipates that the price of ABC stock will increase. Consequently, she initiates 10 diagonal bull call spreads on June 9. Calculate the profit/loss on June 19, based on the following prices:

Date	Stock	Strike	June	July
June 9	90½	90	1⁷⁄₁₆	2⅞
		95	³⁄₁₆	⅞
June 19	95	90	4⅞	5¾
		95	¹⁄₁₆	2¼

*15-12   Bear Put Spread

A speculator sets up a bear put spread using P&G options, with a 47½ strike selling for 1⅜ and a 50 strike selling for 2½. The P&G stock price is at 50. Given this information, what is the actual profit, maximum profit, and maximum loss?

*15-13 Buying a Strap

Compute the break-even prices and maximum loss when a strap is purchased on CBS stock. The stock price is 194⅜, the strike price of the options is 200, and the July call and put are priced at 1⅜ and 6½, respectively. If the stock price increases to 208⅝, determine the rate of return for the strap's owner.

*15-14 Strips

US Surgical sells for 104. The August 105 call sells for 5¼, while the 105 put is priced at 5⅞. Determine the break-even, profit, and maximum loss if a strip is purchased.

Chapter 16

HEDGING WITH OPTIONS

Overview

The purpose of hedging strategies is to reduce downside risk. In addition, using options to implement hedging strategies achieves risk-return characteristics that are not available when other hedging strategies are undertaken. Two basic option hedging strategies are selling a call option while buying/owning the stock, and buying a put option while owning the stock. Selling the call and buying stock is a popular institutional strategy called covered option writing. This strategy reduces the downside risk moderately, while providing the hedger with an income equal to the price of the option. However, covered call writing eliminates most of the upside potential of the stock. Evidence concerning this strategy shows that its risk-return characteristics are often superior to owning the stock or speculating in options. Another hedging strategy, buying a put while owning the stock, protects the hedger from a decline in the price of the stock while keeping the upside potential intact. This protection creates a cost to the hedger, this cost being the price of the put.

Terminology

*Covered option writing (covered call)   The sale of a call option in conjunction with the purchase or ownership of the underlying stock. The time value received from the sale of the call option enhances the total portfolio return, while the option price received provides partial downside protection against a decline in the value of the stock. However, this strategy does not fully participate in stock price increases.

*Hedging (with options)   Taking a position in options which reduces the potential downside loss of the combined asset/option portfolio in comparison to the asset-only position.

Opportunity loss   Foregoing a gain (or reducing a loss) by not taking a specific action.

*Protective put   An option hedging strategy where a put is purchased in order to provide protection against a decline in the value of the currently held stock position.

Ratio writing   The sale of call options such that the number of options sold is a multiple of the number of stock shares owned.

COVERED OPTION WRITING

The Concepts

Covered option writing involves the sale of a call option and the ownership of the underlying stock, with the covered writer receiving the option price from the buyer when the option is *sold*. Covered option writing is often referred to as a covered call. A simple example of a covered call is when a stock is purchased at 100 and an at-the-money call option is sold for a price of 4. If the stock price is above 100 at option expiration, then a profit of 4 is made on the transaction.

The payoff diagram shown in Figure 16-1 illustrates the basic characteristics, advantages, and disadvantages of this **hedging** procedure. The dashed line in Figure 16-1 represents the stock-only position, which is useful for comparison purposes. The solid line shows the payoff diagram for a covered call initiated with a strike price of K, with the stock being purchased at price K. Three important points are highlighted in the graph:

- The maximum profit for a covered call when the stock is purchased at the strike price is the price of the call option.
- The stock-only and covered call graphs cross when the option price equals the profit on the stock-only position. When the stock price is greater than this value, the stock-only position provides greater profits, and vice versa.

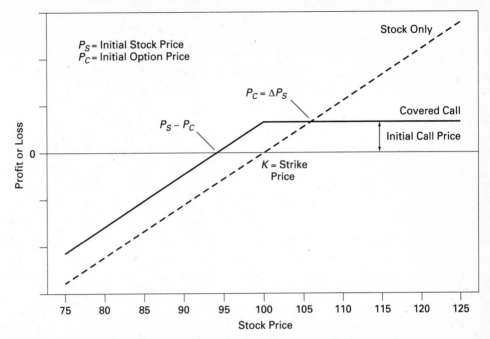

Figure 16-1 Payoff diagram at expiration for writing a covered call option. Figure depicts stock purchased at option strike price.

- The break-even of the covered call occurs at the stock price less the call option price. This break-even occurs at a price that is *less* than the corresponding break-even for the stock.

A covered call is like "selling insurance": The writer receives a premium to protect the call option buyer from a decline in price. Another way to think of covered calls is in terms of replicating the position with a dynamic stock position. In this case, the hedger would *decrease* the number of shares as stock prices rise, and increase the number of shares as prices decline. Figure 16-2 shows how the payoff diagrams for a long stock position and selling a call combine to make the payoff diagram of a covered call. Thus, if one adds the profits/losses of the two individual positions shown by the dashed lines in Figure 16-2, one obtains the covered call position shown by the solid line. The advantages and disadvantages of covered calls are explained in more detail below.

Advantages. The advantages of covered call writing are:

- Covered writing reduces the potential downside loss when compared to a stock-only position. For example, when the stock is bought at 100 and a call with a strike price of 100 is sold for 4, the covered call reduces the downside loss by 4 points. This protection occurs because the seller receives the call option price.
- Writing call options that are overpriced increases the option income received, although the writer must consider whether the higher time value is simply reflecting a higher volatility for the stock.
- The option writer keeps any dividends issued on the stock before the option is exercised.

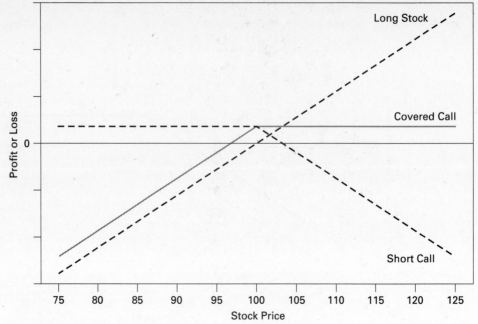

Figure 16-2 Components of the payoff diagram of a covered call.

Disadvantages. The disadvantages of covered call writing are:

- The option writer does *not* participate in any *stock price gains* above the strike price since the stock is called away at the strike price by the option buyer. Thus, covered option writing provides inferior profits to the stock-only position when the stock price rises to a point above the strike price plus the time value. In other words, a covered writer experiences an **opportunity loss** when the stock price increases significantly above the strike price. For our example this occurs at any price above 104—that is, the strike price of 100 plus the time value of 4. Consequently, traders who can correctly forecast major upward moves for stocks on a consistent basis, while simultaneously avoiding losers, should not include call option writing as a strategy for their portfolios.

- Retail commissions eliminate most of the profits generated by covered writing positions executed by individuals.

An Example. Covered option writing reduces downside risk and provides income to the writer. Therefore, option writing is superior to a stock-only strategy *if* prices decline or if stocks trade in a relatively narrow price range. The disadvantage of option writing is that it is inferior to owning the stock when prices increase significantly, as occurred from 1982 to 1987 and during certain periods in the early 1990s. Example 16-1 shows the components of an in-the-money covered call transaction. Notice that the projected return for the example depends *only* on the stock price remaining above the strike price.

EXAMPLE 16-1
An Example of Covered Call Writing

The following represents actual prices for an at-the-money covered call position:

Buy IBM stock 2/25	$51.75
Sell July 70 call (receive funds 2/25)	− 5.125
Net cost per share	$46.625

Since the writer receives the option price at the initiation of the trade, it is often considered a reduction in the net cost of the combined stock/option covered call position, as shown above. The break-even point on this position is 46⅝, or a 9.9% downside protection from 51¾. The option expires in 141 days (4¾ months).

The maximum potential profit on the position is:

Stock sold via exercise of option	$50.00
Net cost of position	− 46.625
Gain from stock/option position	3.375
Dividend received (5/7)	+ .54
Total profit per share	3.915

The annualized rate of return on the covered call strategy is:

$$\text{Return} = (\text{Profit/Net cost})\,(365/\text{Number of days position held})$$

$$\text{Return} = (3.915/46.525)\,(365/141)$$

$$= 21.8\%$$

The Relationships for Covered Writing

The following discussions elaborate on the break-even point, profits, and losses for covered option writing in the more general case when the initial stock price does not equal the strike price:

- The break-even point for a covered call at option expiration exists at the point where the stock price is equal to the original stock price minus the original option price, as shown by Equation (16-1) (ignoring dividends):

$$\text{BE}_{CC} = P_S - P_C \qquad (16\text{-}1)$$

where BE_{CC} = the break-even point for the covered call

P_C = the price of the call option when it is originally sold—that is, the proceeds from the sale of the call option

P_S = the price of the stock purchased when the call is sold

A profit for the covered call occurs whenever the stock price at option expiration is above this break-even point. Example 16-2 illustrates the break-even and other equations given in this section.

- The maximum profit for selling a covered call that was originally at-the-money occurs when the stock trades at or above the strike price at option expiration. The size of this maximum profit in this situation equals the option price received. The writer of an *out-of-the-money* option benefits from any positive stock price change up to the strike price. In general, the maximum profit for a covered call is given in Equation (16-2):

$$\text{Max Profit}_{CC} = P_C - (P_S - K) \tag{16-2}$$

where Max Profit$_{CC}$ = the maximum profit from a covered call position

Any dividends per share received while the covered position is held increase the maximum profit.

Equation (16-3) states the *net* profit (loss) from a covered call position:

$$\text{Profit}_{CC} = P_C + \text{Min}[\Delta P_S, K - P_S] \tag{16-3}$$

EXAMPLE 16-2
Covered Call Break-even, Maximum Profits, and Profits

The following illustrates Equations (16-1) through (16-4) to calculate the break-even, maximum profits, and profits for a covered call position, given:

$P_S = 98$ P_S (at option expiration) $= 99$ $P_C = 1\frac{1}{2}$ $K = 100$ $t = 90$ days

Break-even:

$$\text{BE}_{CC} = P_S - P_C \tag{16-1}$$

$$= 98 - 1\frac{1}{2} = 96\frac{1}{2}$$

Maximum profit:

$$\text{Max Profit}_{CC} = P_C - (P_S - K) \tag{16-2}$$

$$= 1\frac{1}{2} - (98 - 100) = 3\frac{1}{2}$$

Profit:

$$\text{Profit}_{CC} = P_C + \text{Min}[\Delta P_S, K - P_S] \tag{16-3}$$

$$= 1\frac{1}{2} + \text{Min}[+1, 100 - 98]$$

$$= 1\frac{1}{2} + 1 = 2\frac{1}{2}$$

Annual return:

$$\text{Annual Return} = [\text{Profit}_{CC}/(P_S - P_C)](365/\text{Number of days position held}) \tag{16-4}$$

$$= [2\frac{1}{2}/(100 - 1\frac{1}{2})](365/90)$$

$$= 10.3\%$$

where Profit$_{CC}$ = the profit on the covered call position

ΔP_S = the change in the price of the stock over the life of the option

Again, dividends received increase the profits for a covered call. The annualized rate of return then can be obtained by Equation (16-4):

$$\text{Annual Return} = [\text{Profit}_{CC}/(P_S - P_C)](365/\text{Number of Days Position Held}) \qquad (16\text{-}4)$$

- In order to increase the likelihood of a profit (the stock trading above the covered call break-even point), analysis of the stock and/or market should eliminate potential "losers" from consideration. This strategy differs from typical security analysis, which attempts to pick winners.

- The option writer suffers a *net* loss if the stock price falls below the break-even point for the covered call—that is, a loss occurs if the stock falls below the original stock price by more than the price of the option. However, losses on the covered call position are less than losses on the stock-only position.

- Figure 16-3 illustrates an alternative way to conceptualize the payoffs of the covered call strategy by using a probability curve. This figure shows that covered calls truncate the upside return at the maximum return of the covered call—namely, 18% for this hypothetical example. However, it also shows that the probability of obtaining an 18% return is 70%.

Exhibit 16-1 shows the OptionVue Matrix when covered calls are employed. Here, 300 shares of ABC stock are purchased and options on the 95, 100, and 105 strikes are sold. The deltas for the long stock (1.00) minus the short option (−.717, −.564, and −.408, respectively) show that covered writing using in-the-money options is a conservative strategy with a net delta of −.283, while an out-of-the-money covered call is more risky with a delta of −.592. The bottom summary of the OptionVue Matrix screen gives the delta, gamma, vega, and theta of the *combined* positions (in this case, long 300 shares and short 3 call options with different strike prices).

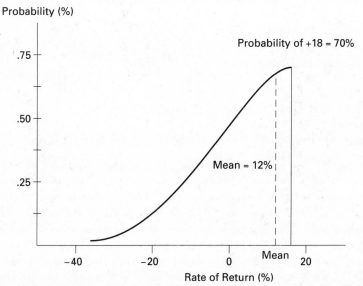

Figure 16-3 Probability diagram of a covered call. (Source: Rubinstein (1991).)

EXHIBIT 16-1
OptionVue Matrix for Covered Calls

ACTUALS							

ABC Com

100	+300
1.00	300

OPTIONS							
Feb (31)		**Apr (90)**		**Jul (181)**		**Oct (273)**	
CALLS	6¼	————	8½	−1	11	————	13¼	————
95	.788		.717	−71.7	.699		.698	
CALLS	3⅛	————	5⅝	−1	8¼	————	10½	————
100	.538		.564	−56.4	.591		.611	
CALLS	1¼	————	3⅜	−1	6	————	8⅛	————
105	.283		.408	−40.8	.481		.522	

SUMMARY							
Orig. Reqmt:	$15,250	Commis:	$0.00	Delta:	+131.0	AvgMIV:	25.2%
Maint. Reqmt:	$10,475			Gamma:	−9.03	Calls:	25.2%
Cash Flow:	−$30,000	Theta:	+$9.87/day	Vega:	−56.1	Puts:	———

Format of numbers with each option/stock of ABC:

(1) Price (3) Long/short position

(2) Delta (4) Position delta

Options are sold on the April 95, 100, and 105 calls (one each). Three hundred common shares ("actuals") are purchased. The summary section shows the net position delta, position gamma, position vega, and the per day theta.

Source: Developed using OptionVue IV.

Covered Option Writing: Strategies and Implementation

The Strategies. The strategies and types of participants for covered option writing differ, depending on whether the hedger sells an out-of-the-money for in-the-money call option. Figure 16-4 illustrates the payoff diagrams for in-the-money, at-the-money, and out-of-the-money covered calls—that is, the graphs show the effects of using differing strike prices. Out-of-the-money options are written by individuals and funds preferring to keep the stock and/or wishing to benefit from a stock price increase up to the strike price. Since the writer must pay a stock commission when the call option is exercised, writing out-of-the-money calls reduces the likelihood that such a commission will be required. Out-of-the-money covered writing also produces a larger

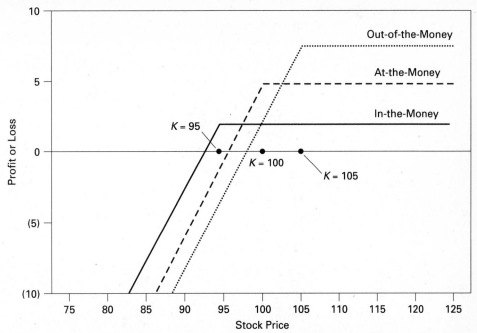

Figure 16-4 Payoff diagrams at expiration for covered call positions with differing strike prices.

overall profit than an in-the-money strategy when the stock price increases sufficiently. This is because the out-of-the-money strategy profits both from the reception of the option price *and* from the stock price increase up to the strike price. The disadvantages of writing out-of-the money calls are that a smaller downside protection exists in relation to an in-the-money strategy, the maximum potential profits are relatively small if the stock does not increase in price, and covered writing in general is inferior to a stock-only strategy for major stock price increases. Example 16-3 compares in-the-money and out-of-the-money covered calls.

An in-the-money covered call strategy is often executed by institutional funds that pay minimal commissions due to large block trading. These small commissions allow the funds to deliver the stock on a consistent basis without adversely affecting the net return from the strategy. In this case, the fund manager expects that the stock will be called away by the option buyer, with the return obtained from the time value plus dividends being larger than the return from a stock-only strategy when there is a stable or declining market. Since the option is in-the-money when initiated, the likelihood of option exericse is much greater than for an out-of-the-money covered call. This larger probability of exercise tends to stabilize the income from writing calls from one period to another. The principal disadvantage of writing in-the-money calls is the lower returns for this strategy in comparison to a stock-only position when a major price increase occurs.

Commissions. Commissions are a major factor affecting the potential profitability of covered option writing. Institutions trading 5,000 or 10,000 share blocks of the stock

EXAMPLE 16-3
Comparing In-the-Money and Out-of-the-Money Covered Calls

To compare an in-the-money covered call to an out-of-the-money position, we continue our use of IBM calls. Here, the shorter-term April options with 50 days until expiration are employed to examine the various scenarios. The April 50 options sell for 3¾, while the April 55 calls sell for 1½. No dividends are received before the April option expires.

Net cost of the options:

	April 50	April 55
Buy IBM stock 2/25	$ 51.75	$ 51.75
Sell April call (receive funds 2/25)	− 3.75	− 1.50
Net cost per share	$ 48.00	$ 50.25

The maximum potential profit on the position is:

	April 50 $P_S > 50$	April 55 no Δ P	April 55 $P_S > 55$
Stock sold via exercise of option	$50.00	–	$55.00
Net cost of position	− 48.00	–	50.25
Gain from stock/option position	2.00	1.50	4.75
Return	30.4%	21.8%	69.0%

The benefits of using an out-of-the-money strategy are: (1) the stock is not called away if the stock price remains below the strike price, saving on stock commissions, and (2) if the stock price does increase, the profit on the covered call increases.

and option typically pay a total of only 10 cents per share *round trip* for all stock and option commissions. Individuals who trade 100 shares at a time through a retail broker pay $1.50 or more per share round trip. Consequently, an annual rate of return of 24% generated by writing three-month in-the-money call options by an institution is reduced to 7% to 13% for an individual who pays retail commissions and only trades 100 shares at a time.

One method individual option writers use to reduce commissions is to use discount brokers, often in conjunction with trading several hundred shares at one time. However, one must take care to select a discount broker who provides executions at good market prices, since option writing returns are sensitive to small changes in the prices obtained for the stock and option transactions.[1] Another approach individuals employ to reduce stock commissions is to write out-of-the-money options, since a stock sale and commission are not required if the option is not exercised. Example 16-4 compares the

[1] A major criticism of discount brokers by traders is that executions are poor—that is, transaction prices are away from the market by ⅛ to ¼ of a point (or more), and the trade is not made quickly after it is received by the broker.

EXAMPLE 16-4
The Effect of Commissions on Covered Calls

Using the information from Example 16-2, the following compares the effect of differing commissions for institutions and individuals on covered calls.

	Institutions	Individuals	
		Full-Service Broker	Discount Broker
For 100 share trades for individuals:			
Profits per share before commissions	$4.455	$4.455	$4.455
Commissions (buy/sell stock and options)	− .10	− 2.08	− .98
Profits after commissions	4.355	2.365	3.475
Annualized return before commissions	24.8%	24.8%	24.8%
Annualized return after commissions	24.2%	13.2%	19.3%
For 1000 share trades for individuals:			
Profits per share before commissions	$4.455	$4.455	$4.455
Commissions (buy/sell stock and options)	− .10	− 1.43	− .35
Profits after commissions	4.355	3.025	4.005
Annualized return after commissions	24.2%	16.8%	22.2%
Break-even protection:			
100 share individual trade	9.7%	5.8%	8.0%
1000 share individual trade	9.7%	7.1%	9.2%

Institutional returns are only marginally affected by commissions, since they pay only 10 cents per share round trip, stocks and options combined. However, the return for individuals trading 100 shares through full-service brokers is substantially reduced. Those who trade through discount brokers and/or who trade large numbers of shares have a smaller reduction in return. Commissions reduce out-of-the-money covered call returns to an even greater extent than they do for in-the-money strategies.

effects of commissions for in-the-money and out-of-the-money covered calls for institutions and individuals.

A third approach is to leverage positions in order to increase the income from selling the options. In other words, the writer buys *twice* as many shares of the relevant stock by buying the stock on margin, while also selling twice as many call options. This procedure often is transacted in conjunction with selling out-of-the-money calls. In fact, if the stock price does increase, then the option writer receives the best of both worlds: additional option income *and* additional profits from the stock price increase. These profits are much greater than the interest paid on the money borrowed on margin. On the other hand, if the stock price *declines,* the option writer has both a loss on twice as many shares of stock *and* the cost of the margin funds, with only the option price and dividends as income. Consequently, this procedure generates leverage that subverts the lower risk characteristic of the typical covered option strategy.

Implementing Covered Writing.   Covered call option writing has become the most popular option strategy for pension funds and specialized mutual funds. Pension funds use covered writing in an attempt to outperform the S&P 500 Index (especially during bear and fluctuating markets). Moreover, since pension funds have few alternatives to holding a major portion of their assets in common stocks, covered writing also provides some downside protection for their stock portfolio investment. However, since aggressive pension funds are oriented toward short-term performance, bull markets such as those in the 1980s discourage these aggressive funds from participating in covered writing. Mutual funds that are authorized to write covered options offer investors the lure of a consistent income higher than short-term interest rates plus downside protection on the stock portfolio. The public seems to have taken the lure, as 15 of the largest public funds that write options have combined assets of over $5.5 billion!

Our discussion of covered option writing implies that this strategy is a passive undertaking: one chooses an appropriate stock and then buys the stock and sells the associated option. However, monitoring and changing the position also can play an important part in increasing the returns for this strategy. For example, if the stock price declines significantly, such that the call option has a value near zero sometime during its life, then this particular option is repurchased and a new near-to-the-money option is sold. Such an action increases the total option income received during the year, although it can result in a net loss if the stock price rebounds and the stock is called away. Similarly, if the stock price increases significantly above the strike price (the time value is near zero), then the current option can be repurchased (at a loss) and another option at a higher strike price sold in order to receive additional option income. Consequently, the choices concerning which option strike price is optimal at a given time depend on forecasts of future stock prices and a tradeoff decision concerning risk versus return. These decisions, in conjunction with selecting the stocks that are the best candidates for option writing, make covered option writing an active strategy. Focus 16-1 discusses factors stated by institutional money managers that help provide above-average returns for their covered writing programs.

The Evidence Concerning Covered Option Writing

The Merton, Scholes, Gladstein Simulation.   The evidence concerning covered option writing is mixed, reflecting the differing assumptions and methodologies employed in the studies on this subject. The Merton, Scholes, Gladstein (1978) research discussed in connection with buying call options also examines covered calls. One advantage of the Merton et al. analysis is that it involves an extensive time period, although this time span is available only because the authors employ simulated Black-Scholes option model prices rather than actual call option prices.[2]

Table 16-1 summarizes the Merton et al. results, showing that a simulated call writing program using 12 years of data provides inferior returns compared to a stock-only

---

[2] Gastineau's (1979) and Gastineau and Madansky's (1979) criticisms of the Merton et al. approach are covered in Chapter 15. These criticisms suggest that the Merton et al. results are biased against covered option writing, as well as reflecting the upward trend of the market during the period in question. In addition, the use of six-month options in the Merton et al. study negates the possibility of generating additional time values after three months if the stock price increases or decreases significantly.

FOCUS 16-1
Factors Affecting the Returns for Institutional Covered Option Writing

Institutional option writers claim that the following factors allow them to obtain above-average returns when using an option writing strategy:

- Call options are overpriced (which is the general consensus on Wall Street), causing call option buyers to pay more for call options than they are worth. If call options are overpriced, then the option writers benefit by receiving larger time values. Overpriced calls may be due to supply and demand factors, or call buyers may simply be paying for potential jumps in the stock price. A ¼ to ⅜ difference in the price on a three-month option is sufficient to make a 2½% to 3% difference in the annual returns from covered writing.

- Short-term option expirations need to be sold in order to obtain higher per-day time values (longer-term options have smaller per-day time values due to a lesser demand from speculators).

- Trading in large blocks reduces per-share commissions significantly, allowing higher returns for this high-turnover strategy.

- Selecting high-quality stocks causes in-the-money options to be exercised 85% of the time. In other words, selecting high-quality stocks with an in-the-money strategy is almost equivalent to "pre-selling" the stock at a profit. Ignoring the quality of the stock creates "losers" in the portfolio, which reduces the overall portfolio return.

- Stipulating the net cost of the combined stock/option position when transactions are made increases the profitability. Thus, the money manager makes an agreement with a block trader to buy, say, 5000 shares of a stock *and* to sell 50 call options of a particular strike price, with the total net cost for *both* positions being agreed on before the transaction is finalized. Such an agreement eliminates price risk and provides the money manager with an opportunity to negotiate a favorable net cost in order to maximize profits. The block trader often agrees to these terms in order to unload large blocks of the stock with only a small price concession from the current market price.

- Receiving the cash dividend on the stock increases the return to the covered strategy by 2% to 5% per year. Thus, options are often written on stocks with moderate to large dividends. While early exercise can keep the fund from obtaining a given dividend, this effect is partially offset by the reinvestment of these funds at an earlier date than possible if the buyer waited until the expiration date of the option to exercise the right to buy the stock.

- A consistent and moderate rate of return policy via a covered writing program typically generates higher compound returns over a complete market cycle than an erratic strategy that has both large gains and large losses. The erratic strategy is often inferior, because the large losses create a lower base of investment funds.

position. However, even though the option prices are most likely biased downward, the results do illustrate one important characteristic of covered option writing: This strategy is *less* risky than holding only stocks, with the risk decreasing as one goes from an out-of-the-money strategy to an in-the-money strategy. In fact, the risk/reward ratio calculated in this table shows that covered writing is at least as good as the stock-only

Table 16-1 Simulated Covered Call Results

	10% In-the-money	At-the-money	10% Out-of-the-money	20% Out-of-the-money	Stock
136 stock portfolio:					
Average rate of return (%)	3.3	3.7	4.5	5.3	7.9
Standard deviation (%)	4.9	7.1	9.3	11.2	16.6
Standard deviation/return	1.48	1.92	2.07	2.11	2.10
Highest return (%)	14.6	19.3	24.7	30.4	54.6
Lowest return (%)	−9.9	−14.4	−17.4	−19.2	−21.0
Dow Jones stocks:					
Average rate of return (%)	2.9	2.9	3.2	3.5	4.1
Standard deviation (%)	3.7	6.2	8.6	10.4	13.7
Standard deviation/return	1.28	2.13	2.68	2.97	3.34
Highest return (%)	12.3	16.9	22.9	29.5	49.1
Lowest return (%)	−5.4	−9.2	−11.9	−13.8	−16.4

Source: Merton, Scholes, and Gladstein (1978), p. 207.

position, if not better. (Smaller risk/return ratios are better, since they indicate the risk per unit of return is smaller.) Table 16-1 shows the adverse effect of an upward trending market on the covered writing results during much of this time period—that is, the stock position has a 7.9% average return, and out-of-the-money covered calls provide better returns than at-the-money and in-the-money covered calls.[3]

Other Covered Call Results. Pounds (1978) also studies covered call writing by employing simulated Black-Scholes option prices. Pound's study examines *three*-month covered positions for seven years for 43 active stocks by using out-of-the-money, at-the-money, and in-the-money covered option positions. All of the covered positions have higher returns than the stock-only position, with the out-of-the-money strategy

---

[3] Merton, Scholes, and Gladstein estimate that each 10% error in the estimate of the option price affects the covered writing returns by 1% for the 136 stock sample and .8% for the Dow Jones sample. Thus, the simulated option prices would need to be 40% too low for an at-the-money covered strategy to beat the stock-only strategy for the 139 stock portfolio, and 15% too low for the Dow Jones sample to beat the stock-only strategy. Gastineau (1979) suggests that errors in the input factors for the Merton et al. simulation could account for errors of this magnitude in the option prices. Such errors would then adversely affect the covered writing results. Moreover, the covered call strategy is handicapped by the bull market that occurred during a major part of the time period in question.

registering the best results. In addition, all of the covered call results possess lower risk than the stock-only position, with the in-the-money strategy being the least risky. During specific subperiods either a stock-only, an out-of-the-money, or an in-the-money strategy generates superior returns, depending on the trend of the market. While commissions reduce the net returns, the covered strategies still outperform the stock-only position. Moreover, the commissions employed in this study were the pre-1975 rates, which reduced returns by 2%–4% below those of the current commission structure. Overall, the out-of-the-money strategy is superior, because it participates in stock price increases and is affected least by the large commissions employed in the study. An examination of the effect of the level of time values on the returns shows that a *decrease* of 10% to 20% in the size of the time value would be critical in determining whether the covered writing program is superior to a stock-only strategy.[4]

Grube, Panton, and Terrell (1979) found that implementing a covered call strategy reduces unsystematic risk more efficiently than a simple diversification policy of buying more stocks. Thus, a portfolio of 5 covered call stock positions eliminates as much unsystematic risk as buying 12 to 15 stocks.

Institutional Results. Table 16-2 shows the performance for an actual managed covered option writing program over the past 14 years by Loomis, Sayles Inc. The Loomis, Sayles program for pension funds exceeds $400 million in asset value. The strategy includes writing three-month call options on individual stocks. The table compares these managed covered writing results to the S&P 500 and stock indexes and the Solomon bond index. The covered writing program was superior to the indexes from 1975 through 1981 for almost every year. From 1982 to 1987, the stock and bond indexes were superior to the covered writing results. Over the entire period the covered writing results (after all costs) and the stock indexes had nearly equivalent returns, with the bond index lagging behind. The summary results for this table provide other interesting information: The covered writing strategy experienced fewer years below an 8% return than the indexes, and it had fewer losing quarters. But the covered writing approach also had only six quarters with returns above 9%, while the indexes experienced 11 to 14 such quarters.

The standard deviations for the results in Table 16-2 provide evidence concerning the variability of returns for the covered writing results versus the indexes: The annual and

---

[4] Pounds also examines the profitability of using a "roll-up/roll-down" strategy of changing the strike price of the option employed when the time value substantially declines due to stock price movements. This "active portfolio strategy" for six-month options is inferior to a "passive strategy" of no readjustments, since the former strategy generates additional commissions. Trennepohl and Dukes (1979) examine the performance of three-, six-, and nine-month near-the-money covered calls by using actual market prices for a four-year period of time. These strategies earn 12.5% to 15.5% before commissions, compared to a stock-only return of .1%. However, market trends affect these results in a manner similar to other studies. After commissions, these returns decline to 6.0%, 4.5%, and 10.0% for the three-, six-, and nine-month strategies, respectively. However, pre-1975 commissions are employed in the study, which adversely affects the results for anyone dealing in multiple contracts. In addition to obtaining superior returns, the covered call positions are less risky than the stock position. Similarly, Roenfeldt, Cooley, and Gombola (1979) find covered writing to be superior to buying stocks on both a return and risk basis. However, these covered writing returns are only 8% to 10% on an annualized basis, and the stock-only strategy is slightly superior during bull market periods.

Table 16-2 Covered Option Writing: Actual Performance Results vs. the Indexes

Year	Covered Option Writing*	S&P 500 Stock Index	Solomon High Grade Bond Index
1975	25.2%	11.6%	9.4%
1976	30.9	23.9	18.6
1977	−.6	−7.2	1.7
1978	8.7	6.3	0.0
1979	19.9	18.6	−4.2
1980	25.7	32.4	−2.8
1981	9.2	−5.3	−1.2
1982	15.6	21.4	42.5
1983	14.0	22.6	6.3
1984	5.0	6.2	16.9
1985	15.4	31.7	30.1
1986	13.6	18.6	19.9
1987	−5.8	5.3	0.0
1988	17.4	16.5	10.8
1989	27.8	31.7	16.2
1990	8.3	−3.1	6.8
1991	24.3	30.5	19.9
1992	14.4	7.6	9.4
Compounded Annual Returns	14.94	14.98	11.11
Annual σ	9.85	12.91	12.33
Quarterly σ	5.03	7.83	6.24
Number of:			
Years < 8%	3	7	8
Quarters < 0%	16	21	20
Quarters > 9%	6	14	11

*Results from the covered writing program of Loomis, Sayles & Co.
Results are quarterly returns compounded to obtain annual returns; all returns include dividends or interest, as appropriate. Number of quarters < 0% and > 9% are actual quarterly returns.
Source: Performance results from Loomis, Sayles & Co.

quarterly standard deviations show that covered writing is less risky than owning portfolios of stocks or bonds. Thus, these results support our general contentions concerning covered writing: Its return is more stable than a noncovered position and it has fewer losing periods, but it does not participate fully in a bull market.

Covered Writing with Options on Indexes. Covered writing with Index options creates the difficulty of generating a portfolio of stocks with the same exact weights as the index option. Using a portfolio of fewer stocks or using different weights creates a crosshedge. Alderson and Zivney (1989) compare naive and optimal crosshedge portfolios for covered writing, finding that the optimal portfolios outperformed the naive portfolios. More important, they find that portfolios of 25 stocks can match the performance of a 100-stock portfolio for covered writing.

Ratio Writing

Ratio writing is the sale of call options in a multiple of the number of shares of stock owned. For example, when two call options (options on 200 shares of stock) are sold for each 100 shares of stock owned, one obtains a ratio writing position of 2 to 1. Figure 16-5 illustrates the payoff diagram at expiration of a ratio writing strategy, which shows how call ratio writing provides a larger profit to the call writer if stock prices remain stable, but how it causes significant losses if the stock price *either* increases or decreases sharply. Figure 16-5 shows that ratio writing has a payoff diagram similar to selling a straddle. Ratio writing is often initiated by individuals who want to capture additional option time values. However, this strategy also increases downside risk.

PROTECTIVE PUTS

The Concepts and Payoff Diagrams

A hedger who wants to eliminate the risk of a downward price movement in a currently held stock can purchase a put. Similarly, a market index put option is purchased to protect a portfolio of stocks. This strategy is called a **protective put,** because it protects the user against declines in the stock price below the strike price, while still allowing the hedger to participate in a major upward movement in prices.

Figure 16-6 illustrates the payoff diagram for a protective put. The protective put provides an advantage over a stock-only position if the stock price (at option expiration)

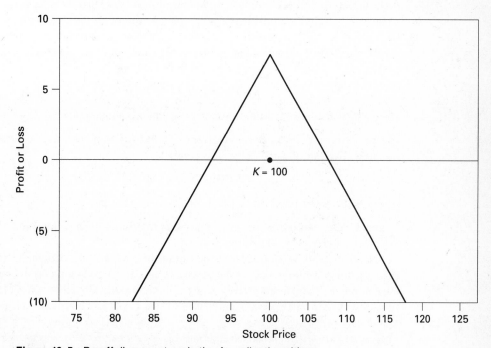

Figure 16-5 Payoff diagram at expiration for call ratio writing.

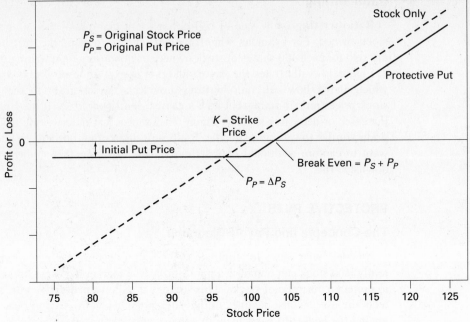

Figure 16-6 Payoff diagram at expiration for a protective put. Stock purchased at option strike price.

is to the left of where the dashed and solid lines cross. Since the original stock price equals the strike price in this example, the maximum loss is simply the initial cost of the put. In general, the maximum *loss* on a protective put position is the put price less the intrinsic value for an in-the-money put, or the put price plus the amount the stock is above the strike price for an out-of-the-money put:

$$\text{Max loss}_{PP} = P_P + P_S - K \qquad (16\text{-}5)$$

where Max loss_{PP} = the maximum loss on the protective put

The break-even point of the protective put is the price of the stock at the initiation of the protective put plus the price of the put:

$$\text{BE}_{PP} = P_S + P_P \qquad (16\text{-}6)$$

where BE_{PP} = the break-even point for the protective put

Example 16-5 compares the maximum loss and break-even points for in-the-money and out-of-the-money protective puts.

A protective put is *equivalent* to the figure for buying a call option: At the expiration date, there is a limited loss on the downside and unlimited gains on the upside.[5] However, a long call and a protective put are initiated by two different types of market participants. A long call option is purchased by a speculator who invests a limited amount

---

[5] Puts tend to be exercised before the expiration date more often than calls, thus the return distribution differs slightly between a protective put and a long call position.

EXAMPLE 16-5
In-the-Money and Out-of-the-Money Protective Puts

The maximum loss and break-even point for protective puts are affected by whether the put is in-the-money or out-of-the-money.

In-the-money	Out-of-the-Money
$P_S = 97$	$P_S = 97$
$K = 100$	$K = 95$
$P_P = 5\ 3/4$	$P_P = 3$

Maximum loss:

$$\text{Max loss}_{PP} = P_P + P_S - K \tag{16-5}$$

In-the-money: $= 5\frac{3}{4} + 97 - 100 = 2\frac{3}{4}$

Out-of-the-money: $= 3 + 97 - 95 = 5$

Break-even:

$$BE_{PP} = P_S + P_P \tag{16-6}$$

In-the-money: $= 97 + 5\frac{3}{4} = 102\frac{3}{4}$

Out-of-the-money: $= 97 + 3 = 100$

Thus, the maximum loss is smaller for an in-the-money protective put, but the break-even is less for an out-of-the-money protective put.

of capital with the expectation of obtaining large gains within a short period of time. A protective put is purchased by a hedger who desires "insurance" against a drop in the price of a currently held asset.[6] The hedger purchasing a put may wish to be protected against a possible adverse court case announcement, a potential poor earnings report, or a failed merger. The hedger is willing to pay the insurance cost for this protection, that cost being the price of buying the put option. However, *continuously* purchasing puts for protection becomes costly, reducing the net return from the stock position significantly. Figure 16-7 shows the components of a protective put—that is, how the profits/losses on the long stock and long put positions combine to equal the payoff of a protective put position.

The figure for a protective put illustrates its advantages. When prices increase, the hedger owns a position with a beta risk that is equivalent to the stock. When prices decrease substantially, the hedger ends up holding a position with a beta equal to 0. The disadvantage is that buying a put creates a cost. Another way of viewing a protective put is in terms of a dynamic replicating portfolio of stock and cash. In this case,

---

[6] This "insurance" is similar to other types of insurance. For example, an owner of a house pays an insurance premium to protect the value of the house against a loss due to fire, flood, or accidents. Similarly, purchasing a put protects against a loss due to a declining stock price.

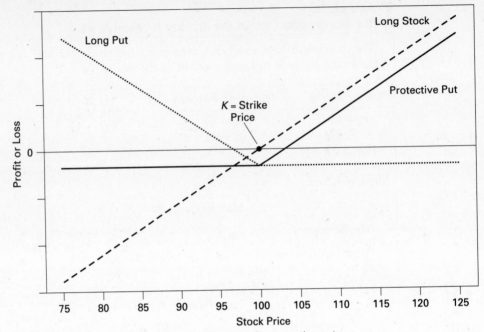

Figure 16-7 Components of the payoff diagram of a protective put.

the number of shares of stock are increased as stock prices increase, and stock shares are sold as prices decrease. This concept is the basis of the strategy called "portfolio insurance."

As with a call option (the protective put has the same payoff diagram as a long call), the profit/loss on a protective put depends on the ending stock price. The equation for the profit on a protective put is:

$$\text{Profit}_{PP} = P_P + \text{Max}[\Delta P_S, K - P_S] \qquad (16\text{-}7)$$

where Profit_{PP} = the profit on the protective put position

P_S = the original stock price

For example, if the original stock price is 103 when the strike price is 100, and the put price is 2, then the profit of the protective put is −5 (a loss) when the final stock price is 99.

The protective put strategy provides a guaranteed minimum selling price for the stock, although this guaranteed price is purchased for a cost. The cost of the guarantee and the level of the selling price are determined by the exercise price of the put and the current price of the stock. Thus, the hedger can choose an in-the-money, near-the-money, or out-of-the-money put. These options provide a tradeoff between cost and the minimum price guarantee. Equivalently, the strike price acts like a deductible on an

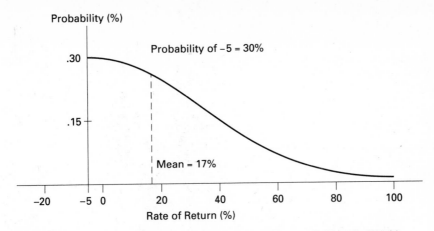

Figure 16-8 Probability diagram of a protective put. (Source: Rubinstein (1991).)

insurance policy: A larger deductible (lower strike price) means that the hedger has more risk, but the cost of the insurance is lower.[7]

Figure 16-8 illustrates the probability distribution for buying a protective put. A protective put (long put plus the stock position) truncates the losses from the stock portfolio, eliminating losses below the strike price. This is achieved at a cost: There is a large probability that a loss of about 5% will occur when the protective put strategy is employed (the 5% loss shown in the figure varies according to the situation).

Exhibit 16-2 shows the OptionVue Matrix for protective puts. The net deltas for the long stock in combination with the 95, 100, and 105 put strike prices are .782 (1 − .212), .538 (1 − .462), and .283 (1 − .717). Thus, an in-the-money 105 protective put is the most conservative strategy, while an out-of-the-money protective put will react most to stock price increases. The combined position delta, gamma, vega, and per day theta appear under the summary part of the screen.

Using Index Puts

Using index put options with a portfolio provides additional benefits in comparison to a protective put strategy for individual stocks. If the fund or individual believes that the market will experience a short-term decline, then buying a put provides downside protection for the systematic risk component of the portfolio. The alternative—selling all of the stocks in the portfolio when a market decline is anticipated—is not usually

---

[7] The insurance aspect of a protective put strategy can also be implemented by "dynamic portfolio insurance." A well-publicized concept, dynamic portfolio insurance advocates emphasize the downward protection and upward potential offered by such a strategy. The differences between a dynamic put strategy and the protective put concept discussed here are twofold. First, in order to reduce the costs associated with buying puts, the dynamic put strategy is implemented only when the stock/market is forecasted to decline (or is implemented gradually as the market starts to decline). Second, due to the cost of buying puts, and since put options often are not liquid enough to implement such a strategy, stock index futures are often employed to simulate a dynamic portfolio insurance strategy.

EXHIBIT 16-2
OptionVue Matrix for Protective Puts

ACTUALS

ABC Com

100	+300
1.00	300

OPTIONS

	Feb (31)		Apr (90)		Jul (181)		Oct (273)	
PUTS	$3/16$	——	$1\frac{1}{8}$	——	$2\frac{1}{4}$	——	$3\frac{1}{8}$	——
90	−.061		−.156		−.204		−.221	
PUTS	$15/16$	+1	$2\frac{3}{8}$	——	$3\frac{3}{4}$	——	$4\frac{3}{4}$	——
95	−.212	−21.2	−.283		−.301		−.302	
PUTS	$2\frac{3}{4}$	+1	$4\frac{3}{8}$	——	$5\frac{3}{4}$	——	$6\frac{3}{4}$	——
100	−.462	−46.2	−.436		−.410		−.389	
PUTS	$5\frac{3}{4}$	+1	$7\frac{1}{8}$	——	$8\frac{3}{8}$	——	$9\frac{1}{4}$	——
105	−.717	−71.7	−.592		−.519		−.478	
PUTS	10	——	$10\frac{5}{8}$	——	$11\frac{1}{2}$	——	$12\frac{1}{4}$	——
110	−1.00		−.728		−.623		−.564	

SUMMARY

Orig. Reqmt:	$15,937	Commis:	$0.00	Delta:	+160.8	AvgMIV:	24.7%
Maint. Reqmt:	$11,412			Gamma:	+14.1	Calls:	25.2%
Cash Flow:	−$30,937	Theta:	−$10.11/day	Vega:	+30.0	Puts:	24.5%

Format of numbers with each option/stock of ABC:

(1) Price   (3) Long/short position

(2) Delta   (4) Position delta

Put options are purchased on the February 95, 100, and 105 puts (one each). Three hundred common shares ("actuals") are purchased. The summary section shows the net position delta, position gamma, position vega, and the per day theta.

Source: Developed using OptionVue IV.

feasible, given the transactions costs involved, the loss of dividends, potential liquidity problems, and the tax consequences. The put option strategy works well if the forecast is correct *and* if the portfolio is highly correlated with the market index. The number of index puts purchased generally should have a total stock value equal to the total value of the portfolio. However, if the portfolio has a significantly different degree of risk than the market (the portfolio beta differs significantly), then the index value is multiplied by the portfolio beta in order to determine the number of puts to buy.

Protective Puts Versus Covered Calls

Figure 16-9 compares the payoff diagrams of a protective put to a covered call at option expiration. Both strategies involve hedge positions, but this diagram shows that their characteristics vary significantly. The covered call reduces the downside loss when compared to a stock-only position, because the option price is received by the writer. On the other hand, a protective put eliminates *any* loss below the strike price less the cost of the put, as well as allowing the protective put hedger to participate in gains on the stock. Thus, for large stock price gains or losses, the protective put outperforms the covered call. For moderate changes in the stock price, the covered call is superior. Consequently, the type of hedge position to undertake depends on the forecast of the *volatility* of the underlying stock price.

The Evidence

Merton, Scholes, and Gladstein (1982) examine the historical performance of protective puts by using simulated option prices for a 14-year period. The methodology of this study is essentially equivalent to their companion study on buying call options and covered call writing discussed earlier. Merton, Scholes, and Gladstein find that protective puts provide an inferior return to a stock-only strategy over the entire time period for the 136-stock portfolio. In-the-money, at-the-money, and out-of-the-money strategies earn 5.9%, 6.7%, and 7.3%, respectively, during this time period, as compared to a 7.7% return for a stock-only position. However, the risk for a protective put is significantly less than the risk for the stock position: The standard deviations for the in-the-

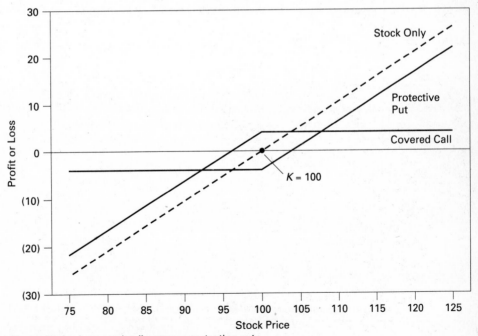

Figure 16-9 A covered call versus a protective put.

money, at-the-money, and out-of-the-money position are 7.1%, 9.5%, and 12.0%, respectively, as compared to a standard deviation of 16.1% for the stock position. The same results for the Dow Jones stock sample show that the returns for the protective put strategies are essentially equivalent to the stock-only portfolio, but the protective puts are significantly less risky. Thus, the ending values for the Dow Jones portfolios hedged with protective puts are larger than the value for the stock-only portfolio. Moreover, the upward trend in the market for the majority of the period of the study biases the results against a protective put strategy.

Other Hedging Strategies

Exhibit 16-3 lists several other option strategies used in conjunction with stocks. These strategies are similar to the strategies discussed above and/or are used less

EXHIBIT 16-3
Summary of Other Stock-Option Hedging Strategies

		Call		Put	
	Strike	Jan	Feb	Jan	Feb
Stock A (P = 100)	95	B	C	D	E
	100	F	G	H	I
	105	J	K	L	M

Strategy	Combination of Positions Needed*	Advantage	Disadvantage
Buy stock, sell put	Buy A and sell H	If A increases, then profit from A as well as keep put price	If A declines moderately, then do worse than A (downside leverage)
Buy stock, sell call, sell put	Buy A, sell F and H	Similar to covered call in shape, but keep both call *and* put time values; profit larger than A only for moderate changes in A	Inferior to A only for *large* changes in A
Sell stock short, buy call (covered short-sale)	Sell A, buy F	Graph same as buying put: profit when A declines moderately	If A increases or stays the same

*Often many different combinations are relevant; only one combination is given here.

frequently than the more popular strategies examined previously. The important characteristics of these strategies are given in the exhibit.

One conservative strategy involving options is called "dividend capture." Corporations buy stock in other companies paying large dividends in order to exclude 85% of these dividends from income taxes. In order to avoid the risk associated with a drop in the stock price over the required 15-day holding period of the stock, the corporation sells a deep-in-the-money call option to execute a hedge.

SUMMARY AND LOOKING AHEAD

This chapter discusses hedging with options. Covered option writing is one type of hedging strategy. Covered writing reduces the downside loss as compared to owning the stock, but it also limits the upside gain. Option writers benefit from receiving the price of the option. The protective put strategy eliminates the majority of the downside risk from holding a stock position, with the hedger paying the cost of the put to receive the required protection. The following chapters deal with applications of futures and options contracts. Chapter 17 involves applying futures to portfolio and financial institution problems. Chapters 18 to 20 involve options applications such as options on futures, currency options, and over-the-counter options.

BIBLIOGRAPHY

Alderson, Michael J., and Terry L. Zivney (1989). "Optimal Cross-Hedge Portfolios for Hedging Stock Index Options," *Journal of Futures Markets,* Vol. 9, No. 1, February, pp. 67–76.

Gastineau, Gary L. (1979). *The Stock Options Manual,* 2d ed. New York: McGraw-Hill.

Gastineau, Gary L., and Albert Madansky (1979). "Why Simulations Are an Unreliable Test of Option Strategies," *Financial Analysts Journal,* Vol. 35, No. 5, September–October 1979, pp. 61–76.

Grube, R. Corwin, Don B. Panton, and J. Michael Terrell (1979). "Risks and Rewards in Covered Call Positions," *Journal of Portfolio Management,* Vol. 5, No. 2, Winter 1979, pp. 64–68.

Merton, Robert C., Myron S. Scholes, and Mathew L. Gladstein (1978). "The Returns and Risk of Alternative Call Option Portfolio Investment Strategies," *Journal of Business,* Vol. 51, No. 2, April, pp. 183–242.

Merton, Robert C., Myron S. Scholes, and Mathew L. Gladstein (1982). "The Returns and Risk of Alternative Put Option Portfolio Investment Strategies," *Journal of Business,* Vol. 55, No. 1, January, pp. 1–56.

Pounds, Henry M. (1978). "Covered Call Option Writing: Strategies and Results," *The Journal of Portfolio Management,* Vol. 4, No. 2, Winter, pp. 31–42.

Roenfeldt, Rodney L., Philip L. Cooley, and Michael J. Gombola (1979). "Market Performance of Options on the Chicago Board Options Exchange," *Journal of Business Research,* Vol. 7, pp. 95–107.

Rubinstein, Mark (1991). "Classnotes," The University of California at Berkeley.

Trennepohl, Gary L., and William P. Dukes (1979). "Return and Risk from Listed Option Investments," *Journal of Financial Research,* Vol. 2, No. 1, Spring, pp. 37–49.

PROBLEMS

* Indicates more difficult problems.

16-1 Break-even for a Covered Call

Mr. Smith owns 100 shares of ABC stock. Its price has been relatively stable recently at about 21½. Predicting that this trend will continue for the next several months, Smith writes a call option on ABC stock to generate additional income. The option has a strike price of 20 and sells for 3½. At option expiration, determine the break-even stock price needed in order to avoid a loss from this covered writing position. (No dividends are paid on the stock.)

16-2 Covered Call

The MJF mutual fund periodically writes call options on selected stocks in its portfolio. Listed below are the results from a 90-day covered call on LBV stock, originally initiated June 1. (Dividends are not relevant.)

	June 1	90 days later (at option expiration)
stock price	23.75	25.50
exercise price	20	20
option price	5.25	5.50

a. What is the profit from the covered call at option expiration?

b. If the stock sells for 30 at option expiration, what would be the profit to the call writer?

c. Calculate the annualized return on the covered call from (a). Is this return greater than that from simply buying the stock on June 1 and selling it 90 days later?

16-3 Covered Call Returns

	At initiation of trade	180 days later (at option expiration)
stock price	7.50	9.75
exercise price	10	10
option price	1.00	0.00

a. Calculate the return from writing an out-of-the-money covered call.

b. Assume that the stock price at expiration falls to 6.75. Calculate the rate of return.

16-4 Protective Put

An investor who owns 100 shares of General Electric is contemplating the purchase of a put option on the stock in order to protect its value, since she is concerned that negotiations on a planned merger with another firm will fall through. After careful consideration, she decides to purchase one put option controlling 100 shares of GE. As predicted, the negotiations break down. The results are provided below.

	Before merger cancellation announcement	After merger cancellation announcement
stock price	33.00	25.00
exercise price	35	35
put price	4.50	10.25

a. Calculate the investor's total loss for 100 shares with and without a protective put.
b. Determine the minimum share price (at option expiration) that would allow the investor to break-even with a protective put.

16-5 Protective Put

Last Chance Associates is an institutional holder of XYZ Corp. stock. A protective put was initiated on September 2 on the expectation that an upcoming quarterly report would reveal weaker earnings. To their surprise, the news was just the opposite: The report disclosed stronger earnings, causing the stock price to increase.

	Sept. 2	Sept. 27
stock price	19.25	21.00
exercise price	20	20
put price	1.00	.25

Calculate the annualized return from the protective put, assuming the report was issued on September 27th and the position was closed at that time.

16-6 Protective Puts, Break-even, and Maximum Loss

On July 6, the following quotation exists for LA Gear and its puts:

LA Gear	Strike	Jul	Aug	Sep
$12\frac{3}{4}$	$12\frac{1}{2}$	$\frac{5}{8}$	$^{13}\!/_{16}$	$1\frac{3}{8}$

A Sep $12\frac{1}{2}$ put and 100 shares of stock are purchased. The option expires September 19.
a. Find the maximum loss and break-even if the stock goes to $11\frac{1}{2}$.
b. Find the maximum loss and break-even if the stock was originally purchased at $12. Why do these results differ from those obtained in (a)?

*16-7 Protective Put Versus Covered Call

Ms. Grey owns 500 shares of Marriott stock, which is currently selling for $16\frac{1}{8}$. The price of the July $17\frac{1}{2}$ call is $\frac{1}{16}$, and the price of the July $17\frac{1}{2}$ put is $1\frac{5}{8}$. Should she choose the protective put or the covered call, assuming the stock price will be between 16 and 19 at option expiration?

Chapter 17

APPLYING FUTURES TO PORTFOLIO MANAGEMENT AND FINANCIAL INSTITUTIONS ISSUES

Overview

The increased volatility of stock and bond markets in the past decade has made the management of these assets difficult. This chapter discusses strategies for dealing with stock and bond portfolio risk and return and the risk of financial institutions by using futures contracts. Money managers of stock and bond portfolios and executives employ these techniques to alter the risk and return characteristics of their portfolios or balance sheets quickly and cheaply.

Bond applications to futures markets include adjusting the risk of the bond portfolio by using duration and creating synthetic instruments to enhance returns. Employing futures to adjust bond durations manages the risk of a bond portfolio. If the duration is reduced, then the sensitivity of the portfolio to changes in interest rates declines. Similarly, if the duration is increased, then the portfolio sensitivity increases. Futures can change this sensitivity quickly and inexpensively. Synthetic securities are generated by an appropriate combination of futures and cash instruments. Synthetic securities often provide a higher rate of return than a similar cash instrument.

Stock applications to futures include using stock betas to adjust risk, using futures to manage portfolio cash flows, and portfolio insurance. Stock index futures are used to alter the risk of a stock portfolio by adjusting the effective beta of the portfolio; that is, hedging reduces the market risk of a portfolio. Pension fund sponsors can use futures to separate the functions of timing the market and selecting individual issues. Such a separation of functions helps to manage large inflows and outflows of cash and to smooth the transition from one money manager to another. Portfolio insurance is a strategy that attempts to keep the portfolio value from falling below a given floor while still allowing the portfolio to participate in market rallies. Portfolio insurance products were among the fastest growing products on Wall Street until the crash of October 1987 when they did not adequately protect the portfolio value from the market decline.

A combination strategy employing stock, bonds, and T-bills is called asset allocation. Asset allocation strategies are a form of active portfolio management in which portfolio managers change the makeup of the portfolio between stocks, bonds, and cash to benefit from their forecasts of these markets. These strategies are performed faster and cheaper by employing futures contracts. Diversification with commodity futures contracts is another combination strategy. Commodity funds can be used for such diversification.

This chapter also examines the use of futures instruments by financial institutions. The major emphasis of this section is the issue of asset-liability management by financial institutions. In particular, the concept of "gaps" is examined; a gap exists when the amount of rate sensitive assets differs from the amount of rate-sensitive liabilities within a given maturity range. When no gaps exist, the institution is perfectly matched. Otherwise, interest rate risk exists. Futures are used to manage gaps. One decision that must be made is whether specific assets should be hedged (microhedges) or whether the net gap position of the institution should be hedged (macrohedges). The considerations relating to this decision are explored.

Hedging Money Market CD (MMCD) rollovers is one of the easiest and most popular uses of futures markets for adjusting the gap structure of a financial institution. The financial manager employs a short hedge to lock in the cost of funds for the subsequent time period in order to reduce the effect of short-term interest rate fluctuations. Another application is using a sell hedge to create a synthetic fixed-rate loan. This synthetic instrument provides the financial institution with a variable-rate loan, while allowing the corporation to possess a fixed-rate loan.

Terminology

*Asset allocation Structuring the portfolio of stocks, bonds, and T-bills to correspond to the forecast of returns and risks in these markets. Futures are employed to change these allocations quickly and inexpensively.

*Basis point value (BPV) The price change in the debt instrument associated with a one-basis-point change in interest rates; BPV is used to determine the size of the position to take with futures contracts in order to alter the structure of a portfolio.

Beta A measure of the relative price movement in the asset (portfolio) in relation to the market movement.

Commodity fund A type of mutual fund in which investors pool money so that a trading manager can speculate in futures positions.

Duration See Chapter 10.

***Dynamic trading strategy** A strategy that changes the proportions of two or more assets as the market price changes.

***Gap** The size of the difference between rate-sensitive assets and rate-sensitive liabilities for a given maturity range.

Intermediation The process by which financial institutions obtain funds from one segment of the economy (individual depositors) and lend to another segment of the economy (corporations); or by which they obtain short-term funds and lend on a long-term basis. Intermediation often causes the amount of rate-sensitive assets to differ from the amount of rate-sensitive liabilities within a given maturity range.

***Microhedging** Hedging specific assets or liabilities on the balance sheet.

***Macrohedging** Hedging the net interest margin.

***Net interest margin (NIM)** The amount of "earnings" for the financial institution, that is, the difference between interest income and interest expense. NIM depends on the size and direction of the gap and the relative spread of interest rates between assets and liabilities.

***Portfolio insurance** See Chapter 8.

***Rate-sensitive assets/liabilities** Assets and liabilities that mature are rolled over to a new maturity, or are repriced at a given time period in association with a specific rate-sensitive instrument.

***Spread (asset-liability) management** Controlling the relationship between rate-sensitive assets and rate-sensitive liabilities to obtain the desired risk-return tradeoff. The return objective is to obtain a return on assets that is greater than the cost of the liabilities. Risk occurs when the assets mature or are repriced at a different time than the liabilities.

Strips A series of futures with consecutive expirations.

***Synthetic fixed-rate loan** Combining a short futures transaction with a variable-rate loan in order to create a synthetic instrument that acts similar to a fixed-rate loan.

***Synthetic security** Generating a position by combining a cash instrument and a futures contract that replicates the characteristics of a different cash instrument. Such positions can provide higher returns than "equivalent" cash securities.

FIXED-INCOME APPLICATIONS

Adjusting Bond Durations[1]

Purchasing a T-bond or T-note futures contract increases the sensitivity of the combined asset/futures portfolio to a change in interest rates, thereby increasing the effective duration; selling long-term debt futures decreases the portfolio sensitivity to interest rate changes and thus decreases the duration.[2] A money manager who adjusts the duration of the portfolio as forecasts of the direction of interest rates change could accomplish this strategy more effectively by using futures contracts. Specifically, the alternative of changing the cash position of the fund—for example, selling bonds and holding T-bills if prices are forecasted to move lower—is not typically a feasible alternative for a fund since restrictions on portfolio composition often hamper the bond manager. Moreover, such a major change in the bond portfolio is expensive in terms of transaction costs, liquidity costs, and potential short selling and tax costs.

In general, a careful choice of the number, position (long or short), and type of futures contracts allows the money manager to replicate the duration of any pure cash bond portfolio. Thus, the specific price reaction of a bond portfolio to a change in interest rates is dictated by adjusting the duration of the bond portfolio with futures contracts. Reducing the duration of the bond portfolio is equivalent to short hedging. Thus, hedging decisions for bonds are essentially duration decisions.[3]

The first step in changing a bond portfolio's duration is to find the **basis point values (BPVs)** for the current cash portfolio, the target duration adjusted portfolio, and the futures contract. The BPV is the *total* dollar price change that is associated with a 1-basis-point change in the interest rate. Thus, BPV is related to the dollar equivalency concept described in Chapter 7. The BPV is determined from Equation (17-1), which employs duration to calculate the change in the value of the portfolio resulting from a change in interest rates of 1 basis point:

$$\text{BPV} = \frac{D(\text{PMV})(.0001)}{1 + (i/k)} \tag{17-1}$$

---

[1] The basic concepts of using duration in conjunction with futures contracts are covered in Chapter 10. The following discussion relates to the *application* of futures to adjust bond duration. The example and application concepts given here follow the "Concepts and Applications: Using Interest Rate Futures in Pension Fund Management" (1987).

[2] Note that purchasng futures *always* increases the sensitivity of the combined cash/futures portfolio, *regardless* of whether the duration of the futures position is less than or greater than the duration of the original cash position. The reason is that futures do not require any investment of funds. Thus, the value of the combined position changes to a greater extent with futures than without, making the portfolio more sensitive to interest rate changes. A similar situation is true for the sale of futures contracts; that is, a sale decreases the sensitivity regardless of the relative durations of the futures and cash instruments. *Averaging* durations is appropriate only when all the positions involve a cash investment of funds *or* when only futures are employed.

[3] Recall that the Macaulay duration measure assumes a flat yield curve with parallel shifts to the term structure. When nonparallel shifts occur, the Macaulay measure of duration provides biased results. Consequently, the relationship of a cash portfolio with a given duration value to a futures-adjusted portfolio with the same calculated duration depends on the type of interest rate shift that occurs and the cash flow characteristics of the two portfolios (i.e., the cash and futures adjusted portfolios can act differently when a nonparallel shift in the term structure occurs). See Chapter 10 for in-depth discussions of this topic.

where BPV = basis point value

D = duration, typically the Macaulay duration

PMV = the portfolio market value

i = the annualized yield to maturity

k = the number of payments per year; that is, $k = 2$ for semiannual coupons

.0001 = 1 basis point (.01%)

Note that Equation (17-1) is simply a rephrasing of the equation given in Chapter 10 for a ΔP due to a Δi; that is, $\Delta P = -DP\,\Delta i/(1 + i)$. The formulation in Equation (17-1) is employed more frequently in the practitioner community because of its ease of use for the purpose of finding the number of required futures contracts.

The determination of the BPV for the *current cash* portfolio, which includes individual cash bonds, is calculated in one of two ways:

- The composite duration of the portfolio is determined, if ease of calculation is the primary factor.
- The BPV for each bond is calculated and the weighted sum of the individual BPVs is determined, if greater accuracy is important.

The BPV of the *target* portfolio is determined by plugging the duration desired by the portfolio manager into Equation (17-1). Finally, the BPV for the futures contract is found by obtaining the duration associated with the cheapest-to-deliver cash bond, since this bond is the one tracked by the futures market in the pricing process. The futures BPV on a *per contract* basis is then determined by dividing the BPV of the cheapest-to-deliver cash bond by the appropriate conversion factor:[4]

$$\text{BPV of futures} = \frac{\text{BPV of the cheapest-to-deliver cash bond}}{\text{conversion factor}} \qquad (17\text{-}2)$$

Given the relevant BPVs from Equations (17-1) and (17-2), the number of futures contracts needed to obtain the desired portfolio duration is determined as follows:

$$N = \frac{\text{BPV target} - \text{BPV current}}{\text{BPV futures}} \qquad (17\text{-}3)$$

where the target and current BPV values are in total dollar values for the portfolio, and the BPV futures value is per contract.

Example 17-1 shows how the above concept is applied in order to adjust a bond portfolio **duration.** In particular, the example shows how to increase the effective duration from the current cash portfolio value of 4.6 years to a 10-year duration. Since interest rates move in the forecasted direction (downward) for the example, the longer duration increases the rate of return on the portfolio. If rates increase, however, then a longer duration provides inferior results to the original (shorter) portfolio duration. This example shows that in addition to being a low-cost and quick way to extend the duration

---

[4] Since multiplying the futures price by the conversion factor changes a futures price into a cash price equivalent (Chapter 9), one finds the relevant futures price BPV by dividing the cash price by the conversion factor.

EXAMPLE 17-1
Changing the Duration of a Portfolio

On January 2, an internal pension plan manager expects a steep decline in bond yields over the next two-month period. The manager's conviction concerning the decrease in yields is so strong that the duration of the fixed-income portfolio is more than doubled. Because the underlying portfolio is tied to a broad-based bond index, and since the internal manager wants to avoid disrupting the externally managed cash bond portfolio, futures contracts are purchased in order to increase the duration of the portfolio rather than buying bonds.

Data Inputs	January 2	February 28
Portfolio duration	4.6	
Target duration	10	
T-bond futures price	85–00	94–26
Cash portfolio value	$100,000,000	$104,535,095
BPV (basis point value) of T-bond		
futures (cheapest-to-deliver cash)	$115.61	
Portfolio yield to maturity	9.27%	

There are three steps to be followed. See Equation (17-1) for steps 1 and 2 and Equation (17-3) for step 3.

1. Convert cash portfolio duration to a BPV:

$$\frac{4.6}{(1 + .0927/2)} \times \$100,000,000 \times .0001 = \$43,962$$

2. Convert target portfolio duration to a BPV:

$$\frac{10}{1 + .0927/2} \times \$100,000,000 \times .0001 = \$95,570$$

3. Determine the number of contracts required to achieve the desired portfolio duration:

$$\frac{\$95,570 - \$43,962}{\$115.61} = 446 \text{ contracts}$$

Results	January 2	February 28
Without futures:		
Cash portfolio value	$100,000,000	$104,535,095
Return		4.54%
With futures:		
Cash portfolio value	$100,000,000	$104,535,095
Futures gain ($9^{26}/_{32}\% \times 446 \times \$100,000$)		$4,376,375
Return		8.91%

Source: "Concepts and Applications: Using Interest Rate Futures in Pension Fund Management," Chicago Board of Trade, 1987, p. 3.

of the cash portfolio, futures allow the portfolio manager to obtain durations that are difficult to structure solely in the cash market, at least without using zero-coupon bonds.[5]

Synthetic Debt Securities and Return

A **synthetic security** replicates a cash security by purchasing a different cash instrument and either buying or selling a futures contract. Creating a synthetic security for long-term debt is very similar to changing the duration of a bond portfolio by using futures. However, the *purpose* of creating a synthetic security is to obtain a higher return than is available for an almost equivalent cash market security, whereas adjusting a bond duration changes the sensitivity of the portfolio to movements in interest rates. This section describes how to generate a synthetic debt instrument and how to compare the returns for such an instrument to a nearly equivalent cash security.

The two basic procedures for creating a synthetic debt instrument are:

- To buy a cash T-bill and then buy T-bond or T-note futures in order to generate a synthetic long-term debt instrument.
- To buy a long-term T-bond and sell T-bond or T-note futures in order to generate a synthetic short-term debt instrument.

The primary reason for creating a synthetic security is to obtain a rate-of-return advantage over a cash security with the same duration. Such an advantage is possible to construct if (1) the futures contract is mispriced, (2) futures price changes lead the cash market changes, or (3) differences exist in the price patterns of the cash and synthetic securities because of the differing cash flow characteristics of the two instruments in conjunction with a favorable twist in the shape of the term structure.[6]

Example 17-2 shows how a synthetic security made up of cash T-bills and a long T-bond futures position can outperform a ten-year cash instrument, with both positions having the same duration. The superiority of the synthetic position depends on a beneficial change in the shape of the yield curve. Thus, the combination of a cash T-bill with a duration of three months, with the appropriate number of T-bond futures contracts with a duration of approximately nine years, provides a combined synthetic security with a duration that is equivalent to the cash T-note position. Moreover, a flattening of the long-term portion of the yield curve illustrated in the example generates superior returns for the synthetic security as compared with the cash instrument. This

---

[5] There is no conflict between the BPV for futures of $115.61 in Example 17-1 and the $31.25 value of a $\frac{1}{32}$-point price change for the T-bond futures contract. The former states the *total dollar* change for a $100,000 par value T-bond with a .01% change in *yield*. This total dollar change is affected by the duration of the bond: the greater the duration, the greater the change in price for a given *yield* change. The $\frac{1}{32}$ states the value of the change in *price* for the futures contract. Thus, BPV states the total change in value of the bond per .0001 change in *yield,* while $\frac{1}{32}$ simply reflects the price change due to a change in the quotation of the bond (a percentage of par of the bond). Stated differently, a 1% change in yields creates a change of 4% to 5% in the price of a longer-duration bond.

[6] Mispricing of the futures contract is determined either by (1) comparing the futures price with the price from a theoretical model or by (2) comparing the implied repo rate from the futures arbitrage transaction with the current repurchase rate for the equivalent term. Both procedures are complicated by the pricing effects of the futures delivery options that exist for the bond and note futures. The type of "favorable twist" in the yield curve necessary to obtain superior returns depends on the relative characteristics of the cash and synthetic instruments.

EXAMPLE 17-2
Creating a Synthetic Instrument

A manager has received a $20 million cash inflow and wants to purchase ten-year Treasury notes in order to keep the portfolio duration constant. The money manager expects a flattening of the long end of the yield curve in the next month such that long-term bonds will outperform ten-year notes. A synthetic ten-year security using cash T-bills and T-bond futures contracts is created that will outperform the cash security if these expectations prove to be true, as shown below.

Inputs	January 22	February 21
T-bill yeild	5%	5%
10-year T-note yield	7%	6.8%
20-year T-bond yield	8%	7.5%
T-bill invoice price (cash)	98.78	99.18
10-year T-note price (decimal)	101.74	103.15
T-bond futures price	99-01	103-26
BPV for T-bill: $20 MM	$464.60	
BPV for 10-year T-note: $20 MM	$14,185.88	
BPV for T-bond futures	$94.82	

Determine how many futures contracts must be added to the cash T-bill position to replicate the duration of a ten-year security:

$$\text{Number of contracts} = \frac{\text{10-year BPV} - \text{T-bill BPV}}{\text{T-bond futures BPV}}$$

$$\frac{\$14,185.88 - \$464.60}{\$94.82} = 144 \text{ contracts}$$

Results	January 22	February 21
Ten-year cash T-note:		
Ten-year T-note	$20,000,000	$20,277,177
Accrued interest	$270,879	$390,384
One-month return		1.98%
Synthetic instrument:		
Purchase cash T-bills	$20,000,000	$20,080,988
T-bond futures gain		$688,500
One-month return		3.85%

Source: "Concepts and Applications: Using Interest Rate Futures in Pension Fund Management," Chicago Board of Trade, 1987, p. 9.

superiority occurs because the synthetic security is made up of a long position in T-bond futures that benefits more from the flattening of the yield curve than does the ten-year cash T-note instrument. That is, the price of the bond futures increases more than the price of the T-note when the yield curve becomes flatter. On the other hand, if the yield curve had become *less* flat, then the synthetic security would have performed *worse* than the cash instrument.[7,8]

Futures as Synthetic Money Market Instruments

A basic use of T-bill (or Eurodollar) futures for a money market trader is to provide an alternative for investing short-term funds by creating synthetic money market instruments. As an example, let us assume that a money manager desires to invest funds for six months in an instrument with the credit risk and liquidity of a T-bill. The various alternatives for such an investment are

1. Buy a 180-day cash T-bill.
2. Buy two successive 90-day cash T-bills (as one T-bill matures, the funds are used to purchase a second 90-day T-bill).
3. Buy a long-term T-bill and sell it after 180 days, with the sale occurring before the T-bill matures.
4. Buy a 90-day T-bill and buy a T-bill futures contract now that expires when the cash T-bill expires.
5. Buy a long-term cash T-bill (say a 270-day T-bill) and sell short a T-bill futures now, for a combined synthetic security with a maturity of 180 days (the futures contract would have to expire when the cash T-bill has 90 days left to maturity).

The above six-month investment alternatives include three combinations involving cash securities and two combinations of cash and futures instruments. Several factors affect the final decision for several of the alternatives. Specifically, alternatives 2 and 3 involve price risk, since one must buy or sell the securities before maturity. The price risk causes the final return for these alternatives to be affected by the interest rates occurring within the investment period, since a change in interest rates affects the prices of the instruments.

---

[7] The duration of a T-bill, as shown in Example 17-2, is simply the maturity of the T-bill. T-bills are zero-coupon bonds since they have no intermediate cash flows. The duration of a zero-coupon bond is its maturity.

[8] Changes in carrying costs and potential crosshedges are major factors affecting the basis risk of a synthetic position. Carrying costs are dominant when the cash and synthetic securities have similar characteristics. However, if the durations are significantly different, or the assumptions of the duration procedure are not met, then the crosshedge risk is often the dominating effect. For example, recall from Chapter 10 that a bond portfolio made up of short-term and long-term securities (a "dumbell" portfolio) changes its duration significantly if a nonparallel change in the shape of the term structure occurs. Although a short hedge for such a situation still shortens the effective duration of the bond portfolio substantially, the behavior of the combined cash-futures position is more difficult to analyze and acts differently than a pure short-term instrument.

Only alternatives 1, 4, and 5 are risk-free strategies. Of course, the basic rule for the money manager is to choose the alternative with the highest rate of return in relation to the risk. Theoretically, if the cash and futures markets are completely linked, then these three alternatives provide equivalent returns.[9] But the existence of different types of participants in the cash and futures markets, who have different expectations concerning interest rate behavior, can cause prices and rates in the two markets to diverge. Alternatively, other considerations such as commissions, bid-ask spreads, or liquidity cause a money manager to prefer one alternative over another.[10] If interest rates or costs do differ significantly between the two markets, then one of the three remaining alternatives provides the highest return. In summary, the existence of T-bill futures provides additional investment alternatives with potentially higher returns for those who have the choice of dealing in either the cash or the futures markets.[11]

A Strip of Futures as a Synthetic Instrument

The futures money market alternative described above is extended here to examine the benefits of a **strip** of futures. A strip of futures is created when one purchases sequential expirations of several T-bill (or Eurodollar) futures contracts. The purchase and subsequent expiration of four sequential Eurodollar futures provides the investor with a series of four 91-day Eurodollar time deposits. Moreover, the total return and price of these time deposits is determined when the four futures contracts are originally purchased. Therefore, one can compare a strip of four Eurodollar futures to a one-year cash Eurodollar deposit in order to determine which investment provides a better return. Of course, other strips of futures are employed for other investment horizons.[12]

Example 17-3 compares a cash alternative with a futures strip; that is, the following are equivalent strategies:

- Invest in a long-term cash Eurodollar time deposit for the entire holding period.
- Alternatively, buy a sequence of futures plus invest in a short-term Eurodollar time deposit now, such that the cash time deposit matures exactly when the nearby futures contract

---

[9] In fact, if markets were perfect and in equilibrium, then all five alternatives would provide the same returns. However, new information and changing expectations cause interest rates to fluctuate, causing price risk for alternatives 2 and 3.

[10] For the situation in question, the T-bill futures combinations do have a disadvantage in comparison with the cash alternative. Specifically, since futures contracts expire only four times per year, using futures poses a significant restriction on matching desired maturity combinations. Consequently, for most situations, the money manager would need flexibility for the length of the investment in order to benefit from the futures/cash alternatives as viable investment opportunities. When the maturity is flexible, the potential higher returns often associated with a futures/cash alternative, or the other potential benefits associated with futures markets listed in the text, could be an important consideration.

[11] In addition to the strategies noted here, pension and investment funds use futures to convert stock or bond positions into equivalent short-term risk-free positions *without* selling the stocks or bonds. The benefits of such an opportunity in terms of commissions and liquidity risk are obvious. The sale of the futures contract is equivalent to an arbitrage position if the cash securities fulfill the specifications of the futures contract. This situation represents a risk-free position where the return is typically equivalent to or higher than a short-term risk-free asset.

[12] Since the expiration date of T-bill futures now varies from one expiration month to another, a perfect strip of futures is not attainable. Strips with Eurodollar futures do not have this problem.

EXAMPLE 17-3
Alternative Returns: Comparing a Cash Eurodollar Rate
to a Strip of Futures

ALTERNATIVE 1: On September 20 place $1 million in a one-year cash Eurodollar time deposit at a money market rate of 5.87% and keep the time deposit until it matures in one year.

ALTERNATIVE 2: Before September 20 buy one contract of Eurodollar futures expiring September 20, December 20, March 20, and June 20. (*Note:* Assume that funds are not available for a time deposit until September 20. Also, actual futures expirations vary by several days from one expiration month to another.) Futures rates locked in at the time of purchase are 5.57%, 5.79%, 5.81%, and 6.10%. For this alternative, the original cash amount of $1 million is invested in a three-month Eurodollar time deposit on September 20, with the rate on this time deposit being locked in with the purchase of the September futures contract. This procedure is repeated in December, March, and June. Since all futures contracts are purchased at the same time, the exact cost is known on that date.

The portfolio manager would choose the alternative with the higher return.

Alternative 1: One-year Eurodollar deposit

$$\$1,000,000(1 + .0587) = \$1,058,700$$

Alternative 2: Strip of futures

$$\$1,000,000(1 + .0557/4) = \$1,013,925$$

$$\$1,013,925(1 + .0579/4) = \$1,028,602$$

$$\$1,028,602(1 + .0581/4) = \$1,043,542$$

$$\$1,043,542(1 + .0610/4) = \$1,059,456$$

The strip of futures provides the highest total interest.

expires. When the first cash time deposit matures, place the funds in another 90-day Eurodollar time deposit; the rate on this second (and subsequent) time deposit is locked in via the original purchase of the futures contracts. In this way the strip of Eurodollar futures purchases guarantees the exact cost and yield of this investment at the time of the original purchase of the strip.

If the futures and cash markets are equivalently priced, then the ending dollar value for the futures strip strategy will equal the ending dollar value for the long-term cash Eurodollar time deposit that has the same maturity as the strip of futures. Alternatively, if one strategy produces a higher yield than the other, then one can undertake a quasi-arbitrage transaction (alternative return strategy) and choose the alternative with the highest ending dollar value.

Another use of the futures strip occurs when an institution always desires three-month cash T-bills for liquidity, but forecasts that interest rates are going to drop drastically over the next (say) year. Purchasing the strip of futures now provides higher returns for the one-year period than buying cash T-bills every three months, since the cash T-bills will have significantly lower interest rates (higher prices) after the interest rates decrease. Of course, the relative success of this futures strategy relates to the money manager's forecasting ability.

Stock Index Arbitrage as a Synthetic Instrument

Stock index arbitrage also creates a synthetic position, as discussed in Chapter 8. Thus, the sale of overpriced futures and the purchase (or ownership) of stocks create a synthetic risk-free position. The purchase of underpriced futures and sale of stocks from a portfolio also creates a synthetic risk-free position. These synthetic instruments are implemented only if they earn a return above the risk-free rate. Consequently, stock index arbitrage becomes an alternative to money market investments.

STOCK MARKET APPLICATIONS

Hedging and Adjusting Stock Portfolio Betas

The basic procedure for hedging a portfolio of stocks is described in Chapter 6: One sells stock index futures to reduce the potential loss from a decline in stock prices. In Chapter 6 we examine regression analysis, using the cash asset and the futures contract to determine the importance of the relative volatilities of the cash stock portfolio and the futures contract in order to maximize the performance of the risk-minimizing hedge.

There is another tool that evaluates the importance of the stock portfolio volatility, namely **beta**. Beta is the (regression) measure of the relative volatility between the currently held stock portfolio and the relevant cash stock *index*.[13] Consequently, a beta hedge is an alternative method for estimating the *minimum-risk* futures hedge ratio. The number of futures contracts needed for the beta hedge is determined by multiplying beta (representing the hedge ratio) times the relative dollar amounts of the stock and futures positions; that is,

$$N_b = (V_S/V_F)\beta_p \tag{17-4}$$

where N_b = the number of futures contracts for a stock beta hedge

V_S = the value of the stock position

V_F = the value of one futures contract, that is, the futures price times its multiplier

β_p = the beta of the portfolio

---

[13] Betas were originally developed as a measure of the relative risk of individual stocks versus the market index. A beta is determined by regressing the stock (or portfolio) returns against the stock index returns, with the slope of the regression line being the beta. A portfolio beta also is obtained by finding the weighted average of the individual stock betas:

$$\beta_p = \sum_{i=1}^{n} W_i \beta_i$$

where β_p = the beta of the portfolio

n = the number of stocks in the portfolio

W_i = the proportion of the total funds in stock i (i.e., $\Sigma W_i = 1$)

β_i = the beta of stock i

Most investment and security analysis textbooks discuss betas in detail.

A study by Lindahl, Boze, and Ferris (1987) shows that using portfolio betas as discussed here provides less basis risk than employing the minimum-variance regression method between the cash portfolio and futures contract.[14]

Futures also are employed to *change* the relative risk of the portfolio. A small alteration in Equation (17-4) determines the number of futures contracts needed to change the portfolio beta to a different relative risk value:[15]

$$N_b = (V_S/V_F)(\beta_t - \beta_p) \tag{17-5}$$

where β_t is the target beta for the portfolio. If N_b is negative, a short hedge is appropriate; a positive N_b relates to a long futures position. Example 17-4 shows how to calculate a stock beta hedge and how to change a portfolio beta with the use of futures.

Portfolio Management of Funds

Timing and Selectivity. One example of using futures markets for timing purposes is related to the strategy of creating a synthetic risk-free instrument with futures. Specifically, one sells futures to create an equivalent risk-free position when a market downturn is expected and lifts the futures position when an upturn is anticipated. This use of futures contracts reduces trading and liquidity costs significantly as compared to cash trades, and allows the manager to keep the desired selection of individual securities. Thus, being able to "buy and sell the market" via futures transactions separates the broad asset allocation decision relating to stocks and bonds from the investment decisions for individual assets. In addition, those who have superior selection abilities but minimal market timing abilities benefit from being able to hedge the market. In fact, one money manager can concentrate on market timing via the use of futures while another manager concentrates on the selection of individual securities. Moreover, once a decision concerning the appropriate relative volatility of the portfolio is made, that decision is executed via going long or short in futures rather than having to choose the individual securities in accordance with the risk of that security.

Additions and Reductions to the Portfolio. Pension funds and insurance companies experience periods during which large cash inflows or outflows to the investment funds occur. Futures can benefit the timing process by allowing the money manager to invest (or disinvest) large sums of money without being affected by the liquidity of individual securities. Over time, the individual securities can be purchased or sold and the futures positions covered.

---

[14] Some hedgers further modify Equation (17-4) by multiplying N_b by the slope of the regression line between the cash *stock* index and the stock index *futures* contract. However, this relationship is near unity and therefore has only a minimal effect on the number of futures contracts used for a hedge. Another consideration is whether β_p changes over time. In general, the betas for large portfolios of stocks are stable over time, whereas individual stock betas and the betas of portfolios of a small number of stocks do change over time. The interval used to measure the beta (i.e., daily or weekly or monthly returns) and the length of time employed affect the beta measure. Moreover, the portfolio beta can differ between an up-market and a down-market because of the reaction of the individual stocks to bull-and-bear market factors; see Kawaller (1987) for a brief discussion. Investments books examine the question of beta stability in some detail.

[15] In effect, the hedge obtained from Equation (17-4) attempts to change the portfolio beta to zero.

EXAMPLE 17-4
Stock Beta Hedges

HEDGING A STOCK PORTFOLIO

A wealthy investor wishes to hedge her stock portfolio against a potential down-turn in the market until she can decide how to rearrange her portfolio. Currently, the stock portfolio is risky since it includes a large number of high-technology stocks. The beta of the portfolio is 1.4 and the current value of the S&P 500 Index is 275.00. The dollar value of the investor's portfolio is $1,250,000. The number of futures contracts needed for a hedge with the S&P futures contract is calculated as follows:

$$N_b = (V_S/V_F)\beta_p \qquad (17\text{-}4)$$

$$N_b = [1,250,000/(275)(500)]1.4$$

$$N_b = 9.091(1.4) = 12.73 = 13 \text{ contracts}$$

ADJUSTING A PORTFOLIO BETA

The investor above decides that her porftolio is more volatile than she desires. She wants to sell the stocks and put the money in utilities and bonds. However, her broker convinces her that the stocks in the portfolio will outperform the market by more than their extra risk warrants if products currently in the research stage prove successful. The broker convinces her to keep the individual stocks but to reduce the effective market risk of the stock portfolio to .6 β by using futures to reduce the beta of the combined cash/futures portfolio. The number of contracts needed is:

$$N_b = (V_S/V_F)(\beta_t - \beta_p) \qquad (17\text{-}5)$$

$$N_b = [1,250,000/(275)(500)][.6 - 1.4]$$

$$N_b = -9.091(.8) = -7.27 = 7 \text{ contracts (short)}$$

Sponsor Activities.   Pension funds typically allocate funds to money managers to invest. The overall investment policy is set by the pension fund and implemented by the managers.[16] Futures allow the pension fund unique opportunities to separate the various functions of the money managers. Separate managers can be hired who excel at market timing and security selection. The fund can override asset allocation, relative risk, or market timing decisions made by the individual money managers by employing futures. When a fund changes managers, futures can help ease the transition.[17]

Portfolio Insurance

The Objective and Concept.   The *objective* of **portfolio insurance** is to "guarantee" a floor for the ending value of the portfolio if the market declines in value while

---

[16] Sharpe (1981) examines the timing and allocation functions of money management. He shows how the pension fund sponsor can separate and allocate these functions to different managers. In particular, the advantages and disadvantages of active versus passive portfolio management are discussed.

[17] Switching money managers often creates large pools of cash and/or a wholesale restructuring of the individual securities in the portfolio. Futures ease the difficulties encountered in such transitions.

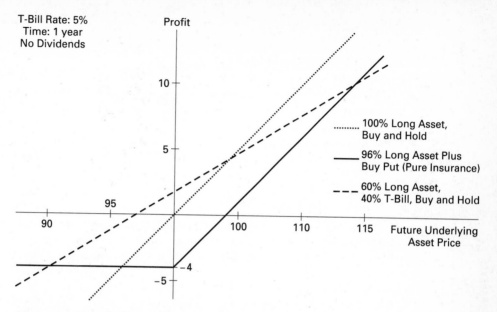

Figure 17-1 Pure portfolio insurance.

allowing the portfolio to participate in market increases. A portion of the potential returns of an uninsured portfolio are foregone in order to obtain the minimum floor value. Portfolio insurance is useful for pension funds, whose managers do not want the value of their assets to fall below their designated floor, as defined by the present value of their liabilities. Notice that portfolio insurance has similar characteristics to other forms of insurance. For example, fire insurance on a house protects the original value of the house to the insurer (for a cost), while any appreciation in the value of the house accrues to the insurer.[18]

Figure 17-1 illustrates the concept of pure portfolio insurance as compared to (1) placing all of one's funds in the asset, or (2) placing 60% of the funds in the asset and 40% in T-bills. The pure insurance portfolio is best described by buying a put option to guarantee the minimum asset value. A put option allows the buyer to *sell* the asset at a prespecified price (the strike price) until the option expires. There is a cost to buying the put option.

Figure 17-1 illustrates how the initial asset price of $100 changes for the alternative investments described above. In particular, the pure insurance alternative loses a maximum of $4 if the asset price falls ($4 is the cost of the put) but participates in upside gains. The 100% long alternative has superior profits on the upside, but larger losses when the asset falls below $96. The 60% long–40% T-bill alternative creates smaller gains and smaller losses than the 100% long case.[19]

---

[18] As with homeowners' or auto insurance, one can create portfolio insurance with a "deductible"; that is, the guaranteed floor can be below the current value.

[19] One can specify a minimum future value *above* the current portfolio value. In this case, one purchases a put for which the exercise price is *above* the current value. The cost of the put is larger since it includes the current value of exercising the put now. The cost of the option is typically reduced by using interest from funds invested in T-bills.

Portfolio Insurance and Dynamic Trading Strategies.   Buying puts to obtain downside protection (one method for obtaining pure portfolio insurance[20]) has the following disadvantages:

- Buying puts creates an ongoing cost (the cost of the put).
- Only the funds remaining after purchasing the put are invested in the cash asset.
- Insufficient liquidity and open interest exist to execute large pure portfolio insurance trades.
- Listed options have short lives and limited exercise prices (these factors limit choices for the minimum desired value of the portfolio). The recent addition of leaps (long-term options) reduces this problem, but leaps do not yet have sufficient liquidity to use for portfolio insurance.
- Initiating pure portfolio insurance for a complicated mix of assets, such as a stock portfolio without a listed option, is difficult.

As an alternative, the portfolio manager can generate a *synthetic* put option with a **dynamic trading strategy;** that is, the proportions of the long asset and a risk-free instrument can be varied to replicate the payoff of buying a put and holding the long asset. As prices increase, more funds are placed in the asset. As prices decrease, more funds are placed in T-bills. Unlike buying a put, no cash outlays for the portfolio protection are required to initiate a dynamic strategy.

Two approaches to implementing a dynamic trading strategy are (1) to buy and sell the asset, or (2) to buy and sell futures on the asset. Since transactions costs for futures are one-tenth the size of the costs of trading the asset itself and liquidity is greater for futures, most institutional funds that implement a dynamic trading strategy employ stock index futures contracts.

Figure 17-2 illustrates the payoffs of a dynamic portfolio insurance strategy in comparison to a 60% asset–40% T-bill buy-and-hold strategy. The dynamic portfolio insurance strategy is superior for large price increases and for moderate to large price decreases of the asset. The shape of the portfolio insurance curve is similar to a long asset plus put position, but at a lower cost. The lower cost occurs because the portfolio insurance strategy replicates a portfolio that is less than fully invested. Thus, on the downside, the loss on the (declining) equity portion of the portfolio is mostly offset by the interest earned on the (increasing) T-bill position.

Futures and Portfolio Insurance.   Dynamic portfolio insurance is implemented by using futures. The equity exposure is actively managed by shorting stock index futures contracts as the market declines in order to reduce losses, and lifting part or all of the short hedge as the market increases in value so as to benefit from the upside potential. The extent of the dynamic hedge varies with the market movement and depends on how close the portfolio's value is to the desired minimum value.[21] When the entire stock portfolio is hedged, the portfolio represents a synthetic T-bill. The number of futures contracts to employ for the hedge is determined using the portfolio beta approach given in Equation (17-4).

---

[20] Another method for creating equivalent payoffs for pure portfolio insurance is to purchase a call option and invest the remaining funds in T-bills. This strategy generates a payoff curve equivalent to the put strategy in Figure 17-1.

[21] This model is similar to the dynamic bond portfolio model of Fong, Pearson, and Vasicek (1983) and bond contingent immunization models.

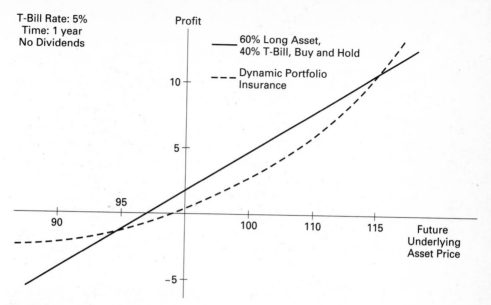

T-Bill Rate: 5%
Time: 1 year
No Dividends

Profit

——— 60% Long Asset,
40% T-Bill, Buy and Hold

– – – Dynamic Portfolio
Insurance

Figure 17-2 Dynamic portfolio insurance.

Although the basic dynamic portfolio insurance model is simple to apply, its effectiveness is determined by the portfolio manager's care in considering the factors that affect the hedge. In addition, if the model is used without market judgment or forecasts, then the size of the futures short hedge simply increases as the market declines and decreases as the market rises. An effective manager realizes when to reduce the risk of the portfolio either by changing the hedge position when the market is overbought or by changing the minimum floor value (and hence the hedge value) to increase the portfolio's protection. Hence, the overall performance of a portfolio insurance program ultimately depends on the judgment of the money manager. The benefit of such a program is to reduce risk in a downward trending market and provide additional equity exposure in an upward trending market.[22]

Dynamic Strategies and Market Crashes. Dynamic portfolio insurance was an important strategy employed by funds before the 1987 market crash. At that time, stock index futures fell so rapidly that portfolio insurers could not effectively reduce the exposure of the equity position fast enough by shorting futures contracts. In addition, since futures prices fell much faster than *reported* cash prices fell, the apparent

[22] Using futures to implement portfolio insurance is basically a type of asset allocation strategy (which is discussed shortly) except that the key decision for other asset allocation strategies is the asset mix, whereas with dynamic portfolio insurance the asset mix is determined by the floor value and the time horizon. The advantage of undertaking a futures portfolio insurance strategy rather than a static cash asset allocation procedure is that the fund can participate in rallies to a greater extent with portfolio insurance because of the greater equity exposure; in addition, the portfolio typically is protected from significant market declines by the hedging activity. However, to be effective, the futures hedge ratio must be dynamically adjusted to compensate for changing market levels and volatilities. For example, the static cash asset allocation strategy often outperforms the dynamic portfolio insurance strategy when the market declines *rapidly,* since the dynamic strategy cannot change the asset mix fast enough to protect the portfolio against sharp drops in the asset price.

cost of hedging a position typically represented a 10% premium, making portfolio insurance seem to be very expensive for those trading on that day. The alternative, trading the cash stocks, was difficult due to liquidity problems for large blocks, the late opening of many stocks, and rapidly changing prices. Moreover, Chapter 8 discusses how cash stock prices were artificially higher than futures prices.

The 100-point decline in the Dow Jones Index on Friday, October 16 should have generated $12 billion in portfolio insurance sales, but only $4 billion were sold. This created an overhang in potential sales for Monday, October 19. Other market participants seemed to sense this potential problem and sold stock and futures on Monday's open, creating additional downward pressure on the market. Given that $80 billion were in existence by 1987, while only $15 to $20 billion existed in 1986, the potential effect of portfolio insurance trades on the market was important.[23]

The market crash highlighted the disadvantages of dynamic portfolio insurance, namely:

- Implementing portfolio insurance assumes the market will have continuous price changes, and that alterations in the portfolio can be made daily without being affected by large jumps in prices.

- If the hedge strategy is not monitored and changed *before* major downward moves, greater risk exists for portfolio insurance than for alternative strategies involving options or for the traditional cash asset allocation position.

- A futures-oriented portfolio insurance model is based on low transactions costs (commissions, bid-ask spread, market impact costs, and small futures basis). These did not occur during the crash.

- The option strategy often cannot be replicated effectively with futures, especially when a large basis occurs due to a delinking of the cash and futures market, causing larger basis risk for the futures strategy than desired for the portfolio. The potential for a larger basis risk with futures is associated with errors in the use of the model employed to generate the hedge ratio; that is, the model can calculate an inappropriate hedge ratio or an incorrect volatility value.

A Dynamic Portfolio Insurance Model. A dynamic portfolio insurance strategy indicates when the money manager should trade, how much to trade, and how the trade will affect the portfolio's performance. Portfolio insurance allocates and switches funds between a risky portfolio (stocks) and a risk-free asset (T-bills). Although a portfolio could be invested in T-bills in an amount equal to the minimum floor value desired for the fund, this practice typically leaves very little leeway for investing in assets promising higher returns. Portfolio insurance provides the advantage of guaranteeing the floor value while allowing the fund to trade in the risky assets to obtain higher returns.

One portfolio insurance model is based on option concepts that are equivalent to a protective put (owning stock and buying a put). The future payoff equation for a protective put that changes due to dynamic portfolio insurance is:

$$\text{future payoff} = \text{Max}[\alpha P_{S,E}, \text{K}] \tag{17-6}$$

where α = upside capture

   K = the floor

   $P_{S,E}$ = the portfolio value at "option expiration" or investment horizon

---

[23] In fact, Jacklin, Kleidon, and Pfleiderer (1992) simulate how a market in which the amount of portfolio insurance is unknown can create a temporary run-up in prices and precipitate a market crash.

The upside capture, α, is set so that the present value of the protective put equals the current value of the underlying portfolio. One finds α by a trial-and-error search (e.g., by a Newton-Raphson search technique). The result of this process is to create a hedge ratio that is used in the dynamic hedging procedure. However, one problem with the procedure is that an estimate of the future volatility is needed. If the future volatility does not equal the expected volatility, the actual results will differ from what was expected.

Black and Jones (1987) present a straightforward application of portfolio insurance that does not involve option pricing theory and does not have a definite expiration date. The Black and Jones model is implemented as follows:

$$eq = m(TA - F) \tag{17-7}$$

where eq = the equity exposure desired
  m = the multiple
  TA = total assets available
  F = the desired floor

The multiple is a function of the total assets, the floor chosen, and the initial equity exposure; that is,

$$m = eq/(TA - F) \tag{17-8}$$

For an example of the above approach let us assume that the total portfolio asset value is $100 million, the desired floor value is $80 million, and the initial equity *exposure* desired is $50 million (50% of total assets). An initial multiple of 2.5 is created (the $50 million desired equity exposure divided by the cushion of $20 million). The money manager rebalances after the market moves 2% (the tolerance factor), or, equivalently, when the cushion changes by 2% times the multiple of 2.5 = 5%.

The multiple chosen determines the volatility of the portfolio, with the multiple typically being the ratio of the initial exposure to the initial cushion. The higher the multiple, the faster the portfolio value increases *and* the faster it decreases toward the floor value. Each *trade* brings the exposure back to the same multiple *of the cushion*. As the cushion approaches zero, the exposure approaches zero. The portfolio falls below the floor value desired only if a large drop in asset prices occurs before the money manager can make a trade to adjust the exposure. As the exposure approaches the maximum limit desired in the portfolio, the money manager is fully invested and does not trade. When the exposure is less than the maximum limit, a significant market move causes the ratio of the exposure to the cushion to differ from the initial multiple desired. When this ratio exceeds some predetermined "tolerance" value, a trade is initiated to bring the multiple back to its initial value. The smaller the tolerance value, the more trades executed (and the more commissions generated). Hence, tolerance values often attempt to reduce transactions costs.

In conclusion, portfolio insurance provides a means for creating a floor for the portfolio value (if trading is continuous), while allowing participation in upward trending markets. Although dynamic portfolio insurance did not perform well during the 1987 market crash—and subsequently, pension funds lost interest in the tool—some funds have recently returned to using this method to provide structured returns for stock market portfolios.

COMBINATION STRATEGIES: ASSET ALLOCATION

An **asset allocation** strategy is another term for active portfolio management. Asset allocators adjust the relative proportions of the portfolio between stocks, bonds, T-bills, and other asset classes when changes in aggregate stock prices and interest rates are forecasted. This strategy has received increased attention in the past few years as money managers attempt to discover methods to enhance short-term portfolio performance. Asset allocation differs from portfolio insurance in that the former typically *reduces* exposure when prices increase (and vice versa), whereas portfolio insurers *increase* exposure as prices increase.

Changes in asset allocations with cash assets have the typical problems of trading costs, liquidity, timeliness, and adjustments to individual asset positions associated with trading cash assets. Employing stock index and interest rate futures contracts reduces these problems for asset allocation. The use of futures contracts to execute asset allocation strategies is a natural extension of cash-only allocation strategies:

- The short- to intermediate-term reallocation of funds between stock and bond portfolios is executed at a lower cost with futures than if attempted in the cash market. In addition, this reallocation is completed with no disruption of the core stock and bond portfolios. For example, when a pension fund employs passive portfolio management (i.e., a core of securities or an index fund is used to mirror the market), futures adjust the asset allocation among the different asset categories without requiring the trading of individual cash assets.
- The long-term reallocation of the cash portfolio among stocks, bonds, and T-bills is *initially* undertaken in the futures market in order to avoid the liquidity and timing problems associated with making the adjustments immediately in the cash market. The cash categories are then adjusted when the liquidity of the individual securities allows such changes *and* in conjunction with security analysts' recommendations concerning which individual stock or bond issues to emphasize in the portfolio.
- When a pension fund allocates the assets of the fund to different money managers, the fund can change the asset allocation exposure itself by using futures contracts. This technique does not unduly restrict the individual stock and bond selections of the individual money managers.

The procedure for implementing an asset allocation strategy using futures markets is straightforward:

1. Determine the amount of cash bonds and stocks one wants to "purchase" or "sell."
2. Find the number of stock index futures to buy/sell by the portfolio beta procedure given in Equation (17-4).
3. The *BPV* (basis point value) and the number of bond futures to buy/sell are determined using Equations (17-1) to (17-3) and the current duration of the bond portfolio.

The performance of an asset allocation procedure is dependent on the timing signals given to change the proportions of the asset categories. Simple timing signals based on publicly available information often provide inferior results. Most asset allocation models employ forecasts of the performance of each asset category based on analysis of the risks and potential rewards of that category. In conclusion, the benefits of using futures to implement an asset allocation model are that futures provide lower commissions and bid-ask spread costs, and futures have greater liquidity and market depth.

COMMODITY FUNDS

An Overview of Commodity Funds

Commodity funds are managed pools of money to which individual speculators contribute in order to obtain professional management of futures transactions. Unlike stock funds, which usually reduce risk by substantial diversification and by prudent management, commodity funds typically speculate in futures by trading often, using trading models, and holding only a small number of different positions. Commodity funds are either public or private. Public funds are sold by brokerage houses to any interested speculator. Private funds are restricted to those who put large sums of money into these accounts.

Commodity funds have received a great deal of attention in the past few years for two reasons. First, many funds claimed very large rates of return. Second, the use of computer trading models by these funds is alleged by traders to cause disruption on the trading floor because these funds often enter the market in large volume, frequently simultaneously.

Commodity Futures and Diversification

In order to diversify risks and to enhance returns more effectively, pension funds have added assets previously ignored as potential investments. Such assets include foreign stocks and bonds, metals, real estate, and commodity futures. Futures on foreign stocks and bonds and on metals can be used for hedging and for implementing an adaptation of the asset allocation models discussed above.

Buying commodity futures provides a way to participate in the diversification benefits of agricultural and other commodity products. As shown in Chapter 3, Bodie and Rosansky (1980) illustrate the benefits of such diversification in reducing risk. In fact, a diversified portfolio of nonfinancial commodity futures contracts provides a risk-return combination comparable to a portfolio of common stocks. Moreover, a portfolio of 60% stocks and 40% commodity futures possesses the same return as the stock portfolio with two-thirds of the risk.

Commodity Fund Operation

The first commodity funds appeared in the mid 1970s, but the concept of commodity funds received widespread interest only from the early 1980s. A commodity fund typically requires $5000 from a speculator, with the fund providing professional management, the benefits of pooled funds, and diversification in trading positions.

Fifty-two public commodity funds hit a peak investment of $620 million in 1984, up from $65 million in 1979. The public funds are offered mostly by the well-known brokerage firms, but the actual management of the positions are given to individual trading firms. The trading partners often obtain large fees and/or a percentage of the trading profits in return for their management expertise. The brokerage house receives a sales fee for the fund and typically receives commissions for trades placed by the fund. Total annual costs are typically 10% to 35% of average annual equity. Trading partners typically are chosen on the basis of their performance with private commodity funds.

However, it is often more difficult to be profitable with a public fund since it is much larger and there are limits on the number of futures contracts one fund can hold at a given time. Public funds are regulated by the CFTC. State regulations require that investors have a minimum net worth and annual income before participating.

Limited Risk and Diversification

A principal selling point of a commodity fund is its "limited risk." Thus, even if the fund goes bankrupt, the investor is liable only for the initial investment. However, this concept is misleading. Commodity funds typically speculate with only 20% to 30% of the total funds available, using the remaining funds as a "cushion" for losses. Hence, the leverage factor in a commodity fund is reduced significantly. Many funds have reported their "returns" based on funds invested in futures positions, rather than on funds *available* to invest, and thus reported rates of return were boosted significantly.

Diversification of trading positions across various types of futures contracts is another reported benefit of using a fund. Although such diversification is typical for stock funds, commodity funds trade in only a few positions at one time. Therefore, minimal diversification occurs, and the risk and profits of the fund are affected solely by the trading model's ability to pick winners.

Fund Performance

The performance of commodity funds has ranged from a very high average return of 45% for all funds in 1979 to significant losses in 1980. In 1983, 56 of the 61 largest funds lost money, with the average loss being 14.5%. In the first 11 months of 1991, funds lost 7.7%. Commodity newsletters also provided poor recommendations. Angrist (1992) states that four of 26 newsletters were profitable in 1991, 14 in 1990, and six in 1989. In addition, private funds outperform public funds. Several explanations for the superiority of private funds have been suggested: (1) public funds have higher costs of setup and operation; (2) private funds take greater risks; (3) since only funds with successful track records go public (combined with random performance of these funds), these public funds perform poorly after they go public; (4) funds have control over the performance numbers they publish—thus, as they go public they select the time period showing the best results from the time when the funds were private. Elton, Gruber, and Rentzler (1989) show that the last two reasons dictate why public funds have poor performance results.

The large rates of return claimed by the commodity funds have been disputed. Some funds used inappropriate methods for determining their rates of return, whereas other funds reported returns achieved by the fund managers on *other* managed money. In addition, many funds ignored trading costs in their calculations. Moreover, the performance of the funds has been inconsistent from year to year in the past decade and are typically inferior over recent years. The decline in returns may be the result of more accurate accounting for returns, but it might also reflect the fact that traders on the floor now seem to know how to outsmart the funds. Since most of the computer trading models used by the funds hit a trading signal at the same price, and since the floor traders now seem to be able to predict this price, the traders automatically change their bids and offers when they anticipate commodity fund activity. Such changes in the price in the pits benefit the floor traders while creating losses for the commodity funds. Although more definitive evidence is needed on the past and future profitability of these funds, current thought suggests that they are not the tremendous profit vehicle once believed by the public.

FINANCIAL INSTITUTIONS AND FUTURES

Factors Affecting Financial Institutions

Earnings of financial institutions are affected significantly by a combination of factors that have increased in importance since the late 1970s:

- Financial institutions possess more short-term liabilities than short-term assets; thus, their liability costs increase faster than their return on assets when interest rates increase.
- Deregulation of financial institutions created a competitive environment that encourages institutions to offer new instruments to customers. These instruments are often short-term in nature and offer interest rates that are higher and more volatile than those of savings accounts, which previously provided most of the financial institutions' funds. Specifically, financial institutions sell money market certificates of deposit (CDs) that are tied to the rates of short-term instruments such as T-bills. Moreover, while deregulation of the liability side of the balance sheet was occurring, the issuance of longer-term fixed-rate loans continued as usual.
- The increasing level and volatility of interest rates created a reduction and instability of earnings.
- The executives of financial institutions did not possess sufficient expertise for effective risk management, mainly because of the highly regulated environment that existed before deregulation.

Because of the above factors, the earnings of financial institutions are often negative when interest rates increase. Since the history of financial institutions is one of stable and positive earnings, this turn of events concerned shareholders, the Federal Reserve, the Federal Deposit Insurance Corporation, and the Comptroller of the Currency.

Financial futures can both alleviate the volatility of earnings of financial institutions and reduce the negative effects of a mismatched asset-liability balance sheet structure. Futures also help manage the risk environment of the institution, given that a rapid restructuring of the cash balance sheet of such institutions is a difficult and/or costly undertaking when interest rates change. As early as 1981, Sanford Rose (1981, p. 185) claimed that "Banks are damaging their own and their customers' profit potential by failing to see the possibilities of the financial futures markets." In reference to the risk of using financial futures, Richard Sandor states: "Clearly, the main risk is ignorance of risk-management fundamentals and of how current structural change in banking's products requires altering them" (Anon., 1984, p. 72).

Asset-Liability Management Concepts

Assets and Liabilities. Financial institutions obtain funds from deposits, savings accounts, and by selling certificates of deposit. They lend out these funds to corporations and individuals, and invest funds in T-bills, T-bonds, and municipal bonds. The process of obtaining funds from one segment of the economy and lending funds to another segment of the ecomony (or obtaining short-term funds and lending on a long-term basis) is known as **intermediation.** This process is the key to asset-liability management as practiced by financial institutions, and is alternatively known as **spread management.**

The maturity and interest rate relationships between the assets of the financial institution (the loans and investments) and the liabilities of the institution (the funds received from depositors plus funds from selling CDs) determine both the profitability and the risk of the bank or savings and loan. Logically, when the average interest rate on the assets exceeds the average rate on the liabilities, the "spread" is positive and the institution is profitable. When the cost of liabilities exceeds the returns from assets, the spread is negative and losses occur. Spread management is the control of the assets and liabilities to obtain a desirable rate of return on assets in relation to the risk.

Maturity Structure. The relationships between the maturities of the assets and the liabilities for different maturity ranges have a significant effect on the variability of the earnings of the institution; that is, the maturity relationships are the important factors affecting risk.[24] The amount of assets in each maturity range (called **rate-sensitive assets**) typically does not equal the amount of **rate-sensitive liabilities** in the same range. Thus, if interest rates increase in the economy, then a maturity range in which more liabilities than assets exist creates a loss when the currently existing liabilities mature and are "rolled over" into new liabilities at a higher cost.[25]

Gaps. The importance of the relative dollar size of the rate-sensitive assets (RSA) to the rate-sensitive liabilities (RSL) in each maturity range is seen by examining a situation in which the amounts differ. Exhibit 17-1 presents a breakdown of the RSA and RSL into their major components, with a net RSA − RSL (or "**gap**") given for each maturity range. The maturity ranges less than 90 days possess positive gaps; that is, the values of RSA − RSL are positive. The ranges from 91 days to 180 days have negative gaps. A positive gap has a direct relationship between interest rate changes and earnings: Earnings increase when interest rates increase, since more assets than liabilities in a given maturity range are repriced at the current (higher) interest rate. A negative gap has an inverse relationship between interest rates and earnings: Earnings increase

---

[24] Chapter 12 examines the use of duration as a measure of the sensitivity of a fixed-income asset to changes in interest rates. Therefore, duration can be employed to measure the average asset and liability sensitivities instead of using maturity ranges. Maturities are employed here for several reasons. First this practice is the industry convention. Second, duration ignores the effects of changes in the shape of the yield curve. Finally, most financial institutions concentrate on the effect of short-term maturity ranges on earnings, rather than the entire asset-liability structure measured by a duration analysis.

[25] When rate-sensitive assets and rate-sensitive liabilities are perfectly balanced, changes in the interest rate have no effect on the earnings stream. The following conditions are needed for a perfectly hedged situation:

- The spread between the returns generated by the assets and the cost of the liabilities remains stable.
- The average maturity of the assets equals the average maturity of the liabilities in each maturity range.
- The distribution of the risk of the asset returns remains the same; the asset-liability maturity ranges include any intermediate cash flows from assets-liabilities that mature later, *or* one analyzes the situation by using duration instead of maturity.

EXHIBIT 17-1
A Gap Analysis

(000,000s)	Over-night	1–30 Days	31–60 Days	61–90 Days	91–135 Days	136–180 Days
Investments	$1750	$ 390	$ 484	$1428	$ 580	$ 440
Loans	—	2230	1780	1802	1440	1590
Total rate-sensitive assets:	$1750	$2620	$2264	$3230	$ 2020	$2030
Money market certificates	—	$1020	$1300	$1500	$ 2610	$1100
Other liabilities	—	530	475	515	900	850
Total rate-sensitive liabilities:	—	$1550	$1775	$2015	$ 3510	$1950
RSA − RSL ("gap")	$1750	$1070	$ 489	$1215	$(1490)	$ (80)

Source: "Inside T-bill Futures," CMEX, p. 13.

when interest rates decrease, since more liabilities than assets are repriced at the lower interest rate. These associations are shown by the following, with E representing earnings:

		i+	i−
Positive gap	RSA − RSL > 0	E+	E−
Negative gap	RSA − RSL < 0	E−	E+

Net interest margin (NIM) is often used as the measure of "earnings" for financial institutions. Net interest margin is the difference between interest income and interest expense. Of course, net earnings would also include operating expenses and other charges. For our purposes, we use earnings and net interest margin interchangeably.[26]

HEDGING MATURITY GAPS

The following discussion on hedging maturity gaps concentrates on the *factors* affecting these hedges. The methods used to identify the type and size of the appropriate hedge are discussed in Chapters 10 to 14. Many financial institutions employ the dollar equivalency hedges described in Chapter 9 when the cash instrument underlying the futures contract is equivalent to the cash instrument being hedged. If the cash instrument differs in kind from the underlying futures instrument (e.g., CDs versus

---

[26] Summing the size of the changes in the interest rates for each maturity times the gap for that maturity provides an approximation for the change in net interest margin. The change in the rate of return for the institution is determined by dividing this change in NIM by the amount of assets or by the capital of the institution.

T-bills), then the relative sensitivities of these instruments to changes in interest rates are determined.[27]

Microhedges and Macrohedges

An institution can hedge either individual assets or the total gap of the institution. This distinction is important. A hedging program that deals with the interest rate sensitivity of the balance sheet by hedging *only* the specific instruments associated with the largest gaps is called **microhedging.** The largest microgaps are typically those related to the shorter-term maturities.[28] More sophisticated hedging programs that determine the overall net effect of a change in interest rates on NIM and then hedge the net gap are called **macrohedging** programs. The success of macrohedging depends on the care used to identify the true NIM volatility inherent in the balance sheet and the sophistication of the hedge procedure.

Theoretically, regulators require that banks employ macrohedging procedures, wherein the bank determines the net interest rate exposure for the entire balance sheet and then hedges this exposure. An extreme version of macrohedging is called "blind macrohedging," which occurs when the entire gap is hedged without concern for the maturity or volatility characteristics of the underlying assets or liabilities that make up the maturity mismatch. A blind macrohedge could provide inferior results as compared to a more analytical approach.

Microhedging occurs when specific assets or liabilities are identified to be hedged. The extreme situation for this procedure is "blind microhedging," in which hedges are placed on specific assets or liabilities without regard for the relevant gap or effect on NIM. Consequently, blind microhedging often *increases* the risk of the institution.

In reality, many financial institutions use a type of microhedge whereby specific assets or liabilities are hedged in relation to the objective of reducing the effect of interest rate changes on NIM. Regulators accept this type of hedge if there is proof that the hedge reduces NIM exposure to changes in interest rates.

Kolb, Timme, and Gay (1984) note that banks use microhedges rather than macrohedges for two reasons. First, bankers associate "hedge" accounting with specific assets or liabilities that can be tracked in price; in fact, many bankers believe that hedge accounting is allowed only when a specific asset (liability) or well-defined set of assets (liabilities) is hedged. Thus, accounting procedures are geared toward microhedging. Second, macrohedging requires a significant amount of information in order to determine the correct gaps. Consequently, gathering and processing this information affects the relative cost of macrohedging versus microhedging. Moreover, the information requirements for macrohedging necessitate a centralized operation, whereas a decentralized operation could institute microhedges for each area of control.

[27] When gaps involve a number of different instruments and maturities, the problem becomes complicated. Some institutions use a combination of short-term and long-term futures contracts to hedge intermediate-term gaps. One may use duration or regression to find the sensitivity of the combined futures position to the cash position in order to determine the appropriate hedge ratio. However, this type of combined futures position creates additional basis risk *if* the shape of the term structure changes, especially if a hump appears in the term structure.

[28] Hedging only the shorter-term maturities simplifies the problem of dealing with the maturity and expiration restrictions of the available futures contracts.

Interest Rate Risk

The objective of hedging gaps is to reduce interest rate risk—that is, to reduce the effect of changes in interest rates on NIM. At the extreme, a program to hedge the entire gap could create a perfectly matched balance sheet. Although such a situation eliminates all interest rate risk, it also reduces the rate of return to below-average or marginal levels. Hence, it is the function of the financial executive to manage the gap structure in order to achieve the desired balance between interest rate risk and rate of return. In essence, the financial executive must consider timing the implementation of hedges by forecasting interest rates.

Selectively hedging because of correct interest rate predictions provides a superior risk-return relationship for the institution. Unfortunately, there is no simple equation that determines *when* to hedge; such a decision is based on judgment and knowledge of the factors affecting interest rates. However, once a decision is formulated concerning the direction of interest rates, the executive can determine *whether* a futures hedge will benefit the institution and determine the size of the hedge and which futures contracts to use. One compromise to the extremes of either completely hedging the gap position or formulating a purely selective hedging program is to hedge a "core" position on a consistent basis and then use selective hedging on the remaining exposed position.

HEDGING CERTIFICATES OF DEPOSIT

The MMCD Short Hedge

The purchase of money market certificates of deposit (MMCD) by the public creates large short-term negative gaps, thereby causing a decline in NIM when interest rates increase. A savings and loan may easily have positive earnings one period and negative earnings the next if short-term rates increase from, say, 7% to 11%. Thus, if the institution believes that short-term rates will increase before the current MMCDs mature and are reissued, or if the institution wants to eliminate routinely this MMCD rollover risk, the future interest rate on these certificates should be hedged.[29]

Let us assume for simplicity that all MMCDs are issued for six months. The MMCD rate is linked directly to the six-month T-bill auction rate. A short hedge with T-bill futures offsets losses resulting from changes in the MMCD rate between the time the hedge is initiated and when existing MMCDs are rolled over. As the MMCDs are rolled over, the futures are repurchased. The gains on the short T-bill futures contracts resulting from the higher interest rates will offset most of the higher interest expense on the MMCDs. Focus 17-1 illustrates the procedure for using T-bill futures for a short hedge of MMCDs.[30]

---

[29] Much of this section is adapted from Parker and Daigler (1981).

[30] This use of interest rate futures markets by national banks is authorized by the Office of the Comptroller of the Currency's revised bank circular no. 79, falling under the category of general asset-liability management hedges.

FOCUS 17-1
A Procedure for Hedging MMCDs

A short hedge with T-bill futures locks in the cost of future MMCDs so as to avoid the adverse effects of potentially higher future interest rates. The higher cost of the MMCDs is offset by the gain in the short futures position. The following procedure is followed during those quarters when a short hedge with T-bill futures is implemented for six-month MMCDs:

- The amount of the negative (90-day) gap that exists and the amount that the institution *decides* to hedge must be determined. Quarters are used because they represent the typical forecast period for most financial institutions.

- On the first day of the quarter, futures are sold to hedge that portion of the gap due to the MMCD rollovers during the quarter. *Two* futures contracts must be sold to hedge each $1 million of cash MMCDs, since T-bill futures are based on 90-day cash T-bills, whereas the MMCDs are six-month instruments. This two-to-one hedge ratio is based on the relative maturity of the cash MMCDs and the futures contract.

- Each week a given portion of the hedged MMCDs is rolled over and reissued. For each $1 million of MMCDs, two futures contracts are repurchased to offset the previous sale. Hence, an increase in MMCD costs due to an increase in interest rates during the quarter (especially large, unanticipated rate increases) is offset by a decrease in futures prices. For each basis point increase in interest rates, the hedge saves $50 in interest rxpense per $1 million in MMCDs—that is, $1 million × (½ year) × .0001 = $50.

- The new MMCDs are no longer hedged after they are rolled over. In addition, under the procedure discussed here, MMCDs being rolled over in a quarter other than the current quarter will not be covered by the hedge. A more encompassing hedge can be devised.

- In general, it is advisable to close out the short positions in T-bill futures only once a week, rather than spreading the closing transactions throughout the week to correspond to the exact issuance date of the MMCDs. The weekly closing is appropriate because the MMCD rate is fixed for the entire week. Monday's closing price of T-bill futures should correspond most closely to the information used to determine the T-bill auction rate, which in turn fixes the weekly MMCD issuance rate. Moreover, closing the shorts only once a week saves on transactions costs if the trades are made in volume.

The decision at the beginning of the quarter to determine whether the bank should hedge the gap is made by one of several methods:

- **Automatically hedge each quarter:** This procedure reduces the variability of earnings as the institution locks in the future MMCD rates.

- **Selectively hedge:** Based on some mechanical rule that attempts to forecast the direction of interest rates.

- **Selectively hedge based on market judgment:** Correct selective hedge decisions provide the highest returns, since profits based on this method include market forecasting returns. However, incorrect hedge decisions adversely affect the variability of returns as well as earnings themselves.

Two tables that provide the basis for analysis and record-keeping purposes are found in Parker and Daigler (1981). The tables show how to set up the hedge positions and rollovers each week, the unhedged and hedged interest expense, and the relevant futures prices.

Considerations in Implementing the MMCD Hedge

Several considerations exist for using T-bill futures to hedge the MMCD position:

- The size of the gap for the period must be forecasted. This is not easy since a number of factors affect the demand for MMCDs. In particular, the size of this gap is affected by the direction of interest rates and the state of the economy. Moreover, the overall basis risk of the gap is affected by the forecasting error of the amount of MMCDs that will be rolled over.

- The procedure employed for this type of hedge affects the risk of the position. Specifically, the procedure for hedging MMCDs presented in Focus 17-1 assumes that only the following quarter's rollovers are hedged. This only reduces the zero- to three-month gap. Hedging for other gaps is possible if care is taken in setting up the hedge.

- Since the quarterly expirations of the futures contracts are a severe restriction in comparison to the weekly maturities of the MMCDs, the basis risk for the procedure used here is affected, although most of the forward rates typically do not vary significantly from one another.

- If hedge accounting is not employed, the futures changes affect earnings in the current quarter, while the higher interest cost does not occur until the six-month period after the MMCDs are rolled over. This timing difference could adversely affect the variability of earnings, although it reduces the overall cost of funds during periods when interest rates increase.

- As Jacobs (1982) notes, futures prices often include a risk premium or "insurance" cost above the expected spot rate. This extra cost means that the hedge can create a net loss, although this loss is significantly less than the loss of an unhedged position when interest rates increase. In effect, this potential "insurance premium" is the payment required to avoid the risk of unanticipated changes in the future interest rate.

SYNTHETIC FIXED-RATE LOANS

Reasons for the Synthetic Fixed-Rate Loan

An interesting application of financial futures contracts for bank management is the **synthetic fixed-rate loan** (SFRL). An SFRL occurs when a variable-rate loan plus a short futures hedge has the same cash flow characteristics as a fixed-rate loan. The typical practice is for the lender to provide a variable-rate loan to the corporation, which is preferable to the bank for asset-liability maturity matching purposes. However, the corporation desires a fixed-rate loan in order to eliminate interest rate risk. An SFRL provides benefits to both parties, since the SFRL keeps the variable-rate loan on the books of the bank while the corporate borrower receives a fixed-rate loan. An additional benefit to both the financial institution and the corporation is that the SFRL reduces credit risk by placing a ceiling on the interest rate paid by the corporation.[31]

---

[31] The use of variable-rate loans by banks has driven the most creditworthy corporations to the commercial paper market in order to obtain funds, leaving the higher-risk medium-size firms to obtain loans from the commercial banks. Financial institutions offering an SFRL would obtain a competitive advantage over other commercial banks to obtain larger corporate customers. Corporations prefer the commercial paper market to bank loans since they obtain lower rates from commercial paper than from a variable-rate loan. Actually, large corporations still affect the bank's risk exposure, even when the corporations obtain their funds from the commercial paper market, since the corporations obtain lines of credit from the banks in order to sell the commercial paper. Of course, the corporations use these bank lines of credit if funds are not obtainable from the commercial paper market. Banks would like to regain the large corporations as potential customers in order to broaden their portfolio choices. In fact, one reason for the large loan program to lesser developed countries during the 1970s and early 1980s was that there were no feasible domestic loan alternatives for the banks.

The SFRL Hedge

A short sale of a short-term financial futures contract, such as Eurodollar or T-bill futures, is all that is necessary to transform a variable-rate loan from a bank into a fixed-rate loan for the corporation. Thus, if interest rates increase, the profits from the short futures transaction offset the higher interest rate costs from the variable-rate loan. Of course, if interest rates fall, the losses on the futures contract offset the *lower* interest costs from the loan. Consequently, except for basis risk, the corporation receives a (synthetic) fixed-rate loan.

For the SFRL to work, the bank must use a market-based instrument to price the loan. The loan rate is typically based on the market instrument index rate plus a premium of, say, two or three percentage points. The index may be T-bills or the Euro-dollar LIBOR rate, as long as the index is an instrument traded on the futures market. Using T-bills or LIBOR would entail a shift in policy of most banks, since they usually employ the prime rate as the index for loans. Since the prime rate is not a traded futures instrument, and since the prime has a poor association with market interest rates, hedging a prime-based variable-rate loan creates a significant amount of basis risk.[32] In fact, Dew and Martell (1981) state that using T-bill futures to hedge a prime-rate loan eliminates only 30% of the risk for weekly repricing and 39% of the risk for monthly repricing.

Implementing the Hedge

An SFRL typically is generated either by the bank or by the corporation. If the bank provides the opportunity for the borrower to receive an SFRL, the synthetic loan is implemented in one of two ways:

- The bank guarantees a fixed rate for the loan, with the loan rate being several percentage points above the current short-term rate. The premium above the current interest rate would compensate for the default risk of the loan *plus* the basis risk that the bank is assuming. This alternative is particularly useful if the bank wants to generate a competitive edge over other institutions in the origination of loans for corporations.

- The bank uses its expertise in risk management and futures markets to generate the SFRL; changes in the variable-rate portion of the loan to the corporation is offset by the changes in the futures contract, except for the basis risk. The agreement between the bank and the corporation stipulates that the basis risk is passed along to the corporation. In this case, the price of the loan is the current short-term rate plus a premium for the default risk of the loan; no premium is included for the basis risk.

If the financial institution does not provide SFRLs, the corporation generates its own SFRL by implementing its own hedges in the futures market. The crucial element in

---

[32] Using a market instrument such as Eurodollars to price the variable-rate loan also benefits the financial institution, since the lack of association between the prime rate and the actual cost of liabilities to the institution makes asset-liability matching difficult, if not impossible. Thus, using the prime rate instead of a market rate *increases* the volatility of earnings for the financial institution. In fact, the R^2 between the cash CD rate (a major source of funds for the institution) and the prime rate for monthly changes during the volatile 1979–1980 period was less than 50% (Dew and Martell, 1981).

this case is to convince the financial institution that it is in the best interests of the institution to use a market-based rate as the base for the variable-rate loan. As noted above, if the institution uses the prime rate, the basis risk will make the hedge practically infeasible.

Difficulties with the SFRL Hedge

Several difficulties can exist that would reduce the attractiveness of the SFRL concept for financial institutions:

- The historical practice associated with fixed-rate loans to corporations is as follows: If interest rates increase, the fixed-rate loan ramains intact, while if interest rates fall significantly, the corporation asks the bank to renegotiate the loan rate. A renegotiation is often agreed to by the bank to keep the corporate customer happy. Obviously, if a futures hedge is set up to transform a variable-rate loan into a fixed-rate loan, then there can be *no* renegotiation of rates unless the bank suffers significant losses or unless severe and enforceable prepayment penalties exist. This issue could be treated with both legal and education components, since a "no renegotiation" clause is essential for the effective operation of the SFRL by the financial institution. Alternatively, the futures contract can be officially assigned to the corporation, alleviating any potential that the corporation would attempt to renegotiate the contract.
- The tradition of the banking industry is to use the prime rate as the benchmark for loans. This tradition has survived, even though the prime rate no longer reflects the cost of money to the banking industry. Either prime must be abandoned by the bank in order to institute an SFRL program, or a liquid prime-rate futures must be available in order to hedge against changes in the prime rate.
- The length of the SFRL is limited by the liquidity of the deferred futures contracts and the longest expiration of these contracts.
- The marking-to-market requirements for futures create a daily cash outflow when interest rates fall. From an economic standpoint, negative cash flows are coincident with lower interest rates for the variable-rate loan issued by the bank; thus, subtracting the negative cash flow (due to the futures marking-to-market requirement) from the fixed-rate amount received by the bank nets to the variable-rate amount desired by the bank (ignoring basis risk). Therefore, the bank's management must be able to distinguish between the net economic effect and the separate futures and loan accounts. Alternatively, the futures contract can be assigned to the corporation so that they are responsible for the cash flows.
- Without hedge accounting, the effects on the earnings of the bank could vary significantly from quarter to quarter. Thus, the futures price changes would affect earnings in the quarter in which they occur, while the effect of the higher earnings from the synthetic fixed-rate loan would be accounted for over the life of the loan. Again, this problem is avoided if the futures contract is assigned to the corporation.

SUMMARY AND LOOKING AHEAD

This chapter examines the uses of financial futures contracts for portfolio management applications. Such applications include asset allocation strategies, portfolio insurance, adjusting bond durations, and commodity funds. This chapter also discusses spread management for financial institutions. Financial institutions employ futures as a tool for adjusting the interest rate risk associated with spread management. Although the term structure and volatility of interest rates cannot be controlled by the institution and the maturity structure of the balance sheet often cannot be changed quickly, the adverse effects of these factors are reduced by employing financial futures. Topics include hedging MMCD rollovers and creating synthetic fixed-rate loans. The following chapters cover special options topics.

BIBLIOGRAPHY

Angrist, Stanley W. (1992). "Of 26 Commodity Market Newsletters Surveyed, Only Four Gave Profitable Advice Last Year," *The Wall Street Journal,* February 10.

Anon. (1984). "When You're Trading Interest-Rate Futures, Ignorance Is Risk," *ABA Banking Journal,* April, p. 72.

Black, Fischer, and Robert Jones (1987). "Simplifying Portfolio Insurance," *Journal of Portfolio Management,* Vol. 14, No. 1, Fall, pp. 48–51.

Bodie, Zvi, and Victor Rosansky (1980). "Risk and Return in Commodity Futures," *Financial Analysts Journal,* Vol. 36, No. 3, May–June, pp. 27–39.

Chicago Mercantile Exchange, "Inside T-Bill Futures," Pamphlet, No Date.

"Concepts and Applications: Using Interest Rate Futures in Pension Fund Management" (1987). The Chicago Board of Trade, pamphlet.

Dew, James Kurt, and Terrence F. Martell (1981). "Treasury Bill Futures, Commercial Lending, and the Synthetic Fixed-Rate Loan," *The Journal of Commercial Bank Lending,* June, pp. 27–38.

Elton, Edwin J., Martin J. Gruber, and Joel Rentzler (1989). "Commodity Funds: Does the Prospectus Really Tell All?" *AAII Journal,* Vol. 11, No. 9, October, pp. 8–11.

Fong, Gifford, Charles Pearson, and Oldrich Vasicek (1983). "Bond Performance: Analyzing Sources of Return," *Journal of Portfolio Management,* Vol. 9, No. 3, Spring, pp. 46–50.

Jacklin, Charles J., Allan W. Kleidon, and Paul Pfleiderer (1992). "Underestimation of Portfolio Insurance and the Crash of October 1987," *Review of Financial Studies,* Vol. 5, No. 1, pp. 35–64.

Jacobs, Rodney L. (1982). "Restructuring the Maturity of Regulated Deposits with Treasury-Bill Futures," *The Journal of Futures Markets,* Vol. 2, No. 2, Summer, pp. 183–193.

Kawaller, Ira (1987). "The Beta Bogy," *Futures,* July, pp. 64, 66.

Kolb, Robert W., Stephen G. Timme, and Gerald D. Gay (1984). "Macro Versus Micro Futures Hedges at Commercial Banks," *The Journal of Futures Markets,* Vol. 4, No. 1, Spring, pp. 47–54.

Lindahl, Mary, Ken Boze, and Mike Ferris (1987). "Hedging Market Risk with Stock Index Futures and Options," working paper, The University of Alaska, Fairbanks.

Parker, Jack W., and Robert T. Daigler (1981). "Hedging Money Market CDs with Treasury-Bill Futures," *The Journal of Futures Markets,* Vol. 1, No. 4, Winter, pp. 597–606.

Rose, Sanford (1981). "Banks Should Look to the Futures," *Fortune,* April 20, pp. 185–186, 188, 190–192.

Sharpe, W. F. (1981). "Decentralized Investment Management," *Journal of Finance,* Vol. 36, No. 2, May, pp. 217–234.

PROBLEMS

*Indicates more difficult problems.

17-1   Changing the Duration of a Bond Portfolio

On September 10 a portfolio manager forecasts a large decline in bond yields over the next quarter. Due to the forecast, the manager decides to purchase futures contracts as a means of increasing the duration of the portfolio. Given the attached data, determine the number of contracts required to achieve the manager's new duration goal for the portfolio.

	September 10	December
Portfolio duration	3.58	8.0 (target)
Bond futures price	89-16	96-24
Portfolio market value	250,000,000	250,000,000
YTM	8.94%	
BPV of futures	$97.51	

17-2   Creating a Synthetic Instrument

Determine how many long-term futures contracts must be added to a cash T-bill position in order to replicate a ten-year security given the following:

BPV for T-bill ($20MM): $515.20
BPV for 10-year T-note ($20MM): $16,185.88
BPV for T-bond futures: = $104.92

*17-3   Changing the Duration of a Portfolio

It is now March 1, 1991, and over the next three months you expect a steep decline in bond yields. You have decided to buy futures contracts in order to increase the duration of the portfolio.

	March 1, 1991	June 30, 1991
Portfolio duration	4.9	
Target duration	8.0	
Bond cash price	89:16	96:8
Cash portfolio par value	$100,000,000	
BPV of futures	$70.50	
Portfolio yield to maturity	10.4%	8.5%

Convert the cash portfolio duration and target portfolio duration to basis point values and then determine the number of contracts needed to arrive at the desired portfolio duration. Also, give profit and return results with and without using futures. Assume annual coupon payments and that the futures have the same yield change as the cash portfolio.

*17-4   Basis Point Value

A portfolio of high-grade corporate bonds has a current YTM of 11.35%, a market value of $14,235,000, and a BPV of $9887.38. If the investment manager wishes to reduce interest rate sensitivity by 25%, what would be the new portfolio duration?

17-5   Adjusting Portfolio Beta

An investor decides that his stock portfolio is too volatile. He wants to lower the beta of the portfolio from its current value of 1.3 to a target of .7. What is the number of futures contracts needed to reduce the portfolio beta, given that the dollar value of the portfolio is $1 million and the current value of the S&P 500 Index is 270.00?

*17-6   Asset Allocation

A pension fund portfolio manager forecasts that within the next month long-term interest rates will decline. He also forecasts that the S&P 500 Index will decrease within the following month. The current composition of the portfolio is: bonds, 40%; stocks, 40%; T-bills, 20%. In view of the expected changes, the portfolio manager proposes to change the portfolio's composition to 60%, 20%, and 20%. Bonds pay interest semiannually. The following information is available on the current portfolio and includes forecasted values for a target portfolio.

	Current Portfolio	Target Portfolio
Bonds: market value	$40,000,000	$60,000,000
Stocks: market value	$40,000,000	$20,000,000
T-bills: market value	$20,000,000	$20,000,000
Portfolio beta	.97	.97
Nearby S&P 500 futures	336.95	305.20
Nearby T-bond futures	88-22	94-16
Duration of T-bond portfolio	6	10
Portfolio YTM	10.00%	
Duration of cheapest-to-deliver bond	7	
Conversion factor	1.1111	

a. How many T-bond futures contracts are needed to achieve the targeted results?
b. How many stock index futures contracts are needed to alter the asset allocation?
c. Show the profits arising from the transactions.

17-7   Portfolio Insurance

A manager has an insurance portfolio with a value of $100 million and has chosen a floor value of $80 million; the multiple to be used is 2.5. Determine the equity exposure desired.

17-8   Alternative Returns with Eurodollar Strips

Based on the following, would it be more profitable to invest in a one-year Eurodollar time deposit or to employ a strip of futures? Find the ending dollar amounts for each possibility; the current date is March 20. LIBOR rates: 3 months, 8.5%; 1 year, 9.0%.

Eurodollar Futures	Settle
June	91.28
September	91.17
December	91.02

17-9   Alternative Returns with Strips with Eurodollar Futures

On December 19 a portfolio manager in Europe has $1 million to invest the next day in a short-term fixed-rate investment. The portfolio manager has narrowed the selection to two options:

- Place the $1 million cash in a Eurodollar time deposit for one year.
- Place the $1 million cash in a 3-month Eurodollar time deposit expiring in March *and* at the same time purchase a strip of three Eurodollar futures contracts expiring in March, June, and September. (Assume that the original time deposit matures when the first futures expire.)

The following conditions exist in December:

	Yield/Index
One-year Eurodollar time deposit	7.98
Three-month Eurodollar time deposit	7.95
Eurodollar futures expiring in March	92.18
Eurodollar futures expiring in June	92.19
Eurodollar futures expiring in September	92.09

  a. What is the total dollar value from choosing option 1?
  b. What is the total dollar value from choosing option 2?
  c. Which alternative should the portfolio manager choose and why?

17-10   Asset-Liability Hedge

Eagle Savings and Loan has an $800 million mortgage portfolio. $400 million of the portfolio has an $8\frac{3}{4}\%$ fixed rate with 25 years to maturity. The other $400 million in mortgages is in variable-rate loans based on the 90-day T-bill rate plus a 2% premium. Liabilities consist of $800 million three-month certificates of deposit. The interest rate on these CDs is the 90-day T-bill rate plus $\frac{5}{8}\%$.

How would you hedge this portfolio to offset the potentially higher cost of the CDs to be issued in the future? How many futures contracts are needed for the hedge? Set up a table for the cash and futures transactions on March 12 and September 12 given the following:

March 12 cash T-bill rate:	$7\frac{5}{8}\%$
September T-bill futures index:	92.40
September 12 cash T-bill rate:	$11\frac{5}{8}\%$
September T-bill futures index:	88.55

17-11   Asset-Liability Management (Hedging)

Amerifirst Bank wishes to hedge $10 million in six-month money market CDs.
  a. Which futures contract should be used? How many contracts should be sold? Why?
  b. If the futures price fell by 100 basis points, what would be the savings to Amerifirst from hedging?

17-12 MMCDs Creation of Earnings Volatility

Bank of Boston has $10 million in fixed-rate mortgages at 10½%. It is funding these mortgages with the bank's MMCDs presently at 9¾%. For the next five periods of six months each the MMCD rate changes to 9½%, 9%, 9⅜%, 10½%, and 11%, respectively.

a. What will happen to the bank's earnings as the MMCD rate fluctuates?

b. How could the change in interest rates be offset?

Chapter 18

OPTIONS ON FUTURES

Overview

Options on futures provide the buyer the right to buy (call option) or sell (put option) a futures contract at a specific strike price for a specific period of time. Options on stock index futures, T-bond and T-note futures, Eurodollar futures, energy futures, and certain agricultural futures are active contracts, with each contract having its own characteristics. Each option on futures has a specific futures contract as the underlying security, with a call option buyer receiving a long position in the futures and the put buyer receiving a short futures position at option expiration (if the option is exercised).

The pricing of options on futures typically is based on the Black model, which adapts the Black-Scholes model to options on futures. However, the early exercise provision of American options on futures creates pricing problems for the Black European pricing model. In particular, traders often exercise in-the-money options on futures early in order to invest the proceeds at the risk-free interest rate. Put-call parity is also useful for pricing options on futures. Moreover, put-call parity in combination with the Black model for call options creates a model for pricing put options on futures. The basic speculative and hedging applications of options on futures parallel those of options on stocks, including covered option writing and using protective puts.

Terminology

*Option on futures   An option contract having a futures contract as the underlying asset; thus, the futures contract changes hands at delivery.

A BACKGROUND TO OPTIONS ON FUTURES

What Are Options on Futures?

An option on an asset, such as a stock, provides the right to buy the asset (a call option) or the right to sell the asset (a put option) at the strike price until the option expires. If the option is exercised, the asset changes hands at the strike price.[1] **Options on futures** (or, equivalently, futures options) are contracts for which *futures* are the underlying asset that changes hands at the time of delivery. As with other options, the option buyer has the right (but not the obligation) to execute the option. Thus, the call buyer can choose to exercise the option to buy the futures contract at the strike price (take a long position in the futures at the strike price), while the put buyer can choose to sell the futures contract at the strike price (take a long position in the futures at the strike price). All of the typical option concepts apply. For example, the owner of a call option will exercise the right to buy the futures contract only if doing so produces a profit or reduces a loss.

Options on futures were banned from exchange trading in 1936. During the late 1970s and early 1980s, before options on futures trading were allowed on organized exchanges in the United States, over-the-counter options houses sold options on international commodities such as sugar. While commodity options trading in London was a respectable enterprise, many of the U.S. options houses doubled or tripled the London price of these options, used hard-sell telephone pitches to unsophisticated customers, and abruptly closed offices when their customers' options became profitable, subsequently reopening under a new name. In response to these illegal over-the-counter practices, the Commodity Futures Trading Commission allowed each exchange to trade one option on futures contract, starting in 1982. The success of this program caused permanent authorization for options on futures in 1987. Currently, options on futures are traded on futures exchanges for many types of futures contracts, including stock index futures, interest rate futures, currency futures, and agricultural and commodity futures. Options on financial futures constitute over 40% of the entire futures options

---

[1] Index options settle by means of a cash transfer of the difference in price between the final asset price and the strike price since delivering a portfolio of assets is too cumbersome.

volume, with currency options on futures contributing around 20% and agricultural futures options less than 20%. Energy futures options have a volume of about 15%.

What Are the Advantages of Options on Futures?

Options on futures have the following benefits over futures contracts:

- Options have a limited loss feature that futures do not possess.
- A long call and a short put position create a synthetic long futures position (as discussed later).[2]
- Although both futures options and futures have equivalent price limits that restrict the maximum price change for a given day, a number of the futures options continue to trade after futures hit their price limits, since near-the-money option prices move less than the underlying futures contracts. For example, during the October 1987 market crash, T-bond futures hit their daily price limit, but options on T-bond futures continued to trade. However, stock index futures stop trading when the circuit breakers become effective.
- Options on futures allow producers of commodities to hedge quantity risk as well as price risk, while futures allow only one to hedge price risk. Since agricultural producers do not know the size of the harvest, futures options provide a less risky method for hedging.

However, futures options need futures contracts to exist, since futures are the delivery and pricing instrument needed for the futures options to trade.

Options on futures also provide these benefits that typically do not exist for an option on the underlying cash asset:

- Futures contracts are liquid and trade continuously when the futures exchange is open, allowing option traders access to the prices of an actively traded underlying asset. This characteristic is beneficial for the pricing of the options contract.[3]
- Implementing option strategies involving the underlying security, such as covered call and protective put hedges, are often easier with futures options. This is because options on the cash asset could require a complicated portfolio of stocks, an illiquid bond, or options on many different grades of wheat.
- Delivery of the futures contract when the option is exercised is a simple wire transfer of a standardized futures contract with no quality variations. Moreover, exercise of a futures option results in a futures position with limited margin requirements, while exercise of a cash option requires purchase of the cash asset.
- The regulations of the exchanges provide safeguards for the option trader that do not exist for the over-the-counter version of these options.
- The ability to exercise options on futures contracts early allows the trader to invest accumulated profits in a risk-free asset without needing cash to buy the asset. (This characteristic of options on futures is discussed below.)

[2] Similarly, a long put and a short call create a synthetic short futures position. However, futures can create option positions only if a dynamic hedging program with futures is initiated. A dynamic hedge involves constantly revising the hedge position. Moreover, this strategy assumes that large jumps in the underlying futures price do not occur, since such jumps negate the ability to revise the hedge position quickly.

[3] One reason futures options can provide more accurate pricing than exchange-traded options on cash assets is because the futures options trade alongside the fututres contracts on the exchanges. Hence, the floor traders know the current price of the underlying futures contracts.

Despite the advantages of options on futures over options on cash assets, cash options have a high volume for certain securities, such as the S&P 100 Index and foreign currencies.

CHARACTERISTICS AND QUOTATIONS OF OPTIONS ON FUTURES

The characteristics and quotation procedures for options on futures are stated below. Currency options on futures are discussed in conjunction with cash currency options in Chapter 19. Exhibit 18-1 provides an example of the quotations of options on futures contracts.

EXHIBIT 18-1
Options on Futures Quotations

INDEX

S&P 500 STOCK INDEX (CME)
  $500 times premium

Strike Price	Calls–Settle			Puts–Settle		
	May	Jun	Jly	May	Jun	Jly
425	....	16.70	....	2.40	4.75	6.40
430	10.50	13.10	....	3.50	6.15	....
435	7.10	9.80	....	5.10	7.80	9.60
440	4.35	7.00	....	7.35	10.00	11.75
445	2.35	4.70	....	10.30	12.65	14.30
450	1.10	3.05	4.95	14.05	15.95	17.35

Est. vol. 7,374;
Thur vol. 4,104 calls; 6,925 puts
Op. int. Thur 28,968 calls; 92,068 puts

INTEREST RATE

T-BONDS (CBT)
  $100,000; points and 64ths of 100%

Strike Price	Calls–Settle			Puts–Settle		
	May	Jun	Sep	May	Jun	Sep
108	4-04	3-55	3-42	...	0-10	1-15
110	2-04	2-14	2-30	...	0-32	2-01
112	0-07	1-00	1-36	0-05	1-18	3-07
114	...	0-23	0-59	2-08	2-41	4-29
116	...	0-05	0-33	...	4-22	7-39
118	...	0-01	0-17	...	6-18	...

Est. vol. 115,000;
Thur vol. 57,061 calls; 41,220 puts
Op. int. Thur 321,142 calls, 330,023 puts

continued next page

continued

T-NOTES (CBT)
$100,000; points and 64ths of 100%

110	3-01	2-59	2-41	0-01	0-13	1-04
111	2-00	2-02	2-02	0-01	0-28	1-29
112	1-01	1-18	1-33	0-01	0-55	1-59
113	0-05	0-45	1-06	0-05	1-31	2-30
114	0-01	0-21	0-50	. . .	2-17	3-09
115	0-01	0-08	0-34	. . .	. . .	3-56

Est. vol. 25,000;
Thur vol. 10,256 calls; 10,810 puts
Op. int. Thur 99,041 calls; 135,972 puts

EURODOLLAR (CME)
$ million; pts. of 100%

Strike Price	Calls–Settle			Puts–Settle		
	Jun	Sep	Dec	Jun	Sep	Dec
9625	0.54	0.46	0.27	.0004	0.03	0.18
9650	0.30	0.25	0.14	0.01	0.07	0.30
9675	0.08	0.09	0.06	0.04	0.16	0.46
9700	0.01	0.02	0.03	0.22	0.34	0.68
9725	.0004	.0004	0.01	0.46	0.57	0.91
9750	.0004	.0004	.0004	0.71	. . . .	. . .

Est. vol. 51,488;
Thur vol. 34,089 calls; 59,702 puts
Op int. Thur 526,390 calls; 561,143 puts

METALS
GOLD (CMX)
100 troy ounces; $ per troy ounce

Strike Price	Calls–Settle			Puts–Settle		
	Jun	Jly	Aug	Jun	Jly	Aug
330	17.70	19.60	20.30	.30	1.00	1.50
340	9.00	11.50	12.50	1.50	2.60	3.60
350	3.30	5.50	6.80	5.80	6.60	7.80
360	1.30	2.30	3.70	12.60	13.50	14.60
370	.70	1.30	2.00	22.50	22.70	22.70
380	.30	.80	1.40	32.50	31.70	31.50

Est. vol. 12,000;
Thur vol. 2,400 calls; 1,464 puts
Op. int. Thur 101,355 calls; 29,260 puts

continued next page

Stock Index Options

The most active stock index option on futures is the S&P 500 contract. This contract has strike prices differing by 5 points and active options for the first three expirations.

continued

SILVER (CMX)
5,000 troy ounces; cts per troy ounce

Strike	Calls–Settle			Puts–Settle		
Price	Jun	Jly	Sep	Jun	Jly	Sep
350	48.3	48.9	52.0	0.1	0.7	1.5
375	24.5	26.4	32.0	1.3	3.2	6.2
400	7.5	12.0	17.8	9.3	13.8	17.0
425	2.2	5.6	10.8	29.0	32.4	35.0
450	0.7	2.8	6.3	52.5	54.6	55.0
475	0.4	2.0	4.5	77.2	78.8	78.0

Est. vol. 5,000;
Thur vol. 3,037 calls; 901 puts
Op. int. Thur 65,249 calls; 14,723 puts

OIL

CRUDE OIL (NYM)
1,000 bbls.; $ per bbl.

Strike	Calls–Settle			Puts–Settle		
Price	Jun	Jly	Aug	Jun	Jly	Aug
18	2.35	2.54	2.67	.01	.04	.06
19	1.37	1.61	1.78	.03	.11	.16
20	.51	.79	.98	.17	.28	.35
21	.08	.25	.45	.74	.74	.82
22	.01	.09	.17	1.67	1.57	. . .
23	.01	.03	.05	2.67	2.51	. . .

Est. vol. 15,184;
Thur vol. 11,166 calls; 17,083 puts
Op. int. Thur 374,312 calls; 189,800 puts

HEATING OIL No.2 (NYM)
42,000 gal.; $ per gal.

Strike	Calls–Settle			Puts–Settle		
Price	May	Jun	Jly	May	Jun	Jly
52	.0382	.0384	.0432	.0001	.0007	.0018
54	.0182	.0209	.0266	.0001	.0032	.0051
56	.0001	.0085	.0139	.0018	.0107	.0123
58	.0001	.0029	.0065	.0218	.0250	.0248
60	.0001	.0010	.0025	.0418	.0431	.0407
62	.0001	.0003	.0010	. . . .	. . . .	. . . .

Est. vol. 2,343;
Thur vol. 422 calls; 834 puts
Op. int. Thur 26,143 calls; 21,963 puts

continued next page

continued

GASOLINE–Unlead (NYM)
42,000 gal.; $ per gal.

Strike Price	Calls–Settle			Puts–Settle		
	May	**Jun**	**Jly**	**May**	**Jun**	**Jly**
56	.0435	.0454	.0469	.0001	.0009	.0022
58	.0241	.0275	.0301	.0001	.0030	.0053
60	.0001	.0135	.0180	.0006	.0089	.0123
62	.0001	.0051	.0095	.0206	.0205	.0245
64	.0001	.0019	.0044	....	....	....
66	.0001	.0009	.0020	.0606	....	....

Est. vol. 4,968;
Thur vol. 3,207 calls; 1,730 puts
Op. int. Thur 38,797 calls; 27,383 puts

AGRICULTURAL

CORN (CBT)
5,000 bu.; cents per bu.

Strike Price	Calls–Settle			Puts–Settle		
	May	**Jly**	**Sep**	**May**	**Jly**	**Sep**
200	25	29¾	35	c1	⅛	¼
210	15¼	20½	26¼	c1	¼	1¾
220	5¼	11¾	19½	c1	2¼	4¾
230	c1	6⅝	13¾	4¾	6¾	9
240	c1	3⅝	10	14½	13¾	15½
250	c1	1⅞	7½	24½	21½	22½

Ext. vol. 10,000;
Thur vol. 7,306 calls; 3,284 puts
Op. int. Thur 109,472 calls; 56,255 puts

SOYBEANS (CBT)
5,000 bu.; cents per bu.

Strike Price	Calls–Settle			Puts–Settle		
	May	**Jly**	**Aug**	**May**	**Jly**	**Aug**
550	42	45¼	48¾	c1	1	3½
575	16¾	25	32	c1	5¾	11½
600	c2	12¾	21¼	8¼	18¼	25¾
625	c1	6⅞	15¼	33	37½	44¾
650	c1	4	12	...	59¾	65¾
675	c1	2½	8¾	...	83	...

Est. vol. 5,000;
Thur vol. 5,528 calls; 1,631 puts
Op. int. Thur 113,307 calls; 49,179 puts

continued next page

continued

WHEAT (CBT)
5,000 bu.; cents per bu.

Strike Price	Calls–Settle			Puts–Settle		
	May	Jly	Sep	May	Jly	Sep
330	22	2⅜	6½	⅛	27½	28¾
340	12	1½	4¾	⅛	36½	...
350	1½	1	3½	⅜	45½	...
360	⅛	⅝	2½	9	55¼	...
370	⅛	⅜	1¾	19½	65	...
380	⅛	⅛	1¼	29	...	...

Est. vol. 4,000;
Thur vol. 1,707 calls; 2,024 puts
Op. Int. Thur 31,107 calls; 19,532 puts

SUGAR–WORLD (CSCE)
112,000 lbs.; cents per lb.

Strike Price	Calls–Settle			Puts–Settle		
	Jun	Jly	Oct	Jun	Jly	Oct
11.50	1.00	1.32	1.26	0.15	0.44	0.90
12.00	0.71	0.95	1.09	0.33	0.60	1.23
12.50	0.50	0.74	0.90	0.62	0.89	1.54
13.00	0.33	0.57	0.76	0.95	1.19	1.90
14.00	0.10	0.35	0.55	1.72	1.97	2.69
15.00	0.08	0.20	0.39	2.70	2.82	3.53

Est. vol. 9,244;
Thur vol. 3,686 calls; 2,463 puts
Op. int. Thur 41,616 calls; 30,467 puts

Source: Futures Exchanges, April 23.

Expirations exist for the current and next month and two additional expirations in the financial cycle of March, June, September, and December. The total cost of the option is 500 times the quoted option price. Thus, each .05 price change (the minimum tick size) results in a change of $25 for the option. For example, the 440 call for the May S&P 500 futures options in Exhibit 18-1 cost 4.35, or $500 × 4.35 = $2175 per option. Options also exist on the Major Market Index futures, the NYSE Composite Index futures, and the Nikkei 225 Stock Average futures; however, their option volumes are 200 or fewer contracts per day.

Each option expires in the last half of the expiration month. The S&P 500 options on futures that expire during a financial futures cycle month stop trading on the Thursday prior to the third Friday of the expiration month. Options that expire during other months stop trading on the third Friday of the month. When an option on a stock index futures contract is exercised, the call option buyer receives a long position (the put buyer takes a short position) in the *next* futures expiration. Thus, if a January S&P 500 options futures is exercised, a call buyer receives the March S&P 500 futures contract.[4]

Interest Rate Options

Active options on futures trade for the following contracts: T-bonds, Ten-year T-notes, Five-year T-notes, Eurodollars, and the British Long Gilt bond. Low-volume options on futures trade for the Municipal Bond Index, the one-month LIBOR contract, T-bills, and Two-year T-notes. The T-bond and Eurodollar futures options have open interest that exceeds 400,000 and 600,000 options contracts, respectively, making these options the most successful contracts traded.

The T-bond and T-note interest rate futures options have expirations within 30 days (the nearby option) plus options for the following two months in the financial cycle. The Municipal bond, Eurodollar, T-bill, and Long Gilt contracts trade options that expire only for the financial cycle. T-bond and T-note options on futures expire during the month *previous* to the futures expiration (specifically, on the Friday at least five business days before the first notice day for the futures delivery). Hence, a September option on T-bond futures actually expires in August. Similarly, the nearby option month actually expires during the month previous to the month quoted in the paper (an August option expires in July, etc.).

The prices of long-term interest rate options on futures (T-bonds, T-notes, Municipal bonds, and the Gilt contract) are quoted in $1/64$ths of a point. Thus, a quoted price of 1-10 represents 1 and $10/64$ths points. Each point is 1% of the par value of the $100,000 futures contract, or $1000. For example, the June 110 T-bond futures options in Exhibit 18-1 are quoted at 2 and $14/64$, or $2218.75 per option. The strike prices for T-bonds are in units of two points. Ten-year T-notes and the Municipal bond contract have strike price intervals of one point. The five-year T-note options on futures have strike price intervals of $1/2$ point. The short-term interest rate options on futures have strike price intervals of $1/4$ to $1/2$ of a percentage point, depending on the contract and the level of interest rates. The par value for the Eurodollar, LIBOR, and T-bill contracts is $1,000,000. Therefore, options on futures par values are based on the par values of the underlying futures contracts. Exhibit 18-2 provides the contract specifications for the options on financial futures contracts.

One major advantage of active interest rate futures options as compared to over-the-counter debt options is the liquidity of the exchange-traded contracts. Hence, those wishing to trade a large volume or those who want to offset a current position quickly and at a fair price are more likely to achieve their aims if an active interest rate futures option contract exists. In addition, futures options can be exercised at any time, while over-the-counter options are European-style options that can be exercised only on the expiration date.

---

[4] If an option that expires in March, June, September, or December is exercised on the last trading day, then the option is settled via cash since the futures contract is no longer trading. The cash settlement is based on the S&P 500 Index value on the open of the next day, the third Friday of the contract month. This is the same procedure used to settle the futures contract.

EXHIBIT 18-2
Contract Specifications for Major Financial Options on Futures

Option Contract on:	Price Interval	Strike Intervals	Daily Price Limit	Contract Months*	Last Trading Day	Automatic Exercise
S&P 500 futures	.05 = $25	5 points	Close when S&P 500 futures close	(1)	(2)	(5)
T-bond futures	1/64 = $15.625	2 points (1 point nearby)	3 points	(3)	(4)	(5)
10-year T-note futures	1/64 = $15.625	1 point	3 points	(3)	(4)	(5)
5-year T-note futures	1/64 = $15.625	1/2 point	3 points	(3)	(4)	(5)
Eurodollar futures	.01 = $25	.25 of an index point (7)	None	FC	(6)	(5)
Gold	$.10 = $10	$10 (below $500)	$75	monthly	(8)	(5)

(1) The current month and the next calendar month plus the financial cycle.
(2) During a futures expiration month, trading stops on the Thursday before the third Friday of the month. For a non-futures expiration month, trading stops on the third Friday of the month.
(3) A contract with less than 30 days until expiration plus the financial cycle.
(4) Noon on the Friday preceded by at least five business days before the first notice day of delivery of the futures contract.
(5) All in-the-money options at expiration are automatically exercised (as of late 1993).
(6) The last day and time as the underlying futures expire.
(7) The strike interval is .50 when the index is below 91.00 (the interest rate is above 9%).
(8) Second Friday of the month before futures expiration.

*FC = the financial cycle of March, June, September, and December
Source: Exchange booklets.

Agricultural and Commodity Options

Options on futures for agricultural items, oil, livestock, and metals exist for a number of different commodities, but many of these options on futures contracts have volume below 1000 contracts per day. The most active agricultural options on futures are for corn, soybeans, wheat, coffee, and sugar, with 2000 to 12,000 options contracts traded per day for these contracts. Live cattle options are the only active livestock options on futures contract. Each option has its own quotation procedures, size of contract, expiration months, and strike price intervals. Newspapers such as *The Wall Street Journal* specify these characteristics (or see Exhibit 18-1).

The crude oil options on futures is a very active market, with option volume of 30,000 to 50,000 contracts per day. Heating oil and gasoline options on futures trade 3000 to 4000 contracts per day. The strike price interval for crude oil options is $1.

Gold and silver options on futures are active, with copper and platinum options being less active. The price of the gold options is in dollars times 100 troy ounces per contract. Gold has strike price intervals of 10 dollars. Silver options are in cents times 5000 troy ounces per contract. Silver has strike intervals of 25 cents.

General Characteristics

The underlying security for an option on futures contract is a futures contract. Hence, the size of the option contract is equivalent to the underlying futures contract. A long position in a call option on futures gives the buyer the right to take a long position in the underlying futures contract at the strike price. A long position in a put gives the buyer the right to take a short position in the underlying futures contract. Conversely, the seller (writer) of a call assumes the obligation to take a short position in the futures (if the buyer exercises the option), while the seller of a put has the obligation to take a long futures position. Futures options are American options; therefore, they can be exercised on any day that the exchange is open. When an option is exercised, the clearinghouse randomly chooses the seller to take the futures position opposite the option buyer.

Options on futures buyers do not require a margin payment, since the most they can lose is the cost of the option. However, the seller of an option on futures must put up margin on the option account, because a loss can occur for the seller (the seller must be ready to take a futures position at a price that immediately creates a loss). The margin needed in the account for the seller is calculated daily. When an option on futures is exercised, the previous owner of the option receives the profit (the difference between the futures price and the strike price), while the previous short on the option must pay this amount. For example, if the strike price of an S&P 500 futures option is 430 and the futures contract trades at 437 when the call option on the futures is exercised, then the call buyer receives a payment of $3500 (7 points × 500) from the seller; in addition, the call buyer receives a long futures position and the seller takes a short futures position. Since a futures position is undertaken, both the new long and new short for the futures must put up futures margins (unless the futures contract is covered immediately). Exhibit 18-3 summarizes the positions and cash flows when futures options are exercised.

EXHIBIT 18-3
Positions and Cash Flows When Futures Options Are Exercised

Option	Futures Position	Cash Flows
Call		
Owner	Receives long futures position	Receives $P_F - K$
Seller	Takes short futures position	Pays $P_F - K$
Put		
Owner	Takes short futures position	Receives $K - P_F$
Seller	Receives long futures position	Pays $K - P_F$

P_F = the futures price when option is exercised
K = the option exercise price

The option position is created with the clearinghouse of the exchange (but there must be both a buyer and a seller of the option to create the position). The clearinghouse *automatically* exercises expiring in-the-money futures options if the option is sufficiently in-the-money and if the corresponding futures are also expiring, unless specific instructions are given not to exercise the contract. Such automatic exercises are executed because the in-the-money options have value. For example, in-the-money options on S&P 500 futures during the expiration month are automatically exercised. Options on T-bond and T-note futures must be at least two points in-the-money to be automatically exercised.

Trading Options on the Exchange

Futures options are traded on the futures exchanges next to the associated futures contracts. While most of the futures traders are scalpers—that is, they buy at the bid and sell at the ask price—only about 10% of the options on futures traders are scalpers. Most of the option floor traders are spreaders between different strike prices or generate a synthetic position by an appropriate combination of the options and the futures contracts. Such trades reduce the risk for the option floor traders, since typically there is insufficient liquidity in any one option for many traders to operate as scalpers.

Since the floor traders use spreads and synthetic trades, finding the fair option price and the option deltas and thetas become important trading tools. These sensitivities allow the floor trader to limit risk and to determine whether options are mispriced. Implied volatilities also provide important information concerning whether certain options are mispriced and the market attitude about future changes in the underlying futures contract.

THE PRICING OF OPTIONS ON FUTURES CONTRACTS

In general, the pricing relationships explained for options on stocks are also valid for options on futures. In fact, at expiration a European call on a futures contract provides a price that is equivalent to a European call on the cash asset, if both can be exercised at the same time and at option expiration. This equivalent price occurs because the exercise of the call provides a futures contract that expires immediately.[5] However, several exceptions do exist for an American option on futures, which is the type of contract traded in the United States. For example, if the futures option is sufficiently in-the-money, it can be more profitable to exercise the option early than to wait until option expiration. Thus, in this case, an American option on the futures is worth more than an American option on the cash asset (when the latter has no cash flows). The effect of early exercise and other differences in pricing between options on futures and options on the cash asset are explored in conjunction with the pricing equations discussed below.

The Black Model for Calls

Fisher Black (1976) developed a model to price options on futures. The model is based on the Black-Scholes model for options on cash assets without intermediate cash flows. When the option and corresponding futures contracts expire simultaneously, Equation (18-1) determines the fair value of a call option on futures:

$$P_C = e^{-rt}[P_F N(d_1) - KN(d_2)] \qquad (18\text{-}1)$$

where

$$d_1 = \frac{\ln(P_F/K) + (.5\sigma^2)t}{\sigma\sqrt{t}} \qquad (18\text{-}2)$$

$$d_2 = d_1 - \sigma\sqrt{t} \qquad (18\text{-}3)$$

The equation for d_1 above does not contain the risk-free rate, as it does in the Black-Scholes option equation for stocks. For stocks one must consider the opportunity cost of funds invested in the stock, while for futures no investment funds are needed.[6] Normal distribution and natural logarithm tables are found in Appendices A and B at the back of the book. Example 18-1 illustrates the usage of the Black model.

The prices obtained from the Black model can be slightly smaller than the actual option market prices. The reason for this is that futures contracts involve a daily resettlement on the profits/losses of the contract. This is equivalent to a continuous dividend for a stock option. Since the Black model is based on a European model, which assumes that intermediate cash flows such as dividends and marking-to-market do not exist and

---

[5] The value of a European option on futures calculated via a model could differ from the option on the cash asset, since the futures contract typically is more volatile than the cash asset.

[6] Margin on the futures can be posted in T-bills rather than cash so that no immediate cash investment is needed. The Black-Scholes and the Black models can be shown to be equivalent if $P_F e^{-rt}$ is substituted for P_S in the Black-Scholes model. Thus, the two models will give equivalent results *if* the volatilities of the cash and futures instruments are equivalent *and* intermediate cash flows such as marking-to-market of the futures are ignored. Moreover, note that if no uncertainty existed—that is, $N(d_1)$ and $N(d_2)$ equal 1.0—then the Black model is $P_C = e^{-rt}[P_F - K]$, which means that the value of the call option when certainty exists equals the present value of the proceeds when the option is exercised.

EXAMPLE 18-1
The Black Model and S&P 500 Options on Futures

The Black model for finding the fair value of a call option on futures is:

$$P_C = e^{-rt}[P_F N(d_1) - KN(d_2)] \tag{18-1}$$

where

$$d_1 = \frac{\ln(P_F/K) + (.5\sigma^2)t}{\sigma\sqrt{t}} \tag{18-2}$$

$$d_2 = d_1 - \sigma\sqrt{t} \tag{18-3}$$

The inputs for an option on the S&P 500 futures are as follows:

$$P_F = 442.15 \qquad K = 445 \qquad \sigma_S = .21 \qquad r = 3.3\% \qquad t = 82/365 = .22466$$

$$d_1 = \frac{\ln(442.15/445) + .5(.21)^2(.22466)}{.21\sqrt{.2247}}$$

$$= \frac{\ln(.9935955) + .5(.0441)(.22466)}{.21(.474025)}$$

$$= \frac{-.00643 + .00495375}{.0995453} = -.01483$$

$$d_2 = -.01483 - .21\sqrt{.2247}$$

$$= -.01483 - .0995463$$

$$= -.11438$$

$$N(d_1) = .4941$$

$$N(d_2) = .4544$$

$$P_C = e^{-.033(.2247)}[442.15(.4941) - 445(.4544)]$$

$$= e^{-.007415}[218.466 - 202.208]$$

$$= .99261(16.258)$$

$$= \$16.14$$

early exercise is not possible (i.e., a forward contract), the Black model is not completely accurate.[7] Figure 18-1 shows the implied and historical volatility of the S&P 500 futures options. Here the implied volatility is consistently higher than the historical volatility.

---

[7] American options on futures are equivalent to a series of European options. In other words, the early exercise of an option on futures contract obtains the intrinsic value of the option, but forfeits the remaining daily opportunities to exercise the option at a later time. Because it is difficult to value a series of European options in a simple manner, there is no closed-form solution for the value of an American option on futures contract. Only an approximate solution exists.

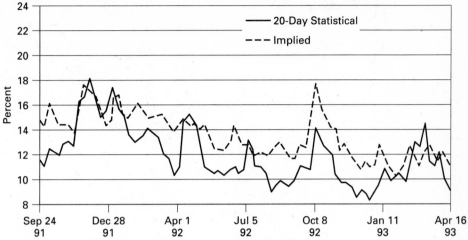

Figure 18-1   Implied and historical volatility for the S&P 500 futures options. (*Source: OptionVue IV.*)

Early Exercise of Options on Futures Contracts

The discussion of options on stocks determined that call options are typically "worth more alive than dead"—that is, it is more profitable to trade a call option than to exercise it, due to the existence of the option time value. In particular, using the Black-Scholes model for European options to value stock options provides an accurate value for an American option as long as the stock does not pay dividends. When a stock pays dividends, the call option buyer might exercise the American option early to obtain the dividend. This early exercise characteristic affects the option value. Put options on stocks are also exercised early, if the option is sufficiently in-the-money, in order to invest the proceeds at the risk-free interest rate.

Both call and put options on futures are exercised early if the option is sufficiently in-the-money. A deep-in-the-money option has a minimal option time value and changes point-for-point with the underlying futures contract. If the option is exercised, the resulting futures position will behave equivalently to the option, but the value of the option when exercised can be invested in a risk-free instrument to earn extra income. This is not possible with a stock option, since the purchase of the underlying stock requires funds. In fact, Gay, Kolb, and Yung (1989) show that over 55% of all futures options exercised are early exercises.[8]

One aspect of the early exercise question is whether options on futures are priced differently from options on cash, and if so, by how much. This is important for certain situations in which both types of options exist, such as for stock indexes, currencies, and debt. This question arises because of the benefit of exercising an option on futures

---

[8] To avoid arbitrage for a European call on futrues, $P_C \geq \text{Max}[0, P_F(1 + r)^{-t} - K(1 + r)^{-t}]$. The exercisable value for an American call on futures is $\text{Max}[0, P_F - K]$. Since $(1 + r)^{-t} \leq 1$, we have: $\text{Max}[0, (1 + r)^{-t}(P_F - K)] \leq \text{Max}[0, P_F - K]$. Therefore, it *may* be beneficial to exercise an in-the-money American call at any time. A similar argument holds for puts on futures.

contract early to invest the profits from the option. The following relationships exist between the two types of options:

- If the cash asset does not have a cash flow (e.g., a dividend), then the call futures option is worth more than the cash option.
- If the rate of return on any cash flow is less than the risk-free interest rate for investing funds, then the call futures option is worth more than the cash option.
- If the return on the cash flow equals the risk-free rate, then the two options have equivalent values.
- If the rate of return on cash flow is more than the risk-free rate, then the call futures option is worth less than the cash option.

Put futures options have the opposite relationships to put cash options. Table 18-1 shows the size of the difference between call futures options and call cash options when no intermediate cash flows exist.

Table 18-1 Percentage Differences Between
Call Options on Futures and Call Cash
Options

P_S/K	Days Until Option Expiration				
	30	**60**	**90**	**180**	**270**
.80	0.00	0.00	0.00	1.20	2.20
.90	0.00	0.00	0.47	1.58	3.15
1.00	0.29	0.56	1.02	2.48	4.51
1.10	0.61	1.15	1.72	3.79	6.34
1.20	1.22	2.13	2.89	5.52	8.70

Note: Cash asset has no intermediate cash flows; interest rate = 15%; standard deviation = .25
Source: Brenner, Courtadon, and Subrahmanyam (1985).

Comparing Options on Futures Prices

The early exercise provision of an American option provides a benefit over the European option that should be reflected in the option's price. However, the Black model prices the European (no early exercise) version of options on futures. Table 18-2 uses the results from Barone-Adesi and Whaley (1987) to compare hypothetical European and approximate American options on futures values for a six-month option with a strike price equal to 100.[9] This table shows that European out-of-the-money model values are approximately the same as their American counterparts. However, in-the-money option values reflect the benefit of exercising the American option early.

Another aspect of the futures option pricing process is comparing actual market prices to model prices. Table 18-3 uses results from Whaley (1986) to provide a

---

[9] Adesi and Whaley use several approximation methods to value options on futures. The method they propose is superior on a computational basis for obtaining these values.

Table 18-2 Call Values for European and American Options on Futures

Futures Price	European Call	Approximate American Call
80	$ .30	$ .30
90	1.70	1.72
100	5.42	5.48
110	11.73	11.90
120	19.91	20.34
strike price = 100		standard deviation = .20
interest rate = .08		time to expiration = ½ year

Source: Barone-Adesi and Whaley (1987).

summary of the market/model comparison for options on S&P 500 futures. This table shows that differences between market and model prices are not large. However, out-of-the-money and near-the-money options do have market prices that are generally less than the model price, while in-the-money options have market prices that are above model prices. Studies on more recent data, such as those by Jordan, Seale, McCabe, and Kenyon (1987) on soybean futures options and Bailey (1987) on gold futures options, find even smaller differences between market and model prices. Moreover, one difficulty in interpreting differences in market versus model prices based on empirical studies is whether the differences occur because the market is mispricing the options or because the model is incorrect.

Pricing Options on T-Bond Futures

In addition to the early exercise problem, the Black model has difficulty in pricing options on T-bond futures. This problem results from two characteristics of this contract: First, options on T-bond futures expire more than one month prior to the futures expiration. Second, this contract prices an interest-sensitive asset. The Black model assumes a constant interest rate, while T-bond prices directly reflect changing interest rates. Merville and Overdahl (1986) illustrate the pricing problems associated with applying the Black model to options on T-bond futures. Investment houses in New York are actively attempting to solve this pricing problem.

Put-Call Parity

The concept of put-call parity for options on futures is equivalent to put-call parity for stocks. Exhibit 18-4 shows how the payoffs from a long futures, long put, short call, and risk-free bond position with a face value of $P_F - K$ generate a payoff of zero, whether the futures are above or below the strike price at option expiration.[10] Since the entire portfolio has a payoff of zero at option expiration, the initial value of the portfolio must also be zero. Consequently,

$$P_P - P_C + (P_F - K)e^{-rt} = 0 \qquad (18\text{-}4)$$

where P_F = the original futures price

---

[10] If the exercise price is greater than the futures price, then one issues rather than buys bonds.

Table 18-3 Market Less Model Prices for Options on S&P 500 Futures

	Calls				Puts			
	$t < 6$	$6 < t < 12$	$t > 12$	All t	$t < 6$	$6 < t < 12$	$t > 12$	All t
$P_F/K < 0.98$	−0.063	−0.137	−0.087	−0.103	−0.106	−0.091	−0.106	−0.101
$.98 \leq P_F/K \leq 1.02$	−0.123	−0.076	0.007	−0.092	−0.082	−0.020	0.134	−0.041
$P_F/K > 1.02$	0.058	0.118	0.070	0.081	0.129	0.191	0.306	0.193
All strikes	−0.076	−0.056	−0.012	−0.061	−0.019	0.081	0.229	0.053

Table depicts the average pricing difference for the market price less the American model price. P_F/K is the ratio of the futures price to the option strike price—that is, the extent to which it is out-of-the-money ($P_F/K < 1$) or in-the-money ($P_F/K > 1$); t is the number of weeks until option expiration.
Source: Whaley (1986).

EXHIBIT 18-4
Put-Call Parity Payoffs for Options on Futures

		Payoffs at Option Expiration	
Instrument	Current Value	$P_{F,E} < K$	$P_{F,E} > K$
Long futures	0	$P_{F,E} - P_F$	$P_{F,E} - P_F$
Long put	P_P	$K - P_{F,E}$	0
Short call	$-P_C$	0	$-(P_{F,E} - K)$
Bonds	$(P_F - K)e^{-rt}$	$P_F - K$	$P_F - K$
Portfolio		0	0

P_F = original futures price
$P_{F,E}$ = futures price at option expiration
Bond face value = $P_F - K$

Solving for the put price:[11]

$$P_P = P_C - (P_F - K)e^{-rt} \qquad (18\text{-}5)$$

Since traded options on futures are American options, the European model in Equation (18-5) can give answers slightly different from actual exchange prices. However, Jordan and Seale (1986) and Blomeyer and Boyd (1988) find that deviations for actual options on futures prices from Equation (18-5) are unusual and most deviations are not large enough to obtain a profit.

Figure 18-2 shows the implied and historical volatility for Eurodollar futures options. Notice the large increase in volatility in October, and the relationship between the implied and historical volatility during this time period.

The Black Model for Puts

Employing put-call parity from Equation (18-5) and the Black model for call options on futures from Equations (18-1) to (18-3) results in the Black equation for put options on futures with continuously compounded interest rates:

$$P_P = Ke^{-rt}[1 - N(d_2)] - P_F e^{-rt}[1 - N(d_1)] \qquad (18\text{-}6)$$

where d_1 and d_2 are defined as Equations (18-2) and (18-3) on page 563.

The Delta and Theta Sensitivities

As with stock options, the pricing model for options on futures creates option sensitivities. The sensitivity values for options on cash and options on futures are almost

---

[11] Since $P_F = P_C(1 + r)^t$ when no intermediate cash flows are relevant, substituting P_C for $P_F(1 + r)^{-t}$ results in the put-call parity equation for stocks without dividends.

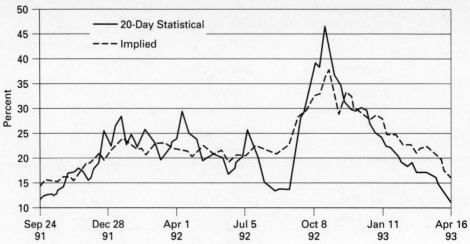

Figure 18-2 Implied and historical volatilities for Eurodollar futures options. (*Source:* OptionVue IV.)

identical when one employs the same underlying price and option strike price.[12] Recall that delta represents the hedge ratio and the extent to which the option price changes for a given change in the underlying futures price. For example, call delta values for an S&P 500 options on futures contract state the change in the option price for a 1-point change in the futures price. The deltas for an out-of-the-money option such as the 445 strike price in Exhibit 18-1 are smaller in value than in-the-money options, since an in-the-money strike price changes almost point-for-point with the futures price change.

Options are a wasting asset over time, as measured by theta. Shorter-term options have less time value, and this time value decreases faster for shorter-term options. Many options on futures contracts, especially options on financial futures, possess expirations within one month of the current date as well as for the financial cycle. The shorter-term options are useful for traders with short-term expectations concerning volatility. Such traders buy options when they expect the volatility to increase and sell options when they expect volatility to decrease.

USES OF OPTIONS ON FUTURES

In general, the strategies used for options on futures parallel those for options on cash assets. The payoff diagrams and basic pricing relationships discussed in Chapters 11 to 14 apply equally well to options on futures contracts. However, options on futures exist for a number of underlying assets that do not trade options on the cash asset, at least on an organized exchange. In addition, the motivations of the users of options on futures contracts can differ from the users of options on cash because of the application needed. Moreover, the model used to price options on futures differs from the standard Black-Scholes model for cash assets.

---

[12] For example, the equation for the delta for options on futures is $e^{-rt}N(d_1)$ which is equivalent to the delta equation for options on cash.

Synthetic Options and Futures Positions

Since futures contracts do not generate dividends or interest, a trader does not need to consider the cost of carrying a cash asset. Consequently, the relationship between call and put options on futures and the futures contracts themselves is straightforward:

$$\text{Long call} + \text{short put} = \text{long futures} \qquad (18\text{-}7)$$

Various combinations of this relationship exist, as given in Exhibit 18-5. Exhibit 18-5 shows that if a trader buys a call option when a short futures position is already held, a synthetic put option is created. The relationships shown in Exhibit 18-5 allow a trader to generate numerous combinations of securities for various risk-return strategies.

Speculation

Options on the S&P 500 futures provide the trader with a means to speculate on the broad market by using the limited loss feature of options. While S&P 100 cash options exist, the S&P 500 options on futures follow a broader market of 500 stocks. Speculators can use options on futures to foretell increased volatility in the underlying cash market. In fact, Bates (1991) shows that the time value on options on S&P 500 futures showed evidence of the 1987 market crash *prior* to October 1987. In particular, out-of-the-money puts became unusually expensive the year before the crash.

The options on debt futures, agricultural futures, and commodity futures provide speculative opportunities that are not available with cash options, at least on organized exchanges. These options on futures provide the advantages of a limited loss, a small cost, and leverage. Trading in the futures themselves involves the possibility of unlimited losses and margin calls.

Hedging

Hedgers, like speculators, can use options on futures in the same manner as options on cash assets. Therefore, strategies such as covered option writing and purchasing a put provide downside protection for an existing asset position.[13]

Covered option writing for stock index options on futures is similar to covered option writing for stocks, except that the hedger often does not have a portfolio of stocks

EXHIBIT 18-5
Synthetic Options-Futures Combinations

Synthetic long futures	= call − put
Synthetic call	= put + futures
Synthetic put	= call − futures
Synthetic short futures	= put − call
Synthetic short call	= −put − futures
Synthetic short put	= −call + futures

Note: A minus sign indicates a short position in the security. The synthetic instrument created here has the same profit and loss characteristics as the actual instrument.

that exactly matches the stock index. In this case, the number of calls sold is adjusted for the beta of the portfolio of stocks and for the size of the portfolio holdings. In addition, if the portfolio is not well diversified, then basis risk exists between the stock portfolio and the stock index. However, the motivation for the writer of the cash option is equivalent to that of the writer of an option on futures position. Thus, option writing can provide additional income if the hedger believes that the market will be relatively flat over the life of the option.[14] Brooks (1991) uses a risk-return evaluation tool called stochastic dominance to show that implementing covered call writing with futures options provides larger returns than using cash index options. Similarly, Brooks finds that using futures put options is superior to using cash put options.

Options on interest rate futures provide opportunities for hedging strategies not explored in previous chapters, since exchange-traded options on cash debt are not active contracts. Exhibit 18-6 lists examples of the more important strategies using interest rate options on futures and the objective of such strategies. One of the examples listed in Exhibit 18-6 is covered option writing on a fixed-income portfolio. Such a strategy is beneficial when interest rate volatility is minimal. Moreover, the portfolio manager can write the covered options on cash bonds, even though a T-bond futures contract is the delivery instrument for the options contract, since the cash T-bond can be delivered into the futures contract. Alternatively, the option position can be closed before the typical exercise time to avoid delivery of the futures.[15] DeRonne (1985) illustrates how to use futures options for hedging interest rate instruments for specific market scenarios. Brophy (1984) discusses some aspects of commercial hedging uses of options on agricultural futures.

SUMMARY AND LOOKING AHEAD

Options on futures contracts extend the benefits of options contracts to an entirely new range of securities. The Black model is often used to price futures options. However, the early exercise opportunities for options on futures create unique pricing problems for these contracts. The lack of a closed-form model to price options contracts provides uncertainties and opportunities for those using these contracts. The following chapter examines currency options on both the cash currency and the futures contract.

---

[13] Covered option writers for stocks have the advantage of receiving the cash dividends on the stocks held. Covered option writers for options on futures do not receive any cash inflows, since futures do not pay dividends or interest.

[14] Short options on futures require that margin be deposited to avoid potential losses. While any such losses on the short call option are offset by gains in the stock portfolio position, margins do require interim cash payments.

[15] While options can be written on over-the-counter cash options on specific T-bonds, it is important to make sure that liquidity exists for the specific T-bond and that the option price does not include a large premium related to its over-the-counter nature. Over-the-counter options on specific T-bonds do avoid the basis risk that is possible with options on T-bond futures. Thus, if futures options are employed and the cash bond used does not correspond to the cheapest-to-deliver bond priced by the T-bond futures contract, then basis risk exists.

EXHIBIT 18-6
Strategies with Interest Rate Options on Futures

Situation	Objective	Strategy
An institutional bond portfolio contains bonds scheduled to mature in three months and the money will be available for reinvestment at that time.	To achieve protection against a possible decline in interest rates and higher bond prices without forgoing the opportunity to benefit from lower bond prices if interest rates should rise.	Buy call options on T-bond futures.
An institution has a substantial portion of its funds in Treasury bills and other money market investments—perhaps to maintain a high level of liquidity and to avoid the risks associated with long-term investments.	To participate in any significant increase in the value of long-term bonds without forgoing the advantages of short-term investments.	Buy call options on T-bond futures.
The management of a bond portfolio is considering an immunization strategy to protect against rising interest rates and declining bond prices.	To protect the market value of the portfolio while retaining the opportunity to profit if bond prices should increase.	Buy put options on T-bond futures.
An investment portfolio includes a substantial number of Treasury bonds. The outlook is for relatively stable interest rates and bond prices.	To increase current portfolio return.	Write call options on T-bond futures against bonds held in the portfolio.
An institution plans, in about three months, to sell bonds that it currently holds in its portfolio. It anticipates that bond prices at that time will be approximately the same as they are now.	To obtain an above-the-market net price when bonds are sold.	Write call options on futures.

Source: "Options on U.S. Treasury Bond Futures for Institutional Investors," Chicago Board of Trade, pp. 9–13. This source has examples of each of the above strategies.

BIBLIOGRAPHY

Bailey, W. (1987). "An Empirical Investigation of the Market for Comex Gold Futures Options," *Journal of Finance*, Vol. 42, No. 5, December, pp. 1187–1194.

Barone-Adesi, G., and Robert Whaley (1987). "Efficient Analytic Approximation of American Option Values," *Journal of Finance*, Vol. 42, No. 2, June, pp. 301–320.

Bates, David (1991). "The Crash of '87: Was It Expected? The Evidence from Options Markets," *Journal of Finance,* Vol. 46, No. 3, July, pp. 1009–1044.

Black, Fischer (1976). "The Pricing of Commodity Contracts," *Journal of Financial Economics,* Vol. 3, No. 1–2, January–March, pp. 167–179.

Blomeyer, Edward C., and James C. Boyd (1988). "Empirical Tests of Boundary Conditions for Options on Treasury Bond Futures," *The Journal of Futures Markets,* Vol. 8, No. 2, April, pp. 185–198.

Brenner, M., G. Courtadon, and M. Subrahmanyam (1985). "Options on the Spot and Options on Futures," *Journal of Finance,* Vol. 40, No. 5, December, pp. 1303–1317.

Brooks, Robert (1991). "Analyzing Portfolios with Derivative Assets: A Stochastic Dominance Approach Using Numerical Integration," *Journal of Futures Markets,* Vol. 11, No. 4, August, pp. 411–440.

Brophy, Daniel F. (1984). "Commercial Use of Options," *Review of Futures Markets,* Vol. 3, No. 2, pp. 174–180.

DeRonne, William A. (1985). "Pension Funds and Futures Markets: Option Hedging of Fixed-Rate Assets," *Review of Futures Markets,* Vol. 4, No. 2, pp. 232–241.

Gay, Gerald D., Robert W. Kolb, and Kenneth Yung (1989). "Trader Rationality in the Exercise of Futures Option Positions," *Journal of Financial Economics,* Vol. 23, No. 2, August, pp. 339–362.

Jordan, James V., W. Seale, N. McCabe, and D. Kenyon (1987). "Transactions Data Tests of the Black Model for Soybean Futures Options," *The Journal of Futures Markets,* Vol. 7, No. 5, October, pp. 535–554.

Jordan, James V., and William E. Seale (1986). "Transactions Data Tests of Minimum Prices and Put-Call Parity for Treasury Bond Futures Options," *Advances in Futures and Options Research,* Vol. 1, Part A, pp. 63–87.

Merville, Larry J., and James A. Overdahl (1986). "An Empirical Examination of the T-bond Futures (Call) Options Markets under Conditions of Constant and Changing Variance Rates," *Advances in Futures and Options Research,* Vol. 1, Part A, pp. 898–118.

"Options on U.S. Treasury Bond Futures for Institutional Investors," Chicago Board of Trade, booklet, no date.

"Using S&P 500 Stock Index Options and Futures," (1987). Chicago Mercantile Exchange, booklet.

Whaley, Robert (1986). "Valuation of American Futures Options: Theory and Empirical Tests," *Journal of Finance,* Vol. 41, No. 1, March, pp. 127–150.

PROBLEMS

*Indicates more difficult problems.

18-1 Quotes and Option Values

Given the following futures option prices, find the dollar value of:
a. The wheat 330 Dec call (5000 bushels per contract; cents per bushel)
b. The wheat 340 Sept put
c. The silver 375 Sept call (500 troy ounces per contract; cents per troy ounce)
d. The T-bond 100 Sept call ($100,000; points and 64ths of 100%)
e. The T-bond 102 Dec put

Strike	Sept Calls	Dec Calls	Sept Puts	Dec Puts
Wheat				
330	24¼	36½	1¾	4¼
340	17½	29¾	4½	7
Silver				
375	26.5	33.7	1.0	3.8
T-bonds				
100	1–36	1–53	0–62	2–23
102	0–41	1–05	2–00	3–36

*18-2 Black Model for Futures Call Options

The price for the S&P 500 futures is 423.35. If the volatility for the futures is 20% and the current interest rate (compounded continuously) is 3.16%, what is the fair price of a 425 call option expiring in 77 days?

18-3 Put-Call Parity

Find the price of a put on the S&P 500 futures using the put-call parity formula and the following information:
$P_F = 414.90$ $P_C = 9.4$ $K = 410$ $r = 3.5\%$ $t = .05$

*18-4 Black Model for Puts

Find the put option price for the September 410 S&P 500 futures option when the futures sell for 412, the continuously compounded risk-free interest rate is 3%, the standard deviation of the S&P 500 futures is 13%, and the option has 77 days until it expires.

Chapter 19

CURRENCY OPTIONS

Overview

Options on currency take two forms: options on cash and options on futures. A currency call option on cash provides the right to buy the foreign exchange at a specific strike price in the domestic currency for a specified period of time. A put option on a foreign currency provides the right to sell the foreign exchange at a specific strike price in the domestic currency for a specified period of time. Options on currency futures provide the right to take a long position in a currency futures contract at a specific strike price (call) or a short position in a currency futures (put).

The pricing equation for cash currency options parallels the stock Black-Scholes model, except that both U.S. and foreign interest rates must be considered. Consequently, the values of the cash options and any possible mispricings are affected by these relative interest rates. The Black model is employed for options on futures pricing. Strategies with currency options parallel those used for stock options, except that one is speculating or hedging the relative value of a foreign currency in relation to the dollar.

Terminology

*Currency option** Owning an option on a foreign currency provides the right to buy (call) or the right to sell (put) the foreign exchange at a specific strike price in the domestic currency for a specific period of time.

*Option on currency futures** Owning an option on currency futures provides the right to take a long position (call) or the right to take a short position (put) in a currency futures contract at a specific strike price for a specific period of time.

TYPES AND CHARACTERISTICS OF CURRENCY OPTIONS

Both **currency options** on cash and **options on currency futures** are actively traded in the United States. Currency options on cash trade over 10 million contracts per year, while options on currency futures trade more than 6 million contracts. Currency options are treated separately from other options because of their specialized nature, the need to understand the quotation procedure of the underlying cash asset, and the pricing formula for each option. However, the basic pricing relationships for currency options are equivalent to the pricing relationships for stock options.

Cash currency quotations and currency forwards are covered in Appendix 2A. One must know how the underlying cash currencies are quoted in order to understand the meaning of the quotations of currency options.

Options on Currency

A call option on a foreign currency provides the right to buy the foreign exchange at a specific strike price in the domestic currency for a specific period of time. For example, a call on British pounds provides the right (but not the obligation) to buy pounds at the dollar strike price of the option until the option expires (American option) or at option expiration (European option). Similarly, a put option on a foreign currency provides the right to sell the foreign exchange at a specific strike price in the domestic currency for a specific period of time.

American options dominate the trading of exchange-traded options since these options provide the benefit of allowing exercise on any day that the exchange is open. The Philadelphia and London exchanges actively trade American options on cash foreign currency. European options are traded on the Philadelphia Exchange and are issued by over-the-counter dealers; exchange-traded European options have substantially less liquidity than the American options. Options on cash currencies expire on the Friday prior to the third Wednesday in the option expiration month (as of October 1993), except for the options designated "EOM" (which expire on the last Friday of the month). Expiration months are the next two calendar months plus the financial cycle of March, June, September, and December. (Long-term options with expirations of 18 and 24 months also exist, but have minimal volume.) The Philadelphia Exchange trades currency options from 7:00 P.M to 2:30 P.M. the next day (6:00 A.M. during daylight savings time)—20½ hours total. This extensive time period provides access to the Japanese market. Exhibit 19-1 provides contract size, strike price increments, and minimum price changes for the active currency option contracts.

Exhibit 19-2 shows the quotations for cash currency options traded on the Philadelphia Exchange. Options on foreign currencies exist for those countries that have an important international trading activity. These options on foreign currencies include the Australian dollar, British pound, Canadian dollar, French franc, German mark, Japanese yen, and Swiss franc. Cross-rate options exist between the German mark and Japanese yen (as well as for the British pound and mark), but they have minimal volume. The "r" designation in the quotes means that the option in question did not trade during the day; an "s" means that particular option has never traded. The size of the cash option contracts is one-half the size of both the corresponding futures contracts and the options on futures contracts. Thus, cash currency options are less expensive than the equivalent currency options on futures contracts.

As an example of how to interpret these quotations, let us use the British pound call option with a strike price of 160 ($1.60). Since the pound trades at 157.48 ($1.5748) in the cash market, this is a near-the-money (or technically an out-of-the-money) option. The June call for this option sells for 2.20. Since the British pound trades in U.S. cents per unit of the foreign currency, the quote of 2.20 represents 2.20 cents per pound, or equivalently $.0220 per pound. Multiplying this cost by the 31,250 pounds per option contract provides the total cost of $687.55 for one cash option on British pounds. Similarly, the 155 British pound call option is an in-the-money option, since the current

EXHIBIT 19-1
Currency Option Characteristics

Contract	Contract Size*	Strike Price Increment	Minimum Price Change*	Opening Price Limit**
Australian dollar	50,000AD	$0.01	$0.0001 = $5.00	$.02
British pound	31,250BP	$0.025	$0.0001 = $3.125	$.02
Canadian dollar	50,000CD	$0.005	$0.0001 = $5.00	$.02
German mark	62,500DM	$0.005***	$0.0001 = $6.25	$.02
Japanese yen	6,250,000JY	$0.0005***	$0.000001 = $6.25	$.0002
Swiss franc	62,500SF	$0.005***	$0.0001 = $6.25	$.02

*Futures options are twice these sizes.

** For futures options only.

***These strike intervals are called "half-strikes." They exist only for the three nearest months. Half-strikes futures options exist for the first four expiration months and for the five nearest-to-the-money options including the Australian dollar. Otherwise full strike prices exist, which are twice the size of the half-strikes. The creation of new strikes as currency prices change depends on the decision of the specialist. European options can have fewer strike prices.

EXHIBIT 19-2
Options on Currency Quotations

		Calls–Last			Puts–Last		
Option & Underlying	Strike Price	May	Jun	Sep	May	Jun	Sep
50,000 Australian Dollars-cents per unit.							
ADollr..........	68	r	r	r	r	0.15	r
71.43	71	r	r	r	r	0.97	r
71.43	72	0.25	r	r	r	r	r
31,250 British Pound-German Mark cross.							
BPd-GMk	240	r	9.50	r	r	r	r
249.29	242	r	8.00	r	r	r	r
249.29	252	1.00	r	r	r	r	r
31,250 British Pounds-European Style.							
BPound	150	r	r	r	r	r	2.97
157.48	152½	r	4.66	r	r	r	r
157.48	155	r	r	r	1.93	r	r
157.48	170	r	0.30	r	r	14.85	r
157.48	145	r	r	r	r	r	1.88
31,250 British Pounds-cents per unit.							
BPound	140	r	r	17.40	r	r	0.70
157.48	142½	r	r	15.10	r	0.18	1.08
157.48	145	r	r	12.90	r	r	1.50
157.48	147½	r	9.90	r	0.10	0.52	2.40
157.48	150	r	r	r	0.23	0.95	2.80
157.48	152½	5.33	r	r	0.62	1.60	r
157.48	155	3.60	4.15	r	1.20	r	5.03
157.48	157½	2.00	2.84	r	3.36	3.65	r
157.48	160	1.10	2.20	r	r	r	r
157.48	162½	0.38	1.04	r	r	r	r
157.48	165	r	r	2.25	r	r	r
157.48	167½	r	0.46	1.32	r	r	r
50,000 Canadian Dollars-cents per unit.							
CDollr..........	78½	r	0.89	r	r	r	r
79.26	79½	r	0.40	r	r	r	r
79.26	80	0.13	r	r	r	r	r
79.26	81½	r	r	r	r	2.45	r
62,500 European Currency Units-cents per unit.							
ECU............	120	r	r	r	0.53	r	r
123.40	124	1.05	r	r	r	r	r
250,000 French Francs-European Style.							
FFranc..........	16½	r	r	r	r	0.10	r
187.11	16¾	r	r	r	r	0.18	r
187.11	17	r	r	r	r	0.24	r
187.11	17¼	r	r	r	r	0.32	r

continued next page

continued

Option & Underlying	Strike Price	Calls–Last			Puts–Last		
		May	Jun	Sep	May	Jun	Sep
187.11	18	r	7.20	r	r	r	r
187.11	19	r	1.50	r	r	r	r
187.11	19¼	s	1.10	r	s	r	r
62,500 German Mark-Japanese Yen cross.							
GMk-JYn	68½	r	r	s	0.48	r	s
62,500 German Marks-European Style.							
DMark..........	59	r	3.85	r	r	r	r
63.19	60	r	r	r	r	0.31	r
63.19	60½	2.54	r	s	0.12	r	s
63.19	61	r	2.18	r	r	0.50	r
63.19	61½	1.62	1.90	s	r	r	s
63.19	62	1.40	1.52	r	0.56	r	r
63.19	62½	1.04	r	s	0.60	r	s
63.19	63	r	1.10	r	r	r	r
63.19	64½	r	r	s	r	2.30	s
63.19	66	0.08	r	r	r	r	r
62,500 German Marks-cents per unit.							
DMark..........	58	r	r	r	r	r	0.55
63.19	58½	r	r	s	0.04	r	s
63.19	59	r	r	r	0.05	r	0.80
63.19	60	r	r	r	0.08	0.29	1.10
63.19	60½	r	2.71	s	0.11	r	s
63.19	61	2.23	r	r	0.20	0.55	1.46
63.19	61½	r	r	s	0.31	0.72	s
63.19	62	1.43	1.64	r	0.44	0.88	1.97
63.19	62½	1.09	r	s	0.61	1.11	s
63.19	63	0.81	1.11	1.48	0.86	r	r
63.19	63½	0.61	0.75	s	r	r	s
63.19	64	0.43	r	r	1.32	r	r
63.19	64½	0.32	0.62	s	1.80	r	s
63.19	66	r	0.27	r	r	r	r
63.19	67	r	0.16	r	r	r	r
6,250,000 Japanese Yen-100ths of a cent per unit.							
JYen............	85	r	r	r	r	r	0.52
90.51	87	r	r	r	r	r	0.98
90.51	88	2.50	2.80	r	0.23	0.59	1.40
90.51	89	r	r	r	0.46	0.86	r
90.51	90	1.22	r	r	0.89	1.25	2.20
90.51	90½	1.06	r	s	1.00	r	s
90.51	91	r	r	2.10	1.23	r	r
90.51	91½	r	1.01	s	r	r	s
90.51	92	0.41	0.80	r	r	r	r
90.51	93	r	r	1.32	r	r	r
90.51	94	r	r	1.08	r	r	r

continued next page

continued

Option & Underlying	Strike Price	Calls–Last			Puts–Last		
		May	Jun	Sep	May	Jun	Sep
90.51	96	r	r	0.60	r	r	r
90.51	97	r	0.10	r	r	r	r
6,250,000 Japanese Yen-European Style.							
JYen............	87	r	r	r	r	r	0.95
90.51	93	r	0.60	r	r	r	r
90.51	94	r	r	0.96	r	r	r
62,500 Swiss Francs-European Style.							
SFranc	65	r	r	r	r	0.14	r
70.04	67	r	r	r	r	0.43	r
70.04	68	1.55	r	r	0.31	r	r
70.04	69	1.49	1.91	r	0.63	r	r
70.04	71	0.49	r	r	r	r	r
62,500 Swiss Francs-cents per unit.							
SFranc	65	r	r	r	r	0.24	0.94
70.04	66	r	r	r	0.09	0.31	1.00
70.04	66½	r	r	s	0.13	r	s
70.04	67	r	2.56	r	0.13	r	1.30
70.04	67½	r	r	s	0.22	0.81	s
70.04	68	r	2.53	r	r	1.00	r
70.04	68½	1.40	r	s	r	0.95	s
70.04	69	r	1.85	r	0.65	1.11	2.06
70.04	69½	1.06	r	s	r	r	s
70.04	70	r	0.70	r	r	r	r
70.04	70½	0.73	r	s	r	r	s
70.04	71	0.46	r	r	r	r	r
70.04	72	r	0.60	1.45	r	r	r
70.04	80	s	r	0.19	s	r	r

Option & Underlying	Strike Price	Calls–Last			Puts–Last		
		Apr	May	Jun	Apr	May	Jun
31,250 British Pound-German mark EOM.							
Bpd-GMk	250	0.88	2.68	r	r	r	r
31,250 British Pound EOM-cents per unit.							
BPound	147½	r	r	r	0.04	r	r
157.48	150	r	r	r	0.06	r	r
157.48	152½	r	r	r	0.28	r	r
157.48	155	r	r	r	0.48	r	r
157.48	157½	0.64	r	r	r	r	r
50,000 Canadian Dollars EOM-cents per unit.							
CDollr	79½	0.08	r	r	r	r	r
250,000 French Francs EOM-10ths of a unit per unit.							
FFranc	18¾	r	r	r	r	3.80	r
62,500 German Marks EOM-cents per unit.							
DMark	61	r	r	r	0.08	r	r
63.19	62	1.05	r	r	0.17	r	r

continued next page

continued

		Apr	May	Jun	Apr	May	Jun
63.19	63	0.52	0.94	r	0.60	1.16	r
63.19	64	0.19	r	r	r	r	r
63.19	60½	r	r	r	0.03	0.33	r
63.19	61½	r	r	r	0.07	0.52	r
63.19	62½	0.90	r	r	0.28	r	r
63.19	63½	0.30	0.60	r	r	r	r
63.19	64½	0.10	r	r	r	r	r

6,250,000 Japanese Yen EOM-100ths of a cent per unit.

		Apr	May	Jun	Apr	May	Jun
JYen...........	85	5.35	r	r	r	r	r
90.51	88	2.30	r	r	r	r	r
90.51	89	r	r	r	0.20	r	r
90.51	90	r	1.34	r	0.50	1.14	r
90.51	88½	1.95	r	r	0.11	r	r
90.51	91½	0.38	r	r	r	r	r

62,500 Swiss Franc EOM-cents per unit.

		Apr	May	Jun	Apr	May	Jun
SFranc..........	68	r	r	r	0.11	r	r
70.04	70	r	r	r	0.62	r	r
70.04	67½	r	r	r	0.06	r	r
70.04	68½	1.44	r	r	0.15	r	r

| Total Call Vol | 48,562 | | | | Call Open int 604,938 |
| Total Put Vol | 73,759 | | | | Put Open int 505,326 |

r = option not traded on this day
s = option does not exist.
Source: option exchange, April 23.

value for the pound is 157.48 and the strike price of this option is only 155. The June 155 call sells for 4.15 cents per pound. Multiplying by 31,250 pounds provides the $1296.87 cost of this option.

In the foreign exchange market, British pounds are quoted in terms of the number of U.S. dollars per one pound. This is the same convention used by the options market— that is, options are quoted as the cost of *one unit* of the foreign exchange in U.S. currency (often in terms of one U.S. cent). However, other foreign currencies, such as the German mark and Japanese yen, are quoted in the cash market in terms of the number of foreign currency units (mark or yen) per one U.S. dollar. Thus, a yen quote would be 110 yen/$. The options market, to maintain consistency across all options and to reduce confusion, quotes all currency options as the cost in U.S. currency for one unit of the foreign currency. In other words, an option on the mark is quoted as a cost in U.S. cents per one mark (to obtain the total cost, one multiplies by the 62,500 marks for one option contract). Similarly, an option on the yen is quoted in ¹⁄₁₀₀ths of a U.S. cent per yen (due to the large number of yen per one U.S. dollar); the total cost of a yen option contract is found by multiplying this cost by the 6,250,000 yen for one option contract.

EXHIBIT 19-3
Relationships Between U.S. and Foreign Currency Values

Option Position	Value of U.S. $	Value of Foreign Currency	Direction of $/FC Quote (and Futures Price)	Direction of FC/$ Quote	Direction of Option Position	Profit or Loss on Option Position
Long Call	↑ (strengthens)	↓ (weakens)	↓	↑	↓	Loss
	↓ (weakens)	↑ (strengthens)	↑	↓	↑	Profit
Short Call	↑	↓	↓	↑	↓	Profit
	↓	↑	↑	↓	↑	Loss
Long Put	↑	↓	↓	↑	↑	Profit
	↓	↑	↑	↓	↓	Loss
Short Put	↑	↓	↓	↑	↑	Loss
	↓	↑	↑	↓	↓	Profit

Exhibit 19-3 illustrates the various currency option positions, the possible changes in currency values, and the resultant profit/loss on the option.[1]

Options on Currency Futures

Call options on currency futures provide the right to take a long position in a currency futures contract at a specific strike price for a specific period of time. Put options on currency futures provide the right to take a short position in a currency futures contract at a specific strike price for a specific period of time. Active futures options on currency trade for the Japanese yen, German mark, British pound, and Swiss franc. Less active futures options exists for the Canadian dollar, Australian dollar, mark/yen cross-rate, and the U.S. dollar index. Each futures option has a size in foreign currency units that is equivalent to the underlying futures contract size. All futures options are American options. Expiration months are the next two calendar months and the financial cycle. Strike price intervals depend on the currency. The British pound has intervals of ¼ of a cent, the mark has intervals of ½ of a cent, and the yen has intervals of ½ of 1/100th of a cent. Other currency futures options strike price intervals are evident from the quotations given.

Exhibit 19-4 shows the quotes for the currency futures options. The quotation procedures are equivalent to the quotes for cash currency options, except that the appropriate decimal for the strike price is omitted. Thus, the strike price for the British pound futures option is listed as 1600 rather than 160.0 cents (or $1.60). Similarly, the yen strike price of 9000 is actually 90.00 cents per 100 yen (or .9000 cent per yen). The correct placement of the decimal can be determined by looking at the equivalent cash currency option quotation.

[1] One note of caution is needed when one reads cash option currency quotes from older versions of *The Wall Street Journal*. The value given in older *Journals* for the underlying cash currency value did *not* correspond to the end-of-day quote for the currency. In fact, the currency quote given with the option more closely corresponded to the *previous* day's currency value. This timing difference between the currency's quotation and the option's quote led to difficulties, such as the apparent violations of the pricing relationships given in Chapters 11 and 12. Thus, one often found a currency option that was apparently selling for less than its intrinsic value, *if* one employed the underlying cash currency value provided with the option quotes. Currently, the cash currency quotes more accurately reflect true cash prices.

EXHIBIT 19-4
Options on Currency Futures Quotations

CURRENCY

JAPANESE YEN (CME)
12,500,000 yen; cents per 100 yen

Strike Price	Calls–Settle			Puts–Settle		
	May	Jun	Jly	May	Jun	Jly
8950	1.41	1.88	....	0.40	0.87	....
9000	1.09	1.59	1.99	0.58	1.08	....
9050	0.82	1.33	1.74	0.81	1.32	....
9100	0.61	1.11	....	1.10	1.60	....
9150	0.44	0.92	....	1.43	....	....
9200	0.32	0.75	1.13	1.81	2.23	....

Est. vol. 5,840;
Thur vol. 4,947 calls; 5,492 puts
Op. int. Thur 37,335 calls; 36,982 puts

BRITISH POUND (CME)
62,500 pounds; cents per pound

Strike Price	Calls–Settle			Puts–Settle		
	May	Jun	Jly	May	Jun	Jly
1525	4.90	5.72	5.92	0.44	1.28	2.58
1550	3.02	4.12	4.46	1.06	2.16	3.60
1575	1.54	2.78	3.30	2.08	3.30	....
1600	0.76	1.78	2.38	....	4.80	....
1625	0.34	1.10	1.68	....	6.62	....
1650	0.14	0.64	....	....	8.64	....

Est. vol. 4,349;
Thur vol. 197 calls; 1,040 puts
Op. int. Thur 15,970 calls; 11,521 puts

DEUTSCHEMARK (CME)
125,000 marks; cents per mark

Strike Price	Calls–Settle			Puts–Settle		
	May	Jun	Jly	May	Jun	Jly
6200	1.14	1.56	1.56	0.35	0.77	1.40
6250	0.83	1.29	1.33	0.54	1.00	....
6300	0.57	1.03	1.13	0.78	1.24	....
6350	0.40	0.82	0.95	1.11	1.53	....
6400	0.26	0.66	0.80	1.47	1.86	....
6450	0.16	0.50	....	....	....	....

Est. vol. 28,000;
Thur vol. 7,659 calls; 6,141 puts
Op. int. Thur 178,294 calls; 132,712 puts

SWISS FRANC (CME)
125,000 francs; cents per franc

Strike Price	Calls–Settle			Puts–Settle		
	May	Jun	Jly	May	Jun	Jly
6900	1.34	1.83	2.12	0.42	0.91	....
6950	1.02	1.54	....	0.60	1.12	....
7000	0.76	1.29	1.61	0.84	1.37	....
7050	0.54	1.06	....	....	....	....
7100	0.38	0.87	1.21	....	1.95	....
7150	....	0.57	....	....	2.64	....

Est. vol. 3,914;
Thur vol. 687 calls; 660 puts
Op. int. Thur 11,701 calls; 15,315 puts

CANADIAN DOLLAR (CME)
100,000 Can.$; cents per Can.$

Strike Price	Calls–Settle			Puts–Settle		
	May	Jun	Jly	May	Jun	Jly
7800	....	1.28	....	0.07	0.23	....
7850	0.72	0.93	....	0.16	0.37	....
7900	0.40	0.63	....	0.34	0.57	....
7950	0.18	0.41	....	0.62	0.85	....
8000	0.07	0.25	....	1.01	1.19	....
8050	0.02	0.15	....	....	1.58	....

Est. vol. 502;
Thur vol. 91 calls; 111 puts
Op. int. Thur 3,580 calls; 4,496 puts

U.S. DOLLAR INDEX (FINEX)
1,000 times index

Strike Price	Calls–Settle			Puts–Settle		
	May	Jun	Jly	May	Jun	Jly
88	....	....	....	0.18	0.57	....
89	....	....	....	0.43	0.91	....
90	....	1.28	....	0.85	1.37	....
91	0.38	0.86	....	1.47	1.94	....
92	0.16	0.55	....	2.25	2.63	....
93	0.06	0.33	....	3.14	3.41	....

Est. vol. 660;
Thur vol. 118 calls; 104 puts
Op. int. Thur 1,230 calls; 2,421 puts

.... means not traded.
Source: futures exchanges, April 23.

Let us use the July yen futures option for an example of how to interpret the quotes for options on currency futures contracts. The quote for the July 9000 in-the-money yen futures option is 1.99. This quote is cents per 100 yen or, equivalently, .0199 cents per yen. Converting to dollars, we have $.000199 per yen, or a total option cost of $2487.50 when we multiply by the contract size of 12,500,000 yen.

Taking Positions in Currency Options

Currency options, unlike most other markets, have an active over-the-counter (OTC) market. OTC options allow the option trader to customize the strike price, expiration date, and amount of the option. OTC currency options also exist on currencies not traded on the exchanges. However, the cost of these options will include a premium to the writer for the extra risk undertaken, since the option cannot be hedged with traded options. In addition, OTC options typically are written for amounts of $1 million or more. OTC currency options also allow the creation of unique options to meet specialized needs. These options and their uses are discussed in Chapter 20.[2]

One interesting aspect of exchange-traded currency options is that different option positions provide equivalent positions once the option is exercised. Thus, for cash currency options the following obtain equivalent positions:

- Both the long call and short put positions obtain a long position in the foreign currency if the options are exercised (this position is paid for using the domestic currency, in our case, U.S. dollars). However, the long call holder decides if and when to exercise, while the short put trader does *not* determine when to exercise.
- Both the short call and long put obtain the domestic (U.S.) currency and pay out the foreign currency. The long put has the exercise option, while the short call does not.[3]

For currency options on futures the following obtain equivalent positions:

- Both a long call and a short put take a long position in the associated futures contract.
- Both a short call and a long put take a short position in the associated futures contract.

THE PRICING OF CURRENCY OPTIONS

The pricing relationships discussed in Chapter 12 are relevant for currency options and currency futures options (except for the early exercise issues for futures options discussed in Chapter 18). Cash currency options can be priced with a modified Black-Scholes model. Currency options on futures are priced with the Black model discussed in Chapter 18.

---

[2] Another type of option contract involving currencies is futures-style options. Futures-style options used to trade in London and differ from typical options in that they are marked-to-market daily. Thus, the futures-style call buyer pays the call writer daily an amount equal to the decrease in the market value of the call, while the call writer pays the buyer daily any amount equal to the increase in the market value of the call. In addition, the call buyer has the right to purchase one currency at the strike price stated in terms of a second currency. A futures-style put is similar in nature, except that it gives the owner the right to sell the currency.

[3] Equivalent positions are also possible between options traded in the United States and those traded in other countries. For example, exercising a long call on British pounds with strike price K in the United States generates the same long position in British pounds as does either a long put with strike price 1/K on U.S. dollars obtained in London *or* a short call on U.S. dollars obtained in London (if exercised). Moreover, these type of options also can be obtained over-the-counter in the United States.

The Modified Black-Scholes Model

Garman and Kohlhagen (1983) and Grabbe (1983) develop modified Black-Scholes models for currency options. The important modification is to consider the risk-free interest rate in both the foreign country and the domestic (U.S.) country. The resultant interest rates can be stated either in terms of the rates themselves, or (more commonly) in terms of the value of a discount bond that earns the risk-free rate over the life of the option. Thus, the value of the U.S. (domestic) discount bond is defined as:

$$B = 1/[1 + i(T/360)] \qquad (19\text{-}1)$$

where B = the domestic discount bond, which has a value of one unit of the domestic currency at maturity

i = the domestic risk-free simple interest rate

T = the number of days until the bond matures

Correspondingly, the value of the foreign bond is:

$$B^* = 1/[1 + i^*(T/360)] \qquad (19\text{-}2)$$

where B^* = the foreign discount bond, which has a value of one unit of the foreign currency at maturity

i^* = the foreign risk-free simple interest rate

The above simplification allows us to state the modified Black-Scholes model for currency call options in terms of the discrete values of B and B^*, as follows:[4]

$$P_C = P_S B^* N(d_1) - KBN(d_2) \qquad (19\text{-}3)$$

where $d_1 = \dfrac{\ln(P_S B^*/KB) + .5\sigma_S^2 t}{\sigma_S\sqrt{t}} \qquad (19\text{-}4)$

$$d_2 = d_1 - \sigma_S\sqrt{t} \qquad (19\text{-}5)$$

P_S = the currency exchange rate in terms of cost in domestic (U.S.) currency for one unit of the foreign currency

σ_S = the annualized standard deviation of the continuously compounded return on the cash exchange rate[5]

---

[4] Interest rates for the option equations in this chapter are treated as simple discount rates. The equivalent continuously compounded interest rate formula according to Garman and Kohlhagen (1983), which is a more direct adaptation of the Black-Scholes approach, is:

$$P_C = P_S\, e^{-r^*t} N(d_1) - Ke^{-rt} N(d_2)$$

where $d_1 = \dfrac{\ln(P_S\, e^{-r^*t}/K) + [r + .5\sigma_S^2]t}{\sigma_S\sqrt{t}}$

$d_2 = d_1 - \sigma_S\sqrt{t}$

and r = the domestic risk-free continuously compounded interest rate

r^* = the foreign risk-free continuously compounded interest rate

In this continuous model, the foreign interest rate acts like a continuously compounded dividend yield for stocks. Thus, the only difference between this formula and the Black-Scholes formula for a non–dividend-paying stock is the substitution of $P_S\, e^{-r^*t}$ for P_S.

[5] As with stock options, the continuously compounded standard deviation is calculated by employing the logarithmic percentage change of each observation and then finding the standard deviation of this series.

EXAMPLE 19-1
Finding the Call Value on Foreign Exchange

The modified Black-Scholes equation for finding the fair value of a call option on currency is as follows:

$$P_C = P_S B^* \mathrm{N}(d_1) - KB\mathrm{N}(d_2) \tag{19-3}$$

where
$$d_1 = \frac{\ln(P_S B^*/KB) + .5\sigma_S^2 t}{\sigma_S \sqrt{t}} \tag{19-4}$$

$$d_2 = d_1 - \sigma_S \sqrt{t} \tag{19-5}$$

Given the input information, we can find the fair value of an option on German marks.

$P_S = \$.6131$ (the current cost of one mark in U.S. dollars—that is, the \$/DM quote)
$K = \$.61$ (the strike price of the option in \$/DM)
Time to expiration = 80 days ($t = 80/365 = .21918$; $T = 80/360 = .22222$)
$\sigma_S = .25$ (the standard deviation of the \$/DM value)
$i = 3.5\%$ (the domestic U.S. annual interest rate)
$i^* = 6.5\%$ (the foreign annual interest rate)

To employ Equation (19-3), we need the discount bond values for B and B^*:

$$B = 1/[1 + i(T/360)] \tag{19-1}$$

$$B^* = 1/[1 + i^*(T/360)] \tag{19-2}$$

For this example:

$$B = 1/[1 + .035(.22222)] = 1/1.00777 = .992290$$

$$B^* = 1/[1 + .065(.22222)] = 1/1.014444 = .985762$$

Therefore,

$$d_1 = \frac{\ln[(.6131)(.985762)/(.61)(.992290)] + .5(.25)^2(.21918)}{(.25)(\sqrt{.21918})}$$

$$= \frac{\ln(.9984698) + .006849}{.1170417}$$

$$= (-.00153 + .006849)/.1170417$$

$$= +.0454$$

$$d_2 = -.04543 - .25\sqrt{.21918}$$

$$= +.04543 - .11704$$

$$= -.0716$$

From normal distribution tables (after interpolating)

$$\mathrm{N}(d_1) = .5181$$

$$\mathrm{N}(d_2) = .4722$$

continued next page

continued

The call fair value is:

$$P_C = \$.6131(.985762)(.5181) - \$.61(.992290)(.4722)$$

$$= \$.31312 - \$.28582$$

$$= \$.0273 \text{ or } 2.73 \text{ cents}$$

Table 19-1 The Effect on Relative Interest Rates on Foreign Exchange Call Options

Inputs: $\sigma = .20$ $\qquad$ $P_C = \$1.50/£$ $\qquad$ $t = 90$ days

K = 145	*i** (British Interest Rate)			
i (U.S. Interest Rate)	3%	5%	7%	9%
3%	8.62	8.15	7.69	7.24
5%	9.06	8.58	8.11	7.65
7%	9.52	9.02	8.54	8.06
9%	9.98	9.47	8.98	9.49

K = 150	*i** (British Interest Rate)			
i (U.S. Interest Rate)	3%	5%	7%	9%
3%	5.90	5.53	5.17	4.82
5%	6.26	5.88	5.50	5.14
7%	6.64	6.23	5.85	5.47
9%	7.02	6.61	6.21	5.82

K = 155	*i** (British Interest Rate)			
i (U.S. Interest Rate)	3%	5%	7%	9%
3%	3.84	3.56	3.30	3.04
5%	4.12	3.82	3.55	3.28
7%	4.41	4.10	3.81	3.53
9%	4.71	4.39	4.08	3.79

Source: Developed using OptionVue IV.

Example 19-1 shows how to find the value of a call option on foreign exchange.

The principal difference between the option model in Equation (19-3) and the Black-Scholes model for stock options is in the use of the interest rates in *both* countries of the currency quotation. Consequently, Table 19-1 shows simulated values for a call option on British pounds showing the effect of differing interest rates on the call option value.

FOCUS 19-1
Option Tables and the Simulator

The Option Simulator allows the user to examine relationships among different options in a number of ways. One method is to create a table of option values (or sensitivities) as the input variables change. As shown in the table below, an Option Simulator table allows four variables to change: the strike price and time to expiration (see the two left vertical columns) and the exchange rate and volatility (see the top two rows). Note that the domestic and foreign interest rates are described by DIntRate and FIntRate, respectively. The user chooses from the list of input variables provided. Once the table is created, all the user has to do to create a table of delta, gamma, and so on, sensitivities is to move the arrow key to the desired output. In the table below, the option values are given in dollars, that is, an option worth 8 cents is shown as .08 rather than the typical representation of 8.00 shown in other tables in this chapter and in the newspaper.

FOREIGN-EXCHANGE EUROPEAN OPTIONS (LOGNORMAL)

Call
DIntRate = .040   FIntRate = .060

Strike	YrsToExp	ExchRate = 1.45			ExchRate = 1.50			ExchRate = 1.55		
						Volatility				
		.150	.200	.250	.150	.200	.250	.150	.200	.250
1.45	.10	.03	.04	.04	.06	.07	.07	.10	.10	.11
	.20	.04	.05	.06	.06	.08	.09	.10	.11	.12
	.30	.04	.06	.07	.07	.09	.10	.11	.12	.13
1.50	.10	.01	.02	.02	.03	.04	.05	.06	.07	.07
	.20	.02	.03	.04	.04	.05	.06	.07	.08	.09
	.30	.02	.04	.05	.04	.06	.08	.07	.09	.10
1.55	.10	.00	.01	.01	.01	.02	.03	.03	.04	.05
	.20	.01	.02	.03	.02	.03	.04	.04	.05	.07
	.30	.01	.02	.04	.03	.04	.06	.05	.06	.08

(Source: Created from The Options and Futures Trading Simulator by Mark Rubinstein and Gerald Gennotte (1992).)

In addition, in-the-money, near-the-money, and out-of-the-money options are shown. Examination of this table shows the following:

- If $i = i*$ then *higher* rates of interest are associated with *lower* call option prices.
- Call values increase as the domestic U.S. interest rate increases (for a constant foreign interest rate).

As with the option pricing models for other assets, the above modified Black-Scholes equation is for European call options. American options, which can be exercised any time before option expiration, do not have a closed-form solution to their value. The key pricing relationships for American versus European currency options are as follows:

- The greater the differential of the foreign interest rate over the domestic interest rate, the greater the value of the American call option in comparison to the European call option.
- The greater the differential of the foreign interest rate over the domestic interest rate, the smaller the difference in value between the American put option and the European put option (an American option is worth at least as much as a European option).
- If the domestic interest rate is above the foreign interest rate, the above relationships are reversed.

Tests of the currency option model by Tucker (1985) find a large number of pricing errors that could be exploited by floor traders, but not by others. Shastri and Tandon (1986) compare the European currency option model with an American version. They find that a high foreign interest rate causes the European-modified Black-Scholes model to misprice currency options because of the probability of early exercise.

The concepts of the pricing sensitivities for currency options are equivalent to those examined in earlier chapters. However, the foreign and domestic interest rates do affect the equations specifying these sensitivities.[6]

Pricing Options on Currency Futures

Currency futures options are priced in the same manner as other futures options (see Chapter 18). Since the underlying security is a futures contract, we do not need to worry about the relative interest rates in the two countries (although this factor does affect the futures price). Other characteristics of options on futures apply to currency futures options, including the effect of early exercise of the American options on the pricing process of these options. Figure 19-1 shows the implied and historical volatility

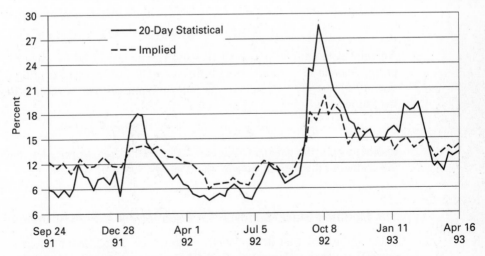

Figure 19-1 Implied and historical volatility for the British pound call options. (*Source:* OptionVue IV.)

[6] In particular, the delta for a call on a currency when continuous discounting is employed is $e^{-i^*t}N(d_1)$.

of the British pound call option on futures. This figure illustrates the significant change in volatility for the pound that can occur and the relationship between the historical and implied volatility associated with such changes.

Interest Rate Parity

The values of currency options are affected by the relative interest rates for the two currencies relevant for the option. These same interest rates are the key factors used to develop interest rate parity in Appendix 4A. Interest rate parity provides the pricing relationship for currency forward and futures contracts. Interest rate parity is also used in the pricing of currency options. The equation describing the price of a forward/futures value in terms of the current currency exchange rate and the interest rates in the two countries is:

$$P_F = \frac{P_S[1 + i(T/360)]}{1 + i^*(T/360)} \tag{19-6}$$

Equation (19-6) shows that the relative interest rates i (the domestic or U.S. rate) and i^* (the foreign rate) affect the futures/forward rate. Thus, when funds are invested in a foreign currency, i^* can be earned, while i is foregone. This difference in interest earned can be viewed as the cost of carry, and is similar to the dividend yield for stock index positions. This relationship is used in one form of the put-call parity relationship discussed below.

Put-Call Parity

Put-call parity for currency options can be developed by employing two equivalent strategies, as shown in Exhibit 19-5. The resultant put-call parity equation is:

$$P_P = P_C - P_S[1 + i^*(T/360)]^{-1} + K[1 + i(T/360)]^{-1} \tag{19-7}$$

An equivalent put-call parity relationship can be developed by using the interest rate parity theorem in conjunction with Equation (19-7). Thus, substituting P_S from Equation (19-6) into (19-7) results in the following put-call parity relationship in terms of the futures rate:

$$P_P = P_C + [K - P_F][1 + i(T/360)]^{-1} \tag{19-8}$$

In other words, the put and call prices differ by the exercise price less the futures price discounted to the present time by the domestic risk-free interest rate.

The Modified Black-Scholes Put Equation for Currency Options

Using the modified Black-Scholes equation for a call option on currencies and the put-call parity equation results in the following modified Black-Scholes put equation:

$$P_P = KB[1 - N(d_2)] - P_S B^*[1 - N(d_1)] \tag{19-9}$$

This equation is calculated in the same manner as the call option for currencies.

EXHIBIT 19-5
Developing Put-Call Parity for Currency Options

Let us examine strategies (A) and (B) concerning foreign currencies:

(A) Buy a put on one unit of a foreign currency (priced in terms of the domestic currency) with a strike price of K, resulting in a put price of P_P.

(B) Initiate each of the following three trades:

- Sell (that is, issue or sell short) a discount bond denominated in the foreign currency, which pays interest at i^*, with the bond maturing at the end of the period, with a value of one unit of the foreign currency. The foreign currency proceeds received from selling the bond are converted into the domestic (U.S.) currency at the exchange rate P_S. Thus, the total amount of domestic currency received is $P_S[1 + i^*(T/360)]^{-1}$.

- Buy K domestic (U.S.) discount bonds at a price of $1/[1 + i(T/360)]$ each for a total price of $K[1 + i(T/360)]^{-1}$.

- Buy a currency call option at the domestic (U.S.) price of P_C for one unit of the foreign currency with strike price K.

The total investment for strategy (B) in terms of the domestic currency is:

$$P_C - P_S[1 + i^*(T/360)]^{-1} + K[1 + i(T/360)]^{-1}$$

The following table shows that at the expiration of the options (which corresponds to the maturity of the discount bond), both strategies (A) and (B) provide the same profits—that is, they are equivalent strategies.

Strategy	$P_S < K$	$P_S \geq K$
(A): buying put	$K - P_S$	0
(B): selling foreign bonds	$-P_S$	$-P_S$
buying domestic bonds	K	K
buying a call	0	$P_S - K$
Total for strategy (B)	$K - P_S$	0

Since the two strategies provide equivalent payoffs at option expiration, we can equate the investments to define put-call parity as:

$$P_P = P_C - P_S[1 + i^*(T/360)]^{-1} + K[1 + i(T/360)]^{-1} \qquad (19\text{-}7)$$

USES OF CURRENCY OPTIONS

Speculation

Speculating in currency options requires care in order to understand when a profit or loss will occur. Buying a call option means that the speculator receives the foreign exchange—say, British pounds. The trader wants the pounds to increase in value. Thus, if the pound increases from $1.55 to $1.70, then a call option with a $1.55 strike price becomes valuable (the speculator can use the call to buy pounds at the strike of $1.55 and then sell the pounds in the open market for $1.70). Therefore, the value of the foreign currency *increases* if the price in dollars (per one unit of the foreign currency) increases. The equivalent benefit occurs for any other currency call option—that is, if the quotation of the U.S. currency (cents) per one unit of the foreign currency (FC) *increases,* then the value of the call position increases.[7]

Puts are the opposite. Owning a currency put provides the right to *sell* the foreign currency. Thus, one benefits if the value of the foreign currency declines. Consequently, if the $/FC declines, then owning a put is worth more money, since it takes fewer dollars to buy one unit of the foreign currency.

Hedging

Buying a protective put as insurance is one method for hedging against declines in the foreign currency value when one owns the foreign currency. Thus, if the foreign exchange falls below the put strike price, the buyer of the put is protected below the strike price of the option. Such a position is useful if the put buyer has (or will have) *foreign exchange to sell.* On the other hand, if one has to *buy foreign exchange in the future,* buying a call option provides protection against the value of that foreign exchange increasing above the option strike price. An example of buying a call option as a hedge is when goods are imported from another country to sell in the United States, but the goods must be paid for in the foreign currency at some time in the future. Without protection from an increase in the value of the foreign currency, the importer could profit from the sale of the goods but lose money on the foreign exchange transaction. Hence, while buying a call option and creating a protective put have the same profit diagram, a long call is useful as a hedge when the foreign currency is needed in the future, while a protective put is needed for a hedge if one currently owns the foreign currency.

A covered call provides another strategy for hedging a foreign currency position. Unlike a protective put, a covered call *receives* the option time value instead of paying it. However, as discussed in Chapter 18, a covered call has a maximum upside gain but potentially large downside losses (although smaller downside losses than owning the foreign exchange without selling a call). A covered call is used for protection when the trader already has the foreign currency (or an asset denominated in the foreign currency) and will sell the foreign currency in the future. Buying a call option is employed for protection when one must *pay* for a security or asset in the future *in terms of the foreign currency.*

SUMMARY AND LOOKING AHEAD

Options on currencies and options on currency futures are distinguished from other options because of the unique characteristics of the underlying cash asset: the foreign currency value relative to the dollar. Thus, the quotation, uses, and pricing of these options are based on the relative value of the foreign currency, which in turn is affected by the foreign and domestic interest rates. Chapter 20 examines financial engineering concepts, including debt and other over-the-counter options, exotic options, and swaps.

---

[7] Recall that foreign currency other than the British pound is quoted as the number of units of FC per one U.S. dollar, the *inverse* of how currency options are quoted. Thus, care must be taken when determining the strength or weakness of a foreign currency. If the $/FC increases, then the value of the FC increases; however, if the FC/$ increases, then the value of the FC *weakens* (since one must pay more units of the FC for one U.S. dollar).

BIBLIOGRAPHY

Garman, Mark B., and Steven W. Kohlhagen (1983). "Foreign Currency Option Values," *Journal of International Money and Finance,* Vol. 2, No. 3, December, pp. 231–237.

Grabbe, J. Orlin (1983). "The Pricing of Call and Put Options on Foreign Exchange," *Journal of International Money and Finance,* Vol. 2, No. 3, December, pp. 239–253.

Rubinstein, Mark, and Gerard Gennotte (1992). *Options and Futures Trading Simulator,* Version 2.0.

Shastri, Kuldeep, and Kishore Tandon (1986). "On the Use of European Models to Price American Options on Foreign Currency," *The Journal of Futures Markets,* Vol. 6, No. 1, Spring, pp. 93–108.

Tucker, Alan (1985). "Empirical Tests of the Efficiency of the Currency Option Market," *Journal of Financial Research,* Vol. 8, No. 4, Winter, pp. 275–285.

PROBLEMS

*Indicates more difficult problems.

19-1 Speculating in Currency Futures Options

Mr. King buys a September 1900 put on British pound futures for 2.04. What is the total dollar cost of this option? If the price of this put declines to 1.04, what is the profit or loss on the position?

*19-2 Currency Call Value

Given the data below, calculate the call option price using the modified Black-Scholes model.

Risk-free interest rate in U.K.	10.24%
Risk-free interest rate in U.S.	3.10%
Current exchange rate	$1.9235/pound
Standard deviation of the exchange rate	0.25
Strike price	190
Time to option expiration	130 days

19-3 Put-Call Parity

The December 64 German mark call option with 135 days left until expiration is selling for 3.62. The exchange rate is $.6778/DM. The risk-free interest rate is 3.1% in the United States and 8.86% in Germany. According to put-call parity, what is the put price of the December 64 mark option?

*19-4 Black-Scholes Currency Put Option Price

The current exchange rate for British pounds is $1.9210. The current rate of interest on 180 day U.S. Treasury bills is 3.26% and the equivalent U.K. rate of interest is 5.45%. If the volatility for the currency exchange is 20%, using the modified Black-Scholes model for currency options, what is the fair price for a put option on this exchange rate with a strike price of 1875 that expires in 180 days?

19-5 Covered Call

Miss Meine buys 62,500 DM for her portfolio at an exchange rate of $.6778/DM. She thinks the exchange rate will remain stable for the next few months and decides to write covered calls to generate income. Therefore, she sells a September 68 call option for 0.77. Fifty days later, the option expires with an unchanged exchange rate. What is the incremental rate of return from the covered call strategy? (Assume the deposit interest rate for DM is 8%.)

19-6 Hedging Foreign Exchange

A bank that holds pounds wants to hedge against a decline in the pound. The price of the pound on July 14 is $1.9211. The put price of a September 187.5 option is 2.45, and the price of the September 195 call is 4.15. What is the appropriate hedge? What is the maximum loss of the hedging transaction? What is the profit or loss of this transaction if the pound increases in value to $2.0107?

19-7 Using a Put to Lock in FC Value

As an importer who has to sell 6,250,000 Japanese yen in October, you decide to hedge by buying a put with a strike price of 76½ and a cost of .21.
a. What will your proceeds be if the yen goes to .0073 yen/$?
b. What would your proceeds be if you had not bought the put?

Chapter 20

FINANCIAL ENGINEERING: SYNTHETIC INSTRUMENTS AND EXOTIC OPTIONS

Overview

Financial engineering uses futures, options, and other financial instruments to control risk and maximize the value of financial strategies. Financial engineering includes developing new financial products to meet a need, as well as combining existing products to meet a specific goal. Synthetic instruments and portfolio insurance are examples of financial engineering.

Swaps have become an important tool in the interest rate market. An interest rate swap is a financial agreement to exchange interest payments on a fixed-rate loan with those of a variable-rate loan. The *net* difference in interest payments exchanges hands for each payment period. Parties use swaps for risk management, for example, to exchange fixed interest rates for floating rates, and to obtain a better interest rate. Eurodollar futures are often used by dealers to hedge swap positions. "Swaptions" are options on swaps.

Over-the-counter options are created and traded by major financial institutions to meet the specific needs of firms that are not met by conventional options. Popular over-the-counter options involve interest rates and energy. Caps, floors, and collars are interest rate options that provide a *series* of call and/or put options on interest rates over a period of time that lock in interest rate costs. Sycurves are options on the slope of the yield curve.

Exotic options are options with unusual characteristics. Range forwards are combinations of options that involve a zero initial cost. Average rate options provide a payoff on an average asset price. Other exotic options include compound options (call on a call), lookback options, down-and-out options, and two-color rainbow options.

Terminology

*Average rate option   An option that pays the difference between the strike price and the *average* rate (or price) of the asset over the life of the option.

Barrier option   An option that becomes either active or inactive when the cash asset crosses a threshold.

Cacall   A call on a call option that pays the value of *another* call option at expiration.

*Cap   A series of call options on the interest rate that locks in a maximum interest rate.

Caput   A call on a put option that pays the value of a put at option expiration.

Cylinder option   A range option in which the call price does not equal the put price.

*Collar   A combination of a cap and a floor.

Compound option   An option on an option (see cacall and caput).

Down-and-in call option   An option that activates only if the cash asset price reaches or crosses a threshold.

Down-and-out call option   An option that becomes worthless if the cash asset price reaches or crosses a threshold.

*Exotic option   An option with unusual characteristics concerning exercise or the underlying security.

*Financial engineering   The development and creative application of products to solve financial problems and to maximize the value of financial techniques.

*Floor   A series of put options on the interest rate that locks in a minimum interest rate.

Interest rate option   An option that has a payoff based on the underlying interest rate.

*Interest rate swap   A financial agreement to exchange interest payments of a fixed-rate loan with those of a variable-rate loan.

Lookback call   An option that is identical to a standard European call except that the strike price is equal to the *minimum* price of the underlying asset during the life of the option.

Lookback put   An option that is identical to a European put except that the strike price is equal to the *maximum* price of the asset during the life of the option.

*Range forward   The purchase of a call with a strike price of K_1 and the sale of a put with a strike price of K_2 (with $K_1 > K_2$) such that the total initial cost of the foward contract is zero.

Swaption   An option on a swap.

*Sycurve option   An option on the slope of the yield curve.

Two-color rainbow option   An option in which the payoff is based on two underlying asset prices.

Up-and-out put option   An option that becomes worthless if the cash asset price reaches or goes above a threshold price.

Up-and-in put option   An option that activates only if the cash price reaches or crosses a threshold.

WHAT IS FINANCIAL ENGINEERING?

The Concepts

Financial engineering involves the development and creative application of products to solve financial problems and to maximize the value of financial techniques. A financial engineer uses financial models, statistics, mathematics, accounting, and tax knowledge to determine how to reduce risk exposure, enhance portfolio management, and solve liquidity, funding, and other problems of the firm. A number of securities are used by the financial engineer. Futures, options, swaps, bonds, stocks, and hybrids of these securities are relevant to the problems encountered by those managing risk and solving corporate problems. The applications of these instruments to financial engineering problems are broad-based and far-reaching, requiring a concrete knowledge of financial models and related areas, plus an ability to create new solutions for new problems. The subject matter of financial engineering is diverse and cannot be adequately described here. The interested reader should see one of the books in this area, such as *Financial Engineering* by Marshall and Bansal (1993). Here, we outline financial engineering in relation to its basic uses with futures, options, and related securities.

Uses of financial engineering include implementing and enhancing arbitrage strategies, developing new products, and managing the risk of new products sold to customers (new products are called financial innovations). A financial innovation can be a major new product that solves a problem not addressed by current products (such as the introduction of financial futures or index options) or a novel twist on an existing product (such as making stock index arbitrage operational by reducing risk through instantaneous purchase of all stocks in a cash index). Three types of financial engineering applications are:

- **Deal making (marketing):** structuring a solution with a currently existing product to solve a particular need of a client.
- **New product generation:** developing a new product or procedure to solve existing problems for a number of firms.
- **Finding loopholes:** finding accounting, tax, or regulatory loopholes to create a benefit to the firm.

Futures, Options, and Financial Engineering

A number of the applications of futures and options contracts discussed in previous chapters are examples of financial engineering:

- Appendix 12A showed how the proper combination of options contracts is equivalent to a futures contract.
- Chapter 13 examined the creation of synthetic calls and puts by floor traders for conversions and reverse conversions.
- Combinations of options (such as straddles, spreads, and strangles) discussed in Chapter 16.
- Chapter 17 examined a number of applications of futures in order to create synthetic instruments that enhance the return of the position above the equivalent cash return.
- Portfolio insurance (Chapter 17) is a dynamic futures trading strategy that creates payoffs equivalent to an option contract (if price changes are continuous).
- Chapter 18 showed how synthetic futures, calls, or puts could be generated using futures and options on futures.

In general, most applications of futures and options to risk management could be considered financial engineering. However, the financial engineering phrase typically is reserved for newer or more creative applications of financial instruments. For example, a major source of profits on Wall Street during the past few years has been the development of new risk management instruments that are sold over-the-counter. Many of these instruments are options: options on products that do not have an exchange-traded equivalent, options that have unusual characteristics, or options with a longer life than exists for exchange-traded options. These over-the-counter options are examined later in this chapter.

SWAPS AND SWAPTIONS

Swap Concepts

Swaps are financial instruments that are typically associated with financial engineering. An **interest rate swap** is a financial agreement to exchange interest payments of a fixed-rate loan with a variable-rate loan. The *net* difference in interest payments exchanges hands for each payment period. Principal amounts are *not* swapped. Swaps often are arranged between financial institutions in the United States and Europe, since U.S. institutions prefer fixed-rate loans but the demand is for variable-rate loans; however, the opposite situation exists in Europe. The purpose of these basic "vanilla" swaps is to change the interest rate risk of the institution. For example, a savings and loan often is forced to issue fixed-rate mortgages, especially during low interest rate environments, because of consumer demand. In order to control its interest rate risk, the savings and loan converts the fixed-rate mortgage to a variable-rate loan via a swap.

An interest rate swap also can create interest savings compared to alternative agreements. To create such a benefit, both parties must be creditworthy, since the net interest

EXAMPLE 20-1
An Interest Rate Swap

	Firm A	Firm B	Differential
Fixed-rate loans	8.5%	9.1%	60 bp
Variable-rate loans	LIBOR + 15 bp	LIBOR + 35 bp	20 bp
Net differential			40 bp

where bp stands for basis points.

Firm A has a better credit rating than firm B; therefore, its cost of funds is lower for both fixed- and variable-rate loans. However, the differential between firms A and B for the fixed-rate loan is 60 basis points, whereas it is only 20 basis points for a variable-rate loan. The initiation of a swap can generate total savings of 40 basis points for the two firms and any broker who acts as an intermediary. Thus, let us assume that the following loans are initiated, including an agreement between the two firms on how to split the benefits:

	Firm A	Firm B
Fixed-rate loans	Obtains loan at 8.5%	Pays swap rate of 8.9% fixed to Firm A
Variable-rate loans	Pays swap rate of LIBOR + 30 bp to Firm B	Obtains loan at LIBOR + 35 bp
Net payment	LIBOR + 30 bp + (8.5 − 8.9) = LIBOR − 10 bp	8.9 + [LIBOR + 35 bp − (LIBOR + 30 bp)] = 8.95
Savings	LIBOR + 15 bp − (LIBOR − 10 bp) = 25 bp	9.10 − 8.95 = 15 bp

The swap saves Firm A 25 basis points as compared with a variable-rate loan taken directly by Firm A, and it saves Firm B 15 basis points on a fixed-rate loan. If a broker is involved, then a fee of 5 to 10 basis points is paid to the broker.

payments are transferred only when the interest is due. Example 20-1 shows how an exchange of payments can benefit the two parties in a swap when a relative credit risk premium exists between the parties.

Originally, the motivation for swap agreements was to obtain a *lower* interest rate than that available without a swap, as shown in Example 20-1. Since fixed and floating rates were priced differently, such benefits were available in the swap market. However, the swap market is more efficient now, eliminating many of the benefits from simple swaps. The motivation for current swaps is to achieve risk management goals, such as matching floating interest rates of assets to liabilities and obtaining tax or institutional benefits. An example of a tax swap occurs when zero coupon bonds are taxed differently in different countries. Institutional factors include financial institutions that are required to have a specified asset-liability structure.

Swaps directly relate to futures markets, since it can be shown that swaps are equivalent to a portfolio of forward contracts. Thus, swaps are essentially equivalent to futures, if the time period is equivalent. The liquidity of these markets and the usefulness of changing the risk factors of a loan show the importance of swaps for firms and financial institutions. In fact, market makers who take on one side of a swap temporarily until they find the other side of the swap will hedge their positions with futures, typically with the Eurodollar futures market. Three-year and five-year swap futures were started by the Chicago Board of Trade, but were not successful.

The size of the over-the-counter swap market has grown from zero in 1981 to more than $3 trillion in outstanding swaps by the early 1990s. Currently, over 300 different *types* of swaps are offered by financial institutions. While interest rate swaps are the most used swap instrument, currency swaps are also an active market, with over $800 million of such swaps in force by the early 1990s. One use for currency swaps is dual currency bonds. A dual currency bond pays interest in one currency and the principal in a second currency. Swaps can create the equivalent of a dual currency bond. More recently, equity swaps have been popular. Macroeconomic swaps are predicted as the next major innovation in the swap market. An example of a macroeconomic swap is a swap that pays a floating rate that is pegged to GNP while receiving a fixed rate. Such a swap would be beneficial to firms such as General Motors, whose profits are related to the business cycle.

Swap Risk and Pricing Swaps

Risk exists for interest rate swap contracts, because funds are transferred only when an interest payment is due. Since the swap contract is a good faith agreement, with no principal amount changing hands, the potential default by one of the parties creates swap risk. Swap risk is actually a compound risk. The initial risk is whether the counterparty to the swap agreement will default. Second, if a default occurs, the cost of creating a replacement swap generates a market risk for the swap. Those who enter into swap agreements need to check the credit risk of the counterparty carefully in order to minimize swap risk.

To price swaps, one needs a model of forward rates (the term structure). Term-structure models used on Wall Street are proprietary, sophisticated applications of financial theory. However, swap models also must consider the potential default risk of the parties. The more sophisticated swap contracts are very difficult to price.[1]

Swaptions

A **swaption** is an option on a swap. A call buyer has the right to enter into a swap agreement to receive fixed payments based on a fixed interest rate and pay floating interest rates.[2] A put buyer has the right to pay the fixed interest rate and receive the floating interest rate. Thus, a swaption buyer is buying insurance (at a cost) to enter into a swap if the interest rate changes in an unfavorable direction.

OVER-THE-COUNTER OPTIONS

Reasons for the Existence of Over-the-Counter Options

Corporations have specific needs to control their risk posture. Therefore, corporations approach investment houses and major financial institutions to inquire about what type of specialized instruments can be devised so that the corporation can hedge its risks. The investment house investigates how it can devise a synthetic instrument, such as an option to meet client needs; how it can hedge its own risk; the appropriate pricing of the instrument; and how much interest the instrument will create in the financial community. If all of these factors indicate a feasible financial instrument, then a new option (or other instrument) is born. This process is one application of financial engineering.

Many types of over-the-counter options exist. Interest rate options are an important type of over-the-counter option, since exchange-traded options on debt are not liquid (although futures options on certain debt options are actively traded), and interest rate options are linked to the movement of rates rather than to prices in order to better hedge against changes in loan interest rates. Options on specific commodities, such as energy products, are also issued over-the-counter. Finally, certain so-called **exotic options** trade over-the-counter. Exotic options have unusual characteristics, such as when the option is valuable only if the asset changes significantly in price.

Pricing of Specialized Options

Options on new products are created because of customer demand to control risk. Wall Street firms determine how they can hedge their risks of creating such an option, often by dynamically trading an existing futures contract, and then add an appropriate premium for risk and profit to the fair price of the option. The fair option price is determined by creating an option pricing model based on the characteristics of the option. Such models are often binomial models. These products typically carry a large premium.

---

[1] A good source for additional information on swaps is *The Swaps Market* by Marshall and Kapner (1993).

[2] This is called the right to go short a swap, since the call buyer receives the fixed interest rate.

Most over-the-counter options are European in nature—that is, they can be exercised only at option expiration. This characteristic helps limit the risk of the investment house that issues the option. Given the specialized nature of these contracts, and how they are hedged by the investment house, it is typically difficult to trade over-the-counter options before they expire.

INTEREST RATE OPTIONS

An **interest rate option** is an option that has a payoff based on the underlying interest rate. Thus, an interest rate option differs from an option on debt, with the latter having a payoff based on the *price* of the underlying debt instrument. Interest rate options are useful for hedging variable-rate loans by both the debtholder and the issuer of the loan. Other interest rate options are based on the spread between long- and short-term interest rates. Exchange-traded interest rate options trade only a few options a day, while their over-the-counter equivalents have an active new issue market.

Caps, Floors, and Collars

Corporations and financial institutions often wish to limit their risk of changing interest rates. If a corporation has a loan at a variable interest rate (such as LIBOR), then the risk of higher interest rates is an important consideration. The corporation therefore wants to limit the maximum interest rate it will pay over the life of the loan. A financial institution that lends funds at a variable interest rate has a risk of lower interest rates. The financial institution wants to limit the minimum interest rate it will receive for the loan.

A **cap** is a series of call options on an interest rate, typically LIBOR. If interest rates increase, the seller of the cap pays the cap buyer the difference between the interest rate and the strike price at *each payment date* of the option. Thus, the strike price is the cap on the interest rate. The strike price is often the interest rate at the time the option is issued. The buyer of the cap pays for the interest rate option when the cap is initiated. The payment of an in-the-money option is usually made at the payment date of the interest on the underlying cash instrument rather than at the expiration of the option. Thus, an option expiring in 30 days that is based on the 90-day LIBOR rate pays off in 120 days, after the LIBOR instrument matures. The payoff amount of the cap at any specific payment date is determined as follows:

$$\text{payoff} = F\frac{t}{360}\frac{\text{Max}[0, \text{LIBOR} - \text{K}]}{100} \tag{20-1}$$

where F = the face value of the underlying instrument

t = the length of time of the interest period

K = the interest rate strike price

Thus, if LIBOR rises to 8% and a corporation buys a cap with K = 6% for a 90-day interest rate period, then the payoff per $1 million is:

$$payoff = \$1,000,000 \ (90/360) \quad Max \ [0, 8 - 6]/100$$

$$= \$1,000,000 \ (.25) \ (.02) = \$5,000$$

A **floor** option is a series of put options on the interest rate. If the interest rate decreases after the puts are obtained, then the seller of the floor pays the floor buyer the difference between the strike price and the interest rate. The strike price is the floor. A floor is useful to a bank that lends money at LIBOR and wishes to protect itself against interest rates falling below the strike price.[3]

A **collar** is a combination of a cap and a floor.[4] Buying both a cap and a floor would give the buyer protection against both an increase and a decrease in the interest rate. However, since most firms only need protection against a change in rates in one direction, buying a cap and *selling* a floor at different interest rates (or vice versa) provides the necessary protection *and* reduces the cost of the option. Of course, in this situation the option hedger reduces the benefits from an advantageous interest rate change because of the sale of one side of the collar.[5]

Options on the Slope of the Yield Curve

Sycurve options are options on the slope of the yield curve. Sycurve options have generated interest in the financial community for hedging mismatches in short-term versus long-term interest rates. For example, a bond portfolio manager who attempts to have a portfolio of interest-sensitive securities to match the behavior of the yield curve can use a sycurve option to overcome mismatches between the portfolio and the current

---

[3] A long swap contract at a fixed rate K is simply a long cap at K and a short floor at K. Similarly, a short swap at a fixed rate K is a short cap at K and a long floor at K.

[4] If one is long a cap and short a floor, then this is equivalent to a series of range forward contracts if the strike prices differ (range forwards are discussed shortly).

[5] A collar also is defined as buying a call at a lower strike price K_1, selling a call at a higher strike price K_2, and lending the present value of K_1. The value of the collar at option expiration is defined as:

$$Min[Max \ (P_{S,E}, K_1), K_2]$$

where $0 < K_1 < K_2$

or alternatively:

$$K_1 + Max[0, P_{S,E} - K_1] - Max[0, P_{S,E} - K_2]$$

such that the payoffs become:

Price of P_S	Payoff
$P_{S,E} < K_1$	K_1
$K_1 \leq P_{S,E} \leq K_2$	$P_{S,E}$
$K_2 < P_{S,E}$	K_2

yield curve. Alternatively, an extreme example of a mismatch is a portfolio in which the bonds are mostly of one maturity, while the performance of the portfolio is measured against a bond benchmark made up of only long-term and short-term bonds (a "barbell" portfolio). In addition, a financial institution whose asset and liability structure differs from the yield curve can use a sycurve option to change the effective composition of the balance sheet.

An example of a sycurve option is a 2/10 sycurve call. This call option represents the right to "buy" the curve—that is, to buy the 2-year end of the yield curve and sell the 10-year end of curve—at a specified yield spread. Since yields are the inverse of prices, a sycurve call option profits when the difference between the 10-year and 2-year yields *increases in value*. The payoff to the 2/10 sycurve becomes:

$$\text{Max}\{[(Y_{10} - Y_2) - K], 0\} \tag{20-2}$$

where Y_{10} and Y_2 are the 10-year and 2-year yields from the term structure

If the strike price (in basis points) is 20, then a 6-month price for a 2/10 sycurve could be 10 basis points (or $100,000 = 10 bp × .01 × $1,000,000 face value). If the spread widens to 40 basis points at option expiration, then the payoff is (40 − 20) bp × 0.1 × $1,000,000 or $200,000, with a net profit of $100,000.

Payoff diagrams of interest rate options and sycurve options show the interesting payoffs that can be obtained. Buying a sycurve call produces the typical call option payoff diagram: As the *spread* between the long-term and short-term yields increases above the strike price, the profit of the call increases. However, combining a sycurve with other interest rate options creates complex profit graphs. Figure 20-1 shows a call

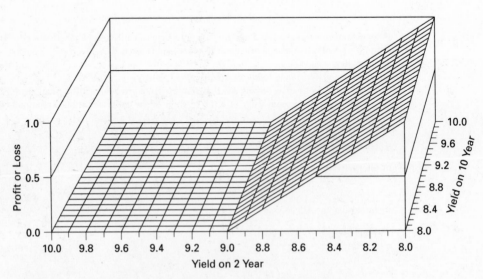

Figure 20-1 Payoff diagram for a long call on a two-year bond yield.

on a simple 2-year interest rate option in relation to both the 2-year and 10-year yields. This simple call profits as yields increase on the 2-year call; changes in the 10-year yield have no effect on the option. Figure 20-2 shows a put on a 10-year yield. Here, changes in the 10-year yield affect the put value. Figure 20-3 shows how a *combination* of the 2-year call and 20-year put creates a more complex payoff structure. This combination profits if *either* the 2-year yield falls below the 9% strike *or* the 10-year yield rises above 9%; if both situations exist, then both parts of the option are in-the-money (the upper-right portion of the graph). Finally, Figure 20-4 adds a *short* position in a sycurve 2/10 call to the long 2-year call and 10-year put positions. This combination is in-the-money for the following combinations:

- Low 2-year yields and low 10-year yields
- High 10-year yields and high 2-year yields.

When 10-year yields are high and 2-year yields are low (when both the 2-year call and 10-year put are in-the-money), the short 2/10 sycurve loses the exact amount of money gained by the other options. Of course, the benefit of this combined position is a lower cost, since one is short the sycurve option.

Pricing Interest Rate Options

One cannot use the Black-Scholes model to price interest rate options because of its assumption that interest rates are constant. Often, the binomial model is used for these types of options. Investment houses are attempting to find a closed-form equation to accurately price these types of options.

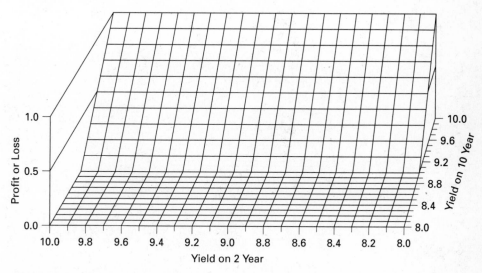

Figure 20-2 Payoff diagram for a long put on a ten-year bond yield.

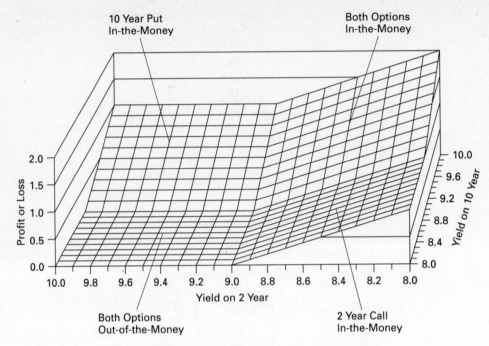

Figure 20-3 Payoff diagram for a long two-year call and long ten-year put.

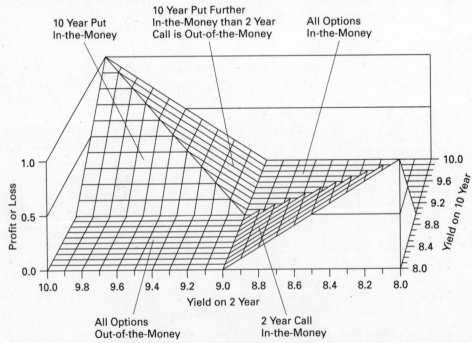

Figure 20-4 Payoff diagram for a long two-year call, long ten-year put, short a sycurve ²⁄₁₀ call.

COMPOUND AND EXOTIC OPTIONS

Exotic options have unusual characteristics: for example, when they become in-the-money; combining several simple options into one complex option; or forming an option on an option. The interest rate options defined above as caps, floors, and collars are technically exotic options, but their widespread use makes them no longer "exotic" in nature. Similarly, some of the options discussed below have extensive use in some markets, but are not yet widespread in all markets.

Range Forwards

A **range forward** for an asset (often foreign exchange) is the purchase of a call option with a strike price of K_1 and the sale of a put option with a strike price of K_2 ($K_1 > K_2$), such that the total initial cost of the transaction is zero. The purpose of a range forward is to have the cost of an asset fall within a designated range, without adding an extra cost to the transaction. Thus, the strike prices are chosen such that the forward price of the asset is between K_1 and K_2 and the cost of the call is equal to the cost of the put. These characteristics cause the total cost of the range option to be zero for the buyer at option initiation. The first three columns of Exhibit 20-1 show the option payoffs at option exercise for a range forward.

FOCUS 20-1
The Options Simulator and Exotic Options

One of the most unique and interesting aspects of the Options Simulator is its inclusion of exotic options and the choices to examine the characteristics of these options. The Simulator includes 34 different options, such as:

- Various versions of the European model, with choices as to the distribution of price changes (for example, the jump process)
- Binomial models of various types of options.
- Exotic options, including compound options, four versions of the average price options, lookback, barrier, two-color rainbow, and all-or-nothing options.

For each of the available options, one can generate tables for the values and the option sensitivities. The program lets you decide what variables to include in the tables and the range of inputs for these variables. The tables of option values used in this book, including the lookback option table in this chapter, are created from the Option Simulator.

The Simulator also allows the user to view and print two- and three-dimensional graphs based on these options. Thus, once you choose the variables and data ranges to use, the program calculates and displays the relationships in graphical format. The orientation of the graph and the colors for the three-dimensional curves can even by changed. Finally, the Simulator runs option replication strategies for several types of options, as well as graphing the results of these strategies.

EXHIBIT 20-1
Payoff Table for a Range Forward

Price of *FC*	Value of a Long Call	Value of a Short Put	Option Payoffs at Expiration	Total Cost of the Asset
$P_{FC} \geq K_1$	$P_{FC} - K_1$	0	$P_{FC} - K_1$	K_1
$K_1 > P_{FC} > K_2$	0	0	0	P_{FC}
$K_2 \geq P_{FC}$	0	$-[K_2 - P_{FC}]$	$P_{FC} - K_2$	K_2

P_{FC} = value of the foreign currency

Figure 20-5(a) illustrates buying a call with a K_1 strike price and selling a put with a K_2 strike, which creates a range forward. Figure 20-5(b) shows the resultant effect of combining the two positions: A profit occurs when $P_{FC} > K_1$ and a loss occurs if $P_{FC} < K_2$. Figure 20-5(c) shows the effect when the range forward is exercised (the asset is purchased via the exercise of the call or the asset is received when the put is exercised by the buyer), or when the asset is purchased if the range option is not exercised. Thus, Figure 20-5(c) is a *total cost* diagram of the asset at option expiration; this payoff diagram is equivalent to a bull spread diagram. The last column of Exhibit 20-1 shows the total cost of the asset for the three possible states of nature given for the final asset price.[6]

Solomon Brothers started to issue range forwards on foreign currency in 1985. The range forward is useful for corporations wanting to guarantee that the cost of the future foreign exchange will be between K_1 and K_2 without having to pay for the protection afforded by the range forward. For a range forward, the buyer chooses one of the strikes and the seller calculates the other strike such that the total cost of the range forward is zero. Range forwards can also be applied to other assets. When K_1 and K_2 are chosen so that the call price does not equal the put price, this combination is called a **cylinder option.** For a cylinder option, the buyer chooses both strike prices and then pays or receives the net value of the options. Citicorp and other investment houses sell cylinder options.

Average-Rate Options

An **average rate option** pays at option expiration the difference between the strike price and the *average* rate or price, A, of the asset over the life of the option. Thus, an average rate call option pays the Max $[0, A - K]$, while an average rate put option pays the Max$[0, K - A]$, where A is the average price of the asset. The average A can be either an arithmetic average or a geometric average of the asset price over the life of the option. Average-rate options are most common for foreign exchange and interest rate assets. They are used by corporations that have daily (or periodic) responsibilities for foreign exchange or interest rates. For example, if a firm wishes to convert 10 million

---

[6] Another definition of a range forward is buying a forward contract, buying a put with strike K_2 and selling a call with strike K_1.

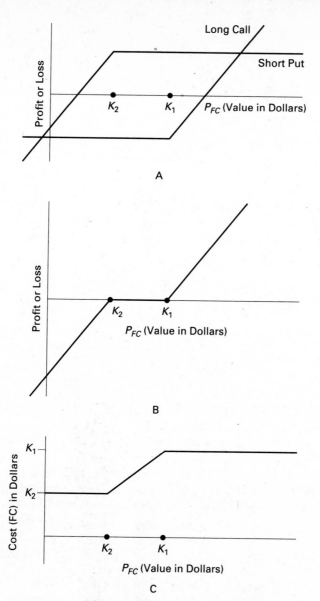

Figure 20-5 Range forward payoff and cost diagrams.
(A) The range forward components, (B) The net range forward diagram, (C) The cost of purchasing the asset with a range forward.

marks to dollars per day and avoid the adverse effect of exchange-rate risk, then average rate options can be used for this periodic exchange. Similarly, if a financial institution has sold certificates of deposit that will mature weekly for the next six months (the institution will then resell CDs at the going interest rate), and it believes interest rates will increase steadily over the period, then an average rate option can control the future interest rate cost. These average rate options provide similar protection to obtaining separate hedging instruments each day or week of the time period over which the option is active.

Compound Options

A **compound option** is an option on an option. A **cacall** is a call on a call option—that is, it is a call that pays the value of *another* call option at expiration. A **caput** is a call on a put—that is, it is a call that pays the value of a put at option expiration. The cost of an option on an option is lower than a simple call or put *if* the option holder does *not* receive the underlying option at expiration of the cacall or caput. The cost of an option on an option is higher if the underlying option is received. The value of a call compound option at the expiration of the compound option on either a call or a put is:

$$\text{cacall: } \text{Max} \{0, PV_t[\text{Max}(0, P_{\hat{s}}^* - K|T)] - k\} \tag{20-3}$$

Table 20-1 Lookback Call Values

		$P_S = 100$							
		$r = .10$		$d = .03$		$r = .03$		$d = .10$	
		European				European			
σ	M	1	3	6	12	1	3	6	12
	70	30.31	30.91	31.81	33.66	30.72	32.09	33.96	37.12
	75	25.35	26.04	27.12	29.46	25.83	27.41	29.60	33.38
	80	20.39	21.20	22.62	25.60	20.94	22.75	25.34	29.80
.2	85	15.43	16.54	18.53	22.27	16.05	18.20	21.31	26.52
	90	10.58	12.45	15.18	19.68	11.24	14.04	17.81	23.75
	95	6.50	9.53	12.95	18.02	7.06	10.88	15.27	21.80
	100	4.78	8.46	12.15	17.44	5.19	9.61	14.28	21.05
	70	30.31	30.96	32.24	35.19	30.72	32.12	34.20	37.89
	75	25.35	26.23	28.06	31.84	25.83	27.54	30.18	34.72
	80	20.41	21.77	24.33	28.99	20.95	23.16	26.50	31.92
.3	85	15.59	17.84	21.23	26.72	16.17	19.20	23.33	29.57
	90	11.25	14.73	18.91	25.06	11.81	15.98	20.86	27.78
	95	8.12	12.75	17.48	24.06	8.57	13.83	19.26	26.65
	100	6.97	12.07	17.01	23.73	7.34	13.06	18.70	26.26
	70	30.31	31.31	33.53	38.02	30.73	32.38	35.14	39.81
	75	25.38	26.97	30.02	35.44	25.86	28.12	31.69	37.32
	80	20.57	23.11	27.05	33.33	21.09	24.27	28.70	35.21
.4	85	16.11	19.90	24.69	31.70	16.64	21.01	26.27	33.53
	90	12.41	17.52	22.99	30.55	12.89	18.53	24.48	32.31
	95	9.96	16.06	21.98	29.88	10.36	16.97	23.38	31.58
	100	9.11	15.58	21.65	29.66	9.46	16.44	23.00	31.33

Payoff: Max[0, S_n − Min(S_0, S_1, ..., S_n)] d = dividend yield
Source: Rubinstein (1991).

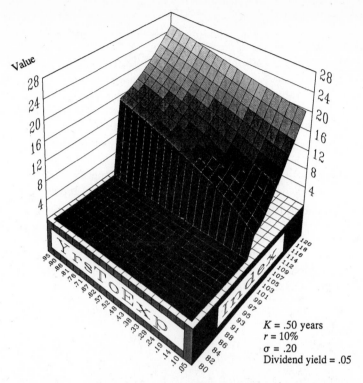

$K = .50$ years
$r = 10\%$
$\sigma = .20$
Dividend yield = .05

Figure 20-6 Lookback call option values. Yrs toExp = years (or time) to expiration; Index = index value or stock price (Source: Created from The Options and Futures Trading Simulator by Mark Rubinstein and Gerard Gennotte (1992).)

$$\text{caput: Max}\{0, \, PV_t[\text{Max}(0, \, K - P_S^*|T] - k\} \qquad (20\text{-}4)$$

where the compound option has a strike price k and time to expiration t and the underlying option has a strike price K and time to expiration $T > t$. P_S^* is the value of the underlying asset at time t and PV_t is the present value at time t of the quantity in brackets.

Lookback and Barrier Options

A **lookback call** is identical to a standard European call except that the strike price is equal to the *minimum* price of the underlying asset during the life of the option. A **lookback put** is identical to a European put except that the strike price is equal to the *maximum* price of the asset during the life of the option. Thus, lookback options are always exercised at option expiration, since they are always in-the-money. The only question concerning a lookback option is the final strike price, which will determine the payoff of the option.[7] The payoff at option expiration of lookback call is:

$$\text{Max}[0, \, P_{S,n} - \text{Min}(P_{S,1}, P_{S,2}, \dots, P_{S,n})] = P_{S,n} - \text{Min}(P_{S,1}, P_{S,2}, \dots, P_{S,n}) \qquad (20\text{-}5)$$

where $P_{S,t} = P_S$ at time t

---

[7] A forward-start call has its strike price determined at a prespecified time in the future, called the grant date. At this date, the strike price is set equal to a prespecified percentage of the market price of the underlying asset.

Lookback options have become an active over-the-counter option, with several billion dollars being traded. Table 20-1 shows the values of lookback call options as time, volatility, dividends, interest rate, and strike prices change. Comparing these values to option values of typical call options (such as in Table 12-2) shows that lookback calls have values approximately twice that of regular calls. Figure 20-6 (see page 613) illustrates the value in a three-dimensional graph as the underlying asset value and the time to expiration change. The benefit of such a graph is to show the relevant relationships when an intuitive understanding is difficult to obtain without such a figure. This is even more relevant for the option sensitivities for exotic options; for example, Figure 20-7 provides the gamma for a lookback option.

A **down-and-out call option** is an option that becomes worthless if the cash asset price reaches or falls below a threshold price, often called a **barrier**; thus, the alternative name **barrier option**. A **down-and-in-call option** is an option that becomes active only if the cash asset price reaches or crosses the threshold. An **up-and-out put option** is an option that becomes worthless if the cash asset price reaches or goes above a threshold price. An **up-and-in put option** activates only if the cash price reaches or crosses the threshold. Figure 20-8 illustrates the value of a barrier call option in relation to the time to expiration and the asset value.

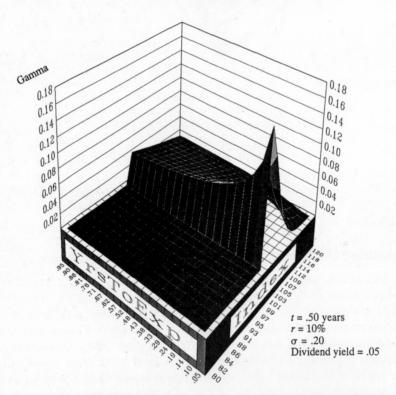

Figure 20-7 Lookback gammas. Yrs To Exp = years (or time) to expiration; Index = index value or stock price. (Source: Created from The Options and Futures Trading Simulator by Mark Rubinstein and Gerard Gennotte (1992).)

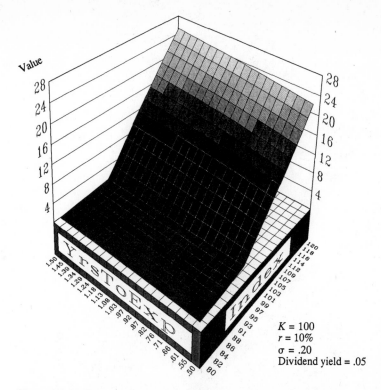

Value

$K = 100$
$r = 10\%$
$\sigma = .20$
Dividend yield = .05

Figure 20-8 Barrier option values. Yrs To Exp = years (or time) to expiration; Index = index value or stock price. (Source: Created from The Options and Futures Trading Simulator by Mark Rubinstein and Gerard Gennotte (1992).)

Rainbow Options

Two-color rainbow options are options in which the payoff is based on two underlying asset prices. For example, one type of a two-color rainbow option is based on the product of two underlying asset prices. Thus, this call rainbow option payoff is:

$$\text{Max}[0, (P_{S1} P_{S2}) - K] \qquad (20\text{-}6)$$

where P_{S1} and P_{S2} equal the prices of the two underlying cash assets at option expiration

A guaranteed exchange rate call on a foreign stock index is a rainbow option in which the payoff from the normal option on the foreign stock index is converted into the domestic currency using a prespecified exchange rate. Other rainbow options include the option to exchange one risky asset for another, options to deliver the worse (or better) of two risky assets, and options on the minimum (or maximum) of two risky assets. Figure 20-9 shows how the value of a two-color rainbow option changes in relation to the values of the two underlying assets. The graph clearly shows how the *interrelationship* between the asset values are important to the option value.

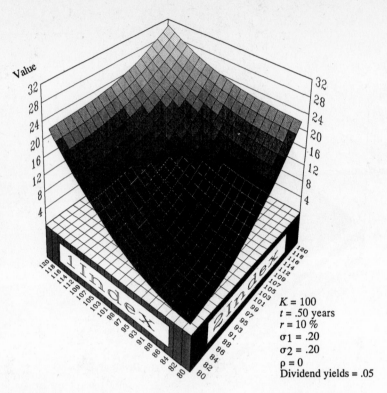

$K = 100$
$t = .50$ years
$r = 10\%$
$\sigma_1 = .20$
$\sigma_2 = .20$
$\rho = 0$
Dividend yields = .05

Figure 20-9 Two-color rainbow values. Index = index value or stock price;
(Source: Created from The Options and Futures Trading
Simulator by Mark Rubinstein and Gerard Gennotte (1992).)

SUMMARY

Financial engineering provides solutions for risk management situations that cannot be handled by exchange-traded securities. Swaps are one type of financial product that can effectively control interest rate (and other types of) risk without the use of futures or options contracts. Over-the-counter options meet needs not adequately met by options traded on the exchanges. Interest rate over-the-counter options include caps, collars, and floors. Exotic options are options with unusual characteristics, such as a call on a call or a down-and-out option.

BIBLIOGRAPHY

Marshall, John F., and Kenneth R. Kapner (1993). *The Swaps Market,* 2d ed. Miami: Kolb Publishing.

Marshall, John, and Vipul Bansal (1993). *Financial Engineering,* 2d ed. Miami: Kolb Publishing.

Rubinstein, Mark, and Gerard Gennotte (1992). *Options and Futures Trading Simulator,* Version 2.0.

PROBLEMS

*Indicates more difficult problems.

20-1 Buying and Paying Off on a CAP

You took out a loan for $1,000,000 with a variable interest rate. The current LIBOR rate is 3%. At the end of three months, when the payment is due, LIBOR is 9.5%. However, you purchased a CAP with a strike price of 5%. What is the payoff on the loan?

20-2 Average Rate Call Option

You bought 100 average rate call options on a stock with a strike price of 95. Throughout the 90 days during which you hold the option, the stock has the following price movements relevant for the average rate call: 100, 105, 110, 90, and 85. What is the value of the option?

*20-3 Range Forward

September British pound futures are trading at $1.8650/£. The options on futures prices are: 1850 Sept. call = 7.16 cents and the 1875 Sept. call = 5.46 cents. An investment manager involved with currency trades wants to implement a range forward position. What should he do and what are the payoffs?

APPENDIX A

Values for the Probabilities from the Normal Distribution

This table presents the values for the normal distribution N(*d*). The value for N(*d*) is needed to solve option pricing models. N(*d*) represents the probability associated with a specific value of "*d*". The values for "*d*" in statistics books are often labeled as the "z-statistic". Values for N(−*d*) are found by taking 1.0 − N(*d*) from this table.

z	0.00	0.01	0.02	0.03	0.04	0.05	0.06	0.07	0.08	0.09
0.0	.5000	.5040	.5080	.5120	.5160	.5199	.5239	.5279	.5319	.5359
0.1	.5398	.5438	.5478	.5517	.5557	.5596	.5636	.5675	.5714	.5753
0.2	.5793	.5832	.5871	.5910	.5948	.5987	.6026	.6064	.6103	.6141
0.3	.6179	.6217	.6255	.6293	.6331	.6368	.6406	.6443	.6480	.6517
0.4	.6554	.6591	.6628	.6664	.6700	.6736	.6772	.6808	.6844	.6879
0.5	.6915	.6950	.6985	.7019	.7054	.7088	.7123	.7157	.7190	.7224
0.6	.7257	.7291	.7324	.7357	.7389	.7422	.7454	.7486	.7517	.7549
0.7	.7580	.7611	.7642	.7673	.7704	.7734	.7764	.7794	.7823	.7852
0.8	.7881	.7910	.7939	.7967	.7995	.8023	.8051	.8078	.8106	.8133
0.9	.8159	.8186	.8212	.8238	.8264	.8289	.8315	.8340	.8365	.8389
1.0	.8413	.8438	.8461	.8485	.8508	.8531	.8554	.8577	.8599	.8621
1.1	.8643	.8665	.8686	.8708	.8729	.8749	.8770	.8790	.8810	.8830
1.2	.8849	.8860	.8888	.8907	.8925	.8943	.8962	.8980	.8997	.9015
1.3	.9032	.9049	.9066	.9082	.9099	.9115	.9131	.9147	.9162	.9177
1.4	.9192	.9207	.9222	.9236	.9251	.9265	.9279	.9292	.9306	.9319
1.5	.9332	.9345	.9357	.9370	.9382	.9394	.9406	.9418	.9429	.9441
1.6	.9452	.9463	.9474	.9484	.9495	.9505	.9515	.9525	.9535	.9545
1.7	.9554	.9564	.9573	.9582	.9591	.9599	.9608	.9616	.9625	.9633
1.8	.9641	.9649	.9656	.9664	.9671	.9678	.9686	.9693	.9699	.9706
1.9	.9713	.9719	.9726	.9732	.9738	.9744	.9750	.9756	.9761	.9767
2.0	.9772	.9778	.9783	.9788	.9793	.9798	.9803	.9808	.9812	.9817
2.1	.9821	.9826	.9830	.9834	.9838	.9842	.9846	.9850	.9854	.9857
2.2	.9861	.9864	.9868	.9871	.9875	.9878	.9881	.9884	.9887	.9890
2.3	.9893	.9896	.9898	.9901	.9904	.9906	.9909	.9911	.9913	.9916
2.4	.9918	.9920	.9922	.9925	.9927	.9929	.9931	.9932	.9934	.9936
2.5	.9938	.9940	.9941	.9943	.9945	.9946	.9948	.9949	.9951	.9952
2.6	.9953	.9955	.9956	.9957	.9959	.9960	.9961	.9962	.9963	.9964
2.7	.9965	.9966	.9967	.9968	.9969	.9970	.9971	.9972	.9973	.9974
2.8	.9974	.9975	.9976	.9977	.9977	.9978	.9979	.9979	.9980	.9981
2.9	.9981	.9982	.9982	.9983	.9984	.9984	.9985	.9985	.9986	.9986
3.0	.9987	.9987	.9987	.9988	.9988	.9989	.9989	.9989	.9990	.9990

APPENDIX B

Natural Logarithms

x	ln x	x	ln x	x	ln x	x	ln x
.01	−4.60517	.43	.84397	.85	−0.16252	1.27	.23902
.02	−3.91202	.44	.82098	.86	.15032	1.28	.24686
.03	.50656	.45	.79851	.87	.13926	1.29	.25464
.04	.21888	.46	.77653	.88	.12783	1.30	.26236
.05	−2.99573	.47	.75502	.89	.11653	1.31	.27003
.06	.81341	.48	.73397	0.90	−0.10536	1.32	.27763
.07	.65926	.49	.71335	.91	.09431	1.33	.28518
.08	.52573	0.50	−0.69315	.92	.08338	1.34	.29267
.09	.40795	.51	.67334	.93	.07257	1.35	.20010
0.10	−2.30259	.52	.65393	.94	.06188	1.36	.30748
.11	.20727	.53	.63488	.95	.05129	1.37	.31481
.12	.12026	.54	.61619	.96	.04082	1.38	.32208
.13	.04022	.55	.59784	.97	.03046	1.39	.32930
.14	−1.96611	.56	.57982	.98	.02020	1.40	.33647
.15	.89712	.57	.56212	.99	.01005	1.41	.34359
.16	.83258	.58	.54473	1.00	0.00000	1.42	.35066
.17	.77196	.59	.52763	1.01	.00995	1.43	.35767
.18	.71480	0.60	−0.51083	1.02	.01980	1.44	.36464
.19	.66073	.61	.49430	1.03	.02956	1.45	.37156
0.20	−1.60944	.62	.47804	1.04	.03922	1.46	.37844
.21	.56065	.63	.46024	1.05	.04879	1.47	.38526
.22	.51413	.64	.44629	1.06	.05827	1.48	.39204
.23	.46968	.65	.43708	1.07	.06766	1.49	.39878
.24	.42712	.66	.41552	1.08	.07696	1.5	0.40547
.25	.38629	.67	.40048	1.09	.08618	1.6	7000
.26	.34707	.68	.38566	1.10	.09531	1.7	0.53063
.27	.30933	.69	.37106	1.11	.10436	1.8	8779
.28	.27297	0.70	−0.35667	1.12	.11333	1.9	0.64185
.29	.23787	.71	.34249	1.13	.12222	2.0	9315
0.30	−1.20397	.72	.32850	1.14	.13103	2.1	0.74194
.31	.17118	.73	.31471	1.15	.13976	2.2	8846
.32	.13943	.74	.30111	1.16	.14842	2.3	0.83291
.33	.10866	.75	.28768	1.17	.15700	2.4	7547
.34	.07881	.76	.27444	1.18	.16551	2.5	0.91629
.35	−1.04982	.77	.26136	1.19	.17395	2.6	5551
.36	.02165	.78	.24846	1.20	.18232	2.7	9325
.37	−0.99425	.79	.23572	1.21	.19062	2.8	1.02962
.38	.96758	0.80	−0.22314	1.22	.19885	2.9	6471
.39	.94161	.81	.21072	1.23	.20701	3.0	9861
0.40	−0.91629	.82	.19845	1.24	.21511	4.0	1.38629
.41	.89160	.83	.18633	1.25	.22314	5.0	1.60944
.42	.86750	.84	.17435	1.26	.23111	10.0	2.30258

CREDITS

We gratefully acknowledge the use of the following material.

Examples, Exhibits, and Tables

Chapter 3   Table 3-3, Michael Hartzmark, "Returns to Individual Traders of Futures: Aggregate Results," *Journal of Political Economy,* Vol. 95, No. 6, December 1987, pp. 1292–1306. Reprinted by permission of The University of Chicago Press. / Table 3-5, Zvi Bodie and Victor Rosansky, "Risk and Return in Commodity Futures," *Financial Analysts Journal,* Vol. 36, No. 3, May–June 1980, pp. 27–39.

Chapter 7   Table 7-1, S. P. Hegde, "The Impact of Interest Rate Level and Volatility on the Performance of Interest Rate Hedges," *The Journal of Futures Markets,* Vol. 2, No. 4, Winter 1982. Reprinted by permission of John Wiley & Sons, Inc. / Table 7-2, Joanne Hill and Thomas Schneeweis, "Risk Reduction Potential of Financial Futures for Corporate Bond Positions," originally in *Interest Rate Futures: Concepts and Issues,* edited by Gay and Kolb, 1982. Reprinted with permission of the authors. / Table 7-3, Steven Figlewski, "Hedging with Stock Index Futures; Theory and Applications in a New Market," *Journal of Futures Markets,* Vol. 5, No. 2, Summer 1985, pp. 183–200. Reprinted by permission of John Wiley & Sons, Inc.

Chapter 9   Table 9-2, "Conversion Factor Tables," *Financial Instruments Guide.* Copyright © Board of Trade of the City of Chicago.

Chapter 10   Tables 10-3 and 10-4, Richard McEnally, "How to Neutralize Reinvestment Rate Risk," *The Journal of Portfolio Management,* Vol. 6, No. 3, Spring 1980, pp. 59–63. This copyrighted material is reprinted with permission of *The Journal of Portfolio Management.*

Chapter 12   Table 12-2 and Exhibits 12A-1 and 12B-1 Reprinted with permission of Mark Rubinstein from "Classnotes, University of California, Berkeley," 1991.

Chapter 13   Tables 13-1, 13-2, 13A-1, and 13A-2 and Exhibits 13-2 and 13-3 Reprinted with permission of Mark Rubinstein from "Classnotes, University of California, Berkeley," 1991. / Focus 13-1 reprinted with permission of Mark Rubinstein, created from The Options and Futures Trading Simulator, Version 2.0, by Mark Rubinstein and Gerald Gennotte, copyright © 1992. / Table 13-3 and Focus 13-2 reprinted with permission of OptionVue Systems International from OptionVue IV.

Chapter 14   Tables 14-1, 14-2, 14-3, 14-4, 14-5, 14-6, and 14-7 and Focus 14-2 reprinted with permission of OptionVue Systems International from OptionVue IV.

Chapter 15   Exhibit 15-1 reprinted with permission of Mark Rubinstein, created from the Options and Futures Trading Simulator, Version 2.0, by Mark Rubinstein and

Gerald Gennotte, copyright © 1992. / Exhibits 15-2, 15-3, and 15-4 reprinted with permission of OptionVue Systems International from OptionVue IV. / Table 15-1, Robert C. Merton, Myron S. Scholes, and Mathew L. Gladstein, "The Returns and Risk of Alternative Call Option Portfolio Investment Strategies," *The Journal of Business,* Vol. 51, No. 2, April 1978, p. 219. Reprinted with permission of The University of Chicago Press. / Exhibits 15-8 and 15-9, *Futures and Options Strategy Guide,* p. 1, 11. The Chicago Mercantile Exchange.

Chapter 16 Exhibits 16-1 and 16-2, reprinted with permission of OptionVue Systems International from OptionVue IV. / Table 16-1, Robert C. Merton, Myron S. Scholes, and Mathew L. Gladstein, "The Returns and Risk of Alternative Call Option Portfolio Investment Strategies," *The Journal of Business,* Vol. 51, No. 2, April 1978, P. 207. Reprinted by permission of the University of Chicago Press. / Table 16-2, Used by permission of William T. Mullen, Loomis, Sayles & Co.

Chapter 17 Examples 17-1 and 17-2, "Concepts and Applications: Using Interest Rate Futures in Pension Fund Management," Chicago Board of Trade Pamphlet. Copyright © 1987 Board of Trade of the City of Chicago. / Exhibit 17-1, "Inside T-Bill Futures," p. 13, Chicago Mercantile Exchange pamphlet.

Chapter 18 Table 18-1, M. Brenner, G. Courtadon, and M. Subrahmanyam, "Options on the Spot and options on Futures," *The Journal of Finance,* Vol 40, No. 5, December 1985, pp. 1303–1317. Reprinted by permission of *The Journal of Finance.* / Table 18-2 G. Barone-Adesi and Robert Whaley, "Efficient Analytic Approximation of American Option Values," *The Journal of Finance,* Vol. 42, No. 2, June 1987, pp. 301–320. Reprinted with permission of *The Journal of Finance.* / Table 18-3 Robert Whaley, "Valuation of American Futures Options: Theory and Empirical Tests," *The Journal of Finance,* Vol. 41, No. 1, March 1986, pp. 127–150. Reprinted with permission of *The Journal of Finance.* / Exhibit 18-6, "Options on U.S. Treasury Bond Futures for Institutional Investors," pp. 9–13. Copyright © Board of Trade of the City of Chicago.

Chapter 19 Table 19-1 reprinted with permission of OptionVue Systems International from OptionVue IV. / Focus 19-1 reprinted with permission of Mark Rubinstein, created from The Options and Futures Trading Simulator, Version 2.0, by Mark Rubinsten and Gerald Gennotte, copyright © 1992.

Chapter 20 Table 20-1 reprinted with permission of Mark Rubinstein from "Classnotes, University of California, Berkeley," 1991.

Figures

Chapter 3 Figure 3-5, Robert T. Daigler, "The S&P Index Futures: A Hedging Contract," *CME Financial Strategy Paper,* 1990, Chicago Mercantile Exchange.

Chapter 4 Figure 4-2, Charles T. Howard, "Are T-Bill Futures Good Forecasters of Interest Rates?," *The Journal of Futures Markets,* Vol. 2, No. 4, Winter 1982, pp. 305–315. Reprinted by permission of John Wiley & Sons, Inc.

Chapter 5 Figure 5-1, "A World Marketplace," 1985, p. 9. Chicago Mercantile Exchange.

Chapter 7 Figure 7-3, Robert C. Kuberek and Norman G. Pefley, "Hedging Corporate Debt with U.S. Treasury Bond Futures," *The Journal of Futures Markets,* Vol. 3, No. 4, Winter 1983, pp. 345–353.

Chapter 8   Figures 8-1 and 8-2, "Dividend Payouts and the MMI," *Financial Futures Professional,* Vol. 14, No. 4, April 1990. Copyright © Board of Trade of the City of Chicago.

Chapter 10   Figure 10-4, Richard McEnally, "How to Neutralize Reinvestment Rate Risk," *The Journal of Portfolio Management,* Vol. 6, No. 3, Spring 1980, pp. 59–63. This copyrighted material is reprinted with permission of *The Journal of Portfolio Management.*

Chapter 12   Figure 12-3 reprinted with permission of Mark Rubinstein, created from the Options and Futures Trading Simulator, Version 2.0, by Mark Rubinstein and Gerald Gennotte, copyright © 1992. / Figure 12-4 reprinted with permission of Mark Rubinstein from "Classnotes, University of California, Berkeley," 1991.

Chapter 13   Figures 13-3 and 13-4 reprinted with permission of OptionVue Systems International from OptionVue IV.

Chapter 14   Figures 14-1, 14-2, 14-3, 14-4, 14-5, 14-6, 14-7, 14-8, 14-9, 14-10, 14-11, 14-12, 14-14, 14-15 reprinted with permission of Mark Rubinstein, created from The Options and Futures Trading Simulator, Version 2.0, by Mark Rubinstein and Gerald Gennotte, copyright © 1992. / Figure 14-13 Espen Gaardner Haug, "Opportunities and Perils of Using Option Sensitivities," *The Journal of Financial Engineering,* Vol. 2, No. 2, September, 1993.

Chapter 15   Figure 15-1 reprinted with permission of Mark Rubinstein from "Classnotes, University of California, Berkeley," 1991. / Figures 15-2, 15-3, 15-4, 15-5, 15-9, 15-11, 15-13, 15-17, 15-18 reprinted with permission of Mark Rubinstein, created from The Options and Futures Trading Simulator, Version 2.0, by Mark Rubinstein and Gerald Gennotte, copyright © 1992.

Chapter 16   Figures 16-3 and 16-8 reprinted with permission of Mark Rubinstein from "Classnotes, University of California, Berkeley," 1991.

Chapter 18   Figures 18-1 and 18-2 reprinted with permission of OptionVue Systems International from the background database of OptionVue IV.

Chapter 19   Figure 19-1 reprinted with permission of OptionVue Systems International from the background database of OptionVue IV.

Chapter 20   Figures 20-6, 20-7, 20-8, and 20-9 reprinted with permission of Mark Rubinstein, created from The Options and Futures Trading Simulator, Version 2.0, by Mark Rubinstein and Gerald Gennotte, copyright © 1992.

INDEX

Page numbers in bold indicate pages on which terms are defined.